ABRAHAM AND THE CHALLENGE OF FAITH
ACCORDING TO THE MIDRASH RABBAH

ABRAHAM AND
THE CHALLENGE OF FAITH

according to the
MIDRASH RABBAH

Rabbi Dr.
WILFRED SHUCHAT

DE**V**ORA
PUBLISHING
NEW YORK◆JERUSALEM◆LONDON

Abraham and the Challenge of Faith
According to the Midrash Rabbah
by Wilfred Shuchat

Typeset by Ariel Walden

Printed in Israel

First Edition
ISBN 978-965-524-273-7

Urim Publications   Lambda Publishers, Inc.
P.O.Box 52287   527 Empire Blvd.
Jerusalem 91521 Israel   Brooklyn, NY 11225 U.S.A.
                                      Tel: 718-972-5449
                                      Fax: 718-972-6307

www.UrimPublications.com

Library of Congress Cataloging-in-Publication Data
Names: Shuchat, Wilfred, author.
Title: Abraham and the challenge of faith according to the Midrash Rabbah /
    Rabbi Dr. Wilfred Shuchat.
Other titles: Midrash rabbah. Genesis XXXIX-LVII. English.
Description: First edition. | New York ; Jerusalem ; London : Urim Publications,
    [2017] | Includes bibliographical references.
Identifiers: LCCN 2017031025 | ISBN 9789655242737 (hardcover : alk.
    paper)
Subjects: LCSH: Abraham (Biblical patriarch)—In rabbinical literature. |
    Midrash rabbah. Genesis XXXIX-LVII. | Faith (Judaism)
Classification: LCC BM518.A2 S2017 58 | DDC 4206/296.1—dc23 LC record
    available at https://lccn.loc.gov/2017031025

*D*edicated to the seventieth anniversary of my rabbinate,

including as Rabbi Emeritus, at Congregation Shaar Hashomayim,

Westmount, Quebec, Canada.

CONTENTS

Midrash Rabbah follows the cycle of the Pentateuch. In my books, there are two titles, one of which is the name of the scriptural portion, with the other title hinting at some aspect of the content. My first book in this respect was *The Creation*. It did not have a subtitle because the word "creation" is self-explanatory to the first two chapters of the Pentateuch. My second volume was *The Garden of Eden*, and its subtitle was *The Struggle to be Human*. My third book was entitled *Noah*, with the subtitle of *The Failure of Man*. I am about to publish the fourth volume, which will be entitled *Abraham*, and the subtitle will be *The Challenge of Faith*.

Every person's life is affected by so many unpredictable forces. It was always my hope that when I retire from the Shaar Hashomayim congregation, my main effort would be dedicated to the study of Midrash. Publication never entered into my mind. It so happened, however, that I discovered a cousin whose business was publishing. When he read an excerpt from my Midrash preparation in English, he liked it and offered to publish it as early as possible. I told him that I would think about it. Unfortunately, he was overcome by a serious illness and left this world long before his time. Somehow or another, I and others felt that we wanted to do something in his memory, and it was that concern which determined my decision to publish my first book – that is *The Creation*. Publication turned out to be a good decision. When you realize that many others will read what you have written, you make a much stronger effort to be correct in language, punctuation, and whatever other element goes on the printed page.

The readers may have noticed that reference is made in the present document to the fact that I have just completed my seventieth year at Congregation Shaar Hashomayim. I was the active rabbi for 47 years, but since 1993, I retired with the title Rabbi Emeritus. For some people, certain dates in the calendar have tremendous meaning. I recall offering congratulations to a friend of mine who observed her 97th birthday; she thanked me for the good wishes but then added that this birthday would not be nearly as meaningful as the one three years from today, which would be her 100th birthday. I found it hard to understand that. I knew that at such moments, the birthday person receives a letter from the Queen. I knew of no other development. Probably, however, it was her personal intention to create a mammoth celebration which she could well afford and invite as many people as she wished. Unfortunately, she did not live very long after our conversation, and her hope was never fulfilled.

My own reaction to these special events is that the most important person is God. He decides how old we will be, and He decides whether we will have a long-time career in our profession or not. The celebration of this kind of anniversary, therefore, should be devoted entirely to an expression of thanksgiving in many areas.

The average book takes several years in order to compose and complete. This requires not only participants who share a loyalty but individuals who offer help beyond the call of duty.

I shall like to begin by thanking the publisher of my fourth book, Tzvi Mauer. He was tremendously interested in our publication, very strict in his demands, and very devoted to the highest principles in this kind of publication. I also wish to thank the editor, Batsheva Pomerantz, who also helped us very much to produce a volume of which we could be truly proud.

As well, I would like to thank Yosef Robinson, who has been with the latest literary project almost since its very beginning. He has been responsible for all the computer work that this particular volume demanded. He has offered many suggestions, some of which have been incorporated into this book, and in general he has made it become a better volume. I also wish to thank Yarom Pincovich for his continued interest.

I also wish to thank my son, Rabbi Bernard Raphael Shuchat. My son has become one of the great scholars of Judaica not only in Israel but wherever Jewish scholars find themselves. I wanted him to have the title of co-author, but he declined. Let me therefore thank him for writing the introduction to this volume and for doing all the rewriting that was necessary wherever corrections had to be made. As one who lives in Jerusalem, he was in close contact with our publisher, also based in Jerusalem, making the development of this volume so much more successful. Rabbi Raphael's publications in both Hebrew and English have been outstanding and more of them are on their way. I thank him with all my heart.

My rabbinate was centered in one city, Montreal, and one congregation, Shaar Hashomayim. Most rabbis do not have this good fortune and very often have to move from place to place, from community to community. My seventieth anniversary, therefore, acknowledges only one source, and that is Congregation Shaar Hashomayim of Westmount, Quebec. I wish to express my appreciation not only to the present generation of leadership, but to the generation before and to the second generation before this, with whom I worked in very close association. I am trying to prepare a detailed chronology of my seventy years at the Shaar, but it is taking longer than I had anticipated. When and if I complete this document, I shall send it first to the president and the board of trustees, and they will decide if it should be forwarded to others as well.

My thanks are directed not only to today's president, Claire Berger Fagen, but to all the presidents who preceded her. At the same time, I wish to acknowledge the spiritual leadership of the congregation. I wish to start by mentioning my predecessor, Rabbi Herman Abramowitz, whose rabbinate was close to fifty years at the Shaar Hashomayim and who enabled it to grow from a little synagogue to one of the largest and most important congregations in Canada. I also wish to acknowledge the present spiritual leadership of the congregation to whom all of us are indebted. This includes Rabbi Adam Scheier, Maharat Rachel Kohl Finegold, Cantor Gideon Zelermyer, Rabbi David Woolfson (the ritual director), Cantor Emeritus Sidney Dworkin, and Roï Azoulay (the music director). None of the above were with me when I was the official rabbi of the congregation, with the exception of Cantor Sidney Dworkin. We should now include Yossi Even-Hen, who will become ritual director when Rabbi Woolfson completes his retirement arrangements. We are very lucky to have this kind of religious talent in the spiritual leadership of the congregation and we extend to them every single measure of blessing.

I cannot allow these moments without including members of my family circle. I think of my late daughter Elizabeth, so full of talent, who was taken from us in the prime of her life. I think of my late dear wife Miriam, who transformed my life completely from the time we were together. My children – Margola Shuchat, Bryna and Joshua Landes,

Rabbi Raphael Shuchat – were all brought up within the circles of Shaar Hashomayim, and to this day, all of them, no matter where they live, have wonderful memories of growing up in Shaar Hashomayim.

One of the last requests of the publisher, was to go over the entire manuscript as quickly as possible, one more time. Rafi accepted to do the first half of the volume and I accepted to do the second half. Not only did I enjoy reading it, but I must admit my pleasure at the fact that there is so much Torah with the comments which I wrote and which I read at that moment. To be in a position to add holy thoughts to the remarkable spiritual literature of the Jewish people is an important achievement, and I hope that others will feel the same way. Let me now conclude with one of my favorite verses, ה' חפץ למען צדקו יגדיל תורה ויאדיר – *Hashem hafetz le-maan tzidko yagdil Torah ve-yaadir.* This is how the Hebrew should be understood: ה' חפץ למען צדקו של ישראל, שישראל תכבד ותשמור את התורה – *Hashem hafetz le-maan tzidko shel Yisrael, she-Yisrael tekhabed ve-tishmor et ha-Torah.* In other words, God wanted Israel to justify its existence by honoring the Torah and being honored by it.

INTRODUCTION:
ABRAHAM AND THE CHALLENGE OF FAITH

The midrashic material of this book is a commentary on the life of Abraham. The text which provokes the commentary is taken from two scriptural portions. In Hebrew, the first portion is called *Lekh Lekha*, which means "leave," as in to leave your land and your birthplace and go forward to establish a new community in a place which God will choose. We will read about the youth of Abraham, his military victories, and his leadership qualities. His success was such that communities, even those who he defeated, wanted him to be their king. He, however, declined this invitation.

The second scriptural portion is called *Vayera* in Hebrew, which means "to appear," and it deals with three visitors who came to see Abraham to comfort him on his recent decision to achieve circumcision. We will learn later on that these visitors were angelic beings who were dressed in human form. One of them as indicated was meant to comfort Abraham. The second was intended to bring about the destruction of Sodom and Gomorrah. The third was to inform Abraham and Sarah that they would be blessed with a son. One of the exciting aspects of this scriptural portion is that it deals with one of the most famous and most complicated scriptural stories, namely the binding of Isaac. I was wondering how this remarkable story would be handled by the Midrash. Would it enlighten its readers or would it make the behavior of Abraham even more enigmatic than it was? There is much that can be learned from these messages which I will summarize briefly. In the first midrashic comments, God is quoted as telling Abraham that it was not his intention to slaughter his son but only to have him go through the motions of the sacrificial offering. It turns out that he wanted the world to know that slaughtering life in the name of religion is a terrible thing. He even told Abraham that when he gave the commandment for Abraham to slaughter his son, he ordered his special angel to watch

Abraham carefully so that if Abraham did not properly understand the message, the angel would intervene and stop him from doing the wrong thing, as actually happened.

There are several other midrashic commentaries which are also of great interest. In the biblical story, Abraham's son, Isaac, says to his father, "We now have the fire and the wood but where is the lamb for the slaughter?" This is how the Midrash answers that question: "God will provide the lamb, and if he does not, you will be the lamb for the slaughter." Isaac listened, and the verse then continues "The two walked together," which means that Isaac accepted what his father had said. The Midrash then continues in a similar vein with Isaac saying to his father: "Dear father, Because of your age, the knife may not be as firmly held as it should be, so I would like you to be very careful and tie me tightly so that the pain will be less." So here we have the remarkable situation where the Jewish people have not one but two leaders capable of the most self-sacrificing actions because of what they were convinced was the commandment of God to them. We now know, of course, that such a great sacrifice was never required of them. But the fact that they were prepared for this ordeal is most exceptional.

We now come to a situation where something should be said because of what is missing from the story and not included, whether in the Midrash or in the actual biblical text. How come Abraham and Sarah, who not only loved each other, but were blessed with the birth of their son Isaac, did not discuss together the Divine commandment to slaughter their son? They discussed everything else with each other; in fact, God went out of his way to inform Abraham that whatever Sarah wanted was to be followed. Why, then, did this conversation not take place? Let me suggest at least one possibility. Suppose Abraham had informed Sarah that God wanted him to slaughter his favorite son, whose birth in their old ages had been arranged by God. Her response would certainly have been negative. She would probably have said something to the effect that she would rather die herself and have Abraham die with her rather than have anything bad of this sort happen to their son Isaac. Abraham, then, would have had to choose between what God wanted him to do and what Sarah wanted him to do, a terrible decision. However, Abraham knew about these possibilities – choosing between Sarah and God – and he knew that he would have to make this decision alone.

MIDRASHIC THINKING
AND THE USE OF SYMBOLISM

Written by Rabbi Dr. B. Raphael Shuchat

Rabbinic thinking in general does not use only the regular modes of logical patterns as described by the Greeks. Aristotle argued that all rational thought is based on syllogistic patterns. This reductionist description helped create the basis of modern theories of logic but also closed the door to other modes of thought. The Babylonian Talmud uses logical patterns in its analysis of halakhic problems but does not shy away from symbolic thinking as well. This can be seen in the inductive method it uses to create categories. Greek logic is based on the deductive method. A general rule is established from which one deduces the particulars. For example: If all men are mortal and Socrates is a man, then Socrates must be mortal too. The problem with deductive thinking is establishing the general rule. How do I know if all men are mortal? Have I met every man? But after meeting a certain amount of men I conclude that the general characteristic is "most probably correct." However, to reach the rule, I had to induce from all the individual men I met who were mortal that this must be a general principle. This means that even deductive logic, which goes from the universal to the particular, begins with an inductive method from the particular to the universal.

In Talmudic thinking, the particular, therefore, is used as the universal rule. For example, there are four categories of damages in the Tractate of *Baba Kama*, but they are referred to in the particular form: a trampling ox, a pit, a devouring ox, and fire (Mishnah, *Baba Kama* 1:1). These are four particular examples that when analyzed, develop into multiple universal categories of damage. Another example: "If an egg is laid on Yom Tov," there is an argument between Beit Shammai and Beit Hillel about whether it is allowed for consumption on the Yom Tov or not. (*Beit-*

zah 1:1) The particular case begins both the discussion of *muktzeh* and the preparing from the Sabbath to Yom Tov, representing two general principles from one particular example. In other words, the particular is substituted for the general categories and also demonstrates their use at the same time. Sometimes the Mishnah will say: "This is the general rule" (*zeh haklal*, see Mishnah *Sukkah* 1:4 and *Berakhot* 6:7), and then one can ask whether the general rule now adds to the original rule since we already know that there is a general rule from the particular cases.

We can therefore say that the particular case, in rabbinic halakhic thought, is a symbolic representation of the general rule.

In midrashic thinking as in aggadic literature of the Talmud, the use of symbolism and metaphoric language is more common and sometimes taken to an extreme. Maimonides in his introduction to *Helek* (commentary to the Mishnah *Sanhedrin*, chapter 11) argues that this is the way of the wise in general to use metaphors to explain difficult issues which cannot always be explained in regular logical thinking. Maimonides quotes the beginning of Proverbs which states: "To understand analogies and hints, the words of the wise and their riddles" (Proverbs 1:6).

Maimonides brings examples of metaphoric passages in the Bible, such as, Ecclesiastes, chapter 12; II Kings 23:15–17, 20–22, concerning the warriors of King David and his request for water from the cistern of Bethlehem. Even the Song of Songs is a metaphor according to Rabbi Akiba. For Maimonides, the metaphoric languages is utilized by *Midrashim* that are describing metaphysical issues such as: God, the human soul, prayer, the afterlife, etc. However, it is possible that this is also an extension of the rabbinic mode of thinking of using symbols and particulars representing general ideas. Let me begin by examples from aggadic material and then proceed to the Midrash: The Talmud says that Moses was ten cubits tall (about 5 meters, *Berakhot* 54b). This it deduces from the fact that the verse says, "He [Moses] spread the covering over the Tabernacle" (Exodus 40:19). Now since the Tabernacle is ten cubits high the Talmud assumes that Moses was that tall as well. This seems puzzling since it is possible that Moses used a ladder. In addition, if Moses was so exceptionally tall, why wasn't this mentioned in the Bible as was the case with King Saul (I Samuel, 9:2) and Og the King of Bashan? In addition, the Talmud assumes that Pharaoh of the Exodus story was only one cubit high (about half a meter, *Moed Katan* 18a). This of course would seem quite amusing in every case where we are told that Moses and Pharaoh met. The Maharal of Prague, who tends to follow the Maimonidean guideline of the metaphoric language of the Aggadah, argues that these descriptions are to be seen as metaphors. Moses who was the greatest of prophets, reaching the epitome of human spiritual height, should have been ten cubits high, he states. Since ten represents a complete entity and therefore the universe was created in Ten Utterances and the Torah was given in Ten Utterances. Therefore, spiritually, Moses was ten cubits, however physically it is possible that he was just a bit taller.

The idea of Pharaoh being one cubit tall can also be explained as a metaphor. The Talmud in *Eruvin* states that one can carry up to four cubits in a public area on the Sabbath since this is considered one's domain. Why four cubits? Since the average person is three cubits tall according to the Talmud, and when they lie down they can extend their arm an additional cubit beyond their head, therefore, one takes up four cubits of space. In Chassidic literature, this is seen as metaphoric. The three cubits represent thought, emotions, and action. The higher cubit, beyond the head, represents faith, as is said about Moses in the battle with Amalek, "When Moses raised his hands the Israelites prevailed" (Exodus 17:11). Therefore, his hands were held up by Aaron and Hur and 'were faithful until morning'" (ibid., 12). Pharaoh is called "one cubit" since he obviously lacked faith in God – "Who is God that I shall listen to Him." He lacked reason since it's obvious that if God brought the plagues on him through Moses that this could continue until he complied. He lacked emotions as well since Moses told him that God would smite all the firstborn including his own son and he refused to comply and went to sleep that night (Rashi on Exodus 12:30). So all that was left was the action in which he constantly denied the Israelites their freedom. The metaphors here are subtle – since it is possible that Moses was tall and that Pharaoh was short. However, the extreme language of the Aggadah, making Moses unreasonably tall and Pharaoh unusually short, beg for a metaphoric interpretation. Let us now proceed to the Midrash at hand.

Introduction to the First Midrash

The first Midrash about Abraham in this book (Chapter 39:1) is an opening idea (*ptihta*). "Rabbi Isaac opened." Right away there is a parable about a man who sees a *birah doleket* translated by Soncino as "a building on fire." The man wonders whether there is an owner of the building and the owner reveals himself. Since the verse interpreted is "And God spoke to Abraham," we understand that God reveals Himself to Abraham after Abraham pondered God's existence. The term *birah doleket* is ambiguous lending itself to multiple interpretations. *Birah* literally means "a mansion" or "a palace" – that is, a very large and unique house. *Doleket*, meaning "burning," is usually used in reference to candles. Maimonides interprets this Midrash to mean that Abraham saw the sun and moon and stars and all the wonders of the universe and wondered if they could exist without a creator. Then God appeared to him and told him that he was the creator (Maimonides, *Hilkhot Avodah Zarah* 1:3 and *Guide* 2:39). He interprets this Midrash portraying Abraham as a seeker of God who found God through an intellectual pursuit. Hasdai Crescas, the fourteenth century critic of Aristotle, claims that intellectual reasoning alone cannot bring one to faith. Therefore, God must reveal Himself to Abraham, for him to have real certainty (*Ohr Hashem*, Maamar 1, Klal 3, chapter 6). In the nineteenth century, R. Yehuda Aryeh Leib of Gur interpreted *doleket* in the *biblical* sense, meaning "to chase or run." In other words, Abraham saw that all of the world was running after some sense of meaning subconsciously. They were looking for that Divine spark in man which is at the spiritual epicenter of the soul (*Sfat Emet, Parshat Lekh Lekha*, drasha of 1872). My father interprets: "the house was burning" to mean that the world was becoming morally corrupt and Abraham could not believe that God would forsake His world and leave it to disintegrate morally and socially. At that moment, God gave Abraham the task of beginning the Jewish people in the land of Canaan. We now have one Midrash with four interpretations. The Chassidic interpretation seems farthest from the simple meaning of the words but not so far from the idea the Midrash wants to portray. The metaphor of the burning or the lit up palace is the idea of Abraham pondering the world and human life. God's revelation to him is the beginning of the answer for him and for mankind.

א ויאמר ה' אל אברם לך לך מארצך וגו'. ר' יצחק פתח (תהלים מה): שמעי בת וראי והטי אזנך
ושכחי עמך ובית אביך. אמר רבי יצחק: משל לאחד שהיה עובר ממקום למקום וראה בירה
אחת דולקת. אמר: תאמר שהבירה זו בלא מנהיג? הציץ עליו בעל הבירה, אמר לו: אני הוא
בעל הבירה. כך לפי שהיה אבינו אברהם אומר: תאמר שהעולם הזה בלא מנהיג? הציץ עליו
הקב"ה ואמר לו: אני הוא בעל העולם (שם) ויתאו המלך יפיך כי הוא אדוניך ויתאו המלך יפיך
ליפותיך בעולם והשתחוי לו, הוי, ויאמר ה' אל אברם:

1. NOW THE LORD SAID UNTO ABRAM: GET THEE OUT OF THY COUNTRY,
ETC. (GEN. 12:1). R. ISAAC COMMENCED HIS DISCOURSE WITH, HEARKEN,
O DAUGHTER, AND CONSIDER, AND INCLINE THINE EAR; FORGET ALSO
THINE OWN PEOPLE, AND THY FATHER'S HOUSE (PS. 45:11).

The first question is based on the actual biblical text as has been quoted, namely *lekh lekha me-artzekha*. The question is why in this particular order? Should it not have been first to leave your father's house then the various words that continue and finally you leave your country? The answer is that the verse has to be understood as being written in terms of forgetfulness. When you move from your homeland, first you forget your country, then your birthplace, and the very last thing is your father's house because it is so deep in your mentality. (*Tiferet Tzion*)

Said R. Isaac: This may be compared to a man who was traveling from place to place when he saw a building in flames. Is it possible that the building lacks a person to look after it?, he wondered. The owner of the building looked out and said, "I am the owner of the building." Similarly, because Abraham our father said, "Is it conceivable that the world is without a guide?" The Holy One, blessed be He, looked out and said to him, "I am the Guide, the Sovereign of the Universe." So shall the king desire thy beauty (Ps. 45:12): i.e., to make thee glorious in the world. For He is thy Lord, and do homage unto Him (45:12): hence, THE LORD SAID UNTO ABRAM: GET THEE, etc.

The question can be raised that Abram surely knew that God was the

25

Sovereign of the Universe. Why then was he so amazed when he saw the palace abandoned? The answer was that it was not the abandonment of the palace that bothered him, but the fact that it was burning. How could God allow the world to burn?

—

Seed Thoughts

The main question in this and some of the following Midrashim is why was it necessary for Abram to be ordered to leave his homeland and go to the Land of Israel. The answer is, to quote the parable, because the palace was burning. It was not merely the fact that the environment was hostile. It was always hostile to good people who wanted to live ethical lives. But this time the world was burning, which meant that good people had no chance to remain alive. There was perpetual harassment. The best example was perhaps when Abraham himself was forced by Nimrod to jump into a burning fire. Abraham had to leave, not only to save his mission in life, but to save his life and the lives of his family circle.

—

Additional Commentary

The purpose of these Midrashim

One of the main points being raised by the Midrash is why it was necessary for God to get Abraham to leave his home in order to fulfill his special mission if, as we learn later, his wife converted the women and he converted the men, why could he not have done so in his homeland? Why was that dependent on being in Eretz Israel? Many of the Midrashim of this chapter attempt to answer this question in various ways. (Aryeh Mirkin)

PARASHAH THIRTY-NINE, *Midrash Two*

ב ויאמר ה' אל אברם.

AS WAS INDICATED EARLIER, THE PURPOSE OF THE FIRST SEVERAL MI-
DRASHIM OF *PARSHAT LEKH LEKHA* HAVE TO DO WITH THE QUESTION
WHY IT WAS NECESSARY FOR GOD TO REMOVE ABRAHAM FROM HIS NA-
TIVE LAND. THE FIRST REASON, AS INDICATED ABOVE, WAS DUE TO THE
IMPLACABLE HOSTILITY OF HIS ENVIRONMENT. WE WILL NOW READ
ABOUT A SECOND REASON.

רבי ברכיה פתח (שיר א): לריח שמניך טובים שמן תורק שמך. אמר רבי ברכיה, למה היה
אברהם אבינו דומה? לצלוחית של אפופילסימון מוקפת צמיד פתיל ומונחת בזווית ולא היה
ריחו נודף. כיון שהיתה מיטלטלת היה ריחו נודף. כך, אמר הקדוש ברוך הוא לאברהם אבינו,
טלטל עצמך ממקום למקום ושמך מתגדל בעולם:

2. R. BEREKIAH COMMENCED: THINE OINTMENTS HAVE A GOODLY FRA-
GRANCE (SONG 1:3). SAID R. BEREKIAH: WHAT DID ABRAHAM RESEMBLE?
A PHIAL OF MYRRH CLOSED WITH A TIGHT-FITTING LID AND LYING IN
A CORNER, SO THAT ITS FRAGRANCE WAS NOT DISSEMINATED; AS SOON
AS IT WAS TAKEN UP, HOWEVER, ITS FRAGRANCE WAS DISSEMINATED.
SIMILARLY, THE HOLY ONE, BLESSED BE HE, SAID TO ABRAHAM: "TRAVEL
FROM PLACE TO PLACE, AND THY NAME WILL BECOME GREAT IN THE
WORLD": HENCE, GET THEE, ETC.

In this text, there are two elements that are preventing Abraham's
perfume from being noticed. The first reason is due to the fact that it is
surrounded by a tight-fitting lid. Secondly, because it was in a corner –
where even the good perfume that escaped from it could not be carried
by the wind. Similarly, in the case of Abraham, there were two liabilities
that prevented him from bringing his good perfume to the world, so to
speak. One problem is that he was outside the Land of Israel, where it
was not possible for him to receive any element of prophecy. Secondly,
whatever influence he may have had, there was no one in that world
upon whom he can bestow that influence.

Seed Thoughts

So far two motivations have been given as to why the decision was made to persuade Abraham to leave his native land and go to Israel. The first was the hostility of his environment. This was a very extreme hostility described by the words, "burning of the palace," the point where Abraham's physical life was in danger. The second motivation was internal. It had to do with the spiritual quality of Abraham himself. The beautiful message of justice, peace, and the love of God, which Abraham promulgated and advocated. Both of these elements are relevant today. The State of Israel may not be ideal, but is far more conducive to the Jewish spiritual life than any other place. As for the moral and ethical heritage of Abraham, it is the main element in what we describe as the Jewish way of life anywhere and everywhere in the world.

~

Additional Commentary

The power of the Land of Israel

There are many difficulties that even someone like Abraham had in approaching God for His direction. This was not so in the Land of Israel. From the moment he arrived to the Land of Israel, he was able to build an altar and call upon the name of God. This began his mission to the world. As for the expression, "Your name will become great," the reference is to the possibility of creating converts that would join the spiritual family of Abraham.

PARASHAH THIRTY-NINE, *Midrash Three*

ג ויאמר ה' אל אברם.

THE REASON WHY WE ARE CONTINUING TO STUDY THIS VERSE IS NOT
ONLY BECAUSE OF THE QUESTION OF WHY GOD DECIDED TO REMOVE
ABRAHAM FROM HIS PLACE OF BIRTH. ANOTHER QUESTION TO BE ASKED
IS WHY IT HAPPENED AT THIS PARTICULAR TIME.

רבי ברכיה פתח (שיר ח): אחות לנו קטנה ושדים אין לה וגו'. אחות לנו קטנה, זה אברהם
שאיחה את כל באי העולם.

3. R BEREKIAH COMMENCED: WE HAVE A LITTLE SISTER – *AHOT* . . . (SONG
8:8), THIS REFERS TO ABRAHAM, WHO UNITED (*IHAH*) THE WHOLE
WORLD FOR US.

R. Berekiah was looking for a verse that would explain Abraham's
preeminence. In his opinion, the verse in the Song of Songs was spoken
by the Holy One, blessed be He, to His angelic associates to explain the
role of Abraham. The Hebrew word אחות – *ahot* is based on the word
ihah – "to unite or "to bring together." That was perceived to be Abraham's role in the world – to unite his generation in the service of God.

בר קפרא אמר: כזה שהוא מאחה את הקרע. קטנה, שעד שהוא קטן, היה מסגל מצוות
ומעשים טובים. ושדים אין לה, לא הניקוהו, לא למצוות ומעשים טובים. מה נעשה לאחותנו
ביום שידובר בה, ביום שגזר עליו נמרוד לירד לתוך כבשן האש. אם חומה היא נבנה עליה,
אם מעמיד דברים כחומה, יבנה עליה. ואם דלת היא נצור עליה אם דל הוא במצוות
ובמעשים טובים, נצור עליה לוח ארז. מה הצורה הזו אינה אלא לשעה, כך אין אני מתקיים
עליו אלא לשעה. אמר לפניו, רבון העולמים, אני חומה, מעמיד אני דברי. ושדי כמגדלות, זה
חנניה מישאל ועזריה. אז הייתי בעיניו כמוצאת שלום, שנכנס בשלום ויצא בשלום:

BAR KAPPARA OBSERVED: LIKE A PERSON WHO SEWS A RENT TOGETHER.
"LITTLE": EVEN WHILE YOUNG, HE STORED UP PIOUS ACTS AND GOOD
DEEDS. AND SHE HATH NO BREASTS (SONG 8:8): NO BREASTS SUCKLED
HIM IN PIETY OR GOOD DEEDS. WHAT SHALL WE DO FOR OUR SISTER
IN THE DAY WHEN SHE SHALL BE SPOKEN FOR (8:8), I.E., ON THE DAY
WHEN THE WICKED NIMROD ORDERED HIM TO BE CAST INTO THE FIERY
FURNACE? IF SHE BE A WALL, WE WILL BUILD UPON HER (8:9): IF HE
RESISTS [NIMROD] LIKE A WALL, HE [GOD] WILL BUILD UP [A DEFENSE]

FOR HIM. AND IF SHE BE A DOOR (*DELET*), WE WILL ENCLOSE (*NAZUR*)
HER WITH BOARDS OF CEDAR (8:9): IF HE IS POOR (*DAL*) IN PIETY AND
NOBLE DEEDS, WE WILL ENCLOSE (*NAZUR*) HER WITH BOARDS OF CEDAR,
AND JUST AS A DRAWING (*ZURAH*) [ON BOARDS] IS ONLY TEMPORARY, SO
WILL I PROTECT HIM ONLY FOR A TIME. SAID HE [ABRAHAM] TO HIM:
"SOVEREIGN OF THE UNIVERSE! I AM A WALL (8:10): I STAND AS FIRM AS
A WALL. AND MY BREASTS LIKE THE TOWERS THEREOF (8:10): MY SONS
ARE HANANIAH, MISHAEL, AND AZARIAH. THEN WAS I IN HIS EYES AS
ONE THAT FOUND PEACE" (8:10). HE ENTERED [THE FIERY FURNACE] IN
PEACE AND LEFT IT UNSCATHED: HENCE, NOW THE LORD SAID UNTO
ABRAM: GET THEE.

Bar Kappara points out that Abraham's sewing together was not a new
thing. The people did have a form of unity until idol worship took over.
That was the rent in the garment. Abraham's role was to try to restore
the spirit of unity that had disappeared. Bar Kappara then interpreted
the various phrases in the verse. The idea of a little sister emphasizes the
word "little", in the case of the time when Abraham was himself little,
he was already engaged in good deeds and fulfilled obligations. On the
other hand, others in that generation did not have such opportunities
and learned nothing from their peers. That is the interpretation of, "As
she had no breasts."

Bar Kappara now places the entire event in the context of the decree
of Nimrod to throw Abraham into the furnace for having destroyed his
father's idols. This answers the question as to why the command of לך
לך "leave your land" was ordered at this time, namely, after the ordeal
of Nimrod and the fiery furnace. As for the concepts of wall and door,
the interpretation is as follows: If Abraham is true to his Divine mission and acts like a חומה, wall, protecting God, he will be rewarded with
deliverance from Nimrod. If he is a דלת, he is דל, meaning "weak" (in
observance of the commandments), He will help him temporarily in
the hope that he would eventually return to his spiritual mission. The
Midrash concludes with Abraham's assurance that he is like a wall in
defense of God.

Seed Thoughts

It is very difficult for a modern person to follow some of the midrashic interpretations that are based on verses from the Song of Songs. The Song of Songs is a magnificent literary document. It deals with love between a man and woman on the highest level possible. It deals with love as between children and parents. Its verses and thoughts have to do with beauty, modesty, and morality. It also contains many manifestations of sexuality and even sexual passion depending on how you interpret certain verses. All in all, it is a most compelling and thought-provoking book. To the authors of the Midrash, however, the Song of Songs represented the love between God and Israel. It represented nothing else. The way they read the text, there was no sexuality in the book. As for sexual passion, they would not have dreamed of looking upon it as part of Divine literature. A modern person would find it very difficult to identify "my little sister" as referring to Abraham, and what we would call, various other manifestations of sexuality as referring to other biblical characters who are involved in the love of God and Israel.

It may be difficult for us to adjust to these various elements, but we should understand that our cultural backgrounds are different. In the Western world we see things very differently than the midrashic world of the second and third centuries. Nevertheless, we have to understand that there is this cultural difference, that it should be accepted and understood. It should not be looked upon as a source for criticism in any direction. This is how the Sages interpret it, and if you will, how we may interpret certain sections. But all of us are aware that this involves the love of God for Israel, and the love of Israel for God, all of which we cherish immensely.

Additional Commentary

Abraham uniting the people

What does it mean when it says Abraham united his community? It means that he was able to get his community to accept one religious faith. This is in contrast to the worshippers of idols who established idols any place they wanted. Before Abraham's arrival on the scene, there was a great separation, between the people and God. When Abraham came

to the fore, he closed that separation. He did his best to gather and motivate the doing of commandments and the doing of good deeds.

PARASHAH THIRTY-NINE, *Midrash Four*

ד ויאמר ה' אל אברם לך לך (קהלת ז) החכמה תעוז לחכם מעשרה שליטים אשר היו בעיר.
מעשרה דורות שמנה ועד אברהם ומכולם לא דברתי עם אחד, אלא עמך, ויאמר ה' אל
אברם לך לך:

4. WISDOM MAKETH A WISE MAN STRONGER THAN TEN RULERS (ECCL.
7:19): THIS REFERS TO ABRAHAM, [WHOM WISDOM MADE STRONGER]
THAN THE TEN GENERATIONS FROM NOAH TO ABRAHAM; OUT OF ALL
OF THEM I SPOKE TO THEE ALONE, AS IT IS WRITTEN: NOW THE LORD
SAID UNTO ABRAHAM.

The use of the term "ruler" refers to the head of that generation, whose
names are listed in Scripture as well as in the Ethics of the Fathers. The
use of the word "city," עיר, refers either to the world as experienced by
that particular generation or the environment in which they lived.

—

Seed Thoughts I

The preliminary Midrashim that we have just studied deal with the
question of why God persuaded Abraham to leave his birthplace.
Various reasons were given. Our present Midrash leaps over all of those
arguments to the fundamental question of communication. The important thing is not what God said to Abraham, but the important thing is
that He had said anything at all. The wondrous experience or miracle
was that God communicated with a human being. In Abraham's case
this has not been done since the era of Noah. This discovery of God
communicating with man puts the Abraham story on an entirely different level. Abraham in the biblical story now becomes a most important
person to watch because he will be communicating with God on more
than one occasion.

—

Seed Thoughts II

When I first came to the Shaar Hashomayim synagogue in Montreal, a remarkable debate took place over several evenings. It started at a Kiddush discussion on the Sabbath where the speaker made the point that it was not God Who had chosen Abraham but that it was Abraham who had chosen God. You would not think that this kind of subject matter would interest the average person. But hundreds of people came to this debate over an entire evening. Did God choose Abraham or did Abraham choose God? The truth of the matter is that it does not really matter from the spiritual point of view, and no special meaning is attached to the question as to which side of the argument is right. What has drawn me to this Midrash like a magnet is a statement by the *Tiferet Tzion,* quoted as an Additional Commentary below, that it was pretty obvious that it was Abraham who had chosen God. The Midrash mentions that he possessed not only special Divine wisdom, but also special Torah wisdom. Nobody before him possessed these remarkable attributes which he must have had since his early childhood, because his acknowledgment of God began in his early years.

Whereas in the ultimate sense, it may not really matter who chose who, there is a certain power to the idea that Abraham chose God, because it would mean that others can do the same. Furthermore, we now have a most remarkable interpretation of לֶךְ לְךָ (*lekh lekha*). It is not just a matter of communication in which God communicated with Abraham and did not do so with any of the other leaders of the ten generations. It means that by saying לֶךְ לְךָ, God affirmed Abraham's choice of Him and He responded by making Abraham His disciple, the carrier of His mission and his Tower representative. The preposition לְךָ, therefore, is no longer superfluous, but is the key interpretation that Abraham was accepted to be God's human partner on Earth.

———

Additional Commentary

What wisdom can do

The preposition לְךָ in the expression לֶךְ לְךָ is superfluous. That is why the Midrash brings forward for a consideration the verse that begins, "Wisdom makes a wise man stronger than ten rulers." It can now be explained. The verse mentions that wisdom is greater than the rulers of the ten generations between Noah and Abraham. The explanation is that even though God sometimes requires talking to the rulers so that they should be properly advised on how they should rule, in this particular relationship, God spoke to none of them because they were not properly prepared with good deeds that might eventually prepare them for prophecy. But in the case of Abraham, even though he was not a ruler, he merited prophecy as a result of his special wisdom, because from the very beginning he recognized and acknowledged the Holy One, blessed be He, as a result of his special wisdom. That is what the text meant when it said, "Wisdom makes a man stronger," which means that wisdom is a power or strength to the wise man, far greater than the power that ten rulers can bring. The best proof of this is the life of Abraham, and it is in this respect that God said to Abraham, "Go to Canaan and there you will be a prophet and a guide to life and it will not be difficult for you, because after all, Shem, the son of Noah, was king of Jerusalem for a while and, therefore, he would have the possibility of being a prophet." Therefore, He said לֶךְ לְךָ to you, for there will there be communication between God and man, all because of your special wisdom. (*Tiferet Tzion*)

PARASHAH THIRTY-NINE, *Midrash Five*

ה ר' עזריה פתח (ירמיה נא): רפינו את בבל ולא נרפאת עזבוה ונלך איש לארצו. רפינו את בבל, בדור אנוש. ולא נרפאתה, בדור המבול. עזבוה, בדור הפלגה, ונלך איש לארצו, ויאמר ה' אל אברם לך לך:

5. R. AZARIAH COMMENCED: WE WOULD HAVE HEALED BABYLON, BUT SHE WAS NOT HEALED (JER. 51:9). WE WOULD HAVE HEALED BABYLON – IN THE GENERATION OF ENOSH. BUT SHE WAS NOT HEALED – IN THE GENERATION OF THE FLOOD. FORSAKE HER, AND LET US GO EVERY ONE INTO HIS COUNTRY (51:9), AS IT IS WRITTEN: NOW THE LORD SAID UNTO ABRAM: GET THEE, ETC.

Seed Thoughts

The text indicates that Babylon, which was the great political and military power of its day, was guilty of many crimes that warranted its punishment. Its behavior during the time of Enosh merited a severe punishment. Its behavior at the time of the Food had merited great punishment. Finally, due to its behavior at the time of the separation, the era of the Tower of Babel, it was punished, though in a way that would enable it to survive.

How do we account for this kind of behavior? In Midrash, it is easier to ask the question than to motivate the proper answer. Nevertheless, let us attempt to find a response, which although may not be the final answer, may help us resolve the problem.

Babylon was the great power of its day. Not only politically and military, it was also technologically superior. Some of the plans that the Midrash and other writings describe entail tremendous technical knowledge. If a power like Babylon were to repent, or at any rate accept the moral law, it would be a tremendous achievement for the Holy One, blessed be He, in allowing the human being to make a choice, which is what freedom is all about. When, however, in the time of Enosh, Babylon did not repent, the Holy One, blessed be He, held back the punishment in the hope that at the next crisis Babylon would behave in a better way. When at the time of the Flood, Babylon was as guilty as anyone else, the Almighty held back again. To punish a great power like Babylon would weaken the moral fiber of the whole human race. When the repentance did not happen, then the Holy One, blessed be He, threw all restraint aside, and in the story of the Tower of Babel, the description of the punishment meted out to the world is in great detail.

Parashah Thirty-Nine, *Midrash Six*

ו רבי עזריה משום רבי אחא פתח (תהלים מה): אהבת צדק ותשנא רשע על כן משחך אלהים
אלהיך שמן ששון מחבריך. רבי עזריה פתר קרייה באברהם: בשעה שעמד אברהם אבינו
לבקש רחמים על הסדומים, מה כתיב: תמן (בראשית יח) חלילה לך מעשות כדבר הזה להמית
צדיק עם רשע והיה וגו'. א"ר אחא: נשבעת ואמרת שאין אתה מביא מבול לעולם, ומה אתה
מערים על השבועה אתמהא? מבול של מים אין אתה מביא, מבול אש אתה מביא? א"כ
לא יצאת ידי השבועה. אמר רבי לוי: השופט כל הארץ לא יעשה משפט? אם עולם אתה
מבקש, אין דין. ואם דין אתה מבקש, אין עולם. ומה אתה תופש חבל בתרין ראשין, את בעי
עלמא, ובעי דינא. סב לך חדא מנייהו, ואם לית את מוותיר, ציבחר לית עלמא יכול קאים.
א"ל הקב"ה: אברהם אהבת צדק ותשנא רשע וגו', מחבריך מהו? מחבריך מנח ועד אצלך י'
דורות, ומכלם לא דברתי עם אחד מהם, אלא עמך:

6. R. AZARIAH COMMENCED IN R. AHA'S NAME THUS: THOU HAST LOVED
RIGHTEOUSNESS, AND HATED WICKEDNESS, ETC. (PS. 45:8). R. AZARIAH
IN R. AHA'S NAME REFERRED THE VERSE TO OUR FATHER ABRAHAM.
WHEN ABRAHAM OUR FATHER STOOD TO PLEAD FOR MERCY FOR THE
SODOMITES, WHAT IS WRITTEN THERE? THAT BE FAR FROM THEE TO DO
AFTER THIS MANNER (GEN. 18:25). R. AHA EXPLAINED THIS: THOU HAST
SWORN NOT TO BRING A DELUGE UPON THE WORLD. WOULDST THOU
EVADE THINE OATH! NOT A DELUGE OF WATER WILT THOU BRING BUT
A DELUGE OF FIRE? THEN THOU HAST NOT BEEN TRUE TO THINE OATH.
R. LEVI COMMENTED: SHALT NOT THE JUDGE OF ALL THE EARTH DO
JUSTLY (18:25)? IF THOU DESIREST THE WORLD TO ENDURE, THERE CAN
BE NO ABSOLUTE JUSTICE, WHILE IF THOU DESIREST ABSOLUTE JUSTICE
THE WORLD CANNOT ENDURE, YET THOU WOULDST HOLD THE CORD
BY BOTH ENDS, DESIRING BOTH THE WORLD AND ABSOLUTE JUSTICE.
UNLESS THOU FORGOEST A LITTLE, THE WORLD CANNOT ENDURE. SAID
THE HOLY ONE, BLESSED BE HE, TO ABRAHAM: "THOU HAST LOVED
RIGHTEOUSNESS, AND HATED WICKEDNESS; THEREFORE GOD, THY
GOD, HATH ANOINTED THEE WITH THE OIL OF GLADNESS ABOVE THY
FELLOWS (PS. 45:8): FROM NOAH UNTIL THEE WERE TEN GENERATIONS,
AND OUT OF ALL OF THEM I SPOKE WITH THEE ALONE."

Seed Thoughts

If I were speaking in public, I would tell the audience that on the one hand I am going to share with them one or the outstanding Midrashim that I have ever studied. But I am also going to tell them that they will not like what they hear. Whereas many of the teachings relating to God and Abraham are full of hope and aspiration, this one is realistic. It hits the very gut of the human being and fills us, not only with hope, but with trepidation and fear.

Consider the following: We are dealing with what at first glance appears to be one of the most beautiful verses in all of Scripture. Shall not the Judge of the world do justly? At the end of this commentary, I will repeat this beautiful sentence with a different punctuation and you will then see what the Midrash has done to this verse.

The first point raised by the sages is that God promised that never again will the floodgates be opened to destroy the world. But now look at what is happening. Sodom and Gomorrah are about to be destroyed. How could the Almighty contradict Himself? You might suggest that God meant that He would never use a flood to destroy the world, but the use of fire might be alright. That is the kind of verbal trickery that human beings use. But surely God meant that He would not destroy the entire world because of the behavior of some. Furthermore, the verse says that God should act justly. What do we mean by justly? Since we are talking about God, this must be a reference to absolute justice. Human beings can tolerate a justice less than absolute, but surely not God. Abraham himself says, "Should the innocent suffer with the guilty?" The answer can only be yes because the innocent with the guilty, the children did suffer with the old and absolute justice did not prevail. You might then add, how can absolute justice prevail when we are dealing with human beings who are not capable of living in terms of absolute justice? Either we have absolute justice and forget about the human being and the human race and the possibility of peace and compassion with justice, or we have a world where justice is not absolute and human beings have to make do with righteousness that has to compromise with compassion, mercy, and humility.

The world cannot have it both ways and God Himself cannot have it both ways. Abraham's rhetorical question was, "Shall not the Judge of all the earth do justly?" The analysis of the Midrash and the startling conclusion is no, the Judge of all the earth shall not do justly because He cannot by the very nature of the conditions on the basis of which men and women were created and given a Torah.

———

Additional Commentary

Thou hath sworn not to bring a deluge

In the light of the promise not to destroy to the world, how can You justify breaking the promise in connection with Sodom and Gomorrah? You have desecrated a sacred promise. How can that possibly be allowed to stand? (Aryeh Mirkin)

If Thou desirest the world to endure

Shall not the Judge of all the earth do justice? The truth is that the Judge of all the earth cannot do absolute justice. Surely, You do not wish to destroy all the earth, but rather to judge it. Therefore, you cannot do absolute justice because the world is not capable of sustaining itself by these absolute principles. How can You pull a rope by both ends? You seem to want a world and also absolute justice. This is like pulling a rope by both ends.

This is very similar to other expressions that can be found in rabbinic writings. For example, in Tractate *Ketubbot* 58b, it says, "break the jar but preserve the wine." Or, "cut off the head and make sure it does not die." You have to choose one of these alternatives and only one. If You do not give in on any one of these alternatives, there is no possibility for the world to survive. (Aryeh Mirkin)

PARASHAH THIRTY-NINE, *Midrash Seven*

ז ויאמר ה' אל אברם לך לך

THIS IS ONE OF A SERIES OF MIDRASHIM THAT WILL QUESTION THE USE
OF THE TERM לך – *LEKHA.* THE WORD לך – *LEKH,* WHICH MEANS "TO GO,"
IS OBVIOUSLY THE KEY WORD ORDERING ABRAHAM TO GO TO THE LAND
OF ISRAEL. BUT WHAT QUALIFICATION IS ADDED BY THE TERM *LEKHA*?
THE MIDRASH WILL EVENTUALLY MAKE A PROPOSAL IN THIS REGARD.

מה כתיב למעלה מן העניין, וימת תרח בחרן. א"ר יצחק: אם לעניין החשבון ועד עכשיו
מתבקש לו עוד ששים וחמש שנים?

7. NOW WHAT PRECEDES THIS PASSAGE? AND TERAH DIED IN HARAN
(GEN. 11:32), [WHICH IS FOLLOWED BY] NOW THE LORD SAID UNTO
ABRAM: GET THEE (*LEKH LEKHA*). R. ISAAC SAID: FROM THE POINT OF
VIEW OF CHRONOLOGY, A PERIOD OF SIXTY-FIVE YEARS IS STILL RE-
QUIRED.

The Midrash points out that the death of Terah took place 65 years
after Abraham left Haran (see Additional Commentary), so then why
does the Torah imply that Terah died before Abraham left Haran?

אלא בתחילה אתה דורש הרשעים קרויים מתים בחייהן, לפי שהיה אברהם אבינו מפחד
ואומר: אצא ויהיו מחללין בי שם שמים ואומרים: הניח אביו והלך לו לעת זקנתו אמר ליה
הקב"ה: לך! אני פוטרך מכיבוד אב ואם, ואין אני פוטר לאחר מכיבוד אב ואם.

BUT FIRST YOU MAY LEARN THAT THE WICKED, EVEN DURING THEIR
LIFETIME, ARE CALLED DEAD. FOR ABRAHAM WAS AFRAID, SAYING,
"SHALL I GO OUT AND BRING DISHONOR UPON THE DIVINE NAME,
AS PEOPLE WILL SAY, 'HE LEFT HIS FATHER IN HIS OLD AGE AND DE-
PARTED?'" THEREFORE, THE HOLY ONE, BLESSED BE HE, REASSURED HIM:
"I EXEMPT THEE (*LEKHA*) FROM THE DUTY OF HONORING THY PARENTS,
THOUGH I EXEMPT NO ONE ELSE FROM THIS DUTY."

Attempts were now made by the Midrash to confront this challenge.
The first was the rabbinic saying that an idol worshipper is considered
dead, even when he is alive. Abraham was also very sensitive to the
charge that he would be criticized for leaving his father in his old age.

ולא עוד, אלא שאני מקדים מיתתו ליציאתך. בתחלה וימת תרח בחרן ואח"כ ויאמר ה' אל
אברם:

MOREOVER, "I WILL RECORD HIS DEATH BEFORE THY DEPARTURE."
HENCE, "AND TERAH DIED IN HARAN" IS STATED FIRST, AND THEN, NOW
THE LORD SAID UNTO ABRAM, ETC.

There is a view in a later Midrash that Abraham may have left Haran
twice, returning the first time for reasons already stated (i.e., his feelings
of guilt). The second time, the situation had changed and Terah had
died before Abraham left Haran.

―

Seed Thoughts

The *Tiferet Tzion* makes the point that Abraham was very uncomfortable
with the exemption that God had given him from fulfilling the commandment of honoring one's parent. A person who observes the Torah
can only find complete fulfillment when he observes a commandment
to the best of his ability. It does something spiritually affirmative to his
very being and even to his bodily comforts. The true fulfillment of a
mitzvah is one of the goals of Judaism and being exempt is not equal to
fulfilling a commandment. The fact that you do not have to do something does not mean that you have done it. Abraham understood that
and so should we.

The whole idea of a commandment in Judaism is the method in
which the Torah reaches into the life of an individual and both demands
and makes possible a response to the duty of the commandment. When
the response is affirmative in as maximum a way as possible, the true
fulfillment of a Jew, therefore, becomes possible at that point. That is
how the individual approaches God. You might say the system of the
commandments is the manner in which God approaches the individual.
Both together are a most unusual combination and make of Judaism a
spiritual reality.

―

Additional Commentary

The mathematical problem

If the purpose is to resolve this question by means of mathematical calculation, how could it have been said that Terah died in Haran? The text says specifically that Terah died just before Abraham left Haran. Therefore, there is a difference of 65 years between the first mention of the death of Terah and the second mention. Terah lived 205 years, and in his seventieth year, Abraham was born. Furthermore, Abraham himself was 70 years old when he first left Haran as written in Genesis 12:4. His second departure from Haran, as will be indicated in the next Midrash, happened when he was 75. As far as the first mention of Terah's death, we can use the interpretation that an idol worshipper is considered dead even though he may be alive. (Mirkin)

לְךָ – *Lekha*

Abraham returned to Haran very quickly because of his sense of guilt that people would think he was desecrating the Divine name by not honoring his father. The Almighty tried to make Abraham feel better by exempting him from the duty of honoring his father, but not exempting anybody else. That is the meaning of *lekha*, only for *you* and nobody else. (Mirkin)

On being exempt from a commandment

Abraham was very uncomfortable with God's decision to exempt him from honoring his father. The average person would not know the value of going to the Land of Israel, which as a great mitzvah was the reason why God exempted Abraham from the duty of honoring one's father and mother. Abraham would feel that the people would see him as dishonoring his father. Therefore, he did not rush to fulfill God's commandment of leaving, but waited until he was specifically ordered to do so. Furthermore, he was worried that the people would look upon honoring one's parent as being of less importance. That is what God meant by using the word *lekha*. "Only for *you* Abraham, do I make an exemption, and no one else." Despite this fact, Abraham felt very bad, that by leaving Haran he would not be honoring his father properly, because a person cannot find complete fulfillment unless he fulfills as many commandments as possible – in action and not only in theory. The mere fact that he was exempt does not mean that he had fulfilled the commandment. That is when God said to him, "I will see to it that Terah's death will precede your leaving of Haran." (*Tiferet Tzion*)

PARASHAH THIRTY-NINE, *Midrash Eight*

ח רבי יהודה ורבי נחמיה, רי"א: לך לך שתי פעמים, אחד מארם נהרים ואחד מארם נחור.

8. GET THEE (*LEKH LEKHA*). R. JUDAH SAID: *LEKH LEKHA* (GO, GO) IS WRITTEN TWICE, ONE PASSAGE [REFERRING TO HIS DEPARTURE] FROM ARAM NAHARAIM, AND THE OTHER [TO HIS DEPARTURE] FROM ARAM NAHOR.

This is one of several Midrashim that deals with the phrase *lekh lekha*, and the question is why the extension, and is only *lekh* enough? R. Judah and R. Nehemiah differ as to why it is written twice. R. Judah interprets the phrase as though it is *lekh lekh*, meaning that Abraham was commanded to leave twice and he did. Once from Aram Naharaim and once from Aram Nahor.

רבי נחמיה אמר: לך לך שתי פעמים, אחד מארם נהרים ומארם נחור ואחד שהפריחו מבין הבתרים והביאו לחרן, הה"ד (תהלים קי): עמך נדבות ביום חילך. עמך, הייתי בעת שנדבת לשמי לירד לכבשן האש. ביום חילך, בעת שכנסת אתה לי כל החיילות והאוכלסים.

R. NEHEMIAH SAID: *LEKH LEKHA* IS WRITTEN TWICE, ONE PASSAGE [REFERRING TO HIS DEPARTURE] FROM ARAM NAHARAIM AND ARAM NAHOR, AND THE OTHER INTIMATING THAT HE MADE HIM FLY FROM THE COVENANT BETWEEN THE PIECES AND BROUGHT HIM TO HARAN. IT IS WRITTEN: THY PEOPLE (*AMMEKHA*) OFFER THEMSELVES WILLINGLY (*NEDABOTH*) IN THE DAY OF THY WARFARE (*HELEKHA*), ETC. (PS. 110:3). THIS MEANS: I WAS WITH THEE (*IMMEKHA*) WHEN THOU DIDST WILL-INGLY OFFER (*NADABTA*) FOR MY NAME'S SAKE TO ENTER THE FIERY FURNACE. IN THE DAY OF THY WARFARE [LIT. "RETINUE"] – WHEN THOU DIDST BRING ME ALL THOSE BANDS.

R. Nehemiah also interprets it as though it is *lekh lekh*. The first *lekh* refers to the departure from both Aram Naharaim and Aram Nahor. The second *lekh* refers to when Abraham was restored to Haran at the Covenant of the Pieces, בין הבתרים. A series of verses are now brought from Psalm 110, all of which have been interpreted by the various commentators as referring to Abraham. What our Midrash has done is to change the punctuation style (i.e., *amekha* to *imekha*) which indicates that God was with Abraham and saved him from the fiery furnace. At the same time, God acknowledged the large number of people that Abraham brought with him who had been converted as a result of his being saved by God from the fiery furnace.

בהדרי קדש, מהדרו של עולם. הקדשתיך מרחם משחר, מרחמו של עולם. שחרתיך לי לך
טל ילדותך, לפי שהיה אבינו אברהם מתפחד ואומר תאמר שיש בידי עוון, שהייתי עובד
עבודת כוכבים כל השנים הללו. א"ל הקב"ה: לך טל ילדותך, מה טל זה פורח אף עוונותיך
פורחים. מה הטל הזה סימן ברכה לעולם אף אתה סימן ברכה לעולם. הה"ד (שם נה): ואומר
מי יתן לי אבר כיונה אעופה ואשכונה.

IN THE MOUNTAINS OF HOLINESS: FROM THE ANCIENT MOUNTAIN DID I
SANCTIFY THEE. FROM THE WOMB OF THE DAWN – *MEREHEM MISHEHAR*
(PS. 110:3): FROM OUT OF THE WOMB OF THE WORLD HAVE I SOUGHT
THEE (*SHIHARTIKHA*) FOR ME. THINE IS THE DEW OF THY YOUTH (110:3):
BECAUSE ABRAHAM WAS AFRAID AND SAID TO HIMSELF, "PERHAPS I
BEAR GUILT FOR HAVING WORSHIPPED IDOLS ALL THESE YEARS," GOD
REASSURED HIM: "THINE IS THE DEW OF THY YOUTH": EVEN AS DEW
EVAPORATES, SO HAVE THY SINS EVAPORATED [DISAPPEARED]; AS DEW
IS A SIGN OF BLESSING TO THE WORLD, SO ART THOU A SIGN OF BLESS-
ING TO THE WORLD. IT IS WRITTEN: AND I SAID: OH THAT I HAD WINGS
LIKE A DOVE! THEN I WOULD FLY AWAY, AND BE AT REST (55:7).

The verses go on to explain that God saw in Abraham the possibility of influencing the entire world. This is one of the meanings of לך לך. Through Abraham, a world will be redeemed. Abraham had a sense of guilt at the fact that so much of his life was concerned with the worship of idols. God had reassured him not to be concerned – just as the dew eventually disappears as part of the nature of growth, so has Abraham's early life disappeared in the light of his greater spiritual commitment.

למה כיונה? ר' עזריה בשם רבי יודן אמר: לפי שכל העופות בשעה שהם יגעים הן נחין על
גבי סלע, או על גבי אילן, אבל היונה הזו, בשעה שהיא פורחת ויגיעה קופצת באחד מאגפיה,

ופורחת באחד מאגפיה. (שם) הנה ארחיק נדוד, נדנוד טלטול אחר טלטול. אלין במדבר
סלה, מוטב ללון במדברות של א"י ולא ללון בפלטריות של חו"ל. וא"ת שלא גהן אברהם
ושמח על דיבור המקום ולמה לא יצא? שעדיין לא הורשה, אבל משהורשה, וילך אברם
כאשר דבר אליו ה' וילך אתו לוט.

WHY LIKE A DOVE? SAID R. AZARIAH IN THE NAME OF R. JUDAN B. R.
SIMON: BECAUSE ALL OTHER BIRDS, WHEN TIRED, REST ON A ROCK OR
A TREE, BUT WHEN A DOVE IS TIRED SHE DRAWS IN ONE OF HER WINGS
AND FLIES ON WITH THE OTHER. LO, THEN I WOULD WANDER FAR OFF
(PS. 55:8): EXILE AFTER EXILE, JOURNEY AFTER JOURNEY. I WOULD
LODGE IN THE WILDERNESS. *SELAH* (55:8): BETTER IS IT TO LODGE IN
THE DESERTS OF ERETZ ISRAEL THAN IN PALACES ABROAD. AND SHOULD
YOU OBJECT, IF HE [ABRAHAM] HAD NO QUALMS BUT REJOICED [TO GO
TO ERETZ ISRAEL], WHY DID HE NOT EMIGRATE [SOONER]? BECAUSE HE
HAD NOT YET BEEN PERMITTED, BUT AS SOON AS HE WAS PERMITTED,
IT IS WRITTEN, SO ABRAM WENT, AS THE LORD HAD SPOKEN UNTO HIM,
AND LOT WENT WITH HIM (GEN. 12:4).

The symbol of the dove is very meaningful. Unlike other birds, the
dove does not have to stop flying when it is tired. It merely rests one
wing allowing the other to take over. Naturally, in this condition, the
dove does not fly as fast as the other birds. However, that is the main lesson. Abraham wanted to see the Land of Israel, as the dove flies, meaning slowly, carefully, with the opportunity of watching every aspect of
nature as well as human nature.

אמר רבי לוי: בשעה שהיה אברהם מהלך בארם נהרים ובארם נחור, ראה אותן אוכלים
ושותים ופוחזים. אמר: הלוואי לא יהא לי חלק בארץ הזאת וכיון שהגיע לסולמה של צור,
ראה אותן עסוקין בניכוש בשעת הניכוש, בעידור בשעת העידור, אמר: הלוואי יהא חלקי
בארץ הזאת. אמר לו הקב"ה: לזרעך אתן את הארץ הזאת:

R. LEVI SAID: WHEN ABRAHAM WAS TRAVELLING THROUGH ARAM NAHA-
RAIM AND ARAM NAHOR, HE SAW ITS INHABITANTS EATING AND DRINK-
ING AND REVELING. "MAY MY PORTION NOT BE IN THIS COUNTRY!", HE
EXCLAIMED. BUT WHEN HE REACHED THE PROMONTORY OF TYRE AND
SAW THEM ENGAGED IN WEEDING AND HOEING AT THE PROPER SEA-
SONS, HE EXCLAIMED, "WOULD THAT MY PORTION MIGHT BE IN THIS
COUNTRY!" SAID THE HOLY ONE, BLESSED BE HE, TO HIM: UNTO THY
SEED HAVE I GIVEN THIS LAND (GEN. 15:18).

T raveling with the symbol of the dove in mind enabled Abraham to observe what ordinarily would not be visible. This enabled Abraham to see through the people of Aram Naharaim and Aram Nahor, his birthplace. They were more interested in having a good time than in helping the country to develop the land in a helpful way. However, when he came to Tyre, the northernmost point of Israel, and saw the people engaged in every manner of work that would benefit each other and the very land they occupied, he chose that as a place where he wanted to live. This desire was granted to him.

—

Seed Thoughts

In an earlier Midrash, we are told that Abraham chose God. But in God's point of view, that was not good enough because God Himself would have to have chosen someone, and to approve of it, in order to be a carrier of His prophetic mission. According to the Ethics of the Fathers, ten such difficult challenges were created for Abraham, all of which he succeeded in accomplishing. By the same token, God chose the land of Canaan to be the environment that would be suitable as it was described as the land of milk and honey. According to the Midrash, that too was not good enough. The story could not begin until Abraham himself fell in love with the Land of Israel. It did not happen the first time he left Haran. But it did happen the second time he left Haran when in the vicinity of Tyre he said that that would be the place where he would like to live. God answered, "To thy seed will I give this land."

—

Additional Commentary

R. Judah and R. Nehemiah

Their difference of opinion has to do with the kind of legal system that our ancestors followed – from Abraham up to the time of the giving of the Torah? Did they follow the system of the sons of Noah or that of Bnei Israel? R. Judah was of the opinion that they followed the law of Bnei Israel. The laws applied to Abraham as גר שנתגייר, a person who had just been converted. This can also be seen as a child that was just born. Therefore, it was not necessary for God to have transported him back to Haran from the Covenant of the Pieces. R. Nehemiah claims that the law of Noah was the system that Abraham followed, and whatever commandments they followed were those that they chose themselves without being commanded. With the exception of "go to the Land of Israel," because Abraham did not wish to belittle his father and leave him, and, therefore, God had to motivate him to leave. (*Tiferet Tzion*)

The land must be desired

Note that the verse says, *Lekh lekha,* meaning, "go forth, to the land which I will show you, *areka.*" But He did not say at that point, *asher eten lekha,* meaning "which I will give you," the purpose being that he should see the land and that it should find favor in his eyes. In other words, that he should desire it. Only after he expressed his desire for the land, that he wanted to live among its people, did God say, "To your descendants will I give this land." (*HaMidrash HaMevo'ar*)

PARASHAH THIRTY-NINE, *Midrash Nine*

ט אמר רבי לוי: שתי פעמים כתיב לך לך ואין אנו יודעים אי זו חביבה, אם השנייה אם הראשונה. ממה דכתיב: אל ארץ המוריה, הוי השנייה חביבה מן הראשונה.

9. R. LEVI SAID: "GET THEE" IS WRITTEN TWICE, AND WE DO NOT KNOW WHICH WAS MORE PRECIOUS [IN THE EYES OF GOD], WHETHER THE FIRST OR THE SECOND.

This Midrash continues to search for meanings of the extra word *lekha* in the expression *lekh lekh,* "get thee out." It is mentioned twice in Scripture, and the first question raised is: Which of these is more important? The word "precious" should be understood as being important and not that God favors one procedure over another.

אמר רבי יוחנן: לך לך מארצך, מארפכי שלך. וממולדתך, זו שכונתך. ומבית אביך, זו בית אביך. אל הארץ אשר אראך. ולמה לא גלה לו? כדי לחבבה בעיניו, וליתן לו שכר על כל פסיעה ופסיעה.

R. JOHANAN SAID: GET THEE OUT OF THY COUNTRY MEANS, FROM THY PROVINCE; AND FROM THY KINDRED — FROM THE PLACE WHERE THOU

ART SETTLED; AND FROM THY FATHER'S HOUSE – LITERALLY, THY FA-
THER'S HOUSE. UNTO THE LAND THAT I WILL SHOW THEE: WHY DID HE
NOT REVEAL IT TO HIM [THERE AND THEN]? IN ORDER TO MAKE IT MORE
BELOVED IN HIS EYES AND TO REWARD HIM FOR EVERY STEP HE TOOK.

The view of R. Johanan is that one of the reasons why God did not reveal the specific goal of Abraham's pilgrimage is so that he might receive
a special spiritual reward for every step that he took in the fulfillment of
God's commandment.

הוא דעתיה, דרבי יוחנן דאמר: ר' יוחנן (בראשית כב) ויאמר קח נא את בנך את יחידך. א"ל:
זה יחיד לאמו, וזה יחיד לאמו. אמר לו: אשר אהבת. א"ל: ואית תחומין במעיא? א"ל: את
יצחק. ולמה לא גלה לו? כדי לחבבו בעיניו, וליתן לו שכר על כל דבור ודבור.

THIS AGREES WITH ANOTHER TEACHING OF R. JOHANAN, FOR R. JO-
HANAN SAID: AND HE SAID: TAKE NOW THY SON (GEN. 22:2) – "WHICH
ONE?" "THINE ONLY SON." "EACH IS THE ONLY ONE OF HIS MOTHER?"
"WHOM THOU LOVEST." "I LOVE THEM BOTH: ARE THERE LIMITS TO
ONE'S EMOTIONS?" SAID HE TO HIM: "EVEN ISAAC." AND WHY DID HE
NOT REVEAL IT TO HIM [WITHOUT DELAY]? IN ORDER TO MAKE HIM
EVEN MORE BELOVED IN HIS EYES AND REWARD HIM FOR EVERY WORD
SPOKEN.

R. Yohanan adds the same thought in connection with the second *lekh
lekha,* whose goal was to bring Abraham to Mount Moriah and the *Akeidah,* the Sacrifice of Isaac, by not revealing immediately that the person
to be sacrificed was Isaac. God added even more spiritual rewards to
Abraham's character.

דאמר רב הונא משם רבי אליעזר בנו של רבי יוסי הגלילי: משהה הקב"ה ומתלא עיניהם של
צדיקים, ואח"כ הוא מגלה להם טעמו של דבר. כך אל הארץ אשר אראך. על אחד ההרים
אשר אומר אליך. (יונה ג) וקרא אליה את הקריאה אשר אני דובר אליך. (יחזקאל ג) קום צא אל
הבקעה ושם אדבר אתך:

FOR R. HUNA SAID IN R. ELIEZER'S NAME: THE HOLY ONE, BLESSED
BE HE, FIRST PLACES THE RIGHTEOUS IN DOUBT AND SUSPENSE, AND
THEN HE REVEALS TO THEM THE MEANING OF THE MATTER. THUS IT
IS WRITTEN, TO THE LAND THAT I WILL SHEW THEE; UPON ONE OF THE
MOUNTAINS WHICH I WILL TELL THEE OF (GEN. 22:2); AND MAKE UNTO
IT THE PROCLAMATION THAT I BID THEE (JONAH 3:2); ARISE, GO FORTH
INTO THE PLAIN, AND I WILL THERE SPEAK WITH THEE (EZEK. 3:22).

The Midrash then enlists a number of places in Scripture where God did not reveal exact details of His mission to His disciples, but motivated them gradually until the full meaning was achieved.

Seed Thoughts

What is involved in this Midrash is an attempt to show how the relationship between Abraham and God developed. At the outset, Abraham was only beginning to learn, and God was not yet completely certain of him. He had to be tempted and motivated just as a good teacher tries to create new challenges for his best pupils. Finally, however, Abraham passes all the tests, ten of them as listed in the Ethics of the Fathers, and he then becomes a full-fledged dedicated disciple. The first *lekh lekha* from "your land, your birthplace, your father's house," is the opening movement in the symphony between God and Abraham. The climax is the *Akeidah*, which is the second *lekh lekha*, where God tells him specifically that he will go to Mount Moriah, the holiest place in Israel. The meaning of *lekha*, therefore, now becomes, 'for your spiritual benefit,' *le-tovatkha*.

PARASHAH THIRTY-NINE, *Midrash Ten*

י רבי ברכיה בשם רבי נחמיה אמר: למלך שהיה עובר ממקום למקום ונפלה מרגלית
מעל ראשו, עמד המלך והעמיד פמליא שלו שם, ועשה צבורים והביא מכברות, וכבר את
הראשונה ולא מצא, השני ולא מצא, ובג' מצאה. אמרו: מצא המלך מרגליות שלו. כך אמר
הקב"ה: מה צורך היה לי לייחס שם, ארפכשד, שלח, עבר, פלג, רעו, שרוג, נחור, תרח, אלא
בשבילך, (נחמיה ט) ומצאת את לבבו נאמן לפניך. כך אמר הקב"ה: לדוד, מה צורך היה לי
ליחס, פרץ, חצרון, רם, עמינדב, נחשון, שלמון, בועז, עובד, ישי, דוד, לא בשבילך? (תהלים
פט) מצאתי דוד עבדי בשמן קדשי משחתיו:

10. R. BEREKIAH B. R. SIMON SAID IN R. NEHEMIAH'S NAME: THIS MAY
BE ILLUSTRATED BY A KING WHO WAS PASSING FROM PLACE TO PLACE,
WHEN A GEM FELL FROM HIS HEAD. WHEREUPON THE KING HALTED
AND STATIONED HIS RETINUE THERE, GATHERED THE SAND IN PILES,
AND BROUGHT SIEVES. HE SIFTED THE FIRST PILE, BUT DID NOT FIND
IT; THE SECOND, BUT DID NOT FIND IT; BUT IN THE THIRD, HE FOUND

IT. SAID THEY: "THE KING HAS FOUND HIS PEARL." SIMILARLY, THE HOLY
ONE, BLESSED BE HE, SAID TO ABRAHAM: "WHAT NEED HAD I TO TRACE
THE DESCENT OF SHEM, ARPACHSHAD, SHELAH, EBER, PELEG, REU, SE-
RUG, NAHOR, AND TERAH? WAS IT NOT ON THY ACCOUNT?" THUS IT IS
WRITTEN: AND FOUNDEST HIS HEART [ABRAHAM'S] FAITHFUL BEFORE
THEE (NEH. 9:8). IN LIKE MANNER, GOD SAID TO DAVID: "WHAT NEED
HAD I TO TRACE THE DESCENT OF PEREZ, HEZRON, RAM, AMINADAB,
NACHSHON, SHALMON, BOAZ, OBED, AND JESSE? WAS IT NOT ON THY
ACCOUNT?" HENCE IT IS WRITTEN: I HAVE FOUND DAVID MY SERVANT;
WITH MY HOLY OIL HAVE I ANOINTED HIM (PS. 89:21).

What we should try to understand is the interpretation of the parable.
The *Tiferet Tzion* expresses the view that the pearl that the king lost was
referring to Adam, the first man who had been especially prepared by
the Divine power Himself and ultimately did not live up to the divine
expectations. Abraham was able to replace Adam in God's eyes and
begin again to fill the purpose of Creation. However, this interpretation
leaves out the three stages of the parable. In the view of the *Midrash
HaMevo'ar*, these refer to the children of Noah who became the basis for
all of humanity, namely, Shem, Ham, and Japheth. In this interpretation,
Japheth and Ham were discarded because the pearl was not found in
their midst, but Shem saved the pearl. This means that the great descendant of Shem was Abraham and he was able to restore God's design for
mankind.

Seed Thoughts

I have recently been reading some mystical literature, particularly that
involving the great debate between the Ari (R. Luria) and the Ramhal
(Luzatto). The ideas has to do with the doctrine of צמצום – *tzimtzum*,
whereby God voluntarily relinquishes some of His power and authority,
in order that humankind can exist within the limited spiritual possibilities.

Thus we see in the present Midrash that God does not control history. Generation after generation emerged among the descendants of
Shem that God had no interest in them until Abraham arose. God also
seemed to have no special interest in the descendants of Perez until the
arrival of David, the king.

One cannot use words like struggle in connection with God, but we might add that even God, the Almighty, Who had limited His power for the sake of mankind, has to wait and allow history to happen, until the one He wants arrives on the scene.

―

Additional Commentary

The meaning of Lekha

The parable of the king offers a new interpretation of the meaning of *lekha* in the expression *lekh lekha*. God is waiting for someone to appear in the families of Japheth and the right one did not appear. Similarly was the case in the families of Ham. However, in the family of Shem, Abraham appeared and even though he was brought up in a home dedicated to the worship of idols, his character shrugged off all of these negative influences and he was the one God had been waiting for. It is as though the Almighty said to him, "I have been waiting for you. I was hoping for *lekha*, for you, and you have now fulfilled My expectations." (*HaMidrash HaMevo'ar*)

PARASHAH THIRTY-NINE, *Midrash Eleven*

יא ואעשך לגוי גדול. אמר לו: ומנח לא העמדת ע' אומות? אמר לו: אותה אומה אומר שכתוב בה
(דברים ד): כי מי גוי גדול, אני מעמיד ממך. אמר רבי ברכיה: אתנך ואשימך אין כתיב כאן,
אלא ואעשך, משאני עושה אותך בריה חדשה, את פרה ורבה.

11. AND I WILL MAKE OF THEE A GREAT NATION (GEN. 12:2). SAID HE TO HIM: "YET HAST THOU NOT CAUSED THE SEVENTY NATIONS TO SPRING FROM NOAH?" HE REPLIED: "THAT NATION OF WHICH IT IS WRITTEN: FOR WHAT GREAT NATION IS THERE, THAT HATH GOD SO NIGH UNTO THEM (DEUT. 4:7), THEM WILL I RAISE UP FROM THEE." R. BEREKIAH SAID: IT IS NOT WRITTEN: AND I WILL GIVE THEE, OR AND I WILL SET THEE, BUT, AND I WLLL MAKE THEE: I.E., AFTER I HAVE CREATED THEE AS A NEW CREATION, THOU WILT BE FRUITFUL AND MULTIPLY.

The point to be made here is not that Abraham will found another people, just like the other nations of the world that were descended from Noah. On the contrary, the goal will be a unique nation that would fulfill the role as described in *Devarim* (Deuteronomy 4:7), "For what great nation is there that God is intimate with them?"

רבי לוי בר חוויות ורבי אבא בריה דרבי חייא בר אבא אמרו: שלשה גדולות וארבע ברכות כתיב כאן. בישרו שהן שלש אבות וארבע אמהות. אמר רבי חייא: לפי שהדרך מגרמת לשלשה דברים: ממעטת פריה ורביה, וממעטת את היציאה, וממעטת את השם. ממעטת פריה ורביה, ואעשך לגוי גדול. ממעטת את היציאה, ואברכך. ממעטת את השם, ואגדלה שמך. ולפום דאמרין אינשי, מבית לבית חלוק, מאתר לאתר נפש. ברם, את לא נפש את חסר ולא ממון

R. LEVI B. HAVYATH AND R. ABBA SON OF R. HIYYA BAR ABBA SAID: THRICE IS "GREATNESS" MENTIONED HERE, AND "BLESSINGS" FOUR TIMES: HE THUS INFORMED HIM THAT THERE WOULD BE THREE PATRIARCHS AND FOUR MATRIARCHS. R. BEREKIAH SAID: BECAUSE TRAVELLING HAS THREE ADVERSE EFFECTS – DIMINISHING PROCREATION, AND REDUC-ING ONE'S WEALTH AND ONE'S FAME – [GOD GAVE HIM COUNTER ASSUR-ANCES]. SINCE IT DIMINISHES PROCREATION [HE SAID TO HIM], AND I WILL MAKE OF THEE A GREAT NATION; IT DECREASES ONE'S WEALTH, HENCE, AND I WILL BLESS THEE; IT DIMINISHES ONE'S NAME [FAME], HENCE, AND MAKE THY NAME GREAT. AND THOUGH THE PROVERB SAYS, "WHEN YOU TRAVEL FROM ONE HOUSE TO ANOTHER, YOU LOSE A SHIRT; FROM ONE COUNTRY TO ANOTHER, YOU LOSE A LIFE," YET IN TRUTH THOU WILT LOSE NEITHER LIFE NOR PROPERTY.

The Midrash discerned in the various blessings, three that were pa-triarchal and four that were matriarchal. At the same time the Midrash gave assurances that while travel leads to serious negative consequences, three of which are mentioned, the blessings contained specific assur-ances that Abraham will be protected from all the negative factors that are to be found in traveling.

רבי ברכיה בשם ר' חלבו אמר: שיצא מוניטין שלו בעולם. ארבעה הם שיצא להם מוניטין בעולם: אברהם, ואעשך לגוי גדול. יצא לו מוניטין. ומהו מוניטין שלו? זקן וזקנה מיכן, בחור ובתולה מיכן. יהושע. יהושע (יהושע ו): ויהי ה' את יהושע ויהי שמעו בכל הארץ. יצא לו מוניטין בעולם. מהו? שור מיכן וראם מיכן. ע"ש (דברים לג): בכור שורו הדר לו וקרני ראם קרניו. דוד (ד"ה א יד): ויצא שם דוד בכל הארצות. יצא לו מוניטין בעולם. ומה היה מוניטין שלו? מקל

ותרמיל מיכן ומגדל מיכן. ע"ש (שיר ד): כמגדל דויד צוארך. מרדכי (אסתר ט): כי גדול מרדכי
בבית המלך ושמעו הולך בכל המדינות. יצא לו מוניטין. ומה מוניטין שלו? שק ואפר מיכן
ועטרת זהב מיכן. א"ר יודן: קובע אני לך ברכה בשמונה עשרה, אבל אין את יודע אם שלי
קודמת, אם שלך קודמת? א"ר אחויה בשם רבי זעירא: שלך קודמת לשלי. בשעה שהוא
אומר מגן אברהם, אחר כך מחיה המתים. רבי אבהו אמר: הבט נא שמים אין כתיב כאן,
אלא השמימה. אמר הקב"ה: בה"א בראתי את העולם, הריני מוסיף ה"א על שמך, ואת פרה
ורבה. ואמר רבי יודן: והיו אותותיך מנין אברככה, מאתים וארבעים ושמונה. אמר ר' לוי: לא
שם אדם פרה מאברהם עד שנתברך, ולא שמה לו, עד שנתברך מאברהם. כיצד אברהם
היה מתפלל על עקרות והם נפקדות ועל החולים והם מרויחים? רב הונא אמר: לא סוף דבר.
אברהם הולך אצל החולה, אלא החולה רואה אותו ומרויח. א"ר חנינא: אפילו ספינות שהיו
מפרשות בים הגדול היו ניצולות בזכותו של אברהם, ולא של יין נסך היו אתמהא? אלא הלא
מזיל חמרא בכ"מ, שיין עובדי כוכבים מצוי, יין של ישראל נמכר בזול. א"ר יצחק: אף לאיוב
עשה כן שנאמר (איוב א): מעשה ידיו ברכת. לא נטל אדם פרוטה מאיוב ונצטרך ליטול ממנו
פעם שנייה. והיה ברכה, קרי ביה בריכה, מה בריכה זו מטהרת את הטמאים, אף את מקרב
רחוקים ומטהרם לאביהם שבשמים.

R. BEREKIAH SAID IN R. HELBO'S NAME: IT MEANS THAT HIS COINAGE WAS
CURRENT IN THE WORLD. THERE WERE FOUR WHOSE COINAGE BECAME
CURRENT IN THE WORLD: (I) ABRAHAM, AS IT IS WRITTEN: AND I WILL
MAKE OF THEE, ETC. AND WHAT EFFIGY DID HIS COINAGE BEAR? AN OLD
MAN AND AN OLD WOMAN ON ONE SIDE, AND A BOY AND A GIRL ON THE
OTHER. (II) JOSHUA, AS IT IS WRITTEN: SO THE LORD WAS WITH JOSHUA,
AND HIS FAME WAS IN ALL THE LAND (JOSH. 6:27), WHICH MEANS THAT
HIS COINAGE WAS CURRENT IN THE WORLD. AND WHAT WAS ITS EFFIGY?
AN OX ON ONE SIDE AND A WILD-OX ON THE OTHER, CORRESPONDING
TO: HIS FIRSTLING BULLOCK, MAJESTY IS HIS, AND HIS HORNS ARE THE
HORNS OF A WILD-OX (DEUT. 33:17). (III) DAVID, AS IT IS WRITTEN: AND
THE FAME OF DAVID WENT OUT INTO ALL THE LANDS (I CHRON. 14:17),
WHICH MEANS THAT HIS COINAGE WAS CURRENT. AND WHAT WAS ITS
EFFIGY? A STAFF AND A WALLET ON ONE SIDE, AND A TOWER ON THE
OTHER, CORRESPONDING TO: THY NECK IS LIKE THE TOWER OF DAVID,
BUILDED WITH TURRETS (SONG 4:4). (IV) MORDECAI, AS IT IS WRIT-
TEN: FOR MORDECAI WAS GREAT IN THE KING'S HOUSE, AND HIS FAME
WENT FORTH THROUGHOUT ALL THE PROVINCES (EST. 9:4) – THIS TOO
MEANS THAT HIS COINAGE WAS CURRENT. AND WHAT WAS ITS EFFIGY?
SACKCLOTH AND ASHES ON ONE SIDE AND A GOLDEN CROWN ON THE
OTHER. R. ISAAC SAID: [GOD PROMISED ABRAHAM]: "I WILL SET THEE
AS A BLESSING IN THE EIGHTEEN [BENEDICTIONS]. YET THOU DOST NOT
KNOW WHETHER MINE IS FIRST OR THINE IS FIRST." SAID R. AHA IN R.
ZE'IRA'S NAME: THINE IS BEFORE MINE; AFTER HAVING RECITED "THE

SHIELD OF ABRAHAM," WE THEN RECITE "WHO RESURRECTEST THE
DEAD." [AND I WILL MAKE THY NAME GREAT; THIS MEANS, I WILL ADD
THE LETTER *HEH* TO THY NAME.] R. ABBAHU COMMENTED THEREON:
IT IS NOT WRITTEN, "LOOK NOW *HASHAMAYIM*" (AT THE HEAVEN), BUT,
"LOOK NOW *HASHAMAYMAH*"– E.V. "TOWARD HEAVEN" (GEN. 15:5): WITH
THIS *HEH*, I CREATED THE WORLD; BEHOLD, I WILL ADD IT TO THY NAME,
AND THEN THOU WILT BE FRUITFUL AND MULTIPLY.

The interesting thing in this section is that unique figures in biblical
history had coinage created for themselves with special symbols that
related either to their character, their achievement or their destiny. In
Abraham's case for example there was an old man and old woman on
one side, and a young boy and young girl on the other side. This means
that his faith in God was as strong towards the end of his life as it was in
the beginning.

Note that the change in Abraham's name consisted of the addition
of the Hebrew letter *heh*, ה. This was mentioned earlier in the Creation
story that God created the world as easily as one pronounces the letter
heh, which is the easiest to pronounce of all the Hebrew letters.

R. Judan said: The numerical value of the letters of thy name will
equal those of Wa-abarekeka (And I will bless thee): Just as Wa-abarekeka amounts to two hundred and forty-eight, so do the letters of thy
name amount to two hundred and forty-eight. R. Levi said: No man
ever priced a cow belonging to Abraham [in order to buy it] without
becoming blessed, nor did a man ever price a cow [to sell] to him without his becoming blessed. Abraham used to pray for barren women, and
they were remembered [i.e., they conceived]; and on behalf of the sick,
and they were healed. R. Huna said: It was not necessary for Abraham
to go to the sick person, for when the sick person merely saw him he
was relieved. R. Hanina said: Even ships travelling the sea were saved
for Abraham's sake. But did they not contain forbidden wine? [There
is a proverb]: "Vinegar cheapens wine": wherever gentile wine is available, Jewish wine is cheap. R. Isaac said: To Job too He did thus, as it
is written: Thou hast blessed the work of his hands (Job 1:10): no man
who took a farthing from Job had to take a second one from him. And
be Thou a blessing (*berakah*): this means, be thou a *berekah* (pool): Just
as a pool purifies the unclean, so do thou bring near [to Me] those who
are afar.

The addition of the letter *heh*, made it possible for his name to have the same numerical value as the phrase, "And I will bless you." Thus Abraham became a source of blessing to everyone with whom he came into contact.

א"ר ברכיה: כבר כתוב ואברככה, מה תלמוד לומר והיה ברכה? אלא, א"ל: עד כאן הייתי זקוק לברך את עולמי, מיכן ואילך הרי הברכות מסורות לך. למאן דחזי לך למברכא, בריך:

R. BEREKIAH SAID: SEEING THAT IT IS ALREADY WRITTEN, AND I WLLL BLESS THEE, WHY IS AND BE THOU A BLESSING ADDED? HE [GOD] SAID TO HIM: "HITHERTO, I HAD TO BLESS MY WORLD; HENCEFORTH THE BLESSINGS ARE ENTRUSTED TO THEE: WHOM IT PLEASES THEE TO BLESS, DO THOU BLESS."

This is a beautiful interpretation of *hayeh berakhah*, "be thou a blessing." It means that he should be a source of blessing. God had blessed Abraham and now Abraham will have the ability to bless others.

—

Seed Thoughts

The verse in our text says, "And I will make of thee a great nation, and I will bless thee, and make thy name great; and be though a blessing." The question arises: If it says that God will bless you, what does it mean to then say, "And you should make of yourself a blessing?" Over the years, many preachers of sermons have given these phrases many types of interpretations. What the Midrash does, however, is something absolutely unique. It says first, "and I will bless you." It then goes on to say, "And you will be a blessing." But let us understand what that means. What God is saying means that as a result of "My blessing, you Abraham, in the future, you will be a source of blessing and be able to bless others." The Midrash then goes on to say that the most remarkable thing that happens is that Abraham and his name did indeed become the most important source of blessing. Every time we recite the *Amidah* or *Shmoneh Esreh* or whenever a *minyan* gets together to recite the daily service, no matter how, when or where, the very first blessing is always *Magen Avraham*. What this means is that God blesses us through Abraham.

—

Additional Commentary

What does it mean to be great?

"And I will make you into a great nation." (Gen. 12:2) This is one of several phrases where greatness is ascribed to Abraham. Another phrase is, "and thou shalt be the father of a multitude of nations" (17:4). It also says in 18:18, "seeing that Abraham shall surely become a great and mighty nation." We have to understand that the greatness that we are talking about is not bigness. The promise was not that the descendants of Abraham would be another Babylon, Assyria, or Rome. The term "great" has to do with quality and character, a great nation in terms of morality and a great nation in terms of culture. (Mirkin)

PARASHAH THIRTY-NINE, *Midrash Twelve*

יב ואברכה מברכיך. א"ר ירמיה: החמיר הקב"ה בכבודו של צדיק יותר מכבודו. בכבודו כתיב: (שמואל א ב): כי מכבדי אכבד ובוזי יקלו ע"י אחרים. ובכבודו של צדיק, כתיב: ואברכה מברכיך ומקללך אאור.

12. AND I WILL BLESS THEM THAT BLESS THEE (GEN. 12:3). R. JEREMIAH B. ELEAZAR SAID: THE HOLY ONE, BLESSED BE HE, WAS STRICTER IN DEFENSE OF THE HONOR OF THE RIGHTEOUS THAN OF HIS OWN HONOR. FOR IN RESPECT TO HIS OWN HONOR, IT IS WRITTEN: FOR THEM THAT HONOR ME I WILL HONOR, AND THEY THAT DESPISE ME SHALL BE DISGRACED (I SAM. 2:30), WHICH MEANS THROUGH OTHERS; WHEREAS CONCERNING THE HONOR OF THE RIGHTEOUS, IT IS WRITTEN: AND I WILL BLESS THEM THAT BLESS THEE, AND HIM THAT CURSETH THEE WILL I CURSE – I MYSELF.

The proof text here is based on the grammar of the words in the case of honor due to God, etc. It does not say enemies will be cursed by Him but by others.

אנא תניא אלו ברכות שאדם שוחה בהם? באבות תחלה וסוף. מודים תחלה וסוף. והשוחה על כל ברכה וברכה מלמדין אותו שלא לשוח. רבי יצחק בר נחמן בשם רבי יהושע בן לוי אמר: כהן גדול תחלת כל ברכה שוחה, והמלך בתחלת כל ברכה וסוף כל ברכה שוחה. רבי

סימון בשם רבי יהושע בן לוי אמר: המלך משהיה כורע לא היה נזקף עד שהיה גומר כל
תפלתו, הה"ד (מלכים א ח): ויהי ככלות שלמה להתפלל אל ה' את כל התפלה והתחנה הזאת,
קם מלפני מזבח ה' מכרוע על ברכיו וכפיו פרושות השמים.

IT WAS TAUGHT: AT THESE BENEDICTIONS ONE MUST BOW: AT THE BE-
GINNING AND END OF THE FIRST, AND AT THE BEGINNING AND END OF
"WE GIVE THANKS"; AND IF A MAN BOWS AT EACH BENEDICTION, HE
MUST BE INSTRUCTED TO REFRAIN. R. ISAAC B. R. NAHMAN SAID IN THE
NAME OF R. JOSHUA B. LEVI: THE HIGH PRIEST BOWS AT THE BEGINNING
OF EACH BENEDICTION, AND A KING MUST BOW AT THE BEGINNING AND
THE END OF EACH BENEDICTION. R. SIMON SAID IN THE NAME OF R.
JOSHUA B. LEVI: ONCE HE [THE KING] HAD BENT THE KNEE, HE DID NOT
STRAIGHTEN HIMSELF UNTIL HE FINISHED HIS ENTIRE PRAYER, AS IT
IS WRITTEN: AND IT WAS SO, THAT WHEN SOLOMON HAD MADE AN END
OF PRAYING ALL THIS PRAYER AND SUPPLICATION UNTO THE LORD, HE
AROSE FROM BEFORE THE ALTAR OF THE LORD, FROM KNEELING ON HIS
KNEES, ETC. (I KINGS 8:54).

We learn from this section that kneeling was the basic form of Jewish
worship in the Temple. In the case of the average person, he would kneel
at the beginning of a major prayer and at the end. Very special people,
such as the High Priest and the king would kneel much more often and
in a much more pretentious way. This kneeling was eventually replaced
with bowing (*shoheh*) as the Midrash states here and as we will explain
later.

ואיזו כריעה ואיזו בריכה? רבי חייא רבה הראה כריעה לפני רבי ונפסח ונתרפא. ובר סיסי
הראה בריכה לפני רבי ונפסח ולא נתרפא.

WHAT IS *KERI'AH* AND WHAT IS *BERIKHAH*? R. HIYYA THE ELDER
SHOWED RABBI THE ACTION OF *KERI'AH*, AND BECAME LAME, BUT WAS
SUBSEQUENTLY HEALED. LEVI B. SUSI SHOWED RABBI THE ACTION OF
BERIKHAH; HE BECAME LAME AND WAS NOT HEALED.

You have here a description of the difference between בריכה, kneeling,
and כריעה, prostrating. Kneeling has to do with the weight being carried
by the knees. Prostrating means having the body stretched out on the
floor.

ונברכו בך, הגשמים בזכותך, הטללים בזכותך, הה"ד (אסתר ב): ויודע הדבר למרדכי ויגד
לאסתר המלכה וגו', זה מהול וזה ערל וחם עליו, אתמהא? ר"י ור"נ ר"י אומר (תהלים קיט):

מזקנים אתבונן כי פקודיך נצרתי. אמר: יעקב בירך את פרעה, שנאמר (בראשית מז): ויברך
יעקב את פרעה יוסף. גילה לו, דניאל גילה לנבוכדנצר, אף אני כן (אסתר ב): ויגד לאסתר
המלכה. ור' נחמיה אמר: אמר הקב"ה לאברהם אבינו: ונברכו בך כל משפחות האדמה
ובזרעך, אין תימר דלהוי עתירין, הרי עתירין אנון מינן? אלא? לשאלה כשהן נכנסין לצרה,
הם נשאלים לנו, ואנו מגלין להם:

AND IN THEE SHALL BE BLESSED: RAIN AND DEW SHALL COME FOR THY
SAKE. NOW IT IS WRITTEN: AND THE THING BECAME KNOWN TO MOR-
DECAI, WHO TOLD IT UNTO ESTHER THE QUEEN, ETC. (EST. 2:22): HE
[MORDECAI] WAS CIRCUMCISED WHILE THE OTHER [AHASUERUS] WAS
UNCIRCUMCISED, YET HE HAD PITY ON HIM! R. JUDAH QUOTED: FROM
MY ELDERS I RECEIVE UNDERSTANDING (PS. 119:100): HE [MORDECAI]
REASONED THUS: JACOB BLESSED PHARAOH, AS IT IS WRITTEN: AND
JACOB BLESSED PHARAOH (GEN. 47:7); MOREOVER, DID NOT JOSEPH
REVEAL HIS DREAMS TO HIM, AND DID NOT DANIEL REVEAL HIS DREAMS
TO NEBUCHADNEZZAR? SO I TOO; HENCE, AND HE TOLD IT UNTO ESTHER
THE QUEEN. R. NEHEMIAH SAID: THE HOLY ONE, BLESSED BE HE, SAID
TO ABRAHAM: AND IN THEE SHALL ALL THE FAMILIES OF THE EARTH
BE BLESSED. NOW IF THAT IS MEANT IN RESPECT OF WEALTH, THEY
ARE SURELY WEALTHIER THAN WE! BUT IT WAS MEANT IN RESPECT OF
COUNSEL: WHEN THEY GET INTO TROUBLE THEY ASK OUR ADVICE, AND
WE GIVE IT TO THEM.

The question is raised about Mordecai helping Achashverosh even to
the point where his life was saved. The problem is that we are dealing
with one that is circumcised and one that is not. Should they be helping
each other? The Midrash lists a number of individuals who helped non-
Jewish associates. The general feeling seems to be that non-Jews should
be helped when they are in trouble. The only question left unresolved is
whether they should celebrate together.

—

Seed Thoughts

One of the most fascinating aspects of Jewish life is the liturgy. How do
they develop, who developed it and how did it reach the form that it
now possesses?

One can phrase the question in a more abrupt way. How come after
the destruction of the Temple was it possible for the Jewish people and
its spiritual leaders to recreate a form of worship almost instantaneously?

The answer is that it was not instantaneous, but that it was based on a form of worship highly developed, highly perfected, and well-known by a group of professionals such as the priests and Levites as well as the general Jewish population who patronized the form of worship based on the sacrificial system. Thus, in the Midrash we are now dealing with, we begin to understand how it is that when traditional Jews *daven* today, they bow at various points in the service, namely, at the beginning of the *Avot* in the Eighteen Benedictions and end it with *Magen Avraham*. There is also a procedure for bowing at the beginning of *Modim* and again at its *berakhah*.

Why the *Avot*? Because there is the use of *Barukh Atah* at the beginning and the end of the *Avot*. Why the *Modim*? Because it represents the deepest and most profound message of the prayer service, namely the complete and unconditional gratitude to God.

The main point, however, is that at the beginning and at the end, these prayers were featured dramatically by kneeling and prostration. When the Temple was destroyed, these acts were eliminated and were replaced with bowing as detailed by the *Shulhan Arukh*. The whole idea is that this was not a new invention or a new style. It was simply an adaptation of the Temple service to the new needs of the Jewish people.

—

Additional Commentary

Why does the righteous man need special help?

The *tzaddik* suffers more when he is hurt because he does not understand why it should happen since he is a good man, has hurt no one, and betrayed no one. Why should bad things happen to him? God understands this particular feeling of the tzaddik and, therefore, He puts the care and concern for the tzaddik before His concern for Himself. (*Tiferet Tzion*)

PARASHAH THIRTY-NINE, *Midrash Thirteen*

יג וילך אברם כאשר דבר אליו ה' וגו' ולוט טפל לו.

13. SO ABRAM WENT, AS THE LORD HAD SPOKEN UNTO HIM; AND LOT
WENT WITH HIM (GEN. 12:4): LOT WAS MERELY JOINED ON WITH HIM.

The point that the Midrash is trying to establish is that Lot was not
included in the orders that were issued to Abraham, such as לך לך, or
whether he was included in the special blessings to Abraham and in any
other possibility projected for Abraham in the Midrash. He was there
of his own accord and Abraham looked after him in the same way that
Mordecai looked after Esther. When the time came that Lot felt that he
would no longer be beholden to Abraham and had accumulated enough
wealth to support himself, he left Abraham's community to forge a unit
of his own.

ואברם בן שבעים וחמש שנים. הה"ד (שם): ויהי אומן את הדסה היא אסתר. רב אמר: בת
מ' היתה. ושמואל אמר: בת שמונים שנה. רבנן אמרי: בת שבעים וחמשה. רבי ברכיה בשם
רבנן דתמן אמר: אמר הקב"ה לאברהם: אתה יצאת מבית אביך בן שבעים וחמשה שנים,
חייך! אף גואל שאני מעמיד ממך, יהיה בן שבעים וחמשה שנים, כמנין הדסה:

AND ABRAM WAS SEVENTY-FIVE YEARS OLD. THUS IT IS WRITTEN, AND
HE BROUGHT UP HADASSAH (EST. 2:7). RAB SAID: SHE WAS FORTY YEARS
OLD; SAMUEL SAID: SHE WAS EIGHTY YEARS OLD; THE RABBIS OF THAT
PLACE [I.E., BABYLONIA] SAID: SHE WAS SEVENTY-FIVE YEARS OLD. R.
BEREKIAH OBSERVED IN THE NAME OF THE RABBIS: THE HOLY ONE,
BLESSED BE HE, ASSURED ABRAHAM: "THOU DIDST LEAVE THY FATHER'S
HOUSE WHEN SEVENTY-FIVE YEARS OLD; BY THY LIFE, THE REDEEMER
WHOM I WILL RAISE UP FROM THEE SHALL BE SEVENTY-FIVE YEARS
OLD," THIS BEING THE NUMERICAL VALUE OF HADASSAH.

This is the calculation in accordance with which Esther is described
as being 75 or 80 years old, way beyond the age of a youngster. A more
elaborate calculation is given by Aryeh Mirkin below.

Seed Thoughts I

One of the saddest outcomes of this Midrash is the manner in which Lot is characterized. At the beginning of the Midrash, there is a question whether he was included in God's order to Abraham to leave Ur Casdim or not included. It appears that Lot joined Abraham, you might say, because his room and board was looked after. By the same token, Abraham felt an obligation to Lot who was his brother's son. What happened as time went on is that Abraham favored Lot with much of his abundance and allowed him to choose where he would prefer to live and which sheep he would want to look after. The result was that Lot became wealthy in his own right. When that happened, Lot chose to separate himself from Abraham. The separation, however, was not only personal but included a separation from his religion and from God.

Seed Thoughts II

It will certainly come as a surprise to most people in the world that the midrashic text does not believe that Esther was a young girl when she won the beauty contest and married King Ahashverosh. Based on various textual readings, which will be listed elsewhere, there are those who feel that she was 75, others say that she was 80. One of the support sources of her being 75, is her other name Hadassah, which numerical value is close to 75 (it's actually 74, but one is sometimes added for the word).

This is one of several occasions where the text comes into conflict with life. It really does not matter what the rabbis are saying in the scriptural proof texts. Life will simply not accept them. The Jewish people will continue to celebrate Purim and continue to adore Esther and continue to regard her as one who won the beauty contest at a younger age. They will also continue to regard her as one of the great heroines of the Jewish people, who saved her community and people from a terrible calamity and move them from darkness to light, which lasted for several generations.

Seed Thoughts III

Since reading the Midrash about the possibility of Esther being a much older person, 40, 75, or 80, I have been waiting to see whether or not there is an important commentator who would feel as negative about these commentaries and their textual proof as my own. I finally found one such important personality in the writings of the *Tiferet Tzion*. He begins by saying that the Book of Esther talks about Esther and then simply says that she was formerly known as Hadassah. But who was Hadassah and why did she have the name of Hadassah and what was so special about being called Esther? The main conclusion of the *Tiferet Tzion* is that Esther describes the heroine from the point of view of her actual place in society. She was, as the book says, a נערה – *naarah*, a young woman, very beautiful, who competed in the beauty contest against her will and who was chosen by the king to be his queen. The name Hadassah interprets Esther from an entirely different point of view. Mordecai, who adopted her, was her model. She did everything possible to refine her character, to do as many commandments and good deeds as was possible for her. The sage who said that she was 40, used that number as a synonym for wisdom as mentioned in the Ethics of the Fathers, ארבעים לבינה – *arba'im lebinah*. He did not mean that she was 40 years, but that she had the wisdom of a 40 year-old although she was a young girl. The sage who said that she was 80 did not mean that she was 80 years old chronologically but that the age of 80 is associated with גבורות – *g'vurot*, meaning extraordinary accomplishments spiritually. The one who used the term 75 had in mind the numerical values of the letters in the name Hadassah (74 plus the word itself).

The *Tiferet Tzion* says that this is one way of looking at this paragraph of which he approves. There is another direction which some Sages advocate. For those who believe in reincarnation, she already existed in the world before that time and thus brought with her the learning and the achievements of 40, 75, or 80.

Additional Commentary

How old was Esther in the Purim story?

Esther married Ahashverosh in the seventh year of his reign. Haman's evil decree was in the twelfth year of the reign of King Ahashverosh.

That same year, the deliverance of the Jews took place. The calculation of the rabbis was that she was at least 75 when she married Ahashverosh. The verse quoted from the Megillah, chapter 2:5–7, describes how Mordecai came to Jerusalem when King Yechanyah was driven out of Jerusalem. Starting then and all the years that followed, he looked after Hadassah. Thirty-seven years after *galut Yechanyeh* until the reign of Eveel Meroda'h, who was king for 23 years (*Megillah* 11:2) was followed by Belshatzar, who was king of Persia for 3 years. You would have to add at this point 5 years of Daryavesh (Darius) and Cirus (Cyrus), all of which are mentioned in the Megillah and the Talmud. Furthermore, to this calculation, you would have to add the seven years in which Ahashverosh was king until he was married to Esther. It all adds up to 75 years from the *galut Yechanyeh* to the marriage of Esther to the king. All of this is substantiated by Rabbi Zev Wolf Einhorn. Or we could say that this follows the numerical value of Hadassah which is 74, when Esther entered the contest and married one year later at 75. (Aryeh Mirkin)

PARASHAH THIRTY-NINE, *Midrash Fourteen*

יד ואת הנפש אשר עשו בחרן. אמר רבי אלעזר בן זימרא: אם מתכנסין כל באי העולם
לברוא אפילו יתוש אחד, אינן יכולין לזרוק בו נשמה, ואת אמר ואת הנפש אשר עשו? אלא,
אלו הגרים שגיירו. ואם כן שגיירו למה אמר עשו? אלא ללמדך, שכל מי שהוא מקרב את
העובד כוכבים ומגיירו כאלו בראו. ויאמר אשר עשה, למה נאמר אשר עשו? אמר רב הונא:
אברהם היה מגייר את האנשים ושרה מגיירת את הנשים:

14. AND ABRAM TOOK SARAI HIS WIFE, AND LOT THEIR BROTHER'S SON, AND ALL THEIR SUBSTANCE WHICH THEY HAD GATHERED, AND THE SOULS THAT THEY HAD MADE IN HARAN (GEN. 12:5). R. ELAZAR OBSERVED IN THE NAME OF R. JOSE B. ZIMRA: IF ALL THE NATIONS ASSEMBLED TO CREATE ONE INSECT THEY COULD NOT ENDOW IT WITH LIFE, YET YOU SAY, AND THE SOULS THAT THEY HAD MADE! IT REFERS, HOWEVER, TO THE PROSELYTES [WHICH THEY HAD MADE]. THEN LET IT SAY, THAT THEY HAD CONVERTED; WHY THAT THEY HAD MADE? THAT IS TO TEACH YOU THAT HE WHO BRINGS A GENTILE NEAR [TO GOD] IS AS THOUGH HE CREATED HIM. NOW LET IT SAY, THAT HE HAD MADE; WHY THAT THEY HAD MADE? SAID R. HUNA: ABRAHAM CONVERTED THE MEN, AND SARAH THE WOMEN.

Seed Thoughts

In this Midrash, we learn that Abraham and Sarah had succeeded in converting many non-Jewish individuals to Judaism and the Torah. There are those who say that the people they converted were actually their servants, but that does not alter the fact that they indeed converted to Judaism one-hundred percent.

I would like to point out to the attention of the reader that in the previous Midrash, they described Abraham's dealing with Lot. Abraham was unusually generous towards Lot, both personally and financially. And yet, when the time came and Lot left Abraham with his assets in order to live separately as the master of his own estate, he not only deserted Abraham, he also deserted the God of Abraham.

Here we have a situation which in modern times we observe time and time again, but in Scripture it seems quite unusual. The great Abraham and Sarah who were able to convert hundreds, and maybe more, to the spiritual life of Judaism, did not succeed with their flesh and blood nephew, Lot. Abraham's nephew lived in his household, watched Abraham and Sarah and learned many things from them, but did not learn and did not accept what Abraham wanted him most to love, namely the God of Israel and His statutes. This is not a criticism. It only shows that Abraham was also a human being. You cannot win everything. Sometimes you lose. The greatest of our heroes and leaders sometimes do not succeed. In this one instance, Abraham did not succeed. But even his failure was an important lesson in that if at first you do not succeed you must try and try again.

PARASHAH THIRTY-NINE, *Midrash Fifteen*

טו ויעבור אברם בארץ וגו'. עד עכשיו נתבקש להם זכות בארץ.

15. AND ABRAM PASSED THROUGH THE LAND UNTO THE PLACE OF SHECHEM . . . AND THE CANAANITE WAS THEN IN THE LAND (GEN. 12:6): SO FAR THEY STILL HAD A RIGHT IN THE LAND.

The question that is raised is, why didn't Abraham settle there immediately? Why did he pass through? This will be handled in a more detailed fashion as we go along.

וירא ה' אל אברם ויאמר לזרעך וגו'. לא בנה מזבח, אלא על בשורת א"י.

AND THE LORD APPEARED UNTO ABRAM, AND SAID: UNTO THY SEED WILL I GIVE THIS LAND; AND HE BUILDED THERE AN ALTAR (GEN. 12:7): WHAT IS STATED HERE IS ON ACCOUNT OF THE GOOD TIDINGS ABOUT ERETZ ISRAEL.

The question that is being raised here by the *Tiferet Tzion* and others is why did God promise the Land of Israel to Abraham's descendants? Only to his descendants and not himself? Why did He simply not give the land to Abraham so that he would settle it immediately with himself as the authority? Nevertheless, so important was the promise to his descendants that he immediately built an altar in praise of God and in thankfulness for the gift of the Land of Israel.

ויעתק משם ההרה מקדם לבית אל. לשעבר היתה נקראת בית אל, ועכשיו היא נקראת בית און. אר"א: לא זכה להקראות בית העמוד, הרי היא נקראת בית העמל. תמן קריין לפועלא טבא עמידא, ולהרהון של מימי רגלים עמילה.

AND HE REMOVED FROM THENCE UNTO THE MOUNTAIN ON THE EAST OF (MI-KEDEM) BETH EL (GEN. 12:8): ORIGINALLY IT WAS CALLED BETH EL (HOUSE OF GOD), BUT NOW IT IS CALLED BETH AWEN (HOUSE OF IN-IQUITY). R. LIEZER SAID: HE WHO DOES NOT MERIT BEING CALLED *BEN HE-AMAL* IS CALLED *BEN HE-AMAD*. R. ISAAC B. NAHMAN SAID: THERE [IN PALESTINE], A GOOD WORKER IS CALLED *AMELA* (INDUSTRIOUS), WHILE URINE-SOAKED DUNG IS CALLED *AMIDAH*.

B eth El was considered as one of the holiest of places in Israel, almost as much as Jerusalem. However, Jeroboam, who took over the northern kingdom by revolution after the days of King Solomon, placed idols in Beth El to divert people from going to the Temple in Jerusalem. It was this event that changed the character of Beth El and gave it the very names listed in our Midrash that cheapened its reputation and removed its sanctity.

ויט אהלה. אהלה כתיב, מלמד שנטע אהל שרה תחלה, ואח"כ נטע אהלו:

AND PITCHED HIS TENT (*AHALO*). R. HANINA SAID: *AHALAH* (HER TENT) IS WRITTEN; AFTER HAVING PITCHED SARAH'S TENT HE PITCHED HIS OWN.

T he fact that the word אהלה is written with a ה – *heh*, and not with a ו – *vav*, is interpreted by the Midrash as being a feminine ending. They concluded from this that Abraham first looked after Sarah's tent and saw to it that all her belongings were placed in a way that would contribute to her well-being. This, it is hoped, would be a lesson to all married couples of the primacy of the Jewish woman in the Jewish home.

⁓

Seed Thoughts

I am always amazed when I come across material in the Midrash that reads like an editorial in the twentieth-century. What are the greatest concerns of the Jewish people today who love Israel? The struggle for rights in the Land of Israel. The rights of the Jewish people have been preserved for centuries in documents such as the Bible and prayer book. The Palestinians and other Arabs claim rights of centuries of residence, but it is obviously not a new thing. The Midrash interprets the story of Abraham and his entrance into the Land of Israel as a triumph of the Jewish understanding of their rights to the land. The truth of the matter is that the Canaanites who were dominant at the time were idol worshippers of one form or another. The real danger is that these beliefs were not just theological, but rather the immoral way of life seemed to be associated with the worship of idols. It was this that justified conquering and building in the land in the time of Abraham. There is no idol worship today, but the absence of a real national need on the part of the Palestinians who never had a nation state, and who could, if so desired, identify with twenty-one other Arab states, is quite different than the story of Abraham and the Canaanites.

—

Additional Commentary

Rights to the land – Part 1

The difficulty in the text is that when God appeared to Abraham, it was not with the intention of him settling the land immediately, as was originally promised to him. What was happening at this point was that they were looking for some rights that would justify his taking over of the land, because the Holy One, blessed is He, does not deprive any human being of their rights. The Canaanites had a right to be in the land until that particular moment. For this reason God's appearance to Abraham was to tell him about his descendants who would receive the land and not himself. However, when Abraham and his entire entourage passed through the land, they were completely ignored. After all, Abraham was known throughout the area, not only as a leader but as one with great intelligence who offered a very important way of life. Nobody sought his opinion; nobody offered him help or assistance, not even lending a bowl of oil. This is one of the reasons that justified removing their rights to the land. (*Tiferet Tzion*)

Rights to the land – Part 2

The verse says specifically, "The Canaanites were then in the land," which meant that the Canaanite had political sovereignty and the Children of Israel were looking for such authority בדין שמים – *bedin Shamayim*, by a decisive law that would come from Heaven. They did receive such a right when God said to Abraham at the Covenant of the Pieces. This was alluded to in a text which says that they were not sufficiently punished for the sin of the anti-Israel behavior over many years. That was now to come. (*HaMidrash HaMevo'ar*)

Parashah Thirty-Nine, *Midrash Sixteen*

טז ויבן שם מזבח לה'. אר"א: ג' מזבחות בנה. אחד לבשורת א"י, וא' לקנינה, וא' שלא יפלו
בניו. הה"ד (יהושע ז): ויקרע יהושע שמלותיו ויפול על פניו ארצה לפני ארון ה' עד הערב,
הוא וזקני ישראל ויעלו עפר על ראשם. אר"א בן שמוע: התחילו מזכירים זכותו של אברהם
אבינו, שנאמר (בראשית יח): ואנכי עפר ואפר: כלום בנה אברהם מזבח בעי? אלא שלא יפלו
בניו בעי.

16. AND HE BUILDED THERE AN ALTAR UNTO THE LORD (GEN. 12:16). R.
LEAZAR SAID: HE BUILT THREE ALTARS – ONE ON ACCOUNT OF THE GOOD
TIDINGS ABOUT ERETZ ISRAEL, ANOTHER FOR HIS POSSESSION THEREOF,
AND A THIRD [AS A PRAYER], THAT HIS DESCENDANTS MIGHT NOT FALL
AT AI, AS IT IS WRITTEN: AND JOSHUA RENT HIS CLOTHES, AND FELL TO
THE EARTH UPON HIS FACE BEFORE THE ARK OF THE LORD UNTIL THE
EVENING, HE AND THE ELDERS OF ISRAEL, AND THEY PUT DUST UPON
THEIR HEADS (JOSH. 7:6). R. LEAZAR B. SHAMUA SAID: THEY BEGAN RE-
CALLING THE MERIT OF OUR FATHER ABRAHAM, WHO SAID, I AM BUT
DUST AND ASHES (GEN. 18:27). ABRAHAM THEN BUILT THEE AN ALTAR AT
AI FOR AUGHT BUT THAT HIS CHILDREN SHOULD NOT FALL THERE!

Although it is quite true that Abraham created and offered in prayer
three altars – only two of them commemorated an event. The third had
to do with his hope that the people of Ai, who were in a confrontation
with the people of Beth El should not be victimized by war and similar
uprisings.

ויקרא בשם ה'. מלמד שהקריא שמו של הקב"ה בפי כל בריה. ד"א: ויקרא, התחיל מגייר
גרים ולהכניסם תחת כנפי השכינה. ויסע אברם הלוך ונסוע הנגבה, מחקה והולך ומכוין כנגד
ביהמ"ק:

AND CALLED UPON THE NAME OF THE LORD: WITH PRAYER. ANOTHER
INTERPRETATION OF AND CALLED: HE BEGAN TO MAKE CONVERTS. AND
ABRAM JOURNEYED, GOING ON STILL TOWARD THE SOUTH (GEN. 12:9):
HE DREW A COURSE AND JOURNEYED TOWARD THE [FUTURE] SITE OF
THE TEMPLE.

"Called upon the Name of the Lord" is interpreted as Abraham's efforts to convert men and women to his understanding of God and of
what we know today as monotheism.

⌢

Seed Thoughts

Based on the Additional Commentary by the *Tiferet Tzion*, it should be said that the goal of life is not to rest but to be creative spiritually at all times.

⌢

Additional Commentary

Abraham in relationship to the Land of Israel

מחקה והולך – *mehakeh veholekh*. One of the problems is that the text says *halokh venaso'a*, to walk and travel in the land, after it had already said *vayisa Avraham*, and Abraham traveled. It should only have said "Abraham traveled south." What was the point of his traveling south? After all, he had already carried out God's command the moment he entered Eretz Israel. And God said to him, "To your seed will I give this land." He should have, therefore, stayed in the place where he created the altar. In this connection the Midrash says, מחקה והולך – *mehakeh veholekh*. The interpretation is that when it comes to the holiness of the land, there are levels of holiness. The portion of Yehuda is holier than the portion of the Galilee. The holiness of Jerusalem is greater than the holiness of Yehuda. The Temple Mount is holier than even Jerusalem. The place of the Temple, which is interpreted as being the gate of Heaven, is the holiest of all. A tzaddik feels this. He feels that the place is especially holy when he is standing there, because from that particular holy place he receives an abundance of spiritual holiness. As the rabbis said, the prophets began prophesying in Jerusalem because of the tremendous holiness of the place. The result was that they were able to feel personally the elevation of their prophecy.

When Abraham came to Israel, he arrived first in the Galilee, and then, heading south, he arrived in the Shomron where Shechem is. He already felt the power of prophecy far more than in חוץ לארץ – *hutz laAretz*, out of the Land (of Israel). In the beginning, it says about his relationship with God, "And God said . . ." After coming to Israel it said, "God appeared to Abraham . . ." That is a much higher level. Abraham felt this spirit of holiness and realized that there are some places that are holier than others, so that is where he went. Whenever he went, it says, הלוך ונסוע – *halokh venaso'a*, which means that when a person moves up from one level to another level, this is called הליכה – *halikhah*. The meaning is that even when a person is in a world of angels, often described as those who stand in their own place, Abraham is among those who walk among the angels – from one level to another. Even in the World to Come, a sage will have no rest because he will be motivated to continue his path from one level to another. That is how Abraham felt – he was moving from one level to another in holiness. That is why he moved in the direction of the Negev, towards the south. (*Tiferet Tzion*)

Parashah Forty, *Midrash One*

א ויהי רעב בארץ וירד אברם מצרימה לגור.

1. AND THERE WAS A FAMINE IN THE LAND, ETC. (GEN. 12:10).

This Midrash is concerned with the fact that there was a famine in the land of Canaan which forced Abraham to emigrate to Egypt, not merely as a visitor but to live there and to inhabit the land with all of its belongings. The question that concerns the Midrash is why does God allow this to happen – that Abraham should be forced to seek his bread elsewhere after being given the greatest possible blessings by God?

כתיב (תהלים לג): הנה עין ה' אל יראיו למיחלים לחסדו. הנה עין ה' אל יראיו, זה אברהם,
שנאמר (בראשית כב): כי עתה ידעתי כי ירא אלהים אתה. למיחלים לחסדו, שנאמר (מיכה ז):
תתן אמת ליעקב חסד לאברהם וגו'. להציל ממות נפשם, ממיתתו של נמרוד. ולחיותם
ברעב, ויהי רעב בארץ:

IT IS WRITTEN: BEHOLD, THE EYE OF THE LORD IS TOWARD THEM THAT FEAR HIM (PS. 33:18): THIS ALLUDES TO ABRAHAM, OF WHOM IT IS WRITTEN: FOR NOW I KNOW THAT THOU ART A GOD-FEARING MAN (GEN. 22:12). TOWARD THEM THAT WAIT FOR HIS MERCY (PS. 33:18), THUS IT IS WRITTEN: THOU WILT SHOW FAITHFULNESS TO JACOB, MERCY TO ABRAHAM (MICAH 7:20). TO DELIVER THEIR SOUL FROM DEATH (PS. 33:19), FROM THE DEATH DECREED BY NIMROD. AND TO KEEP THEM ALIVE IN FAMINE (33:19), THUS IT IS WRITTEN: AND THERE WAS A FAMINE IN THE LAND; AND ABRAM WENT DOWN INTO EGYPT TO SOJOURN THERE.

The development of the Midrash indicates God's relationship to man – especially unusual leaders like Abraham. Even their suffering is part of their training for leadership. When the allotted degree of painfulness and restrictions like famine are completed, God would elevate them as they completed the challenges of life and leadership with great credit to themselves.

~

Seed Thoughts

The average person would read the text of the Torah which mentions that there was a famine in the land and Abraham moved to Egypt where there was food. Millions of Jews have read this line without any problem. Along comes the Midrash and asks how is this possible?! God had just said to Abraham, "I will bless you, I will make your name great and you will be a blessing." How, then, could He allow Abraham to search for bread, leading him into Egypt? The answer is that Abraham went to Egypt of his own accord. He did not believe that he or anyone else who look upon themselves as righteous has a claim for miracles. Miracles are God's department, not man's. God does not need any advice concerning miracles or should there be any such request. He has given us the whole world including its possibilities and challenges. Abraham understood this, accepted it and tried to be a role model for others. There is a famine, so he went to Egypt where there is food. He did not ask for permission, he did not ask God what to do. He used his common sense which told him what to do. There is a tremendous lesson in all of this, and among other things, it has the power of making those who consider themselves to be good people and are looked upon as such by others. Their spiritual challenge is no different of that of others, and they have to keep trying to do their best and be their best. We are taught the meaning of humility.

~

Additional Commentary

Miracles or no miracles?

The verse we are quoting refers to, "The eye of the Lord is towards those who fear Him." (Ps. 33:18) This verse speaks about the righteous who follow in the way of Abraham, who did not want to benefit from the divine way of miracles. For this reduces a person's merit. He and they wanted to benefit from the natural order of things which God grants to the entire world with His love and mercy. For example, Abraham said to the Holy One, blessed be He, I saw in the astrological signs that I was not going to have a son. This is a problem in the sense of – what was the point of him referring to astrology in light of the fact that the Holy One, blessed be He, Who directs the entire world, including the *mazalot* (constellations), had already promised him of having a son? However, this was due to the fact that he did not want to benefit from a miraculous life that he made use of the astrological formula. God, therefore, advised him that He would adjust the mazalot, which control the natural world so that there will be no problems giving birth to a son. Furthermore, this would not be against the natural world. In this sense, the verse said, "The eye of the Lord is upon those who fear Him," meaning that even though God sometimes relates with the righteous with the assistance of miracles, nevertheless, those *hassidim* who long for His mercy do not wish to benefit from these miracles but from the benefits of the natural world. (*Tiferet Tzion*)

What kind of fear is the fear of Heaven?

The Midrash makes a point that in the very last challenge to Abraham at the *Akeida* – now at last He knows that Abraham fears Him. The reason why this is spoken about is because we are dealing with יראת הרוממות – *yirat haRomemut*, the fear of the Majesty of God, which means that fear which exists only because of the honor and the glory that is due to God and has nothing whatsoever to do with the kind of fear that makes the person afraid for his life. This is the highest possible level of religious experience. It is much higher than love and, therefore, the verse says, עין ד' אל יראיו – *eyin Elohim el yireav*, "The eye of the Lord is towards those who fear Him" (and not those who are fearful). (*Tiferet Tzion*)

PARASHAH FORTY, *Midrash Two*

ב ויהי רעב בארץ. רבי פנחס בשם רבי חנין דציפורין פתח: (תהלים צד) אשרי הגבר אשר
תיסרנו יה ואם בא להקפיד, ומתורתך תלמדנו. מה כתיב? באברהם, ואברכך ואגדלה שמך,
כיון שיצא, קפץ עליו רעבון ולא קרא תגר, ולא הקפיד, אלא וירד אברם מצרימה לגור שם.

2. R. PHINEHAS COMMENCED HIS DISCOURSE IN THE NAME OF R. HANAN
OF SEPPHORIS: HAPPY IS THE MAN WHOM THOU CHASTISEST, O LORD
(PS. 94:12): YET SHOULD HE OBJECT, THEN, "AND TEACHEST OUT OF THY
LAW" (94:12): WHAT IS WRITTEN OF ABRAHAM? AND I WILL BLESS THEE,
AND MAKE THY NAME GREAT (GEN. 12:2). AS SOON AS HE SET OUT, FAM-
INE ASSAILED HIM, YET HE DID NOT PROTEST NOR MURMUR AGAINST
HIM, BUT, AND ABRAM WENT DOWN INTO EGYPT, ETC.

It is of interest to note that R. Pinhas quoted the verse from Psalms
acknowledging that chastisement can't be good and it should have then
said, "this is learned from Your Torah." But it does not use that language.
Instead it says that from the Torah we can learn all about this phenomenon. In other words, it is possible to have Torah without suffering but
in this verse the suffering is given primacy to show that the suffering
and or the chastisement is for the welfare of the person. As we learned
earlier, if the person protests this arrangement, he should be reminded
that Abraham who was much greater than he, also suffered, never complained, and went about the situation with the best of his ability.

ויהי רעב בארץ. רבי יהושע בן לוי פתח: (שם קיא) טרף נתן ליראיו, טירוף נתן ליראיו בעולם
הזה, אבל לעתיד לבא, יזכור לעולם. מה כתיב באברהם: ואברכך ואגדלה שמך, כיון שיצא
קפץ עליו רעבון ולא הקפיד ולא קרא תגר, אלא ויהי רעב בארץ:

R. JOSHUA B. LEVI COMMENCED THUS: HE HATH GIVEN *TEREF* [E.V.
"FOOD"] UNTO THEM THAT FEAR HIM; HE WILL BE EVER MINDFUL OF HIS
COVENANT (PS. 111:5). SAID R. JOSHUA B. LEVI: IN THIS WORLD, HE HATH
GIVEN WANDERINGS (*TIRUF*) UNTO THEM THAT FEAR HIM; BUT IN THE
MESSIANIC FUTURE, "HE WILL BE EVER MINDFUL OF HIS COVENANT."
FOR WHAT IS WRITTEN OF ABRAM? AND I WILL BLESS THEE, AND MAKE
THY NAME GREAT (GEN. 12:2). AS SOON AS HE SET OUT, FAMINE ASSAILED
HIM, YET HE DID NOT PROTEST NOR MURMUR AGAINST HIM, BUT, AND
THERE WAS A FAMINE IN THE LAND, ETC.

T he Midrash repeats the situation of Abraham, who after receiving the greatest possible blessing was forced to experience a terrible famine which he accepted without complaint. All of this is written in the Torah in order to teach the future generations how to receive such difficulties in the spirit of love, for this is the only purpose of the suffering. The Midrash has an explanatory note as to why the word טרף – *teref* is used in place of ordinary words like לחם – *lehem* for bread, or מזון – *mazon* for food. The expression *teref* is usually used for wild or domestic animals. This is now used in the Midrash as טירוף של גלות – *teruf shel galut*, meaning the additional insecurity of living in exile. It is as though the struggle for bread and food was made that much more difficult, almost animalistic and therefore the expression *teruf*.

R. Joshua b. Levi makes the point that there is no true מנוחה – *menuhah*, exceptional rest, for the human being on this earth. That can only happen in the time to come and in the World to Come.

***

Seed Thoughts

This Midrash deals with one of the most ethical problems in human life. Why do human beings suffer, and specifically, why do Jews who do not sin and who do good deeds suffer pain or discomfort and experiences that make it harder and harder for them to live a good life?

Both Midrashim that we have just covered describe the fact that many good people suffer. When and if they question this suffering, they are immediately reminded of the biography of Abraham whom they all admit was far superior to them in moral and ethical living as well as in other areas of the human experience. He suffered and never complained. Why can they not emulate him and suffer in silence?

This, however, begs the question, why should even Abraham have had to suffer? He was the person who received the tremendous blessing, "I will bless you and make your name great." He of all people should have been spared suffering. The *Tiferet Tzion* offers a particular explanation. From time to time, God withdraws His presence from the world or at any rate does not interfere with the decision-making process. In Hebrew, this is called הסתר פנים – *haster panim*. The *Tiferet Tzion* goes on to say that the good people will be blessed and receive a reward, in proportion to God's removal from the world, with all its difficulties.

This is a beautiful ideal, but we have to acknowledge that this is a

belief. Beliefs as a general rule cannot be proven. That does not necessarily lessen their impact, their goal, and their hope.

⁓

Additional Commentary

Famine and the Land of Israel

Although Abraham was forced to suffer the kind of famine that forced
him down to Egypt, he did not complain. He had already left Haran, his
original starting place, to a life in the land of Canaan which was God's
will and experienced a great famine, but he did not turn back and did
not protest. We can now see that this was the purpose of the events that
happened to him, so that others would follow his example and accept
similar challenges without falling into despair. (*HaMidrash HaMevo'ar*)

The suffering of good people

In the case of Abraham, we read in the text that after he was blessed with
some outstanding blessings of which language was capable of expressing, he was suddenly punished with famine and was forced to seek bread
for his family in other ways. We learn from this that even a person who
is free from sin, who also did very good deeds, and who deserves to be
blessed, was nevertheless deprived of this blessing which was replaced
with pain and suffering. There is no greater seeming divine withdrawal
from the world – הסתר פנים, *haster panim* – than this. It is in this respect
that the verse says, "God will forever remember His covenant."יזכור לעולם
בריתו – *yizkor le-olam brito*. What is that covenant? The reward of doing
the commandments is in relationship to the power, the frequency, and
the length of God's seeming withdrawal from the world. Despite this, a
person should not stumble in his faith, but should continue to perform
the commandments in the spirit of joy and love. In this manner, his reward will grow in the World to Come forever. In conclusion, God who
does all the good in the world, הטוב והמטיב – *hatov vehametiv*, has given
this challenge to those who fear Him, in order to increase the reward in
the world to come for this is the true good, the true end, and the true
fulfillment. (*Tiferet Tzion*)

PARASHAH FORTY, *Midrash Three*

ג וירד אברם מצרימה לגור שם. י' רעבון באו לעולם. אחד בימי אדם הראשון, וכוליה עניינא
עד ואחד לעתיד לבא (עמוס ח): לא רעב ללחם ולא צמא למים כי אם לשמוע את דברי ה'.
כדלעיל מן האדמה אשר אררה כו'.

3. AND THERE WAS A FAMINE IN THE LAND, ETC. TEN FAMINES HAVE
COME UPON THE EARTH. ONE IN THE DAYS OF ADAM: CURSED IS THE
GROUND FOR THY SAKE (GEN. 3:17); ONE IN THE DAYS OF LAMECH:
WHICH COMETH FROM THE GROUND WHICH THE LORD HATH CURSED
(5:29); ONE IN THE DAYS OF ABRAHAM: AND THERE WAS A FAMINE IN
THE LAND; ONE IN THE DAYS OF ISAAC: AND THERE WAS FAMINE IN THE
LAND, BESIDE THE FIRST FAMINE THAT WAS IN THE DAYS OF ABRAHAM
(26:1); ONE IN THE DAYS OF JACOB: FOR THESE TWO YEARS HATH THE
FAMINE BEEN IN THE LAND (45:6); ONE IN THE DAYS WHEN THE JUDGES
JUDGED: AND IT CAME TO PASS IN THE DAYS THAT THE JUDGES JUDGED,
THAT THERE WAS A FAMINE IN THE LAND (RUTH 1:1); ONE IN THE DAYS
OF DAVID: AND THERE WAS A FAMINE IN THE DAYS OF DAVID (II SAM.
21:1); ONE IN THE DAYS OF ELIJAH: AS THE LORD, THE GOD OF ISRAEL,
LIVETH, BEFORE WHOM I STAND, THERE SHALL NOT BE DEW NOR RAIN
THESE YEARS (I KINGS 17:1); ONE IN THE DAYS OF ELISHA: AND THERE
WAS A GREAT FAMINE IN SAMARIA (II KINGS 6:25); AND THERE IS ONE
FAMINE THAT TRAVELS ABOUT THE WORLD, AND ONE WILL BE IN THE
MESSIANIC FUTURE – NOT A FAMINE OF BREAD, NOR A THIRST FOR WA-
TER, BUT OF HEARING THE WORDS OF THE LORD (AMOS 8:11).

One of the surprising names in the list is the famine in the time of
Adam. After all, there is ample food and drink in the Garden, and wherever Adam and Eve lived. This is why the verse that appears later on in
Scripture applies to them, that there will come a day of famine. "Not
a famine of bread and water but of listening to the Lord." This kind of
famine will appear again in the future world. Some of the listings also
change the character and meaning of famine. For example, during the
time of Elijah, the famine was due to lack of rain. During the time of
Elisha, the famine was caused by a siege of soldiers of a superior army or
police of a conquering nation (Aram – Assyria) who demanded certain
gifts and privileges from the community at large at the threat of their
demise.

ר' הונא ור' ירמיה בשם ר' שמואל בר רבי יצחק: עיקר אוותנטיאה שלו, לא היתה אלא
בימי דוד, ולא היה ראוי לבא אלא בימי שאול, אלא ע"י שהיה שאול גרופות של שקמה,
וגלגלו הקב"ה והביאו בימי דוד. שילו חטייא וויחנה משתלמא? לפיכך, כלם לא באו אלא
בימי בני אדם גבורים, שהם יכולים לעמוד בהן ולא בימי בני אדם שפופים, שאינן יכולים
לעמוד בהן. א"ר חייא רבה: משל לזוג שהיה בידו קופה מלאה כוסות ודייטרוטין, ובשעה
שהיה מבקש לתלות את קופתו היה מביא יתד ותוקעה ונתלה בה, ואח"כ היה תולה את
קופתו. לפיכך, לא באו בימי בני אדם שפופים, אלא בימי בני אדם גבורים, שהן יכולים
לעמוד בהם.

R. HUNA AND R. JEREMIAH IN THE NAME OF R. SAMUEL B. ISAAC SAID:
THE PROPER TIME FOR ITS MANIFESTATION WAS IN THE DAYS OF DA-
VID, AND IT OUGHT REALLY TO HAVE COME IN THE DAYS OF SAUL, BUT
BECAUSE SAUL WAS THE SHOOT OF A SYCAMORE TREE, THE HOLY ONE,
BLESSED BE HE, POSTPONED IT AND BROUGHT IT IN THE DAYS OF DA-
VID. SHILA SINS AND JOHANA IS PUNISHED! SAID R. HIYYA: IMAGINE A
GLASS-WORKER HOLDING A BASKET FULL OF GOBLETS AND CUT GLASS;
WHEN HE WISHED TO HANG THE BASKET UP, HE BROUGHT A NAIL AND
DROVE IT [INTO THE WALL], AND HELD ON TO IT WHILE HE HUNG UP
HIS BASKET. FOR THAT REASON ALL THESE [FAMINES] CAME NOT IN THE
DAYS OF LOWLY [WEAK] MEN BUT IN THE DAYS OF THE MIGHTY ONES,
WHO COULD WITHSTAND IT.

The Midrash at this point seems to indicate that a famine is closely
connected with a powerful person such as David, rather than Saul. The
reason for this will be discussed later on in this commentary.

רבי ברכיה הוי קרי עליהון (ישעיה מ): נותן ליעף כח. רבי ברכיה בשם ר' חלבו אמר: שנים
באו בימי אברהם. רבי הונא בשם ר' אחא: א' בימי למך וא' בימי אברהם. רעב שבא בימי
אליהו, רעב של בצורת היה. רעב שבא בימי אלישע, רעב של מהומה היה. רעב שבא בימי
שפוט השופטים,

R. BEREKIAH APPLIED TO THEM THE VERSE, HE GIVETH POWER TO
THE FAINT (ISA. 40:29). R. BEREKIAH SAID IN R. HELBO'S NAME: THERE
WERE TWO FAMINES IN THE DAYS OF ABRAHAM. R. HUNA SAID IN R.
AHA'S NAME: THERE WAS ONE IN THE DAYS OF LAMECH AND ONE IN
THE DAYS OF ABRAHAM. THE FAMINE OF ELIJAH'S TIME WAS ONE OF
SCARCITY, ONE YEAR BEING PRODUCTIVE AND THE NEXT YEAR UNPRO-
DUCTIVE. THE FAMINE IN THE DAYS OF ELISHA WAS ONE OF PANIC,
UNTIL AN ASS'S HEAD WAS SOLD FOR FOURSCORE PIECES OF SILVER,
ETC. (II KINGS 6:25). AS FOR THE FAMINE DURING THE DAYS OF THE
JUDGES,

In general, the Midrash interprets the ten famines that have been listed. Not all have to do with the lack of bread and water. Some have to do with various types of physical discomfort which made living very difficult.

רבי הונא בשם רבי דוסא: מ"ב סאין היו ונעשו מ"א. והא תני, לא יצא אדם לחו"ל, אא"כ סאתים של חטים הולכות בסלע. אר"ש בן יוחאי: אימתי? בזמן שאינו מוצא ליקח, אבל אם היה מוצא ליקח אפי' סאה בסלע, לא יצא לחו"ל:

R. HUNA SAID IN R. DOSA'S NAME: FROM THE PRICE OF TWO SE'AHS [OF WHEAT PER SELA] IT ADVANCED TO ONE SE'AH [PER SELA], WHEREAS IT WAS TAUGHT: A MAN MUST NOT EMIGRATE ABROAD UNLESS TWO SE'AHS COST A SELA. R. SIMEON OBSERVED: THAT IS ONLY WHEN IT IS ALTO-GETHER UNOBTAINABLE, BUT IF IT IS OBTAINABLE, EVEN AT A SE'AH PER SELA, ONE MUST NOT GO ABROAD.

See the Additional Commentary for this section on the relationship between the economic factors and emigration.

Seed Thoughts

We have been dealing in some of the opening Midrashim of this section with the challenge of famine as it appeared in various parts of the biblical narrative. The most important question of all, however, is not raised by the Midrash. Why was famine necessary in the first place? Why does God need a famine to exercise His categories of Justice and Mercy? After all, in a famine, not only are the evil ones suffering, but also the good, the righteous *tzaddikim*, and the leadership. Maybe the response to this question can be found in another question. That question is: Why is a famine identified with a particular person? What is the point of saying that the famine should have been in the time of Saul but because he was a lesser personality, it occurred in the time of David? Did Saul's body have a harder time fasting than David's body? The answer seems to be on an entirely different level. God did not order the famine in the time of King Saul because of his inability to handle it – he did not know how to organize the people in the community. In the case of David, however, his kingship was very strong. He not only knew what to do, but he was able to enforce a rule over the people and sustain them. Like his ancestor Joseph, King David used every possible means to provide food for the people, provide them with the necessities of life, so that the famine was not replaced with prosperity but was controlled in a special way that the people were able to survive. This interpretation applies to all the names that were listed in the ten famines, which were given the names of particular biblical personalities to which the famines can be identified.

—

Additional Commentary

Under what economic conditions is emigration from Israel allowed?

"The famine that took place in the time of the Judges." R. Huna in the name of R. Dosa said that they did not take place as an actual famine. What happened was that all the grain increased in price. Formerly, in the days of the Judges, 42 *sayim* could be sold for 1 *sela*. (1 *seah* equals 144 eggs or about 6776 liters, and 1 *sela* equals the weight of 1 silver coin, 19.2 grams.) That was very inexpensive. To show the comparison, in the days of the Sages, 4 *sayim* were sold for 1 *sela*. That is 10 times the value. A person should not leave the Land of Israel because of the high cost of grain unless 2 *sayim* of wheat is sold for a *sela*. R. Shimon b. Yochai modifies this section mentioning that one should not leave even if the price is double unless it cannot be obtained in the marketplace. The proof he uses concerns Elimelech, the husband Naomi, who was very wealthy but left the land to search for a better trade. This resulted in his death and complete loss of a family – for he was able to attain produce in the Land of Israel. (*HaMidrash HaMevo'ar*)

PARASHAH FORTY, *Midrash Four*

ד ויהי כאשר הקריב לבא מצרימה. כל השנים הללו הוא עמה, ועכשיו הוא אומר לה הנה נא
ידעתי כי אשה יפת מראה את? אלא, שע"י הדרך אדם מתבזה וזו עמדה ביפיה.

4. AND IT CAME TO PASS, WHEN HE WAS COME NEAR TO ENTER INTO
EGYPT, ETC. (GEN. 12:11). SHE WAS WITH HIM ALL THESE YEARS, YET NOW
HE SAYS TO HER, BEHOLD, NOW I KNOW THAT THOU ART A FAIR WOMAN
TO LOOK UPON! THE REASON, HOWEVER, IS BECAUSE TRAVELING TAKES
TOLL OF ONE'S BEAUTY.

Over the years, countless numbers of readers of the Torah narrative ask the same question that the Midrash now asks. Abraham and
Sarah were married all these years. Surely he knew how beautiful she
was. The answer is that he had in mind what they were now doing.
They were engaged in traveling to Egypt under circumstances that
were terribly difficult and any opportunity for make-up, such as that
which women use, was out of the question. Most people look their
worst under these circumstances. Not Sarah. She was as beautiful
even under those circumstances and as the commentators put it,
עמדה ביפיה – *amdah beyaphya*; here, beauty was as significant now as
earlier. What Abraham was saying was not only how beautiful she
was, but it was the kind of beauty to which others cannot possibly
compare.

ר' זעירא בשם רבי סימון אמר: הלכנו בארם נהרים ובארם נחור ולא מצאנו אשה נאה
כמותך, עכשיו שאנו נכנסים למקום כעורים ושחורים, אמרי נא אחותי את וגו'.

R. AZARIAH SAID IN THE NAME OF R. JUDAH B. R. SIMON: [ABRAHAM
SAID TO SARAH:] WE HAVE TRAVERSED ARAM NAHARAIM AND ARAM
NAHOR AND NOT FOUND A WOMAN AS BEAUTIFUL AS YOU; NOW THAT
WE ARE ENTERING A COUNTRY WHOSE INHABITANTS ARE SWARTHY AND
UGLY, SAY, I PRAY THEE, THOU ART MY SISTER, THAT IT MAY BE WELL
WITH ME FOR THY SAKE, ETC. (GEN. 12:13).

Nevertheless, her very beauty could have been their undoing and that
is why Abraham asked Sarah for her help. Namely that she should say
that she is his sister.

ר' פנחס בשם רבי אבון אמר: ב' בני אדם היו עיקר ועשו עצמן טפילה ונעשו טפילה. אברהם
וברק. ברק (שופטים ד): ותשלח ותקרא לברק בן אבינועם מקדש נפתלי, ותאמר אליו הלא
צוה ה' אלהי ישראל, לך ומשכת בהר תבור ולקחת עמך עשרת אלפים וגו'. ויאמר אליה
ברק: אם תלכי עמי והלכתי ואם לא תלכי עמי לא אלך. רבי יהודה ורבי נחמיה. רי"א: אם
תלכי עמי לקדש, אלך עמך לחצור. ואם לא תלכי עמי לקדש, לא אלך עמך לחצור. רבי
נחמיה אמר: אם תלכי עמי לשירה, אלך עמך למלחמה. ואם לא תלכי עמי לשירה, לא אלך
עמך למלחמה. ותאמר: הלוך אלך עמך, אפס כי לא תהיה תפארתך.

R. PHINEHAS SAID IN THE NAME OF R. REUBEN: TWO PEOPLE WERE
PRINCIPAL ACTORS AND YET MADE THEMSELVES SUBORDINATE, VIZ.
ABRAHAM AND BARAK. BARAK, AS IT IS WRITTEN: AND SHE SENT AND
CALLED BARAK . . . AND BARAK SAID UNTO HER: IF THOU WILT GO WITH
ME, THEN I WILL GO; BUT IF THOU WILT NOT GO WITH ME, I WILL NOT
GO (JUDG. 4:6FF.). R. JUDAH EXPLAINED: IF THOU WILT GO WITH ME
TO KADESH, I WILL GO WITH THEE AGAINST HAZOR; WHILST IF THOU
WILT NOT GO WITH ME TO KADESH, I WILL NOT GO WITH THEE AGAINST
HAZOR. R. NEHEMIAH EXPLAINED IT: IF THOU WILT GO WITH ME IN
SONG, I WILL GO WITH THEE TO BATTLE; BUT IF THOU WILT NOT GO
WITH ME IN SONG, I WILL NOT GO WITH THEE TO BATTLE. AND SHE
SAID: I WILL SURELY GO WITH THEE, NOTWITHSTANDING (*EFES*) THE
JOURNEY THAT THOU TAKEST SHALL NOT BE FOR THY HONOR (4:9).

The Midrash now points out that there were two important biblical
personalities that willingly made themselves secondary to women. The
first was Abraham who asked Sarah for her help in preserving his life.
The second was Barak who asked Deborah the Prophetess for her help
in preparing the war against Sisra.

א"ר ראובן: לשון יווני היא אפס. אמרה לו: מה את סבור שתתפארתה של שירה נמסרה לך
לבדך אתמהא? ונעשה טפילה. ותשר דבורה וברק בן אבינועם. אברהם היה עיקר ויקח
אברהם את שרי אשתו עשה עצמו טפילה. אמרי נא אחותי את, ונעשה טפילה לה ולאברם
היטיב בעבורה:

R. REUBEN SAID: [*EFES*] IS A GREEK WORD, AS THOUGH TO SAY *HAFES*
(LET ALONE). SAID SHE TO HIM: "WHAT THINKEST THOU? THAT THE
GLORY FOR THE SONG SHALL BE GIVEN TO THEE ALONE!" HE RETIRED
INTO THE SECOND PLACE, AS IT IS WRITTEN, THEN SANG DEBORAH
AND BARAK THE SON OF ABINOAM, ETC. (JUDG. 5:1). ABRAHAM WAS THE
PRINCIPAL, AS IT IS WRITTEN: AND ABRAM TOOK SARAI HIS WIFE (GEN.
12:5), BUT HE MADE HIMSELF OF SECONDARY IMPORTANCE, SAYING, SAY,

I PRAY THEE, THOU ART MY SISTER, WHEREUPON HE REALLY BECAME
SUBORDINATE TO HER, AS IT IS WRITTEN, AND HE DEALT WELI WITH
ABRAM FOR HER SAKE (12:16).

See the comment by Mirkin below.

—

Seed Thoughts

The story of Deborah and Barak as told in Scripture is beautiful, idyllic, and inspiring. Never until this moment did I ever question what Barak said to Deborah and what Deborah responded. They were both almost angelic characters in human form. How could they do anything wrong? The commentary by Aryeh Mirkin changes all of that. He introduces a sense of realism and reality that we do not usually find in biblical literature.

Concerning Abraham and Sarah: Are there marriages where husband and wife vie with each other for recognition, who want to show that they are tops in certain areas of life more so than their marriage partner?

Concerning Barak and Deborah, we see two people here who were chosen by God for the fulfillment of a purpose. Deborah was chosen to deliver God's message to Barak – to lead the army against Midian. Barak was the person chosen by God to lead the army of Israel in the war against the Midianites. Is that not enough for any two individuals – to be chosen by the Divine? Apparently it is not enough. The competitiveness and the childish desires to be number one and not number two is very hard to associate with such popular biblical characters. But the arguments appear to be true. Deborah with all her gifts as a prophetess was self-centered and was arrogant and did have a strong ego. All these are reflected in the song that she sang when subject to the scrutiny of a scholarly mind. Does that lessen the importance of the biblical writings? That is a matter of opinion. Many of us are grateful whenever it is brought to our attention that a popular biblical character is also human and can also make mistakes. But somehow or other s/he will eventually find their way and remain role models for all of us.

—

Additional Commentary

A completely different interpretation

The text above says, "If you do not go with him to Kadesh, etc . . ." It could have just said, "If you go with me, I will go," and it would be understood that if she does not go with him, he would not go. Why did the text have to conclude with the negative? We are talking here about two types of going. According to R. Judah, Barak said: "If you go with me to Kadesh to rouse the people to take part in the war, then I will go with you to Hazor, where the war will take place. But if you do not go with me to Kadesh, I will not go to Hazor with you but myself, to the war." (Mirkin)

Deborah's arrogance

Deborah was very arrogant as we can see from the text in the song that says: "Until I (Deborah) arose, until I came forward as a mother in Israel," she sought the glory of the war. The ordinary routines of arousing the people to participate never interested her. That kind of thing was left to Barak. Barak was actually the key personality in this whole affair, because, after all, Deborah approached him. He came and made himself secondary to Deborah because he said he would go with her to the war. As we can see from the song where it says, "and Deborah and Barak sang," Barak is mentioned second. Barak roused the people by himself and went to war by himself. But the song that gave them the publicity mentioned his name after Deborah. He was willing to make himself secondary in the song, but she should be secondary to him in the war. As to the fact that she wanted to make him secondary in some things, he says to stop doing it, אפס – *efes*, stop doing it. Although in general the Sages try to treat everybody equally, in the case of husband and wife, the sages take the husbands' side. Barak and Deborah were husband and wife. (Mirkin)

Were Deborah and Barak husband and wife?

In the previous Additional Commentary, it should be noted that the source stating their relationship is found in *Yalkut Shoftim*. I first became interested in their relationship as a result of the fact that the Malbim, possibly the greatest commentator after Rashi, had a note on the very first line of the chapters on Deborah where she is described as אשת לפידות – *eshet lapidot*. The Malbim noted that this does not mean that she was the wife of someone called Lapidot. There is no document that describes a person called Lapidot. The word *lapidot* is based on the word *lapid*, meaning a torch, and the expression *eshet lapidot* should be translated as a woman on fire, and means that she was utterly devoted to God and utterly zealous as a prophetess. Once this interpretation is accepted, the confusion of the term *eshet lapidot* is removed, and so it becomes much easier to agree with Aryeh Mirkin that they were husband and wife.

Say you are my sister

The scheme whereby Sarah would be presented as Abraham's sister was not only meant to save his life but also to prevent Sarah from being forced into an immoral situation. With her beauty, there would be many offers of marriage. All of these would come to her brother who was really Abraham, her husband. He would see to it that the conditions would be so difficult, especially the financial ones, that no marriage, even of convenience, would take place with Sarah so long as Abraham had something to do with it. If he announced a high sum of money and someone was willing to pay it, he would immediately raise the amount and continue to do so until he would be quite certain to prevent any kind of relationship. (*Tiferet Tzion*)

Why were the two cities mentioned?

There is a tradition that if after ten years of marriage, no child is born, the husband has to take a second wife. However, the second wife has to look and be of at least the same status as the first wife. They went to the two major centers, Aram Nahor and Aram Naharaim, and could find no one as beautiful as Sarah and as capable. That is what prompted Abraham to say that there is no one as beautiful as Sarah in the whole world. When they went to live in the land of Canaan, this did not apply, because the years of exile are not counted. (*Tiferet Tzion*)

ה ויהי כבא אברם מצרימה ויראו המצרים. ושרה היכן היתה? נתנה בתיבה ונעל בפניה.
5. AND IT CAME TO PASS, THAT, WHEN ABRAM WAS COMING INTO EGYPT,
ETC. (GEN. 12:14). AND WHERE WAS SARAH? HE HAD PUT HER IN A BOX
AND LOCKED HER IN IT.

All of this was done with Sarah's consent as it was something that both discussed together and she agreed that this was the way to go.

כיון דמטא למכסא, אמרין ליה: הב מכסא. אמר: אנא יהיב מכסא. אמרין ליה: מאנין את
טעין? אמר: אנא יהיב דמאנין. אמרין ליה: דהב את טעין. אמר: אנא יהיב מן דדהב. אמרו
ליה: מטכסין את טעין. אמר: דמטכסי אנא יהיב. מרגלין את טעון. אמר: אנא יהיב דמרגלין.
אמרין ליה: לא אפשר.
WHEN HE CAME TO THE CUSTOMS-HOUSE, HE [THE CUSTOMS OFFICER]
DEMANDED, "PAY THE CUSTOM DUES." "I WILL PAY," HE REPLIED. "YOU
CARRY GARMENTS IN THAT BOX," SAID HE. "I WILL PAY THE DUES ON
GARMENTS." "YOU ARE CARRYING SILKS," HE ASSERTED. "I WILL PAY
ON SILKS." "YOU ARE CARRYING PRECIOUS STONES." "I WILL PAY ON
PRECIOUS STONES." "IT IS IMPERATIVE THAT YOU OPEN IT AND WE SEE
WHAT IT CONTAINS," HE INSISTED.

Abraham's goal at the border was to do everything possible that they should not open the box. Therefore, he was ready to pay any custom duties that they demanded. However, the more he agreed to pay, the more they suspected that he was a spy. Finally, the officials lost patience and demanded that the box should be opened.

אלא דפתחת וחמית לן מה בגוה, כיון שפתחה הבהיקה כל ארץ מצרים מזיוה. ר' עזריה
ור' יונתן בר חגי משם רבי יצחק אמרי: איקונין של חוה נמסרו לראשי הדורות. להלן כתיב:
והנערה יפה עד מאד, מגעת עד איקונין של חוה. ברם הכא, כי יפה היא מאד מאד, מאיקונין
של חוה. ויראו אותה שרי פרעה. רבי יוחנן אמר: מתעלה והולכת. חד אמר: אנא יהיב מאה
דינרין, ואיעלל עמה. וחד אמר: אנא יהיב מאתן, ואיעלל עמה. אין לי אלא בעליתן. בירידתן
מניין? תלמוד לומר (ירמיה לח): וימשכו את ירמיהו בחבלים, ויעלו אותו מן הבור. מעלין אותו
אין לי אלא בעולם הזה. בעולם הבא מנין? תלמוד לומר (ישעיה יד): ולקחום עמים והביאום
אל מקומם:

AS SOON AS HE OPENED IT, THE LAND OF EGYPT WAS IRRADIATED WITH
HER LUSTER [BEAUTY]. R. AZARIAH AND R. JONATHAN IN R. ISAAC'S NAME
SAID: EVE'S IMAGE WAS TRANSMITTED TO THE REIGNING BEAUTIES OF
EACH GENERATION. ELSEWHERE IT IS WRITTEN: AND THE DAMSEL WAS
VERY FAIR – AD ME'OD (I KINGS 1:4), WHICH MEANS THAT SHE ATTAINED
TO EVE'S BEAUTY; BUT HERE IN TRUTH IT IS WRITTEN, THE EGYPTIANS
BEHELD THE WOMAN THAT SHE WAS VERY FAIR (ME'OD) – WHICH MEANS,
EVEN MORE BEAUTIFUL THAN EVE'S IMAGE. AND THE PRINCES OF PHA-
RAOH SAW HER, AND PRAISED HER (GEN. 12:15). R. JOHANAN SAID: THEY
WENT ON OUTBIDDING EACH OTHER FOR HER: ONE SAID, "I GIVE A
HUNDRED DINARS THAT I MAY ENTER [PHARAOH'S PALACE] WITH HER,"
WHEREUPON ANOTHER BID, "I GIVE TWO HUNDRED DINARS TO ENTER
WITH HER." I KNOW THIS ONLY OF THEIR ADVANCEMENT; WHENCE DO
WE KNOW IT OF THEIR DEGRADATION? BECAUSE IT SAYS: THEN TOOK
THEY JEREMIAH, AND CAST HIM INTO THE PIT (JER. 38:6): THEY RAISED
HIS PRICE. WE KNOW IT ONLY OF THIS WORLD. WHENCE DO WE KNOW
IT OF THE MESSIANIC FUTURE? BECAUSE IT IS SAID: AND THE PEOPLES
SHALL TAKE THEM, AND BRING THEM TO THEIR PLACE (ISA. 14:2).

When the box was opened, Sarah's beauty transfigured everyone. All
felt that only Pharaoh deserved that Sarah be brought to him. When
some of the officers realized that they could not outbid Pharaoh, they
offered money to be allowed to accompany her to the palace gates and
even from the gates to Pharaoh's personal quarters. The text spends a
little time in trying to appraise Sarah's beauty. There is a play on words
here from the Book of Kings. Avishag, King David's companion at a later
age, was described as being beautiful עד מאד – *ad me-od,* very beautiful (until beautiful), meaning up to the beauty of Eve. In the case of
Sarah, her beauty was described as מאד מאד – *me-od me-od,* more than
very beautiful (very very). This means that Sarah was described as being
more beautiful than Eve.

—

Seed Thoughts

This is one of many places in Midrash and Talmudic literature where
a woman's beauty is discussed, particularly in connection with women
leaders of the biblical stories, all of whom are described as very beautiful. I must confess that I reacted to some of these discussions with a

certain amount of sadness. Why is it so important that Sarah has to be the most beautiful and how is it possible to compare the beauty of a woman who lived in the sixth century before the common era to that of one who lived four centuries later? Even had there been photography at that time, photography can reproduce all kinds of emotional moods which may not be absolute guides to what is or is not beautiful.

In general, why is it important that Avishag should be as beautiful as Eve, or less so or more so? Furthermore, why should beauty be used as a form of competition? It is as though to say, since we have more beautiful women than you, we are better than you.

These views seem to be infantile, but at the same time they should not be allowed to affect the concept of beauty which is real and can be authentic if belonging to a good person. The use of the text as being the form and the basis of which we learn who is or is not, who was or was not beautiful, is a very weak form of logical support. The use of the term *ad me-od*, which in its literal interpretation differs from its use in Modern Hebrew, points out the weakness of this kind of interpretation. This Midrash should be understood therefore as saying that real beauty is only valuable when it is used by an ethical person such as Sarah and Eve.

PARASHAH FORTY, *Midrash Six*

ו ולאברם היטיב בעבורה ויהי לו צאן ובקר וגו' ויצו עליו פרעה אנשים וישלחו אותו

6. AND HE DEALT WELL WITH ABRAM, ETC. (GEN. 12:16). IT IS WRITTEN:
AND PHARAOH GAVE MEN CHARGE CONCERNING HIM, ETC. (12:20).

The point of this Midrash is to make a connection between the departures of Abraham from Egypt and the departure of the Hebrews at a later stage from Egypt under the leadership of Moses. Lacking in this Midrash are one or two sages who are usually introduced to provide meaning to the text. Is it important that the Children of Israel follow the traveling tours of Abraham? If so, why?! The Midrash itself did not offer meaning; the individual reader has the right or even the duty, if he has an insight, to share it with all.

ר' פנחס בשם רבי הושעיא רבה אמר: אמר הקב"ה לאברהם אבינו: צא וכבוש את הדרך לפני בניך. את מוצא כל מה שכתוב באברהם, כתיב בבניו. באברהם כתיב (שם יב): ויהי רעב

בארץ. בישראל כתיב (שם מח): כי זה שנתים הרעב בקרב הארץ. באברהם כתיב (שם יב):
וירד אברם מצרימה לגור שם. ובישראל כתיב (במדבר כ): וירדו אבותינו מצרימה. באברהם
כתיב: לגור שם. ובישראל כתיב: לגור בארץ באנו. באברהם כתיב: כי כבד הרעב בארץ
כנען. בישראל כתיב: והרעב כבד בארץ. באברהם כתיב: ויהי כאשר הקריב. בישראל כתיב:
ופרעה הקריב. באברהם כתיב (בראשית יב): והרגו אותי ואותך יחיו. ובישראל כתיב (שמות א):
כל הבן הילוד היאורה תשליכוהו. באברהם כתיב: אמרי נא אחותי את למען ייטב לי בעבורך
וגו'. ובישראל כתיב: וייטב אלהים למילדות. באברהם כתיב: ויהי כבוא אברם מצרימה.
ובישראל כתיב (שם): אלה שמות בני ישראל הבאים מצרימה. באברהם כתיב (בראשית יג):
ואברם כבד מאד במקנה. ובישראל כתיב (תהלים קה): ויוציאם בכסף וזהב. באברהם כתיב:
ויצו עליו פרעה. ובישראל כתיב: ותחזק מצרים על העם. באברהם כתיב: וילך למסעיו.
ובישראל כתיב: אלה מסעי בני ישראל:

R. PHINEHAS COMMENTED IN R. HOSHAYA'S NAME: THE HOLY ONE,
BLESSED BE HE, SAID TO OUR FATHER ABRAHAM: "GO FORTH AND TREAD
OUT A PATH FOR THY CHILDREN." FOR YOU FIND THAT EVERYTHING
WRITTEN IN CONNECTION WITH ABRAHAM IS WRITTEN IN CONNEC-
TION WITH HIS CHILDREN. IN CONNECTION WITH ABRAHAM, IT IS
WRITTEN: AND THERE WAS A FAMINE IN THE LAND (GEN. 12:10), WHILE
IN CONNECTION WITH ISRAEL IT IS WRITTEN: FOR THESE TWO YEARS
HATH THE FAMINE BEEN IN THE LAND (45:6). ABRAHAM: AND ABRAM
WENT DOWN INTO EGYPT; ISRAEL: AND OUR FATHERS WENT DOWN
INTO EGYPT (NUM. 20:15). ABRAHAM: TO SOJOURN THERE; ISRAEL: TO
SOJOURN IN THE LAND ARE WE COME (GEN. 47:4). ABRAHAM: FOR THE
FAMINE WAS SORE IN THE LAND; ISRAEL: AND THE FAMINE WAS SORE IN
THE LAND (43:1). ABRAHAM: AND IT CAME TO PASS, WHEN HE WAS COME
NEAR (*HIKRIB*) TO ENTER INTO EGYPT; ISRAEL: AND WHEN PHARAOH
DREW NIGH – *HIKRIB* (EX. 14:10). ABRAHAM: AND THEY WILL KILL ME,
BUT THEE THEY WILL KEEP ALIVE; ISRAEL: EVERY SON THAT IS BORN
YE SHALL CAST INTO THE RIVER, AND EVERY DAUGHTER YE SHALL SAVE
ALIVE (1:22). ABRAHAM: SAY, I PRAY THEE, THAT THOU ART MY SISTER,
THAT IT MAY BE WELL WITH ME; ISRAEL: AND GOD DEALT WELL WITH
THE MIDWIVES (1:20). ABRAHAM: AND IT CAME TO PASS, THAT, WHEN
ABRAM WAS COME INTO EGYPT; ISRAEL: NOW THESE ARE THE NAMES OF
THE SONS OF ISRAEL, WHO CAME IN EGYPT (1:1). ABRAHAM: AND ABRAM
WAS VERY RICH IN CATTLE, IN SILVER, AND IN GOLD (GEN. 13:2); ISRAEL:
AND HE BROUGHT THEM FORTH WITH SILVER AND GOLD (PS. 105:37).
ABRAHAM: AND PHARAOH GAVE MEN CHARGE CONCERNING HIM, AND
THEY SENT HIM AWAY; ISRAEL: AND THE EGYPTIANS WERE URGENT
UPON THE PEOPLE, TO SEND THEM OUT (EX. 12:33). ABRAHAM: AND HE

WENT ON HIS JOURNEYS (GEN. 13:3); ISRAEL: THESE ARE THE JOURNEYS
OF THE CHILDREN OF ISRAEL (NUM. 33:1).

Aryeh Mirkin, the commentator, makes the point that the Sages were
looking into the journeys of Abraham and trying to make a connection
between them and the journeys of Israel later on.

Seed Thoughts

Why is it important to know the manner in which Abraham left Egypt?
Why, from the midrashic point of view is it important to identify those
journeys as being the very ones used by the Children of Israel several
centuries later on? Abraham was the founder of the Jewish people. How
appropriate that a way should be found to include him in the Exodus
from Egypt, the most important event in Jewish history, which transformed the families of Abraham into the people of Israel. Could it be that
this is why a famine forced Abraham into Egypt, so that his departure
from Egypt might become an important lesson for the Jewish people?
Even if we were to grant that all this was truly happening, how would the
generation of Moses know which route Abraham took and why? The
answer is not far to seek. The pillar of cloud by day and the pillar of
fire by night, which directed the Children of Israel, would surely have
known the way that Abraham followed. This chapter of *Midrash Rabbah*
opened with a series of interpretations of *lekh lekha*, which teaches that
the term *lekha* means that something very important would happen to
Abraham personally as a result of many challenges. Surely, the highest
form of *lekh lekha* in the last Midrash of this chapter where the mission
of Abraham is catapulted into the Exodus of the Jewish people from
Egypt and the transformation into a great nation and according to the
blessings of Abraham, "I will bless and make your name great, and you
shall certainly become a great blessing for the Jewish people."

א וינגע ה' את פרעה נגעים גדולים וגו'. כתיב (שם צב) צדיק כתמר יפרח.

1. AND THE LORD PLAGUED PHARAOH AND HIS HOUSE WITH GREAT
PLAGUES, ETC. (GEN. 12:17). IT IS WRITTEN: THE RIGHTEOUS SHALL
FLOURISH LIKE THE PALM TREE; HE SHALL GROW LIKE A CEDAR IN
LEBANON (PS. 92:13).

The Midrashim that follow contain interpretations that help us understand how the symbol of the palm tree makes it easy to understand
the symbol of the righteous.

מה התמרה הזו וארז אין בהם לא עקומים ולא סיקוסים, כך הצדיקים אין בהם לא עקומים
ולא סיקוסים. מה התמרה וארז צילן רחוק, כך מתן שכרן של צדיקים רחוק. מה התמרה
וארז לבן מכוון למעלן, כך הצדיקים לבן מכוון להקב"ה, הה"ד (שם כה): עיני תמיד אל ה'
כי הוא יוציא מרשת רגלי. מה תמרה וארז יש להן תאוה, אף צדיקים יש להן תאוה. ומה
היא תאותן? הקב"ה, שנאמר (שם מא): קוה קויתי ה'. א"ר תנחומא: מעשה בתמרה אחת
שהיתה עומדת בחמתן ולא היתה עושה פירות. עבר דקלי אחד וראה אותה. אמר: תמרה זו
צופה מיריחו, כיון שהרכיבו אותה עשתה פירות. אי מה התמרה הזו אין עושין ממנה כלים,
יכול אף הצדיקים כן, אתמהא? תלמוד לומר: כארז. א"ר הונא: תמן עבדין מיניה מאנין, אי
מה הארז אינו עושה פירות, כך הן צדיקים אתמהא? תלמוד לומר: יפרח. מה תמרה זו אין
בה פסולת, אלא תמריה לאכילה, ולולביה להלל, חריות לסכוך, סיבים לחבלים, סנסנים
לכברה, שפעת קורות להקרות בהם את הבית. כך הם ישראל, אין בהם פסולת, אלא: מהם
בעלי מקרא, מהם בעלי משנה, מהם בעלי תלמוד, מהם בעלי הגדה. מה תמרה זו וארז, כל
מי שהוא עולה לראשן ואינו משמר את עצמו הוא נופל ומת. כך כל מי שהוא בא להזדווג
לישראל, סוף שהוא נוטל את שלו מתחת ידיהם. תדע לך שכן, שהרי שרה, על ידי שמשכה
פרעה לילה אחת, לקה הוא וביתו בנגעים, הה"ד (בראשית יב): וינגע ה' את פרעה נגעים
גדולים וגו':

AS THE PALM AND THE CEDAR HAVE NEITHER CROOKED CURVES NOR
EXCRESCENCES, SO THE RIGHTEOUS HAVE NEITHER CROOKEDNESS NOR
EXCRESCENCES; AS THE SHADOW OF THE PALM AND THE CEDAR IS CAST
AFAR, SO IS THE REWARD OF THE RIGHTEOUS FAR AWAY [IN THE FUTURE

WORLD]; AS THE HEART OF THE PALM AND THE CEDAR IS DIRECTED
UPWARD, SO ARE THE HEARTS OF THE RIGHTEOUS DIRECTED TOWARD
THE HOLY ONE, BLESSED BE HE, AS IT IS WRITTEN: MINE EYES ARE EVER
TOWARD THE LORD, FOR HE WILL BRING FORTH MY FEET OUT OF THE
NET (PS. 25:15); AS THE PALM AND THE CEDAR HAVE DESIRE, SO HAVE
THE RIGHTEOUS DESIRE. AND WHAT IS THEIR DESIRE? THE HOLY ONE,
BLESSED BE HE. R. TANHUMA SAID: THERE WAS ONCE A PALM TREE IN
AMATHO THAT DID NOT YIELD FRUIT. A PALM-GARDENER PASSED AND
SAW IT; SAID HE: "THIS UNGRAFTED TREE LOOKS TO [A MALE PALM]
FROM JERICHO." AS SOON AS THEY GRAFTED IT, IT YIELDED FRUIT. OR
[SHOULD YOU ARGUE]: AS WE CANNOT MAKE UTENSILS FROM A PALM
TREE, SO ARE THE RIGHTEOUS! THEREFORE, IT SAYS "LIKE A CEDAR."
R. HUNA OBSERVED: THERE [IN BABYLONIA] UTENSILS ARE MANUFAC-
TURED FROM IT [THE PALM TREE]. THEN WILL YOU SAY: AS THE CEDAR
DOES NOT PRODUCE FRUIT, SO ARE THE RIGHTEOUS? THEREFORE IT IS
STATED, "THE RIGHTEOUS SHALL FLOURISH LIKE THE PALM TREE": AS
NO PART OF THE PALM HAS ANY WASTE, THE DATES BEING EATEN, THE
BRANCHES USED FOR *HALLEL*, THE TWIGS FOR COVERING [BOOTHS], THE
BAST FOR ROPES, THE LEAVES FOR BESOMS, AND THE PLANED BOARDS
FOR CEILING ROOMS, SO ARE THERE NONE WORTHLESS IN ISRAEL, SOME
BEING VERSED IN SCRIPTURE, OTHERS IN MISHNAH, SOME IN TALMUD,
OTHERS IN HAGGADAH. AND AS WHOEVER CLIMBS TO THE TOP OF THE
PALM AND THE CEDAR AND DOES NOT TAKE CARE OF HIMSELF FALLS
AND IS KILLED, SO WHOEVER COMES TO ATTACK ISRAEL EVENTUALLY
RECEIVES HIS DESERTS ON THEIR ACCOUNT, THE PROOF BEING THAT
BECAUSE PHARAOH TOOK POSSESSION OF SARAH FOR ONE NIGHT HE
AND HIS HOUSEHOLD WERE SMITTEN WITH PLAGUES, AS IT IS WRITTEN,
AND THE LORD PLAGUED PHARAOH, ETC.

Seed Thoughts

One of the characteristics of the palm tree is that one cannot make utensils from it, although there is a different interpretation from that of the
Sages in Babylonia. As for those who say that utensils cannot be made
from the palm tree, there is an interesting twist in the interpretation. We
are told that it is for this reason, among others, that the righteous are
compared to both the palm tree and the cedar. In those areas where one

cannot find an interpretation from the palm tree, the Midrash is able to offer a parallel from the symbol of the cedar. For example, the cedar is tall and majestic and its shadow can be reflected over a long distance. Similarly, the influence of a tzaddik is very great and it covers not only areas in this world but also in areas of the World to Come.

When I first read this interpretation, a window opened up in my mind. There is no such thing as only one symbol whose meaning interprets another. There has to be more than one. My thought and reaction to the interpretation just described can be stated as follows. What the tzaddik needs most is a non-tzaddik. The latter term is a play on words that I have created, simply to describe the good person who, for whatever reason, is no longer guided by or accepting of a religious tradition but, nonetheless, observes the moral principles based on their human reason, but also since it was introduced to them through a religious tradition. Is it possible to think of a partnership around the world between those who observe the moral law for the sake of God and those for the sake of man? This would still be a minority group throughout the world, though still quite powerful.

Unfortunately, the challenges appear to be great for this beautiful relationship to happen. Perhaps we ought to begin with the first step of what should be called tolerance. Those who observe the moral law for its own sake and not as a religious commandment should be grateful for the creation of these moral traditions, and others who observe the moral law as a religious commandment should be grateful that there are those who fulfill the demands of the moral challenge. These divisions have already been noted in the Hebrew tradition as being the difference between being אדם למקום – *adam laMakom*, between man and God, and between אדם לחברו – *adam la'haveiro*, between man and his fellow human being. Both together are the best relationship, but there is great spiritual power even when observed separately.

———

Additional Commentary

The palm tree that did not produce fruit

The fact that the tree did not produce fruit implies that the world was not benefiting from it because even in its growth, it was growing only for itself, becoming very tall. Similarly, one can say the same about a tzaddik – much of what he does is also for himself in order to appear better in this world than in the World to Come. But others are not better than the tzaddik, which is why the palm tree is being described as being beneficial only when it is fruitful. For so long as the palm tree is fruitful, the whole world benefits from it. Similarly, the world benefits from what the tzaddikim do. The whole world is spiritually fed. The *talmidei hakhamim* engage themselves in the transmission of Torah in all its various forms, which are the fruits that they produce for the world and the World to Come. (*Tiferet Tzion*)

PARASHAH FORTY-ONE, *Midrash Two*

ב ריש לקיש בשם בר קפרא אמר: פרעה בראתן לקה.

2. R. SIMEON B. LAKISH SAID IN BAR KAPPARA'S NAME: PHARAOH WAS SMITTEN WITH LUPUS.

The word "leprosy" is usually used for this disease that Pharaoh had because of the fact that the word נגע – *nega* is usually associated with leprosy.

אמר רשב"ג: מצאני זקן אחד מוכה שחין בציפורין, ואמר לי: כ"ד מיני שחין הם, ואין לך קשה מכולם, שהאשה רעה לו, אלא ראתן בלבד, ובו לקה פרעה.

R. SIMEON B. GAMALIEL SAID: AN OLD MAN SUFFERING WITH BOILS MET ME IN SEPPHORIS; SAID HE TO ME: "THERE ARE TWENTY-FOUR VARIETIES OF BOILS, AND OUT OF ALL THESE THE ONLY ONE UPON WHICH A WOMAN HAS AN INJURIOUS EFFECT IS LUPUS"; AND THEREWITH WAS THE WICKED PHARAOH SMITTEN. AND HIS HOUSE.

Apparently what is implied is that the disease of boils or lupus, as is mentioned, is at its worst when an individual attempts a sexual relationship, which is why Pharaoh was so severely stricken. All of these terms, including leprosy, are diseases that relate to the skin and, therefore, are usually interchangeable since no modern diagnosis is available.

אמר רבי אחא: אפילו קורות ביתו לקון, והכל היו אומרין: על דבר שרי אשת אברם.

R. AHA SAID: EVEN THE BEAMS OF HIS HOUSE WERE SMITTEN, AND ALL EXCLAIMED, "IT IS BECAUSE OF SARAI, ABRAM'S WIFE."

The fact that certain aspects of the house became infected is not un-usual in certain types of diseases. The important phrase that we shall soon see is that everyone seems to understand that all this was due to Pharaoh's relationship with Sarah.

אמר רבי ברכיה: עלו דטולמוסין למקרב למסאנא דמטרונא, וכל אותו הלילה היתה שרה שטוחה על פניה ואומרת: רבון העולמים! אברהם יצא בהבטחה, ואני יצאתי באמונה, אברהם יצא חוץ לסירה ואני בתוך הסירה.

R. BEREKIAH SAID: BECAUSE HE DARED TO APPROACH THE SHOE OF THAT LADY. AND THE WHOLE OF THAT NIGHT SARAH LAY PROSTRATE ON HER FACE, CRYING: "SOVEREIGN OF THE UNIVERSE! ABRAHAM WENT FORTH [FROM HIS LAND] ON THINE ASSURANCE, AND I WENT FORTH WITH FAITH; ABRAHAM IS WITHOUT THIS PRISON WHILE I AM WITHIN!"

Even at this stage Sarah looked upon herself as secondary to Abraham. While he had many promises of greatness that awaited him, all she had was a simple faith of God and in her husband. She still believed at this point that Pharaoh was being punished because of Abraham and not because of her.

אמר לה הקב"ה: כל מה שאני עושה, בשבילך אני עושה. והכל אומרים: על דבר שרי אשת אברם. אמר רבי לוי: כל אותו הלילה היה מלאך עומד ומגלב בידו. הוה אמר לה: אין אמרת מחי, מחינא. אין אמרת נישבק, שביקנא. וכל כך למה? שהיתה אומרת לו: אשת איש אני, ולא היה פורש.

SAID THE HOLY ONE, BLESSED BE HE, TO HER: "WHATEVER I DO, I DO FOR THY SAKE, AND ALL WILL SAY, 'IT IS BECAUSE OF SARAI, ABRAM'S WIFE.'"

R. Berekiah said: Because he dared to approach the shoe of that lady. R. Levi said: The whole of that night an angel stood with a whip in his hand; when she ordered, "Strike," he struck, and when she ordered, "Desist," he desisted. And why such severity? Because she told him [Pharaoh]: "I am a married woman," yet he would not leave her.

God's response to Sarah was that if Pharaoh had succeeded in what he wanted to do, she would have been victim. That changes the entire re-lationship. Sarah thus became the person of priority. Everything, there-fore, that happened to Pharaoh was because of Sarah and not because of Abraham. The interesting point of this Midrash at this stage was that Sarah wanted justice to be applied even to Pharaoh. In his country, the king had the right to take anyone for his wife, except a married woman. However, when the moment of truth came, and Sarah told him that she was a married woman, it did not change his intention. It was only then that Sarah ordered the angel to punish the king.

רבי אלעזר תני לה בשם ר"א בן יעקב: שמענו בפרעה שלקה בצרעת ואבימלך בעיצור. מנין ליתן את האמור של זה בזה, ושל זה בזה? ת"ל על דבר שרה, על דבר על דבר לגזירה שוה:

R. ELAZAR SAID (THE SAME WAS ALSO TAUGHT IN THE NAME OF R. ELIEZER B. JACOB): WE KNOW THAT PHARAOH WAS SMITTEN WITH LEPROSY AND ABIMELECH WITH THE CLOSING UP [OF THE ORIFICES]: HOW DO WE KNOW THAT WHAT IS SAID HERE IS TO BE APPLIED THERE, AND VICE VERSA? BECAUSE "FOR THE SAKE OF" OCCURS IN BOTH PLACES, THAT AN ANALOGY MAY BE DRAWN.

Seed Thoughts

The important point of this Midrash is that Sarah is now singled out not only for her devotion and dedication, but also for her leadership in thought and deed. She maintained that her position was secondary to Abraham as befit her modesty. She also insisted that Pharaoh be treated with justice, which finally happened when he did not live up to his promises. From this point on in the biblical story, Sarah becomes and remains a great leader in Judaism.

PARASHAH FORTY-ONE, *Midrash Three*

ג ואברם כבד מאד במקנה בכסף ובזהב. הה"ד (תהלים קה): ויוציאם בכסף וזהב וגו'.

3. AND ABRAM WAS VERY RICH IN CATTLE, IN SILVER, AND IN GOLD (GEN. 13:2). THUS IT IS WRITTEN, AND HE BROUGHT THEM FORTH WITH SILVER AND WITH GOLD; AND THERE WAS NONE THAT STUMBLED AMONG HIS TRIBES (PS. 105:37).

Apparently, this verse is meant to indicate that something similar will happen to the children and offspring of Abraham. Indeed, this is what we learn in the Exodus from Egypt in the days of Moses. Every one of them left with some important things that they took from Egypt, not necessarily silver and gold, but other types of possessions, given to them by the residents of Egypt. In this respect, they too left Egypt with many material assets.

וילך למסעיו, במסעות שהלך בהן חזר. אמר רבי אלעזר ברבי מנחם: הלך לפרוע הקפותיו.

AND HE WENT ON HIS JOURNEYS (GEN. 13:3): HE RETURNED BY THE SAME ROUTE BY WHICH HE HAD COME. R. ELIEZER SON OF MENAHEM SAID: HE WENT TO SETTLE HIS DEBTS.

What is apparently meant here is that on his way to Egypt, Abraham made an arrangement with the innkeepers which today is like having credit for not having adequate cash to pay for his room and board. On his way out of Egypt, however, he made sure to revisit these places to pay the money owed and what they deserved. Here, the Midrash brings the folk saying, trying to favor the same hotels that one stayed in before. This, however, was not explained, unless it was a way of helping the hotel industry maintain itself.

וגם ללוט ההולך את אברם וגו'. ד' דברים טובים היו ללוט בעבור אברם. וילך אברם וגו' וילך אתו לוט. וגם ללוט ההולך את אברם, וישב את כל הרכוש וגם את לוט. ויהי בשחת אלהים וגו', ויזכור אלהים את אברהם וישלח את לוט מתוך וגו'. וכנגדו היו בניו צריכים לפרוע לנו טובות, לא דיין שלא פרעו לנו טובות אלא רעות.

AND LOT ALSO, WHO WENT WITH ABRAM, ETC. (GEN. 13:5). LOT ENJOYED FOUR BOONS (I.E., BENEFITS) ON ACCOUNT OF ABRAHAM: (I) AND LOT WENT WITH HIM (12:4); (II) AND LOT ALSO, ETC., (III) AND HE ALSO

BROUGHT BACK HIS BROTHER LOT, AND HIS GOODS (14:16); AND (IV)
AND IT CAME TO PASS, WHEN GOD DESTROYED THE CITIES OF THE
PLAIN, THAT GOD REMEMBERED ABRAHAM, AND SENT LOT OUT OF THE
MIDST OF THE OVERTHROW (19:29). NOW IN RETURN FOR THESE HIS
DESCENDANTS SHOULD HAVE REQUITED US WITH KINDNESS, YET NOT
ALONE DID THEY NOT REQUITE US WITH KINDNESS, BUT THEY EVEN DID
US EVIL.

The remainder of the Midrash is explained through the following
literary style. It lists the four most important areas where Lot benefited
from Abraham. It then goes on to quote four prophets who criticize Lot
and his behavior very vigorously.

הה"ד (במדבר כב): וישלח מלאכים אל בלעם בן בעור וגו'. ועתה לכה נא ארה לי את העם.
(שופטים ג) ויאסף אליו את בני עמון ועמלק וילך ויך את ישראל ויירשו את עיר התמרים. (ד"ה
ב כ): ויהי אחרי כן באו בני מואב ובני מדין ועמהם מן העמונים על יהושפט. ועוד כתיב (איכה
א): ידו פרש צר על כל מחמדיה. ונכתב חטא שלהם בארבעה מקומות: (דברים כג) לא יבוא
עמוני ומואבי על דבר אשר לא קדמו אתכם בלחם ובמים. וכתיב (מיכה ו) עמי זכר נא מה יעץ
בלק מלך מואב ומה ענה וגו'.

THUS IT IS WRITTEN: AND HE SENT MESSENGERS UNTO BALAAM ...
COME NOW THEREFORE, I PRAY THEE, CURSE ME THIS PEOPLE (NUM.
22:5F.); AGAIN, AND HE GATHERED UNTO HIM THE CHILDREN OF AMMON
AND AMALEK, AND HE WENT AND SMOTE ISRAEL (JUDG. 3:13); ALSO, AND
IT CAME TO PASS AFTER THIS, THAT . . . THE CHILDREN OF AMMON, AND
WITH THEM SOME OF THE AMMONITES, CAME AGAINST JEHOSHAPHAT
TO BATTLE (II CHRON. 20:1); ALSO THIS VERSE, THE ADVERSARY HATH
SPREAD OUT HIS HAND UPON ALL HER TREASURES (LAM. 1:10). THEIR
SIN IS RECORDED IN FOUR PLACES: AN AMMONITE OF A MOABITE SHALL
NOT ENTER INTO THE ASSEMBLY OF THE LORD . . . BECAUSE THEY MET
YOU NOT WITH BREAD AND WATER IN THE WAY, ETC. (DEUT. 23:4F.);
BECAUSE THEY MET NOT THE CHILDREN OF ISRAEL WITH BREAD AND
WATER, ETC. (NEH. 13:2); O MY PEOPLE, REMEMBER NOW WHAT BALAK
KING OF MOAB DEVISED (MICAH 6:5).

Everything quoted now in the Midrash is stated explicitly in the Torah.
But the average reader either does not make the various connections
or does not take them too seriously. This Midrash emphasizes most
dramatically that Ammon and Moab were the great enemies of Israel
and of the Jewish people of that day. Yet they were the children and

grandchildren of Lot, the great beneficiaries of Abraham's love, generosity, and family loyalty. They betrayed him as completely as anyone could have been.

עמדו ד' נביאים וחתמו גזר דינם, אלו הם: ישעיה וירמיה צפניה ויחזקאל. ישעיה אמר (ישעיה טו): משא מואב כי בליל שודד ער מואב נדמה כי בליל שודד קיר מואב נדמה. ירמיה אמר (ירמיה מט): לכן הנה ימים באים נאם ה', והשמעתי אל רבת בני עמון תרועת מלחמה, והיתה לתל שממה ובנותיה באש תצתנה, וירש ישראל את יורשיו אמר ה'. יחזקאל אמר (יחזקאל כה): לבני קדם על בני עמון, ונתתיה למורשה, למען לא תזכר בני עמון בגוים, ובמואב אעשה שפטים, וידעו כי אני ה'. צפניה אמר (צפניה ב): לכן חי אני נאם ה' צבאות אלהי ישראל, כי מואב כסדום תהיה, ובני עמון כעמורה וגו':

FOUR PROPHETS AROSE AND SEALED THEIR DOOM, VIZ. ISAIAH, JEREMIAH, EZEKIEL, AND ZEPHANIAH. ISAIAH SAID: THE BURDEN OF MOAB, ETC. (ISA. 15:1); JEREMIAH: THEN I WILL CAUSE AN ALARM OF WAR TO BE HEARD AGAINST RABBAH OF THE CHILDREN OF AMMON, ETC. (JER. 49:2); EZEKIEL: I WILL OPEN THE FLANK OF MOAB . . . TOGETHER WITH THE CHILDREN OF AMMON, UNTO THE CHILDREN OF THE EAST . . . AND I WILL EXECUTE JUDGMENTS UPON MOAB, ETC. (EZEK. 25:9FF.); ZEPHANIAH: SURELY MOAB SHALL BE AS SODOM, AND THE CHILDREN OF AMMON AS GOMORRAH, ETC. (ZEPH. 2:9).

As we can see, the prophets sealed the doom of the descendants of Lot and their families. The prophets used Lot as an example of one who repaid the most beautiful goodness of the world with the most horrible reaction. This is the perfect example of רעה תחת טובה – *raah tahat tovah*, rewarding goodness with evil.

Seed Thoughts

We read this material like most people read Scripture. We also do not make the connections between Moab and Ammon and their original generation. It takes a Midrash like this one to hit us so directly, so to speak, and to point out that we are dealing with enemies of Israel who are indeed members of Abraham's family – who turned against him, his progeny, and his people.

There is a word to describe this phenomenon, but most of us think that it applies only to modern times. But we are wrong. The word is self-hatred.

Why does this happen? Why are there people who are always jealous of what is on the other side of the fence, who always diminish their own background, and end up hating their people, their families, and very often themselves?

We have many examples of Jewish self-hatred, but we should not imagine that this applies only to Jews. In the history of the world, self-hatred can be identified with many individuals of many cultures. In the case of the Jews, one could find, if not a justification, at least an attempt to understand why some people are filled with self-hatred. The Holocaust is probably the most terrible event of an effort to eliminate a people by death – not only in modern times but probably in the history of the world. It was not only the Jews who were put to death that suffered. So were many of their families left behind. I know personally of families who gathered every Jewish document in their families and destroyed them so that no one should ever know they were Jews. Why did they do it? Because they were afraid that their lives were in danger. Can we describe this as self-hatred? We have to be careful with the answer. These families felt that their lives would be in danger if they were discovered to be Jewish. This is more self-preservation than self-hatred. But we have to be very careful before casting judgments on others. It is enough to assert that there are many people, Jews among them, who are filled with the attitude of self-hatred. And now we can add scriptures to this devastating subject. Ammon and Moab were guilty of self-hatred. They fought the Jews who were their brothers and fought to dominate the Land of Israel, which they thought was as much theirs as it was others. It is a sad story, and this additional knowledge makes it even sadder.

───

Additional Commentary

What was the sin of Lot?

In discussing the sin of Lot, Scripture makes the point that the criticism of Moab and Ammon was that when the Children of Israel wanted access to their land, they refused to give them bread and water. Granted, this was a bad thing to do. Can it really be the worst thing to do? It seems that Moab and Ammon did much worse than this at other times. How then can we explain the fact that not giving them bread and water was the real dividing line between them and Israel? The explanation of this fact is that we are dealing with symbols. Not giving them bread and wa-ter is a symbol that the covenant between Lot and his uncle Abraham was now weak, if not broken. This was a signal to the outside world that this was the perfect time to attack Israel and get rid of them. Lot thought that through this device, he would assume leadership of the whole world and not just of his belongings. It did not turn out that way, but could have. That is why this reason is given the prominence it now has. (*Tiferet Tzion*)

PARASHAH FORTY-ONE, *Midrash Four*

ד היה צאן ובקר ואהלים.

4. HAD FLOCKS, AND HERDS, AND TENTS.

The Sages saw a problem that might be described as grammatical. The Hebrew word צאן – *tzon*, does not necessarily describe one sheep, but can cover a flock of sheep. The same goes for בקר – *bakar* – cattle. If the intent of the Midrash had been to describe the tents and their inhabit-ants, the word אוהל – *ohel*, meaning "tent," could have been enough. It could stand for one or many. Why choose *ohalim* which is a minimum of two?

רבי טוביה בר יצחק אמר: שני אהלים: רות המואביה ונעמה העמונית. דכוותה: קום קח את אשתך ואת שתי בנותיך וגו'. רבי טוביה בר רבי יצחק אמר: ב' אוהלים. רבי יוסי ברבי יצחק אמר: שתי מציאות: רות המואביה ונעמה העמונית. א"ר יצחק (תהלים פט): מצאתי דוד עבדי. היכן מצאתיו? בסדום:

R. TOBIAH B. R. ISAAC SAID: HE HAD TWO TENTS, VIZ. RUTH THE MOABITESS AND NAAMAH THE AMMONITESS. SIMILARLY IT IS WRITTEN: ARISE, TAKE THY WIFE, AND THY TWO DAUGHTERS THAT ARE FOUND (GEN. 19:15): R. TOBIAH SAID: THAT MEANS TWO "FINDS", VIZ. RUTH AND NAAMAH. R. ISAAC COMMENTED: I HAVE FOUND DAVID MY SERVANT (PS. 89:21): WHERE DID I FIND HIM? IN SODOM.

R. Tobiah b. R. Isaac interprets the *ohalim* as referring to the two off-spring of Lot, Ruth and Naamah who possessed the highest talents of morality and ethics and who deserved to be singled out in this fashion.

As to the reference of David and Sodom, it is simply an acknowledgment that because Ruth was saved from the destruction of Sodom, David (who is her descendant) was also saved as a result of Sodom.

⁓

Seed Thoughts

In this and several other Midrashim, we detect a concern about the household of Lot and the general disapproval of many of the events and relationships that happened in the family circle. How could Lot have lived so close to Abraham and neither he nor his offspring appear to have been influenced by his moral and spiritual stature? The importance of this Midrash is that at last the Sages found two descendants who resemble the characters of Abraham and Sarah in the most delicate detail – namely Ruth, the descendant of Moab, and Naamah, the descendant of Ammon. Ruth's descendants eventually included King David. Naamah was the mother of Rehoboam, who was one of the kings of Israel.

PARASHAH FORTY-ONE, *Midrash Five*

ה ויהי ריב בין רועי מקנה אברם ובין רועי מקנה לוט. רבי ברכיה בשם רבי יהודה ב"ר סימון
אמר: בהמתו של אברהם אבינו היתה יוצאה זמומה, ובהמתו של לוט לא היתה יוצאה
זמומה. היו אומרים להם רועי אברהם: הותר הגזל?

5. AND THERE WAS A STRIFE BETWEEN THE HERDSMEN OF ABRAM'S CATTLE AND THE HERDSMEN OF LOT'S CATTLE (GEN. 13:7). R. BEREKIAH SAID IN R JUDAN'S NAME: ABRAHAM'S CATTLE USED TO GO OUT MUZZLED, BUT LOT'S DID NOT GO OUT MUZZLED. SAID ABRAHAM'S HERDSMEN TO THEM: "HAS THEN ROBBERY BEEN PERMITTED?"

The purpose of wearing a muzzle is to prevent the animal from damaging the harvest or property of the neighbor. Abraham was careful while Lot was not. However, this appears to be too trivial an interpretation. It exists all the time among people in this kind of work. Why did this have to be mentioned in the Holy Scripture? For this reason, the Sages sought another reason and found it.

היו אומרים להם רועי לוט: כך אמר הקב״ה לאברהם: לזרעך אתן את הארץ הזאת. ואברהם
פרדה עקרה ואינו מוליד, למחר הוא מת ולוט בן אחיו יורשו, ואין אכלין, מדידהון אינון
אכלין. אמר להם הקב״ה: כך אמרתי לו: לזרעך נתתי. אימתי? לכשיעקרו שבעה עממים
מתוכה. והכנעני והפרזי אז יושב בארץ, עד עכשיו מתבקש להם זכות בארץ:

TO WHICH LOT'S HERDSMEN REPLIED: "THUS DID THE HOLY ONE,
BLESSED BE HE, SAY TO ABRAHAM: UNTO THY SEED WILL I GIVE THIS
LAND (GEN. 12:7); NOW ABRAHAM IS A BARREN MULE, WHO CANNOT
BEGET CHILDREN, THEREFORE LOT WILL BE HIS HEIR; IF THEY EAT,
THEY ARE EATING THEIR OWN." SAID THE HOLY ONE, BLESSED BE HE,
TO THEM: "THUS DID I SAY TO HIM: UNTO THY SEED HAVE I GIVEN THIS
LAND" (15:18): WHEN? WHEN THE SEVEN NATIONS ARE UPROOTED FROM
IT. NOW, HOWEVER, AND THE CANAANITE AND THE PERIZZITE DWELT
THEN IN THE LAND, ETC. SO FAR THEY STILL HAVE A RIGHT IN THE LAND.

The Sages have discovered that the problems were ideological. The
servants of Lot concluded that Abraham and Sarah were too old to have
children and, therefore, Lot would inherit all of Abraham's properties.
Since he would inherit everything eventually, it did not seem wrong to
act like the owner even now. What happened, however, was that they
did not foresee the miracle of the birth of Isaac, which changed the
entire picture.

~

Seed Thoughts

In the midrashic material that we have gone over so far, references have
been made to the claims of the native people for ownership of what
we accept as the Land of Israel. They had in mind the seven original
Canaanite nations whose rights and claims were based on longevity and
on the fact that they occupied this land long before the promise was
made to Abraham that his seed would inherit it.

We then witnessed in the scriptural narrative the eventual elimination of these nations, usually by means of war. At the time of this
Midrash, two of these nations still remained, the Canaanites and the
Perizzites, and Lot would never have inherited the land without a war
which he may not have won. The situation of Abraham was different. He
had saved them in many wars and returned their land and possessions
to them. They would have never quarreled with Abraham's right to the
Land of Israel.

PARASHAH FORTY-ONE, *Midrash Six*

ו ויאמר אברם אל לוט: אל נא תהי מריבה ביני ובינך וגו'. רבי עזריה בשם ר"י ב"ר סימון
אמר: כשם שהיה ריב בין רועי אברם ובין רועי לוט כך היה ריב בין אברם ללוט, הדא הוא
דכתיב: ויאמר אברם אל לוט אל נא תהי מריבה ביני ובינך וגו', וכי אחים היו? אלא שהיה
קלסתר פניו דומה לו.

6. AND ABRAM SAID UNTO LOT: LET THERE BE NO STRIFE, I PRAY THEE,
BETWEEN ME AND THEE, ETC. (GEN. 13:8). R. AZARIAH SAID IN R. JU-
DAH'S NAME: JUST AS THERE WAS STRIFE BETWEEN THE HERDSMEN OF
ABRAHAM AND THE HERDSMEN OF LOT, SO WAS THERE STRIFE BETWEEN
ABRAHAM AND LOT, AS IT SAYS: AND ABRAM SAID UNTO LOT: LET THERE
BE NO STRIFE, ETC. FOR WE ARE BRETHREN. WAS HE THEN HIS BROTHER?
IN FACT, HE CALLED HIM SO BECAUSE HIS FEATURES RESEMBLED HIS
OWN.

The main problem facing the Midrash at this point is whether we are
dealing with one or two quarrels. Was the quarrel between Abraham
and Lot the same as the quarrel between their shepherds? See the Additional Commentary below for two different points of views.

הלא כל הארץ לפניך הפרד נא מעלי. אמר רבי חלבו: הבדל נא אין כתיב כאן, אלא הפרד.
מה הפרדה הזו אינה קולטת זרע, כך א"א לאותו האיש להתערב בזרעו של אברהם.

IS NOT THE WHOLE LAND BEFORE THEE? SEPARATE THYSELF (*HIPPARED*)
I PRAY THEE (GEN. 13:9). R. HELBO SAID: NOT *HIBBADELL* IS WRITTEN,
BUT *HIPPARED*: JUST AS A *PEREDAH* (MULE) CANNOT DEVELOP SEMEN,
SO IS IT IMPOSSIBLE FOR THIS MAN [LOT] TO MIX WITH THE SEED OF
ABRAHAM.

The nature of the quarrel between Abraham and Lot eventually led
to their separation. There are many things about Lot that did not meet
Abraham's qualification for leadership and the future of the Jewish
people. Therefore, at this stage of the relationship, he made preparations
for the ultimate separation.

אם השמאל ואימינה ואם הימין ואשמאילה. אמר ליה: אם את לשמאילה, אנא לדרומה.
ואם אנא לדרומה, את לשמאלה. אמר רבי יוחנן: לשני בני אדם שהיו להם שתי כורים,
אחד של חטים ואחד של שעורים. אמר ליה: אם חטייא דידי, שערי דידך. ואם שערי דידך,

חטייא דידי. מן כל אתר חטייא דידי! כך, אם השמאל ואימינה, ואם הימין ואשמאילה. אמר
רבי חנינא בר יצחק: ואשמאלה אין כתיב כאן, אלא ואשמאילה מן כל אתר, אנא משמאיל
לההוא גברא:

IF THOU WILT TAKE THE LEFT HAND, THEN I WILL GO TO THE RIGHT; OR
IF THOU TAKE THE RIGHT HAND, THEN I WILL GO TO THE LEFT. HE SAID
TO HIM: "IF THOU GOEST TO THE LEFT, I GO TO THE SOUTH, WHILE IF I
GO TO THE SOUTH, THOU GOEST TO THE LEFT, SO THAT IN EITHER CASE
I GO TO THE SOUTH." R. JOHANAN SAID: THIS MAY BE COMPARED TO
TWO MEN WHO HAD TWO STACKS, ONE OF WHEAT AND THE OTHER OF
BARLEY. SAID ONE TO THE OTHER: "IF THE WHEAT IS MINE, THEN THE
BARLEY IS YOURS, WHILE IF THE BARLEY IS YOURS THE WHEAT IS MINE;
IN EITHER CASE THEN THE WHEAT IS MINE." R. HANINA B. ISAAC SAID:
IT IS NOT WRITTEN, *VE-ASME'ELAH* BUT *VE-ASME'ILAH*: IN ALL EVENTS, I
WILL MAKE THAT MAN [LOT] GO TO THE LEFT.

The example of the two men, one with a stack of wheat and the other
with barley, was more than an exchange of words. The person who
wanted the wheat insisted no matter what. By the same token, Abraham
said that if Lot would take either the left or right, then Abraham would
take the opposite. But that was not Abraham's real intention. His real
intention was that Lot should not share an inheritance in the Land of
Israel. After all, God said, "To thy seed will I give this land." And the very
text states that neither a male member of Ammon nor of Moab can be
counted within the community of Israel because they were the children
of Lot.

~

Seed Thoughts

There is an unusual and intriguing example in our text of what the Midrash can do with the biblical script by changing the meaning without
changing any part of the text itself. In the biblical text, Abraham gives
Lot the right to choose the fields either to the right or the left and claim
them as his own. Presumably he does so, and Lot becomes a person of
great material wealth. But this is not what the Midrash is bringing to our
attention. It was never Abraham's intention to give up any portion of the
Land of Israel in light of the blessing from God of giving it to his seed.
The Midrash changes the meaning of left and right as not having to do
with physical direction but with moral direction. "Your direction has

been wrong and my direction has been right and I want this to continue." Abraham knew that the quarrel between the shepherds had to do with stealing and becoming bad neighbors. He wanted to separate himself from this kind of behavior. When he said that he wants him to move to the left, he really meant that he wanted to be separated to the extent that the text says (Deuteronomy 23:4): "An Ammonite or Moabite shall not enter into the congregation of the Lord; to their tenth generation shall they not enter into the congregation of the Lord forever."

Additional Commentary

One quarrel or two quarrels?

Just as there was a quarrel between the shepherds, etc., it should not be understood that when Abraham said, "Let there not be a quarrel between us," this was a result of the quarrel between their shepherds. On the contrary, there was a quarrel between Abraham and Lot personally. Lot had permitted many forms of immorality, including theft. Were it not for this, why else would there be a necessity for the separation of the two peoples? (Aryeh Mirkin)

One quarrel or two quarrels?

R. Azariah's point of view was that the quarrel between Abraham and Lot was the same as the one between the shepherds. It was the very same quarrel. We can derive from Abraham's statement, "Let there not be a quarrel between our shepherds," the following: Why was it necessary for Abraham to make reference of this quarrel, while saying to Lot to not let there be such a quarrel? The answer is that it was Abraham's intention – by saying this statement – that he had in mind the quarrel between the shepherds. In general, important people usually have quarrels between themselves but find some way to resolve them. However, when ordinary people have quarrels, it is very hard for the important people to intervene. That is what Abraham meant when saying something like "Let us not have a quarrel over the same reasons that bother the shepherds." (*Tiferet Tzion*)

PARASHAH FORTY-ONE, *Midrash Seven*

ז וישא לוט את עיניו וירא את כל ככר הירדן. אמר רבי נחמן בר חנין: כל מי שהוא להוט
אחר בולמוס של עריות, סוף שמאכילים אותו מבשרו. א"ר יוסי בר חנינא: כל הפסוק הזה
לשון ערוה הוא, היך מה דאת אמר (בראשית לט): ותשא אשת אדוניו את עיניה וגו'. וירא את
כל ככר הירדן כי כלה משקה. היך מה דאת אמר (משלי ו): כי בעד אשה זונה עד ככר לחם כי
כולה משקה, היך מה דאת אמר (במדבר ה): והשקה את האשה את מי המרים. לפני שחת ה',
היך מד"א (בראשית לח): והיה אם בא אל אשת אחיו ושחת ארצה.

7. AND LOT LIFTED UP HIS EYES, ETC. R. NAHMAN B. HANAN SAID: WHO-
EVER IS FIRED WITH IMMORAL DESIRE IS EVENTUALLY FED WITH HIS
OWN FLESH. R. JOSE B. R. HANINA SAID: THE WHOLE OF THIS VERSE CON-
NOTES IMMORAL DESIRE. THUS: AND LOT LIFTED UP HIS EYES, AS YOU
READ: AND HIS MASTER'S WIFE LIFTED UP HER EYES TO JOSEPH (GEN.
39:7). AND BEHELD ALL THE PLAIN (*KIKKAR*) OF THE JORDAN, AS YOU
READ: FOR ON ACCOUNT OF A HARLOT A MAN IS BROUGHT TO A LOAF
(*KIKKAR*) OF BREAD (PROV. 6:26). THAT IT WAS WELL WATERED (*MASH-
KEH*) EVERYWHERE, AS YOU READ: AND HE SHALL MAKE THE WOMAN
DRINK – *VEHISHKAH* (NUM. 5:24); BEFORE THE LORD DESTROYED (*SHA-
HETH*) SODOM, AS YOU READ: AND IT CAME TO PASS, WHEN HE WENT IN
UNTO HIS BROTHER'S WIFE, THAT HE SPILLED ON THE GROUND (GEN.
38:9).

This Midrash subjects the character of Lot to a criticism that can only be described as devastating. He is interpreted as one of the most immoral personalities of the Bible. It is very rare that this happens to a biblical character where the text itself uses personality from an entirely different and positive perspective.

The *Tiferet Tzion* wants to know on what basis the phrase is used in comparing Lot and the wife of Potiphar. He notes in this connection that the phrase, "He lifted up his eyes . . . ," was completely unnecessary. Lot could simply have said that he wanted the fruitful area of the Jordan valley. But these words seem to be inserted in order to become provocative and allow for a comparison between Lot and Potiphar's wife, and what he has to say is interpreted as having negative sexual connotations.

כגן ה', לאילנות. כארץ מצרים, לזרעים. ויבחר לו לוט. א"ר יוסי בר זימרא: כאינש דבחר
פורנא דאימיה.

LIKE THE GARDEN OF THE LORD, LIKE THE LAND OF EGYPT: LIKE THE
GARDEN OF THE LORD IN TREES, AND LIKE THE LAND OF EGYPT IN CERE-
ALS. SO LOT CHOSE FOR HIMSELF ALL THE PLAIN OF THE JORDAN, ETC.
(GEN. 13:11). R. JOSE B. ZIMRA SAID: HE WAS LIKE A MAN WHO COVETS
HIS MOTHER'S DOWRY.

The use of the term "Egypt" seems to be appropriate because not only
was it a fruitful land, but it also possessed its share of immoral sexual
behavior. In this respect, it was like Sodom, since it was very beautiful,
fruitful, and evil.

As for the interpretation of his mother's dowry, it is simply that Sodom was something he wanted very much and very badly.

ויסע לוט מקדם, הסיע עצמו מקדמונו של עולם. אמר: אי אפשי לא באברם ולא באלוהו.
ויפרדו איש מעל אחיו, אברם ישב. ר"מ אומר: אין לך בכרכים רע כסדום, כשאדם רע קורין
אותו סדומי, ואין לך בעממים קשה מאמורי, כשאדם קשה הן קוראין אותו אמורי. א"ר יוסי:
אין לך בכרכים יפה מסדום, שחזר לוט על כל ערי הככר ולא מצא מקום יפה כסדום. ואלו
היו החשובין שבהן. ואנשי סדום רעים וחטאים לה' מאד. רעים, אלו לאלו. חטאים, בגילוי
עריות. לה', בעבודת כוכבים. מאד, בשפיכות דמים:

AND LOT JOURNEYED EAST (*MI-KEDEM*): HE BETOOK HIMSELF FROM THE
ANCIENT (*KADMON*) OF THE WORLD, SAYING, I WANT NEITHER ABRAHAM
NOR HIS GOD. AND THEY SEPARATED THEMSELVES THE ONE FROM THE
OTHER. ABRAM DWELT IN THE LAND OF CANAAN, ETC. (GEN. 13:11F.).
RABBI SAID: THERE WAS NO CITY MORE WICKED THAN SODOM: WHEN
A MAN WAS EVIL HE WAS CALLED A SODOMITE; AND THERE WAS NO NA-
TION MORE CRUEL THAN THE AMORITES; WHEN A MAN WAS CRUEL HE
WAS CALLED AN AMORITE. R. ISSI SAID: THERE WAS NO CITY [IN THE
PLAIN] BETTER THAN SODOM, FOR LOT SEARCHED THROUGH ALL THE
CITIES OF THE PLAIN AND FOUND NONE LIKE SODOM. THUS THESE
PEOPLE WERE THE BEST OF ALL, YET, THE MEN OF SODOM WERE WICKED
AND SINNERS (13:13) – THEY WERE WICKED TO EACH OTHER; SINNERS
IN ADULTERY; AGAINST THE LORD IN IDOLATRY; WHILE EXCEEDINGLY
REFERS TO BLOODSHED.

The conclusion of the Lot story is simply that Lot wanted no part of
Abraham and no part of the God of Abraham. If a Sodomite stood for an
evil person, that is the name he wanted. The same goes for the Amorite,
if the Amorites would accept him as part of their nation.

Seed Thoughts

It is hard to imagine how absolutely serious is the criticism of Lot. By comparison, the Torah text was tender. He slept with his daughters because he was in a drunken stupor. The Midrash does not agree with this at all. It later says that he knew what he was doing and did what he desired to do. Wherever the text seems to justify or apologize for Lot's behavior, the Midrash tears those observations apart and replaces them with an absolute criticism. There is a magnificent opportunity at this point to realize what a great literature the Midrash is, because the next one will show that God was angry with this kind of criticism and expected more from Abraham in terms of Lot's spiritual welfare. More of this information will be forthcoming later. What other literature would include this kind of criticism and its almost justification by the Almighty?!

PARASHAH FORTY-ONE, *Midrash Eight*

ח וה' אמר אל אברם וגו'. ר' יודה אומר: כעס היה לאבינו אברהם בשעה שפירש לוט בן
אחיו מעמו. אמר הקב"ה: לכל הוא מדבק וללוט אחיו אינו מדבק?

8. AND THE LORD SAID UNTO ABRAM, AFTER THAT LOT WAS SEPA-
RATED FROM HIM (GEN. 13:14F.). R. JUDAH SAID: THERE WAS ANGER
[IN HEAVEN] AGAINST OUR FATHER ABRAHAM WHEN HIS NEPHEW LOT
PARTED FROM HIM. "HE MAKES EVERYONE CLEAVE [TO ME]," SAID THE
HOLY ONE, BLESSED BE HE, "YET HE DOES NOT CAUSE HIS BROTHER'S
SON TO CLEAVE [TO ME]!"

The first part of this Midrash describes God's criticism of how Lot was treated. Here, you have people like Abraham and Sarah who converted the whole of their world but who were not able to handle Lot. Why was that? It was because they obviously did not give him the time necessary. They were too interested in converting others and not sufficiently interested in looking after Abraham's brother's son Lot, for whom he was *in loco parentis* (a substitute parent).

רבי נחמיה אמר: כעס היה לו להקב"ה, בשעה שהיה מהלך לוט עם אברהם אבינו. אמר
הקב"ה: אני אמרתי לו: לזרעך נתתי את הארץ הזאת, והוא מדביק את לוט בן אחיו, כדי
לירשו? א"כ ילך ויביא לו שני פרסתקין מן השוק, ויורישם את שלו, כמו שהוא רוצה בן
אחיו? הה"ד (משלי כב): גרש לץ ויצא מדון. גרש לץ, זה לוט. ויצא מדון, ויהי ריב בין רועי
אברם וגו'. וישבות דין וקלון. ויאמר אברם אל לוט: אל נא תהי מריבה וגו' (שם), אהב טהר לב
וחן שפתיו רעהו מלך. הקב"ה אוהב כל מי שהוא טהר לב, ומי שיש לו חן בשפתיו. מלך הוא
רעהו, זה אברהם, שהיה תמים וטהר לבב, ונעשה אוהבו של מקום, שנאמר: זרע אברהם
אוהבו, ולפי שהיה לו חן בשפתיו, שנאמר (איוב מא): ודבר גבורות וחין ערכו, נעשה לו הקב"ה
כריע, שמתוך אהבה שאהבו. אמר לו: לזרעך נתתי את הארץ הזאת:

R. NEHEMIAH SAID: THERE WAS ANGER [IN HEAVEN] AGAINST THE PATRIARCH ABRAHAM WHEN LOT, HIS BROTHER'S SON, WENT WITH HIM. "I PROMISED HIM, UNTO THY SEED HAVE I GIVEN THIS LAND" (GEN. 15:18), SAID GOD, "YET HE ATTACHES LOT TO HIMSELF; IF SO, LET HIM GO AND PROCURE TWO COMMON SOLDIERS!" THIS EXPLAINS THE TEXT: CAST OUT THE SCORNER (PROV. 22:10), WHICH ALLUDES TO LOT; AND CONTENTION WILL GO OUT (22:10), ALLUDING TO: AND THERE WAS A STRIFE BETWEEN THE HERDSMEN OF ABRAHAM'S CATTLE, ETC. YEA, STRIFE AND SHAME WILL CEASE (22:10), AS IT SAYS: AND ABRAM SAID TO LOT: LET THERE BE NO STRIFE. HE THAT LOVETH PURENESS OF HEART, THAT HATH GRACE IN HIS IIPS, THE KING SHALL BE HIS FRIEND (22:11): HENCE, AND THE LORD SAID UNTO ABRAM: ... FOR ALL THE LAND WHICH THOU SEEST, TO THEE WILL I GIVE IT, ETC.

There is a second form of criticism by God of Abraham. It probably would be more appropriate to say in this connection, not that God was angry in Abraham, but that He was disappointed in him. The shepherds of Lot made fun of the fact that Abraham could not produce a child at this age, and therefore their employer Lot would inherit everything that belonged to the Patriarch Abraham. The disappointment of God was the fact that Abraham did not protest these arguments and might even have agreed with them – considering the fact that childbirth at their age was very difficult. God was disappointed that Abraham showed a lack of faith, and he should have been positive in affirming God's promise that only Abraham's flesh and blood would inherit and no one else. The verse concerning the scorner indicates that the fool creates argument after argument which have no basis in facts or life. Lot was a great scorner of this biblical promise.

Seed Thoughts

When God realized that Abraham was hesitating about affirming the promise that he would have a child, and he seemed to go along with the scornful views of Lot and his shepherds, why did God not reach out to Abraham and call this behavior to his attention? According to the *Tiferet Tzion*, this is not the way God relates to man. It is very important that Abraham, who is a truly righteous person – both in actual practice and great potential – to have come to this conclusion on his own. It may involve a struggle or hardship, but the good person has to come to his important spiritual position by his own effort, by his own decision, by his own sacrifices, and – if necessary – by his own suffering. Abraham eventually did realize what he was doing, and his great reward was the birth of Isaac.

Additional Commentary

When God did not speak to Abraham

"And the Lord said unto Abram when Lot was separated from him" (Genesis 13:14). It should be pointed out that during the entire time of the quarrels and separation between Abraham and Lot, God did not speak to Abraham because He was angry with him. He said, in effect, that Abraham reached out to everyone, but to Lot, his brother's son, he did not reach out. R. Nehemiah then added that during this entire time the Holy One did not speak to Abraham because he permitted Lot to walk with him in leadership – without converting him to have an awareness of God. When Lot separated from Abraham, God spoke to him again. (Mirkin)

PARASHAH FORTY-ONE, *Midrash Nine*

ט וה' אמר אל אברם אחרי הפרד לוט כי את כל הארץ אשר אתה רואה לך אתננה גו' ושמתי
את זרעך כעפר הארץ, מה עפר הארץ מסוף העולם ועד סופו, כך בניך יהיו מפוזרים מסוף
העולם ועד סופו.

9. AND I WILL MAKE THY SEED AS THE DUST OF THE EARTH (GEN. 13:16).
JUST AS THE DUST OF THE EARTH IS FOUND FROM ONE END OF THE
WORLD TO THE OTHER, SO SHALL THY CHILDREN BE FOUND FROM ONE
END OF THE EARTH TO THE OTHER.

T he main interest in this verse is the comparison or rather the difference between this parable and the original version which compared the
children of Abraham to the stars in the sky. Both are blessings of fertility
and a large population. Our Midrash, however, will be concerned with
the special meanings the dust of the earth might have.

ומה עפר הארץ אינו מתברך אלא במים, אף ישראל אינן מתברכין אלא בזכות התורה,
שנמשלה למים. ומה עפר מבלה את כלי מתכות והוא קיים לעולם, כך ישראל כל עובדי
כוכבים בטלים והם קיימים. ומה עפר עשויה דייש, אף בניך עשויין דייש לעובדי כוכבים,
הדא הוא דכתיב (ישעיה נא): ושמתיה ביד מוגיך וגו'. מה הוא מוגיך? אילן דממיגין מכתיך,
דמלחלחין מחתיך, אפילו כן לטובתיך משקשקין ליך מן חוביך. היך מה דאת אמר (תהלים
סה): ברביבים תמוגגנה. (ישעיה נא) אשר אמרו לנפשך שחי ונעבורה. מה היו עושים להם?
מרביצים אותן בפלטריות ומעבירין רדיה עליהם.

AND AS THE DUST OF THE EARTH CAN BE BLESSED ONLY THROUGH
WATER, SO WILL THY CHILDREN BE BLESSED ONLY FOR THE SAKE OF
THE TORAH, WHICH IS LIKENED TO WATER; AND AS THE DUST OF THE
EARTH WEARS OUT EVEN METAL UTENSILS YET ITSELF ENDURES FOR-
EVER, SO WILL ISRAEL EXIST [FOREVER] WHILE THE NATIONS OF THE
WORLD WILL CEASE TO BE; AND AS THE DUST OF THE EARTH IS TROD-
DEN UPON, SO WILL THY CHILDREN BE DOWNTRODDEN UNDER THE
HEEL OF [FOREIGN] POWERS, AS IT IS WRITTEN: AND I WILI PUT IT INTO
THE HAND OF THEM THAT AFFLICT THEE (ISA. 51:23); WHICH MEANS,
THOSE WHO MAKE THY WOUNDS FLOW. NEVERTHELESS, IT IS FOR THY
BENEFIT, FOR THEY PURIFY THEE OF GUILT, AS YOU READ: THOU MAK-
EST HER SOFT WITH SHOWERS, ETC. (PS. 65:11). THAT HAVE SAID TO THY
SOUL: BOW DOWN, THAT WE MAY GO OVER (ISA. 51:23). WHAT DID THEY

DO TO THEM? THEY MADE THEM LIE DOWN IN THE STREETS AND DREW
PLOUGHS OVER THEM.

The metaphor of the dust of the earth has a meaning that goes beyond
numbers and population. It includes also the negative aspect of Jewish
and human life. It includes the exile of the Jewish people and its various problems. At the same time, it stresses that what may seem to be a
serious negative aspect also has some good points. For example, earth
appears everywhere in the world. Nevertheless, Jewish people may
be persecuted in one area of the world and saved by living elsewhere.
Sometimes, therefore, a dispersion might be helpful for their survival.
Another asset of the earth is that seeds can be planted in it and vegetation for food and floral power can emerge to sustain mankind and
beautify it. Furthermore, with the Temple destroyed, all the various
areas where Jews could find consolation, forgiveness, or redemption are
closed, and all that remains is the Torah. Therefore, this became a way in
which the Torah became the only source of redemption for the Jewish
people, and therefore it is significantly studied.

רבי עזריה משם ר' אחא: סימן דא סימן טב. מה פלטייא זו מבלה את העוברים ואת השבים
והיא קיימת לעולם, כך בניך מבלים את כל העובדי כוכבים, והן קיימים לעולם:

R. AZARIAH SAID IN R. AHA'S NAME: THAT IS A GOOD AUGURY: AS THE
STREET OUTLIVES THOSE WHO TRAVEL ON IT, YET ITSELF REMAINS
FOREVER, SO SHALL THY SONS, [SAID GOD TO ABRAHAM], OUTLIVE THE
NATIONS OF THE WORLD WHILE THEY WILL REMAIN FOREVER.

Seed Thoughts

The traditional biblical text was made much more powerful by including as a blessing for Israel, a blessing in the form of the dust of the earth.
It makes us realize that the blessings of the stars in the sky was not good
enough. It was too positive and offered something too easy to be successful. In the case of the dust of the earth, there is strong realism. This
is far more gripping than the stars in the sky, and this made not only
the Jewish people but all other human beings more cognizant and more
careful of their way of life. The dust of the earth symbolized exile and
oppression. It also made possible challenge, resistance, and survival.

Additional Commentary

What dispersion cannot do

The dispersion around the world may appear to be something very negative, since Israel is eliminated from its homeland. On the other hand, it has this one advantage. Persecution in one area of the world need not take place everywhere. Some communities can be spared from this persecution by virtue of their separation in distance and communication. (Mirkin)

PARASHAH FORTY-ONE, *Midrash Ten*

י קום התהלך בארץ. תני הלך בשדה בין לארכה בין לרחבה, קנה עד מקום שהלך, כדברי רבי
אליעזר, שהיה ר"א אומר: הילוך קנה. וחכ"א: לא קנה עד שיהלך לארכה ולרחבה. א"ר יעקב
בן זבדי: טעמיה דר"א: קום התהלך בארץ וגו':

10. ARISE, WALK THROUGH THE LAND, ETC. (GEN. 13:17). IT WAS TAUGHT: IF HE WALKS IN THE FIELD, WHETHER ALONG ITS LENGTH OR ITS BREADTH, HE ACQUIRES IT AS FAR AS HE WALKS. THIS IS THE VIEW OF R. LIEZER, BUT THE SAGES MAINTAIN: HE DOES NOT ACQUIRE IT UNTIL HE TAKES POSSESSION. R. JACOB SAID: R. ELIEZER'S VIEW IS BASED ON THE VERSE, ARISE, WALK THROUGH THE LAND.

Seed Thoughts

The question in this Midrash is what is the legal method by which one acquires property? Two views are given. One view is that one has to go over the property lengthwise and breadthwise, if it is for the sake of acquisition, it is accepted. The Sages felt that this was not good enough and required a document and witnesses. R. Jacob felt that the arguments of the Sages were not convincing. The text says to walk through the land without mentioning the purpose of acquisition – this should be enough, due to the power of the text itself.

א ויהי בימי אמרפל מלך שנער. ר' יהושע דסכנין בשם רבי לוי פתח (תהלים ל"ז): חרב פתחו
רשעים וגו' חרבם תבא בלבם וגו'. מעשה בר"א בן הורקנוס, שהיו אחיו חורשים במישור
והוא חורש בהר ונפלה פרתו ונשברה, אמר: לטובתי נשברה פרתי, ברח והלך לו אצל רבן
יוחנן בן זכאי, והיה אוכל קוזזות אדמה עד שעשה פיו ריח רע. הלכו ואמרו לרבי יוחנן בן
זכאי: ריח פיו של ר"א קשה לו. א"ל: כשם שהבאיש ריח פיך על התורה, כך יהיה ריח
תלמודך הולך מסוף העולם ועד סופו. לאחר ימים עלה אביו לנדותו מנכסיו, ומצאו יושב
ודורש וגדולי מדינתו יושבים לפניו: בן ציצית הכסת, ונקדימון בן גוריון, ובן כלבא שבוע.
ומצאו יושב ודורש הפסוק הזה: חרב פתחו רשעים וגו', זה אמרפל וחביריו. להפיל עני
ואביון, זה לוט. לטבוח ישרי דרך, זה אברהם, חרבם תבא בלבם, ויחלק עליהם לילה הוא
ועבדיו ויכם. א"ל אביו: בני! לא עליתי לכאן אלא לנדותך מנכסי, עכשיו הרי כל נכסי נתונים
לך מתנה. אמר: הרי הם עלי חרם, ואיני אלא שוה בם כאחי. ד"א: חרב פתחו רשעים ודרכו,
זה אמרפל וחביריו:

1. AND IT CAME TO PASS IN THE DAYS OF AMRAPHEL, ETC. (GEN. 14:1).
R. JOSHUA COMMENCED HIS DISCOURSE IN THE NAME OF R. LEVI: THE
WICKED HAVE DRAWN OUT THE SWORD, ETC. (PS. 37:14). R. LIEZER'S
BROTHERS WERE ONCE PLOUGHING IN THE PLAIN, WHILE HE WAS
PLOUGHING ON THE MOUNTAIN, WHEN HIS COW FELL AND WAS
MAIMED. IT PROVED FORTUNATE FOR HIM THAT HIS COW WAS MAIMED,
FOR HE FLED TO R. JOHANAN B. ZAKKAI. HE ATE THERE CLODS OF
EARTH UNTIL HIS MOUTH EMITTED AN OFFENSIVE ODOR, AND WHEN
THEY WENT AND TOLD R. JOHANAN B. ZAKKAI THAT THE BREATH FROM
R. ELIEZER'S MOUTH SMELT FOUL, HE SAID TO HIM: "AS THE SMELL OF
YOUR MOUTH BECAME UNPLEASANT FOR THE SAKE OF THE TORAH, SO
WILL THE FRAGRANCE OF YOUR LEARNING BE DIFFUSED FROM ONE END
OF THE WORLD TO THE OTHER." AFTER SOME TIME, HIS FATHER CAME
UP TO DISINHERIT HIM, AND FOUND HIM SITTING AND LECTURING
WITH THE GREATEST OF THE LAND SITTING BEFORE HIM. BEN ZIZZITH
HAKESETH, NIKODEMON BEN GURION, AND BEN KALBA SHABUA. HE WAS
EXPOUNDING THIS VERSE: "THE WICKED HAVE DRAWN OUT THE SWORD,
AND HAVE BENT THE BOW"; THIS ALLUDES TO AMRAPHEL AND HIS

COMPANIONS; TO CAST DOWN THE POOR AND NEEDY (37:14) – TO LOT;
TO SLAY SUCH AS ARE UPRIGHT IN THE WAY (37:14.) – TO ABRAHAM.
THEIR SWORD SHALL ENTER INTO THEIR OWN HEART (37:15), AS IT IS
WRITTEN: AND HE FOUGHT AGAINST THEM BY NIGHT, HE AND HIS SER-
VANTS, AND SMOTE THEM, ETC. (GEN. 15:15). SAID HIS FATHER TO HIM,
"MY SON, I CAME UP ONLY TO DISINHERIT THEE; NOW, HOWEVER, ALL
MY PROPERTY IS GIVEN TO THEE AS A GIFT." "BEHOLD," HE REPLIED, "LET
IT BE *HEREM* [ACCURSED] TO ME; I WILL TAKE ONLY AN EQUAL SHARE
WITH MY BROTHERS." (ANOTHER INTERPRETATION: "THE WICKED HAVE
DRAWN OUT THE SWORD" ALLUDES TO AMRAPHEL AND HIS ALLIES, AS IT
IS WRITTEN, AND IT CAME TO PASS IN THE DAYS OF AMRAPHEL).

Let us begin with the story that is told. A young man used an accident
with one of the cattle as a way of escaping from his father's authority in
following the agricultural way of life on the family farm. He ultimately
became a great scholar. His father came to the academy with the goal of
eliminating his right to inheritance, and ended up being so impressed
that he designated his learned son to be the one to inherit everything.
The son, however, refused to do so and insisted on being equal to his
siblings. The question one can now ask of the Midrash is why was this
story presented in connection with the text concerning Amraphel? Why
was the text brought down in connection with the sword? The answer is
that the story of Amraphel and the kings was the first example of war in
the Torah. We have many examples of violence, such as Cain, Lamech,
and others. But this is the first record of a war between peoples and
nations. Just as throughout the Creation story (whenever something
new was created) the text said that it was the first, so too, in the case of
Amraphel, the Midrash is now telling us that this is the first example of
war in the Torah.

The place of the story in this Midrash can be explained as follows.
R. Eliezer interpreted the verse that is quoted as referring to Amraphel,
who was interested, not only in fighting against the other kings, but in
going after the poor and the upright, such as Lot and Abraham. In the
end, this came back to haunt them, and they were punished as a curse;
they were made to suffer as much as the intended victims. This interpretation was admired so much by his colleagues and his father.

Parashah Forty-Two, *Midrash Two*

ב ויהי בימי אמרפל. ר' שמואל בר שילת פתח (קהלת ה): וגם זו רעה חולה כל עומת שבא
כן ילך. א"ר שמואל בר שילת: כמה דאתא בחליטין, כן הוא אזיל בחליטין. א"ר אבון: כשם
שפתח בד' מלכיות, כך אינו חותם אלא בד' מלכיות. את כדרלעומר מלך עילם ותדעל
מלך גוים ואמרפל מלך שנער ואריוך מלך אלסר, כך אינו חותם אלא בד' מלכיות: מלכות
בבל ומלכות מדי ומלכות יון ומלכות אדום. רבי פנחס בשם רבי אייבו פתח (מיכה ד): והמה
לא ידעו מחשבות ה' ולא הבינו עצתו, כי קבצם כעמיר גרנה. למה כל אלה חברו אל עמק
השדים? כדי שיבואו ויפלו ביד אברהם, הה"ד: ויהי בימי אמרפל וגו':

2. R. SAMUEL COMMENCED HIS DISCOURSE: AND THIS ALSO IS A GRIEV-
OUS EVIL, THAT IN ALL POINTS AS HE CAME, SO SHALL HE GO (ECCL.
5:15). SAID R. SAMUEL: AS HE COMES WITH SLOPS, SO HE GOES WITH
SLOPS. R. ABIN SAID: JUST AS HE COMMENCED WITH FOUR KINGS, SO
WILL HE CONCLUDE WITH FOUR KINGS. [HE COMMENCES WITH FOUR
KINGS, VIZ.]: WITH CHEDORLAOMER KING OF ELAM, AND TIDAL KING
OF GOIIM, AND AMRAPHEL KING OF SHINAR, AND ARIOCH KING OF EL-
LASAR (GEN. 14:9); SO HE ENDS WITH FOUR KINGDOMS: THE KINGDOM
OF BABYLON, THE KINGDOM OF MEDIA, THE KINGDOM OF GREECE, AND
THE EMPIRE OF EDOM [I.E., ROME]. R. PHINEHAS QUOTED IN R. ABIN'S
NAME: BUT THEY KNOW NOT THE THOUGHTS OF THE LORD, NEITHER
UNDERSTAND THEY HIS COUNSEL, FOR HE HATH GATHERED THEM AS
THE SHEAVES TO THE THRESHING-FLOOR (MICAH 4:12). THUS, WHY
CAME ALL THESE AS ALLIES (GEN. 14:3)? IN ORDER THAT THEY MIGHT
COME AND FALL BY THE HANDS OF ABRAHAM; HENCE IT IS WRITTEN,
AND IT CAME TO PASS LN THE DAYS OF AMRAPHEL, ETC.

This Midrash is a continuation of the one before it. It has reference
to the fact that the various kings engaged not in one war between them,
but in two wars. This prompted the various Sages to say that there are
some people who are destined to repeat themselves at all times. If they
are born in a certain way, they will continue to be that way. So it was that
four kings fought against five kings, and later on the same four kings
fought against the same five kings with various results until Abraham
came along and changed the course of their history.

Seed Thoughts

The vast majority of readers of this section of the Torah, and in particular children, are convinced that Abraham is a great military general. They were convinced that it was Abraham's military genius that conquered Chedorlaomer and evoked the public thanksgiving of the king of Sodom. A more careful reading of the story indicates that it was not Abraham's victory, but that it was God's victory. Whether there is or is not *mazal le-Yisrael*, that is to say, lucky things that happen to Israel, this story was perfectly set up to make Abraham as a military general. He was not. Events had so unfolded that the kings who were the real military power were weakened considerably. This was the perfect opportunity for Abraham's staff and younger generation of his community to step in and subdue even the then so-called military powers. It was God's miracle of which Abraham was God's beneficiary.

Additional Commentary

The miracle of Abraham's victory

Many readers make the mistake of thinking that Abraham was a military power, that his household and his staff were trained soldiers who knew how to achieve military victories. Nothing could be farther from the truth. What happened in this section was not a military victory but a miraculous development.

Consider the following. Four kings went to war to achieve more land and they were militarily successful. After the passage of a number of years, however, the five kings whom they attacked rebelled against the victors who were headed by Chedorlaomer. Their rebellion was unsuccessful and they became wards and servants of the conquering powers. In this situation, you might say, that there was peace between them. Their military preparations were forgotten and they had no reason for the soldiers to be trained for imminent war. It was at this moment of relatively military weakness that Abraham appeared on the scene. The immediate reason was to rescue Lot, his nephew. But God so arranged the historical situation that Abraham and his staff were able to conquer the kings militarily because of their weakened condition. Abraham thus became the leading power of his generation and the most important occupier of the land promised to him. (*Tiferet Tzion*)

PARASHAH FORTY-TWO, *Midrash Three*

ג ד"א ויהי בימי אמרפל. ר' תנחומא בשם ר' חייא רבה ור' ברכיה בשם ר"א: זה המדרש
עלה בידינו מהגולה. בכל מקום שנאמר: ויהי בימי צרה, ויהי בימי אמרפל. ומה צרה היתה
שם? עשו מלחמה. א"ר שמואל בר נחמן: וחמשה הן. משל לאוהבו של מלך, שהיה שרוי
במדינה ובשבילו נזקק המלך למדינה, וכיון שבאו בדברים ליזקק לו, אמרו: אוי לנו! שאין
המלך נזקק למדינה, כמו שהוא למוד אם נהרוג את אוהבו, הדא הוא דכתיב: וישובו אל
עין משפט, היא קדש. אמר רבי אחא: לא באו להזדווג אלא לתוך גלגל עינו של עולם. עין
שעשתה מדת הדין בעולם, הם מבקשים לסמותה, הוא קדש. א"ר אחא: הוא כתיב, הוא,
שקדש שמו של הקב"ה בכבשן האש, וכיון שבאו בדברים להזדווג לו, התחילו הכל צווחים
ווי, הה"ד: ויהי בימי אמרפל.

3. AND IT CAME TO PASS (*WAYYEHI*) IN THE DAYS OF AMRAPHEL. R. TAN-
HUMA SAID IN THE NAME OF R. HIYYA THE ELDER AND R. BEREKIAH
SAID IN R. ELEAZAR'S NAME: THE FOLLOWING TEACHING CAME TO US
FROM THE EXILE: WHEREVER "AND IT CAME TO PASS IN THE DAYS OF"
(*WAYYEHI BIYEME*) OCCURS, IT DENOTES TROUBLE. R. SAMUEL B. NAH-
MAN SAID: "AND IT CAME TO PASS IN THE DAYS OF" OCCURS FIVE TIMES:
(I) AND IT CAME TO PASS IN THE DAYS OF AMRAPHEL: THAT THEY MADE
WAR. THIS MAY BE COMPARED TO A KING'S FRIEND WHO DWELT IN A
PROVINCE, AND ON HIS ACCOUNT THE KING USED TO VISIT THE PROV-
INCE AND SHOWED IT FAVOR. BUT WHEN BARBARIANS CAME TO ATTACK
HIM [THIS FRIEND], THEY LAMENTED, "WOE TO US, FOR THE KING WILL
NO LONGER SHOW FAVOR TO THIS PROVINCE AS WAS HIS WONT, [IF HIS
FRIEND IS KILLED]." THUS IT IS WRITTEN: AND THEY TURNED BACK AND
CAME TO EN-MISHPAT, ETC. (GEN. 14:7): R. AHA SAID: THEY CAME ONLY
IN ORDER TO ATTACK THE EYEBALL OF THE WORLD; THE EYE WHICH
EXECUTED JUDGMENT IN THE WORLD THEY DESIRE TO BLIND! THE SAME
(*HI*) IS KADESH: R. AHA SAID: THIS IS WRITTEN *HU* (HE): IT WAS HE
[ABRAHAM] THAT SANCTIFIED (*KIDDASH*) THE NAME OF THE HOLY ONE,
BLESSED BE HE, IN THE FIERY FURNACE. HENCE WHEN BARBARIANS
CAME TO ATTACK HIM, ALL BEGAN LAMENTING, "WOE!": THUS, THERE
WAS WOE IN THE DAYS OF AMRAPHEL.

The opening content explains the direction of the entire Midrash. It is
based on the tradition that wherever you have the expression ויהי בימי –
vayehi bimei, meaning "and it happened in the days of," it spells trouble.
The contents of the Midrash then go on to explain the five different

occasions where this expression occurs. It then describes the trouble associated with these occasions together with a parable that helps explain it. The fact that this interpretation is something that was taught in the communities of the exile is also something to note since it is a tribute to the high degree of learning that was possible in the diaspora.

In the case of Amraphel, he was attacked by the barbarians, who did not succeed in their conquest because of Abraham, the real master of the land.

(ישעיה ז) ויהי בימי אחז. מה צרה היתה שם? (שם ט) ארם מקדם ופלשתים מאחור. משל לבן שרים שנזדווג לו פדגוגו להמיתו. אמר: אם אני הורגו עכשיו אתחייב מיתה לשר, אלא הריני מושך מניקתו ממנו, ומעצמו הוא מת. כך אמר אחז: אם אין גדיים אין תישים, אם אין תישים אין צאן, אם אין צאן אין רועה, אם אין רועה אין עולם. כך היה סבור בדעתו לומר: אם אין קטנים אין תלמידים, אם אין תלמידים אין חכמים, אם אין חכמים אין זקנים, אם אין זקנים אין נביאים, אם אין נביאים אין הקב"ה משרה שכינתו עליהם, הה"ד (שם ח): צור תעודה חתום תורה בלמודי. רבי חוניא בר אלעזר אמר: למה נקרא שמו אחז? שאחז בתי כנסיות ובתי מדרשות. ר' יעקב בר אבא בשם ר' אחא אמר: ישעיה (שם): וחכיתי לה' המסתיר פניו מבית יעקב. אין לך שעה קשה כאותה שעה שכתב בה (דברים לא): ואנכי הסתר אסתיר פני בעת ההיא. ומאותה שעה קויתי לו שאמר: כי לא תשכח מפי זרעו. ומה הועיל לו? (ישעיה ח) הנה אנכי והילדים אשר נתן לי ה' לאותות ולמופתים. וכי ילדיו היו והלא תלמידיו היו? אלא מלמד שהיו חביבים עליו כבניו, וכיון שאחז בתי כנסיות ובתי מדרשות, התחילו צווחים ווי! ויהי בימי אחז.

(II) AND IT CAME TO PASS IN THE DAYS OF AHAZ (ISA. 7:1): [WHAT]? THE ARAMEANS ON THE EAST, AND THE PHILISTINES ON THE WEST (9:11). THIS MAY BE COMPARED TO THE SON OF A KING AGAINST WHOM HIS TUTOR PLOTTED IN ORDER TO KILL HIM. SAID HE TO HIMSELF: "IF I SLAY HIM NOW, MY LIFE WILL BE FORFEIT TO THE KING. THEREFORE I WILL RATHER WITHDRAW HIS FOSTER-MOTHER FROM HIM, AND HE WILL DIE OF HIMSELF." AHAZ SAID LIKEWISE: IF THERE ARE NO KIDS THERE ARE NO WETHERS; IF THERE ARE NO WETHERS THERE ARE NO SHEEP; IF THERE ARE NO SHEEP THERE IS NO SHEPHERD; IF THERE IS NO SHEPHERD THERE IS NO WORLD. HE REASONED THUS TO HIMSELF: NO CHILDREN, NO ADULTS; NO ADULTS, NO DISCIPLES; NO DISCIPLES, NO SAGES; NO SAGES, NO ELDERS; NO ELDERS, NO PROPHETS; AND IF THERE ARE NO PROPHETS, THE HOLY ONE, BLESSED BE HE, WILL NOT CAUSE HIS SHECHINAH TO REST UPON THEM. THUS IT IS WRITTEN: BIND UP THE TESTIMONY, SHUT UP THE INSTRUCTION AMONG MY DISCIPLES (8:16). R. HUNIA SAID IN R. LEAZAR'S NAME: WHY WAS HE CALLED AHAZ? BECAUSE HE SEIZED (AHAZ) THE SYNAGOGUES AND SCHOOLS. R. JACOB SAID IN

R. AHA'S NAME: ISAIAH SAID: AND I WILL WAIT FOR THE LORD, THAT
HIDETH HIS FACE FROM THE HOUSE OF JACOB AND I WILL LOOK FOR
HIM (8:17). NO HOUR IS AS GRIEVOUS AS THAT WHEREOF IT IS WRITTEN:
AND I WILL SURELY HIDE MY FACE, ETC. (DEUT. 31:18), AND SINCE THAT
HOUR I HAVE HOPED FOR HIM, FOR HE SAID TO ME: FOR IT SHALL NOT
BE FORGOTTEN OUT OF THE MOUTHS OF THEIR SEED (31:21). AND WHAT
DID IT AVAIL HIM [SC. AHAZ]? BEHOLD, I AND THE CHILDREN WHOM THE
LORD HATH GIVEN ME SHALL BE FOR SIGNS AND FOR WONDERS (ISA.
8:18). WERE THEY THEN HIS CHILDREN? SURELY THEY WERE HIS DIS-
CIPLES! THIS, HOWEVER, TEACHES THAT THEY WERE DEAR TO HIM, AND
SO HE CALLED THEM HIS CHILDREN. BUT AS SOON AS HE SEIZED THE
SYNAGOGUES AND SCHOOLS, ALL BEGAN LAMENTING, "WOE": THUS,
THERE WAS WOE IN THE DAYS OF AHAZ.

King Ahaz was very sensitive to the fact that the sages of Israel and
the entire Torah network opposed his reign, and would have been very
happy with his departure. He felt that he could not oppose them directly, only indirectly. He, therefore, ultimately closed the schools, the
academies, and the *yeshivot*. This caused great trouble for which Ahaz
was responsible.

ויהי בימי יהויקים. ומה צרה היתה שם? (ירמיה ד) ראיתי את הארץ והנה תהו ובהו. משל לשר
ששלח פרסטגמא שלו במדינה. מה עשו לה בני המדינה? נטלו אותה וקרעו אותה ושרפו
אותה באש, שנאמר (שם לו): ויהי ככרוא יהודי שלש דלתות וארבעה. תלת ארבע פסוקי,
כיון שהגיע לפסוק (איכה א): היו צריה לראש, קרעה בתער הסופר, והשלך אל האש עד תום
כל המגלה, על האש אשר על האח, כיון שראו הכל כן, התחילו הכל צווחים: ווי! ויהי בימי
יהויקים.

(III) IT CAME TO PASS IN THE DAYS OF JEHOIAKIM (JER. 1:3) – I BEHELD
THE EARTH, AND LO, IT WAS WASTE AND VOID (4:23). THIS MAY BE COM-
PARED TO A KING WHO SENT AN ORDINANCE TO A PROVINCE: WHAT
DID ITS INHABITANTS DO? THEY TOOK IT, TORE IT UP, AND BURNT IT IN
FIRE. [SIMILARLY WE READ]: AND IT CAME TO PASS, WHEN JEHUDI HAD
READ THREE OR FOUR COLUMNS, THAT HE CUT IT WITH THE PENKNIFE,
AND CAST IT INTO THE FIRE (36:23). WHEN THEY SAW THIS ALL BEGAN
CRYING, "WOE": THUS, THERE WAS WOE IN THE DAYS OF JEHOIAKIM.

During the days of Jehoiakim, a document was discovered that spelled
out in detail the mission of the Children of Israel as the people of God.
The people wanted very much to hear this document, to study it, and

above all, to obey it. Not only did Jehoiakim oppose the teaching of this document, but he ultimately tore it and destroyed it by throwing it in the fire. That was the great trouble of his reign and of his personality.

(רות א) ויהי בימי שפוט השופטים. ומה צרה היתה שם? ויהי רעב בארץ. למדינה שהיתה חייבת ליפס לשר, שלח השר גבאי טימיון לגבותה. מה עשו לו בני המדינה? נטלו אותו, והכו אותו, ואח"כ אמרו: אוי לנו! כשירגיש השר בדברים הללו, מה שבקש לעשות לנו, עשינו לו! כך, בימי שפוט השופטים, היה אדם מישראל עובד עבודת כוכבים, והיה הדיין מבקש להעביר עליו מדת הדין, והיה הוא בא ומלקה את הדיין. אמר: מה שבקש לעשות לי, עשיתי לו! אמרו: אוי לו לדור ששפטו את שופטיהם, הה"ד: ויהי בימי שפוט השופטים, ויהי רעב בארץ.

(IV) AND IT CAME TO PASS IN THE DAYS WHEN THE JUDGES JUDGED (RUTH 1:1) – THAT THERE WAS A FAMINE IN THE IAND (1:1). THIS MAY BE COMPARED TO A PROVINCE THAT OWED ARREARS TO THE KING, AND THE KING SENT A TREASURY OFFICER TO COLLECT THEM. WHAT DID THE INHABITANTS DO? THEY SEIZED HIM, BEAT HIM, AND MULCTED HIM. THEN THEY CRIED: "WOE TO US WHEN THE KING LEARNS OF THIS: WHAT HE WISHED TO DO TO US, WE HAVE DONE TO HIM": SIMILARLY, WOE TO THE GENERATION THAT JUDGED ITS JUDGES! THUS, THERE WAS WOE IN THE DAYS WHEN THE JUDGES WERE JUDGED.

In the case of the fourth expression, we are dealing with the verse that says, "In the days when the Judges judged." The trouble that is connected with this fourth expression happens to be in the very text itself. The text says that in the days of the Judges, there was a famine in the land. What we have to ask ourselves is what caused the famine? What caused the famine was illustrated by the tax collector who was beaten by those from whom he requested the payment of taxes. It was this kind of behavior – where people attacked the authorities – that caused famine in the land.

(אסתר א) ויהי בימי אחשורוש. ומה צרה היתה שם? להשמיד להרוג ולאבד. משל לשר שהיה לו כרם אחד ונזדווגו לו ג' שונאים: הראשון מתחיל מקטף בעוללות. והב' מזנב באשכולות. והג' מעקר בגפנים. כך פרעה (שמות א): כל הבן הילוד היאורה תשליכוהו. נבוכדנצר (מלכים ב כד): החרש והמסגר אלף. ר' ברכיה אמר: החרש אלף והמסגר אלף. רבנן אמרין: כלם אלף. המן ביקש לעקור הגפן כלה, שנאמר (אסתר ג): להשמיד להרוג ולאבד את כל היהודים וגו'. וכיון שראו שהכל, כן התחילו צווחים ווי, הה"ד: ויהי בימי אחשורוש.

(V) AND IT CAME TO PASS IN THE DAYS OF AHASUERUS (EST. 1:1) – WHEREFORE HAMAN SOUGHT TO DESTROY ALL THE JEWS (3:6). THIS MAY BE

COMPARED TO A KING WHO HAD A VINEYARD, WHICH THREE ENEMIES
ATTACKED: THE FIRST PLUCKED OFF SINGLE GRAPES, THE SECOND
THINNED THE CLUSTERS, AND THE THIRD UPROOTED THE VINES. THUS,
PHARAOH DECREED: EVERY SON THAT IS BORN YE SHALL CAST INTO THE
RIVER (EX. 1:22); NEBUCHADNEZZAR DEPORTED – THE CRAFTSMEN AND
THE SMITHS A THOUSAND (II KINGS 24:16). (R. BEREKIAH SAID IN R.
JUDAH'S NAME: THAT MEANS, THE CRAFTSMEN A THOUSAND AND THE
SMITHS A THOUSAND. THE RABBIS SAID: IT MEANS A THOUSAND IN ALL.)
BUT HAMAN WISHED TO PULL UP THE VERY ROOTS, AS IT IS WRITTEN:
TO DESTROY, TO SLAY, AND TO CAUSE TO PERISH ALl JEWS (EST. 3:13).
WHEN THEY SAW THIS, ALL BEGAN LAMENTING, "WOE": THUS, THERE
WAS WOE IN THE DAYS OF AHASUERUS.

In the case of the days of Achashverosh, the terrible trouble was
the decree of Haman to not only kill the Jews, but to completely an-
nihilate them. The reason why Achashverosh seemed to go along with
this terrible decree without any question was because it seemed to be
the kind of behavior that was bequeathed to him by his ancestors, as
kings – namely, Pharaoh, Nebuchadnezzar, and finally Haman (who
was not king himself, although he was the person upon whom the king
depended upon his policy).

ר"ש בר אבא משום ר' יוחנן: בכל מקום שנאמר ויהי משמש צרה ושמחה. אם צרה, אין צרה
כיוצא בה, ואם שמחה, אין שמחה כיוצא בה. אתא רבי שמואל ב"נ ועבד פלגא: בכל מקום,
שנאמר ויהי משמש צרה, והיה שמחה.

R. SIMEON [B. R. ABBA] SAID IN R. JOHANAN'S NAME: WHEREVER
WAYYEHI (AND IT CAME TO PASS) IS EMPLOYED, IT CONNOTES EITHER
TROUBLE OR JOY; IF TROUBLE, THERE WAS NONE LIKE IT; IF JOY, THERE
WAS NONE LIKE IT. R. SAMUEL B. NAHMAN CAME AND DREW A DISTINC-
TION: WHEREVER WAYYEHI IS STATED, IT DENOTES TROUBLE; WE-HAYAH
DENOTES JOY.

Apparently the rabbis are asserting that wherever *vayehi* is mentioned,
it symbolizes trouble or joy. In the case of trouble, it is the worst trouble
possible and in the case of joy, the best joy possible. However, there
is disagreement. Another sage says that *vayehi* introduces trouble, but
vehayah introduces joy.

מתיבין ליה: והכתיב (בראשית א): ויהי אור? עוד היא אינה שמחה שלימה, שלא זכה העולם
להשתמש באותה האורה. אמר רבי יהודה בר סימון: אותה האורה שנבראת ביום הראשון,
היה אדם מביט בה מסוף העולם ועד סופו, כיון שצפה הקב"ה בדור המבול ובדור הפלגה,
גנזה לצדיקים לעתיד לבא, הה"ד (משלי ד): ואורח צדיקים כאור נוגה הולך ואור עד נכון היום.

THEY OBJECTED: BUT IT IS WRITTEN: AND GOD SAID: LET THERE BE
LIGHT AND THERE WAS (*WAYYEHI*) LIGHT (GEN. 1:3)? THAT STILL DOES
NOT CONNOTE JOY, HE REPLIED, SINCE THE WORLD WAS NOT PRIVI-
LEGED TO MAKE USE OF THAT LIGHT. (R. JUDAH SAID: BY THE LIGHT
WHICH WAS CREATED ON THE FIRST DAY, MAN COULD HAVE SEEN FROM
ONE END OF THE WORLD TO THE OTHER; BUT WHEN THE HOLY ONE,
BLESSED BE HE, FORESAW THE WICKED, HE HID IT AWAY FOR THE RIGH-
TEOUS, AS IT IS WRITTEN: BUT THE PATH OF THE RIGHTEOUS AS THE
LIGHT OF DAWN, THAT SHINETH MORE AND MORE UNTO THE PERFECT
DAY (PROV. 4:18).)

One of the proof texts that has to do with *vayehi* has to do with the
light that was created included the expression *vayehi* in Genesis. Light,
of course, is something joyous, except that the particular light created
in the first day had such extraordinary powers that it was hidden so that
ordinary people could not use it. It is reserved for the tzaddikim, the
very righteous, in the end of days (See the Additional Commentary
concerning light.)

מתיבין ליה: והכתיב (בראשית א): ויהי ערב ויהי בוקר? אמר להם: עוד אינה שמחה שלימה,
שכל מה שנברא ביום ראשון עתידין לבלות, שנאמר (ישעיה נא): כי שמים כעשן נמלחו
והארץ כבגד תבלה. אתיבין ליה: והכתיב: ויהי ערב ויהי בוקר יום ב' יום ג' יום ד' יום ה' יום
ו'. אמר להם: עוד אינה שלימה, שכל מה שנברא בששת ימי בראשית צריכים עשייה, כגון:
החרדל צריך למתוק, החטים צריכם להטחן, התורמוסין צריכין לימתק.

THEY OBJECTED: BUT IT IS WRITTEN: AND THERE WAS (*WAYYEHI*) EVE-
NING AND THERE WAS (*WAYYEHI*) MORNING, ONE DAY (GEN. 1:4). THAT
TOO WAS NOT AN OCCASION OF JOY, REPLIED HE, FOR EVERYTHING CRE-
ATED ON THE FIRST DAY IS DESTINED TO WEAR OUT, AS IT IS WRITTEN:
FOR THE HEAVENS SHALL VANISH AWAY LIKE SMOKE, AND THE EARTH
SHALL WAX OLD LIKE A GARMENT (ISA. 51:6). THEY OBJECTED: BUT IT
IS WRITTEN: AND THERE WAS (*WAYYEHI*) EVENING AND THERE WAS
(*WAYYEHI*) MORNING, A SECOND DAY (GEN. 1:8) ... A THIRD DAY (1:13)
... A FOURTH DAY (1:19), ETC.? THESE STILL DO NOT CONNOTE JOY, HE
ANSWERED, FOR WHATEVER WAS CREATED IN THE FIRST SIX DAYS OF

CREATION NEEDS FURTHER PREPARATION [BEFORE IT IS FIT FOR USE],
E.G., MUSTARD MUST BE SWEETENED, WHEAT MUST BE GROUND.

Even though *vayehi* is used in the creation of day and night, it has to be understood that following the first six days, the world was not a finished product. Everything had to be developed, trained, and refined, so that it was not complete joy.

מתיבין ליה: והכתיב (בראשית לט): ויהי ה' את יוסף? אמר להם: עוד אינה שמחה שלימה שנזדווגה לו אותה הדוב. מתיבין ליה. מתיבין ליה: והכתיב (ויקרא ט): ויהי ביום השמיני קרא משה? אמר להם: עוד אינה שמחה שלימה שמתו נדב ואביהוא. מתיבין ליה: והא כתיב (במדבר ז): ויהי ביום כלות משה. אמר להם: עוד אינה שמחה שנגנזה בבנין הבית. מתיבין ליה: והכתיב (יהושע ו): ויהי ה' את יהושע. אמר להם: עוד אינה שמחה, שהצריך לקרוע בגדיו. מתיבין ליה: והכתיב (שמואל ב ז): ויהי כי ישב המלך בביתו וה' הניח לו וגו'. אמר להם: עוד אינה שמחה שלמה, שבא נתן ואמר לו (מלכים א ח): רק אתה לא תבנה בית.

THEY OBJECTED: BUT IT IS WRITTEN: AND THE LORD WAS (*WAYYEHI*) WITH JOSEPH (39:2)? THAT TOO WAS NOT AN OCCASION OF JOY, BECAUSE THAT SHE-BEAR [POTIPHAR'S WIFE] ASSAILED HIM. ANOTHER OBJECTION: BUT IT IS WRITTEN: AND IT CAME TO PASS (*WAYYEHI*) ON THE EIGHTH DAY (LEV. 9:1)? THAT DOES STILL NOT CONNOTE JOY, HE REPLIED, BECAUSE ON THAT VERY DAY NADAB AND ABIHU DIED. BUT IT IS WRITTEN: AND IT CAME TO PASS (*WAYYEHI*) ON THE DAY THAT MOSES HAD MADE AN END OF SETTING UP THE TABERNACLE (NUM. 7:1)? THAT STILL DOES NOT CONNOTE JOY, HE ANSWERED, BECAUSE IT [THE TABERNACLE] WAS HIDDEN AWAY AT THE BUILDING OF THE TEMPLE. BUT IT IS WRITTEN: SO THE LORD WAS (*WAYYEHI*) WITH JOSHUA, AND HIS FAME WAS IN ALL THE LAND (JOSH. 6:27)? THAT STILL DOES NOT CONNOTE JOY, HE REPLIED, SINCE HE EVENTUALLY HAD TO REND HIS GARMENTS. BUT IT IS WRITTEN, AND IT CAME TO PASS (*WAYYEHI*), WHEN THE KING DWELT IN HIS HOUSE, ETC. (II SAM. 7:1)? – NATHAN CAME AND INFORMED HIM: NEVERTHELESS, THOU SHALT NOT BUILD THE HOUSE (I KINGS 8:19).

A series of examples are given as to the good things that were produced with the expression *vayehi*. However, as time went on, each one produced results that were less than joyous.

לשמי אמרין ליה: אמרן דידן, אמור דידך! אמר להם: והכתיב (זכריה יד): והיה ביום ההוא יצאו מים חיים וגו'. (ישעיה ז) והיה ביום ההוא יחיה איש עגלת בקר וגו'. (שם יא) והיה ביום

ההוא יוסיף ה' וגו'. (יואל ד) והיה ביום ההוא יטפו ההרים עסיס. (ישעיה כז) והיה ביום ההוא
יתקע בשופר גדול וגו'. מתיבין ליה: והכתיב (ירמיה לח) והיה כאשר נלכדה ירושלים. אמר
להם: עוד היא שמחה שבו ביום נטלו ישראל, אופכי על עוונותיהם. דאמר רבי שמואל ב"ר
אופכי גדולה נטלו ישראל על עוונותיהם, ביום שחרב בית המקדש, שנאמר: תם עוונך בת
ציון וגו':

SAID THEY TO HIM: WE HAVE QUOTED OUR OBJECTIONS: DO YOU QUOTE
YOUR PROOFS? THEREUPON HE CITED: AND IT SHALL COME TO PASS
(*WE-HAYAH*) IN THAT DAY, THAT LIVING WATERS SHALL GO OUT FROM
JERUSALEM (ZECH. 14:8); AND IT SHALI COME TO PASS (*WE-HAYAH*) IN
THAT DAY, THAT A GREAT HORN SHALL BE BLOWN, ETC. (ISA. 27:13);
AND IT SHALL COME TO PASS (*WE-HAYAH*) IN THAT DAY, THAT A MAN
SHALL REAR A YOUNG COW, ETC. (7:21); AND IT SHALL COME TO PASS
(*WE-HAYAH*) THAT THE LORD WILL SET HIS HAND AGAIN A SECOND TIME
TO RECOVER THE REMNANT OF HIS PEOPLE (11:11); AND IT SHALL COME
TO PASS (*WE-HAYAH*) IN THAT DAY, THAT THE MOUNTAINS SHALI DROP
DOWN SWEET WINE (JOEL 4:18). THEY OBJECTED: BUT IT IS WRITTEN:
AND HE (JEREMIAH) WAS THERE (*WE-HAYAH*) WHEN JERUSALEM WAS
TAKEN (JER. 38:28)? EVEN THAT CONNOTES JOY, WAS HIS REPLY, FOR
ON THAT VERY DAY ISRAEL RECEIVED FULL QUITTANCE FOR THEIR
SINS, AS R. SAMUEL B. NAHMAN SAID: ISRAEL RECEIVED QUITTANCE IN
FULL MEASURE FOR THEIR SINS ON THE DAY THAT THE TEMPLE WAS
DESTROYED, AS IT IS WRITTEN: THE PUNISHMENT OF THINE INIQUITY
IS COMPLETE, O DAUGHTER OF ZION, ETC. (LAM. 4:22).

A series of events was listed where *vehayah* was used to mean an expression of joy. The climax of these expressions was the view that even
the destruction of the Temple, which happened in the days of Jeremiah,
had an element about it that can be described as good. The sins of every
Jew were forgiven on that occasion.

—

Seed Thoughts

There is a remarkable statement in this Midrash which I, as one reader,
found it difficult to understand. There it said that the greatest tragedy
of all was the destruction of the Temple. But it also implied that the
greatest *simha* was associated with that tragedy in a sense that every
individual Jew had his sins forgiven. Speaking personally, I found it difficult to accept that statement since the Jews whose sins were forgiven

did not know that their sins were forgiven and, therefore, lacked the motivation that would transform their life into higher moral and ethical ideals. I found it very difficult to understand this teaching until I came across an interpretation by the *Tiferet Tzion*. He says that God was angry at the Jewish people because of their immoral behavior, because they worship false Gods, idols, but He took out His anger, as they say in Hebrew, על העצים ועל האבנים – *al ha-etzim ve-al ha-avanim*, upon the trees and the stones. Basically, the Temple, for all its spiritual meaning was a building. It was made of wood and stones. God destroyed the building but did not destroy the Jewish people. The Jewish people survived the destruction of the Temple and achieved many wonderful things in the areas of Torah, Jewish worship, and the doing of good deeds. This made the tragedy into some sort of blessing (although we have to take care of using such words). The Jewish people survived and that is the lesson that we have to learn.

Unfortunately, one cannot stop at this point because we are living in the twenty-first century. Most of us were witness to what is called the Shoah, the Holocaust of the twentieth century, where one third of the Jewish people were annihilated in the cruelest way possible. The destruction of the people was a tragedy much worse that the destruction of the Temple, much worse than a building being destroyed. If every human life represents a world, millions of worlds were destroyed. The fact that non-European Jews were saved is only a partial consolation. Terrible as the tragedy has been, almost as bad, is the fact that we have not understood, we do not know why it happened, or do not understand why we deserved this to happen, or why the Jewish people of all the people in the world should be made to suffer this humiliation. This is unfinished business. God grant that somehow and in some way that we will learn why it happened to us and much more.

⸺

Additional Commentary

The light of the first day

We were told that the light on the first day was so powerful that it had to be hidden, and received its full possibilities during the days of the tzaddikim. On this subject, the Vilna Gaon had an extraordinary comment. The light that we are now talking about was not something that had to do with the sun or any other physical process. It was the light of human intelligence. That was the greatest of all lights, better that the physical light of day and night. Not everyone can use this intelligence equally. Some know how to use it to a greater extent and others to a lesser extent. This light is the greatest of all lights. It has done and interpreted many remarkable things for us, but the best has yet to come. (Vilna Gaon, quoted from *Tiferet Tzion*)

PARASHAH FORTY-TWO, *Midrash Four*

ד ויהי בימי אמרפל. ג' שמות נקראו לו: כוש ונמרוד ואמרפל. כוש, שהיה כושי ודאי. נמרוד, שהעמיד מרד בעולם. אמרפל, שהיתה אמירתו אפילה, דאמרי ואפלי בעלמא, דאמרי ואפלי באברהם, שאמר שירד לכבשן האש.

4. AND IT CAME TO PASS IN THE DAYS OF AMRAPHEL. HE WAS CALLED BY THREE NAMES: CUSH, NIMROD, AND AMRAPHEL. CUSH, BECAUSE HE WAS INDEED A CUSHITE. NIMROD, BECAUSE HE INCITED THE WORLD TO RE-VOLT (*HIMRID*). AMRAPHEL DENOTES: HE MADE A DECLARATION (*AMAR IMRAH*), "I WILL CAST DOWN (*APPILAH*)." [ANOTHER INTERPRETATION IS] THAT HE MADE SPORT OF (*AMAR WE-AFLEH*) THE WORLD, ALSO THAT HE MADE SPORT OF ABRAHAM; AGAIN, THAT HE ORDERED ABRAHAM TO BE THROWN (*AMAR WE-HIPPIL*) INTO THE FURNACE.

Apparently, the Midrash wants to indicate that the name of the person had something to do either with his character, personality, or his origin. Thus, Cushite – as that is the tribe he comes from; Nimrod – who was responsible for the rebellions in the generation of the Tower of Babel; and Amraphel – because he used his mouth and opinions in various ways, usually to the detriment of others.

ואריוך מלך אלסר. א"ר יוסי ממלחייא: תמן תנינן, איסרין, לשם אלסר. כדרלעומר מלך עילם ותדעל מלך גוים. א"ר לוי: אתר הוא תמן מצטווח ברומי, ונטלו אדם אחד והמליכו אותו עליהם. א"ר יוחנן: ותדעל הוה שמו.

ARIOCH KING OF ELLASAR. R. JOSE OF MILHAYA SAID: WHY ARE THEY [HAZEL-NUTS] CALLED *ELSARIN*? BECAUSE [THEY GROW IN THE TERRI-TORY] OF ELLASAR. CHEDORLAOMER KING OF ELAM, AND TIDAL KING OF GOIIM. R. LEVI SAID: THERE IS A PLACE WHICH IS SO CALLED THERE

[SC. IN BABYLON], AND [ITS INHABITANTS] TOOK A CERTAIN MAN AND MADE HIM KING OVER THEM. R. JOHANAN SAID: AND HIS NAME WAS TIDAL.

Apparently, the monarchy was not in high esteem and the person they chose did not seem to have any special leadership ability.

ד"א: ויהי בימי אמרפל מלך שנער, זו בבל. ואריוך מלך אלסר, זה אנטיוכס. כדרלעומר מלך עילם, זה מדי. ותדעל מלך גוים, זו מלכות אדום, שהיא מכתבת טירוניא מכל אומות העולם. אמר רבי אלעזר בר אבינא: אם ראית מלכיות מתגרות אלו באלו צפה לרגלו של משיח, תדע שכן, שהרי בימי אברהם על ידי שנתגרו המלכיות אלו באלו, באה הגאולה לאברהם:

ANOTHER INTERPRETATION: AND IT CAME TO PASS IN THE DAYS OF AMRAPHEL KING OF SHINAR: THIS ALLUDES TO BABYLON; ARIOCH KING OF ELLASAR: THAT ALLUDES TO GREECE; CHEDORLAOMER KING OF ELAM: THAT IS MEDIA; AND TIDAL THE KING OF GOIIM [LIT. "NATIONS"]: THIS ALLUDES TO THE WICKED POWER [I.E., ROME] WHICH LEVIES TROOPS FROM ALL THE NATIONS OF THE WORLD. R. ELEAZAR B. R. ABINA SAID: WHEN YOU SEE THE POWERS FIGHTING EACH OTHER, LOOK FOR THE COMING [LIT. "FEET"] OF THE KING MESSIAH. THE PROOF IS THAT IN THE DAYS OF ABRAHAM, BECAUSE THESE POWERS FOUGHT AGAINST EACH OTHER, GREATNESS CAME TO ABRAHAM.

The Midrash is now moving in a direction, which is the purpose of this particular teaching. These kingdoms may have been small when Abraham brought them under his control. However, they were never destroyed. They grew and became more powerful, and ultimately each of them created an empire that ruled the world for one generation and was dramatically and consistently anti-Jewish. In fact, the order in which their names are mentioned is the order in which they took over power from their predecessor, and each one in turn took control of the world while at the same hating the Jewish people.

R. Eleazar adds the thought that might encourage the smaller powers not to give up hope. If a way could be found to have these great powers compete with each other, and in this competition weaken each other, it is possible for a person like Abraham, who headed a small nation, to take power even over the big empires.

The story is told of a rabbi who was asked concerning a war between two wicked nations. He said, "May both sides win."

—

Seed Thoughts

When I first began reading the Midrashim having to do with Amraphel, I was not able to understand why the Midrash would spend time with what would seem to me an unimportant detail in the story of Abraham. How wrong I was. As these Midrashim developed, one can see that the midrashic writers did not believe that Abraham's victory over the five nations was something that would remain permanent. On the contrary, not only were they not destroyed as time went on, they grew in importance and in power. The same four and five powers that Abraham controlled in his generation did not remain dependent for too long a time after Abraham's disappearance from the biblical scene. They grew, they developed, and they became politically powerful. One became the empire of Babylonia. A second became the empire of Greece. A third became the empire of Persia. The fourth was the empire of Rome. The more you think about this development, the more it is difficult to accept. Abraham may have had victory, but did not eliminate the enemies of Israel. The little kingdom became a powerful nation which controlled the world and was also against the Jewish people. This can be said of Nebuchadnezzar of Babylon, Antiochus of Greece, Achashverosh of Persia, and finally the kingdom of Rome.

After this point, the Midrash says that all of these will be eliminated when the King Messiah comes to earth. Unfortunately, he has not come forth. He should have come at the time of the Holocaust and many other times. He did not, and as Jews we suffered very much. We have no explanation for this suffering which makes it even worse. We have no knowledge of when it will end, which makes it very demoralizing. All we have left is hope. It is not a strong hope, nor a strong faith, because it has been betrayed many times over the centuries, but it is the only thing we have left. Let us today recognize as the Jewish national anthem is properly translated as "The Hope," *Hatikvah*. It is all we have and we have to cherish it to the very best of our ability.

PARASHAH FORTY-TWO, *Midrash Five*

ה עשו מלחמה את ברע וגו'. רבי מאיר היה דורש שמות, רבי יהושע בן קרחה היה דורש
שמות: ברע, שהיה בן רע: ברשע, שהיה בן רשע. שנאב, שהיה שואב ממון. ושמאבר, שהיה
פורח ומביא ממון. ומלך בלע היא צוער, שנתבלעו דיוריה.

5. THEY MADE WAR WITH BERA, ETC. (GEN. 14:2). R. MEIR USED TO IN-
TERPRET NAMES: BERA SIGNIFIES THAT HE WAS AN EVIL SON (*BEN RA*);
BIRSHA, THAT HE WAS A WICKED SON (*BEN RASHA*); SHINAB, THAT HE
AMASSED WEALTH (*SHO'EB MAMMON*); SHEMEBER, THAT HE FLEW AND
PROCURED RICHES; BELA, THAT ITS INHABITANTS WERE SWALLOWED
UP (*NITH-BAILU*).

The text went out of its way to emphasize the names because we are
dealing with monarchs and regal leadership who were known for their
evil ways. The text wanted to emphasize this very much. The text emphasizes two sages, R. Meir and R. Joshua b. Karcha (see the Hebrew
text). It says about each of them שמות דורש היה – *hayah doresh shemot*,
used to interpret names.

כל אלה חברו אל עמק השדים, ג' שמות נקראו לו: עמק השדים, עמק שוה, עמק סוכות.
עמק השדים, שהוא מגדל סדנים. ד"א: שהוא עשוי שדים, שדים תלמים. ד"א: שהוא מניק
את בנו כשדים. עמק שוה. ועשו לו בימה גדולה והושיבו אותו למעלה ממנה, והיו מקלסין
עובדי כוכבים וקיצצו ארזים, ועשו לו בימה גדולה והושיבו אותו למעלה ממנה, והיו מקלסין
לפניו ואומרים: שמענו אדוני, נשיא אלהים, אתה בתוכנו. אמרו לו: מלך את עלינו. נשיא
את עלינו. אלוה את עלינו. אמר להם: אל יחסר העולם מלכו, ואל יחסר העולם אלוהו. עמק
סוכות, שהוא מסוכך באילנות. א"ר תנחומא: א"ר שם לא היה שם אלא צנורות היאורים, גפן ותאנה ורמון, אגוז ושקד, תפוח ופרסק
.הוא ים המלח. א"ר אייבו: לא היה שם אלא צנורות היאורים ונתבקעו ונעשו ים, הה"ד (איוב
כח): בצורות יאורים בקע:

ALL THESE CAME AS ALLIES UNTO THE VALE OF SIDDIM (GEN. 14:3).
THIS WAS CALLED BY THREE NAMES: THE VALE OF SIDDIM, THE VALE
OF SHAVEH, AND THE VALE OF SUCCOTH. SIDDIM SIGNIFIES THAT OAK
TREES (*SADDANIM*) GREW THERE; AGAIN, THAT IT WAS DIVIDED UP
INTO FIELDS (*SADIM*); AND FINALLY, THAT IT SUCKLED ITS CHILDREN
LIKE BREASTS (*SHADAYIM*). THE VALE OF SHAVEH: R. BEREKIAH AND R.
HELBO IN THE NAME OF R. SAMUEL B. NAHMAN SAID: IT WAS SO CALLED
BECAUSE THERE ALL THE PEOPLES OF THE WORLD BECAME UNANIMOUS
(*HUSHEWU*), FELLED CEDARS, ERECTED A LARGE DAIS FOR HIM [ABRA-

HAM] AND SET HIM ON TOP, WHILE UTTERING PRAISES BEFORE HIM,
SAYING: HEAR US, MY LORD: THOU ART A PRINCE OF GOD AMONG US;
IN THE CHOICE, ETC. (GEN. 23:6). THEY SAID TO HIM: "THOU ART KING
OVER US, THOU ART A GOD TO US." BUT HE REPLIED: "THE WORLD DOES
NOT LACK ITS KING AND THE WORLD DOES NOT LACK ITS GOD." SUC-
COTH, IMPLIES THAT IT WAS OVERSHADOWED (ME-SUKAK) WITH TREES.
R. TANHUMA SAID: THESE WERE THE VINE, FIG, POMEGRANATE, NUT,
ALMOND, APPLE, AND PEACH TREES. THE SAME IS THE SALT SEA. R. AIBU
SAID: THERE WAS NO SEA THERE, BUT THE ROCKY BANKS OF THE RIVER
[JORDAN?] WERE BROKEN THROUGH AND A SEA [LAKE] WAS FORMED, AS
IT IS WRITTEN: HE CUTTETH OUT CHANNELS AMONG THE ROCKS (JOB
28:10).

Although there are three names by which this area is known, ultimately they became what we know today as ים המלח – *yam hamelah*, [lit. "the Salt Sea"] the Dead Sea. What we are now discussing was not a sea or a body of water, although it did contain rivulets and streams that enabled plants and vegetables to grow. Our Midrash lists the different fruit trees contained in this forest. The bottom line is that although Sodom and Gomorrah only existed for a short period of time, since they were ulti- mately destroyed, their region represented the most fertile earth of the entire region.

Seed Thoughts

Many aspects, not only of life in the Land of Israel, but of its geography are unique and have been the subject of interpretation and commentary over the years. Certainly, that which we know by the name of the Dead Sea is one of these unique areas.

Children and adults who come upon the term "the Dead Sea" have wondered about its origin, its content, and its future. Where does the salt come from? Is it really salt? Are there all kinds of chemicals in it? Is there another place in the world equivalent to the Dead Sea? Many scientific interpretations have been offered. But no one seems to take them very seriously. Can anything be done with the Dead Sea? Does it have to be left the way it is?

The interesting aspect of our Midrash and some of its commentaries is that they offer a biblical interpretation of the origin of the Dead Sea and its meaning. Maybe it has scientific value or maybe it does not. But it does have a moral value. That is probably what makes it so significant and important.

We are told that the king of Sodom had his throne in the area that we call today the Dead Sea. That in itself is something quite remarkable. Why would he do that unless that particular area was either very special or very beautiful or very significant or very imposing in the eyes of the world? The Midrash says that the four kingdoms and the five kingdoms that were involved in these wars, and ultimately were defeated by Abraham offered him the leadership of their world. They had built a special platform for him in a special area, and if he would have accepted the kingship or princeship or something that represented divine leadership, that platform would be used by him. He refused their offer and all other offers. But the fact remains that this was the area by which universal agreement in those days was the appropriate place for their leadership to hold sway and carry his message forward.

But the king of Sodom was corrupt, morally and ethically, in just about every area of human behavior and concern. The concept of Abraham presiding over such an immoral league of nations was in itself a tragedy. It had to be overturned as Sodom and Gomorrah were overturned, and as the king of Sodom was overturned. Every aspect of that region including its magnificent fields and gardens and orchards – the finest in the land at that time – were ultimately destroyed.

In light of this background, it is appropriate that the Dead Sea should be salty and therefore not livable, that it should be in every respect undesirable and completely inappropriate forever – to be a living reality – and anything other than a reminder of the terrible events that produced it. The Dead Sea remains a symbol of the need for moral rehabilitation at all times.

⌒

Additional Commentary

Interpreting a name

What is meant by interpreting a name? It means that either by virtue of a meaning that can be found of some other word or concept within the name itself, or that the use of the name over a period of time, in various forms of behavior, affects the character who possesses the name, either for good or for evil. (Mirkin)

The vegetation of Sodom

The important thing to note is that the king of Sodom had his throne in the area which we now call the Dead Sea. Not only that, but the vegetation, the plants and trees, were thick not only with leaves but with produce of the fruit trees which they contained. So thick was the foliage that if one bird was on one side of this beautiful forest, even though high up, it would not be able to see the other side. (*Tiferet Tzion*)

PARASHAH FORTY-TWO, *Midrash Six*

ו שתים עשרה שנה עבדו וגו'. רבי יוסי ורשב"ג, רבי יוסי אומר: שנים עשר ושלש עשרה
הרי עשרים וחמשה. אמר רבי שמעון בן גמליאל: כולהון שלש עשרה שנה היו. מה מקיים
רבי שמעון בן גמליאל ובארבע ובארבע עשרה שנה? אלא בארבע עשר למרדן. ובי"ד שנה בא
כדרלעומר בעל קורה טעין בעוביה. והמלכים אשר אתו. ויכו את רפאים בעשתרות קרנים,
בעשתרא דקרנא. ואת הזוזים בהם, ית זיוותנה דבהון. ואת האמים בשוה קריתים, תרתין
קריין אינון. ואת החורי, זו מטרפולין. ולמה הוא קורא אותו חורי? שבררו אותה ויצאת להם
לחירות בדור הפלגה. עד איל פארן אשר על המדבר, עד משריא דפארן:

6. TWELVE YEARS, ETC. (GEN. 14:4). R. JOSE AND R. SIMEON B. GAMALIEL DISAGREED. R. JOSE SAID: TWELVE YEARS [SERVICE] AND THIRTEEN YEARS [REBELLION], THUS AMOUNTING TO TWENTY-FIVE. R. SIMEON SAID: IT MEANS THIRTEEN IN ALL. HOW THEN DO I EXPLAIN, AND THE FOURTEENTH YEAR? IT MEANS THEIR REBELLION. AND IN THE FOURTEENTH YEAR CAME CHEDORLAOMER. THE OWNER OF THE BEAM HAS TO BEAR THE WEIGHT OF IT. AND THE KINGS THAT WERE WITH HIM, AND SMOTE THE REPHAIM IN ASHTEROTH-KARNAIM: I.E., IN ASHTARTA LYING BETWEEN THE HORNS. AND THE ZUZIM IN HAM: THAT MEANS THE MOST ILLUSTRIOUS OF THEM (*ZIWTANE BA-HEM*). AND THE EMIM IN SHAVEH-KIRYATHAIM: THEY WERE TWIN CITIES BOTH CALLED SHAVEH. AND THE HORITES (14:6): ELEUTHEROPOLIS [FREE-TOWN]. AND WHY WAS IT CALLED ELEUTHEROPOLIS? BECAUSE ITS INHABITANTS CHOSE IT AND MADE THEMSELVES INDEPENDENT [FREE] IN THE GENERATION OF

SEPARATION. UNTO EL-PARAN, WHICH IS BY THE WILDERNESS; I.E., BY
THE PLAIN OF PARAN.

Although the English translation is clear cut, the original Hebrew
lends itself to a possible misinterpretation. We can understand from the
Hebrew why R. Jose and R. Simeon disagreed. The nature of the Midrash is not only to avoid the decision of whose opinion is not correct,
but also the reader is not expected to do so. On the other hand, a reader
like myself living now in the twenty-first century would find it difficult
to understand why a tyrant like Chedorlaomer would allow a rebellion
to continue and not crush it immediately. That, however, is merely an
opinion and the Midrash on the other hand accepts the two possibilities
as indicated.

—

Seed Thoughts

There is an important point to remember whenever the victory of Abraham is spoken of in such glorious terms. This is particularly so in light of
the present series of Midrashim that deal with these episodes. Certainly,
when I first read these stories as a child, Abraham was depicted in my
imagination as a general who defeated all these armies. It is understandable for children to feel this way, but adults should be wary of this kind
of interpretation. Since when did Abraham have an army? Who taught
them and what were their maneuvers? How come we did not hear about
his army before this particular victory? The answer is that we are dealing
with God's victory, and Abraham was chosen by God to represent Him
in these concerns as we have learned from time to time. Not only was
the victory great and Abraham a remarkable leader, but according to
the *Tiferet Tzion*, the generation at the time could have been blessed
with the coming of the Messiah, had they not been guilty of moral and
ethical failures on their own part. Nevertheless, Abraham's leadership
was tremendous and he prepared the Jewish people for much of its
continued survival.

—

Additional Commentary

The conclusion

The various developments and power struggles that have been listed were included in the Midrash for us to understand and comprehend the individuality and strength of this people and from this knowledge to derive a conception of the more advanced individuality and strength of Chedorlaomer who had conquered all of them. This knowledge, however, is meant to have a special meaning for us and that is that we comprehend the power, the strength, and the victorious achievement of Abraham. (Mirkin)

PARASHAH FORTY-TWO, *Midrash Seven*

ז וישובו ויבואו אל עין וגו'. אמר רבי אחא: לא באו ליזדווג אלא בתוך גלגל עינו של עולם. עין שעשתה מדת הדין בעולם, הן מבקשים לסמותה אתמהא? היא קדש. אמר רבי אחא: הוא כתיב, הוא, שקדש שמו של הקב"ה בכבשן האש. ויכו את כל שדה העמלקי, עדיין לא נולד עמלק ואת אמרת ויכו את כל שדה העמלקי? אלא (ישעיה מו): מגיד מראשית אחרית. וגם את האמורי היושב בחצצון תמר ובעין גדי, דתמרייה. ויצא מלך סדום ומלך עמורה את כדרלעומר מלך עילם וגו'. ד' מלכים עשו מלחמה כנגד חמשה ויכלו להם. ועמק השדים בארות בארות חמר, בירין בירין מסקן חמר. וינוסו מלך סדום ועמורה ויפלו שמה. רבי יהודה ור' נחמיה. רבי יהודה אומר: ויפלו שמה, אלו האוכלוסין. הנשארים הרה נסו, אלו המלכים. ורבי נחמיה אמר: ויפלו שמה, אלו המלכים. והנשארים הרה נסו, אלו האוכלוסין. על דעתיה דרבי יהודה ניחא. ועל דעתיה דרבי נחמיה קשיא. רבי עזריה ורבי יונתן בן חגי בשם רבי יצחק אמרו: בשעה שירד אברהם אבינו לכבשן האש וניצול, יש מעובדי כוכבים שהיו מאמינים ויש שלא היו מאמינים, וכיון שירד מלך סדום לחמר וניצול, התחילו מאמינים באברהם למפרע. ויקחו את כל רכוש סדום ועמורה ואת כל אכלם. ר' יהודה אומר: זו עבודה. ורבי נחמיה אמר: אלו הכותבות. ויקחו את לוט וגו', כך עשו ללוט, נתנו אותו בסירה ונטלו אותו עמהם. כל כך למה? והוא יושב בסדום, לקיים מה שנאמר (משלי יג): הולך את חכמים יחכם ורועה כסילים ירוע:

7. AND THEY TURNED BACK, AND CAME TO EN-MISHPAT – THE SAME IS KADESH (GEN. 14:7). R. AHA SAID: THEY CAME ONLY IN ORDER TO ATTACK THE EYEBALL OF THE WORLD; THE EYE WHICH EXECUTED JUDGMENT IN THE WORLD THEY DESIRE TO BLIND! THE SAME (*HI*) IS KADESH: R. AHA SAID: THIS IS WRITTEN, *HU* (HE): IT WAS HE [ABRAHAM] THAT

SANCTIFIED (*KIDDASH*) THE NAME OF THE HOLY ONE, BLESSED BE HE, IN
THE FIERY FURNACE. AND THEY SMOTE ALL THE COUNTRY OF THE AMA-
LEKITES. AMALEK HAD NOT YET ARISEN, YET YOU SAY, AND THEY SMOTE
ALL THE COUNTRY OF THE AMALEKITES! BUT, HE DECLARETH THE END
FROM THE BEGINNING (ISA. 56:10). AND ALSO THE AMORITES, THAT
DWELT IN HAZAZON-TAMAR: THIS MEANS, IN EN-GEDI OF THE PALM-
TREES. AND THERE WENT OUT THE KIND OF SODOM ... FOUR KINGS
AGINST THE FIVE (GEN. 14:8F.). FOUR KINGS WAGED WAR WITH FIVE AND
DEFEATED THEM. NOW THE VALE OF SIDDIM WAS FULL OF SLIME PITS –
HEMOR (14:10): FULL OF PITS PRODUCING ASPHALT (*HAMOR*). AND THE
KINGS OF SODOM AND GOMORRAH FLED, AND THEY FELL THERE, AND
THEY THAT REMAINED FLED TO THE MOUNTAIN. R. JUDAH SAID: AND
THEY FELL THERE REFERS TO THE TROOPS, WHILE AND THEY THAT RE-
MAINED FLED TO THE MOUNTAIN REFERS TO THE KINGS. R. NEHEMIAH
SAID: AND THEY FELL THERE REFERS TO THE KINGS, WHILE AND THEY
THAT REMAINED FLED TO THE MOUNTAIN REFERS TO THE TROOPS. NOW
ON THE VIEW OF R. JUDAH THERE IS NO DIFFICULTY. BUT ON THE VIEW
OF R. NEHEMIA, R. AZARIAH AND R. JONATHAN IN R. ISAAC'S NAME GAVE
THE FOLLOWING FURTHER EXPLANATION: WHEN ABRAHAM DESCENDED
INTO THE FIERY FURNACE AND WAS RESCUED, SOME OF THE NATIONS
BELIEVED [THAT IT HAD HAPPENED], WHILE OTHERS DISBELIEVED. BUT
WHEN THE KING OF SODOM DESCENDED INTO THE FIERY FURNACE AND
WAS RESCUED, SOME OF THE NATIONS BELIEVED [THAT IT HAD HAP-
PENED], WHILE OTHERS DISBELIEVED. BUT WHEN THE KING OF SODOM
DESCENDED INTO THE SLIME AND WAS RESCUED, THEN ALL BELIEVED IN
ABRAHAM RETROSPECTIVELY. AND THEY TOOK ALL THE GOODS OF SO-
DOM AND GOMORRAH, AND ALL THEIR VICTUALS (*OKLAM*), AND WENT
THEIR WAY (14:11). R. JUDAH SAID: WAS IT NOT A BIG THING TO TAKE ALL
THEIR VICTUALS? SAID R. NEHEMIAH: WHAT IS MEANT IS DRY DATES.
AND THEY TOOK LOT ... AND HIS GOODS, ETC. THEY DID THIS TO LOT:
THEY PUT HIM IN A BOAT AND TOOK HIM WITH THEM. AND WHY DID HE
COME TO THIS? BECAUSE HE DWELT IN SODOM (14:12), THUS FULFILLING
THE VERSE, HE THAT WALKETH WITH WISE MEN SHALL BE WISE, BUT
THE COMPANION OF FOOLS SHALL SMART FOR IT (PROV. 13:20).

Seed Thoughts

The text that the Midrash is speaking about is as follows, "And they may turn back." Reference is to the four kings who were defeated by Abraham and who were touring the little world of Israel of their time, along the north and along the south. What was their goal? The answer has been written in a most unusual style not only in English, but in Hebrew. "They came only in order to attack the eyeball of the world; the eye which executed judgement in the world."

R. Aba said it was Abraham who sanctified the name of the Holy One, blessed be He. In other words, the four kings were looking for a method to regain power, and which included opposition to Abraham. In other words, the enemies of Israel never give up. In the Torah text, it was forcefully stated that Abraham's victory over the kings was complete, and that they were subjected to defeat for a very long time.

The Midrash disagrees. The enemies of Israel are never defeated. We think they are defeated, but they reorganize and come back all the time. In modern times we should understand that even better than a Midrash.

The Second World War defeated Nazi Germany and therefore overturned all the anti-Semitic laws of that generation. But here we, are two generations later, and we get reports that this racial hatred is becoming alive again in certain parts of Europe and Asia Minor.

The enemies of Israel never give up and therefore we should never give up. One of our great goals should always be *"Am Yisrael chai,"* that the Jewish people should remain alive and healthy and wholesome from one generation to the next.

Parashah Forty-Two, *Midrash Eight*

ח ויבא הפליט. ריש לקיש בשם בר קפרא הוא עוג, הוא פליט: ולמה נקרא שמו עוג? שבא
ומצא את אברם יושב ועוסק במצות עוגות, הוא לא נתכוון לשם שמים, אלא אמר: אברהם
זה קונinון הוא, ועכשיו אני אומר לו נשבה בן אחיך, והוא יוצא למלחמה ונהרג, ואני נוטל
את שרי אשתו. אמר לו הקדוש ברוך הוא: חייך! שכר פסיעותיך אתה נוטל, שאת מאריך
ימים בעולם, ועל שחשבת להרוג את הצדיק, חייך! שאתה רואה אלף אלפים ורבי רבבות
מבני בניו, ואין סופו של אותו האיש ליפול, אלא בידן, שנאמר (דברים ג): ויאמר ה' אלי אל
תירא אותו כי בידך וגו'. ויגד לאברם העברי. רבי יהודה ורבי נחמיה ורבנן. רבי יהודה אומר:
כל העולם כולו מעבר אחד, והוא מעבר אחד. ר' נחמיה אמר: שהוא מבני בניו של עבר.
ורבנן אמרי: שהוא מעבר הנהר, ושהוא משיח בלשון עברי. והוא שוכן באלוני ממרא. רבי
יהודה ורבי נחמיה. רבי יהודה אמר: במשריא דממרא. ורבי נחמיה אמר: בפלטין דממרא.
על דעתיה דרבי יהודה: אתרא הוא, דשמיה ממרא. על דעתיה דרבי נחמיה: גברא הוא,
דשמיה ממרא. ולמה נקרא שמו ממרא? ר' עזריה בשם רבי יהודה בשם ר' סימון: שהמרה
פנים באברהם, בשעה שאמר הקב"ה לאברהם לימול, הלך ונמלך בג' אוהביו. אמר לו ענר:
כבר בן ק' שנה אתה, ואתה הולך ומצער את עצמך? אמר לו אשכול: מה את הולך ומסיים
את עצמך בין שונאיך? אמר לו ממרא: אלהיך שעמד לך: בכבשן האש, ובמלכים, וברעבון,
והדבר הזה שאמר לך למול, אין אתה שומע לו? אמר לו הקדוש ברוך הוא: אתה נתתה
לו עצה למול, חייך! שאיני נגלה עליו, לא בפלטין של ענר, ולא בפלטין של אשכול, אלא
בפלטין שלך, הה"ד (בראשית יח): וירא אליו ה' באלוני ממרא.

8. AND THERE CAME ONE THAT HAD ESCAPED, AND TOLD ABRAM, ETC.
(GEN. 14:13). R. SIMEON B. LAKISH SAID IN THE NAME OF BAR KAPPARA:
THAT WAS OG; AND WHY WAS HE CALLED OG? BECAUSE HE CAME AND
FOUND ABRAHAM SITTING AND ENGAGED IN THE PRECEPT OF [UNLEAV-
ENED] CAKES (*UGOTH*). HE DID NOT ACT FROM A PIOUS MOTIVE, BUT HE
SAID TO HIMSELF: "THIS MAN ABRAHAM IS VINDICTIVE: I WILL APPRISE
HIM THAT LOT IS CAPTURED; THEN WILL HE GO OUT TO BATTLE AND BE
SLAIN, WHILE I WILL TAKE SARAH." "BY THY LIFE!" SAID THE HOLY ONE,
BLESSED BE HE, TO HIM, "THOU WILT RECEIVE REWARD FOR THEY JOUR-
NEY [FOOTSTEPS] BY LIVING A LONG TIME IN THE WORLD. BUT BECAUSE
THOUGH DIDST INTEND TO SLAY THAT RIGHTEOUS MAN, THOU WILT
SEE MYRIADS OF HIS DESCENDANTS AND WILT ULTIMATELY FALL INTO
THE HANDS OF HIS SONS," AS IT IS WRITTEN: AND THE LORD SAID UNTO
MOSES: FEAR HIM NOT; FOR I HAVE DELIVERED HIM INTO THY HAND,
ETC. (NUM. 21:34). AND TOLD ABRAM THE HEBREW (*HA-IBRI*). R. JUDAH
SAID: [*HA-IBRI* SIGNIFIES THAT] THE WHOLE WORLD WAS ON ONE SIDE
(*EBER*) WHILE HE WAS ON THE OTHER SIDE (*EBER*). R. NEHEMIAH SAID:

[IT DENOTES] THAT HE WAS DESCENDED FROM EBER. THE RABBIS SAID: IT MEANS THAT HE CAME FROM ACROSS THE RIVER; FURTHER, THAT HE SPOKE IN THE LANGUAGE OF THE DWELLERS ACROSS THE RIVER. NOW HE DWELT *BE-ELONE* (E.V. "BY THE TEREBINTHS OF") MAMRE, ETC. R. JUDAH SAID: THAT MEANS, IN THE PLAIN OF MAMRE. R. NEHEMIAH SAID: IN THE PALACE OF MAMRE. ON R. JUDAH'S VIEW A PLACE CALLED MAMRE IS MEANT; ON R. NEHEMIAH'S VIEW, IT REFERS TO A PERSON CALLED MAMRE. AND WHY WAS HE CALLED MAMRE? R. AZARIAH SAID IN THE NAME OF R. JUDAH: BECAUSE HE REBUKED (*HIMRAH*) ABRAHAM. WHEN THE HOLY ONE, BLESSED BE HE, COMMANDED ABRAHAM TO CIRCUMCISE HIMSELF, HE WENT AND TOOK COUNSEL WITH HIS THREE FRIENDS. ANER SAID TO HIM: "YOU ARE ALREADY A HUNDRED YEARS OLD, YET YOU WOULD INFLICT THIS PAIN UPON YOURSELF?" ESCHOL SAID TO HIM: "WHY SHOULD YOU GO AND MAKE YOURSELF DISTINGUISHABLE TO YOUR ENEMIES?" BUT MAMRE SAID TO HIM: "WHEN DID HE NOT STAND BY YOU – IN THE FIERY FURNACE, IN FAMINE, AND IN YOUR WAR WITH THE KINGS? WILL YOU NOT OBEY HIM THEN IN THIS MATTER!" SAID THE HOLY ONE, BLESSED BE HE, TO HIM: "THOU GAVEST HIM GOOD ADVICE, TO CIRCUMCISE HIMSELF: BY THY LIFE! I WILL REVEAL MYSELF TO HIM ONLY IN THY PALACE." HENCE IT IS WRITTEN: AND THE LORD APPEARED UNTO HIM IN THE PALACE OF MAMRE (GEN. 18:1)

～

Additional Commentary

Abraham is for the first time referred to as a Hebrew in Genesis 14:13. Why this connotation? The Midrash gives three possibilities. R. Judah says it comes from the root *ever*, meaning "the side of the river." Abraham came from the other side of the river from Aram Naharaim to reach Israel. But R. Judah is speaking metaphorically as well, since Abraham was a monotheist in a pagan world, as if, on one side of the river and the whole world on the other side. R. Nehemiah says he was referred to as a Hebrew (*Ivri*) since he was descended from Ever (Genesis 11:17). The Rabbis say that it has a few meanings, both that he was from the other side of the river and also that he conversed in Hebrew. The most interesting idea in my opinion is that Abraham was a man of conviction who had the courage to stand up for what he believed in even when it was not politically correct to be a monotheist. It was easy to blame a monotheist of being narrow-minded. For polytheists believe in many gods and were therefore tolerant of a multiplicity of gods, but monotheists claim there can only be one. Isn't that intolerant? Abraham stood up for his beliefs and taught them to all who wished to know about them with patience and understanding. (B.R. Shuchat)

א וישמע אברם כי נשבה אחיו. (תהלים קיב) משמועה רעה לא יירא נכון לבו בטוח בה' סמוך
לבו לא יירא עד אשר יראה בצריו. משמועה רעה לא יירא, זה אברהם, כי עתה ידעתי כי ירא
אלהים אתה. נכון לבו בטוח בה', ומצאת את לבבו נאמן לפניך. סמוך לבו לא יירא, שנאמר
(בראשית טו): אל תירא אברם. עד אשר יראה בצריו, ויחלק עליהם לילה:

1. AND ABRAM HEARD THAT HIS BROTHER WAS TAKEN CAPTIVE (GEN.
14:14). IT IS WRITTEN: HE SHALL NOT BE AFRAID OF EVIL THINGS; HIS
HEART IS STEADFAST, TRUSTING IN THE LORD (PS. 112:7); ALSO, AND
FOUNDEST HIS HEART FAITHFUL BEFORE THEE (NEH. 9:8); ALSO, HIS
HEART IS ESTABLISHED, HE SHALI NOT BE AFRAID (PS. 112:8); ALSO, FEAR
NOT ABRAM (GEN. 15:1); ALSO, UNTIL HE GAZE UPON HIS ADVERSARIES
(PS. 112:7). CONSEQUENTLY, AND HE DIVIDED HIMSELF AGAINST THEM
BY NIGHT, ETC. (GEN. 15:15).

The verse says, "From an evil report, do not fear." This verse reflects
the wonderful attitude of Abraham. The *palit*, messenger, was full of fear
in telling Abraham about the power of the five kings who were defeated
by the even more powerful four kings. Instead of becoming fearful and
running away, Abraham gathered all of his people and attacked the very
power that was described by the refugee messenger. In other words
the fearful message did not make Abraham fearful. With a heart full of
confidence in God, he attacked the tyrants. Some of the other verses are
now brought forward to help him do so.

"Now I know that you truly fear God . . ." (The above is commentary
from Mirkin.)

~

Seed Thoughts

If there were a title to this paragraph, it would be called Fear and Faith.
Many people, including intellectuals and scholars, are of the opinion

that a true person of faith should have no fear. If the life of Abraham is an example, it completely shatters this point of view. He was a man of many fears, some of which will be alluded to in the Additional Commentary. Like so many others in the human race, he had the fear of death, a fear of suffering, a fear of severe illness, a fear of failure, and so on . . . The only difference between Abraham and others is that he was a person with great faith in God. That does not mean that he expected God to remove his fears. It does mean, however, that he had a great reason to fight his fears and try to replace them by hope, faith, longing, and the example of good deeds. He hoped that his good behavior would be rewarded by a gradual elimination of his fears. But none of these things happened in advance. When it did happen, however, he overflowed with thanksgiving and appreciation.

Additional Commentary

What did Abraham fear?

The verse says, "Fear not an evil report." How do you explain the fact that when Abraham heard the report of the special messenger about the capture of Lot and the power of the conquerors, his immediate response was practically to ignore what was said, and do whatever possible to organize his own forces? One answer, of course, is that his nephew Lot was captive. Another answer is that the intention of the captors had nothing to do with Lot, but in actual fact, their goal was Abraham – to attack his leadership and to ultimately defeat him. Abraham knew all of this before it was told to him, and therefore, knew he had to resist. (*Tiferet Tzion*)

What did Abraham fear?

What Abraham really feared was something quite different from what his enemies expected. He feared God. He did not fear man. The moment he heard that his nephew Lot was captured, he asked no questions of anyone but proceeded to organize himself into a force of resistance. But one thing did begin to bother him. Did he do the right thing? Should he not have asked God what to do and waited until he receives Divine permission to organize a force of resistance? This was Abraham's real fear. It is not something he could discuss with anyone. He only hoped that if he did wrong, God would forgive him. He would not feel secure until he received a Divine message or at least some sign that his behavior was acceptable. (*Tiferet Tzion*)

PARASHAH FORTY-THREE, *Midrash Two*

ב וישמע אברם כי נשבה אחיו. הה"ד (ישעיה לג): אוטם אזנו משמוע דמים. וירק את חניכיו.
רבי יהודה ור' נחמיה ר' יהודה אומר: הן הוריקו פנים, כנגד אברהם. אמרו: ה' מלכים לא
יכלו לעמוד בהם, ואנו יכולים לעמוד בהם? רבי נחמיה אמר: אברהם הוריק פנים כנגדן.
אמר: אצא ואפול על קדוש שמו של מקום. אבא בר זבדא אמר: בכלי זיין הוריקן, היך מה
דאת אמר (תהלים לה): והרק חנית וסגור לקראת רודפי. אמר רבי שמעון בן לקיש: באבנים
טובות ומרגליות הוריקן, היך מה דאת אמר (תהלים סח), ואברותיה בירקרק חרוץ. רבי לוי
אמר: בפרשת שוטרים הוריקן, היך מד"א (דברים כ): מי האיש הירא ורך הלבב ילך וישוב
לביתו. חניכיו: בעלי חניכתו. שמם, אברם כשמו. שמנה עשר ושלש מאות. ריש לקיש בשם
בר קפרא: אליעזר לבדו היה, מנין אליעזר, י"א וג' מאות. וירדוף עד דן, שם עבודת כוכבים
היא, ומכה מלפניה ומאחריה. מכה מלפניה, וירדוף עד דן. ומכה מאחריה (ירמיה ח): מדן
נשמע נחרת סוסיו:

2. AND ABRAM HEARD, ETC. THUS IT IS WRITTEN, HE STOPPETH HIS EARS FROM HEARING OF BLOOD, ETC. (ISA. 33:15). HE LED FORTH (*WAYYAREK*) HIS TRAINED MEN, ETC. R. JUDAH SAID: IT WAS THEY WHO TURNED A WRATHFUL COUNTENANCE (*HORIKU PANIM*) UPON ABRAHAM, SAYING: "FIVE KINGS COULD NOT DEFEAT THEM, YET WE ARE TO DEFEAT THEM?" R. NEHEMIAH INTERPRETED IT: HE TURNED A DEFIANT COUNTENANCE (*HORIK PANIM*) TO THEM AND EXCLAIMED: "I WILL GO FORTH AND FALL IN SANCTIFYING THE NAME OF THE HOLY ONE, BLESSED BE HE." R. ABBA B. ZABDA SAID: HE MADE THEM GLITTER (*HORIKAN*) WITH WEAPONS, AS YOU READ: BURNISH (*HAREK*, E.V. "DRAW OUT") ALSO THE SPEAR, AND THE BATTLE AXE, AGAINST THEM THAT PURSUE ME; SAY UNTO MY SOUL: I AM THY SALVATION (PS. 35:3). R. SIMEON B. LAKISH SAID: HE MADE THEM GLITTER WITH PRECIOUS STONES AND PEARLS, AS YOU READ: WITH THE SHIMMER OF (*YERAKRAK*) GOLD (68:14). R. LEVI SAID: HE THINNED THEIR NUMBERS BY READING THE SECTION OF THE HERALDS, AS YOU READ: WHAT MAN IS THERE THAT IS FEARFUL (*YAREH*) AND FAINT-HEARTED (*RAKH*) (DEUT. 20:8)? BORN IN HIS HOUSE. THIS MEANS, THOSE BEARING HIS NAME, THEIR NAME BEING ABRAM, LIKE HIS OWN. THREE HUNDRED AND EIGHTEEN. R. SIMEON B. LAKISH SAID: IT WAS

ELIEZER ALONE, THE NUMERICAL VALUE OF ELIEZER BEING THREE HUN-
DRED AND EIGHTEEN. AND PURSUED AS FAR AS DAN. IDOLATRY SMITES
BOTH BEFORE IT COMES AND AFTER IT HAS DEPARTED. IT SMITES IN AN-
TICIPATION, AS IT IS WRITTEN: AND PURSUED AS FAR AS DAN. IT SMITES
RETROSPECTIVELY, AS IT IS WRITTEN: THE SNORTING OF HIS HORSES IS
HEARD FROM DAN (JER. 8:16).

—

Seed Thoughts I

This Midrash is a very good example of one the unique aspects of midrashic literature, though it is very difficult to give it a name to describe
the phenomenon. I would like to give an example from English literature to describe what I want to share from the Midrash. I know someone
who uses biography for the books that she writes. Although she started
with a real biography, she adds many things from her imagination and
projects many conversations that her hero may have had, whether real
or fictional. The author knows what is real or fictional but the reader
does not, and is equally impressed – whether it is one or the other.

If I now apply this description to the Midrash, I apologize if I am
reducing it to something secular. Abraham decided to oppose the four
kings with force. According to R. Judah, when Abraham announced his
intention to his people that they would go against the four kings, they
protested forcefully. These five kings were beaten by the four kings. How
can we be expected to succeed where five important kingdoms failed?
How did R. Judah know what was said, or was it simply his imagination
that projected what could have happened and therefore, might have
happened?

R. Nehemiah goes a step further. Not only does he accept what R.
Judah said, but adds that Abraham became furious at this protest. He
became so angry that he told his people that he did not want them and
that he did not need them. He said that he would rely on God's mercies
that would look after how to handle the four kings. Abraham would rely
on God's support.

Both R. Judah and R. Nehemiah made this scene much more dramatic and interesting, yet we still do not know the sources which gave
them the authority to say what they said. As a matter of fact, as the
Midrash developed, Abraham did not accept all the volunteers from his

people, but only those whose confidence, love, and friendship he could trust. The example we have here is duplicated many hundreds of times and helps make the midrashic text as interesting as certain bestsellers.

———

Seed Thoughts II

The Midrash has a line which is very impressive but very hard to understand at first glance. It says that every tzaddik represents 318 different worlds, and goes on to say that the גימטריה – *gematria*, the numerical value of the name Eliezer is 318. This means that Eliezer was a tzaddik and we know that from his relationship with Abraham, how important he was for his friend and master Abraham.

I found it hard to understand this development until discovering that a few verses later, the number of troops was 318. We now know the meaning of the number. If the numerical value of the name Eliezer is equal to the number of troops in Abraham's legion, it can only mean one thing. Eliezer was not only a tzaddik, but the true leader of the military operation. As in so many other things, Abraham appointed Eliezer as his right-hand man to conduct his most important and sacred tasks. We do not know in general how important gematria was but it seems that when it can be associated with another value, such as the text we have just read, it can be looked upon by the Sages with tremendous importance.

PARASHAH FORTY-THREE, *Midrash Three*

ג ויחלק עליהם לילה. רבי בנימין בר יפת משם ר' יונתן: הלילה נחלק מאיליו.

3. AND THE NIGHT WAS DIVIDED AGAINST THEM (GEN. 14:15). R. BENJA-
MIN B. JEPHETH SAID IN R. JOHANAN'S NAME: THE NIGHT WAS DIVIDED
OF ITS OWN ACCORD.

T he verse says that the night was divided, presumably up to the time
of the battle and then after the battle. How was it divided? R. Benjamin
says, by itself.

ורבנן אמרי: יוצרו חלקו.

THE RABBIS SAY: ITS CREATOR DIVIDED IT.

T he rabbis, on the other hand, claim that the Holy One, divided the
night. This is meant to foresee what happened in the time of Moses
where the destruction of the firstborn took place as what was described
as "half the night."

אמר הקב"ה: אביהם פעל עמי בחצי הלילה, אף אני פועל עם בניו בחצי הלילה. ואימתי?
במצרים שנאמר (שמות יב): ויהי בחצי הלילה וה' הכה כל בכור וגו'. אמר רבי תנחומא: אית
דמפקין לישנא אחרינא. אמר הקב"ה: אביהם יצא בחצי הלילה, אף אני אצא עם בניו בחצי
הלילה, שנאמר (שם): כה אמר ה' כחצות הלילה אני יוצא.

THE HOLY ONE, BLESSED BE HE, SAID: "ABRAHAM HAS LABORED WITH ME
AT MIDNIGHT; THEREFORE I TOO WILL ACT FOR HIS SONS AT MIDNIGHT."
AND WHEN DID THAT HAPPEN? IN EGYPT, AS IT SAYS: AND IT CAME TO
PASS AT MIDNIGHT (EX. 12:29). R. TANHUMA SAID: SOME STATE THIS IN
A DIFFERENT FORM. THE HOLY ONE, BLESSED BE HE, SAID: "ABRAHAM
WENT FORTH AT MIDNIGHT, THEREFORE I TOO WILL GO FORTH WITH
HIS SONS AT MIDNIGHT," AS IT SAYS: THUS SAITH THE LORD: ABOUT
MIDNIGHT WILL I GO OUT, ETC. (11:4).

R. Tanhuma points out that the language has to be changed because
at the time of the Exodus, the expression was כחצי הלילה – *ka'hatzi halaylah*, "approximately midnight." By using the approximation it gives
the impression that God did not know when half the night took place.
Therefore, the Midrash interprets Him saying בחצי הלילה – *ba'hatzi*

halaylah, at midnight. At midnight the deliverance will take place here as well. According to the *Midrash HaMevo'ar,* the expression "approximately midnight" does not need additional interpretation. God wanted the Egyptians punished at the same time that Abraham did what he had to do in the night. Whatever "approximately midnight" may have meant in the Exodus story was a time for which Abraham did what he had to do with to his enemies.

ויכם וירדפם. וכי יש אדם רודף הרוגים? אמר רבי פנחס: רודפיו של אבינו אברהם הרוגים היו, שנאמר (תהלים סט): כי אתה אשר הכית רדפו, הה"ד (ישעיה מא): מי העיר ממזרח צדק יקראהו לרגלו. מי הוא זה שהעיר לבם של מזרחיים, שיבואו ויפלו ביד אברהם.

AND SMOTE THEM, AND PURSUED THEM. DOES THEN A MAN PURSUE THE SLAIN? SAID R. PHINEHAS: THOSE WHO WERE PURSUED BY ABRAHAM WERE [ALREADY LOOKED UPON AS] SLAIN, AS IT SAYS: FOR THEY PURSUE HIM WHOM THOU HAST SMITTEN (PS. 69:27). IT IS WRITTEN: WHO HATH RAISED UP (*HE'IR*) ONE FROM THE EAST, ZEDEK (RIGHTEOUSNESS) CALLING HIM TO HIS FEET (ISA. 41:2) 2 [THIS ALLUDES TO ZEDEK-THE RIGHTEOUS ONE] THE LIFE OF ALL WORLDS, WHO ILLUMINED (*ME'IR*) HIS PATH WHEREVER HE WENT.

Two points might be mentioned in connection with the interpretation of this passage. The Midrash translates מכה – *makeh,* as being smitten with death. In many of the English translations, such as the JPS and even the King James Version, ויכם – *vayakem* means "smote" or "to smite," which means a serious injury but not necessarily death. Obviously, the Midrash did not accept this translation or it would not have grounds for this commentary. To the authors of this Midrash, the word meant, "put to death," which enabled them to express their wonder that dead people would pursue others. The *Midrash HaMevo'ar* offers an explanation for those who are not satisfied to have miracles interpret a text. In their view, the enemies of Abraham (the four kings and their followers), were sentenced to death by heavenly decree, but it had not yet taken place. When, therefore, the verse says that they were pursued by those who were dead, this is what was really meant. They were marked as dead.

צדק יקראהו לרגלו חי העולמים, שהיה מאיר לו בכל מקום שהיה הולך. אמר רבי ברכיה: מזל צדק היה מאיר לו. אמר ר' ראובן: צדקה היתה צווחת ואומרת: אם אין אברהם אין מי יעשה אותי, הה"ד (שם): יתן לפניו גוים ומלכים ירד. רבי יהודה ור' נחמיה, ר' יהודה אמר: אברהם היה משליך עליהם עפר, והוא נעשה חרבות קש ונעשה חצים. ורבי נחמיה אמר:

יתן עפר לא נאמר אלא, כעפר. הן היו משליכים חרבות על אברהם, ונעשין עפר חצים, והן
נעשים קש, הה"ד (שם מא): ירדפם יעבור שלום. רבי לוי בשם רבי יוסי בר זמרא: פסיעותיו
של אבינו אברהם היו שלש מילין. ר' יודן בר רבי סימון אמר: מיל שנאמר (שם): אורח ברגליו
לא יבא. ר' נחמיה אמר בשם רבי אבהו: לא נתאבקו רגליהן, אלא כזה שהוא הולך מביתו
לבית הכנסת:

R. BEREKIAH SAID: THE PLANET ZEDEK [JUPITER] ILLUMINED HIS PATH.
R. REUBEN SAID: RIGHTEOUSNESS CRIED OUT AND SAID: "IF ABRAHAM
WILL NOT PERFORM ME, NONE WILL PERFORM ME." IT IS WRITTEN: HE
GIVETH NATIONS BEFORE HIM, AND MAKETH HIM RULE OVER KINGS; HIS
SWORD MAKETH THEM AS THE DUST, HIS BOW AS THE DRIVEN STUBBLE
(ISA. 41:2). R. JUDAH AND R. NEHEMIAH DIFFERED. ONE MAINTAINED:
THIS MEANS THAT ABRAHAM THREW DUST AT THEM [THE FOUR KINGS]
WHICH TURNED TO SWORDS; STUBBLE, AND IT TURNED TO ARROWS.
BUT THE OTHER ARGUED: IT IS NOT WRITTEN: "HE MAKETH DUST," BUT
"HE MAKETH THEM AS THE DUST": THEY THREW SWORDS AT ABRAHAM
WHICH TURNED TO DUST; AND ARROWS, WHICH BECAME STUBBLE.
AGAIN, IT IS WRITTEN: HE PURSUETH THEM, AND PASSETH ON SAFELY-
SHALOM (41:3). R. LEVI AND ELEAZAR IN R. JOSE'S NAME SAID: ABRA-
HAM'S STEPS WERE THREE MILES LONG. R. JUDAH B. R. SIMEON SAID:
THEY WERE ONE MILE LONG, FOR IT SAYS: THE WAY WITH HIS FEET HE
TREADETH NOT (41:3). R. NEHUNIA SAID IN R. BIBI'S NAME: THEIR FEET
BECAME NO MORE DUST-STAINED THAN THOSE OF ONE WHO GOES FROM
HIS HOME TO THE SYNAGOGUE.

We note that in this part, R. Judah, R. Nehemia, and the rabbis usually differ on most of the details regarding the connection. Most of the differences do change the meaning of what happened, but they are interesting. Thus, one teacher said that their swords were turned into dust and could not continue to fight, while another said that the dust turned to swords and the other could not fight. The bottom line is that God defeated the enemies of Abraham. It was not the military prowess of Abraham himself.

Additional Commentary

Abraham's planet

"R. Berekiah said: The planet Zedek [Jupiter] illumined his path." This seems to be trivial compared to the previous idea that God showed him the way. However, since the Talmud (*Shabbat* 156b) associates the astrological sign of Jupiter with Abraham, this could possibly mean that this was a good time for him to pursue his enemies. (Mirkin)

PARASHAH FORTY-THREE, *Midrash Four*

ד וישב את כל הרכוש וגם את לוט וגו'. רבי יודן אמר: אנשים ונשים ונשים השיב, וטף לא החזיר. עמדו ונתגיירו וגדרו ערות אבותיהם, הה"ד (יחזקאל ז): והבאתי רעי גוים. מי הם רועי גוים? ר"י בר רבי סימון: אלו אנשי סדום, שנאמר ואנשי סדום:

4. AND HE BROUGHT BACK ALL THE GOODS . . . AND THE WOMEN ALSO, AND THE PEOPLE (GEN. 14:16). R. JUDAN SAID: THEY BROUGHT BACK THE MEN AND THE WOMEN, BUT NOT THE CHILDREN. THEREUPON THEY AROSE AND BECAME PROSELYTES AND CUT OFF THE REPROACH OF THEIR FATHERS. THUS IT IS WRITTEN: WHEREFORE I WILL BRING THE WORST OF THE NATIONS (EZEK. 7:24). WHO ARE "THE WORST OF THE NATIONS"? SAID R. JUDAH: THE PEOPLE OF SODOM, AS IT SAYS: NOW THE MEN OF SODOM WERE WICKED AND SINNERS (GEN. 13:13).

Seed Thoughts

The main point of this Midrash is that all the living protagonists in the struggle were returned with the exception of the children. They were not returned, so that they could be prepared for the life of *mitzvot* and thereby become a blessing not only to their captors but to themselves as well as to their families.

PARASHAH FORTY-THREE, *Midrash Five*

ה ויצא מלך סדום לקראתו וגו'. רבי אבא בר כהנא אמר: התחיל לקשקש לו בזנבו. א"ל: מה
אתה ירדת לכבשן האש וניצלת, אף אני ירדתי לחמר וניצלתי. אל עמק שוה. רבי ברכיה ורבי
חנינא בשם רבי שמואל בר נחמן: ששם השוו כל עובדי כוכבים וקצצו ארזים ועשו בימה
גדולה והושיבו אותו בתוכו למעלה, והיו מקלסין לפניו ואומרים לו: שמענו אדוני וגו'. אמרו
לו: מלך את עלינו! נשיא את עלינו! אלוה את עלינו! אמר להם: אל יחסר העולם מלכו, ואל
יחסר אלוהו:

5. AND THE KING OF SODOM WENT OUT TO MEET HIM (GEN. 14:17). R.
ABBA B. KAHANA SAID: HE BEGAN PUTTING ON AIRS, SAYING TO HIM:
"JUST AS YOU DESCENDED INTO THE FIERY FURNACE AND WERE SAVED,
SO DID I DESCEND INTO THE SLIME AND WAS SAVED." AT THE VALE OF
SHAVEH – THE SAME – IS THE KING'S VALE. R. BEREKIAH AND R. HELBO
IN THE NAME OF R. SAMUEL B. NAHMAN SAID: IT WAS SO CALLED BE-
CAUSE THERE ALL PEOPLES OF THE WORLD BECAME UNANIMOUS, AND
SAID TO ABRAHAM: "BE THOU KING OVER US." BUT HE REPLIED: "THE
WORLD DOES NOT LACK ITS KING AND ITS GOD."

The king of Sodom tried to get closer to Abraham by stating that they
were equally involved in a perilous life threatening-situation: Abraham
in the fiery furnace and the king of Sodom mired in the slime. All kinds
of honors were offered to Abraham, but he declined them all!

―

Seed Thoughts

We learn from this Midrash that Abraham was not impressed by the
social and political honors that could have been showered upon him.
There is only One King in the world and that is the King of kings, the
Holy One, blessed be He. All other office holders were pretenders who
did not possess the character of either leadership or of service. Abraham
understood this and kept away from these honors with scrupulous care.

PARASHAH FORTY-THREE, *Midrash Six*

ו ומלכי צדק מלך שלם וגו'. הה"ד (תהלים מה): ובת צור במנחה פניך יחלו עשירי עם. ומלכי
צדק מלך שלם, המקום הזה מצדיק את יושביו. מלכי צדק, אדוני צדק, צדק נקראת ירושלים.
שנאמר (ישעיה א): צדק ילין בה.

6. AND MELCHIZEDEK KING OF SALEM BROUGHT FORTH BREAD AND
WINE (GEN. 14:18). IT IS WRITTEN: AND, O DAUGHTER OF ZOR [E.V.
"TYRE"], THE RICHEST OF THE PEOPLE SHALL ENTREAT THY FAVOR
WITH A GIFT (PS. 45:13). "DAUGHTER OF ZOR" ALLUDES TO ABRAHAM,
WHO DISTRESSED (*HEZAR*) KINGS AND WHO WAS DISTRESSED BY KINGS.
THEY SHALL ENTREAT THY FAVOR WITH A GIFT, AS IT IS WRITTEN: AND
MELCHIZEDEK KING OF SALEM BROUGHT FORTH BREAD AND WINE.
AND MELCHIZEDEK: THIS PLACE MADE ITS INHABITANTS RIGHTEOUS.
[ANOTHER INTERPRETATION]: AND THE KING OF ZEDEK, THE LORD OF
ZEDEK (JOSH. 10:1). JERUSALEM IS CALLED ZEDEK (RIGHTEOUSNESS), AS
IT IS WRITTEN: ZEDEK (RIGHTEOUSNESS) LODGED IN HER (ISA. 1:21).

At the present stage of this Midrash, where it speaks of the kings of
Zedek and of Shalem, we know that they were important people since
the name of their communities are related to justice and peace.

מלך שלם. רבי יצחק הבבלי אומר: שנולד מהול. הוציא לחם ויין והוא כהן לאל עליון. רבי
שמואל בר נחמן ורבנן רבי שמואל אמר: הלכות כהונה גדולה גילה לו. לחם, זה לחם הפנים.
ויין, אלו הנסכים. ורבנן אמרי: תורה גילה לו שנאמר (משלי ט): לכו לחמו בלחמי ושתו ביין
מסכתי. והוא כהן לאל עליון.

KING OF SALEM (SHALEM). R. ISAAC THE BABYLONIAN SAID: THIS IM-
PLIES THAT HE WAS BORN CIRCUMCISED. BROUGHT FORTH BREAD AND
WINE. R. SAMUEL B. NAHMAN SAID: HE INSTRUCTED HIM IN THE LAWS
OF THE PRIESTHOOD, BREAD ALLUDING TO THE SHEWBREAD, AND WINE
TO LIBATIONS. THE RABBIS SAID: HE REVEALED TORAH TO HIM, AS IT IS
WRITTEN: COME, EAT OF MY BREAD, AND DRINK OF THE WINE WHICH
I HAVE MINGLED (PROV. 9:5). AND HE WAS PRIEST OF THE GOD MOST
HIGH.

We now come to a most interesting development where the Midrash
discusses the important city and the important people without mentioning their names. But the commentators know who we are talking

about. We are talking about Shem, the son of Noah, whose high moral principles were already revealed when he protected his father who had disgraced himself unintentionally. There is a tradition where Shem was born circumcised which meant that he was blessed with holiness and great fulfillment. Shalem was also a name of Jerusalem and it seems quite conclusive that Shem the son of Noah was king of Shalem which is a shortened version of Jerusalem. It was also said about him that he had high priestly honors and was a servant of God most high. So that when he presented to Abraham bread and wine, it was not ordinary food, but those especially blessed by having a share in the priesthood.

רבי אבא בר כהנא אמר: כל יין שכתוב בתורה עושה רושם, חוץ מזה. א"ר לוי: אף זה לא
יצאנו מידו, שמשם קרא עליו: ועבדום וענו אותם ארבע מאות שנה:

R. ABBA B. KAHANA SAID: WHEREVER "WINE" IS MENTIONED IN THE TO-
RAH, IT LEAVES ITS MARK, EXCEPT IN THE PRESENT INSTANCE. R. LEVI
SAID: HERE TOO WE HAVE NOT ESCAPED UNSCATHED, FOR IMMEDIATELY
AFTER THIS, IT WAS REVEALED TO HIM: AND THEY SHALL SERVE THEM;
AND THEY SHALL AFFLICT THEM, ETC. (GEN. 15:13)

We know from the experience of Noah what terrible affects wine can have if it is consumed in an uncontrollable fashion. Even here it seems innocent enough that wine and bread were presented to Abraham. R. Abba b. Kahana calls us to our attention that not long after this experience, tragedy was foretold with the expression that there would be an affliction for 400 years (Genesis 15:13).

Additional Commentary

Jerusalem, City of Righteousness

"Malki Zedek the king of Shalem." It would appear from the verse that Shalem refers to Jerusalem. However, the Midrash implies that Zedek was a name of Jerusalem since it brings righteousness to its inhabitants, as it says: "The nation residing in it are forgiven of sin" (Isaiah 33:24). Therefore, the king was *shalem*, meaning born circumcised since he was saintly. (Mirkin)

PARASHAH FORTY-THREE, *Midrash Seven*

ז ויברכהו ויאמר ברוך אברם לאל עליון קונה שמים וארץ. ממי קנאן?

7. AND HE BLESSED HIM, AND SAID: BLESSED BE ABRAM OF THE GOD
MOST HIGH, WHO HAS ACQUIRED (*KONEH*) HEAVEN AND EARTH (GEN.
14:19). FROM WHOM THEN DID HE ACQUIRE THEM?

If the translation of קונה – *koneh* is to acquire or to buy, from whom was
it acquired? If Abraham had said "Creator" of (instead of "acquired")
Heaven and Earth than it would have been obvious. But the use of the
word "acquire" begs a question which has to be responded to.

רבי אבא בשם רב כהנא ור' יצחק רבי אבא אמר: כאינש דאמר: פלן, עינוהי יאי, שעריה יאי.
א"ר יצחק: היה מקבל את העוברים ואת השבים, ומשהיו אוכלים ושותין היה אומר להן,
ברכו: והן אומרים לו: מה נאמר? והוא אומר להם: אמרו, ברוך אל עולם שאכלנו משלו! א"ל
הקב"ה: אני, לא היה שמי ניכר לבריותי, והכרת אותי בבריותי, מעלה אני עליך כאילו אתה
שותף עמי בברייתו של עולם, הה"ד (בראשית יד): קונה שמים וארץ:

SAID R. ABBA: ["ACQUIRED" IS ATTRIBUTIVE,] AS ONE SAYS: SO-AND-SO
HAS BEAUTIFUL EYES AND HAIR. R. ISAAC SAID: ABRAHAM USED TO EN-
TERTAIN WAYFARERS, AND AFTER THEY HAD EATEN, HE WOULD SAY TO
THEM, "SAY A BLESSING." "WHAT SHALL WE SAY?" THEY ASKED. "BLESSED
BE THE GOD OF THE UNIVERSE OF WHOSE BOUNTY WE HAVE EATEN,"
REPLIED HE. THEN THE HOLY ONE, BLESSED BE HE, SAID TO HIM: "MY
NAME WAS NOT KNOWN AMONG MY CREATURES, AND THOU HAST MADE
IT KNOWN AMONG THEM: I WILL REGARD THEE AS THOUGH THOU WAST
ASSOCIATED WITH ME IN THE CREATION OF THE WORLD." HENCE IT IS
WRITTEN, AND HE BLESSED HIM, AND SAID: BLESSED BE ABRAM OF THE
GOD MOST HIGH, WHO [SC. ABRAHAM] HAS ACQUIRED HEAVEN AND
EARTH.

Abraham's behavior made him a partner with God in repairing or
recreating the world.

—

Seed Thoughts

God did not create the world for Himself. He created it for mankind and
for all those elements mentioned in the poem of ברכי נפשי – *Barhi Nafshi*
(Psalms 104). When, therefore, someone with the talents and character
of Abraham appears and shows such love for mankind as to motivate
him to look after all their needs, God realizes that such a person has
eternalized the purpose of the world. He deserves to share in its acquisition and perfection.

PARASHAH FORTY-THREE, *Midrash Eight*

ח וברוך אל עליון אשר מגן צריך בידך. רבי הונא אמר: שהופך מגנגין שלך על צריך. רבי יודן
אמר: כמה מגנגנאות עשיתי להביאן תחת ידיך, אוהבים היו זה לזה, זה משלח לזה כתבים וזה
משלח לזה דורונות, והמרדתי אותם אלו על אלו, כדי שיבואו ויפלו תחת ידיך.

8. AND BLESSED BE GOD THE MOST HIGH, WHO HATH DELIVERED
(*MIGGEN*) THINE ENEMIES INTO THY HAND (GEN. 14:8). R. HUNA IN-
TERPRETED IT: WHO HATH TURNED THY WEAPONS AGAINST THINE
ENEMIES. R. JUDAN INTERPRETED: BY HOW MANY CONTRIVANCES DID I
BRING THEM UNDER THY HANDS! THEY WERE CLOSE FRIENDS AND USED
TO INTERCHANGE GIFTS OF DRY DATES AND OTHER PRESENTS; YET I
INCITED THEM TO REBEL AGAINST EACH OTHER, SO THAT THEY MIGHT
FALL INTO THY HANDS.

At first glance, it seems to be a natural development. Certain kings
were friendly with each other for a number of years. Then something occurred that interfered with that friendship, and it ultimately developed
into a hostile relationship. We are now told that this was not a natural
development. It was the Almighty Who had intervened. His introduc-
ing civil unrest into their relationship enabled Abraham to destroy their
power.

ויתן לו מעשר מכל. רבי יהודה בר סימון אמר: מכח אותה ברכה, אכלו ג' יתידות גדולות
בעולם. אברהם יצחק ויעקב. באברהם, כתיב (בראשית כד): וה' ברך את אברהם בכל, בזכות
ויתן לו מעשר מכל. ביצחק, כתיב (שם כז): ואוכל מכל, בזכות ויתן לו מעשר מכל. ביעקב
כתיב (שם לג): כי חנני אלהים וכי יש לי כל, בזכות ויתן לו מעשר מכל.

AND HE GAVE HIM A TENTH OF ALL. R. JUDAH SAID IN R. NEHORAI'S
NAME: IN VIRTUE OF THAT BLESSING, THE THREE GREAT PILLARS OF
THE WORLD, ABRAHAM, ISAAC, AND JACOB, ENJOYED PROSPERITY. IN
THE CASE OF ABRAHAM IT IS WRITTEN: AND THE LORD BLESSED ABRA-
HAM IN ALL THINGS (GEN. 24:1), AS A REWARD FOR, AND HE GAVE HIM
A TENTH OF ALL. OF ISAAC IT IS WRITTEN: AND I HAVE EATEN OF ALL
(27:33), AS A REWARD FOR, AND HE GAVE HIM A TENTH OF ALL. OF JACOB
IT IS WRITTEN: BECAUSE GOD HATH DEALT GRACIOUSLY WITH ME, AND
BECAUSE I HAVE ALL (33:11), AS A REWARD FOR, AND HE GAVE HIM A
TENTH OF ALL.

See the Seed Thoughts for this section.

מהיכן זכו ישראל לברכת כהנים? רבי יהודה ור' נחמיה ורבנן ר"י אמר: מאברהם, כה יהיה
זרעך כה תברכו את בני ישראל. ר' נחמיה אמר: מיצחק, שנאמר (בראשית כב): ואני והנער
נלכה עד כה, לפיכך אמר המקום: כה תברכו את בני ישראל. ורבנן אמרי: מיעקב שנאמר
(שמות יט): כה תאמר לבית יעקב, וכנגדו,כה תברכו את בני ישראל.

WHENCE WERE ISRAEL PRIVILEGED TO RECEIVE THE PRIESTLY BLESSING?
R. JUDAH SAID: FROM ABRAHAM, [FOR IN HIS CASE, IT IS WRITTEN:] SO
(*KOH*) SHALL THY SEED BE (GEN. 15:5), WHILE THERE IT IS WRITTEN: SO
(*KOH*) SHALL YE BLESS THE CHILDREN OF ISRAEL (NUM. 6:23). R. NEHE-
MIAH SAID: FROM ISAAC, FOR IT IS WRITTEN: AND I AND THE LAD WILL
GO YONDER – AD KOH (GEN. 22:5); THEREFORE THE HOLY ONE, BLESSED
BE HE, PROMISED: SO (KOH) SHALL YE BLESS THE CHILDREN OF LSRAEL.
THE RABBIS TAUGHT: FROM JACOB, FOR IT SAYS: SO (*KOH*) SHALT THOU
SAY TO THE HOUSE OF JACOB (EX. 19:3), TO WHICH CORRESPONDS, SO
SHALL YE BLESS THE CHILDREN OF ISRAEL.

The sages, R. Judah, R. Nehemiah and the rabbis whose names are
featured so prominently differ in their interpretation of who or what
is the source of the Priestly Blessing? The Priestly Blessing begins with
כה תברכו את בני ישראל – *koh tevarhu et Bnei Yisrael*. R. Judah claims that
the source is Abraham based on his vision of the stars of the sky, and
the blessing of *koh yihyeh zaraha*, so will be your seed. R. Nehemiah
offers a different explanation based mainly on the fact that Abraham
had another son, Ishmael, who eventually was not part of the house of
Israel, for whom the Priestly Blessing was intended. In the case of Isaac,
the blessing was, *ve-ani vehanaar nelha ad koh*. The rabbis felt that even
R. Nehemiah's view was inadequate because Esav was descended (from

Isaac) and not part of the house of Israel. We, therefore, come to Jacob from whom the house of Israel dates its origin. In his case it says, *koh tomar lebeit Yaakov.* (*HaMidrash HaMevo'ar*)

רבי אליעזר ור' יוסי בר חנינא. ר"א אמר: אימתי אני מגדל את בניך ככוכבים? כשאגלה
עליהם, בכה, כה תאמר לבית יעקב. ור' יוסי ב"ר חנינא אמר: כשאגלה על מנהיגם בכה,
שנאמר (שם ד): כה אמר ה': בני בכורי ישראל:

WHEN WILL I MAGNIFY THY SONS LIKE THE STARS? R. ELEAZAR AND R.
JOSE B. R. HANINA GAVE DIFFERENT REPLIES. ONE MAINTAINED: WHEN
I REVEAL MYSELF TO THEM WITH A MESSAGE "SO," VIZ. SO SHALT THOU
SAY TO THE HOUSE OF JACOB. THE OTHER MAINTAINED: WHEN I REVEAL
MYSELF TO THEIR LEADERS WITH A MESSAGE "SO", VIZ. SO (*KOH*) SAITH
THE LORD: ISRAEL IS MY SON, MY FIRSTBORN (EX. 4:22).

The question being raised by the two Sages R. Eleazar and R. Jose, is how to treat God's blessing to Abraham when He showed him the stars in the sky and said that Abraham's descendants be similar. The question they were investigating is how to understand the blessing: Is it quantitative? If so, this did not happen up to that point, nor has it happened up to the point of those writing this thought. One of the Sages, R. Eleazar, said that this blessing would be fulfilled at Mount Sinai. The relevant verse with the expression is *koh tomar leBeit Yaakov,* "So shall thou say to the House of Jacob," which means that the greatness of Israel begins with the giving of the Torah. Therefore, the blessing of Abraham has to be understood as not quantitative but as qualitative – referring to the quality of Torah. R. Jose says that the blessing of Abraham will be fulfilled when God reveals Himself to the leaders who were responsible for the Exodus. Israel was referred to as God's firstborn which is the greatest compliment that a people could receive. This is also not quantitative but qualitative.

—

Seed Thoughts I

One of the remarkable developments in the story of the Patriarchs is that in addition to each of them being blessed with everything – this was spelled out in a way that was not only beautiful, but one of the predominant motivations in their life. Each of the Patriarchs, we are told, had everything. But in the Hebrew language, the grammar was slightly changed to indicate that each of them did something, which was at the same time wonderful and unique in terms of their heritage. In the case of Abraham, "everything" was written in Hebrew as בכל – *bakol*, meaning "with everything." In the case of Isaac, "everything was written as מכל – *mikol*, meaning "from everything." That is to say that whatever needs he discovered in others, he tried to fulfill from everything which he possessed. In the case of Jacob, "everything" was written simply as כל – *kol*, "everything." He needed or wanted nothing more for he had everything.

What has just been written about the Patriarchs is very beautiful. But when they are applied to the Midrash we are now reading, they become not only more fascinating, but more revolutionary – if we can use such an expression. They become far more profound. Their "everything" is related in our Midrash to מעשר – *maaser*. This is the tithe that people working in agriculture had to give the authorities in various times of the year. It was a tax, but with great authority and power. To explain this in a more popular fashion, everything that the Patriarchs represented and possessed was judged by how they related themselves to giving to charity. These are qualities in which the *maaser* challenges every individual. The text of the Torah and its commentary allowed the Patriarchs to act as they could with their "everything," since our opinion of their judgment is very high. Our present Midrash, however, does not act that way at all. They have to be tested by the *maaser*. The way that they act towards their giving, their charity and philanthropy, and everything related to these concepts, is the way in which they are called upon to justify their having everything.

～

Seed Thoughts II

We, who write this column, live 3,000 years after the discussion that has just been quoted. The Jewish people have remained a minority ever since, and do not even look forward to a revolution in terms of numbers. What should interest us is character and not numbers. Let us examine carefully God's message to Abraham. Counting the stars can no longer be seen as a quantitative blessing because it has not appeared in 4000 years. It has to be understood differently. What is a star? If through some device, the stars were automatically extinguished in the heavens and only one remained, would it give light? Of course it would. However, the greatness of Israel cannot be a giver of physical light. But we can be a giver of light on a much higher moral level: the light of love, the light of learning, the light of understanding, and the light of tolerance. Many more values can be added to this list, but it is enough to indicate the real blessing God gave to Abraham is for his descendants to become givers of light. That light which adds meaning and significance to human life.

PARASHAH FORTY-THREE, *Midrash Nine*

ט ויאמר מלך סדום אל אברם תן לי הנפש וגו'. ויאמר אברם אל מלך סדום הרימותי ידי וגו'.

9. AND THE KING OF SODOM SAID UNTO ABRAM . . . AND ABRAM SAID TO THE KING OF SODOM: I HAVE LIFTED UP (*HARIMOTHI*) MY HAND UNTO THE LORD (GEN. 14:21F.).

The question that will now be raised by the Midrash is how we inter-pret the verse that says "and I have lifted up my hand . . ." What does it mean and what was Abraham trying to express?

ר' יהודה ור' נחמיה ורבנן. ר"י אמר: עשאן תרומה, היך מד"א (במדבר יח): והרמותם ממנו תרומת ה'. ורבי נחמיה אמר: עשאן שבועה, היך מה דאת אמר (דניאל יב): וירם ימינו ושמאלו אל השמים, וישבע בחי העולם. ורבנן אמרי: עשאן שירה, היך מה דאת אמר (שמות טו): זה אלי ואנוהו אלהי אבי וארוממנהו.

R. JUDAH SAID: HE HAD SEPARATED *TERUMAH* THEREOF, AS YOU READ: THEN YE SHALL SET APART (*WA-HAREMOTHEM*) OF IT A GIFT (*TERUMAH*) TO THE LORD (NUM. 18:26). R. NEHEMIAH INTERPRETED IT: HE HAD TAKEN AN OATH IN RESPECT OF IT, AS YOU READ: AND HE LIFTED UP HIS RIGHT HAND AND HIS LEFT HAND UNTO HEAVEN, AND SWORE (DAN. 12:7). THE RABBIS SAID: HE HAD UTTERED SONG [TO GOD] ON ITS ACCOUNT, AS YOU READ: MY FATHER'S GOD, AND I WILL EXALT HIM – *AROMEMENHU* (EX. 15:2).

R. Judah said that he was doing what many Jewish agriculturalists did with *terumah*. That is to say, they would set aside a certain amount of produce to be given to the Kohanim, and this would be treated in holi-ness. Only *terumah* would have those special rules and none of the other agricultural produce. R. Nehemiah said that lifting the hands was an ex-pression of an oath. Abraham rose up his hands in testimony. Therefore, he was taking an oath. The Sages differed with both interpretations and said that Abraham was merely expressing the majesty of God. This was his way of formulating a sincere thanksgiving.

רבי ברכיה ור' חלבו ור' אמי בשם ר"א אמרו: אמר משה: בל' שאמר אבא שירה. הרימותי ידי אל ה'. בו בלשון אני אומר שירה, שנאמר: אלהי אבי וארוממנהו.

R. BEREKIAH SAID IN R. ELEAZAR'S NAME: MOSES SAID: "WITH THE VERY SAME LANGUAGE IN WHICH MY ANCESTOR UTTERED SONG, VIZ. *HARIMOTHI*, WILL I UTTER SONG, VIZ. 'MY FATHER'S GOD, AND I WILL EXALT HIM – *AROMEMENHU*'" THAT I WILL NOT TAKE A THREAD NOR A SHOE-LATCHET (GEN. 14:23).

There are many other occasions where the thanksgiving of God is found.

אם מחוט: א"ר אבא בר ממל: א"ל הקב"ה: את אמרת אם מחוט, חייך! שאני נותן לבניך מצוות ציצית, היך מה דאת אמר (במדבר טו): ונתנו על ציצית הכנף פתיל תכלת, ומתרגמינן חוטא דתכלתא.

R. ABBA B. MAMMEL SAID: THE HOLY ONE, BLESSED BE HE, ASSURED HIM: "BECAUSE THOU SAIDEST, I WILL NOT TAKE A THREAD, BY THY LIFE! I WILL GIVE THY CHILDREN THE PRECEPT OF FRINGES," AS YOU READ: AND THAT THEY PUT WITH THE FRINGE OF EACH CORNER A THREAD OF BLUE (NUM. 15:38), WHICH IS RENDERED, A THREAD OF BLUE WOOL.

The second part of Abraham's declaration was also idealized by several of the Sages. Because Abraham said that he would not take even a thread that belongs to the king of Sodom, his children were blessed with the mitzvah of *tzitzis*, where the male population was enveloped in fringes to remind them of God's commandments.

ועד שרוך נעל. חייך! שאני נותן לבניך מצוות יבמה, היך מה דאת אמר (דברים כה): וחלצה נעלו מעל רגלו.

NOR A SHOE-LATCHET: I SWEAR TO THEE THAT I WILL GIVE THY CHILDREN THE PRECEPT OF *YEBAMAH*, IN CONNECTION WITH WHICH YOU READ: THEN SHALL SHE LOOSE HIS SHOE FROM OFF HIS FOOT (DEUT. 25:9).

Because Abraham said that he would not touch even a shoe lace, his children would be blessed with the mitzvah of *yibum*, which is the levirate

marriage to protect the woman whose husband died without children.
The rule was that the husband's brother had to marry the widow or be
subject to the ceremony of *halitzah,* whereby she would remove a shoe
from the brother as a sign that he refused to carry on his brother's name.

ד"א. אם מחוט, זה המשכן שהוא מצוייר בתכלת וארגמן. ועד שרוך נעל, אלו עורות
התחשים. ד"א: אם מחוט, אלו הקרבנות כההיא דתנן: וחוט של סקרא חוגרו באמצע,
להבדיל בין דמים העליונים לדמים התחתונים. ועד שרוך נעל, אלו פעמי רגלים, היך מה
דאת אמר (שיר ז): מה יפו פעמיך בנעלים.

ANOTHER INTERPRETATION: NOT A THREAD: THIS IS AN ALLUSION
TO THE TABERNACLE, WHICH WAS ADORNED WITH BLUE WOOL AND
PURPLE WOOL; NOR A SHOE-LATCHET ALLUDES TO THE BADGER SKINS.
ANOTHER INTERPRETATION: NOT A THREAD ALLUDES TO SACRIFICES,
AS WE LEARNED: A THREAD OF SCARLET GIRDLED IT [THE ALTAR] ABOUT
THE MIDDLE. NOR A SHOE–LATCHET: THIS ALLUDES TO THE FEET OF
THE [FESTIVAL] PILGRIMS, AS IT SAYS: HOW BEAUTIFUL ARE THY STEPS
IN SANDALS (SONG 7:2).

These are not popular interpretations, but they are the view of emi-
nent sages.

בלעדי, רק אשר אכלו הנערים הה"ד (שמואל א ל): ויען כל איש רע ובליעל, מהאנשים אשר
הלכו עם דוד, ויאמרו: יען אשר לא הלכו עמי, לא נתן להם מהשלל אשר הצלנו, כי אם איש
את אשתו ואת בניו, וינהגו וילכו, ויאמר דוד: לא תעשון כן אחי! את אשר נתן ה' לנו וישמור
אותנו ויתן את הגדוד הבא עלינו בידינו, ומי ישמע לכם לדבר הזה! כי כחלק היורד במלחמה
וכחלק היושב על הכלים יחדו יחלוקו.

SAVE ONLY THAT WHICH THE YOUNG MEN HAVE EATEN AND THE POR-
TION OF THE YOUNG MEN WHICH WENT WITH ME; [ALSO] LET ANER,
ESCHOL, AND MAMRE TAKE THEIR PORTIONS (GEN. 14:24). THUS IT IS
WRITTEN: THEN ANSWERED ALL THE WICKED MEN AND BASE FELLOWS,
OF THOSE THAT WENT WITH DAVID, AND SAID: BECAUSE THEY WENT NOT
WITH US, WE WILL NOT GIVE THEM AUGHT OF THE SPOIL . . . THEN SAID
DAVID: YE SHALL NOT DO SO, MY BRETHREN . . . FOR AS IS THE SHARE OF
HIM THAT GOETH DOWN TO BATTLE, SO SHALL BE THE SHARE OF HIM
THAT TARRIETH BY THE BAGGAGE; THEY SHALL ALL SHARE ALIKE.

Although Abraham would not take a thing from the victory, he would
not deny the share nor equal portion from his confederates (*Hertz Chu-
mash,* 2nd edition on Genesis 14:24)

ויהי מהיום ההוא ומעלה, וישימה דוד לחוק ולמשפט לישראל עד היום הזה אמר. רבי יודן:
והלאה אין כתיב כאן, אלא ומעלה. וממי למד? מאברהם זקינו שאמר: בלעדי, רק אשר
אכלו הנערים וחלק האנשים וגו':

AND SO IT WAS FROM THAT DAY AND ABOVE, THAT HE MADE IT A STAT-
UTE (L SAM. 30:22–25). R. JUDAH SAID: IT IS NOT WRITTEN: "[FROM
THAT DAY] AND ONWARD," BUT "[FROM THAT DAY] AND ABOVE": FROM
WHOM DID HE LEARN? FROM HIS ANCESTOR ABRAHAM, WHO SAID, SAVE
ONLY THAT WHICH THE YOUNG MEN HAVE EATEN . . . [ALSO] LET ANER,
ESCHOL, AND MAMRE TAKE THEIR PORTION.

Seed Thoughts

There is an interesting use of two Hebrew words. The word הלאה – *halah*,
which can be translated as "continuous" and the word מעלה – *maalah*,
which usually means "something above." In this case, it means something that goes back into history. King David refused to allow those
soldiers who stayed home to protect the camp and the community to be
discriminated against financially. He changed the law to make it manda-
tory that all participants in war, whether on the battlefield or off, should
participate equally in the spoils of the battle. He did not attribute this
to himself but to his ancestor Abraham. Therefore, the law was not only
halah, "continuous" but *maalah*, something which had already been
done and was revived by King David.

א אחר הדברים האלה היה דבר ה' אל אברם במחזה לאמר וגו'. (תהלים יח): האל תמים דרכו אמרת ה' צרופה מגן הוא לכל החוסים בו. אם דרכיו תמימים, הוא על אחת כמה וכמה! רב אמר: לא נתנו המצוות אלא לצרף בהן את הבריות. וכי מה איכפת ליה להקב"ה למי ששוחט מן הצואר או מי ששוחט מן העורף? הוי, לא נתנו המצוות אלא לצרף בהם את הבריות. ד"א: האל תמים דרכו, זה אברהם, שנאמר (נחמיה ט): ומצאת את לבבו נאמן לפניך. אמרת ה' צרופה, שצרפו הקב"ה בכבשן האש. מגן הוא לכל החוסים בו, אל תירא אברם אנכי מגן לך:

1. AFTER THESE THINGS THE WORD OF THE LORD CAME UNTO ABRAM IN A VISION, ETC. (GEN. 15:1). IT IS WRITTEN: AS FOR GOD, HIS WAY IS PERFECT; THE WORD OF THE LORD IS TRIED (PS. 18:31). IF HIS WAY IS PERFECT, HOW MUCH THE MORE HE HIMSELF! RAB SAID: THE PRECEPTS WERE GIVEN ONLY IN ORDER THAT MAN MIGHT BE REFINED BY THEM. FOR WHAT DOES THE HOLY ONE, BLESSED BE HE, CARE WHETHER A MAN KILLS AN ANIMAL BY THE THROAT OR BY THE NAPE OF ITS NECK? HENCE ITS PURPOSE IS TO REFINE [TRY] MAN. ANOTHER INTERPRETATION: HIS WAY IS PERFECT, ALLUDES TO ABRAHAM, FOR IT IS WRITTEN: AND THOU FOUNDEST HIS [SC. ABRAHAM'S] WAY FAITHFUL BEFORE THEE, ETC. (NEH. 9:8). THE WORD OF THE LORD IS TRIED, INTIMATES THAT THE HOLY ONE, BLESSED BE HE, TRIED HIM IN A FIERY FURNACE. HE IS A SHIELD UNTO ALL THEM THAT TAKE REFUGE IN HIM (PS. 18:31); HENCE, FEAR NOT. ABRAM, I AM THY SHIELD, ETC.

God appears in this Midrash as the protector of Abraham. This has remained not only in Jewish literature, but in the very act of religious worship, in the very first blessing of the eighteen blessings in the *Amidah – Magen Avraham*. This description is detailed in the verse that is quoted, that "God's way is perfect" and, therefore, it follows that He and He alone can be the protector of all those who have hope in Him. It is of interest to note that the phrase that is quoted reads, האל תמים דרכו – *HaEl tamim darko*, "God's way is perfect." It does not say that "God is perfect," since who are we to make such a judgment. It says that "God's way is perfect," and we discover His ways, either through Scripture or in the ways of the world itself. From these ways, we interpret and/or discover the perfection of God. As the Midrash puts it: If His way is perfect, how much more so is He perfect!

Seed Thoughts

This Midrash presents for our consideration one of the most important statements in the religion of Judaism. It says that God gave mitzvot only so that man should be refined. Let us think about this for a moment. A better definition for צרוף – *tzeruf* should be purified and raised to the highest possible level through the commandments. Sometimes this teaching is self-evident as, for example, the commandment to love thy neighbor as yourself, and many other ethical or moral commandments and teachings. The question is how can these moral teachings, as important as they are, be functional in the life of people so that their behavior would consciously conform to the intent of these laws? The Midrash understands that more is necessary to make these laws and commandments a factor in the life of the individual Jew. That explains the second half of the statement that appears in our Midrash – why should God care how a man kills an animal, either by the throat or the nape of its neck?! From the point of view of reason, the statement is quite correct, that it does not matter to God whether an animal is slaughtered the kosher way or the non-kosher way. But in actual fact, it does matter, and matters very strongly and very strictly. This is because God understands that commandments would not be followed merely because they are spiritual and nice. You cannot touch something that is spiritual, because it is only an idea or a concept. But when it comes to slaughtering an animal the kosher way, you are dealing with something you can see and touch and do something about. In other words, when we describe the term "ritual," it includes so many things that seem to be, if not irrational, then certainly not in accordance with reasonable behavior. The point, however, is that in order to follow commandments, Jews had to be trained to do mitzvot, commandments, which include many that may or may not have reasonable explanations, except that they make the Jews a spiritual people and keep the people alive. From this point of view, we have to say that whether or not man kills an animal by the throat or by the nape of its neck, it is important to God because it is a way of training

Jews in the habit of following the commandments with the greatest possible sacrificial intentions.

There is another statement of the rabbis, not found in this Midrash, but very relevant to this whole discussion. It is the verse that concludes every chapter of the Ethics of the Fathers. God wanted to raise Israel to a higher level. Therefore, He gave them additional commandments, meant only for the Jewish people and no one else. These are the commandments which we introduce with the benedictions because they are listed in the Torah. Whenever we partake in this commandment, we say: "Who has sanctified us with His commandments and commanded us to do this particular mitzvah." This statement, taken together with the one in our Midrash, are an important interpretation in Judaism. They are a development of which all of us can be very proud.

—

Additional Commentary

The word of the Lord is tried

We can say about this statement that the word of God is not only refined, but sanctified and dedicated to the highest purposes of life. Every commandment of God is pure from every fault or defect. Its purpose is to bring the doer of the commandment as distant as possible from the evil in the world, and as close as possible to what is good, pure, and meaningful. (*HaMidrash HaMevo'ar*)

From the throat

The Midrash asks why God should care if one slaughters an animal from the throat or from the back of the neck, after all in both cases you are severing the head. The answer is that the mitzvot were given to for the purification and ethical betterment of man. This is an important point. It is not God who needs the commandment, but man, in order to achieve the correct moral level. Therefore, we must slaughter from the throat which is more compassionate to the animal and not from the back of the neck which is crueler even if in the end it achieves the same result. Even when we take the life of an animal for consumption it must be done with the least amount of pain. (B.R. Shuchat)

PARASHAH FORTY-FOUR, *Midrash Two*

ב ד"א: אחר הדברים וגו'. כתיב (משלי יד): חכם ירא וסר מרע וכסיל מתעבר ובוטח. חכם
ירא, אל תירא אברם, אל תהי חכם בעיניך. ירא את ה' וסר מרע, אל תהי חכם בעיניך במה
שאת רואה בעיניך. תאמר שאני מוליד, תאמר שאין אני מוליד. ירא את ה', אל תירא אברם.

2. A WISE MAN FEARETH, AND DEPARTETH FROM EVIL (PROV. 14:16):
THOUGH THOU ART WISE AND DEPARTEST FROM EVIL, YET THOU FEAR-
EST! [THEREFORE I SAY TO THEE] FEAR NOT, ABRAM. BE NOT WISE IN
THINE OWN EYES; FEAR THE LORD (3:7): BE NOT WISE BY WHAT THOU
SEEST WITH THINE OWN EYES; CANST THOU SAY THAT I WILL CAUSE
THEE TO BEGET OR THAT I WILL NOT CAUSE THEE TO BEGET? FEAR THE
LORD: THUS IT IS WRITTEN: FEAR NOT, ABRAM, I AM THY SHIELD.

One of the important examples of Abraham's fear was his concern of
whether he would be able to father a child or not. Considering his age,
he was probably the object of many snide remarks of many of his coun-
trymen who joked about the fact that the man who wanted to change
the world cannot even become a father. God's help sustained him until
the birth of Isaac, which came as a tremendous relief to him.

רבי אבין בשם רבי חנינא פתח: (משלי יא) רשע עושה פעולת שקר וגו'. רשע עושה פעולת
שקר, זה נמרוד, שהיו פעולותיו על שקר. וזורע צדקה, זה אברהם, שנאמר (בראשית יט):
ושמרו דרך ה' לעשות צדקה ומשפט. שכר אמת, אל תירא אברם וגו':

R. ABIN COMMENCED HIS DISCOURSE IN R. HANINA'S NAME: THE
WICKED DOETH WORK OF FALSEHOOD; BUT HE THAT SOWETH RIGH-
TEOUSNESS HATH A SURE REWARD (PROV. 11:18). THE WICKED DOETH
WORK OF FALSEHOOD, ALLUDES TO NIMROD, WHOSE WORKS WERE OF
FALSEHOOD; BUT HE THAT SOWETH RIGHTEOUSNESS, ALLUDES TO
ABRAHAM, OF WHOM IT IS WRITTEN: THAT THEY MAY KEEP THE WAY OF
THE LORD, TO DO RIGHTEOUSNESS AND JUSTICE (GEN. 18:19); HATH A
SURE REWARD, AS IT IS WRITTEN: FEAR NOT, ABRAM, I AM THY SHIELD,
THY REWARD SHALL BE EXCEEDINGLY GREAT.

Abraham's main concern was not for his own personal well-being or
his own future, but rather the well-being of his family circle that would
come after him. The verse that applies to him most as stated in this Midrash is זורע צדקה – *zore-a zedakah*. He was not merely interested in the

practices of righteousness for himself, but for planting righteousness for the life and souls of his offspring. It meant that there would be continuity to his life which is the whole point of God's choice of Abraham and the change of his name from Abram to Abraham, which implied for him a role among the nations of the world.

⸺

Seed Thoughts

This Midrash and several others that follow deal with the question of Abraham's fear. Why should he fear considering all the successes he had under God's protection? The text says that God said to Abraham not to fear, which implies that he had some fear despite his successes. A unique feature in this Midrash is that the word ירא – *yareh*, which means "fear" also has the meaning "to see." In the verse that describes the wise man, he sees much more than ordinary people do, he sees implications and, therefore, he becomes much more cautious that ordinary people who are not wise. This is a case where both readings of the word *yareh* can be applied.

⸺

Additional Commentary

Fear and Sight

"Fear not, Abram. 'Be not wise in thine own eyes; fear the Lord (Prov. 3:7)': Be not wise by what thou seest with thine own eyes; canst thou say that I will cause thee to beget." The midrash interprets *al tira*, "do not fear" both as "fear" (*yira*) and as "sight" (*re'iyah*). (Mirkin)

PARASHAH FORTY-FOUR, *Midrash Three*

ג אנכי מגן לך. רבי לוי אמר: תרתין. ורבנן אמר: חדא. ר' לוי אמר: לפי שהיה אבינו אברהם
מתפחד ואומר: תאמר אותן אוכלסין שהרגתי, שהיה בהם צדיק אחד, וירא שמים אחד?
משל לאחד, שהיה עובר לפני פרדסו של מלך, ראה חבילה של קוצים וירד ונטלה, והציץ
המלך וראה אותו, התחיל מטמין מפניו. אמר לו: מפני מה אתה מטמן? כמה פועלים הייתי
צריך שיקושו אותה? עכשיו, שקיששת אותה, בא וטול שכר. כך אמר הקדוש ברוך הוא
לאברהם: אותן אוכלסין שהרגת, קוצים כסוחים היו, הדא הוא דכתיב (ישעיה לג): והיו עמים
משרפות סיד, קוצים כסוחים. רבי לוי אמר: אוחרי, לפי שהיה אבינו אברהם מתפחד ואומר:
תאמר אותן המלכים שהרגתי, שבניהם מכנסין אוכלסין ובאים ועושים עמי מלחמה?
אמר לו הקב«ה: אל תירא, אנכי מגל לך! מה המגן הזה, אפילו כל החרבות באות עליה
היא עומדת כנגדן, כך את, אפי' כל עובדי כוכבים מתכנסין עליך, נלחם אני כנגדן. ורבנן
אמרי: חדא, לפי שהיה אבינו אברהם מתפחד ואומר: ירדתי לכבשן האש ונצלתי, ירדתי
למלחמת המלכים ונצלתי, תאמר שנתקבלתי שכרי בעולם הזה ואין לי כלום לעתיד לבא?
אמר הקדוש ברוך הוא: אל תירא, אנכי מגן לך! וכל מה שעשיתי עמך בעולם הזה, חנם
עשיתי עמך, אבל שכרך מתוקן לעתיד לבא, שכרך הרבה מאד! היך מה דאת אמר (תהלים
לא): מה רב טובך אשר צפנת ליראיך:

3. BUT THOU, ISRAEL, MY SERVANT, IF JACOB WHOM I HAVE CHOSEN, THE
SEED OF ABRAHAM MY FRIEND, THOU WHOM I HAVE TAKEN HOLD OF
FROM THE ENDS OF THE EARTH (ISA. 41:8F.) – I.E., FROM MESOPOTAMIA
AND ITS COUNTRY TOWNS; AND CALLED THEE FROM ITS NOBLES (41:9):
I SUMMONED THEE FROM OUT OF ITS DISTINGUISHED MEN. I HAVE
CHOSEN THEE AND NOT CAST THEE AWAY (41:9): I CHOSE THEE WHEN
THOU WAST ABRAM, AND DID NOT CAST THEE AWAY WHEN THOU WAST
ABRAHAM. FEAR NOT, FOR I AM WITH THEE, BE NOT DISMAYED, FOR I AM
THY GOD (41:10).

The fact that the phrase that God assured Abraham to not fear is
repeated often is demonstrated in many ways throughout the lives of
Abraham and his children.

R. Hoshaya said: When Isaac said to Jacob: Come near, I pray thee,
that I may feel thee (Gen. 27:21), perspiration poured over his legs, and
his heart melted like wax; whereupon the Holy One, blessed be He,
provided him with two angels, one at his right and one at his left, and
these supported him by the elbows, that he might not fall. Hence He
said to him: Be not dismayed (*tishta*) – i.e., be not wax-like (*teshawa*),
For I am thy God.

R. Hoshaya said that when Jacob appeared before his father Isaac to receive the blessing that Isaac planned to give to Esau, Jacob began trembling. In fact, he was so afraid that his sweat began to remove his disguise. God sent him angelic help to protect him.

I strengthen thee, yea, I help thee; yea, I uphold thee with My victorious right hand. Behold, they shall all be ashamed and confounded that were incensed against thee (Isa. 41:10f.) – this means, those who are hostile to thee; They that strove with thee shall be as nothing, and shall perish (41:11) – that means, those who engage in strife with thee; Thou shalt seek them, and shalt not find them, even them that contended with thee (41:12) – this refers to those who wage quarrels with thee. For I the Lord thy God hold thy right hand, who say unto thee: Fear not (41:13), as it is written, Fear not, Abram, etc.

God assured Abraham, not only in the case of Jacob, but in all the challenges to his leadership, that never would Abraham be abandoned, that His choice of him would be eternal, and that there would be no compromise when it comes to facing the challenges to the Abrahamic dynasty.

—

Additional Commentary

Michael and Gabriel

"Whereupon the Holy One, blessed be He, provided him with two angels, one at his right and one at his left" – Michael on his right and Gabriel on his left, and He in His glory, May His name be blessed, supported him from behind. (Midrash Tanhuma)

PARASHAH FORTY-FOUR, *Midrash Four*

ד אנכי מגן לך. רבי לוי אמר: תרתין. ורבנן אמרי: חדא. ר' לוי אמר: לפי שהיה אבינו אברהם
מתפחד ואומר: תאמר אותן אוכלסין שהרגתי, שהיה בהם צדיק אחד, וירא שמים אחד?
משל לאחד שהי' עובר לפני פרדסו של מלך, ראה חבילה של קוצים ירד ונטלה, והציץ
המלך וראה אותו, התחיל מטמון מפניו. א"ל: מפני מה אתה מטמון? כמה פועלים הייתי צריך
שיקושו אותך? עכשיו, שקששת אותה, בא וטול שכר. כך אמר הקב"ה לאברהם: אותן
אוכלסין שהרגת, קוצים כסוחים היו: הדא הוא דכתיב (ישעיה לג): והיו עמים משרפות סיד,
קוצים כסוחים. רבי לוי אמר: אוחרי, לפי שהיה אבינו אברהם מתפחד ואומר: תאמר אותן
המלכים שהרגתי, שבניהם מכנסין אוכלסין ובאים ועושים עמי מלחמה? אמר לו הקב"ה:
אל תירא, אנכי מגן לך! מה המגן הזה, אפילו כל החרבות באות עליה היא עומדת כנגדן, כך
את, אפי' כל עובדי כוכבים מתכנסין עליך, נלחם אני כנגדן. ורבנן אמרי: חדא, לפי שהיה
אבינו אברהם מתפחד ואומר: ירדתי לכבשן האש ונצלתי, ירדתי למלחמת המלכים ונצלתי,
תאמר שנתקבלתי שכרי בעולם הזה ואין לי כלום לעתיד לבא? אמר הקב"ה: אל תירא, אנכי
מגן לך! וכל מה שעשיתי עמך בעולם הזה, חנם עשיתי עמך, אבל שכרך מתוקן לעתיד לבא,
שכרך הרבה מאד! היך מה דאת אמר (תהלים לא): מה רב טובך אשר צפנת ליראיך:

4. R. LEVI EXPLAINED THIS IN TWO WAYS, THE RABBIS IN ONE. R. LEVI
SAID: ABRAHAM WAS FILLED WITH MISGIVING, THINKING TO HIMSELF:
MAYBE THERE WAS A RIGHTEOUS OR GOD-FEARING MAN AMONG THOSE
TROOPS WHICH I SLEW. THIS MAY BE COMPARED TO A STRAW-MERCHANT
WHO WAS PASSING THE KING'S ORCHARDS, AND SEEING SOME BUNDLES
OF THORNS, DESCENDED [FROM HIS WAGON] AND TOOK THEM. [THE
KING] CAUGHT SIGHT OF HIM, WHEREUPON HE TRIED TO HIDE HIM-
SELF. "WHY DO YOU HIDE?" HE SAID TO HIM, REASSURINGLY, "I NEEDED
LABORERS TO GATHER THEM; NOW THAT YOU HAVE GATHERED THEM,
COME AND RECEIVE YOUR REWARD." THUS THE HOLY ONE, BLESSED BE
HE, SAID TO ABRAHAM: "THOSE TROOPS THAT THOU SLEWEST WERE
THORNS ALREADY CUT DOWN"; THUS IT IS WRITTEN: AND THE PEOPLES
SHALL BE AS THE BURNINGS OF LIME; AS THORNS CUT DOWN, THAT
ARE BURNED IN THE FIRE (ISA. 33:12). R. LEVI MADE ANOTHER COM-
MENT: ABRAHAM WAS FEARFUL, SAYING, "PERHAPS THE SONS OF THE
KINGS THAT I SLEW WILL COLLECT TROOPS AND COME AND WAGE WAR
AGAINST ME." THEREFORE THE HOLY ONE, BLESSED BE HE, SAID TO HIM:
FEAR NOT, ABRAM, I AM THY SHIELD: JUST AS A SHIELD RECEIVES ALL
SPEARS AND WITHSTANDS THEM, SO WILL I STAND BY THEE.

T he main point of this Midrash is that some of Abraham's fears are on a level quite different and quite elevating from what we have so far been discussing. He was concerned that he may have killed a righteous man who may have been a member of one of the armies of the four kings, and not know about it. One Sage and the rabbis offer interpretations that make Abraham feel much less concerned about what was worrying him. R. Levi says that God assured Abraham that the armies of the four kings had no righteousness and by killing them, he paved the way for a place for righteousness to evolve. He gave another opinion in that Abraham feared that a descendant of the kings may return and attack the seed of Abraham. God assured him the He will be a shield and protect him from such attacks.

The Rabbis explained it thus: Abraham was filled with misgivings, saying to himself: "I descended into the fiery furnace and was delivered; I went through famine and war and was delivered: perhaps then I have already received my reward in this world and have nought for the future world?" Therefore, the Holy One, blessed be He, reassured him: Fear not, Abram, I am thy shield (*magen*), meaning, a gift of grace (*maggan*) to thee, all that I have done for thee in this world I did for nought; but in the future that is to come, Thy reward shall be exceeding great, even as you read: Oh how abundant is Thy goodness, which Thou hast laid up for them that fear Thee, etc. (Ps. 31:20).

God assures Abraham that not only was he rewarded in this world, but he shall be rewarded in the World to Come.

—

Seed Thoughts I

Midrashim 2, 3, and 4 talk about the fears of Abraham and God's as-surances to him. The more we read the contents of his fears, the more we should understand that these are the kinds of fears that any human being of stature and intellectual accomplishment could fear. Even though there is an assurance that God would help, it does not change the reality of the fear. What are his fears about? Whether he can be a father, whether he has to fear a cautious life, whether Jacob should fear his brother Esav, the fear of other family relationships, or whether he killed another righteous person. One does not have to be as Moses was described, as the man of God in order to have such fears. Everybody has them in greater or lesser degree. We have to understand this and realize that we can easily put ourselves in Abraham's position and experience the very same fears. We are dealing with human fears. This is the main lesson.

—

Seed Thoughts II

What sometimes makes the readers feel is that we are dealing with a phenomenon that is more than what a human being can deal with. It is a fact that at every opportunity available, God says not to fear. It is this which makes us feel that what happened in the biblical story cannot happen in the reality of today. However, perhaps we are wrong to feel that way. We may not have prophets in the authentic sense, but we have the equivalent of prophecy on a slightly lower level. There is the book of Psalms and many other types of literature that deals with man in an almost prophetic sense. What greater source of inspiration is there than the last line of אדון עולם – *Adon Olam* which is "God is with me, I shall not fear." This is just as powerful as the lines we have just commented concerning the early verses of Scripture. We have much more material of this type in our liturgical and poetic literature that can inspire and fulfill all of us.

Parashah Forty-Four, *Midrash Five*

ה רבי יודן ורבי הונא, תרוויהון בשם רבי יוסי בן זימרא, רבי יודן אמר: בכל מקום שנאמר
אחרי, סמוך אחר מופלג. ור' הונא אמר: בכל מקום שנאמר אחר, סמוך אחרי מופלג..
5. AFTER (*AHAR*) THESE THINGS. R. JUDAN AND R. HUNA BOTH SAID IN
THE NAME OF R. JOSE B. R. JUDAN: WHEREVER *AHARE* OCCURS IT DE-
NOTES "IN IMMEDIATE CONNECTION WITH," WHEREAS *AHAR* DENOTES
THAT THERE IS NO CONNECTION. R. HUNA SAID: WHEREVER *AHAR* IS
STATED IT DENOTES "IN IMMEDIATE CONNECTION WITH," WHEREAS
AHARE IMPLIES THAT THERE IS NO CONNECTION.

אחר הדברים האלה. אחר הירהורי דברים שהיו שם. מי הרהר? אברהם הרהר. אמר לפני
הקב"ה: רבון העולמים, כרת ברית עם נח, שאינך מכלה את בניו, עמדתי וסיגלתי מצוות
ומעשים טובים יותר ממנו, ודחתה בריתי לבריתו. תאמר שאחר עומד ומסגל מצוות
ומעשים טובים יותר ממני, ותדחה בריתו לבריתי? א"ל הקב"ה: מנח לא העמדתי מגינים
של צדיקים, אבל ממך אני מעמיד מגינים של צדיקים. ולא עוד אלא בשעה שיהיו בניך באים
לידי עבירות ומעשים רעים, אני רואה צדיק אחד שבהם, ומכריעו עליהם, שהוא יכול לומר
למדת הדין: די! אני נוטלו ומכפר עליהם:
AFTER THESE THINGS. MISGIVINGS WERE ENTERTAINED THERE. WHO
ENTERTAINED THEM? ABRAHAM. HE SAID TO GOD: "SOVEREIGN OF THE
UNIVERSE! THOU MADEST A COVENANT WITH NOAH NOT TO EXTERMI-
NATE HIS CHILDREN; THEN I AROSE AND ACCUMULATED MERITORIOUS
ACTS AND PIOUS DEEDS, WHEREUPON MY COVENANT SUPERSEDED HIS.
PERHAPS ANOTHER WILL ARISE AND ACCUMULATE EVEN A GREATER
STORE OF PRECEPTS AND GOOD DEEDS, AND THEN A COVENANT WITH
HIM WILL SUPERSEDE THY COVENANT WITH ME?" SAID THE HOLY ONE,
BLESSED BE HE, TO HIM: "FROM NOAH – I DID NOT SET UP SHIELDS OF
THE RIGHTEOUS, BUT FROM THEE I SET UP SHIELDS OF THE RIGHTEOUS.
MOREOVER, WHEN THY CHILDREN TAKE TO TRANSGRESSIONS AND EVIL
DEEDS, I WILL SEE ONE RIGHTEOUS MAN AMONGST THEM WHO WILL BE
ABLE TO SAY TO MY ATTRIBUTE OF JUSTICE," ENOUGH! "WHEREUPON I
WILL TAKE HIM AND MAKE HIM ATONE FOR THEM."

The use of *ahar* without any special connection to what follows is
the case of Abraham in relationship to Noah and his followers. Abraham's problem was his belief that there was a covenant between God

and Noah. He is probably referring to the magnificent revelation of the rainbow and its message to mankind to remain moral. Abraham is bothered by a number of things. Was there a covenant between God and Noah? If so, why were certain branches of the family in rebellion against the covenant? Is that what happens with every covenant? Will it also happen with Abraham's covenant although he devoted his life to commandments and good deeds? God's answer to Abraham was in a series of revelations informing him that because of his own personal behavior, his family will consist of many tzaddikim, who are the real shields of the Abrahamic covenant. Granted that many of Noah's followers perished in the war against the four kings, but that has to be understood as referring to the fact that the majority of the population of that time were of the family of Noah. Abraham had מגינים – *maginim*, spiritual defenders. Noah's family had none.

Seed Thoughts

The first section of our Midrash is concerned with the words אחרי – *aharei* and אחר – *ahar*, both of which mean "after" or "afterwards." These appear in many places and at different times. R. Judan believes that *aharei* is usually followed by a thought or an incident that is connected, סמוך – *samuh*, where as *ahar* is usually followed by something not connected. This would be a good principle of interpretation except that the two Sages disagree with each other completely as the text indicates. Under these circumstances, writes the *Tiferet Tzion*, there is no room for the acceptance of a principle. You simply have to judge the meaning of the word in reference to the context in which it appears.

Additional Commentary

The Covenants of Noah and of Abraham

"Thou madest a covenant with Noah not to exterminate his children; then I arose and accumulated meritorious acts and pious deeds, whereupon my covenant superseded his. Perhaps another will arise and accumulate even a greater store of precepts and good deeds, and then a covenant with him will supersede Thy covenant with me?"

Abraham wondered: Noah was promised that God would not destroy his offspring, but I, (Abraham) got a new treaty with God and was allowed to destroy many of Noah's offspring in the war against the four kings. Will the same happen to my children if a new treaty arises? God answered that Noah had no righteous people in his offspring to protect his children, but Abraham would have many and they would protect his children. (Mirkin)

PARASHAH FORTY-FOUR, *Midrash Six*

ו היה דבר ה' אל אברם במחזה לאמר.

6. THE WORD OF THE LORD CAME UNTO ABRAM IN A VISION, ETC.

The Midrash raises the question, why are there ten Hebrew names for the prophetic experience? Prophecy is undoubtedly one of the unique features of Scripture. Without prophecy, we would have a series of laws and stories unrelated to a divine source. Prophecy is the great connection to God. We do not know who He chooses as prophets and why they were chosen, except in special circumstances. The Midrash is asking the question why ten names were needed, but the text itself does not provide an answer. The ten Hebrew words for the different manifestations of prophecy are beautifully expressed in the Hebrew language and each word contains a source which helps us understand what it is trying to say. However, in the present state of the midrashic text, its only concern is which kind of prophecy is most severe. We have three answers, but they are not comparative. They do not explain why one is better than the other.

עשרה לשונות נקראת נבואה: חזון, הטפה, דבור, אמירה, צווי, משא, משל, מליצה, חידה.

[PROPHECY] IS EXPRESSED BY TEN DESIGNATIONS: PROPHECY, VISION, PREACHING, SPEECH, SAYING, COMMAND, BURDEN, PARABLE, META-PHOR, AND ENIGMA.

The *Tiferet Tzion* asks the question of why there are ten names for prophecy. His answer is that they are related to the ten *Sefirot* that were expounded by the Kabbalists of the twelfth century. The Sefirot are emanations which apparently are meant to supplement the Creation story. The first three have to do with thought, the second three with the soul, and the last three have to do with human behavior. All of them are related to the *Ein Sof*, which is the infiniteness of God. Only the prophets understand this relationship.

ואיזו היא קשה שבכולן? רבי אליעזר אמר: חזון, שנאמר (ישעיה כא): חזות קשה הוגד לי.
רבי יוחנן אמר: דבור, שנאמר (בראשית מב): דבר האיש אדוני הארץ אתנו קשות. רבנן אמרי:
משא, כמשמעו, שנאמר (תהלים לח): כמשא כבד יכבדו ממני.

AND WHICH IS THE SEVEREST FORM? R. LEAZAR SAID: VISION, AS IT
SAYS: A GRIEVOUS VISION IS DECLARED UNTO ME (ISA. 21:2). R. JOHANAN
SAID: SPEECH (*DIBBUR*), AS IT SAYS: THE MAN, THE LORD OF THE LAND,
SPOKE (*DIBBER*) ROUGHLY WITH US, ETC. (GEN. 42:30). THE RABBIS SAID:
BURDEN, AS IT SAYS: AS A HEAVY BURDEN (PS. 38:5).

The use of the term קשות – *kashot*, meaning "severest," has to be understood to mean "very important" (Mirkin). This applies to all of the rabbis who have just been quoted.

גדול כחו של אברם, שנדבר עמו בדיבור ובחזון, שנאמר (בראשית טו): היה דבר ה' אל אברם
במחזה:

GREAT THEN WAS THE POWER OF ABRAHAM THAT [DIVINE] CONVERSE
WAS HELD WITH HIM IN VISION AND IN SPEECH.

We now come to the main point of this Midrash. The words *dibbur*, "speech," and *hazon*, "vision," have both been mentioned as extremely important. Both happen to be in the main text of our Midrash where the word of God appeared to Abraham in a vision and said to him: "Fear not Abraham." In other words, Abraham was sensitive enough that God had appeared to him by using the most important terms. Abraham was therefore fearful, and that is why God said: "Fear not Abraham." It also explains why this Midrash appears as part of an entire series of Midrashim that try to explain why Abraham was fearful and God helped resolve those fears.

Seed Thoughts

Is there a way of responding to the question as to why so many names
are needed for the phenomenon of prophecy, especially by those who
do not relate well to Kabbalistic theories, since very few commentators
have responded to this question? It simply means that other opinions
can be offered. In the Torah text, there are a few occasions where God
talks to certain individuals on matters which have nothing to do with
prophecy. For example, a Midrash yet to come speaks to King Solomon,
King Ahaz, and King David, and invites them to make whatever request
they have of the Divine. Perhaps the purpose of these special names is to
inform not only the reader of the Bible, but also the prophet that what
follows is prophecy. In other words, if any of those ten words are used,
the prophet should know that prophecy will follow. It is also a way of
explaining that every prophet is unique, and the title of his presentation
expresses that uniqueness. Perhaps this approach makes us more appreciative of this beautiful style which accompanies the prophetic word.

PARASHAH FORTY-FOUR, *Midrash Seven*

ז אל תירא אברם. ממי נתירא? ר' ברכיה אמר: משם נתירא.

7. FEAR NOT, ABRAM. WHOM DID HE FEAR? R. BEREKIAH SAID: HE
FEARED SHEM.

The reason for questioning why Abraham feared was because he had
just defeated four kings, and should have been happy to rest on his lau-
rels. Why, then, did he fear?

הה"ד (ישעיה מא) ראו איים וייראו קצות הארץ יחרדו וגו'. מה איים הללו מסויימים בים,
כך היו אברהם ושם מסויימים בעולם. וייראו, זה נתיירא מזה, וזה נתיירא מזה. זה נתיירא
מזה, לומר: שמא תאמר שם, שיש בלבו עלי, שהרגתי את בניו. וזה נתיירא מזה, לומר: שמא
תאמר אברהם, שיש בלבו עלי, שהעמדתי רשעים.

AS IT IS WRITTEN: THE ISLES SAW, AND FEARED (ISA. 41:5): JUST AS
ISLANDS STAND OUT IN THE SEA, SO WERE ABRAHAM AND SHEM OUT-
STANDING IN THE WORLD. AND FEARED: EACH ONE FEARED THE OTHER.

THE FORMER FEARED THE LATTER, THINKING: PERHAPS HE NURSES
RESENTMENT AGAINST ME FOR SLAYING HIS SONS. AND THE LATTER
FEARED THE FORMER, THINKING: PERHAPS HE NURSES RESENTMENT
AGAINST ME FOR BEGETTING WICKED OFFSPRING.

The verse in Isaiah talks about the fact that Shem and Abraham lived a far distance from each other. One lived on the eastern border of Canaan, and the other lived on the western border, around Jerusalem. In those days, these were the borders. They were not only distant geographically, but also in knowing each other. However, their friendship eventually emerged, as we shall soon see from the text.

קצות הארץ, זה שרוי בקיצו של עולם, וזה שרוי בקיצו של עולם. (שם) קרבו ויאתיון, זה קרב
אצל זה, וזה קרב אצל זה. (שם) איש את רעהו יעזורו, זה עוזר לזה בברכות, וזה עוזר לזה
במתנות. זה עוזר לזה בברכות, ויברכהו, ויאמר: ברוך אברם לאל עליון וגו'. וזה עוזר לזה
במתנות, ויתן לו מעשר מכל. (שם) ויחזק חרש, זה שם, שעשה את התיבה. את צורף, זה
אברהם, שצרפו הקב"ה בכבשן האש. מחליק פטיש את הולם פעם, שהחליק פטישו והלם
את כל באי עולם, בדרך אחת למקום. אומר לדבק טוב הוא, אלו אומות העולם, שהן אומרין
מוטב להדבק באלוה של אברהם, ולא נדבק בעבודת כוכבים של נמרוד. ויחזקהו במסמרים,
החזיק אברהם את שם במצוות ומעשים טובים. ולא ימוט, אברהם:

THE ENDS OF THE EARTH (ISA. 41:5): ONE DWELT AT ONE END OF THE
WORLD AND THE OTHER DWELT AT ANOTHER END OF THE WORLD. THEY
DREW NEAR, AND CAME (41:5): EACH APPROACHED THE OTHER. THEY
HELPED, EVERY ONE HIS NEIGHBOR (41:6): EACH HELPED THE OTHER.
ONE HELPED THE OTHER WITH BLESSINGS, AS IT SAYS: AND HE BLESSED
HIM, AND SAID: BLESSED BE ABRAM, ETC. (GEN. 14:19). AND THE OTHER
HELPED THE FORMER WITH GIFTS, AS IT SAYS: AND HE GAVE HIM A
TENTH OF ALL (14:20). SO THE CARPENTER ENCOURAGED (ISA. 41:7):
THIS ALLUDES TO SHEM, WHO MADE THE ARK; THE REFINER (41:7): THIS
IS ABRAHAM, WHOM THE HOLY ONE, BLESSED BE HE, REFINED [TRIED]
IN THE FIERY FURNACE. AND HE THAT SMOOTHETH WITH THE HAMMER
HIM THAT SMITETH THE ANVIL – PAAM (41:7): HE SMOOTHED WITH THE
HAMMER AND BEAT ALL MANKIND INTO ONE PATH (PAAM). SAYING OF
THE JOIN: IT IS GOOD (41:7): THIS REFERS TO THE NATIONS OF THE
WORLD, WHO SAID: IT IS BETTER TO BE JOINED TO THE GOD OF ABRA-
HAM THAN TO THE IDOL OF NIMROD. AND HE STRENGTHENED IT WITH
NAILS (41:7): ABRAHAM STRENGTHENED SHEM IN RELIGIOUS ACTS AND
PIOUS DEEDS; HE SHALL NOT BE MOVED (41:7): VIZ. ABRAHAM.

A scholar of the Midrash made the point that the verses in Isaiah 41 are basically a prophecy to Abraham, which is the reason why the Midrash interprets those verses in terms of Abraham and Shem. The main point of the prophecy is that Abraham was going to meet someone important. It turned out, according to this scholar, that it was at that point that Abraham met Melchizedek, the king of Jerusalem, who happened to be Shem, the son of Noah. They had feared each other, as was described, without having met, but now that they met, a remarkable friendship occurred despite the differences in their generations. The Midrash describes in detail what each did for the other.

Seed Thoughts

The *Tiferet Tzion* brings to our attention the remarkable phenomenon that Abraham prayed for Sodom and Gomorrah even though they were the most corrupt cities in our areas. Noah, on the other hand, did not pray for the welfare of the world while he was building the ark. That is probably why Isaiah (54:9) sometimes refers to the Flood as מי נח – *mei Noah*, meaning "the waters of Noah," probably because his progeny were partly responsible for the corruption of the time.

Abraham's nephew, Lot, was living in Sodom. Would it not have been enough for Abraham to pray for the relief of his nephew? That, however, was not his intention; he was appalled at the possibility of the destruction of the cities. Granted, the immorality of Sodom and Gomorrah, there had to be some people who were better than others. Why, then, should the innocent suffer with the guilty? He was very saddened when he actually saw the cities being destroyed. The Bible even has a scene where he did not leave right away; possibly, he was trying to figure out why God did not accept his prayers.

Abraham, praying for Sodom and Gomorrah, begins a series of conflicts and relationships that have existed since that time. What is our priority in life – is it the welfare and survival of the Jewish people, or is it our concern for all of humanity and the welfare of the world, or is it both, or is it a little bit of each? The best proof that this is still a modern problem is a debate in Israel whether to be a Jewish state or a democratic state.

Abraham, with this prayer for Sodom and Gomorrah, has set the stage for all of us to follow. Our mandate is to be a kingdom of priests and a holy nation. A holy nation has to do with the survival of Jews with the highest standards possible, but a kingdom of priests implies a relationship to the world at large. Abraham is saying to us that hard as it may seem, we've got to follow both. We have to practice *Am Yisrael chai,* and also that God should be King over all the earth.

⌣

Additional Commentary

What happened to the covenant with Noah?

The first point to be made is that the covenant with Noah was not abrogated – it simply disappeared through lack of use. Noah was not able to create a group of learned men who might be referred to as tzaddikim, but Abraham was. Not only did Abraham create followers wherever he lived, but he produced three generations: his own, Isaac, and Jacob. They were the real creators of the Jewish people. There was no further mention of the covenant of Noah in the Torah because nothing happened, but in the case of Abraham, the covenant was real and active.

PARASHAH FORTY-FOUR, *Midrash Eight*

ח ויאמר אברם: ה' אלהים מה תתן לי. אמר רבי יונתן: ג' הן שנאמר בהם שאל, ואלו הן:
שלמה ואחז ומלך המשיח.

8. AND ABRAM SAID: O LORD GOD, WHAT WILT THOU GIVE ME (GEN. 15:2)? R. JONATHAN SAID: THREE PERSONS WERE BIDDEN "ASK," VIZ.: SOLOMON, AHAZ, AND THE KING MESSIAH.

What concerns the Midrash is that some of the biblical personalities used an expression that God had either given them a gift or promised them a gift. The use of the Hebrew word תתן – *titen,* meaning "give," demonstrates this. By discovering three important personalities to whom God asked to tell Him what they wanted, it justifies the use of the term of a gift. Each of these three personalities had the term שאל – *shaol,* meaning "ask me," and therefore it justifies their response of having something offered to them.

שלמה, דכתיב (מלכים א ג): בגבעון נראה ה' אל שלמה בחלום הלילה, ויאמר אלהים: שאל
מה אתן לך. אחז, דכתיב (ישעיה ז): שאל לך אות מעם ה'. מלך המשיח, דכתיב ביה (תהלים ב):
שאל ממני ואתנה גוים נחלתך. רבי ברכיה ורבי אחא בשם רבי שמואל אומר: אנו מביאים
עוד שנים מן ההגדה. אברהם ויעקב. אברהם, דכתיב ביה: ה' אלהים מה תתן לי? אינו אומר
מה תתן לי, אלא שאמר לו: שאל. יעקב דכתיב (בראשית כח): וכל אשר תתן לי עשר אעשרנו
לך, אינו אומר כן, אלא שאמר לו שאל:

SOLOMON: ASK WHAT I SHALL GIVE THEE (I KINGS 3:5). AHAZ: ASK THEE
A SIGN (ISA. 7:11). THE KING MESSIAH: ASK OF ME, ETC. (PS. 2:8). R.
BEREKIAH AND R. AHI IN THE NAME OF R. SAMUEL B. NAHMAN SAID: WE
CAN CITE ANOTHER TWO FROM THE HAGGADAH: ABRAHAM AND JACOB.
ABRAHAM: WHAT WILT THOU GIVE ME? HE COULD NOT SAY: WHAT WILT
THOU GIVE ME, UNLESS HE [GOD] HAD PREVIOUSLY SAID TO HIM: ASK.
JACOB SAID: AND OF ALL THAT THOU SHALT GIVE ME (GEN. 28:22), AND
HE WOULD NOT SAY: AND OF ALL THAT THOU SHALT GIVE ME, UNLESS
HE HAD PREVIOUSLY SAID TO HIM: ASK.

What is involved here is that Abraham and Jacob have certainly been invited by God to make a request of what their needs might be. However, they were not expressed by the term *shaol* but by other forms of reference. For example, Abraham was told by God: "Your reward shall be very great." Some of the commentators explain that this refers to the World to Come, but even if so, it involves the expression of some kind of reward to Abraham.

—

Seed Thoughts

There is no question that the goal of the Midrash is to interpret the biblical text in the way that would make it most appealing and most inspiring. But it also does this by affirming the tradition and accepting the text without compromise. That is why when one is forced to comment in connection with what the text says about Jacob, the Midrash and other commentators criticize the statement of Jacob where he says: "Whatever You give me, I shall return to You through tithes and other forms of spiritual gifts." But how could Jacob have said "And of all that Thou shalt give me" when the text did not make reference to God inviting him to make such a request? The answer of the Midrash seems to be that even though we cannot find a text that contains God's invitation, we have to assume it. But do we have the right to make such an assumption? Our only response seems to be that the Midrash has introduced here a form of liberalism, probably justified by the fact that it makes this entire text more meaningful, more significant, and more inspiring. Whether the Midrash is justified in doing this is something which deserves everyone's serious reflection.

Additional Commentary

Does this Midrash offer anything new to us?

What new idea did we receive from the statements by King Solomon? We know that the Jewish religion is based on the doctrine of free choice. We could choose to do good or we could choose to do evil. The problem is that after making a choice, the challenge then becomes transforming the choice into a reality. That is why even people with the wisdom of King Solomon have the right to make such requests to God for His assistance even in making their choices possible.

In the case of Ahaz, he was also a king in Israel. What we learn from him is the fact that when God asks what he did most, he answered in terms of a miracle. We learn from this response that even asking for a miracle is a justified request. It probably may not happen, but the person who makes the request should feel that it is justified and does not merit criticism.

In connection with the Messiah who is also described as a king, it might be asked what a Messiah asks for, since he is supposed to have control over everything. Judging by the responses that have been quoted, the Messiah, who the tradition claims is already alive and with us, has accepted his role of being a dominant force among the nations of the world. But how would he go about achieving it? That is the nature of his request. (*Tiferet Tzion*)

PARASHAH FORTY-FOUR, *Midrash Nine*

ט רבי יודן ורבי אייבו בשם רבי יוחנן: ב' בני אדם אמרו דבר אחד, אברהם ודוד.

9. R. JUDAN AND R. AIBU IN R. JOHANAN'S NAME SAID: TWO MEN SAID
THE SAME THING, ABRAHAM AND DAVID.

The Midrash is bothered by the fact that as mentioned with Abraham above, he seemed to have certain doubts as whether the Almighty would fulfill His promise that Abraham would have offspring. They are therefore offering a different interpretation of what in all other respects seemed obvious to the reader. Both of the alternative explanations have been traced by the Midrash to Abraham and David.

אברהם, כתיב ביה: ה' אלהים מה תתן לי. אמר לפניו: רבש"ע, אם עתיד אני להעמיד בנים
ולהכעיסך, מוטב לי, ואני הולך ערירי.

ABRAHAM SAID: O LORD GOD: "SOVEREIGN OF THE UNIVERSE," HE CRIED
OUT TO HIM, "IF I AM DESTINED TO BEGET CHILDREN WHO WILL ANGER
THEE, 'TWERE BETTER FOR ME THAT I GO CHILDLESS."

The alternative interpretation seems to change the obvious meaning of the text. Abraham says that of course he wants offspring, but if his children would turn out to be sinners or rebels against God, if is better not to have them, and he would choose to remain alone. This is the new interpretation of the term ערירי – *ariri*, alone.

דוד אמר (תהלים קלט): חקרני אל ודע לבבי, דע הפורשים ממני וראה, אם דרך עצב בי, ונחני
בדרך עולם. אמר לפניו: רבש"ע. אם עתיד אני להעמיד בנים להעציבך, מוטב לי, ונחני
בדרך עולם.

DAVID SAID: SEARCH ME O GOD, AND KNOW MY HEART, TRY ME, AND
KNOW MY THOUGHTS – *SARAPPAY* (PS. 139:23) – KNOW THOSE WHO HAVE
SPRUNG FROM ME. AND SEE IF THERE BE ANY WAY IN ME THAT IS GRIEV-
OUS, AND LEAD ME IN THE WAY EVERLASTING (139:24): "SOVEREIGN OF
THE UNIVERSE!" HE PLEADED: "IF I AM TO BEGET CHILDREN TO PRO-
VOKE THEE, 'TWERE BETTER FOR ME THAT THOU DIDST LEAD ME IN THE
WAY EVERLASTING."

 King David's situation has been interpreted in a similar fashion. He states in his prayers, "If you examine my heart and soul, You will discover that my desire for children is above all, to honor You and fulfill Your commandments. If it were to turn out that my children would be rebellious against You, I hereby state that I would prefer to be alone and childless rather than have this happen."

ובן משק ביתי. ר"א אומר: בן משק ביתי זה לוט, שנפשו שוקקת עליו, ליורשני.

AND HE THAT SHALL BE POSSESSOR (*BEN MESHEK*) OF MY HOUSE, ETC. (GEN. 15:2). R. LEAZAR SAID IN THE NAME OF R. JOSE B. ZIMRA: BEN MESHEK BETHI (MY HOUSE) ALLUDES TO LOT, WHOSE SOUL, [SAID ABRAHAM,] LONGS (*SHOKEKETH*) TO BE MY HEIR.

In the absence of children, the question then becomes, who will inherit Abraham? The first thought is Eliezer, who was his right-hand man, throughout his life, including bringing a wife for his son Isaac. However, in the case of R. Eliezer in the name of R. Jose, in the absence of a true heir, the inheritance would go to Lot, Abraham's nephew. From the very first, Lot had his eye on this inheritance as something he would cherish very much.

הוא דמשק אליעזר, שבשבילו רדפתי מלכים עד דמשק ועזרני האל. ריש לקיש בשם בר קפרא אמר: בן משק ביתי, בר ביתי הוא אליעזר, שעל ידו רדפתי מלכים עד דמשק. ואליעזר היה שמו, שנאמר: וירק את חניכיו ילידי ביתו שמונה עשר ושלש מאות. מנין אליעזר הוה, י"ח וג' מאות:

IS DAMESEK ELIEZER [E.V. "ELIEZER OF DAMASCUS"]: THIS MEANS, FOR WHOSE SAKE I PURSUED THE KINGS AS FAR AS DAMASCUS AND GOD HELPED ME. R. SIMEON B. LAKISH SAID: BEN MESHEK BETHI MEANS "THE SON OF MY HOUSEHOLD"; IS ELIEZER OF DAMASCUS – I.E., BY HIS ASSISTANCE I PURSUED THE KINGS AS FAR AS DAMASCUS, AND HIS NAME WAS ACTUALLY ELIEZER; FOR IT SAYS: HE LED FORTH HIS TRAINED MEN, THREE HUNDRED AND EIGHTEEN (GEN. 14:14), THE NUMERICAL VALUE OF ELIEZER BEING THREE HUNDRED AND EIGHTEEN.

The Midrash comments on the fact that when Eliezer of Damascus is mentioned, the word הוא – *hu*, "he," follows his name to indicate that he was somebody well-known. It indicates that between him and Lot, Abraham would have preferred Eliezer to inherit, in place of his offspring. Not only did Eliezer accompany Abraham in pursuing the four kings, without an army and only with God's help, but there is even an indication that he did this by himself, even without Abraham. All this is to show the degree of which Abraham relied upon him. Probably, the best proof of all, in the point of view of Abraham, is that the numerical value of name of Eliezer is the same as the number of men he took to fight against the kings.

—

Seed Thoughts I

As readers of the Midrash, we want very much to approve of their teachings and support their views. Sometimes, however, questions arise and it is difficult to come to a conclusion that seems to differ from the Midrash. In my view as a reader, the original interpretation of הולך עירירי – *holekh ariri*, is that Abraham is saying to God, "In the light of the fact that I am so far childless, do not ask me what I want the most, because what I want the most does not make sense unless my original request is granted." If Abraham's main concern is the fact that his future children might rebel against God, the text would have said so unequivocally. It would not have had to hide behind linguistic styles, such as *holekh ariri*, "to walk in a lonesome way." It would, on the other hand, have stated specifically that he was worried about rebellious children. Fortunately, the outcome of Abraham's story was the birth of Isaac, so we do not have to worry too much about these alternative explanations.

—

Seed Thoughts II

The Midrash and indeed much of rabbinic literature, is fond of resorting to gematria, when some additional meaning can be achieved through its use. Gematria is a term used to the assignment of a numerical value to each letter of the alphabet. An example would be the word אהבה – *ahava*, "love" which adds up to the number 13. This can be used by some people to explain why 13 is a popular number in Judaism. Thus in our Midrash, why does it call out to our attention that the numerical value of the name Eliezer is 318, which was the number of men in his army that fought the four kings? In light of the fact that there is a saying in the Midrash, that there was a point in the battle when Abraham and Eliezer were alone in the battle. However, since Eliezer's name was equivalent to 318, it is as though he represented the whole army.

י ויאמר אברם הן לי לא נתת זרע.

10. AND ABRAM SAID: BEHOLD, TO ME THOU HAST GIVEN NO SEED (GEN. 15:3).

The question that a reader might now ask is: Why is this expression used again in light of the fact that Abram had already mentioned that he was alone and lonely – עריר – that he did not have any children? One of the answers is that the use of Hebrew terms like הן and הנה to begin a sentence gives the expression a more serious emphasis.

אמר רב שמואל בר רב יצחק: המזל דוחקני. ואומר לי אברם: אין את מוליד. א"ל הקב"ה: הן כדבריך. אברם לא מוליד, אברהם מוליד! שרי אשתך לא תקרא שמה שרי. שרי לא תלד, שרה תלד:

R. SAMUEL B. ISAAC COMMENTED: [ABRAHAM SAID:] MY PLANETARY FATE OPPRESSES ME AND DECLARES: ABRAM CANNOT BEGET A CHILD. SAID THE HOLY ONE, BLESSED BE HE, TO HIM: LET IT BE EVEN AS THY WORDS: ABRAM AND SARAI CANNOT, BEGET BUT ABRAHAM AND SARAH CAN BEGET.

The use of the term *mazal* lends itself to many interpretations. One view is that every person's destiny is determined by certain information given only to the stars and planets. This view is sometimes explicitly opposed by the rabbis. Another view is that *mazal* refers to the ordinary, natural world as distinct from God's supernatural world. It is as though in modern times, someone in Abram's position might say: "Somehow, something is happening that is not right for me." Thus, Abram is saying: "I have this feeling that I will not have any offspring." The conclusion of the Midrash is the declaration by God that the names of Abram and Sarai will be changed. Abram will become Abraham, and as the Hebrew text explains, it means "father of many nations," and Sarai will become Sarah, which means "princess." Whereas the Torah text does not explain the reason for this change of name, we can now tell from the Midrash that what is really behind the change in name is the change in status. Both Abraham and Sarah are now raised to a much higher level of leadership. Therefore, God's blessings to Abraham will be fulfilled in the life of the Patriarch and Matriarch in accordance with their new names.

—

Seed Thoughts

The change of name that the Midrash refers to should not be strange to a modern reader. Throughout history, names of individuals have been changed for the very same reason – to give them higher status and greater importance. To this day, the House of Lords in Great Britain follows that procedure. A person who is elevated to the House of Lords receives a new name and a title that connects him to a certain property designated by the government. The only difference is that in modern times, the person has the right to choose his own name. Throughout history, especially in those countries where royalty was still part of the country's laws and customs, such practices were very common. The fact that the blessings were removed from Abram and Sarai to Abraham and Sarah should be looked upon as routine.

—

Additional Commentary

Mazal and the new names of our ancestors

This is what Abraham said to the Holy One, blessed be He: "My *mazal* indicates a certain power that resides in the stars of the heavens, that were placed there to direct and teach and influence human beings. Somehow, they have influenced me so I would not father a child. It seems to say to me that my wife and I will not give birth. This is how I interpret what my *mazal* is telling me. I am also confused because I was told that strangers would not inherit me – only my offspring would." The answer of the Holy One to Abraham was: "You seem to be worried about the *mazal* and its meaning, and I will give you something that will startle you more. Your name will now be changed – no longer Abram but Abraham. Your wife's name will no longer be Sarai but Sarah. All the blessings intended for Abram and Sarai will now be offered to Abraham and Sarah, with their new name and their new status." (*HaMidrash HaMevo'ar*)

Did Abraham have any doubts?

The *Tiferet Tzion* is worried that the use of the expression ערירי – "I am alone," seems to indicate that God may not fulfill his promise of a child yet to come. The reason for this speculation is that Abraham was familiar with the life of Shem, the son of Noah, who was known as a very righteous and talented person. Unfortunately, his children rebelled against God, and that forced Abraham to be very concerned and to take notice. If such a thing could happen to Shem, maybe that danger might happen to him as well. So he concluded that rather than produce rebellious children, he would prefer to remain alone in the world, even though he would remain childless.

PARASHAH FORTY-FOUR, *Midrash Eleven*

יא והנה דבר ה' אליו לאמר לא יירשך.

11. AND, BEHOLD, THE WORD OF THE LORD CAME UNTO HIM, SAYING: THIS ONE WILL NOT INHERIT YOU (GEN. 15:4).

The possibility of a new child arising is closely connected to the whole idea of who will inherit Abraham's assets. He definitely did not want to be his nephew Lot, whose life he had protected many times, because Lot acted unworthily to him on many occasions. As for his associate Eliezer, although it does not specify his approval, one assumes he would approve the choice of Eliezer but not to be compared to the birth of a child to Sarah and himself.

רבי יודן ורבי אלעזר בשם ר' יוסי בר זימרא: ה' אליו, דבר ה' אליו, והנה דבר ה' אליו, מלאך אחר מלאך, דבור אחר דבור, אני ושלשה מלאכים נגלים עליך ואומרים לך: לוט לוטא, לא ירית לאברם. ר' הונא ורבי אלעזר בשם רבי יוסי בר זימרא: כתיב, והנה דבר ה' אליו, והנה ה' בא ודבור עמו:

R. JUDAN AND R. LEAZAR IN R. JOSE'S NAME SAID: [WE HAVE HERE,] THE LORD [SPOKE] TO HIM; THE WORD OF THE LORD CAME UNTO HIM; AND,

BEHOLD, THE WORD OF THE LORD CAME UNTO HIM: THIS SIGNIFIES, ANGEL AFTER ANGEL, ANGEL AFTER ANGEL; SPEECH AFTER SPEECH, SPEECH AFTER SPEECH; IMPLYING, I AND THREE OF MY ANGELS REVEAL OURSELVES TO THEE AND SAY TO THEE: LOT IS ACCURSED, HE SHALL NOT BE ABRAHAM'S HEIR. R. HUNA AND R. LEAZAR SAID IN R. JOSE'S NAME: IT IS WRITTEN, AND, BEHOLD, . . . THE LORD: THUS HE CAME AND SPOKE WITH HIM.

The interesting thing about the expression "The Lord spoke to him" is that it appears in the biblical text of this section three times. It is as though God sent one angel to reassure Abraham that Isaac would be born. He then sent a second angel and a third angel, or as one of the commentators said: "God and his Beth Din promised that they would do their best to reassure Abraham." The main thrust of the Midrash is that Lot would not inherit Abraham.

—

Seed Thoughts

God's concern for Abraham

According to the Midrash, the Almighty was terribly interested in the fact that Abraham should maintain the belief that the promise of a child should be forthcoming. He would not allow it to play it cool so that whatever would happen would happen. Abraham was a special person and he would have to act in a special way, and that special way would be to believe in God's promise without any ifs or buts. That is why angel after angel was sent to him to persuade him of this fact, which ultimately became fulfilled.

PARASHAH FORTY-FOUR, *Midrash Twelve*

יב ויוצא אותו החוצה.

12. AND HE BROUGHT HIM FORTH WITHOUT– *HA-HUZAH* (GEN. 15:5).

The word החוצה – *ha-hutzah*, which really means "and he brought him from the outside," is probably the most important word of this part of the Midrash. Was he brought from the outside?

רבי יהושע דסכנין בשם רבי לוי: וכי מחוץ לעולם הוציאו שאמר הכתוב: ויוצא אותו החוצה? אלא אחוי ליה שוקקי שמיא, המד"א: עד לא עשה ארץ וחוצות.

R. JOSHUA SAID IN R. LEVI'S NAME: DID HE THEN LEAD HIM FORTH WITHOUT THE WORLD, THAT IT SAYS: AND HE BROUGHT HIM FORTH WITHOUT? IT MEANS, HOWEVER, THAT HE SHOWED HIM THE STREETS OF HEAVEN, AS YOU READ: WHILE AS YET HE HAD NOT MADE THE EARTH, NOR THE OUTER SPACES – *HUZOTH* (PROV. 8:26).

In the individual biblical text, Rashi makes the point that He took him outside of his temporary dwelling in order to show him the stars above. This is not the view of the Midrash at all; החוצה meant "outside of every-thing." He showed him the universe, the entire universe, and all of its complexities. We do not know from the text whether He took him out of a tent or whether he was already under the heavens. However, it does not seem to matter in terms of what the Midrash has in mind.

אמר רבי יהודה בשם ר' יוחנן: העלה אותו למעלה מכיפת הרקיע, הוא דאמר ליה: הבט נא השמימה. אין הבטה אלא מלמעלה למטה.

R. JUDAH B. R. SIMON SAID IN R. JOHANAN'S NAME: HE LIFTED HIM UP ABOVE THE VAULT OF HEAVEN; HENCE HE SAYS TO HIM, LOOK (*HABBET*) NOW TOWARD HEAVEN [GEN. 15:5], *HABBET* SIGNIFYING TO LOOK DOWN FROM ABOVE.

What the Midrash is now telling us is that Abraham was taken into a position way beyond what we would look upon as the sky. The interest-ing thing is the use of the Hebrew term הבט – *habbet*, which is only used when someone from a higher position looks down on another area. Abraham was placed in such a lofty position that he was commanded not to look up at the stars, but rather to look down upon them. One of the important lessons of this scene is to indicate to Abraham, who had shown an interest in the *mazalot* (the signs of the zodiac which he felt had the power to indicate the future), that this scene of Abraham being placed way above the stars and beyond the mazalot indicates how unimportant the mazalot were, and how only in God is there a future for him and for his spiritual program.

רבנן אמרי: נביא את ואין את אסטרולוגוס, שנאמר (בראשית כ): ועתה השב אשת האיש כי נביא הוא.

THE RABBIS SAID: [GOD SAID TO HIM]: THOU ART A PROPHET, NOT AN ASTROLOGER, AS IT SAYS: NOW THEREFORE RESTORE THE MAN'S WIFE, FOR HE IS A PROPHET (GEN. 20:7).

This Midrash has unusual interpretations of the word נביא – *navi*, which usually means "prophet"; at this stage, it is used to indicate the special powers possessed by Abraham, which should annul his interest in the mazalot. Later on, the term is used again in the Midrash, and it will be commented on.

בימי ירמיה בקשו ישראל לבא לידי מדה זו ולא הניח להם הקב"ה, הה"ה (ירמיה י): כה אמר ה': אל דרך הגוים אל תלמדו, ומאותות השמים אל תחתו וגו'. כבר אברהם אביכם בקש לבא לידי מדה זו ולא הנחתי אותו. וא"ר לוי: עד דסנדלא ברגליך דריס כובא, וכל מי שהוא נתון למטה מהם הוא מתירא מהם, אבל את, שאת נתון למעלה מהם דיישם.

IN THE DAYS OF JEREMIAH, THE ISRAELITES WISHED TO ENTERTAIN THIS BELIEF [IN ASTROLOGY], BUT THE HOLY ONE, BLESSED BE HE, WOULD NOT PERMIT THEM. THUS IT IS WRITTEN: THUS SAITH THE LORD: LEARN NOT THE WAY OF THE NATIONS, AND BE NOT DISMAYED AT THE SIGNS OF HEAVEN, ETC. (JER. 10:2): YOUR ANCESTOR ABRAHAM WISHED TO EN-TERTAIN THIS BELIEF LONG AGO, BUT I WOULD NOT PERMIT HIM. R. LEVI SAID: WHILE THE SANDAL IS ON YOUR FOOT TREAD DOWN THE THORN; HE WHO IS PLACED BELOW THEM FEARS THEM, BUT THOU [ABRAHAM] ART PLACED ABOVE THEM, SO TRAMPLE THEM DOWN [IGNORE THEM].

ר' יודן בשם ר"א אמר: שלשה דברים מבטלים גזירות רעות, ואלו הם: תפלה וצדקה ותשובה, ושלשתן נאמרו בפסוק אחד, הה"ד (ד"ה ב ז): ויכנעו עמי אשר נקרא שמי עליהם. ויתפללו, זו תפלה. ויבקשו פני, הרי צדקה, כמד"א (תהלים יז): אני בצדק אחזה פניך. וישובו מדרכם הרעה, זו תשובה. ואח"כ (ד"ה ב ז): ואסלח לחטאם וארפא את ארצם.

R. JUDAN SAID IN R. LEAZAR'S NAME: THREE THINGS NULLIFY A DECREE [OF EVIL], VIZ. PRAYER, RIGHTEOUSNESS, AND REPENTANCE. AND THE THREE ARE ENUMERATED IN ONE VERSE: IF MY PEOPLE, UPON WHOM MY NAME IS CALLED, SHALL HUMBLE THEMSELVES, AND PRAY (II CHRON. 7:14) – HERE YOU HAVE PRAYER; AND SEEK MY FACE (7:14) ALLUDES TO RIGHTEOUSNESS, AS YOU READ, I SHALL BEHOLD THY FACE IN RIGHTEOUSNESS (PS. 17:15); AND TURN FROM THEIR EVIL WAYS (II CHRON. 7:14) DENOTES REPENTANCE; AFTER THAT, THEN WILL I FORGIVE THEIR SIN (7:14).

W e should note here that the three values have been incorporated into the prayer service in Judaism. They are the goal or the major interpretation of the High Holiday service which ends with this proclamation that penitence, prayer, and righteousness remove the evil decrees. The prayer book has taken these values out of the context of the verse where it originated, and has made them into one of the most important spiritual achievements possible in Judaism.

ר' הונא בר רב יוסף אמר: אף שנוי שם ומעשה טוב. שנוי השם, מאברהם, ולא יקרא עוד שמך אברם. מעשה טוב, מאנשי נינוה, שנאמר (יונה ג): וירא אלהים את מעשיהם כי שבו וגו'.
R. HUNA SAID IN R. JOSEPH'S NAME: ALSO CHANGE OF NAME AND GOOD DEEDS. CHANGE OF NAME IS LEARNED FROM ABRAHAM AND SARAH. GOOD DEEDS, FROM THE PEOPLE OF NINEVEH, FOR IT SAYS: AND GOD SAW THEIR WORKS, THAT THEY TURNED FROM THEIR EVIL WAYS (JONAH 3:10).

T he Midrash holds a few additional possibilities that might be helpful in eliminating a severe decree. One of them is the change of name, which we learn from the story of Abraham and Sarah. They also add the power of good deeds, as demonstrated by the people of Nineveh, who were forgiven because of their penitence.

וי"א: אף שנוי מקום, שנאמר (בראשית יב): ויאמר ה' אל אברם לך לך.
SOME SAY, CHANGE OF PLACE, TOO, FOR IT SAYS: NOW THE LORD SAID UNTO ABRAM: GET THEE OUT OF THY COUNTRY, ETC. (GEN. 12:1).

C hange of location is also a way of escaping an evil decree, and also comes from the story of Abraham and Sarah. We follow the command of לך לך – *lekh lekha*, to go from place to place.

ר' הונא אמר: אף התענית, שנאמר (תהלים כ): יענך ה' ביום צרה וגו'. רבא בר מחסיא ורבי
חמא בן גריון בשם רב אמר: יפה תענית לחלום, כאש בנעורת. א"ר יוסף: ובו ביום ואפילו
בשבת:

R. HUNA SAID: ALSO FASTING, AS IT SAYS: THE LORD ANSWER THEE IN
THE DAY OF TROUBLE (PS. 20:20). RABA B. MEHASIA AND R. HAMA B.
GURIA SAID IN RAB'S NAME: FASTING IS AS EFFECTIVE FOR COUNTER-
ACTING AN EVIL DREAM AS FIRE FOR CONSUMING FLAX. R. JOSEPH SAID:
PROVIDING IT IS DONE ON THE SAME DAY, EVEN ON THE SABBATH.

―

Seed Thoughts I

The second part of the Midrash deals with those procedures which can
protect one from the evil decrees that either affect an individual or a
community. Among the effects that are listed are repentance, prayer,
and charity, to which have been added factors such as a change of name,
a change of location, and fasting. What interested me is to note that
the word for "decree," גזרה – *gezerah*, is written by itself, and one simply
understands that the word *gezerah* means "an evil decree." On the other
hand, very often we are told that the practice of these procedures will
eliminate what is written as רוע הגזרה – *roa ha-gezerah*, which literally
means "the evil of the decree." This is similar to the manner in which
these values are stated in the prayer service. The words that are relevant
here are תשובה – *teshuvah* (repentance), תפילה – *tefillah* (prayer), and
צדקה – *zedakah* (righteousness or charity). The lesson is that the complete decree is not eliminated, but that the evil part of it is. That is to say
such things as pain, suffering, bad dreams, etc. The elimination of such
influences makes the rest of the decree bearable, and that is sufficient for
those who know the power of the decree when the evil is not eliminated.

―

Seed Thoughts II

It is very difficult for a generation that experienced the Holocaust to
react normally to a Midrash which offers remedies for evil decrees that
do not really work. The rabbis of the Midrash knew all about Jewish
suffering over the years, but none have experienced what we call the
Holocaust. Six million Jews were killed during the 1940s; as for those

who survived, commentators have divided them into three categories. One section whose numbers we cannot really calculate have reacted to the Holocaust by lessening their commitment to Judaism, by losing their faith, or changing their way of life from a positive to a negative image of Jewish life. Another section of the survivors have reacted in a completely opposite direction: their Jewish lives have been strengthened, their religious views made stronger, because their position is that the Holocaust was the responsibility of man, not God. In between these two elements, you have the majority of Jewish survivors who are full of questions, full of doubts, completely puzzled by the events, and waiting for someone to offer a reasonable explanation. This is the ideal moment for the Messiah to appear. Let us hope that it may really happen.

Additional Commentary

God's joy in Abraham's talents

All of us are accustomed when we enter a new home or experience some kind of renovation, we enjoy the pleasure of inviting guests to see the new changes and to share with the owner the joys of his new development. This is how the opening phrases of our Midrash should be understood. God invited Abraham to come outside his dwelling. According to the Midrash, however, he showed much more than the stars in the sky. He showed him the entire universe, including those that were not part of our own, such as the stars, the moon, and the various other forms that the astronomers bring to our attention. It is difficult to use the word "pride" in connection to God, but He seemed to be proud of Abraham not only because he was a human being and therefore the highest goal of Creation, but also because he had reached some of the highest possibilities of being a human being. That is how we explain the verse אשר ברא אלהים לעשות – *asher bara Elohim laasot*, meaning that God created the universe in an incomplete fashion, and it was up to human beings to complete it through their thoughts, their actions, and their inspiration. (Mirkin)

PARASHAH FORTY-FOUR, *Midrash Thirteen*

יג ויאמר אליו אני ה' אשר הוצאתיך מאור כשדים וגו'.

13. AND HE BELIEVED IN THE LORD . . . AND HE SAID UNTO HIM: I AM THE
LORD THAT BROUGHT THEE OUT OF UR OF THE CHALDEES, ETC. (GEN.
15:6F.).

The problem facing the Midrash is that nowhere in the biblical text
does it say specifically that God took Abraham out of Ur Kasdim (Ur of
the Chaldees).

ר"א בן יעקב ורבנן ר"א בן יעקב אמר: מיכאל ירד והצילו מכבשן האש.

R. LIEZER B. JACOB SAID: MICHAEL DESCENDED AND RESCUED ABRAHAM
FROM THE FIERY FURNACE.

Rabbi Eliezer and the Rabbis offer different views in explaining this
problem. Rabbi Eliezer claims that the angel Michael liberated Abraham from the fiery furnace, and this took place before the family left for
Ur Kasdim.

ורבנן אמרי: הקב"ה הצילו, הה"ד (בראשית טו): אני ה' אשר הוצאתיך מאור כשדים.

THE RABBIS SAID: THE HOLY ONE, BLESSED BE HE, RESCUED HIM; THUS
IT IS WRITTEN: I AM THE LORD THAT BROUGHT THEE OUT OF UR OF THE
CHALDEES.

The Rabbis maintain that it was God who delivered Abraham from
the fiery furnace, and since this was before the family moved its location,
it can truly be said that God motivated Abraham to leave Ur Kasdim.

ואימתי ירד מיכאל? בחנניה מישאל ועזריה:

AND WHEN DID MICHAEL DESCEND? IN THE CASE OF HANANIAH,
MISHAEL, AND AZARIAH.

This was during the time of Nebuchadnezzar.

Additional Commentary

By Angel or by God

In Daniel 3:28, it says that the angel saved Hanaiah, Mishael, and Aza-riah. Therefore, says R. Eliezer Ben Jacob, this angel must have liberated Abraham as well from the fire of the furnace of Nimrod. However, the Rabbis say it was God himself who saved Abraham since here it states: "I am God who took you out of Ur Kasdim." (Mirkin)

PARASHAH FORTY-FOUR, *Midrash Fourteen*

יד ויאמר ה' אלהים: במה אדע? ר' חייא ברבי חנינא אמר: לא כקורא תגר, אלא אמר לו:
באיזו זכות? א"ל: בכפרות שאני נותן לפניך. ויאמר אליו: קחה לי עגלה משולשת, הראה לו
ג' מיני פרים וג' מיני שעירים וג' מיני אילים. ג' מיני פרים: פר יוה"כ, ופר הבא על כל המצוות,
ועגלה ערופה. וג' מיני שעירים: שעירי רגלים, שעירי ראשי חדשים, ושעירה של יחיד. וג'
מיני אילים: אשם ודאי, ואשם תלוי, וכבשה של יחיד. ותור וגוזל, תור ובר יונה. ויקח לו
את כל אלה. רשב"י ורבנן. רשב"י אומר: כל הכפרות הראה לו, ועשירית האיפה לא הראה
לו. ורבנן אמרי: אף עשירית האיפה הראה לו. נאמר כאן ויקח לו את כל אלה, ונאמר להלן
(ויקרא ב) והבאת את המנחה אשר יעשה מאלה לה'. ואת הצפור לא בתר. הראה לו הקב"ה
שמבדילים בעולת העוף, ואין מבדילים בחטאת העוף:

14. AND HE SAID: O LORD GOD, WHEREBY SHALL I KNOW THAT I SHALL INHERIT IT (GEN. 15:8)? R. HAMA B. HANINA SAID: [HE SPOKE] NOT AS ONE MAKING A COMPLAINT, BUT HE ASKED HIM: THROUGH WHAT MERIT [WILL I INHERIT THE LAND]? GOD REPLIED: "THROUGH THE MERIT OF THE ATONING SACRIFICES WHICH I WILL INSTITUTE FOR THY SONS." AND HE SAID UNTO HIM: TAKE ME A HEIFER OF THREE YEARS OLD (*MESHULSHELETH*), A SHE-GOAT OF THREE YEARS OLD (*MESHULSHE-LETH*), AND A RAM OF THREE YEARS OLD (*MESHULASH*), ETC. (15:9F.). HE SHOWED HIM THREE KINDS OF BULLOCKS, THREE KINDS OF GOATS, AND THREE KINDS OF RAMS. THREE KINDS OF BULLOCKS: THE BULLOCK SACRIFICED ON THE DAY OF ATONEMENT, THE BULLOCK BROUGHT ON ACCOUNT OF [THE UNWITTING TRANSGRESSION OF] ANY OF THE PRE-CEPTS, AND THE HEIFER WHOSE NECK WAS BROKEN. THREE KINDS OF GOATS: THE GOATS SACRIFICED ON FESTIVALS, THE GOATS SACRIFICED ON NEW MOON, AND THE GOAT BROUGHT BY AN INDIVIDUAL. THREE

KINDS OF RAMS: THE GUILT-OFFERING OF CERTAIN OBLIGATION, THE GUILT-OFFERING OF DOUBT, AND THE LAMB [SIN-OFFERING] BROUGHT BY AN INDIVIDUAL. AND A TURTLE-DOVE (TOR) AND A YOUNG PIGEON (GOZAL): THAT IS, A TURTLE-DOVE AND A YOUNG PIGEON. AND HE TOOK HIM ALL THESE, ETC. R. SIMEON B. YOHAI SAID: THE HOLY ONE, BLESSED BE HE, SHOWED ABRAHAM ALL THE ATONING SACRIFICES SAVE THE TENTH OF AN EPHAH [OF FINE MEAL]. THE RABBIS SAID: HE SHOWED HIM THE TENTH OF AN EPHAH [OF FINE MEAL] ALSO; FOR ALL THESE IS STATED HERE, WHILE ELSEWHERE IT IS SAID, AND THOU SHALT BRING THE MEAL-OFFERING THAT IS MADE OF THESE THINGS (LEV. 2:8). BUT THE BIRD DIVIDED HE NOT [GEN. 15:10]. HE INTIMATED TO HIM THAT THE FOWL BURNT-OFFERING IS DIVIDED, BUT THE FOWL SIN-OFFERING IS NOT DIVIDED.

⁓

Seed Thoughts

The question that Abraham was asking was not meant to question God or to test doubts on His ability to foretell the future. Abraham was simply trying to find out what particular merit his children should have so that he would be able to help them achieve this great value, and thereby benefit from the divine promises. The answer given by the Midrash is a listing in miniature of some of the most important offerings that took place in the Temple. The meaning of this answer is that the children of Abraham would do their best to preserve the Temple and its system of offerings, which was the basic religious institution, so long as it remained intact. That would be the merit that would entitle them to God's blessings.

PARASHAH FORTY-FOUR, *Midrash Fifteen*

טו ד"א: קחה לי עגלה משולשת, זו בבל שהעמידה ג' מלכים: נבוכדנצר ואויל מרודך
ובלשצר. ועז משולשת, זו מדי, שהיתה מעמידה ג' מלכים: כורש ודריוש ואחשורוש. ואיל
משולש, זו יון. ר' אלעזר ור' יוחנן. ר"א אמר: כל הרוחות כבשו בני יון, ורוח מזרחית לא
כבשו. א"ל רבי יוחנן: והכתיב (דניאל ח): ראיתי את האיל מנגח ימה וצפונה ונגבה, וכל חיות
לא יעמדו לפניו ואין מציל מידו, ועשה כרצונו והגדיל. הוא דעתיה דר"א: דלא אמר מזרחית.
ותור וגוזל, זו מלכות אדום, תור הוא, אלא שגזלן הוא. ד"א: ויקח לו את כל אלה. ר"י ור'
נחמיה. ר"י אמר: שרי עובדי כוכבים הראה לו. רבי נחמיה אמר: שרי ישראל הראה לו. על
דעתיה דר"י: קתדרין דדין, לקבל קתדרין דדין. על דעתיה דר"נ: ששם היו סנהדרי גדולה
של ישראל יושבת וחותמת דיניהם של ישראל. ואת הצפור לא בתר.

15. ANOTHER INTERPRETATION: TAKE ME A HEIFER THREEFOLD: THIS ALLUDES TO BABYLONIA, WHICH PRODUCED THREE KINGS, NEBUCHADNEZZAR, EVIL-MERODACH, AND BALSHAZZAR; AND A SHE-GOAT THREEFOLD: THIS ALLUDES TO MEDIA, WHICH PRODUCED THREE KINGS: CYRUS, DARIUS, AND AHASUERUS; AND A RAM THREEFOLD: THIS ALLUDES TO GREECE. R. LEAZAR AND R. JOHANAN EXPLAINED HOW. R. LEAZAR SAID: SHE CONQUERED ALL PARTS [OF THE WORLD] SAVE THE EAST. SAID R. JOHANAN TO HIM: EVEN SO IT IS WRITTEN: I SAW THE RAM PUSHING WESTWARD, AND NORTHWARD, AND SOUTHWARD; AND NO BEASTS COULD STAND BEFORE HIM (DAN. 8:4), AND THAT IS HIS [R. ELEAZAR'S] REASON TOO, SINCE EASTWARD IS NOT STATED. AND A TURTLE-DOVE AND A YOUNG PIGEON (*GOZAL*). THIS REFERS TO EDOM [ROME]: IT WAS A TURTLE-DOVE, BUT OF A PREDATORY NATURE. AND HE TOOK HIM ALL THESE. R. JUDAH SAID: HE SHOWED HIM THE PRINCES OF THE GENTILE NATIONS. R. NEHEMIAH SAID: HE SHOWED HIM THE PRINCES OF ISRAEL. ON THE VIEW OF R. JUDAH, [HE LAID EACH HALF OVER AGAINST THE OTHER SYMBOLIZED] THE THRONE OF ONE [PRINCE] OPPOSING THE THRONE OF ANOTHER. ACCORDING TO R. NEHEMIAH, IT SYMBOLIZED THE PLACE WHERE THE GREAT SANHEDRIN [COURT] OF ISRAEL SAT AND DETERMINED THE LAWS OF ISRAEL. BUT THE BIRD DIVIDED HE NOT.

ר' אבא בר כהנא בשם ר' לוי אמר: הראה לו הקב"ה כל מי שהוא מעמיד פנים בגל, הגל
שוטפו, וכל מי שאינו מעמיד פנים בגל, אין הגל שוטפו:

R. ABBA B. KAHANA SAID IN R. LEVI'S NAME: THE HOLY ONE, BLESSED BE HE, INTIMATED TO HIM THAT HE WHO ATTEMPTS TO RESIST THE WAVE

IS SWEPT AWAY BY IT, BUT HE WHO BENDS BEFORE IT IS NOT SWEPT
AWAY BY IT.

～

Seed Thoughts I

The question that Abraham asked in the previous Midrash "What
do my children have to do in order to acquire merit?" should also be
understood as a question that applies to this particular Midrash. The
difference is that, in this Midrash, the various offerings are treated as
symbols – each group of offerings represents kings of a particular period. One thing all of them have in common is that they oppressed the
Jewish community wherever they lived, with the possible exception of
Cyrus, Darius, and Ahasuerus. And even their behavior is sometimes
questionable. However, the answer to Abraham's question lies in the
very fact of the persecution. Jews suffered because they were Jews, and
that is the great merit that all of us and all of them share.

～

Seed Thoughts II

This Midrash includes a thought which is probably the most conten-
tious debate that the Jewish people have ever had throughout their history. It was first stated in the Talmud (Tractate *Taanit* 20a) and now we
find it reflected in this Midrash and a few others that follow. If you were
in the ocean and a big wave comes towards you, if you fight it, sooner or
later other waves will come through and you will eventually lose your
life. By the same token, if you allow the wave to carry you back, you
will be saved. In other words, Jews should not fight their persecutors or
meet violence with violence, because they are sure to lose. They have
to find other ways of fighting, and the Midrash will recommend later
on to move from one location to another, from one country to another.
The Zionist movement was the great protest against this point of view;
it believed in Jewish independence, Jewish sovereignty, and freedom to
act as Jews. It was this view that created the State of Israel, and although
its security is still being sought after, the vast majority of Jews go along
with the Zionist movement. On the other hand, there are still small sec-

tors of Jewry, particularly some of the ultra-Orthodox, who feel that the advice of the Talmudic literature is the best one for the Jews.

PARASHAH FORTY-FOUR, *Midrash Sixteen*

טז וירד העיט על הפגרים. א"ר אסי: נסב אברהם מכישה, והוה מכיש להון, ולא היו מכתשין. אעפ"כ וישב אברם, בתשובה. אמר רבי עזריה: לכשיעשו בניך פגרים, בלא גידים ועצמות, זכותך עומדת להן:

16. AND THE BIRDS OF PREY CAME DOWN UPON THE CARCASSES AND ABRAM DROVE THEM AWAY (GEN. 15:11). R. ASSI SAID: ABRAHAM TOOK A FLAIL AND BEAT THEM, BUT THEY WERE NOT SMITTEN [KILLED], YET EVEN SO, ABRAM DROVE THEM AWAY (*WAYYASHSHEB*) – BY REPENTANCE. R. AZARIAH SAID: [GOD HINTED TO ABRAM]: WHEN THY CHILDREN BECOME AS CARCASSES [CORPSES] WITHOUT SINEWS OR BONES, THY MERIT WILL SUPPORT THEM.

The Midrash is careful to describe that when Abraham tried to eliminate the birds of prey through physical opposition on his part, he did not succeed. It is that fact or description that motivates the text in saying that physical opposition is not the way to eliminate either hatred of Jews or discrimination against Jews. This is the argument that has to be faced by the majority of Jews in our day who disagree with this point of view.

Seed Thoughts

This is the third Midrash which deals with the question of how Jews should oppose their oppressors. If this had happened only once, one could dismiss it as an aberration of their thinking. But when it appears three times in the Midrash in addition to the Talmud in the Tractate of *Taanit*, it has to be taken seriously. We have every right to argue with the *Haredim* ("the pious ones," the term used in Israel for the ultra-Orthodox), if we differ with them politically. On the other hand, they have every right to their opinions, which are backed up by the strong authority of Bible and Midrash. It is not easy to differentiate between political opposition and ideological disagreement, but we have to do that as best as we can.

On the other hand, we can explain that when the rabbis referred to "riding with the wave" and not opposing it, it may have been referring to the Jewish communities in the Diaspora who are at the mercy of the governments under which they live.

PARASHAH FORTY-FOUR, *Midrash Seventeen*

יז ויהי השמש לבא. רבי יהושע דסכנין בשם רבי לוי אמר: תחלת מפלה שינה דמיך ליה,
ולא לעי באורייתא דמיך ליה, ולא עביד עבודה. רב אמר: שלשה תרדמות הן: תרדמת
שינה, ותרדמת נבואה, ותרדמת מרמיטה. תרדמת שינה (בראשית ב): ויפל ה' אלהים תרדמה
על האדם ויישן. תרדמת נבואה (בראשית טו): ויהי השמש לבא ותרדמה נפלה על אברם.
ותרדמת מרמיטה, שנאמר (שמואל א כו): ואין רואה, ואין יודע, ואין מקיץ, כי כלם ישנים, כי
תרדמת ה' נפלה עליהם. ורבנן אמרי: אף תרדמה של שטות, דכתיב (ישעיה כט): כי נסך ה'
עליכם רוח תרדמה וגו'.

17. AND IT CAME TO PASS, THAT, WHEN THE SUN WAS GOING DOWN, ETC. (GEN. 15:12). R. JOSHUA OF SIKNIN SAID IN R. LEVI'S NAME: THE BEGIN-NING OF A MAN'S DOWNFALL IS SLEEP: BEING ASLEEP, HE DOES NOT ENGAGE IN STUDY AND DOES NO WORK. RAB SAID: THERE ARE THREE KINDS OF TORPOR (*TARDEMAH*): THE TORPOR OF SLEEP, THE TORPOR OF PROPHECY, AND THE TORPOR OF UNCONSCIOUSNESS. THE TORPOR OF SLEEP: THEN THE LORD GOD CAUSED A DEEP SLEEP TO FALL UPON THE MAN, AND HE SLEPT (GEN. 2:21). THE TORPOR OF PROPHECY: AND IT CAME TO PASS, THAT, WHEN THE SUN WAS GOING DOWN, A DEEP SLEEP FELL UPON ABRAM. THE TORPOR OF UNCONSCIOUSNESS: AND NO MAN SAW IT, NOR KNEW IT, NEITHER DID ANY AWAKE; FOR THEY WERE ALL ASLEEP; BECAUSE A DEEP SLEEP FROM THE LORD WAS FALLEN UPON THEM (I SAM. 26:12). THE RABBIS SAID: ALSO THE TORPOR OF FOLLY, AS IT IS WRITTEN: STUPEFY YOURSELVES, AND BE STUPID! . . . FOR THE LORD HATH POURED OUT UPON YOU THE SPIRIT OF DEEP SLEEP (ISA. 29:9F.).

This section is self-explanatory, because it is based on stories in Scrip-ture which are well-known and self-evident.

ר' חנינה בר יצחק אמר: שלש נובלות הן. נובלות מיתה – שינה, נובלות נבואה – חלום,
נובלות העוה"ב – שבת. ר' אבין מוסיף תרתין: נובלות אורה של מעלה – גלגל חמה, נובלות
חכמה של מעלה – תורה.

R. HANINA [OR R. HINENA] B. ISAAC SAID: THERE ARE THREE INCOM-
PLETE PHENOMENA: THE INCOMPLETE EXPERIENCE OF DEATH IS SLEEP;
AN INCOMPLETE FORM OF PROPHECY IS THE DREAM; THE INCOMPLETE
FORM OF THE NEXT WORLD IS THE SABBATH. R. ABIN ADDED ANOTHER
TWO: THE INCOMPLETE FORM OF THE HEAVENLY LIGHT IS THE ORB OF
THE SUN; THE INCOMPLETE FORM OF THE HEAVENLY WISDOM IS THE
TORAH.

והנה אימה חשיכה גדולה נופלת עליו. אימה, זו בבל, דכתיב (דניאל ג): באדין נבוכדנצר
התמלי חמא. חשיכה, זו מדי, שהחשיכה עיניהם של ישראל, בצום ובתענית. גדולה, זו יון.
ר' סימון ורבנן. רבי סימון אמר: מאה ועשרים דוכסים, מאה ועשרים אפרכון, מאה ועשרים
אסטרטליטין. ורבנן אמרי: מס' ס', דכתיב (דברים א): נחש שרף ועקרב. נחש, זו בבל. שרף,
זו מדי. עקרב, זה יון. מה עקרב זו יולדת לס' ס', כך העמידה מלכות יון מס' ס'. נופלת עליו,
זו אדום, שנאמר: מקול נפלם רעשה הארץ. נופלת עליו, זו בבל, דכתיב
בה (ישעיה כא): נפלה נפלה בבל. גדולה, זו מדי, דכתיב (אסתר ג): אחר הדברים האלה גדל
המלך אחשורוש. חשיכה, זו יון, שהחשיכה עיניהם של ישראל בגזרותיה, שהיתה אומרת
לישראל: כתבו על קרן השור, שאין לכם חלק באלהי ישראל. אימה, זו אדום, דכתיב (דניאל
ז): וארו חיוא רביעאה, דחילה ואמתני, ותקיפא יתירה:

AND, LO, A DREAD, EVEN A GREAT DARKNESS, FELL UPON HIM (GEN.
15:12). DREAD REFERS TO BABYLON, AS IT IS WRITTEN: THEN WAS NE-
BUCHADNEZZAR FILLED WITH FURY (DAN. 3:19). DARKNESS REFERS TO
MEDIA, WHICH DARKENED THE EYES OF ISRAEL WITH FASTING AND
TRIBULATION; GREAT REFERS TO GREECE. R. SIMON SAID: THE KING-
DOM OF GREECE SET UP ONE HUNDRED AND TWENTY COMMANDERS,
ONE HUNDRED AND TWENTY GOVERNORS, AND ONE HUNDRED AND
TWENTY GENERALS. THE RABBIS SAID: SIXTY OF EACH, FOR IT IS WRIT-
TEN: SERPENTS, FIERY SERPENTS, AND SCORPIONS (DEUT. 8:15): JUST AS
THE SCORPION LAYS SIXTY EGGS AT A TIME, SO DID THE GREEK STATE
SET UP SIXTY OF EACH. FELL UPON HIM ALLUDES TO EDOM [ROME], AS
IT IS WRITTEN: THE EARTH QUAKETH AT THE NOISE OF THEIR FALL
(JER. 49:21). SOME REVERSE IT: FELL UPON HIM (GEN. 15:12) ALLUDES
TO BABYLON, AS IT IS WRITTEN: FALLEN, FALLEN IS BABYLON (ISA.
21:9). GREAT ALLUDES TO MEDIA, AS IT IS WRITTEN: KING AHASUERUS
DID MAKE GREAT, ETC. (EST. 3:1). DARKNESS ALLUDES TO GREECE THAT
DARKENED THE EYES OF ISRAEL WITH ITS DECREES. DREAD ALLUDES

TO EDOM, AS IT IS WRITTEN: AFTER THIS I SAW ... A FOURTH BEAST,
DREADFUL AND TERRIBLE (DAN. 7:7).

~

Seed Thoughts

The *Tiferet Tzion* says that this section has to be understood as relating
to the verse where God says to Abraham: "Fear not for I will protect
you." Why such an interpretation should appear at this point probably
has an explanation, but is not too important to affect the meaning. This
is what the *Tiferet Tzion* says. The first person to experience sleep was
tremendously terrified – he did not know what sleep was, and he did
not know whether he would wake up. When sleep is interpreted simply
as something like death, but far from death itself, this fear is eliminated.
The same thing happened with dreams. A nightmare can be very ter-
rifying. When an individual knows and learns that a dream can be used
for the highest levels of prophecy, his fear becomes manageable and
acceptable. The fact that the Sabbath is looked upon as a preview of the
World to Come is one of the great teachings not only of the Sabbath but
also of the World to Come.

~

Additional Commentary

The three names of the serpent

The serpent (or נחש – *nahash*) is identified with Babylon. The reason
for this is that the serpent was the first creature to oppose Adam and interfere with his life by his attempt to befriend Eve. The fiery serpent (or
שרף – *saraph*) is usually attacked from a distance and is not allowed to
come close. That is why it is identified with the Medes and the Persians,
since Haman added the name "Medes" to his document oppressing the
Jews. The scorpion (or עקרב – *akrab*) is identified with Rome because
they were never successful in eliminating the *akrab* from attacking them,
and similarly, the Rabbis could not foresee the end and/or the defeat of
Rome.

There are three parallels given: sleep to death, dreams to prophecy,
and the Sabbath to the World to Come. Sleep is a little bit like death

since the higher functions of the body are dormant and only the involuntary functions are active. Dreams are a bit similar to prophecy in that they utilize symbols and metaphors to represent ideas. Finally, the Sabbath is a bit like the World to Come since we refrain from toiling in this world and try to just enjoy the benefit of our labors and reach to attain spiritual goals. See also *Berakhot* 57b. (B.R. Shuchat)

PARASHAH FORTY-FOUR, *Midrash Eighteen*

יח ויאמר לאברם ידוע תדע כי גר יהיה זרעך. ידוע, שאני מפזרן, תדע שאני מכנסן. ידוע,
שאני ממשכנן, תדע שאני פורקן. ידוע, שאני משעבדן, תדע שאני גואלן. כי גר יהיה זרעך
בארץ לא להם, משיראה לך זרע. א"ר יודן: גירות בארץ לא להם. עבדות, עינוי לאספטיא
שלהם:

18. AND HE SAID UNTO ABRAM: KNOW, YEA KNOW (GEN: 15:13): KNOW THAT I SHALL DISPERSE THY SEED, KNOW THAT I WILL GATHER THEM TOGETHER; KNOW THAT I WILL GIVE THEM IN PLEDGE, KNOW THAT I WILL REDEEM THEM; KNOW THAT I WILL ALLOW THEM TO BE ENSLAVED, KNOW THAT I WILL FREE THEM. THAT THY SEED SHALL BE A STRANGER IN A LAND THAT IS NOT THEIRS, AND SHALL SERVE THEM, AND THEY SHALL AFFLICT THEM FOUR HUNDRED YEARS: THIS MEANS, UNTIL FOUR HUNDRED YEARS AFTER SEED SHALL BE GRANTED TO THEE. R. JUDAN SAID: THE CONDITION OF BEING STRANGERS, IN SERVITUDE, AND AFFLICTED IN A LAND NOT THEIRS WAS TO LAST FOUR HUNDRED YEARS, WHICH WAS THEIR DECREED TERM.

The key to this Midrash is a special Hebrew grammatical form which combines two formal verbs with each other in order to strengthen and emphasize their message. ידוע תדע – *yadoa teda* – is a means of conveying knowledge to the Children of Israel, whether it says *yadoa* or *teda*, or if both are connected, such as *yadoa teda*. The translation is the same other than the fact that the phrase *yadoa teda*, when it comes together, stands for a much stronger interpretation of the meaning of the words.

That this kind of advice was given to Abraham seems very difficult at first glance. Why would God tell Abraham that his descendants would suffer terribly? The answer is that this is interpreted as the way in which the Egyptians would rule Israel. Since the end of the story marked the delivery of the Jewish people from Egyptian persecution, it was considered appropriate and important enough not to be too surprised. This is obvious from the text that follows: "That thy seed shall be a stranger in a land that is not theirs, etc." As we can see, the important thing is not *yadoa*, that they shall be strangers in a land that is not theirs, but to know and to look forward to the time when the persecution will be over and they will be redeemed.

———

Seed Thoughts I

One of the main concerns of midrashic writers is how to explain the use of the grammatical term of *yadoa teda*. This is the system whereby two forms of verb, both of which mean the same, are translated together. The Rabbis thought that *yadoa teda* was a dangerous term because it meant in a very strong way that the future will include much persecution. The *chidush*, or the novel interpretation of the Midrash, is that *yadoa teda* should be looked forward to not as similar meanings but as two different meanings.

———

Seed Thoughts II

Yadoa refers to events that will have taken place in the past, and *teda* is meant to refer to those events that will ultimately take place in the future. None of these events have yet taken place, but Abraham is informed that some day, his descendants will have to face the difficulties of *yadoa* and the pleasant redemption possibilities of *teda*. (Mirkin)

———

Seed Thoughts III

"And God said to Abraham: '*Yadoa teda* that your offspring will be strangers in a foreign land and will suffer from servitude.'" The text says *yadoa teda* with this double entendre: it talks of the two forms of knowledge. It speaks of three things: (a) that your offspring will be strangers in a strange land, (b) that they will suffer servitude (meaning slavery), and (c) that they will suffer (meaning עינוי – *inuy*). However, just as God will be performing these very bad things, He offers proof that just as

He fulfills one (namely *yadoa* – the evil), so will He have fulfilled *teda*, meaning His good promises.

יט וגם את הגוי אשר יעבודו דן אנכי. היה לומר גם, מאי וגם? אלא גם הוא מצרים, וגם
לרבות ארבעה גליות אשר יעבודו דן אנכי.

19. AND ALSO THAT NATION, WHOM THEY SHALL SERVE, ETC. (GEN. 15:14).
R. HELBO SAID: INSTEAD OF, AND THAT NATION, SCRIPTURE WRITES:
AND ALSO THAT NATION WHOM THEY SHALL SERVE: THIS INDICATES,
ALSO THEY [ABRAHAM'S DESCENDANTS,] ALSO EGYPT AND THE FOUR
KINGDOMS WHICH WILL SUBJUGATE THEE. WILL I JUDGE (*DAN*).

The idea that one letter can make a tremendous difference is a popular method of midrashic analysis. The Midrash uses the additional *vav* to establish a differentiation between the servitude of Egypt and the servitude of the four great Jewish exiles. The text makes no effort to prove these things, but merely to state them in its effort to show that part of the Abrahamic heritage will be negative before it becomes positive.

ר"א בשם ר' יוסי בר זמרא: בשתי אותיות הללו הבטיח הקב"ה לאברהם אבינו שהוא גואל
את בניו, ושאם יעשו תשובה גואלן בשבעים ושתים אותיות.

R. ELEAZAR SAID IN R. JOSE'S NAME: THE HOLY ONE, BLESSED BE HE,
PROMISED OUR FOREFATHER THAT HE WOULD REDEEM HIS CHILDREN
WITH THESE TWO LETTERS; BUT IF THEY REPENTED, HE WOULD REDEEM
THEM WITH SEVENTY-TWO LETTERS.

In the same way that וגם – *vegam* is interpreted as including those powers that were responsible for the great exiles of the Jewish people, the expression דן אנכי – *dan anochi* is interpreted from the positive point of view that the Jewish people will eventually be redeemed and will experience גאולה – *geulah*, which is a combination of independence and national sovereignty. Rabbi Elazar is the one who assures us that the expression *dan anochi* – "I will judge the Jewish people favorably" – applies to the entire Jewish people. However, he adds that the people repent and do something to improve their lives; they will be redeemed on a higher level, with God's name that contains 72 letters.

דא"ר יודן: (דברים ד) מלבא לקחת לו גוי מקרב גוי עד מוראים גדולים. אתה מוצא שבעים ושתים אותיות של הקב"ה. ואם יאמר לך אדם: שבעים וחמשה הם. אמור לו: צא מהם גוי שני, שאינו מן המנין.

R. JUDAN SAID: IN THE PASSAGE, [OR HATH GOD ASSAYED] TO GO AND TAKE HIM A NATION FROM THE MIDST OF ANOTHER NATION, BY TRIALS, BY SIGNS, AND BY WONDERS, AND BY ROAR, AND BY A MIGHTY HAND, AND BY AN OUTSTRETCHED ARM, AND BY GREAT TERRORS (DEUT. 4:34), YOU WILL FIND SEVENTY-TWO LETTERS; AND SHOULD YOU OBJECT THAT THERE ARE SEVENTY-FIVE, DEDUCT THE SECOND "NATION," WHICH IS NOT TO BE COUNTED.

This section introduces for the first time the idea that the name of God, in certain unusual circumstances, consists of 72 letters. The verse from which this teaching is derived is the following in Deuteronomy (4:34): ". . . go and take Him a nation from the midst of another nation, by trials, by signs, and by wonders, and by roar, and by a mighty hand, and by an outstretched arm, and by great terrors." However, if you examine the verse in Deuteronomy, it will be discovered that the number of letters which are supposed to represent the name of God is 75, not 72. The Midrash does not regard that as a problem; all you have to do is not count the second appearance of the word גוי – *goy*, meaning "a nation," since the point of the verse is that the Jewish people were a nation within the nation of Egypt. Since the idea of being within the nation of Egypt is not important in terms of God's name, by not including those three letters (*goy*), you achieve the desired result of 72.

ר' אבין אמר: בשמו גאלן, ששמו של הקדוש ב"ה, שבעים ושתים אותיות:

R. ABIN SAID: HE REDEEMED THEM BY HIS NAME, THE NAME OF THE HOLY ONE, BLESSED BE HE, CONSISTING OF SEVENTY-TWO LETTERS.

Seed Thoughts

The Name of God

For human beings, names are very important. Not only are they used as forms of identity – very often, they have special meanings. They can be a source of inspiration for the owner of the name. For example, אמונה – *emunah*, meaning "faith," can be the name of a person. Indeed, it is considered an important mark of the Creation that names were given to every animal and every star in the sky.

All of this applies to human beings, but it does not apply to God. God has no interest in His own names. All kinds of references are made to His name in the biblical stories, but in all cases, the goal is to influence human beings, and especially the Jewish people, in a certain direction. When we first hear, as in this Midrash, that 72 letters are an ideal form of the name of God, we as humans might regard it as unusual, but to God it is meaningless. There are names of God that consist of two, or three letters. If the letters increase to 72 letters, it does not make any difference to God, although it is important to the rabbinic mind who saw each name as having a unique meaning. This particular name of 72 letters obviously somehow refers to God's power of salvation.

PARASHAH FORTY-FOUR, *Midrash Twenty*

כ ואחרי כן יצאו ברכוש גדול. א"ר אחא: אחר כן אין כתיב כאן, אלא אחרי. משאביא עליהם עשר מכות, ולאח"כ יצאו ברכוש גדול.

20. AND AFTERWARDS (*AHARE KEN*) THEY SHALL COME OUT WITH GREAT SUBSTANCE. R. AHA SAID: NOT *AHAR* IS WRITTEN HERE BUT *AHARE*: THIS TEACHES, WHEN I HAVE VISITED TEN PLAGUES UPON THEM, THEN THEY SHALL COME OUT WITH GREAT SUBSTANCE.

You have here a play on words or numbers according to the system of gematria. Nowhere in the Torah was advance notice given that there would be ten plagues that would bring the Egyptian authorities to submission. But the Midrash found a source in this particular comment. The word אחרי- *aharei* – differs from אחר – *ahar* - in only one respect – namely, the addition of the letter *yod*. Since *yod* is also the number ten, in the system whereby the Hebrew alphabet also attributes numbers to its letters, it is now interpreted by the Midrash as a source that advised the community of Israel that ten plagues will punish the Egyptians after which the Israelites will achieve their independence from their Egyptian masters.

א"ל: אף אני בשיעבוד? א"ל (בראשית טו): ואתה תבא אל אבותיך בשלום וגו'.

SAID HE [ABRAHAM] TO HIM: "SHALL I TOO BE INCLUDED IN THIS SERVI-
TUDE? BUT THOU SHALT GO TO THY FATHERS IN PEACE; THOU SHALT BE
BURIED IN A GOOD OLD AGE (GEN. 15:15)," HE ASSURED HIM.

Upon hearing this prophecy, Abraham wondered whether he, too,
would be involved in the servitude that would ultimately be relieved
as described above. The answer was "Not to worry, that you will leave
this earth in peace, and you will return to your ancestors in the spirit of
shalom." It is this response which motivated a discussion on an interpretation of old age, especially the use of the term שיבה – *saiva* as being an
important way of describing those who leave this world a better place
to live in.

אמר ריש לקיש: ג' הם, שנאמר בהם בשיבה טובה: אברהם היה שוה לו. דוד שוה לו. גדעון
לא שוה לו. למה? (שופטים ח) ויעש אותו גדעון לאפוד לעבודת כוכבים:

R. SIMEON B. LAKISH SAID: OF THREE MEN WAS "IN A GOOD OLD AGE
SAID": ABRAHAM DESERVED IT, DAVID DESERVED IT, BUT GIDEON DID
NOT DESERVE IT. WHY? BECAUSE, AND GIDEON MADE AN *EPHOD* THEREOF
(JUDG. 8:27) – FOR IDOLATRY.

The question still remains, that Gideon was not deserving of the term
saiva. Why was he not deserving of this? The answer seems to be that
the real damage to Gideon's reputation did indeed begin during his
lifetime, but the real damage and the real idolatry that swept over his
kingdom took place after he died, and this seems to justify the use of the
term *saiva* even in terms of Gideon, who left this world as an unworthy
person.

———

Seed Thoughts

The opportunity of old age

The Rabbis and scholars of the Oral Law looked upon old age as a great
blessing. In fact, there is a greeting coined in a very early period of our
history which can be rendered as חיים טובים וארוכים – *hayim tovim va-
arukhim*, which means not just long life, but long life permeated with
good things. The use of the term *saiva* is an indication of this intention.

More than just additional years as the meaning of the blessing, additional years joined together with altruistic behavior is the real meaning of the blessing. The text says in connection with Abraham and David that the word *saiva* was suitable for them, which is the meaning of the expression שוה לו – *shaveh lo*; in other words, *saiva* was supposed to be a standard by which to be monitored. It had to be stopped when Gideon was mistakenly identified as having reached *saiva*, which was very inappropriate and therefore we do not find the word *saiva* used again in this connection.

PARASHAH FORTY-FOUR, *Midrash Twenty-One*

כא ויהי השמש באה ועלטה היה. אמיטתא הות.

21. AND IT CAME TO PASS, THAT, WHEN THE SUN WENT DOWN, AND THERE WAS THICK DARKNESS (GEN. 15:17): THERE WAS INTENSE DARKNESS.

This Midrash begins by establishing a certain mood, which it does by informing us that we are dealing with the setting of the sun. The word עלטה – *alata*, which is a difficult Hebrew word, is translated by an Aramaic word. We have to understand that the reason for this was that Aramaic was a spoken language of the Jewish community at that time. Today, we would have used an English word, or a generation ago, a Yiddish word. However, in those days, the use of the Aramaic word explained everything. The mood, therefore, is the mood of sunset.

והנה תנור עשן ולפיד. שמעון בר אבא בשם ר' יוחנן אמר: ארבעה דברים הראה לו: גיהנם ומלכיות ומתן תורה ובית המקדש. א"ל: כל זמן שבניך עסוקים בשתים, הם ניצולים משתים פירשו משתים, הם נידונין בשתים.

BEHOLD A SMOKING FURNACE AND A FLAMING TORCH. SIMEON B. ABBA SAID IN R. JOHANAN'S NAME: HE [GOD] SHOWED HIM FOUR THINGS: VIZ. GEHENNA, THE [FOREIGN] KINGDOMS, REVELATION, AND THE TEMPLE, WITH THE PROMISE: AS LONG AS THY CHILDREN OCCUPY THEMSELVES WITH THE LATTER TWO, THEY WILL BE SAVED FROM THE FORMER TWO; IF THEY NEGLECT THE LATTER TWO THEY WILL BE PUNISHED BY THE FORMER TWO.

The use of terms like "smoking furnace" or "flaming torch" are meant
to indicate what was going on in Abraham's time, and how much he was
bothered by some of the events and some of the prophecies and visions
that he had experienced. In this connection, Rabbi Simeon tries to add
content to what was bothering Abraham. Four things were shown to
Abraham. The first is Gehenna, a place after death where the souls of
individuals are purified from their sins or punished for them. Second
are the kingdoms, which represent the four empires, ending with Rome,
that were major persecutors of the Jewish people. The third is the Giving
of the Torah, which offered the Jews a way of life as well as inspiration.
Finally, the Temple, whose system of offerings was waged for individual
Jews to seek atonement and the encouragement to continue. Rabbi
Simeon continued that God made known to Abraham that so long as
he concerned himself with two of these four – namely, the Giving of the
Torah and the Temple – he would not have to worry about Gehenna or
anti-Jewish persecution.

Abraham was told: "What would you prefer, that your children
should descend into Gehenna, or should they choose persecution in
this world?" There is a difference of opinion. Rabbi Hanina bar Pappa
said: "Abraham chose anti-Jewish persecution as being preferable to
Gehenna." Rabbi Judan and his associates said: "Abraham actually
chose Gehenna, but God intervened and made him choose anti-Jewish
persecution rather than Gehenna." The Midrash then goes on to explain
that this discussion shows us that Abraham may have been responsible
for anti-Jewish persecution, or at least that the Jews were passive in opposing the persecution, and that God approved of this choice.

א"ל במה אתה רוצה שירדו בניך, בגיהנם או במלכיות? ר' חנינא בר פפא אמר: אברהם ברר
לו את המלכיות. רבי יודן ור' אידי ור' חמא בר חנינא אמרו: אברהם ברר גיהנם, והקב"ה ברר
לו את המלכיות, הה"ד (דברים לב): אם לא כי צורם מכרם, זה אברהם. וה' הסגירם, מלמד
שהסכים הקב"ה לדבריו. ר' הונא בשם ר' אחא אמר: כך היה אבינו אברהם יושב ותמה כל
אותו היום, אמר: במה אברר בגיהנם או במלכיות? א"ל הקב"ה: אברהם קטע הדין מוניטא
מן כדו. ביום ההוא כרת ה' את אברם ברית לאמר. מהו לאמר? באנו למחלוקת. רבי חנינא
בר פפא ור' יודן ור' אידי ור' חמא בר חנינא. רבי חנינא בר פפא אמר: אברהם ברר לו את
המלכיות, הה"ד (תהלים סו): הרכבת אנוש לראשנו באנו באש ובמים.

WOULDST THOU RATHER THAT THY CHILDREN DESCEND INTO GEHENNA
OR INTO THE POWER OF THE [FOREIGN] KINGDOMS? HE ASKED HIM.
R. HANINA B. PAPA SAID: ABRAHAM HIMSELF CHOSE [SUBJECTION TO
FOREIGN] POWERS. R. JUDAN, R. IDI, AND R. HAMA B. R. HANINA SAID:

ABRAHAM CHOSE GEHENNA, BUT THE HOLY ONE, BLESSED BE HE, CHOSE
[SUBJECTION TO FOREIGN] POWERS FOR HIM. THUS IT IS WRITTEN:
HOW SHOULD ONE CHASE A THOUSAND, AND TWO PUT TEN THOUSAND
TO FIGHT, EXCEPT THEIR ROCK HAD GIVEN THEM OVER (DEUT. 32:30)
– THIS ALLUDES TO ABRAHAM; AND THE LORD HAD DELIVERED THEM
UP (32:30)? THIS TEACHES THAT GOD APPROVED HIS CHOICE. R. HUNA
SAID IN R. AHA'S NAME: ABRAHAM SAT WONDERING ALL DAY, THINKING,
WHICH SHOULD I CHOOSE? WHEREUPON THE HOLY ONE, BLESSED BE HE,
SAID TO HIM, MAKE A DECISION WITHOUT DELAY; HENCE IT IS WRIT-
TEN: IN THAT DAY THE LORD MADE A COVENANT WITH ABRAM, ETC.
(GEN. 15:18). IN THIS MATTER WE COME BACK TO THE CONTROVERSY OF
R. HANINA B. PAPA AND R. JUDAN, R. IDI, AND R. HANA B. R. HANINA.
R. HANINA B. PAPA SAID: ABRAHAM HIMSELF CHOSE [SUBJECTION TO
OTHER] POWERS. R. JUDAN, R. IDI, AND R. HAMA B. R. HANINA SAID ON
THE AUTHORITY OF A CERTAIN SAGE IN RABBI'S NAME: THE HOLY ONE,
BLESSED BE HE, CHOSE THE [FOREIGN] KINGDOMS FOR HIM. THUS IT
IS WRITTEN: THOU HAST CAUSED MEN TO RIDE OVER OUR HEADS (PS.
66:12), MEANING: THOU DIDST CAUSE NATIONS TO RIDE OVER OUR
HEADS, WHICH IS AS THOUGH, WE WENT THROUGH FIRE AND THROUGH
WATER (66:12).

This section dramatizes the difference of opinion among the rabbis. One group says that Abraham shows the difficulties in this world and being among the anti-Jewish governments rather than the punishment of Gehenna in the World to Come. Another group of rabbis offer their opinion that on his own, Abraham had chosen Gehenna, but that God intervened and asserted that his choice should be the problems of This World, and naturally, Abraham was forced to accept them.

ר' יהושע בן לוי אמר: אף קריעת ים סוף הראה לו, דכתיב: אשר עבר בין הגזרים האלה. המד"א: (שם קל"ו) לגוזר ים סוף לגזרים:

R. JOSHUA SAID: HE ALSO SHOWED HIM THE DIVIDING OF THE RED SEA, FOR IT IS WRITTEN: THAT PASSED BETWEEN THESE PIECES – *GEZARIM* (GEN. 15:17), *GEZARIM* HAVING THE SAME MEANING] AS IN THE VERSE, [O GIVE THANKS . . .] TO HIM WHO DIVIDED THE RED SEA IN SUNDER – *GEZARIM* (PS. 136:13).

In connection with the interpretation of the Red Sea, there is no relationship to the main argument of the Midrash. It simply indicates that the revelation to Abraham included much more than has been stated in this Midrash; for example, the miracle of the splitting of the Red Sea was already told to Abraham in this same revelation.

—

Seed Thoughts

How can one explain the fact that Abraham, on his own, would have chosen Gehenna (the punishment of the World to Come) for his offspring rather than the possibilities of this world? There are no sources from which we can find any answers to this question, and we can only resort to speculation. What is being written now is not a proof; the argument itself cannot be proven, but it simply helps to arouse curiosity, and maybe someone who reads this will find better answers on his own. Could it be that Abraham felt that what he knows about this world, including its negative aspects, is preferable to something like Gehenna, which exists in the World to Come and about which we know very little? Maybe it is better to worry about what you have rather than allow yourself to be led into strange paths about which you know nothing. However, as we have read in our Midrash, the Holy One, blessed be He, was not satisfied with this kind of speculation, and made the choice for Abraham the choice of this world for which he had to agree.

—

Additional Commentary

The Diaspora as a positive force

We are forced to use terms like "Jewish persecution" and "anti-Jewish behavior" of certain governments, because that is the language used by our Midrash. However, it gives the wrong impression. The idea of God intervening and telling Abraham to choose this world, even with all its difficulties, is the way in which the Holy One, blessed be He, was defining for Abraham the meaning of גלות – *galut* – or what we mean as Diaspora (which means the community of Jews living outside of Israel). Diaspora, or the Exile, should be looked upon as something positive. It is very important that Jewish communities should grow up in many parts of the world. It means that the Jewish people are a worldly people so long as we are here, and the Jewish communities are themselves a tremendous protection of Israel, as we understand today, living as we do with the State of Israel. Granted that there has been great anti-Jewish persecution, there has also been tremendous Jewish achievement. One could list the number of Jews who have won Nobel Prizes, and others who have achieved tremendous things for the welfare of mankind in research in all levels of knowledge. There is another aspect of this interpretation which some of the commentaries have pointed out, and that is that when you choose to live in the *galut* and if you are among those who have suffered persecution, you need not worry about Gehenna. For those who have suffered, Gehenna is totally eliminated. (*HaMidrash HaMevo'ar*)

PARASHAH FORTY-FOUR, *Midrash Twenty-Two*

כב ביום ההוא כרת ה' את אברם ברית לאמר. ר' יודן ורבי יוחנן בן זכאי ור"ע: חד אמר:
העולם הזה גלה לו אבל העולם הבא לא גלה לו. ואוחרנא אמר: אחד העולם הזה ואחד
העוה"ב גלה לו. ר' ברכיה, אר"א ור' יוסי בר חנינא: חד אמר: עד היום הזה גלה לו. ואוחרנא
אמר: עד היום ההוא גלה לו.

22. IN THAT DAY THE LORD MADE A COVENANT WITH ABRAM (GEN.
15:18). R. JUDAN SAID: R. JOHANAN B. ZAKKAI AND R. AKIBA DISAGREE.
ONE MAINTAINS: THIS WORLD HE REVEALED TO HIM, BUT NOT THE
NEXT. THE OTHER MAINTAINS THAT HE REVEALED TO HIM BOTH THIS
WORLD AND THE NEXT. R. BEREKIAH SAID: R. LEAZAR AND R. JOSE B.
R. HANINA DISAGREED. ONE MAINTAINED: HE REVEALED TO HIM [THE
FUTURE] UNTIL THAT DAY; WHILE THE OTHER SAID: HE REVEALED TO
HIM THE FUTURE FROM THAT DAY.

לזרעך נתתי וגו'. ר' הונא ור' דוסתאי בשם רשב"ג: אף מאמרו של הקב"ה מעשה, שנא':
לזרעך נתתי, אתן את הארץ הזאת אין כתיב כאן, אלא נתתי את הארץ הזאת. רבי יודן בשם
רבי אבא בר כהנא אמר: (שם קז) יאמרו גאולי ה', אשר הוא גואלם לא נאמר, אלא אשר
גאלם. א"ר אבון: כי פודה ה' את יעקב, אין כתיב כאן, אלא (ירמיה לא) כי פדה ה' את יעקב.
רבנן אמרי: (זכריה י) אשרקה להם ואקבצם, כי אפדם אין כתיב כאן, אלא כי פדיתים. אמר
רבי יהושע (ישעיה ד): ובראה ה' על כל מכון הר ציון אין כתיב כאן, אלא ברא כבר היא ברואה
ומתוקנת:

UNTO THY SEED HAVE I GIVEN THIS LAND. R. HUNA AND R. DOSTAI SAID
IN THE NAME OF R. SAMUEL B. NAHMAN: THE MERE SPEECH OF THE HOLY
ONE, BLESSED BE HE, IS EQUIVALENT TO ACTION, FOR IT SAYS: UNTO THY
SEED HAVE I GIVEN: NOT I WILL GIVE, BUT HAVE I GIVEN. R. JUDAN SAID
IN R. ABBA'S NAME: IT IS NOT WRITTEN: SO LET THE REDEEMED OF THE
LORD SAY WHOM HE REDEEMETH, BUT, WHOM HE HATH REDEEMED (PS.
107:2). R. ABIN SAID: IT IS NOT WRITTEN: FOR THE LORD RANSOMETH
JACOB, BUT FOR THE LORD HATH RANSOMED JACOB (JER. 31:11). THE
RABBIS SAID: IT IS NOT WRITTEN, I WILL HISS FOR THEM, AND GATHER
THEM, FOR I WILL REDEEM THEM, BUT FOR I HAVE REDEEMED THEM
(ZECH. 10:8). R. JOSHUA SAID: IT IS NOT WRITTEN: AND THE LORD WILL
CREATE (*WE-YIBRA*), BUT, AND THE LORD HAS CREATED (*U-BARA*) . . . A
CLOUD AND SMOKE BY DAY, ETC. (ISA. 4:5): IT HAS LONG BEEN CREATED
AND READY.

The latter part of this Midrash reveals to us many occasions when God established the permanence of various types of actions but interpreted the future by using the past tense. It does not say "He will give the land," but rather "He has given the land." That is demonstrated in the series of phrases that we just read: God has already made His decisions, and nothing that occurs in the future, no matter how dramatic, will change the reality of those decisions.

―――

Seed Thoughts

There is a difference of opinion among the Rabbis as to whether the revelations of Abraham refer to events in This World and not the World to Come, and there is another group of scholars that include not only This World but the World to Come as well. The difference of opinion is based on two words; the scriptural text uses the words ביום ההוא – *bayom ha-hu*, meaning "on that day." It does not say ביום הזה – *bayom ha-zeh* – "on this day." Usually, *bayom ha-zeh* refers to a period of time up to the Exodus from Egypt, because Abraham's offspring were deeply involved in the events that produced the Jewish people during the exile in Egypt. On the other hand, the expression *bayom ha-hu* has the meaning of "on that special day," which includes every aspect of life up to the time of the Messiah, connecting This World to the World to Come.

―――

Additional Commentary

Understanding the future by means of the past

The text reads "to your descendants I have given this land"; "I have given" is written in the past tense, and was said at the time that Abraham did not have any offspring. Therefore, the land could not have possibly been given to them, but that does not matter since sooner or later, it was going to happen. This is based on the principle that even a declaration that comes from God is equivalent to מעשה – *maaseh*, meaning an actual act of creation. This declaration becomes a form of action, and everything will happen when this time comes. (*HaMidrash HaMevo'ar*)

PARASHAH FORTY-FOUR, *Midrash Twenty-Three*

כג רבי דוסתאי בשם רבי שמואל בר נחמן אמר: לפי שאינו מזכיר כאן החוי, לפיכך הוא
מביא רפאים תחתיהם.

23. THE KENITE, AND THE KENIZZITE, AND THE KADMONITE, AND THE
HITTITE, AND THE PERIZZITE, AND THE REPHAIM, AND THE AMORITE,
AND THE CANAANITE, AND THE GIRGASHITE, AND THE JEBUSITE (GEN.
15:19F.). R. DOSTAI SAID IN THE NAME OF R. SAMUEL B. NAHMAN: BE-
CAUSE THE HIVITE IS NOT MENTIONED HERE, THE REPHAIM ARE SUB-
STITUTED IN THEIR STEAD.

The point to know here is that the people known as Hivites were
replaced with those known as Rephaim. We will later discover that both
of these names were used for the same geographic area.

רבי חלבו בשם רבי אבא בשם רבי יוחנן: כך עלה בדעתו של מקום להנחיל להם לישראל,
ארץ עשרה עממים: את הקיני ואת הקנזי ואת הקדמוני, ולא נתן להם אלא ז', את החתי ואת
הפרזי ואת הרפאים ואת האמורי ואת הכנעני ואת הגרגשי ואת היבוסי, הרי שבעה. ולמה
נתן להם שבעה? (פירושן לעיל) ואיזה הם הג' שלא ניתן להם? רבי אומר: ערביה שלמייה
נוטייה.

R. HELBO SAID IN R. ABBA'S NAME IN R. JOHANAN'S NAME: THE HOLY
ONE, BLESSED BE HE, DID AT FIRST CONTEMPLATE GIVING ISRAEL POS-
SESSION OF TEN PEOPLES, BUT HE GAVE THEM ONLY SEVEN, THE OTHER
THREE BEING, THE KENITE, AND THE KENIZZITE, AND THE KADMONITE.
RABBI SAID: THEY ARE ARABIA, THE SHALAMITE, AND THE NABATEAN.

The discussion now centers around which three were eliminated so
that seven remained. The first three names were discarded because they
were Canaanite groups, some of whom lived far away, and in general
were looked upon as strangers to the other seven communities.

רבי שמעון בן יוחאי אומר: דרמוסקוס ואסייא ואספמייא. ר"א בן יעקב אמר: אסיא ותרקי
וקרטגינה. רבנן אמרי: אדום ומואב וראשית בני עמון הם הג' שלא נתן להם בעוה"ז. אדום,
שנאמר (דברים ב): כי לא אתן לך מארצו ירושה כי ירושה לעשו נתתי את הר שעיר. ובמואב,
כתיב (שם): אל תצר את מואב ואל תתגר בם מלחמה. קנזי, הוא מעשו. קיני וקדמוני, הוא
מעמון ומואב. אבל לימות המשיח יחזרו ויהיו לישראל, כדי לקיים מאמרו של הקב"ה. אבל
עכשיו שבעה נתן להם, שנאמר (שם ז): שבעה גוים רבים ועצומים ממך.

R. SIMEON B. YOHAI SAID: THEY ARE THE DAMASCUS REGION, ASIA MI-
NOR, AND APAMEA. R. LIEZER B. JACOB SAID: ASIA MINOR, THRACE, AND
CARTHAGE. THE RABBIS SAID: EDOM, MOAB, AND THE CHIEF OF THE
CHILDREN OF AMMON ARE THE THREE NATIONS THAT WERE NOT GIVEN
TO THEM IN THIS WORLD, AS IT IS SAID: FOR I WILL NOT GIVE YOU OF
THEIR LAND, ETC. (DEUT. 2:5). BUT IN THE DAYS OF THE MESSIAH THEY
SHALL ONCE AGAIN BELONG TO ISRAEL, IN ORDER TO FULFILL GOD'S
PROMISE. NOW, HOWEVER, HE HAS GIVEN THEM BUT SEVEN, AS IT SAYS:
SEVEN NATIONS GREATER AND MIGHTIER THAN THOU (7:1).

It is interesting to note the view that the three communities excluded
from the ten were Edom, Ammon, and Moab. These three groups
were very often competitive, and sometimes even engaged in warfare.
Nonetheless, all of them were originally descended from the offspring
of Isaac, and therefore, had original family connections with each other.
Thus, there was a text that said that these nations are to be protected and
not to be attacked because of the special relationship of their founders
to the descendants of Isaac.

אמר רבי יצחק חזירתא, רעיא בעשרה, ואימרתא ולא בחד כל אילין. אמר הקב"ה לאברהם:
דיהב ליה, את הקיני ואת הקנזי וגו'. ועדיין, ושרי אשת אברהם לא ילדה לו:

R. ISAAC SAID: THE SWINE GRAZES WITH TEN OF ITS YOUNG, WHEREAS
THE SHEEP DOES NOT GRAZE EVEN WITH ONE. THUS, ALL THESE, VIZ.
THE KENITE, THE KENIZZITE, ETC. [WERE PROMISED TO ABRAHAM'S
SEED], YET SO FAR, SARAI, ABRAHAM'S WIFE BORE HIM NO CHILDREN
(GEN. 16:1)!

These lands would ultimately be returned to Israel during the days of
the Messiah.

—

Seed Thoughts

We are about to complete Chapter 44 of the *Midrash Rabbah* and enter
immediately into Chapter 45. Before doing so, I should like to express
a certain interpretation to the readers of our Midrash work, which this
chapter has brought to our particular attention. In the earlier pages
of this chapter, there is a view which states that the Jewish people are
warned not to use violence in their protests against their persecutors.

We are outnumbered in a tremendous way by the majority in whatever country we reside, and such attacks are doomed to failure, as is any attempt to recreate the Jewish state by these methods. These ideas are repeated very often in other forms of language, but basically, they are saying the same thing. If you are living in an area of Jewish persecution, it will get you nowhere, and the best advice is to move elsewhere. These views are stated in several places in the Talmud, but in Chapter 44, they appear again and again in different forms and different guises. Sometimes, they exist in different forms as in the Midrash, where Abraham is forced to choose whether he wants for his offspring Gehenna in the Next World or persecution in This World. The outcome of the Midrash is that he is recommended to choose persecution in This World.

Over the years, two responses have emerged from these messages. The first is the Zionist movement, which is a protest against this point of view. This movement probably has its origin in the failure of the Bar Kokhba revolution, and the terrible losses of the Jewish people inflicted by that failure. A second response was given by a group known as the *Haredim*, the ultra-Orthodox religious group, that some of its more extreme elements, protest the creation of the State of Israel before the Messiah comes.

Having just studied Chapter 44 and many of its commentaries, I feel obliged to point out that both of these responses miss the mark entirely. The views expressed are a statement of affirmation of Jewish survival. We are told that the Jewish people need two things: They need a national home, which the state of Israel was founded in order to create, but they also need a Diaspora (or a *galut*), or "an exile" as it is sometimes translated. The Holy One, blessed be He, is even quoted in one particular Midrash as saying that the Jewish people have to live everywhere it is possible in this world and be related to all the peoples of the world and not live in isolation. This chapter and its teaching has to be seen as an affirmation of the Jewish Diaspora as a form of Jewish survival and not at the expense of any other development. Twice a day, we conclude the *Aleinu* prayer: "And the Lord shall be King over all the Earth, on that day shall the Lord be One and His Name One." How could this happen, unless we are a great people, not great in numbers but great in achievement? With Israel and the Diaspora fulfilling each other's personal national and spiritual needs.

Additional Commentary

Why were the community replacements necessary?

There are many questions that can be asked about this Midrash. If God wanted the society of Israel to be based on ten different peoples who were inhabiting the land at the time, why has that goal changed? Why did the ten become seven, and why were these particular three removed? Furthermore, why does the Midrash end with the phrase "and Sarah had not yet given birth"?

What happened was that Abraham and his generation sinned in the eyes of God, and we are reading about his punishment. God had said: "I have given you this land," as we read in the preceding Midrash. But Abraham's reaction was: "How do I know that I will be able to inherit it?," by which he meant: "How do I know that my children will respect this decision that the leadership will require?" The Holy One, blessed be He, regarded this answer as an expression of doubt in God's ability to fulfill his Divine promise, and Abraham and his children were therefore punished. Three of the communities were removed, and only seven remained. The fact that Sarah was barren for a period of time could also be blamed on Abraham's expression of doubt. Fortunately, many of these punishments were only temporary, and most were restored after a period of time. (*Tiferet Tzion*)

א ושרי אשת אברם לא ילדה לו וגו'. (משלי לא) אשת חיל מי ימצא וגו', ורחוק מפנינים מכרה.
מהו מכרה? ר' אבא בר כהנא אמר: עיבורה, הה"ד (יחזקאל טז): מכורותיך ומולדותיך. אברהם
היה גדול מנחור שנה, ונחור היה גדול מהרן שנה. נמצא אברם גדול מהרן ב' שנים, שנה
לעיבורה של מלכה, ושנה לעיבורה של יסכה, והרן מוליד לשש שנים, ואברם אינו מוליד.
ושרי אשת אברם לא ילדה לו. ר"י ור' נחמיה. ר' יהודה אמר לו: לאברם לא ילדה, אבל אילו
נשאת לאחר ילדה. ורבי נחמיה אמר: לא לו ולא לאחר. ומה דכתיב לא ילדה לו, לו ולה.

1. NOW SARAI ABRAM'S WIFE BORE HIM NO CHILDREN, ETC. (GEN. 16:1).
IT IS WRITTEN: A WOMAN OF VALOR WHO CAN FIND, FOR HER PRICE (*MI-KRAH*) IS FAR ABOVE RUBIES (PROV. 31:10). WHAT DOES *MIKRAH* MEAN? R.
ABBA B. KAHANA SAID: HER PREGNANCY, AS YOU READ: THINE ORIGIN
(*MEKUROTH*) AND THY NATIVITY (EZEK. 16:3). NOW ABRAM WAS A YEAR
OLDER THAN NAHOR, AND NAHOR WAS A YEAR OLDER THAN HARAN;
[HENCE ABRAM WAS] TWO YEARS OLDER [THAN HARAN; DEDUCT] THE
YEAR OF PREGNANCY WITH MILCAH AND THE YEAR OF PREGNANCY WITH
ISCAH, AND YOU FIND THAT HARAN BEGOT CHILDREN AT SIX YEARS OF
AGE, YET YOU SAY THAT ABRAM COULD NOT BEGET? HENCE, NOW SARAI
ABRAM'S WIFE BORE HIM NO CHILDREN. DID NOT BEAR TO HIM. R. JUDAH
SAID: TO HIM TEACHES THAT SHE DID NOT BEAR TO ABRAM, BUT HAD
SHE BEEN MARRIED TO ANOTHER SHE WOULD HAVE BORNE CHILDREN.
R. NEHEMIAH SAID: NEITHER TO HIM NOR TO ANYONE ELSE. HOW THEN
DOES R. NEHEMIAH INTERPRET DID NOT BEAR TO HIM? INTERPRET TO
HIM AND TO HER, THUS: SHE DID NOT BEAR TO HERSELF – ON SARAI'S
OWN ACCOUNT, NOR TO HIM – ON ABRAM'S ACCOUNT.

The interesting comment has to do with the fact that the text says not merely that Sarai did not have children; it says that she did not bring children to him – לו – *lo*. Rabbi Judah makes the interesting point that this text seems to say that Abraham was biologically responsible for Sarah being barren, for it says that she did not bear children to him. Rabbi Judah then says: "Had she later on married someone else, she would probably have borne children to someone else." Rabbi Nehemiah is of a different opinion; she could not have borne children in her condition at that time. There is an interesting play on words; *lo* (to him) is followed in a different context by לה – *la* (to her), meaning that both were equally responsible for her barren condition. The Midrash attempts to offer a different explanation for אשת חיל – *Eishet Hayil*, that מכרה – *mikhra* – does not refer symbolically to the value of a woman of worth, but rather to pregnancy, and is thus related to Sarah's condition of barrenness. The reason for this new translation is that the Rabbis did not think that it was proper to use the word "price" in connection to a woman of worth. However, the new interpretation does not seem to fit in with the rest of the chapter of *Eishet Hayil*.

ולה שפחה מצרית ושמה הגר. שפחת מלוג היתה, והיה חייב במזונותיה, ולא היה רשאי למכרה. בעין קומי ריש לקיש: מהו דתנא עבדי מלוג? אמר להון? כמה דתימא מלוג מלוג: אמר ר"ש בן יוחאי: הגר בתו של פרעה היתה, וכיון שראה פרעה מעשים שנעשו לשרה בביתו, נטל בתו ונתנה לו. אמר: מוטב שתהא בתי שפחה בבית זה, ולא גבירה בבית אחר, הה"ד (בראשית ט): ולה שפחה מצרית, ושמה הגר. הא אגריך, אף אבימלך. כיון שראה נסים שנעשו לשרה בביתו, נטל בתו ונתנה לו. אמר: מוטב שתהא בתי שפחה בבית הזה, ולא גבירה בבית אחרת, הה"ד (תהלים מה): בנות מלכים ביקרותיך, נצבה שגל לימינך, בכתם אופיר:

AND SHE HAD A HANDMAID, AN EGYPTIAN. SHE WAS A HANDMAID OF "PLUCKING" WHOM HE WAS BOUND TO SUPPORT BUT MIGHT NOT SELL. R. SIMEON B. LAKISH WAS ASKED: WHAT IS THE MEANING OF WHAT WE LEARNT!: "SERVANTS OF PLUCKING"? "WHAT YOU PLUCK, YOU PLUCK," HE ANSWERED. R. SIMEON B. YOHAI SAID: HAGAR WAS PHARAOH'S DAUGHTER. WHEN PHARAOH SAW WHAT WAS DONE ON SARAH'S BEHALF IN HIS OWN HOUSE, HE TOOK HIS DAUGHTER AND GAVE HER TO SARAH, SAYING: "BETTER LET MY DAUGHTER BE A HANDMAID IN THIS HOUSE THAN A MISTRESS IN ANOTHER HOUSE"; THUS IT IS WRITTEN: AND SHE HAD A HANDMAID, AN EGYPTIAN, WHOSE NAME WAS HAGAR, HE (PHARAOH) SAYING: HERE IS THY REWARD (AGAR). ABIMELECH, TOO, WHEN HE SAW THE MIRACLES PERFORMED IN HIS HOUSE ON SARAH'S BEHALF, GAVE HIS DAUGHTER TO HER, SAYING: "BETTER LET MY DAUGHTER BE A HANDMAID IN THIS HOUSE THAN A MISTRESS IN ANOTHER," AS IT IS WRITTEN: KINGS' DAUGHTERS ARE AMONG THY FAVORITES (PS. 45:10): VIZ. THE DAUGHTERS OF [TWO] KINGS. AT THY RIGHT HAND DOTH STAND THE QUEEN IN GOLD OF OPHIR (45:10) – THIS ALLUDES TO SARAI.

T his Midrash includes an unusual word מלוג – *melog*, developed by the Talmud to indicate that the handmaiden was entirely hers. The husband, in such cases, had limited rights, such as eating food that she prepared. Sarah was the sole employer in this case. This will help us understand some of the later decisions, such as Sarah's decision regarding Hagar's future.

Seed Thoughts I

It is too bad that the Torah text did not include what we have just learned about the family background of Hagar. She was a princess. Her father was Pharaoh – not the one of Moses's generation – since all kings of Egypt were known as Pharaoh. What happened was that Hagar's father, Pharaoh, was unhappy at the kind of temptations facing unmarried girls in his kingdom. He did know Abraham, however, and felt that Hagar would be much happier in going to Abraham's house than where she was in Egypt. This background answers a lot of questions for us. Why would a wife choose a servant to engage in a sexual life with her husband, even though the goal was to produce a child, which he was not able to do until this point? Not only that – the handmaiden was to become his wife. Since this was a polygamous society, when the handmaiden is a princess, the daughter of Pharaoh, all these doubts are removed. Hagar merited this special treatment. We even understand a little better what happened later on when Sarah and Hagar separated because she did not want Hagar's influence to be too strong on Isaac. Hagar wanted her son Ishmael to be like her father, Pharaoh. Sarah wanted her son to be like her husband, Abraham. In this latter stage, they were incompatible.

Seed Thoughts II

There is, in this Midrash, a wonderful tribute to Sarah. It seems like a mirror detail but it is really important. Either the author of the Book of Proverbs or one of the great scholars of the Midrash felt that the beautiful line "A woman of worth who will find" (from Proverbs) applies to Sarah – that she was the Eishet Hayil that the poet and writer of Proverbs had in mind. The fact that both Pharaoh, king of Egypt, and Abimelech, king of the Philistines, wanted their daughters to be brought up in the household of Sarah is testimony to this fact. It is quite true, as indicated, that the kings were not happy with the behavior to which Sarah was subject by some of their male leaders. On the other hand, it is quite obvious to the two kings that Sarah was the recipient of divine assistance, without which she could not have escaped unscathed from these adventures. If in addition to these midrashic facts, we remember that when Sarah and Abraham had differences of opinion, the Holy One, blessed be He, was always on Sarah's side and always advised Abraham to follow his wife's recommendations in all respects. In short, Sarah (the mother of the Jewish people) was an extraordinary woman and God Himself defined her as such.

~

Additional Commentary

Why was it God's decision for Sarah to remain barren until the appropriate time that He had in mind?

Sarah was brought up in a home that worshipped idols. God was concerned that any child born to Sarah would be greatly influenced by her parents. Grandparents usually have an important influence, and in this case, the results would not have been in the divine interest. So God waited until Sarah had reached the age of זקנה – *ziknah* – roughly translated as 'old age' (at the age of 90), at which time her parents were no longer alive, and Sarah would have every opportunity to bring up Isaac in accordance with God's desire. This is how the new interpretation in Eishet Hayil should be understood. Instead of translating רחוק מפנינים מכרה – *rahok mipeninim mikhra*, meaning 'her value was far above precious pearls', in the new translation, *mikhra* is translated as pregnancy, and פנינים – *peninim* – seems to be from the Hebrew expression מלפנים – *milifnim*, meaning something internal, having to do with their house at home. The interpretation would be her pregnancy – far away from the original possibility. This interpretation, which had first seemed awkward because it interfered with our usual conception of the chapter in Proverbs about the woman of worth, now turns out to be an excellent interpretation. It explains what happened to Sarah in a way far superior to whatever we have learned in the Midrash up until this point. (*Tiferet Tzion*)

Parashah Forty-Five, *Midrash Two*

ב ותאמר שרי אל אברם הנה נא עצרני ה' מלדת. אמרה: ידעת אנא מהיכן היא סבתי, לא
כשם שהיו אומרים לי: קמיע היא צריכה, הימום היא צריכה, אלא הנה נא עצרני ה' מלדת.
2. AND SARAI SAID UNTO ABRAM: BEHOLD NOW, THE LORD HATH RE-
STRAINED ME FROM BEARING, ETC. (GEN. 16:2). SAID SHE: I KNOW THE
SOURCE OF MY AFFLICTION: IT IS NOT AS PEOPLE SAY [OF A BARREN
WOMAN], SHE NEEDS A TALISMAN, SHE NEEDS A CHARM, BUT BEHOLD
NOW, THE LORD HATH RESTRAINED ME FROM BEARING.

In Theodore's commentary, he makes reference to the fact that
Sarah uses the Hebrew words הנה נא – *hineh na*. Usually, this expression is used when one is engaged in debate; therefore, this section of
the Midrash should be looked upon as a debate between Sarah and
her advisors. They are advising her to use various natural means that
other women who are barren use. But Sarah explains that she does
not accept these views. She knows why she is barren, because of God's
decision, and she hopes that some day, this decision will be changed.
Theodore goes on to say that Sarah was a sort of prophetess, and in
some fashion, she had received a message that God was behind it all.
(Mirkin)

תני, כל מי שאין לו בן, כאלו הוא מת, כאלו הוא הרום. כאלו מת, ותאמר רחל אל יעקב הבה
לי בנים וגו'. כאלו הרום, שנאמר: אולי אבנה ממנה, ואין בונין אלא את ההרום.
IT WAS TAUGHT: HE WHO HAS NO CHILD IS AS THOUGH HE WERE DEAD
AND DEMOLISHED. AS THOUGH DEAD: AND SHE SAID UNTO JACOB: GIVE
ME CHILDREN, OR ELSE I AM DEAD (GEN. 30:1). AS THOUGH DEMOLISHED:
IT MAY BE THAT I SHALL BE BUILDED UP THROUGH HER, AND ONLY THAT
WHICH IS DEMOLISHED MUST BE BUILDED UP.

One of the points that could be made is that children, if they are not
a guarantee of the future, are in themselves the future itself. A person
who dies childless is sooner or later forgotten unless he has accomplished something quite extraordinary. Children are a great blessing in
the sense that they can continue the life of a parent in many ways, and
if there are numerous children, it can be guaranteed for more than one
generation.

וישמע אברם לקול שרי. רבי יוסי אמר: לקול רוח הקדש, היך מה דאת אמר: ואתה תשמע
לקול דברי ה':

AND ABRAM HEARKENED TO THE VOICE OF SARAI. R. JOSE SAID: TO THE
VOICE OF THE HOLY SPIRIT, AS YOU READ: NOW THEREFORE HEARKEN
UNTO THE VOICE OF THE WORDS OF THE LORD (I SAM. 15:1).

Theodore points out that the Hebrew word קוֹל – *kol* – meaning
"voice," is sometimes used to indicate something prophetic, so that
when it says that Abraham listened to the voice of his wife, it means
that he recognized that there is something in her message that was prophetic. (Mirkin)

—

Seed Thoughts

This Midrash presents us with an interesting discussion of the word
kol, meaning "voice." It explains that there is something to Sarah's voice
that is being interpreted as being prophetic. Abraham is told to listen to
Sarah's voice and to follow it in the best way he can.

Nowhere does this Midrash draw any conclusions from the use of the
word *kol* in Sarah's life, and the use of one's voice on the part of all others.
I would like to suggest, however, that one of the lessons we should try
to learn from this episode is to take the human voice seriously. In a way,
there has been some original activity in the area of voice. In some of our
modern traditions, among the Ashkenazic Jews, *hazzanut* (which is the
term used to represent the function of the one who leads the service of
prayer) has made extensive use of the ability of one's voice. A great *haz-
zan* was not merely one who interpreted the prayers effectively but also
one whose voice was so beautifully developed that it added a powerful
meaning beyond the significance of the words themselves. For a period
of about 100 years, this kind of vocal *hazzanut* was prevalent in the Ashkenazic communities all over Europe. This tradition has continued in
North America and elsewhere, where new styles of vocal *hazzanut* have
been featured in many congregations, and all of them are associated
with the development of a singing voice. I should like to suggest that
this teaching should motivate us to examine and reflect on use of the
voice in ordinary speech. I am not referring to ordinary conversation.
People in various professions who have to speak in public, and before
a large public, should take the development of the spoken voice very

seriously. There are several wonderful books that explain the use of the voice in a way that is helpful for everyone. Using the voice correctly enhances every presentation, and the spoken voice can become an even greater method of education.

———

Additional Commentary

A permanent inheritance

One of the beautiful messages is the phrase in the wedding benedictions והתקין לו ממנו בנין עדי עד – *ve-hitkin lo mimenu binyan adei ad* – meaning that there was a permanent inheritance prepared for each other. What is this permanent inheritance? There are many answers that could be given to this question. It could be a form of charity, in the form of books, in the form of something heroic done by one of the participants. However, the most natural and most obvious of the permanent inheritances is the *binyan adei ad* – birth of children and bringing them up in the best possible way. The children of a marriage are the real *binyan adei ad*: they are alive, they are functioning, and even when they are gone, their own children can hopefully continue the chain of eternity, if lucky. (*Tiferet Tzion*)

PARASHAH FORTY-FIVE, *Midrash Three*

ג ותקח שרי אשת אברם את הגר המצרית שפחתה. לקחתה בדברים. אמרה לה: אשריך שאת מדבקת לגוף הקדוש הזה.

3. AND SARAI ABRAM'S WIFE TOOK HAGAR THE EGYPTIAN (GEN. 16:3). SHE PERSUADED [TOOK] HER WITH WORDS: "HAPPY ART THOU TO BE UNITED TO SO HOLY A MAN," SHE URGED.

In the previous Midrash, we read that Sarah interpreted her barrenness as God's decision, which she hoped would someday be changed. Some of the commentators suggest that the reason that Sarah helped Hagar accommodate herself to Abraham without any special concern was Sarah's way of doing something moral and ethical, so that by helping

Hagar, God would look with favor upon Sarah, and someday remove her barrenness.

מקץ עשר שנים לשבת אברם בארץ כנען. רבי אמי בשם ריש לקיש: מנין תנינן, נשא אשה
ושהה עמה י' שנים ולא ילדה, אינו רשאי ליבטל מפריה ורביה, אלא, יוציא וישא אשה
אחרת? מהכא, מקץ עשר שנים לשבת אברם בארץ כנען, הדא אמרת: אין ישיבת חוצה
לארץ עולה מן המנין.

AFTER ABRAM HAD DWELT TEN YEARS IN THE LAND OF CANAAN. R. AMMI
SAID IN THE NAME OF RESH LAKISH: WHAT IS THE SOURCE OF WHAT WE
LEARNED: IF A MAN MARRIED A WOMAN AND SPENT TEN YEARS WITH
HER AND SHE DID NOT BEAR A CHILD, HE MAY NOT STAY STERILE? THIS
VERSE: AFTER ABRAM HAD DWELT TEN YEARS: THIS PROVES THAT THE
TIME HE SPENT WITHOUT THE LAND WAS NOT INCLUDED IN THE RECK-
ONING.

The main reason for this section is to establish the primacy of the Land of Israel. Only the years that were spent in Canaan can be calculated to make up the ten years mentioned in the Midrash.

ותתן אותה לאברם אישה, ולא לאחר. לאשה, ולא לפילגש:

AND GAVE HER TO ABRAM HER HUSBAND TO BE A WIFE TO HIM, BUT NOT
TO ANOTHER; TO BE A WIFE, BUT NOT A CONCUBINE.

In the Hebrew idiom, the second wife of a polygamous relationship is called צרה – *tzarah*. The word *tzarah* means "a difficulty" or "a trouble-maker," or it may simply be a nice way of saying that the second wife created difficulties for the first wife. The brief passage that we have just read shows that Sarah did not regard Hagar as a *tzarah* but as an אשה – *isha* – "a full-fledged wife" – to Abraham, and not a פלגש – *pilegesh* – "a concubine."

~

Seed Thoughts

Since we do not live in a polygamous society, we do not know how married women react to each other (to the first wife, second wife, etc.). It is probably very difficult for the first wife to accept that she is being replaced either temporarily or permanently. That is probably one of the reasons why the Hebrew name *tzarah* is applied to this relationship. In

Sarah's case, she took it upon herself to help Hagar as a way of improving her spiritual status in the eyes of the Holy One, blessed be He. It should also be remembered, however, that Hagar was a princess, the daughter of Pharaoh. That was probably an additional major factor in Sarah's care and consideration for her.

PARASHAH FORTY-FIVE, *Midrash Four*

ד ויבא אל הגר ותהר. רבי לוי בר חייתא אמר: מביאה ראשונה נתעברה. אמר רבי אלעזר: לעולם אין האשה מתעברת מביאה ראשונה, והכתיב: ותהרין שתי בנות לוט מאביהן? א"ר תנחומא: שלטו בעצמן והוציאו ערותן ונתעברו, כמביאה שניה.

4. AND HE WENT IN UNTO HAGAR, AND SHE CONCEIVED (GEN. 16:4). R. LEVI B. HAYTHA SAID: SHE BECAME PREGNANT THROUGH THE FIRST INTIMACY. R. ELEAZAR SAID: A WOMAN NEVER CONCEIVES BY THE FIRST INTIMACY. AN OBJECTION IS RAISED: SURELY IT IS WRITTEN: THUS WERE BOTH THE DAUGHTERS OF LOT WITH CHILD BY THEIR FATHER (19:36)? SAID R. TANHUMA: BY AN EFFORT OF WILLPOWER THEY BROUGHT FORTH THEIR VIRGINITY, AND THUS CONCEIVED AT THE FIRST ACT OF INTERCOURSE.

Usually, when something appears in the Midrash dealing either with science or medicine, one tries to relate it to whatever modern developments may have been written on this subject. If the intention of the Midrash is to show that a first intimacy in marriage is something superior, that is not borne out. The only real differences are between pregnancy and barrenness, and nothing in between seems to be of any real importance.

א"ר חנינא בן פזי: הקוצין הללו, אינן לא מתנכשין ולא נזרעים מאיליהן, הן יוצאים ומתמרים ועולים. החטים הללו, כמה צער וכמה יגיע, עד שלא יעלו. ולמה נתעקרו האמהות? ר' לוי משום רבי שילא דכפר תמרתא, ורבי חלבו בשם ר' יוחנן: שהקב"ה מתאוה לתפלתן ומתאוה לשיחתן.

R. HANINA B. PAZZI OBSERVED: THORNS ARE NEITHER WEEDED NOR SOWN, YET OF THEIR OWN ACCORD THEY GROW AND SPRING UP, WHEREAS HOW MUCH PAIN AND TOIL IS REQUIRED BEFORE WHEAT CAN BE MADE TO GROW! WHY WERE THE MATRIARCHS BARREN? R. LEVI SAID

IN R. SHILA'S NAME AND R. HELBO IN R. JOHANAN'S NAME: BECAUSE THE
HOLY ONE, BLESSED BE HE, YEARNS FOR THEIR PRAYERS AND SUPPLICA-
TIONS.

The question of barrenness has always been in the minds of women
who have suffered this difficulty. There are more possibilities in modern
medicine to fight barrenness, but even those possibilities are severely
limited. When the Midrash says that the Matriarchs were barren because God loved to hear their prayers, this would not be considered
satisfactory to the women of today. It is still a very serious problem.

שנאמר: (שיר ב) יונתי בחגוי הסלע. יונתי. בחגוי, למה עקרתי אתכם? בשביל, הראיני את
מראיך השמיעיני את קולך. רבי עזריה משום ר' יוחנן בר פפא: כדי שיהיו מתרפקות על
בעליהן בנויין. רבי הונא משם רבי חייא בר אבא: כדי שיצאו רוב השנים, בלא שיעבוד. רבי
הונא ורבי אבון בשם רבי מאיר אמר: כדי שיהנו בעליהן מהן, שכל זמן שהאשה מקבלת
עוברין היא מתכערת ומתעזבת, שכל תשעים שנה שלא ילדה שרה היתה ככלה בתוך
חופתה, והיו מטרוניות באות לשאול בשלומה של שרה, והיתה שרה אומרת להם: צאו
ושאלו בשלומה של עלובה.

THUS IT IS WRITTEN: O MY DOVE, THOU ART AS THE CLEFTS OF THE
ROCK (SONG 2:14): WHY DID I MAKE THEE BARREN? IN ORDER THAT, LET
ME SEE THY COUNTENANCE, LET ME HEAR THY VOICE (2:14). R. AZA-
RIAH SAID IN R. HANINA'S NAME: SO THAT THEY MIGHT LEAN ON THEIR
HUSBANDS IN [SPITE OF] THEIR BEAUTY. R. HUNA AND R. JEREMIAH IN
THE NAME OF R. HIYYA B. ABBA SAID: SO THAT THEY MIGHT PASS THE
GREATER PART OF THEIR LIFE UNTRAMMELLED. R. HUNA, R. IDI, AND
R. ABIN IN R. MEIR'S NAME SAID: SO THAT THEIR HUSBANDS MIGHT
DERIVE PLEASURE FROM THEM, FOR WHEN A WOMAN IS WITH CHILD
SHE IS DISFIGURED AND LACKS GRACE. THUS THE WHOLE NINETY YEARS
THAT SARAH DID NOT BEAR SHE WAS LIKE A BRIDE IN HER CANOPY. LA-
DIES USED TO COME TO INQUIRE HOW SHE WAS, AND SHE WOULD SAY
TO THEM, "GO AND ASK ABOUT THE WELFARE OF THIS POOR WOMAN"
[HAGAR].

The Midrash states here that there are certain personal advantages to
barrenness. Usually, a woman who is pregnant becomes disfigured, and
after many pregnancies (although it does not always happen), a woman
is not as beautiful as she was before. Women who are barren are able to
retain their beauty for a longer period of time. That is a sort of minor
comfort to those who share the problem of barrenness.

והיתה הגר אומרת להם: שרי גבירתי, אין סיתרה כגלויה. נראית צדקת ואינה צדקת, אילו
היתה צדקת, ראו כמה שנים שלא נתעברה, ואני בלילה אחד נתעברתי! והיתה אומרת: עם
דא אנא מיסב ומיתן? הלואי מיסב ומיתן עם מרה:

HAGAR WOULD TELL THEM: "MY MISTRESS SARAI IS NOT INWARDLY
WHAT SHE IS OUTWARDLY: SHE APPEARS TO BE A RIGHTEOUS WOMAN,
BUT SHE IS NOT. FOR HAD SHE BEEN A RIGHTEOUS WOMAN, SEE HOW
MANY YEARS HAVE PASSED WITHOUT HER CONCEIVING, WHEREAS I
CONCEIVED IN ONE NIGHT!" SAID SARAH: "SHALL I PAY HEED TO THIS
WOMAN AND ARGUE WITH HER! NO, I WILL ARGUE THE MATTER WITH
HER MASTER!"

Hagar seems to have been of the opinion that early intimacy is a sign
of good character, and the fact that Sarah was barren for ninety years
does not justify her reputation as a woman of great righteousness. We
will learn more about this debate in the next Midrash.

⁓

Seed Thoughts

The problem of barrenness is as serious today as it ever was in former
times. Some women use every possible method, whether of medicine or
any other advice they might have received, in order to become pregnant.
Some women have gone through various types of surgery. There are
some women who, as a result of these excessive efforts, have developed
illnesses which on some occasions have even caused their death. People
should be told that the efforts to achieve pregnancy should be limited,
because there are other ways of having children, such as adoption. Some
of the most beautiful cases in social work have to do with children who
have found new parents who love them after their own original parents
suffered either death or various forms of incapacity. Adoption should
become a major priority in any and every society, particularly when
we realize that we live in an age when there are thousands of refugees
around the world, and there are children young and old who are calling
out for this kind of help.

PARASHAH FORTY-FIVE, *Midrash Five*

ה ותאמר שרי אל אברם חמסי עליך. רבי יודן בשם ר' יהודה בר סימון: חוממני אתה בדברים,
למה שאתה שומע בקלוני ושותק? רבי ברכיה בשם ר' אבא בר כהנא אמר: בעי דיני גבך.
משל לשני בני אדם חבושים בבית האסורים. נמצא המלך עובר. א"ל: חד תבע דקיון דידי.
אמר: אפקוהו. אמר ליה חבריה: יבעי דיני גבך! אילו אמרת תבוע דקיון דידן כמה דאפקך
כן אפקני, וכדו דאמרת תבע דקיון דידי, לך אפיק, לי לא אפיק. כך, אילו אמרת ואנו הולכים
עריים, כמה דיהב לך, כן יהב לי, וכדו דאמרת: אנכי הולך עירירי, לך יהיב, ולי לא יהיב.

5. AND SARAI SAID UNTO ABRAM: MY WRONG (*HAMASI*) BE UPON THEE
(GEN. 16:5). R. JUDAN EXPLAINED THIS IN R. JUDAH'S NAME: THOU
WRONGEST ME WITH WORDS, SINCE THOU HEAREST ME INSULTED YET
ART SILENT. R. BEREKIAH EXPLAINED IT IN R. ABBA'S NAME: I HAVE A
GRIEVANCE AGAINST THEE. FOR IMAGINE TWO MEN INCARCERATED IN
PRISON, AND AS THE KING PASSES, ONE OF THEM CRIES OUT: EXECUTE
JUSTICE FOR ME! THE KING ORDERS HIM TO BE RELEASED, WHEREUPON
HIS FELLOW-PRISONER SAYS TO HIM: "I HAVE A GRIEVANCE AGAINST
YOU, FOR HAD YOU SAID, 'EXECUTE JUSTICE FOR US,' HE WOULD HAVE
RELEASED ME JUST AS HE HAS RELEASED YOU; BUT NOW THAT YOU SAID,
'EXECUTE JUSTICE FOR ME,' HE RELEASED YOU BUT NOT ME." SIMILARLY,
HADST THOU SAID, "WE GO CHILDLESS," THEN AS HE GAVE THEE A CHILD
SO WOULD HE HAVE GIVEN ME; SINCE, HOWEVER, THOU SAIDEST: AND I
GO CHILDLESS (15:2), HE GAVE THEE A CHILD BUT NOT ME.

In this section, Sarah was complaining to Abraham, and she was very
disappointed in him. Hagar had forgotten how much she owed Sarah,
and was criticizing her for being less righteous than imagined, and her
being barren was the proof of this. Sarah was mad at Abraham, because
he did not defend her and argue on her behalf. In general, he did not act
as a partner. He complained to God that he was childless, and forgot to
tell Him that Sarah was childless. When Ishmael was born, his childless-
ness ended, but it did not end Sarah's. Abraham did not think of Sarah's
situation. The example of the two men where only one of them asked
for the king's help rather than the king's help for both of them is a good
example of what Sarah was complaining about.

משל לשני בני אדם שהלכו ללוות זרע מן המלך. א"ל: תשאיל לי זרע. אמר: ויהבון ליה. א"ל
חבריה: יבעי דיני גבך. אילו אמרת תשאיל לנו זרע כמה דיהיב לך. כן הוה יהיב לי ה"נ אילו

אמרת הן לנו לא נתת זרע, כמה דיהיב לך, הוה יהיב לי, וכדו דאמרת: הן לי לא נתת זרע, לך
יהיב, לי לא יהיב.

THIS MAY [ALSO] BE COMPARED TO TWO PEOPLE WHO WENT TO BOR-
ROW SEED FROM THE KING. ONE OF THEM ASKED: LEND ME SEED, AND
HE ORDERED, GIVE IT TO HIM. SAID HIS COMPANION TO HIM, I HAVE A
GRIEVANCE AGAINST YOU. HAD YOU ASKED, "LEND US SEED," HE WOULD
HAVE GIVEN ME JUST AS HE GAVE YOU; NOW HOWEVER THAT YOU SAID,
"LEND ME SEED," HE HAS GIVEN YOU BUT NOT ME. SIMILARLY, HADST
THOU SAID: BEHOLD, TO US THOU HAST GIVEN NO SEED, THEN AS HE
GAVE THEE SO HAD HE GIVEN ME. NOW HOWEVER THAT THOU DIDST
SAY, BEHOLD, TO ME THOU HAST GIVEN NO SEED ' (GEN. 5:3), HE GAVE
TO THEE BUT NOT TO ME.

This section continues Sarah's complaints to Abraham that he has not
been acting as a true partner. He was thinking only of himself, assuming
that that would include Sarah, but Sarah insisted that these assumptions
were not verified, that she should be involved in her own right.

ר' נחמיה בשם ר' אבון אמר: חימסה בפניו. ורבנן אמרי: ד' מדות נאמרו בנשים: גרגרניות
ציית-ניות עצלניות קנאניות. גרגרניות, מחוה (בראשית ג): ותקח מפריו ותאכל. ציית-ניות, (שם
יח): ושרה שומעת. עצלניות (שם): מהרי שלש סאים קמח סולת. קנאניות, דכתיב (שם ל):
ותקנא רחל באחותה. רבי יהודה בר נחמיה אמר: אף איסטטניות ודברניות. איסטטניות (שם
טז): ותאמר שרי אל אברם: חמסי עליך. ודברניות (במדבר יב): ותדבר מרים ואהרן במשה.
רבי לוי אמר: אף גנביות שנאמר (בראשית לא): ותגנוב רחל את התרפים. יוצאניות (שם לד):
ותצא דינה.

R. MENAHEMA [NEHEMIAH] SAID IN R. ABIN'S NAME: SHE SCRATCHED
HIS FACE. THE RABBIS SAID: WOMEN ARE SAID TO POSSESS FOUR TRAITS:
THEY ARE GREEDY, EAVESDROPPERS, SLOTHFUL, AND ENVIOUS. GREEDY,
AS IT SAYS: AND SHE TOOK OF THE FRUIT THEREOF, AND DID EAT (GEN.
3:6); EAVESDROPPERS: AND SARAH HEARD IN THE TENT DOOR (18:10);
SLOTHFUL: MAKE READY QUICKLY THREE MEASURES OF FINE MEAL
(18:6); ENVIOUS: RACHEL ENVIED HER SISTER (30:1). R. JOSHUA B. NEHE-
MIAH SAID: SHE IS ALSO A SCRATCHER AND TALKATIVE. A SCRATCHER:
AND SARAI SAID UNTO ABRAM: MY SCRATCH BE UPON THEE. TALKATIVE:
AND MIRIAM SPOKE AGAINST MOSES (NUM. 12:1). R. LEVI SAID: SHE
IS ALSO PRONE TO STEAL AND A GADABOUT. PRONE TO STEAL: AND
RACHEL STOLE THE TERAPHIM (GEN. 31:19). A GADABOUT: AND DINAH
WENT OUT (34:1).

The interpretations that criticize the female personality are most unfair. For example, the text does say that when Abraham was told that he
would definitely have a child, Sarah was listening in the next room. She
happened to be sitting in the next room, so she happened to overhear
the conversation. But this Midrash tries to make the point that Sarah
placed herself there specifically because she wanted to hear what was
being said. There is no basis for this kind of criticism, and all the other
points of this past paragraph can be reinterpreted in a way that they
simply describe normal behavior. The same thing could be said and reinterpreted in the case of the behavior of many of the male personalities
in the biblical story.

רבי תנחומא אמר בשם רבי חייא רבה, ורבי ברכיה אמר בשם רבי חייא: כל מי שהרחיק אחר
מדת הדין, לא יצא שפוי מתחת ידיה. ראויה היתה שרה להגיע לשניו של אברהם ועל ידי
שאמרה (שם טז): ישפוט ה' ביני וביניך, נמנעו מחייה שלשים ושמונה שנה. כתיב ויבא אל הגר
ותהר. ומה ת"ל הנך הרה וילדת בן? אלא מלמד שהכניסה בה שרה עין רעה והפילה עוברה.
א"ר יוחנן: ביני וביניך, ובנך כתיב. א"ר חנינא: אילו אלישע הנביא אמר כן ברוח הקודש דיי,
אלא שזכתה לדבר עמה המלאך:

THE LORD JUDGE BETWEEN ME AND THEE (*UBENEKA*). R. TANHUMA
SAID IN THE NAME OF R. HIYYA THE ELDER, AND R. BEREKIAH SAID IN
R. ELEAZAR'S NAME: WHOEVER PLUNGES EAGERLY INTO LITIGATION
DOES NOT ESCAPE FROM IT UNSCATHED. SARAH SHOULD HAVE REACHED
ABRAHAM'S YEARS, BUT BECAUSE SHE SAID: THE LORD JUDGE BETWEEN
ME AND THEE, HER LIFE WAS REDUCED BY FORTY-EIGHT YEARS. R. HO
SHAYA SAID: *BINKHA* (THY SON) IS WRITTEN. SEEING THAT IT IS ALREADY
WRITTEN: AND HE WENT IN UNTO HAGAR, AND SHE CONCEIVED, WHY IS
IT FURTHER STATED: BEHOLD, THOU WILT CONCEIVE (GEN. 16:11)? THIS,
HOWEVER, TEACHES THAT AN EVIL EYE TOOK POSSESSION OF HER AND
SHE MISCARRIED. R. HANINA OBSERVED: HAD THE PROPHET ELISHA
TOLD HER THAT BY THE HOLY SPIRIT, IT WOULD HAVE SUFFICED HER.

This Midrash is another example of how sometimes, the midrashic
writers are much too critical of Sarah. She said, "Let God judge between
us," which seems to be a fine and honorable thing to say. But the Sages
interpret that most critically, almost as though the writers are trying to
involve her husband in some sort of courtroom. What the Sages should
have written at this point is to attribute to Sarah. They should have said
that Sarah was justified in her complaints. They should have said that

Abraham should have understood the partnership of marriage and should have treated Sarah as equal to himself.

—

Seed Thoughts

Although I realize it is not possible, I would have hoped that this kind of Midrash would not have been written. Since this is being written in the twenty-first century, we currently have many women who are scholars in the Bible and in the Talmud. I am certain that this kind of critical paragraph hurts them although they have been accustomed to this kind of treatment over many generations. Maybe someone should prepare a list of male personalities in the Bible who could be subject to this kind of critical treatment. For example, the voice from the Garden of Eden (Cain): "Am I my brother's keeper?" Or the words that Moses used in addressing the people, which ultimately prevented him from entering the Promised Land – namely: "Listen to me, you rebellious people." I am sure that there is a longer list that could be prepared. We are human beings, and we have human frailties. But we also possess human ideals. Let us not look for frailties in those human beings who have lived a life of idealism and spiritual leadership.

PARASHAH FORTY-FIVE, *Midrash Six*

ו ויאמר אברם אל שרי עשי לה הטוב בעיניך. א"ל: מה איכפת לי? לא בטובתה ולא ברעתה.
כתיב (דברים כא): לא תתעמר בה תחת אשר עניתה.

6. BUT ABRAM SAID UNTO SARAI: BEHOLD, THY MAID IS IN THY HAND
(GEN. 16:6). SAID HE: I AM CONSTRAINED TO DO HER NEITHER GOOD
NOR HARM. IT IS WRITTEN: THOU SHALT NOT DEAL WITH HER AS A
SLAVE, BECAUSE THOU HAST HUMBLED HER (DEUT. 21:14):

This will be mentioned several times in our present Midrash. Abraham insists that he has no special relationship with Hagar, but that she should be protected in accordance with the agreement that brought Hagar into their household.

וזו, מאחר שציערנו אותה, אנו משתעבדין בה? ולא איכפת לי לא בטובתה ולא ברעתה.
כתיב (שמות כא): לעם נכרי לא ימשול למכרה בבגדו בה, וזו, מאחר שעשינו אותה גבירה, אנו
עושין אותה שפחה? לא איכפת לי, לא בטובתה ולא ברעתה.

AFTER WE HAVE VEXED HER, CAN WE NOW ENSLAVE HER AGAIN? I AM
CONSTRAINED TO DO HER NEITHER GOOD NOR HARM. IT IS WRITTEN:
AND SARAH DEALT HARSHLY WITH HER, AND SHE FLED FROM HER
FACE (GEN. 16:6), WHILE IT IS WRITTEN: TO SELL HER UNTO A FOREIGN
PEOPLE HE SHALL HAVE NO POWER, SEEING HE HATH DEALT DECEIT-
FULLY WITH HER (EX. 21:8): AFTER WE HAVE MADE HER A MISTRESS,
SHALL WE MAKE HER A BONDMAID AGAIN? I AM CONSTRAINED TO DO
HER NEITHER GOOD NOR HARM;

Abraham, here, restates his position. Hagar has to be protected, and apparently, she was not protected, since she was treated like a maid from time to time.

ותעניה שרי ותברח מפניה. רבי אבא בר כהנא אמר: מנעתה מתשמיש המטה. רבי ברכיה
אמר: טפחתה בקורדקייסון על פניה. ר' ברכיה בשם רבי אבא בר כהנא: דליים ופנדיות
הוליכה לה למרחץ:

HENCE IT IS WRITTEN, AND SARAH DEALT HARSHLY WITH HER, AND
SHE FLED FROM HER FACE. R. ABBA SAID: SHE RESTRAINED HER FROM
COHABITATION. R. BEREKIAH SAID: SHE SLAPPED HER FACE WITH A

SLIPPER. R. BEREKIAH SAID IN R. ABBA'S NAME: SHE BADE HER CARRY
HER WATER BUCKETS AND BATH TOWELS TO THE BATHS.

This section lists the various ways in which Hagar felt humiliated.
After all, her status was that of the second wife to Abraham, and when
she saw that that status was being lowered, she fled.

⁓

Seed Thoughts

See the Additional Commentary.

⁓

Additional Commentary

Abraham's role

Abraham was put in a difficult position when Sarah seemed to be punishing Hagar. On the one hand, he had to protect Sarah's honor since
she was the chief wife of his household. On the other hand, he felt that
Hagar had to be protected, since there was an agreement made between
Sarah and Hagar's father, Pharaoh, that she would be treated honorably
and definitely not as a slave. Abraham insisted that he had no personal
interest in Hagar; she became his second wife not by his choice but by
arrangements made between Sarah and Hagar themselves. However, he
tried to establish a difference between his personal lack of interest and
his concern that she be treated fairly. (Aryeh Mirkin)

PARASHAH FORTY-FIVE, *Midrash Seven*

ז וימצאה מלאך ה' על עין המים וגו', באורחא דחלוצה. ויאמר הגר שפחת שרי, מתלא
אמר: אם אמר לך חד, אוניך דחמר! לא תיחוש. תרין, עביד לך, פרוכי. כך, אברם אמר:
הנה שפחתך בידך. המלאך אמר: הגר שפחת שרי. ותאמר: מפני שרי גברתי, אנכי בורחת.

7. AND THE ANGEL OF THE LORD FOUND HER ... IN THE WAY TO SHUR
(GEN. 16:7): ON THE ROAD OF HALUZAH. AND HE SAID: HAGAR, SARAI'S
HANDMAID, ETC. (16:8). SO RUNS THE PROVERB: IF ONE MAN TELLS YOU
THAT YOU HAVE ASS'S EARS, DO NOT BELIEVE HIM; IF TWO TELL IT TO
YOU, ORDER A HALTER. THUS, ABRAHAM SAID: BEHOLD, THY MAID IS IN
THY HAND (16:6); THE ANGEL SAID: HAGAR. SARAI'S HANDMAID, ETC.
HENCE, AND SHE SAID: I FLEE FROM THE FACE OF MY MISTRESS SARAI.

The angel used the word שפחה – *shifkha*, meaning maid, on two occasions that we have just read. This was one of Hagar's concerns, because
she did not want to be treated as a "maid." This is what the text means
when it says that if something is repeated, take it very seriously.

ויאמר לה מלאך ה': שובי אל גברתך והתעני וגו'. ויאמר לה מלאך ה': הרבה וגו'. כמה
מלאכים נזדווגו לה? ר' יוסי בר חנינא אמר: חמשה, בכל מקום שנאמר אמירה מלאך. רבנן
אמרי: ארבעה: בכל מקום שנאמר מלאך.

AND AN ANGEL OF THE LORD SAID UNTO HER; RETURN TO THY MIS-
TRESS, ETC ... AND AN ANGEL OF THE LORD SAID UNTO HER: I WILL
GREATLY MULTIPLY THY SEED, ETC. (GEN. 16:9F.). HOW MANY ANGELS
VISITED HER? R. JOSE B. R. HANINA SAID: FIVE, FOR EACH TIME "SPEECH"
IS MENTIONED, IT REFERS TO AN ANGEL. THE RABBIS SAID: FOUR, THIS
BEING THE NUMBER OF TIMES "ANGEL" OCCURS.

Apparently, more than one angel appeared in order to address Hagar.
The evidence for this is that the word מלאך – *malakh* – appears five
times, and it was quite unnecessary for it to be written this way. According to the Rabbis, only four angels appeared, because the first reference
to *malakh* is simply recorded in the text without any special relationship
to Hagar.

א"ר חייא: בוא וראה כמה בין ראשונים לאחרונים. מנוח אמר לאשתו (שופטים יג): מות נמות
כי אלהים ראינו. והגר שפחת שרי רואה ה' מלאכים בזה אחר זה, ולא נתייראה מהם. אמר

רבי חייא: ציפרנן של אבות, ולא כריסן של בנים. א"ר יצחק (משלי לא): צופיה הליכות ביתה.
בני ביתו של אבינו אברהם צופים היו, והיתה רגילה לראות בהם:

R. HIYYA OBSERVED: COME AND SEE HOW GREAT IS THE DIFFERENCE
BETWEEN THE EARLIER GENERATIONS AND THE LATER ONES! WHAT DID
MANOAH SAY TO HIS WIFE? WE SHALL SURELY DIE, BECAUSE WE HAVE
SEEN GOD (JUDG. 13:22); YET HAGAR, A BONDMAID, SEES FIVE ANGELS
AND IS NOT AFRAID OF THEM! R. AHA SAID: THE FINGERNAIL OF THE
FATHERS RATHER THAN THE STOMACH OF THE SONS! R. ISAAC QUOTED:
SHE SEETH THE WAYS OF HER HOUSEHOLD (PROV. 31:27): ABRAHAM'S
HOUSEHOLD WERE SEERS, SO SHE [HAGAR] WAS ACCUSTOMED TO THEM.

The last several sentences are self-explanatory. Manoah and his family seem to show greater reverence to God and was quite fearful of the presence of angels in their life. Hagar did not feel that way, because she was accustomed to seeing and/or hearing angels in the household of Abraham and Sarah. In the same way that one is not bothered by one's fingernails as compared to something that may hurt you in other parts of your body, so Hagar was quite casual about the appearance of angels on this special occasion.

—

Seed Thoughts

A number of questions can be asked based on this Midrash: Why did an angel appear in connection with Hagar's predicament? Was it because of the importance of Abraham and Sarah? Furthermore, why were four or five separate angels required? Nowhere does the Midrash respond to this, but it is a question which the average reader would be concerned with. Another problem is the following: The angels said to her: "You will be pregnant and you will be blessed with a child." What does that mean? Should this be understood in the light of the statement of a previous Midrash that Hagar had a miscarriage? If this is so, does it mean that Ishmael was not a firstborn to Hagar but a second-born? And how do you relate that to the several occasions where Ishmael is mentioned but does not seem to fit in? Not every question can be answered, and we will have to wait and see. The Midrash may once again comment on these matters.

Parashah Forty-Five, *Midrash Eight*

ח ויאמר לה מלאך ה' הנך הרה וגו'.

8. AND THE ANGEL OF THE LORD SAID UNTO HER: BEHOLD, THOU ART
WITH CHILD, ETC. (GEN. 16:11).

The Midrash does not continue the text as it appears in the Pentateuch.
What follows is "and his name shall be called Ishmael." This text already
answers some of our concerns in the commentaries that preceded this
particular Midrash.

א"ר יצחק: שלשה הן שנקראו בשמם לפני הקב"ה, עד שלא נוצרו, ואלו הן: יצחק ושלמה
ויאשיהו. ביצחק, כתיב (בראשית יז): אבל שרה אשתך יולדת לך בן וגו'. בשלמה, מה הוא
אומר? (דה"א כב): הנה בן נולד לך, הוא יהיה איש מנוחה, והניחותי לו מכל אויביו, שלמה יהיה
שמו. ביאשיהו, כתיב (מ"א יג): ויקרא אל המזבח בדבר ה', ויאמר: מזבח מזבח, כה אמר ה'
הנה בן נולד לבית דוד, יאשיהו שמו. וי"א אף ישמעאל באומות, הנך הרה וילדת בן, וקראת
את שמו ישמעאל:

R. ISAAC SAID: THREE WERE CALLED BY THEIR NAMES BEFORE THEY
WERE BORN, ISAAC, SOLOMON, AND JOSIAH. WHAT IS SAID IN THE CASE
OF ISAAC? AND GOD SAID: NAY, BUT SARAH THY WIFE SHALL BEAR THEE
A SON; AND THOU SHALT CALL HIS NAME ISAAC (GEN. 17:19). IN THE
CASE OF SOLOMON? BEHOLD, A SON SHALL BE BORN TO THEE, WHO
SHALL BE A MAN OF REST; AND I WILL GIVE HIM REST FROM ALL HIS
ENEMIES ROUND ABOUT; FOR HIS NAME SHALL BE SOLOMON (I CHRON.
22:9). IN THE CASE OF JOSIAH? AND HE CRIED AGAINST THE ALTAR BY
THE WORD OF THE LORD: O ALTAR, ALTAR, THUS SAITH THE LORD:
BEHOLD, A SON SHALL BE BORN UNTO THE HOUSE OF DAVID, JOSIAH BY
NAME (I KINGS 13:2). SOME ADD ISHMAEL AMONG THE NATIONS [I.E.,
NON-JEWS]: BEHOLD, THOU ART WITH CHILD, AND SHALT BEAR A SON;
AND THOU SHALT CALL HIS NAME ISHMAEL.

The interesting part of this Midrash is that Ishmael is added among
those names of people whose announcements of impending birth
preceded their coming into the world. This seems to confirm what we
learned earlier, that Hagar had suffered a miscarriage from her first pregnancy, and that the joy of this birth will compensate her for her former
suffering.

—

Seed Thoughts

This Midrash is a clear response to those concerns which were stated in the Seed Thoughts of the previous section. One of the concerns was that Hagar suffered a miscarriage, which in retrospect can be interpreted as her punishment for unjustified criticism of Sarah. The commentators also state that Ishmael was a צדיק – tzaddik, a righteous person. Others disagree with this conclusion, and it will have to be investigated further.

PARASHAH FORTY-FIVE, *Midrash Nine*

ט והוא יהיה פרא אדם. רבי יוחנן ורבי שמעון בן לקיש. רבי יוחנן אמר: שהכל יהיו גדלים
ביישוב, והוא יהיה גדל במדבר. רבי שמעון בן לקיש אמר: פרא אדם, ודאי שהכל בוזזים
ממון, והוא בוזז נפשות.

9. AND HE SHALL BE A PERE (E.V. "A WILD ASS") OF A MAN (GEN. 16:12). R. JOHANAN AND RESH LAKISH DEBATED THIS. R. JOHANAN SAID: IT MEANS THAT WHILE ALL PEOPLE ARE BRED IN CIVILIZED SURROUNDINGS, HE WOULD BE REARED IN THE WILDERNESS. RESH LAKISH SAID: IT MEANS A SAVAGE AMONG MEN IN ITS LITERAL SENSE, FOR WHEREAS ALL OTHERS PLUNDER WEALTH, HE PLUNDERS LIVES.

This section begins an entirely different evaluation of Ishmael. He is described as פרא אדם – *pereh adam*. The word *pereh* actually means a "wilderness," whereas the translation uses the adjective "wild" in terms of the behavior of a person in the isolation of a wilderness that can sometimes appear to be wild. Resh Lakish has a different interpretation, which has to do with a person's standards of action. Many people exploit wealth or other forms of acquisition, whereas the term *pereh* applies to those who exploit human lives in many ways.

ידו בכל ויד כל בו, קרי בו כלבו, הוא והכלב שוים. מה הכלב אוכל נבלות, אף הוא אוכל
נבלות. אמר רבי אלעזר: מתי ידו בכל, ויד כל בו? לכשיבא אותו שכתוב (דניאל ב): ובכל
די דארין בני אנשא, חיות ברא, ועוף שמיא, יהב בידך והשלטך בכלהון, הה"ד (ירמיה מט):
לקדר ולממלכות חצור, אשר הכה נבוכדנצר מלך בבל, נבוכד ראצר כתיב, שאצרן במדבר
והרגן. על פני כל אחיו ישכון הכא את אמר: ישכון. והתם כתיב: נפל? אלא כל זמן שהיה

אברהם אבינו קיים, ישכון. וכשמת אברהם, נפל. עד שלא פשט ידו בבית המקדש, ישכון.
כיון שפשט ידו בבית המקדש, נפל. בעולם הזה ישכון, אבל לעתיד לבא נפל:

HIS HAND SHALL BE AGAINST EVERY MAN, AND EVERY MAN'S HAND
AGAINST HIM (KOL BO). HIS HAND AND HIS DOG'S (KALBO) ARE ALIKE.
JUST AS HIS DOG EATS CARRION, SO DOES HE EAT CARRION. R. ELEA-
ZAR SAID: WHEN SHALL HIS HAND BE AGAINST EVERY MAN AND EVERY
MAN'S HAND AGAINST HIM? WHEN HE SHALL COME OF WHOM IT IS
WRITTEN: AND WHERESOEVER THE CHILDREN OF MEN, THE BEASTS OF
THE FIELD, AND THE FOWLS OF THE HEAVEN DWELL, HATH HE GIVEN
THEM INTO THY HAND (DAN. 2:38). HENCE IT IS WRITTEN: OF KEDAR,
AND OF THE KINGDOMS OF HAZOR, WHICH NEHUCHADREZZAR SMOTE
(JER. 49:28): HIS NAME IS WRITTEN "NEBUCHADREZZAR," BECAUSE HE
SHUT THEM UP (AZURAN) IN THE WILDERNESS AND SLEW THEM. AND
HE SHALL DWELL IN THE FACE OF ALL HIS BRETHREN. HERE YOU SAY:
HE SHALL DWELL, WHILE ELSEWHERE YOU READ: HE FELL (GEN. 25:17)?
AS LONG AS ABRAHAM LIVED, HE SHALL DWELL; AS SOON AS HE DIED,
HE FELL. BEFORE HE STRETCHED OUT HIS HAND AGAINST THE TEMPLE,
HE SHALL DWELL; AS SOON AS HE STRETCHED OUT HIS HAND AGAINST
THE TEMPLE, HE FELL. IN THIS WORLD, HE SHALL DWELL; IN THE NEXT
WORLD, HE FELL [SHALL BE APPLICABLE TO HIM].

Additional opinions are recorded as to the meaning of the Hebrew adjective *pereh*. One is that everyone's hand was against him, and his own hands were against everyone else. There is a play on words in terms of this explanation. Everyone's hands against him is written in Hebrew as כל בו – *kol bo*. However, the play on words is to put the two together as *kol bo* in one word, and it could be interpreted as כלבו – *kalbo*, meaning "his dog." In many respects, wilderness living can sometimes reduce a person to the level of a dog, becoming a scavenger when it comes to food, and in general being destructive as dogs are often so destructive. It simply means that he opposed what we call "civilized living." The community, in general, opposed this behavior and took active steps against him. Special names like Kedar and Hazor are place names for regions which were controlled by the descendants of Ishmael. They were his areas where his rules applied, which were quite distinct from other forms of behavior.

There are two additional comments that can be made. The reference to Nebuchadrezzar is based on the charge that the descendants of Ishmael participated in the attack on Jerusalem and possibly even in the attack on the Temple. Two different verbs are associated with Ishmael's community – the word ישכן – *yishkon*, meaning "dwelling in security," and the word נפל – *nafal*, "descending to a very low human level." The interpretation is that so long as Abraham was alive, they dwelled in security. The moment he passed away, their security was jeopardized.

⁓

Seed Thoughts

How does one explain the fact that in the previous Midrash, Ishmael was described as a tzaddik, a righteous person, whereas in the present Midrash, he is described as a wilderness creature? The only explanation appears to be that when Ishmael was young, Abraham (his father) was not only alive, but active in bringing up his son. He loved Ishmael and Ishmael loved him, and Ishmael tried his best to imitate him. The death of Abraham was a serious crisis for Ishmael; he left his parental home, and eventually became involved in the wilderness experience with many negative consequences. Although his descendants were accused of having a share in Nebuchadrezzar's attacks on the Jewish people in Judea, that never involved him, and he kept his distance from those events. On the other hand, many of the commentators write that he did teshuvah, that he repented and changed his lifestyle, so he resembled the earlier Ishmael as his father wanted him to be. There is also the beautiful line in Scripture – that when Abraham died, he was buried by both Ishmael and Isaac, both of whose lives were dedicated to Abraham and his teaching.

PARASHAH FORTY-FIVE, *Midrash Ten*

י ותקרא שם ה' הדובר אליה אתה אל ראי.

10. AND SHE CALLED THE NAME OF THE LORD THAT SPOKE UNTO HER (GEN. 16:13).

One of the main questions with which this Midrash deals is whether God actually spoke to Hagar. If not, what is meant by her expression that to her, God was the one who watched her?

רבי יהודה בר סימון, ורבי יוחנן בשם ר' אלעזר בר שמעון: מעולם לא נזקק הקב"ה להשיח
עם האשה, אלא עם אותה הצדקת, ואף היא ע"י עילה. רבי אבא בשם רבי בירי: כמה
כרכורים כרכר בשביל להשיח עמה? ויאמר: לא, כי צחקת.

R. JUDAH B. R. SIMON AND R. JOHANAN IN THE NAME OF R. ELEAZAR
B. R. SIMEON SAID: THE HOLY ONE, BLESSED BE HE, NEVER CONDE-
SCENDED TO HOLD CONVERSATIONS WITH A WOMAN SAVE WITH THAT
RIGHTEOUS WOMAN [VIZ. SARAH], AND THAT TOO WAS THROUGH A
PARTICULAR CAUSE. R. ABBA B. KAHANA SAID IN R. BIRYA'S NAME: AND
WHAT A ROUNDABOUT WAY HE TOOK IN ORDER TO SPEAK WITH HER, AS
IT IS WRITTEN: AND HE SAID: NAY, BUT THOU DIDST LAUGH (GEN. 18:15)!

The second question being raised by this Midrash as to whether God
communicated with a woman was whether such a conversation was
appropriate. The only exception was his speaking to Sarah, because she
was regarded as righteous. On the other hand, there is a particular reason for God's intervention at that particular time. As to whether Sarah
laughed at the news that she would have a child in her ninetieth year,
God intervened in order to protect Abraham, and did so with a short
conversation to Sarah. In both God's and Abraham's opinions, she did
indeed laugh.

והכתיב: ותקרא שם ה' הדובר אליה? רבי יהושע בר נחמיה אמר: על ידי מלאך. והכתיב:
ויאמר ה' לה? רבי לוי בשם רבי חנינא בר חמא אמר: על ידי מלאך. רבי אלעזר בשם ר' יוסי
בן זמרא אמר: ע"י שם.

BUT IT IS WRITTEN: AND SHE [HAGAR] CALLED THE NAME OF THE LORD
THAT SPOKE UNTO HER? R. JOSHUA B. R. NEHEMIAH ANSWERED IN R.
IDI'S NAME: THAT WAS THROUGH AN ANGEL. BUT IT IS WRITTEN: AND
THE LORD SAID UNTO HER – REBEKAH (GEN. 25:23)? R. LEVI SAID IN THE
NAME OF R. HAMA B. R. HANINA: THAT WAS THROUGH AN ANGEL. R.
LEAZAR SAID IN THE NAME OF R. JOSE B. ZIMRA: THAT WAS THROUGH
THE MEDIUM OF SHEM.

This section tries to respond to the amazing verse where God spoke
to Hagar by saying that he did it through an angel. That would make it
less threatening to the Divine. Another opinion stated is that God spoke
to her through Shem, the son of Noah. He had lived a very long time,
including during the generation that we are now discussing. He had
achieved a high position as a repected priest, and in general, he was a
human being of rare talent, acceptable as a representative of the Divine.

אתה אל ראי. אמר רבי אייבו: אתה הוא רואה בעלבון של עלובין.

THOU ART A GOD OF SEEING (*EL ROI*). R. AIBU EXPLAINED IT: THOU
SEEST THE SUFFERINGS OF THE PERSECUTED.

Rabbi Aibu interpreted Hagar's name for God as the Lord who sees
the insults. He protects those who have been insulted and who no one
else can protect.

כי אמרה: הגם הלום ראיתי אחרי רואי. אמרה: לא דיי שנזקקתי לדיבור, אלא למלכות, היך
מה דאת אמר (שמואל ב ז): כי הביאותני עד הלום. ראיתי אחרי רואי לא דיי שנזקקתי עם
גברתי לראות המלאך, אלא, שאפילו גברתי שהיתה עמי, לא ראתה. ד"א: לא דיי שנזקקתי
עם גברתי, אלא ביני לבין עצמי. אר"ש בר נחמן: משל למטרונה שא"ל המלך: עברי לפני!
עברה לפניו והיתה מסתמכת על שפחתה, וצמצמה פניה, ולא ראתה המלך, והשפחה
ראתה:

FOR SHE SAID: HAVE I EVEN HERE (*HALOM*) SEEN HIM THAT SEETH ME.
SHE SAID: "I HAVE BEEN GRANTED NOT ONLY SPEECH [WITH THE AN-
GEL], BUT EVEN WITH ROYALTY TOO, AS YOU READ: THAT THOU HAST
BROUGHT ME THUS FAR – *HALOM* (II SAM. 7:18). I WAS FAVORED [TO SEE
THE ANGEL] NOT ONLY WHEN WITH MY MISTRESS, BUT EVEN NOW THAT
I AM ALONE." R. SAMUEL SAID: THIS MAY BE COMPARED TO A NOBLE
LADY WHOM THE KING ORDERED TO WALK BEFORE HIM. SHE DID SO
LEANING ON HER MAID AND PRESSING HER FACE AGAINST HER. THUS
HER MAID SAW [THE KING], WHILE SHE DID NOT SEE HIM.

Hagar is quoted as being grateful not only that God spoke to her,
whether through an angel or in any other way, but that the result was
that she was blessed not only with the Divine concern but also with
the promise of royalty. It was prophesized that her son would be among
the leaders of his state. This is the meaning of the Hebrew word הלום --
halom. Does this mean that Hagar experienced God more than Sarah?
Not at all. It means that Sarah was protected not only by her position as
the mistress, but also her very high respect for the Divine. As so often
happens in life, that a servant sees more than a mistress because she has
no inhibitions, so it was that Hagar in Sarah's home may have heard the
voice of God more often, because she had fewer inhibitions about this
than Sarah.

Seed Thoughts

The Midrash raises the question as to whether it was appropriate for God to have conversation with women. The Midrash acknowledges certain exceptions to this rule, such as Sarah, Hagar, and Rebecca. But nowhere does it discuss the reasons why, so that women should not feel the sense of inferiority that these views represent. In modern times, there has been a great rebellion in this regard, whether the terms used are egalitarianism or uniformity. It is not that women want to be like men; it is rather that they would like an interpretation of the meaning of their Jewish existence so that they could prepare for a spiritual role which in every respect would be as important to them as spiritual obligations to Jewish males are.

א ויהי אברם בן תשעים ותשע שנים.

1. AND ABRAM WAS NINETY YEARS OLD AND NINE, ETC. (GEN. 17:1).

This is only part of the verse. The remainder of the verse reads: "Walk before me and be complete." This verse is one of the important interpretations of circumcision, מילה – *milah*. This Midrash is the first of several in this chapter that will deal with the whole question of milah and will try to impress upon the reader to the tremendous importance that the reader assigns to it.

(הושע ט) כענבים במדבר מצאתי ישראל כבכורה בתאנה בראשיתה וגו'.

IT IS WRITTEN, I FOUND ISRAEL LIKE GRAPES IN THE WILDERNESS, I SAW YOUR FATHERS AS THE FIRST-RIPE IN THE FIG-TREE AT HER FIRST SEASON (HOS. 9:10).

The metaphors of grapes and figs are very beautiful. When one travels in any wilderness area, one is surprised to find beautiful flowers or beautiful fruits such as are described. Similarly, when Israel received the Torah in the wilderness, it is as though the wilderness produced the most precious of all possibilities for human life, namely, the spiritual way of life.

אמר רבי יודן: התאנה הזו בתחלה אורים אותה אחת אחת, ואח"כ שתים, ואח"כ שלשה עד שאורים אותה בסלים ובמגריפות. כך, בתחלה אחד היה אברהם וירש את הארץ, ואח"כ שנים אברהם ויצחק, ואח"כ שלשה עד אברהם יצחק ויעקב, ואח"כ ובני ישראל פרו וישרצו וירבו ויעצמו במאד מאד.

R. JUDAN SAID: AT FIRST THE FRUIT OF A FIG-TREE IS GATHERED ONE BY ONE, THEN TWO BY TWO, THEN THREE BY THREE, UNTIL EVENTUALLY THEY ARE GATHERED IN BASKETS AND WITH SHOVELS. EVEN SO, AT THE BEGINNING, ABRAHAM WAS ONE (EZEK. 33:24); THEN THERE

WERE ABRAHAM AND ISAAC; THEN ABRAHAM, ISAAC, AND JACOB. UNTIL
EVENTUALLY: AND THE CHILDREN OF ISRAEL WERE FRUITFUL, AND
INCREASED ABUNDANTLY, AND MULTIPLIED, ETC. (EX. 7:1).

The fig tree is an even more elaborate metaphor. Unlike other fruit
trees where one branch can emerge at one time, such as an apple tree,
the figs emerge only one by one; at the beginning, after a short while,
two can appear at the same time, and three can then appear at the same
time. Ultimately, an entire fig tree can fill several baskets with this product. Similarly, God first chose Abraham to be his special representative,
and Abraham gave birth to Isaac, who gave birth to Jacob, so that there
are two and then three followers and interpreters of God; finally, in
Egypt, they became a people in vast numbers.

אמר ר' יודן: מה התאנה הזו אין לה פסולת, אלא עוקצה בלבד, העבר אותו ובטל המום. כך,
אמר הקב"ה לאברהם: אין בך פסולת, אלא הערלה, העבר אותה ובטל המום, התהלך לפני
והיה תמים:

R. JUDAN SAID: JUST AS A FIG CONTAINS NOTHING INEDIBLE SAVE ITS
STALK, AND WITH ITS REMOVAL EVEN THIS DEFECT CEASES, SO DID
GOD SAY TO ABRAHAM: THERE IS NOUGHT UNWORTHY IN THEE SAVE
THY FORESKIN: REMOVE IT AND THE BLEMISH CEASES: HENCE, WALK
BEFORE ME, AND BE THOU WHOLE.

One of the remarkable attributes of the fig is that all is edible (including its shell), with the exception of its stem. When the stem is removed,
the fig becomes *completely* edible, unlike any other fruit. Similarly, with
regard to Abraham, the Midrash says that God told him: You have most
of the required spiritual values in your personality with one exception,
which is the existence of a foreskin, known in Hebrew as the ערלה – *orlah*. When that is removed by circumcision, you will be as complete as I
would like you to be. That is the great importance of milah.

—

Seed Thoughts

In recent years, the newspapers have brought stories that the practice
of circumcision has been criticized by certain courts of law in European
nations, including Scandinavia. It has been claimed that circumcision is
incompatible with human rights. The charges, particularly in the case

of circumcision of infants, have been that something has been removed
from their bodies without their consent. Naturally, defenders of circumcision have challenged that approach and these decisions. Parents have
every right to do what they think benefits the child. Every pediatrician
will tell you that parents have either accepted or demanded that various
types of surgery be done on their infants' bodies. Knowing in advance
that the infant cannot consent or object in any way – that is the responsibility of the parent. This is not the first time such court challenges have
emerged in the history of the circumcision debate. From the point of
view of the Jewish people, we have never advocated that all non-Jewish
males should be circumcised, though such a thing has been happening
in many countries. From the Jewish point of view, the obligation is
strictly religious. More on this subject will follow.

PARASHAH FORTY-SIX, *Midrash Two*

ב (קהלת ג) לכל זמן ועת לכל חפץ תחת השמים

2. AND WHEN ABRAM WAS NINETY YEARS OLD AND NINE, ETC. IT IS
WRITTEN: TO EVERYTHING THERE IS A SEASON, AND A TIME TO EVERY
PURPOSE UNDER THE HEAVEN (ECCL. 3:1).

This verse does not mean that there is a time for everything and that
you could choose it. It means that everything in this world has a specific
time, and things will only happen when they occur at that designated
time. Our Midrash will illustrate this teaching by certain events in the
life of Abraham.

זמן היה לו לאברהם. אימתי? שניתנה לו מילה, שנאמר (בראשית יז): בעצם היום הזה נימול
אברהם וישמעאל בנו.

THERE WAS A SEASON WHEN CIRCUMCISION SHOULD BE GIVEN TO
ABRAHAM VIZ.: IN THE SELF SAME DAY WAS ABRAHAM CIRCUMCISED
(GEN. 17:26);

The point of this sentence is that Abraham's circumcision was designated to take place in the middle of that particular day. Later on, we will
learn that this was the day on which he turned 89 years old.

זמן היה להם לבניו, שנמולו שתי פעמים. אחד במצרים, ואחד במדבר, שנאמר (יהושע ה): כי
מולים היו כל העם היוצאים וגו'.
THERE WAS A SEASON WHEN HIS DESCENDANTS WERE TO NEGLECT IT,
VIZ. IN THE WILDERNESS, AS IT IS WRITTEN: FOR ALL THE PEOPLE THAT
CAME OUT WERE CIRCUMCISED; BUT ALL THE PEOPLE THAT WERE BORN
IN THE WILDERNESS BY THE WAY AS THEY CAME FORTH OUT OF EGYPT,
HAD NOT BEEN CIRCUMCISED (JOSH. 5:5).

There were two specific occasions when the entire community of
Israel was circumcised in the Bible: just before their departure from
Egypt under the leadership of Moses, and when they were in the wil-
derness prior to entering the Land of Canaan under the leadership of
Joshua.

וימול בן ארבעים ושמונה שנה כשהכיר את בוראו? אלא, שלא לנעול דלת בפני הגרים.
WHY SHOULD HE NOT HAVE CIRCUMCISED HIMSELF AT THE AGE OF
FORTY-EIGHT, WHEN HE RECOGNIZED HIS CREATOR? IN ORDER NOT TO
DISCOURAGE PROSELYTES.

The question that could now be asked is: Why could he not have
been circumcised at the age of 48, which was an age mentioned in
Scripture? The answer is that he did not wish to discourage would-be
converts to the Jewish people. They would have certain fears of circumcision while they were adults, an experience which happens in modern
times as well. So Abraham waited until he had reached advanced years
to show the would-be converts that they have nothing to fear from this
procedure.

ואם תאמר היה לו לימול בן שמונים וחמשה שנה, בשעה שנדבר עמו בין הבתרים? אלא,
כדי שיצא יצחק מטפה קדושה. וימול בן שמונים וששה שנים, בשעה שנולד ישמעאל.
THEN WHY NOT BE CIRCUMCISED AT THE AGE OF EIGHTY-FIVE, WHEN
[GOD] SPOKE WITH HIM BETWEEN THE PIECES? IN ORDER THAT ISAAC
MIGHT ISSUE FROM A HOLY SOURCE. THEN LET HIM BE CIRCUMCISED AT
THE AGE OF EIGHTY-SIX, WHEN ISHMAEL WAS BORN?

The reason in both cases was because Abraham wanted Isaac to be
the first to be born in the holiness created by the fact that his father had
experienced the covenant of circumcision, and therefore, he was born
in sanctity.

אמר ריש לקיש: קנמון אני מעמיד בעולם. מה קנמון הזה כל זמן שאתה מזבלו ומעדרו הוא
עושה פירות, כך משנצרר דמו, משבטל יצרו, משבטלה תאוותו משנקשר דמו:

SAID R. SIMEON B. LAKISH: [GOD SAID]: "I WILL SET UP A CINNAMON
TREE IN THE WORLD: JUST AS THE CINNAMON TREE YIELDS FRUIT AS
LONG AS YOU MANURE AND HOE AROUND IT, SO [SHALL ABRAHAM BE]
EVEN WHEN HIS BLOOD RUNS SLUGGISHLY AND HIS PASSIONS AND
DESIRES HAVE CEASED." [AUTHOR'S NOTE: I. E., ABRAHAM WAS TO BE
LIKE A CINNAMON TREE WHICH, NO MATTER HOW OLD, CAN BE MADE
TO PRODUCE FRUIT; SO WAS CIRCUMCISION TO RENEW HIS VIRILITY.]

אמר: אם חביבה היא המילה, מפני מה לא נתנה לאדם הראשון?

[ABRAHAM] ASKED: IF CIRCUMCISION IS SO PRECIOUS, WHY WAS IT NOT
GIVEN TO ADAM?

See the Seed Thoughts.

—

Seed Thoughts

This is an excellent question. Circumcision is so important – why was
it not made universal? This question is not answered in this particular
Midrash, but it is touched upon in the following several Midrashim. The
question arises, in my mind, as an editor of this literature, as to what
the world would be like if circumcision would be universal today. Medically speaking, the opposition would be very great, as it is from time
to time in modern times when non-Jewish families who have practiced
circumcision on their own without commitment have begun to question that procedure. There have been a few such court cases in modern
times which worry the Jewish community, although they deal largely
with the question of the circumcision of non-Jews. Chances are that
with circumcision, if practiced universally, court cases would multiply
to a very great number. This, however, is not an answer to the question
if circumcision brings with it so many additional spiritual values. A way
would be found even universally to eliminate most of the problems. The
real answer to this question is yet to come.

—

Additional Commentary

Abraham at age 89

Up until the age of 89, Abraham is not commanded to perform circumcision. That is what the text meant in saying when it said: "There is a time for everything under the sun." There is a specific time determined well in advance for every human being, and there is also a certain time set aside for all events yet to take place. What will happen to a particular person, and what particular thing will that person do? Therefore, there is a time established from the very beginning, and in the case of Abraham, that time was established by God as to when he should undergo circumcision, or מילה – milah. (*HaMidrash HaMevo'ar*)

Are there limits to the spiritual life?

Apparently, Abraham thought that there is a limit to human possibilities. Once you achieve a high spiritual level in commandments or in the doing of good deeds, is there a limit beyond which you cannot pass and do more than what you are doing? To this thought or feeling of Abraham, the Holy One, blessed be He, responded that such efforts can continue indefinitely. Since the soul of man is part of the divine heritage, he has the possibility to climb higher in the spiritual life without any limitation whatsoever. (*Tiferet Tzion*)

Parashah Forty-Six, *Midrash Three*

ג אמר לו הקדוש ב"ה לאברהם: דייך אני ואתה בעולם, ואם אין את מקבל עליך לימול, דיי
לעולמי, עד כאן! ודייה לערלה עד כאן! ודייה למילה שתהא עגומה עד כאן!

3. SAID THE HOLY ONE, BLESSED BE HE, TO HIM: LET IT SUFFICE THEE
THAT I AND THOU ARE IN THE WORLD. IF THOU WILT NOT UNDERGO
CIRCUMCISION, IT IS ENOUGH FOR MY WORLD TO HAVE EXISTED UNTIL
NOW, AND IT IS ENOUGH FOR UNCIRCUMCISION TO HAVE EXISTED UNTIL
NOW, AND IT IS ENOUGH FOR CIRCUMCISION TO HAVE BEEN FORLORN
UNTIL NOW.

The first response as to why circumcision did not begin with Adam is
that God had no interest in that subject. He wanted to cement the relationship between Abraham and Himself, and nothing else interested
him other than that subject. The world did not need anything more than
that relationship.

אמר עד שלא מלתי, היו באים ומזדווגים לי. תאמר: משמלתי, הן באין ומזדווגים לי. אמר לו
הקב"ה: אברהם. דייך, שאני אלוהך! דייך, שאני פטרונך! ולא לך לעצמך, אלא דיי לעולמי,
שאני לעולמי שאני פטרונו!

SAID HE: "BEFORE I CIRCUMCISED MYSELF, MEN CAME AND JOINED ME
[IN MY NEW FAITH]. WILL THEY COME AND JOIN ME WHEN I AM CIRCUM-
CISED?" "ABRAHAM," SAID GOD TO HIM, "LET IT SUFFICE THEE THAT I AM
THY GOD; LET IT SUFFICE THEE THAT I AM THY PATRON, AND NOT ONLY
FOR THEE ALONE, BUT IT IS SUFFICIENT FOR MY WORLD THAT I AM ITS
GOD AND ITS PATRON."

Apparently, when Abraham mentioned that people would come to
him and see him, he was concerned that their intention was to attack
him in some fashion. Would not circumcision make him weaker to
oppose their aggression? God's answer is "Not to worry"; He will be
Abraham's protector.

רבי נתן ורבי אחא ורבי ברכיה בשם רבי יצחק: אני אל שדי, אני הוא שאמרתי לעולמי
ולשמים: דיי, לארץ דיי שאלולי שאמרתי להם דיי, עד עכשיו היו נמתחים והולכים. תני
משום רבי אלעזר בן יעקב: אני הוא, שאין העולם ומלואו כדי לאלהותי.

R. NATHAN SAID IN R. AHA'S NAME, AND R. BEREKIAH SAID IN R. ISAAC'S
NAME: I AM EL SHADDAI (GOD ALMIGHTY): IT IS I WHO SAID TO MY
WORLD, *DAI* (ENOUGH)! AND HAD I NOT SAID, *DAI*! TO MY WORLD, THE
HEAVEN WOULD STILL HAVE BEEN SPREADING AND THE EARTH WOULD
HAVE GONE ON EXPANDING TO THIS VERY DAY. IT WAS TAUGHT IN THE
NAME OF R. ELIEZER B. JACOB: IT IS I WHOSE GODHEAD OUTWEIGHS THE
WORLD AND THE FULLNESS THEREOF.

The second response is that God is the one who created the world, and He can just as easily get rid of it without the circumcision of Abraham. That is what he would probably do.

תרגום עקילוס, אכסיום ואנקום:

AKILAS, THE PROSELYTE, AUTHOR OF A TRANSLATION OF THE BIBLE
INTO GREEK IN THE SECOND CENTURY, TRANSLATED IT: SUFFICIENT
AND INCOMPARABLE.

Some commentators render the saying of Akilas as being very honorable, very able, or very talented. The words are *aksios* and *ikanos*. The Targum of *Akilas* translates the first as very important or very valuable, and the second as very honorable. (Mirkin)

⁓

Seed Thoughts I

The last sentence of the previous Midrash asks the most important question that emerges from this series of discussions on the meaning of milah. The question is, if milah is so important in the eyes of God, why was it not given as a commandment to Adam, the first man? Or it can be put in another way: When the human being was created, why was he created with a foreskin? Surely, that would have satisfied the Almighty. This question is taken up in the third chapter that we are discussing. It contains many responses to this question, but no answer. In the first place, God said: "I am only interested in Abraham, I am El Shaddai, the Lord who decides what is enough in the universe." The responses are threefold: My first response is that God and Abraham are enough. My second response is that the world needs Abraham and his family to undergo milah, and if it does not happen, the world loses its purpose as I perceive it. The third response can be put in this ordinary way of speaking; namely: "I am God and I decide everything, and no one has a right to question me, and this is what I want, or I will bring the universe to an end." In other words, these are several responses, but none of them is an answer.

⁓

Seed Thoughts II

It is pretty obvious that God did not want milah to be one of the mitzvot for the first man, Adam. Although no divine answer or explanation was given, let us see if we could figure out why in the eyes of God, circumcision would not have been in the interests of mankind. In the eyes of many commentators, and especially that of Nahmanides (Ramban), the ערלה – *orlah* (foreskin) is the root of all sexuality. It is the view of Nahmanides that milah removes sexual aggressiveness from the life of the practitioner, so that his behavior, even in this important area, is civilized, humanized, and ultimately a source of blessing in marriage and the family. It so happens that in our day (2012), many non-Jews have practiced circumcision voluntarily. There was a time when the royal family in Great Britain invited the *mohel* of the United Synagogue of London to look after the male members of the royal family in this regard. This practice has aroused great controversy mostly in non-Jewish society. The claim is made by many, including physicians, that the body should not be tampered with, and in particular, in the case of an eight-day old baby, who would not be able to give his permission. Certain courts of law in Europe have agreed with this criticism, and have ordered circumcision not to be rendered without the consent of the person, and have added many other restrictions as well. From the Jewish point of view, circumcision is being practiced by the majority of the Jewish people. Nevertheless, we are concerned that somebody's legal decisions will influence certain Jewish families whose Jewish identity is relatively weak. God made the right decision; it is too bad that it did not come in the form of an answer.

PARASHAH FORTY-SIX, *Midrash Four*

ד אמר רבי לוי: למטרונא שאמר המלך עברי לפני ועברה לפניו, ונתכרכמו פניה. אמרה,
תאמר, שנמצא בי פסולת? אמר לה המלך: אין בך פסולת, אלא ציפורן של אצבע קטנה
שלך, גדולה קימעה, העבירי אותו ובטל המום. כך, אמר הקב"ה לאברהם אבינו: אין בך
פסולת, אלא הערלה הזאת, העבר אותה ובטל המום.

4. WALK BEFORE ME, AND BE THOU WHOLE. R. LEVI SAID: THIS MAY BE
ILLUSTRATED BY A NOBLE LADY WHOM THE KING COMMANDED: WALK
BEFORE ME. SHE WALKED BEFORE HIM AND HER FACE WENT PALE, FOR,
THOUGHT SHE, WHO KNOWS BUT THAT SOME DEFECT MAY HAVE BEEN
FOUND IN ME? SAID THE KING TO HER: THOU HAST NO DEFECT, BUT
THAT THE NAIL OF THY LITTLE FINGER IS SLIGHTLY TOO LONG; PARE IT
AND THE DEFECT WILL BE GONE. SIMILARLY, GOD SAID TO ABRAHAM:
THOU HAST NO OTHER DEFECT BUT THIS FORESKIN: REMOVE IT AND
THE DEFECT WILL BE GONE.

התהלך לפני והיה תמים ואתנה בריתי ביני וביניך וגו'. א"ר הונא בשם בר קפרא: ישב אברהם
ודן גזירה שוה. נאמרה ערלה באילן, ונאמרה ערלה באדם. מה ערלה שנאמרה באילן, מקום
שהוא עושה פירות, אף ערלה שנאמר באדם, מקום שהוא עושה פירות.

HENCE, WALK BEFORE ME, AND BE THOU WHOLE. AND I WILL MAKE MY
COVENANT, ETC. (GEN. 17:2). R. HUNA SAID IN BAR KAPPARA'S NAME:
ABRAHAM PONDERED AND DREW AN INFERENCE: *ORLAH* (FORESKIN) IS
SAID HERE (17:11), AND ORLAH OCCURS IN REFERENCE TO A TREE (LEV.
19:23): JUST AS ORLAH IN THE CASE OF TREES REFERS TO THE PLACE
WHERE IT YIELDS FRUIT, SO ORLAH EMPLOYED IN REFERENCE TO MAN
MEANS THE MEMBER WHICH PRODUCES OFFSPRING [FRUIT].

We now begin the rather lengthy discussion as to where in the body the *orlah* should take place. Abraham began by doing some serious thinking. In an earlier portion of the Torah, he discovered the use of the word orlah in connection with the place where the fruit of the tree was produced. The rule is that when a fruit tree is replanted, we wait three years before we are allowed to eat of the fruit. From this knowledge, Jacob deduced that the orlah of a human being should also be done in the place where fruit is produced; in this case, the fruit of infant life. This knowledge from one portion of the Torah to another is called *gezerah shavah*. However, this was only permitted when the Oral Torah was produced and could only be used for specific cases listed by the Talmud. How then was Abraham allowed to make this judgment?

אמר ליה רבי חנינא בר פזי: וכי נתנו גזירות שוות לאברהם אתמהא? אלא רמז רמזה לו,
ואתנה בריתי ביני ובינך וארבה אותך במאד מאד. ואתנה בריתי ביני ובינך, במקום שהוא
פרה ורבה:

SAID R. HANINA TO HIM: HAD THEN REASONING BY ANALOGY (IN HE-
BREW, *GEZERAH SHAVAH*) ALREADY BEEN GIVEN TO ABRAHAM? SURELY
NOT! BUT [HE LEARNED IT FROM GOD S PROMISE]: AND I WILL MAKE
MY COVENANT BETWEEN ME AND THEE, AND WILL MULTIPLY THEE
EXCEEDINGLY: HENCE, WITH [THAT MEMBER THROUGH WHICH] I WILL
MULTIPLY THEE EXCEEDINGLY, I WILL MAKE MY COVENANT BETWEEN
ME AND THEE.

Apparently, one might think that Abraham was privileged to enjoy sections of both Torahs – the Oral Law and the Written Law. That, however, was not the case; the Almighty simply hinted to Abraham from the story of orlah associated with the tree that the place in the body for this to take place is to quote the verse, "I will give my covenant between you and me," as taking place in that part of the body that would fulfill the hope of "I will multiply you very much" – namely, the place to which being fruitful and multiplying applies.

Seed Thoughts

Although the message in the first section of the Midrash is clear – namely, something inconsequential as a longer than usual fingernail to a small finger, which if removed, causes no harm. By the same token, the foreskin which interferes with the almost perfect personality of the human being interferes with that goal. So if it is removed, it causes no harm to the body or the personality. This is the message of the first part of the Midrash, but it is stated in such a way as for it to be difficult to understand. By adding the missing descriptions, this is what has to be imagined, although not actually stated. A king was traveling to a community and he recognized a noblewoman whom he had known, and who a commentator had described as very beautiful. Since the king had known of her beauty, he actually should have come closer so he could see her better. When she realized that they were not speaking to her in his flowery sense of approval, she became embarrassed and thought that he had discovered a defect in her. She apologized to him for the defect, and he immediately responded that she had no defect but that the nail in her small finger, which she was waving with much pride, was too long for the appearance she wanted to create. The king thus corrected her and cut the nail down to size. He said: It will not harm you at all, and your beauty will be completely restored. This is how it was probably meant to be understood, and the Midrash continues with this application to the *orlah*, which is the milah and which has already been explained.

PARASHAH FORTY-SIX, *Midrash Five*

הר' ישמעאל ור' עקיבא. ר' ישמעאל אומר: אברהם כהן גדול היה, שנאמר (תהלים קי): נשבע
ה' ולא ינחם אתה כהן לעולם וגו'.

5. R. ISHMAEL AND R. AKIBA [REASONED AS FOLLOWS]. R. ISHMAEL SAID:
ABRAHAM WAS A HIGH PRIEST, AS IT SAYS: THE LORD HATH SWORN, AND
WILL NOT REPENT: THOU ART A PRIEST FOR EVER AFTER THE MANNER
OF MELCHIZEDEK (PS. 110:4).

We are now dealing with the question of where the place of circumcision should be. To put it another way, how do our ancestors know where circumcision should take place? Rabbi Ishmael offers a new type of answer. It is due to the fact that Abraham was the original *kohen*, or priest. We shall soon see what effect that will have.

ונאמר להלן (בראשית יז): ונמלתם את בשר ערלתכם. מהיכן ימול? אם ימול מן האוזן, אינו
כשר להקריב. מן הפה, אינו כשר להקריב. מן הלב, אינו כשר להקריב. מהיכן ימול ויהיה
כשר להקריב? הוי אומר: זו ערלת הגוף.

AGAIN, IT IS SAID: AND YE SHALL BE CIRCUMCISED TO THE FLESH OF
YOUR ORLAH (GEN. 17:11). IF HE CIRCUMCISED HIMSELF AT THE EAR, HE
WOULD BE UNFIT TO OFFER SACRIFICES; IF AT THE MOUTH, HE WOULD
BE UNFIT TO OFFER; AT THE HEART, HE WOULD BE UNFIT TO OFFER.
HENCE, WHERE COULD HE PERFORM CIRCUMCISION AND YET BE FIT TO
OFFER? NOWHERE ELSE THAN AT THE ORLAH OF THE BODY [THE FORE-
SKIN].

One of the difficulties in examining this problem is that in Scripture itself, the word *orlah,* which is the Hebrew word for "foreskin," appears in many different ways and is applied to many areas other than the human body. The word itself means "edge" or "end," and is usually applied in a critical way to various areas or objects which are situated improperly. The word is applied to the ear, the mouth, and the heart. From what we have just quoted, if either of these areas is affected, meaning that they are departed from their normal positions, they are regarded as being defective, and the person who possesses this defect is not permitted to preside as an offering to God. The conclusion so far is that only the human body is eligible for milah, and we do not yet know where.

ר' עקיבא אומר: ד' ערלות הן. נאמרה ערלה באוזן, (ירמיה ו): הנה ערלה אזנם. ונאמרה ערלה
בפה, (שמות ו): הן אני ערל שפתים. ונאמר ערלה בלב, (ירמיה ט): וכל בית ישראל ערלי לב.
ונאמר ערלה בגוף, וערל זכר. ונאמר לו, התהלך לפני והיה תמים. אם ימול מן האוזן, אינו
תמים. מן הפה, אינו תמים. מן הלב, אינו תמים. ומהיכן ימול ויהיה תמים? הוי אומר: זו
ערלת הגוף. מקרא אמר: ובן שמונת ימים ימול לכם, כל זכר לדורותיכם. אם ימול מן האוזן,
אינו שומע. מן הפה, אינו מדבר. מן הלב, אינו חושב. מהיכן ימול ויהיה יכול לחשוב? זו
ערלת הגוף.

R. AKIBA SAID: THERE ARE FOUR KINDS OF *ORLAH.* THUS, ORLAH IS USED IN CONNECTION WITH THE EAR, VIZ. BEHOLD, THEIR EAR IS ORLAH – [E.V. "DULL"] (JER. 6:10); THE MOUTH, BEHOLD, I AM *ARAL* [E.V. "UNCIRCUMCISED"] OF LIPS (EX. 6:30); THE HEART: FOR ALL THE HOUSE OF ISRAEL ARE *ARLEH* [E.V. "UNCIRCUMCISED"] IN THE HEART (JER. 9:25). NOW, HE WAS ORDERED, WALK BEFORE ME, AND BE THOU WHOLE. IF HE CIRCUMCISED HIMSELF AT THE EAR, HE WOULD NOT BE WHOLE; AT THE MOUTH, HE WOULD NOT BE WHOLE; AT THE HEART, HE WOULD NOT BE WHOLE. WHERE COULD HE CIRCUMCISE HIMSELF AND YET BE WHOLE? NOWHERE ELSE THAN AT THE ORLAH OF THE BODY. SCRIPTURE SAID: IT IS WRITTEN: AND HE THAT IS EIGHT DAYS OLD SHALL BE CIRCUMCISED AMONG YOU, EVERY MALE (GEN. 17:12). NOW IF HE IS CIRCUMCISED AT THE EAR, HE CANNOT HEAR; AT THE MOUTH, HE CANNOT SPEAK; AT THE HEART, HE CANNOT THINK. WHERE THEN COULD HE BE CIRCUMCISED AND YET BE ABLE TO THINK? ONLY AT THE ORLAH OF THE BODY.

Rabbi Akiva uses the same verses in Scripture as Rabbi Ishmael, but he does not apply them to the priesthood at all (Mirkin). As he puts it, if the ear is defective, he cannot hear, if the mouth is defective, he cannot speak, and if the heart is defective, he cannot think. Since the whole idea of milah is to produce an almost morally perfect person, the only conclusion is that somewhere in the human body has to be the source for milah.

א"ר תנחומא: מיסתברא הדא מקרא, וערל זכר. וכי יש ערל נקיבה? אלא ממקום שהוא ניכר אם זכר אם נקבה, משם מוהלים אותו:

R. TANHUMA OBSERVED: THIS ARGUMENT OF SCRIPTURE IS LOGICAL. AND THE UNCIRCUMCISED MALE (GEN. 17:14). IS THERE THEN AN UNCIRCUMCISED FEMALE? THE MEANING, HOWEVER, IS THAT WE MUST PERFORM CIRCUMCISION ON THE MEMBER WHICH MARKS THE DISTINCTION BETWEEN MALE AND FEMALE.

Rabbi Tanhuma concludes this discussion that although Scripture specifies that milah applies only to the male because of two expressions – *arel zakhar*, which means "uncircumcised male"; and the commandment to practice milah when the child is eight days old. When you examine a child at birth to discover whether the child is male or female, that is the place where milah should be practiced; that is, the foreskin of the male.

〜

Seed Thoughts

To those of us in modern times who have known about circumcision and its practices for thousands of years, it might appear somewhat ridiculous to ask where circumcision should take place. We have to understand that the Sages of the Talmud had also practiced circumcision for close to one thousand years. Yet it was their desire to understand the Torah completely. They used their imagination to figure out how one would come to such a ritual conclusion without any precedent. There is a second reason which motivated them, and that was the use of the term *arel*, though in a somewhat different grammatical situation to apply to many other aspects of life, such as the ear, the mouth, and the heart, as the Midrash indicates. At the same time, we have to remember the early Midrashim that preceded this one where circumcision was described as a main resource in civilizing the sexual behaviour of human beings. Our present Midrash emphasizes this point as well; the basic verse that we are discussing is: "Walk before me and become morally whole." A defect in either the ear, the mouth, or the heart would make a person not morally whole, and therefore these parts could not at all be considered as the basis for a milah. The conclusion of the Midrash is that the basic commandment is that a male child should be circumcised on the eighth day, and that the place should be where you look upon an infant to know whether it is male or female. That is of the male organ for which milah is decreed. The conclusion is simple and logical, and that also makes it appear ingenious.

PARASHAH FORTY-SIX, *Midrash Six*

ו ויפול אברם על פניו וידבר אתו אלהים לאמר. ר' פנחס בשם רבי לוי: שתי פעמים כתיב באברהם נפילה על פניו.

6. AND ABRAHAM FELL ON HIS FACE, ETC. (GEN. 17:3). R. PHINEHAS SAID IN R. LEVI'S NAME: ABRAHAM FELL ON HIS FACE ON TWO OCCASIONS.

"Fell on his face" has to be understood as bowing down in worship. It has nothing to do with falling accidentally or otherwise. A person in those days who might have been anxious to express thanksgiving to God might bow down very swiftly, and in the eyes of the beholder it might seem as though they are falling. We are concerned, however, with falling down deliberately and not accidentally.

כנגדן נטלה מילה מבניו שתי פעמים, אחד במצרים ואחד במדבר. במצרים, בא משה ומלן. במדבר, בא יהושע ומלן:

IN CONSEQUENCE, HIS CHILDREN WERE DEPRIVED OF CIRCUMCISION ONCE IN THE WILDERNESS AND ONCE IN EGYPT: IN EGYPT, MOSES CAME AND CIRCUMCISED THEM; IN THE WILDERNESS, JOSHUA CAME AND CIRCUMCISED THEM.

What is involved here is a very complicated interpretation of the verse. Apparently, Abraham knew (or was given to understand) that someday, his descendants would stop practicing milah either on their own or by force of circumstances. His prayer, as he bowed down in thanksgiving, was that in some fashion, the Almighty might help his descendants restore the practice of milah, so that it would become practiced by all male Jews. As it turned out, his prayers were answered positively. Moses (Moshe Rabbeinu) insisted on the Children of Israel to undertake milah in order to be allowed to participate in the Paschal offering as they were about to leave Egypt. They had stopped the practice because of the difficulties provided by their slavery. This was now to be restored. Something similar happened at the time of Joshua. They had been forced to stop the practice of milah in the wilderness because of the danger of the desert and because their lives were always in jeopardy. Joshua ordered that in order to participate in the conquest of the Land of Canaan, milah was an absolute must.

⁓

Seed Thoughts

These words are being written in the twenty-first century. Not only Abraham, but also many of his associates, would be amazed and thankful. and would feel that this forthcoming statement is incredulous. The statement is: Circumcision is still widely practiced by the Jewish people in every part of the world, and is regarded by some as one of the most important commandments in the Torah.

⁓

Additional Commentary

Circumcisions of the Future

Since the biblical text mentions Abraham falling on his face on two occasions and both are next to the section on circumcision, the Midrash connects these falls as relating to a lack of circumcision of his children on two future occasions, and to the acts of Moses and Joshua who corrected this situation. (Mirkin)

PARASHAH FORTY-SIX, *Midrash Seven*

ז ואני הנה בריתי אתך. רבי אבא ורבי ברכיה ורבי שמואל בר אמי הוין יתבין ומקשין: מנין נוטריקון מן התורה?

7. AS FOR ME, BEHOLD, MY COVENANT IS WITH THEE, ETC. (GEN. 17:4). IT IS RELATED THAT R. ABBA, R. BEREKIAH, R. ABBA B. KAHANA, AND R. SAMUEL B. AMMI, WHEN SITTING AND STUDYING, ONCE RAISED THE QUESTION: HOW IS *NOTARIKON* [AS A PERMISSIBLE METHOD OF EXEGESIS] DEDUCED FROM SCRIPTURE?

$\rm T$he word *notarikon* is a method where one adds or subtracts letters to a word or joins one letter to another as a way of presenting an idea in a more abbreviated form. The question that is being asked is not merely whether there is a source for this in the Torah, and if so, what is the source. The second question is whether or not such a notarikon, if it contains thoughts about a scriptural passage, can be used for exegesis – namely, for another interpretation of the Torah.

שנאמר והיית לאב המון גוים, לאבהם, דהוה חסר רי"ש:

WE KNOW IT FROM THIS: AND THOU SHALT BE AB HAMON (THE FATHER OF A MULTITUDE – OF NATIONS), THE *RESH* BEING LACKING.

$\rm W$hat the Rabbis discover is that there is such a natural notarikon in the Torah text itself. That word is the name *Avraham* without the letter *resh,* and it has to be written as אבהם. It is meant to be interpreted as *av hamon goyim* – father of many nations, and the letters *heh* and *mem* are enough to indicate that the name is indicated. His name was changed from אברם (Abram) to אברהם (Abraham), so that it might read *ab* (father of) *ham* (an abbreviation of *hamon,* "multitude"). Hence the letter *resh* must be ignored in a case where Scripture itself provides the exegesis.

⁓

Seed Thoughts

Notarikon is only one of the several methods of speeding up either conversation or the written word, not only in rabbinic literature but wherever the Hebrew language is spoken. One of the most popular forms is the method of shortening names by the use of the initials. For example, the name Rashi (the great commentator) is not Rashi at all, but Rabbi Shlomo Yitzhaki. Maimonides is known as the Rambam based on his full name (including his father's name), Rabbi Moshe ben Maimon. This is one of the most popular forms, and is used by many people in today's society as well. There are other forms not only of shortening conversation, but of emphasizing certain values. For example, in the English language, Shakespeare is always spoken of as Shakespeare in terms of his various works. Very often in general, a person is described by a book and not by himself. For example, "the Shulhan Arukh says" is really "Rabbi Joseph Caro says." The same can be said for any number of traditional books. This kind of thing has enriched the Hebrew language, especially in the confrontation of the language with modern times and with modern words. This has been a major form of enrichment.

PARASHAH FORTY-SIX, *Midrash Eight*

ח ולא יקרא עוד שמך אברם והיה שמך אברהם. בר קפרא אמר: כל מי שהוא קורא לאברהם אברם, עובר בלא תעשה. ר' לוי אמר: בעשה ולא תעשה. ולא יקרא עוד שמך אברם, בל"ת. והיה שמך אברהם, בעשה.

8. NEITHER SHALL THY NAME ANY MORE BE CALLED ABRAM, BUT THY NAME SHALL BE ABRAHAM (GEN. 17:5). BAR KAPPARA SAID: WHOEVER CALLS ABRAHAM "ABRAM," VIOLATES A POSITIVE COMMANDMENT. R. LEVI SAID: A POSITIVE COMMANDMENT AND A NEGATIVE COMMAND-MENT. NEITHER SHALL THY NAME ANY MORE BE CALLED ABRAM – THAT IS A NEGATIVE COMMAND; BUT THY NAME SHALL BE ABRAHAM – THAT IS A POSITIVE COMMAND.

The Midrash is very clear that the commandment being quoted has two aspects. The first is not to do something; in this case, not to use the name "Abram." The second aspect is to do something; namely, to refer to him the name of "Abraham." Not one, but two commandments are at stake.

והרי אנשי כנסת הגדולה קראו אותו אברם, שנאמר (נחמיה ט): אתה הוא ה' האלהים אשר בחרת באברם, והוצאתו מאור כשדים ושמת שמו אברהם.

BUT SURELY THE MEN OF THE GREAT ASSEMBLY CALLED HIM ABRAM, AS
IT IS WRITTEN, THOU . . . WHO DIDST CHOOSE ABRAM (NEH. 9:7).

The fact that the Men of the Great Assembly use the term "Abram" is
not a criticism, because they were merely referring to something historical. That was Abraham's name in the past and no longer in the present.

דלמא שנייה היא, שעד שהוא אברם בחרת בו. דכוותה: הקורא לשרה שרי, עובר בעשה?
אלא, שנצטוה עליה.

THERE IT IS DIFFERENT, AS IT MEANS THAT HE CHOSE HIM WHILE HE
WAS YET ABRAM. THEN, BY ANALOGY, DOES ONE WHO CALLS SARAH
"SARAI" INFRINGE A POSITIVE COMMAND? NO, FOR ONLY HE [ABRAHAM]
WAS ENJOINED WITH RESPECT TO HER.

The Midrash notes that these restrictions do not apply to the change
of name from "Sarai" to "Sarah." The reason is that this was not an announcement to the Jewish people, but merely to Abraham himself.

דכוותה: הקורא לישראל יעקב, עובר בעשה? תני, לא שיעקר שם יעקב ממקומו, אלא, כי
אם ישראל יהיה שמך. ישראל עיקר ויעקב טפילה. ר' זבדא בשם ר' אחא: מכל מקום שמך
יעקב, כי אם ישראל, יעקב עיקר, וישראל מוסיף עליו:

AGAIN, BY ANALOGY, IF ONE CALLS ISRAEL, "JACOB," DOES ONE IN-
FRINGE A POSITIVE COMMAND? [NO, FOR] IT WAS TAUGHT: IT WAS
NOT INTENDED THAT THE NAME JACOB SHOULD DISAPPEAR, BUT THAT
"ISRAEL" SHOULD BE HIS PRINCIPAL NAME, WHILE "JACOB" SHOULD BE
A SECONDARY ONE. R. ZEBIDA INTERPRETED IN R. AHA'S NAME: AT ALL
EVENTS, THY NAME IS JACOB, SAVE THAT, BUT ISRAEL [TOO] SHALL BE
THY NAME (GEN. 35:10): "JACOB" WILL BE THE PRINCIPAL NAME, WHILE
"ISRAEL" WILL BE AN ADDITIONAL ONE.

It is pretty obvious from the above that Israel and Jacob can be used alternatively. Some scholars feel that "Israel" is the chief name and "Jacob"
is supplementary; others feel that "Jacob" is the chief name and "Israel"
is supplementary. It is interesting to note that in the scriptural portion
of *Vayeitzei*, when God speaks to Jacob, it says that he heard the words
"*Yaakov, Yaakov*" ("Jacob, Jacob") and he responded "*hineni*" ("here I
am"). The Almighty Himself used the name Yaakov and not Yisrael (or
Israel).

Seed Thoughts

It is interesting to note that nowhere in the discussion of names does Scripture include a penalty for not following the given instruction. The Rabbis of the Talmud have analyzed the blessings and the warnings very carefully, and have said what the Midrash quotes them as saying. From our point of view, the discussion seems to indicate that the penalties are not to be taken too seriously, particularly in our case when the only way we refer to the biblical characters is from the point of view of history. This is what happened in those days, and that is the only real style in which we refer to the biblical names, especially today, when the Jewish State has adopted the name of Israel. One has to hesitate before knowing whether a person is involved or whether a state is involved. One has to do our best and not be too concerned with the kind of penalties that our Midrash discusses.

PARASHAH FORTY-SIX, *Midrash Nine*

ט ונתתי לך ולזרעך אחריך את ארץ מגוריך.

9. AND I WILL GIVE UNTO THEE, AND TO THY SEED AFTER THEE, THE LAND OF THY SOJOURNINGS, ETC. (GEN. 17:8).

The Midrash begins by establishing that the purpose of the *brit milah*, which implies the covenant of circumcision, is to establish the Almighty as the God of Israel. This, however, is repeated again by similar verses in Scripture – that the purpose of milah (or circumcision) is to bring us closer to God. For that matter, the giving of the Land of Israel is also conditional upon remaining close to God, and all of this (according to our portion) is dependent on milah, which is one of the great commandments in Judaism.

רבי יודן אמר: חמש.

R. JUDAN GAVE FIVE INTERPRETATIONS OF THIS.

It is Rabbi Judan's view that there are five conditions, all of which are dependent on one another and all of which have to do with milah, which make possible not only occupying the Land of Israel, but also having God as our ultimate authority.

אם מקבלים בניך אלהותי – אני אהיה להם לאלוה ולפטרון. ואם לאו – לא אהיה להם לאלוה ולפטרון.

R. JUDAN SAID: GOD SAID: (I) IF THY CHILDREN ACCEPT MY DIVINITY, I WILL BE THEIR GOD AND PATRON; IF NOT, I WILL NOT BE THEIR GOD AND PATRON.

Accepting the burden of the kingdom of heaven is a condition, and without it, God would not accept to be their God. This is the first condition.

אם נכנסין בניך לארץ – הן מקבלין אלהותי. ואם לאו – אינם מקבלים.

(II) IF THY CHILDREN ENTER THE PROMISED LAND, THEY ACCEPT MY DIVINITY; IF NOT, THEY DO NOT ACCEPT MY DIVINITY.

In other words, if Abraham's children enter the Land of Israel in the spirit of love and devotion for the Holy Land, I will be their God. If not, I will not be. This is the second condition.

אם מקיימין בניך את המילה – הן נכנסים לארץ. ואם לאו – אין נכנסים לארץ.

(III) IF THY CHILDREN KEEP CIRCUMCISION, THEY WILL ENTER THE PROMISED LAND; IF NOT, THEY WILL NOT ENTER THE PROMISED LAND.

In other words, milah is an absolute necessity for inheriting the Land of Israel, and this is the third condition.

אם מקבלים בניך את השבת – הם נכנסין לארץ. ואם לאו – אינם נכנסין.

(IV) IF THY CHILDREN ACCEPT THE SABBATH, THEY WILL ENTER THE PROMISED LAND; IF NOT, THEY WILL NOT ENTER THE PROMISED LAND.

In other words, not only is milah a condition for entry to the Promised Land, but so is the Sabbath. It, therefore, becomes an additional condition – both for milah and for entering the Land of Israel. This latter condition [Sabbath], however, is not regarded as the fourth condition but as a separate category. If your children, as indicated in this Midrash, observe the Sabbath fully, it implies that they accept my divine sovereignty as their God. If not, they will be denied their sovereignty.

That is the fourth condition. The acceptance of the kingdom of heaven, together with milah and the occupation of the Land of Israel, are the fifth condition. All of these together are needed to contribute to the salvation of God. (*HaMidrash HaMevo'ar*)

ר' ברכיה ור' חלבו בשם ר' אבון ב"ר יוסי: כתיב (יהושע ה): וזה הדבר אשר מל יהושע. דבר. אמר להם יהושע: ומלן, אמר להם: מה אתם סבורין שאתם נכנסין לארץ ערלים? כך אמר הקב"ה לאברהם אבינו: ונתתי לך ולזרעך אחריך וגו', על מנת, ואתה את בריתי תשמור.

R. BEREKIAH AND R. HELBO IN THE NAME OF R. ABIN B. R. JOSE SAID: IT IS WRITTEN: AND THIS IS THE CAUSE (*DABAR*) WHY JOSHUA DID CIR-CUMCISE" (JOSH. 5:4): JOSHUA SPOKE A WORD (*DABAR*) TO THEM, AND CIRCUMCISED THEM. "WHAT THINK YOU,' SAID HE UPBRAIDING THEM, "THAT YOU WILL ENTER THE LAND UNCIRCUMCISED?" THUS DID THE HOLY ONE, BLESSED BE HE, SAY TO ABRAHAM: AND WILL GIVE UNTO THEE, AND TO THY SEED AFTER THEE, ETC., PROVIDING THAT YOU FULFILL THE CONDITION, AND AS FOR THEE, THOU SHALT KEEP MY COVENANT (GEN. 17:9).

The purpose of the reference to Joshua is to indicate that milah was a condition for the entry of the Children of Israel into the Land of Ca-naan. Forty years in the wilderness, facing challenges of nutrition and homelessness, made it impossible to carry on a program of milah. But Joshua did his best to prepare the people so that they would understand that milah was a condition for their settlement of the Holy Land, and the program that he carried out included all the males that were eligible for this mitzvah.

ואתה את בריתי תשמור. ר' הונא ור' יוחנן. ר' הונא אמר: ואתה, מכאן למוהל שיהא מהול. ורבי יוחנן אמר: המול ימול, מכאן למוהל שיהא מהול. תניא, ישראל ערל אינו מוהל. ק"ו עובד כוכבים ערל:

AND AS FOR THEE, THOU SHALT KEEP MY COVENANT. R. HUNA IN RAB'S NAME AND R. JOHANAN EACH COMMENTED. RAB SAID: AND AS FOR THEE MEANS ONE LIKE THEE [MUST PERFORM THE ACTUAL CIRCUMCISION]; HENCE IT FOLLOWS THAT ONLY HE WHO IS HIMSELF CIRCUMCISED MAY PERFORM CIRCUMCISION. R. JOHANAN SAID: HE MUST NEEDS BE CIRCUM-CISED – *HIMMOL YIMMOL* (GEN. 17:13) TEACHES THAT THE CIRCUMCISER MUST HIMSELF BE CIRCUMCISED. IT WAS TAUGHT: AN UNCIRCUMCISED ISRAELITE [JEW] MAY NOT CIRCUMCISE, AND HOW MUCH MORE SO AN UNCIRCUMCISED GENTILE!

The fact that the one who performs milah should himself be circumcised becomes very important in modern times when sometimes, persons other than official *mohalim* do circumcision, such as physicians and other professional health care providers. The second consideration is that the *mohel* has to be Jewish, and not one who is not commanded in a mitzvah. There is also a play on words here, המול ימול – *himmol yimmol*. The word *himmol* with a few grammatical corrections, could be understood as one who is already circumcised (*mahul*). Therefore, *yimmol* – he is permitted to do onto others. (Mirkin)

Seed Thoughts I

The text of the *midrash* asserts that the person who does milah must be an Israelite and must himself be circumcised. The question that I am now asking is, can a Jewish woman be a *mohel*? I am asking this question because I have heard of a number of situations where this has happened, and the claim is made that this is halakhically very acceptable. (See *Tur* and *Shulchan Aruch, Yoreh Deah* 264:1.) We know, for example, that the wife of Moses herself looked after the milah of her son. A second reference that comes to my mind is the statement in the Grace After Meals where we thank God for many things, including ועל בריתך שחתמת בבשרנו – *ve-al brit'kha she-hatamta b-vsareinu* (the Covenant that has been sealed into our flesh). The question was raised: Can a woman recite this phrase in the Grace? The answer was "yes, definitely," because she is involved in the Covenant, and if among the various interpretations of the ברית – *brit* – is to civilize our sexual behavior, obviously, both sexes are involved in this experience.

Seed Thoughts II

This Midrash seems to have placed the whole concept of circumcision on a level far beyond what we have so far discussed. Up to the present discussion based on the various Midrashim, we have looked upon circumcision as one of the 613 commandments. The present Midrash raises the concept of circumcision from a single commandment to one of the important principles of the Jewish faith. Notice what it says: There are five conditions which have to be fulfilled in order for the Jewish people to be justified in accepting the Land of Israel. The acceptance of God's divinity and the acceptance and observance of Sabbath are conditional to entering the Promised Land, and so is the observance of circumcision. In other words, milah is projected here as a spiritual equivalent of the acceptance of the divinity of God. Can anything be higher than this? From this point of view, it is appropriate that this Midrash should be close to the end of the discussions of milah, since it raises it to the highest possible spiritual position.

PARASHAH FORTY-SIX, *Midrash Ten*

י וּנְמַלְתֶּם אֵת בְּשַׂר עָרְלַתְכֶם, כְּנוּמִי הִיא, תְּלוּיָה בַּגּוּף.

10. AND YE SHALL BE CIRCUMCISED (*U-NEMALTEM*) IN THE FLESH OF YOUR FORESKIN (GEN. 17:11). IT [THE PREPUCE] IS LIKE A SORE (*NUMI*) HANGING FROM THE BODY.

The Sages of the Midrash found much difficulty with this verse. It would have been better if it had been written *u-maltem* and not *u-nimaltem*. They also were concerned that the verse mentioned בשר – *basar* – "flesh." It was not necessary, since by this time, there were many scriptural verses which explained in detail what the circumcision involved. As a result, the verse is interpreted as though there is something involved with the flesh of the male foreskin, and therefore, it had to be removed. This, of course, is contrary to all of the teaching of milah up to this point, and requires an interpretation. In this respect, the stories that now follow are themselves a very adequate explanation.

וּמַעֲשֶׂה בְּמוֹנְבַז הַמֶּלֶךְ וּבְזוֹטוֹס בָּנָיו שֶׁל תַּלְמַי הַמֶּלֶךְ, שֶׁהָיוּ יוֹשְׁבִין וְקוֹרִין סֵפֶר בְּרֵאשִׁית. כֵּיוָן שֶׁהִגִּיעוּ לְפָסוּק הַזֶּה: וּנְמַלְתֶּם אֵת בְּשַׂר עָרְלַתְכֶם, הָפַךְ זֶה פָּנָיו לַכּוֹתֶל וְהִתְחִיל בּוֹכֶה, וְזֶה הָפַךְ פָּנָיו לַכּוֹתֶל וְהִתְחִיל בּוֹכֶה. הָלְכוּ שְׁנֵיהֶם וְנִימוֹלוּ.

ONCE MONABAZ AND IZATES, THE SONS OF KING PTOLEMY, WERE SITTING AND READING THE BOOK OF GENESIS. WHEN THEY CAME TO THE VERSE, AND YE SHALL BE CIRCUMCISED, ONE TURNED HIS FACE TO THE WALL AND COMMENCED TO WEEP, AND THE OTHER TURNED HIS FACE TO THE WALL AND COMMENCED TO WEEP. THEN EACH WENT AND HAD HIMSELF CIRCUMCISED.

The point to remember from this story is that neither brother knew what the other was doing or planning on doing. They did not become circumcised together, but completely separately, and without one's knowledge of the other.

לאחר ימים היו יושבין וקורין בספר בראשית, כיון שהגיעו לפסוק הזה: ונמלתם את בשר ערלתכם, אמר אחד לחבירו: אי לך אחי! א"ל: את, אי לך! לי, לא אוי! גלו את הדבר זה לזה.

SOME TIME LATER THEY WERE SITTING AND READING THE BOOK OF GENESIS, AND WHEN THEY CAME TO THE VERSE, AND YE SHALL BE CIR-CUMCISED, ONE SAID TO THE OTHER, "WOE TO THEE, MY BROTHER!" TO WHICH HE REPLIED, "WOE TO THEE, MY BROTHER, BUT NOT TO ME." THUS THEY REVEALED THE MATTER TO EACH OTHER.

It is important to note that the brothers were very fearful of their father. They did not tell him at all what had happened to them, because they feared the consequences. But they did tell their mother. And this is what happened.

כיון שהרגישה בהן אמן, הלכה ואמרה לאביהן: בניך עלתה נומא בבשרן, וגזר הרופא שימולו. אמר לה: ימולו.

WHEN THEIR MOTHER LEARNED ABOUT IT SHE WENT AND TOLD THEIR FATHER: "A SORE HAS BROKEN OUT ON OUR SONS" FLESH AND THE PHYSICIAN HAS ORDERED CIRCUMCISION.' 'THEN LET THEM BE CIRCUM-CISED,' SAID HE.

We can see from the approach of the mother that she was very careful about how the development of circumcision should be presented to her husband. She used the concept of medical suffering and medical heal-ing. A physician felt that the boys had a medical problem and required circumcision. The father was quite ready to accept that interpretation, and ordered it to happen without, of course, knowing that it had already taken place.

מה פרע לו הקב"ה? אמר רבי פנחס: בשעה שיצא למלחמה, עשו לו סיעה של פסטון, וירד מלאך והצילו:

HOW DID THE HOLY ONE, BLESSED BE HE, REQUITE THEM? SAID R. PHINEHAS: WHEN HE WENT OUT TO BATTLE A BAND OF ENEMIES AT-TACKED HIM, AND AN ANGEL DESCENDED AND RESCUED HIM.

One of the questions posed by a commentator is why the father merited a reward. That same commentator suggested that the reward was due to the fact that he accepted his wife's information and did not ask too many questions about the nature of the circumcision and which part of the body was involved.

—

Seed Thoughts

In this midrashic story, the sons and even the mother did not want to use a religious argument in explanation of the circumcision. They knew in advance that it would be rejected by the father as being opposed to his way of life. The argument used was of medical health by acclaiming that circumcision has certain advantages for the male, such as the claim that it civilizes the sexuality of the person involved, and puts the relationship between the sexes on a more rational and controllable basis. These are not ancient arguments; they have been used in modern times and are still part of the argument, especially on the part of those who advocate the use of circumcision for everybody and not only for Jews. There was a time when this argument was accepted by the official medical profession. Today, the health benefits of circumcision are still officially recognized by the World Health Organization in stemming the spread of AIDS and preventing cancer of the genitals. On the question of circumcision as a universal practice, many courts of law in different countries have come out against this movement for the fact that an infant cannot give his consent. It is of interest to note that in 2012, the German parliament passed a law that religious circumcision is acceptable to us. The decision of parliament in any country is supreme, and it overrules even the judgment of a court.

PARASHAH FORTY-SIX, *Midrash Eleven*

יא ובן שמונת ימים ימול לכם. תניא, הלוקח עובר שפחתו של עובד כוכבים. רבי יוחנן אמר:
ימול לשמונה. ותני ר' חמא בר יוסי: ימול לשמונה. ותני שמואל כן, מה דאמר שמואל: לבן
או לבת מכ"מ:

11. AND HE THAT IS EIGHT DAYS OLD SHALL BE CIRCUMCISED ... HE
THAT IS BORN IN THE HOUSE OR BOUGHT WITH MONEY (GEN. 17:12).
IT WAS TAUGHT: IF A MAN BUYS THE UNBORN CHILD OF A NON-JEWISH
BONDMAID BELONGING TO A GENTILE – R. JOHANAN SAID: HE MUST BE
CIRCUMCISED ON THE EIGHTH DAY [AFTER BIRTH]. IT WAS LIKEWISE
TAUGHT, R. HAMA B. R. JOSE SAID: HE MUST BE CIRCUMCISED ON THE
EIGHTH DAY, WHILE SAMUEL TAUGHT THE SAME. SAMUEL'S STATEMENT
IS BASED ON THE VERSE: FOR A SON, OR FOR A DAUGHTER (LEV. 12:6);
"FOR A SON" MEANS IN ALL CASES, AND "FOR A DAUGHTER" MEANS IN
ALL CASES.

The verse in the Torah text which states that every male child should
be circumcised on the eighth day includes those born in the house
where the gentile mother is the servant or bought within the terms of
the slavery movement of the time. It should be emphasized that "born
in the house or bought with money" refers in this particular case to the
infant being born of a non-Jewish mother. Nevertheless, you circumcise
on the eighth day. The Torah text continues a few verses later to repeat
the same injunction. The infant "born in the house or bought with
money" must certainly be circumcised. Why is this repeated? We might
have thought that the first verse covered all possibilities. But there is
another situation left out, namely that a child acquired by money may
not necessarily be included to be circumcised on the eighth day, but
rather to be circumcised either when it is born or when it is acquired.
Thus, there is the verse that talks about one who acquires a newborn of
his servant who, at that time, was a servant to a non-Jew. That infant is
still regarded as "in the house or bought with money," and he too is to
be circumcised on the eighth day, and not what was originally thought.
Thus, Rabbi Hama and Rabbi Samuel say that the rule in all these cases
is that we follow the status of a child, male or female, and we do not
follow the status of the mother. The child is within the rights, and within

the authority of a Jewish household – that child is treated on the same level as all the Israelite children. (Mirkin)

⁓

Seed Thoughts

A modern reader would certainly be shocked when reading this Midrash for the first time. Was slavery practiced in the Torah? In the second and third centuries when these texts were created, slavery was still the way of the world. Everywhere and at all times, the Jews had to find a way to participate in this situation as best as they could while protecting the legitimacy of the Torah and not of greater ethical idealism. Why then do we study this material now? In the first place, it is part of the original text, and why should we cut up the Midrash simply to illuminate what we do not agree with. On the contrary, there are many parts of the Talmudic tradition which may have outlived the reasons for their existence. Studying this material, however, is an intellectual challenge. Sometimes, we learn many things from it. For example, in this Midrash alone, we have a tremendous sense of liberalism even within the slavery tradition, by which I mean exceptional tolerance for the non-Jewish world through the laws of the practice of milah in the case of non-Jewish infants. This material was not merely a reflection of how the world behaves. In the classic literature of the Bible, one of its most famous stories is how Sarah arranged for two of her maidservants to become the second and third wives of her husband, Abraham. The children born to Leah's and Rachel's maidservants were almost half of Jacob's household and became his children on an equal status of those who were given birth by Leah and Rachel. We do not have to apologize for what has happened in our history, but we do have to try and place Judaism on the highest possibilities of moral life today.

PARASHAH FORTY-SIX, *Midrash Twelve*

יב המול ימול. מילה ופריעה, מילה וציצין.

12. HE SHALL SURELY BE CIRCUMCISED – *HIMMOL YIMMOL* (GEN. 17:13).
THIS MEANS CIRCUMCISION, *PERI'AH*, AND REMOVAL OF THE SHREDS
[*TZITZIN*, OF THE CORONA].

The use of the two terms for circumcision is meant to indicate that
more is involved than the removal of the foreskin. *Peri'ah* is also necessary, which is defined as "the uncovering of the corona by splitting
the membrane and pulling it down" (Soncino). Another action is also
involved, called *tzitzin*, which is defined as the "removal of the shreds of
the corona" (Soncino).

המול ימול, מיכן למוהל שיהא מהול? המול ימול, להביא את שנולד מהול. תני ר"ש ב"א
אומר: לא נחלקו בית שמאי ובית הילל, על שנולד מהול, שהוא צריך להטיף ממנו דם ברית,
מפני שהיא ערלה כבושה. ועל מה נחלקו? על גר שנתגייר מהול, שבש"א שהוא צריך
להטיף ממנו דם, וב"ה אומרים, אינו צריך. ר"א בנו של רבי יוסי הגלילי אומר: ב"ש ובית
הילל לא נחלקו על זה ועל זה שהוא צריך להטיף ממנו דם ברית. ועל מה נחלקו? על מי
שנולד מהול, וכשחל יום שמיני שלו להיות בשבת, שבית שמאי אומרים צריך להטיף ממנו
דם ברית, ובית הילל אומרים, אינו צריך. רבי יצחק בר נחמן בשם רבי הושעיא אמר: הלכה
כדברי התלמיד:

HE SHALL SURELY BE CIRCUMCISED [ALSO MEANS THE FOLLOWING]:
THIS TEACHES THAT THE CIRCUMCISER MUST HIMSELF BE CIRCUM-
CISED. HE SHALL SURELY BE CIRCUMCISED: THIS SIGNIFIES THE INCLU-
SION OF ONE WHO IS BORN CIRCUMCISED. IT WAS TAUGHT, R. SIMEON
B. ELEAZAR SAID: BETH SHAMMAI AND BETH HILLEL AGREE THAT WHEN
ONE IS BORN CIRCUMCISED, THE BLOOD OF THE COVENANT MUST BE
MADE TO FLOW FROM HIM, BECAUSE IT IS A SUPPRESSED FORESKIN.
THEY DISAGREE ONLY ABOUT A MAN WHO BECAME A PROSELYTE WHEN
ALREADY CIRCUMCISED. BETH SHAMMAI MAINTAIN: THE BLOOD OF THE
COVENANT MUST BE MADE TO FLOW FROM HIM, WHILE BETH HILLEL
RULE: IT IS UNNECESSARY. R. ELEAZAR THE SON OF R. ELEAZAR HAKAP-
PAR SAID: BETH SHAMMAI AND BETH HILLEL AGREE THAT IN BOTH OF
THESE CASES THE BLOOD OF THE COVENANT MUST BE MADE TO FLOW.
THEY DISAGREE ABOUT ONE WHO WAS BORN CIRCUMCISED, AND THE
EIGHTH DAY AFTER WHOSE BIRTH FELL ON THE SABBATH. BETH SHAM-

MAI THEN MAINTAIN: THE BLOOD OF THE COVENANT MUST FLOW;
WHILE BETH HILLEL RULE: IT IS UNNECESSARY. R. ISAAC B. NAHMAN
SAID IN R. HOSHAYA'S NAME: THE HALACHAH IS AS STATED BY THE DIS-
CIPLE.

There is another interpretation of the fact that the text includes two verbs to describe circumcision. An additional interpretation makes the point that this means that the one who performs the circumcision should himself be circumcised. This means, of course, that only a Jewish person or one who converts himself to Judaism can perform a circumcision. Additional interpretations have been added to these explanations. Somebody already born without a foreskin still requires the procedure of producing a drop of blood from the sexual organ, putting him on the same level as somebody already circumcised. The question arises as to whether the ritual of removing the drop of blood is such that one is allowed it on the Sabbath in the same way that we are allowed to perform an actual circumcision on the Sabbath. This was one of the differences of opinion between the School of Shammai and the School of Hillel. The School of Shammai insisted that the drop of blood be treated with the same sanctity as an ordinary circumcision. The School of Hillel felt that this was not a requirement. In this regard, it is claimed that both the Schools of Hillel and Shammai agreed – the one born circumcised requires a ritual of removing the drop of blood, but it is not powerful enough to desecrate the Sabbath for its completion. Where, then, did the Schools of Hillel and Shammai differ, if there was a difference? The question still remains: In what areas did the Schools of Shammai and Hillel differ on this question of circumcision? They differ on the question as to whether a person already circumcised by another religion requires the dropping of blood on the Sabbath. The School of Shammai said it is required, but the School of Hillel said it is not required. According to the latter, all that person needs is immersion in a ritual bath. The final conclusion was allowed to rest with an important pupil of Hillel, whose name was Rabbi Shimon ben Elazar. He claimed that the School of Hillel did agree with the School of Shammai that the blood of the covenant was required in all of these cases.

Seed Thoughts

One of the remarkable aspects of these various interpretations is the spirit of liberalism, which is appreciated by all who are commenting on this subject. This applies both to the Schools of Hillel and of Shammai. On the one hand, they wanted to do everything to protect the person who was to become Jewish, and on the other hand, to make it possible for those who have special bodily assets – such as being born circumcised – to function fully as Jews.

～

Additional Commentary

Hatafat Dam Brit on the Sabbath

The halakha follows the view of a disciple of the School of Hillel. The Midrash seemed unable to find a way in which the Schools of Shammai and Hillel can affirm that the convert to Judaism already circumcised by others should require the Covenant of a drop of Blood (*hatafat dam brit*) even on the Sabbath. The debate was resolved by a pupil or disciple of the School of Hillel, whose name was Rabbi Shimon ben Elazar. Why is Rabbi Shimon ben Elazar described as a pupil or disciple? Because he was a pupil (and an excellent one) of the School of Hillel. Rabbi Shimon ben Elazar was a far lesser person than Rabbi Yehuda Ha-Nasi and did not have the status of Rabbi Yehuda Ha-Nasi. The latter, by contrast, was president of the community and the spokesman for Hillel. Because of Rabbi Shimon ben Elazar's strong affirmation, one who was born circumcised must have the Covenant of a drop of Blood done on his body even on the Sabbath. However, a convert who was already circumcised does not require it by the letter of the law. It is only a stringency, and therefore is not done on the Sabbath but postponed to the following Sunday. (Mirkin)

PARASHAH FORTY-SIX, *Midrash Thirteen*

יג וערל זכר. רבי חגי אמר: וכי יש ערל נקבה? אלא ממקום שהוא ניכר, אם זכר אם נקבה
מוהלים אותו.

13. AND THE UNCIRCUMCISED MALE, ETC. (GEN. 17:14). R. HAGGAI SAID
[IN R. ISAAC'S NAME, AND R. BEREKIAH SAID IN R. ISAAC'S NAME]: IS
THERE THEN AN UNCIRCUMCISED FEMALE? THE MEANING, HOWEVER,
IS THAT WE MUST PERFORM CIRCUMCISION ON THE MEMBER WHICH
MARKS THE DISTINCTION BETWEEN MALE AND FEMALE.

The text here uses the expression ערל זכר – *arel zakhar*, meaning
uncircumcised male. The use of the term "male" here was surprising
to the commentators, and so they asked the question: Is there such a
thing as "uncircumcised female?" Of course not, this entire discussion
is elaborated upon in Midrash 5 above, and it is interpreted as helping to
solve what place in the body the circumcision should place. Of course,
the decision was to have it in the male sexual organ.

את בריתי הפר, זה המשוך:

HE HATH BROKEN MY COVENANT. THIS REFERS TO ONE WHOSE CIRCUM-
CISION IS DISGUISED.

The Hebrew term is משוך – *mashukh* (literally, "drawn"). Here, the
term refers to the skin over the prepuce. Under the Hellenizing influence of the pre-Maccabean period, when Greek games were introduced
into Judea, in which the competitors appeared naked, many underwent
operations (i.e., epiplasm) to hide the fact that they were circumcised
(Soncino).

תני המשוך אינו צריך לימול. רי"א: לא ימול, מפני שהיא ערלה כבושה. אמרו לפני ר"י:
והלא הרבה היו בימי בן כוזיבא, לכולהון בנין, חוזרין ומולין. הה"ד: המול ימול. אפילו ד' וה'
פעמים. את בריתי הפר, זה המשוך:

IT WAS TAUGHT: HE WHOSE CIRCUMCISION IS DISGUISED MUST RE-
CIRCUMCISE. R. JUDAH SAID: HE DOES NOT RE-CIRCUMCISE, BECAUSE IT
IS A SUPPRESSED FORESKIN. SAID THEY TO R. JUDAH: YET THERE WERE
MANY IN THE DAYS OF THE SON OF KOSIBA [BAR KOKHBA] WHO RE-CIR-
CUMCISED AND YET GAVE BIRTH TO CHILDREN AFTER THAT. HENCE IT

IS WRITTEN, HE SHALL SURELY BE CIRCUMCISED – EVEN FOUR OR FIVE
TIMES: HE HATH BROKEN MY COVENANT – VIZ. HE WHOSE CIRCUMCI-
SION IS DISGUISED.

At first, the view was that such people should not be re-circumcised
because of the fact that it might involve certain dangers, such as the
elimination of the possibility of having children, or even life-threatening
possibilities. However, when Bar Kokhba (who led the army of Israel)
was successful for a period of two years, many such circumcisions were
performed for those who wanted to return to Judaism. None of the perceived dangers actually happened. The conclusion therefore was חוזרים
ומוהלים – *hozrim u'mohalim* – "let them return to Judaism and let them
be circumcised again."

Seed Thoughts

The various commentaries of this Midrash which deals with the person
who is *mashukh* (whose circumcision is disguised) make reference to
the time of Bar Kokhba. Bar Kokhba led a revolution against the Roman Empire. At first, it was partially successful, and Jerusalem had
independence for about two years. Later on, however, the Roman
legions crushed Bar Kokhba's relatively small army. The historians have
called our attention to a folk saying in this respect: His name was Bar
Kokhba, which means Son of a Star – that was well-deserved when he
was winning. On the other hand, when he lost everything, his name was
changed to Bar Kosiba, which basically means a false leader. Although
some Jewish leaders and historians use Bar Kokhba as some kind of
symbol, Jews were never afraid to use military action to save themselves.
On the other hand, this has been interpreted as one of the great trag-
edies of Jewish life, since many thousands of Jewish soldiers and other
army personnel perished during these battles.

א ויאמר אלהים שרי אשתך וגו'. כתיב (משלי יב): אשת חיל עטרת בעלה.

1. AND GOD SAID UNTO ABRAHAM: AS FOR SARAI THY WIFE, THOU SHALT
NOT CALL HER NAME SARAI, BUT SARAH [I.E., PRINCESS] SHALL HER
NAME BE (GEN. 17:15). IT IS WRITTEN: A VIRTUOUS WOMAN IS A CROWN
TO HER HUSBAND (PROV. 12:4).

The Book of Proverbs contains a wonderful tribute to the woman
of worth (in Hebrew, *Eishet Hayil*). This term has in mind a person
whose talents, values, and character are quite extraordinary. However,
the Book of Proverbs does not identify any specific woman who can
so be designated. Our Midrash, though, identifies Sarah, the wife of
Abraham, as being an excellent model of the Eishet Hayil, who is there
for the adornment of her husband.

אמר רבי אחא: בעלה נתעטר בה, והיא לא נתעטרה בבעלה.

R. AHA SAID: HER HUSBAND WAS CROWNED THROUGH HER, BUT SHE
WAS NOT CROWNED THROUGH HER HUSBAND.

Generally speaking, the average woman in a marriage relationship allows her husband to make many of the family decisions, and her role relates more often to domestic matters. But in the case of an Eishet Hayil,
that role is sometimes reversed. In some cases, therefore, a woman is the
adornment of her husband, but she does not require a similar tribute to
him.

רבנן אמרי: מרתא לבעלה. בכל מקום האיש גוזר, ברם הכא (בראשית כא): כל אשר תאמר
אליך שרה, שמע בקולה.

THE RABBIS SAID: SHE WAS HER HUSBAND'S RULER. USUALLY, THE HUS-
BAND GIVES ORDERS, WHEREAS HERE WE READ: IN ALL THAT SARAH
SAITH UNTO THEE, HEARKEN UNTO HER VOICE (GEN. 21:12).

For *Sarah*, the rabbis use the expression *marta*, which (like *gevira*) means a ruler or prince/princess, whereas Sarai might be translated as resembling the personal grammar in Hebrew as "my wife Sarai." In other words, Sarah became the high authority in the relationship between Abraham and Sarah, and this was treated as a commandment by the Almighty who said to Abraham: "In all that Sarah saith unto thee, hearken unto her voice."

א"ר יהושע בן קרחה: יו"ד שנטל הקב"ה משרי, נחלק חציו לשרה וחציו לאברהם. אמר רבי שמעון בן יוחאי: יו"ד שנטל הקב"ה משרי, היה טס ופורח לפני כסאו של הקב"ה. אמר לפניו: רבש"ע! בשביל שאני קטנה שבאותיות, הוצאתני משרה הצדקת? א"ל הקב"ה: לשעבר היית משמה של נקבה, ובסופן של אותיות, עכשיו אני נותנך בשמו של זכר, ובראשן של אותיות, שנאמר (במדבר יג): ויקרא משה להושע בן נון יהושע.

R. JOSHUA B. KARHAH SAID: THE *YOD* WHICH THE LORD TOOK FROM SARAI SOARED ALOFT BEFORE GOD AND PROTESTED: "SOVEREIGN OF THE UNIVERSE! BECAUSE I AM THE SMALLEST OF ALL LETTERS, THOU HAST WITHDRAWN ME FROM THE NAME OF THAT RIGHTEOUS WOMAN!" SAID THE HOLY ONE, BLESSED BE HE, TO IT: "HITHERTO THOU WAST IN A WOMAN'S NAME AND THE LAST OF ITS LETTERS; NOW I WILL SET THEE IN A MAN'S NAME AND AT THE BEGINNING OF ITS LETTERS," AS IT SAYS: AND MOSES CALLED HOSHEA THE SON OF NUN JOSHUA (NUM. 13:16).

We have here a beautiful play on words often found in the Midrash. The Sages loved to play with Hebrew letters and derive meaning from it. How come the letter *yod* was removed from the name Sarai? One should not feel too badly about the letter *yod*, since the letter *yod* has a numerical value of ten, and ten is made up of 5 + 5, and the number five in Hebrew is the letter *heh*. So, the Torah took the letter *yod* from Sarai, divided it into two – one *yod* was removed from Sarai and replaced with *heh*, and the other *heh* was added to the name Abram, so it became Abraham.

The same letter complained to God why it was removed from *Sarai*, and she was a righteous woman. Was it because *yod* was such a small letter? On the contrary, the letter *yod* would be removed from Sarai and given to Hoshea, so that his name became *Yehoshua*, who was a great leader of the Jewish people.

א"ר מנא: לשעבר, היתה שרי לעצמה. עכשיו, תהא היא שרה לכל באי העולם:

R. MANA SAID: FORMERLY SHE WAS A PRINCESS [SARAI] TO HER OWN PEOPLE ONLY, WHEREAS NOW SHE IS A PRINCESS [SARAH] TO ALL MANKIND.

The name Sarai is very personal, as though Abraham described her as "my Sarah," but the name Sarah is universal and speaks to the world as Sarah and Abraham together spoke to the world.

~

Seed Thoughts

The questions that might occur to the average reader of the Midrash are as follows: How do the Sages actually look upon the game of playing with the letters of the Hebrew alphabet as a source of meaning and teaching? When they ask the question as they did in the present Midrash, what happened to the letter *yod* that was removed from the name of Sarai? How serious were they? Did they actually believe that removing the letter *yod* was a major event that should be explained? Granted that the teaching is very beautiful and highly appreciated especially by children, what are we to say about the great scholars of the Midrash? Did they also take this play of the letters of the alphabet seriously?

After much thinking about this subject, I should like to share the following opinion: We are dealing with poetry. In writing a line of poetry or in reading a poetic line, we understand that the poetic line is not the real intent of the author. The poetic line is a symbol for something else, something very meaningful whose impact on the reader is that much stronger because it is built upon a poetic line which makes the real meaning, the symbolic meaning, much stronger. The fact that the letter *yod* has a numerical value of ten, which can be divided into two fives, means that the letter *heh* (numerically five) is used to create a new meaning. The name Sarai has now been used to elevate the name of Abram to Abraham and Sarai to Sarah. That has been the goal of the game of the Hebrew letters. It is a poetical goal and a very beautiful one.

Parashah Forty-Seven, *Midrash Two*

ב ובְרַכְתִּי אוֹתָהּ וְגַם נָתַתִּי מִמֶּנָּה לְךָ בֵּן וּבֵרַכְתִּיהָ וגו'.

2. AND I WILL BLESS HER, AND MOREOVER I WILL GIVE THEE A SON FROM HER; YEA, I WILL BLESS HER, ETC. (GEN. 17:16).

What is bothering the Sages in the words just read is that the blessing has been repeated twice (Mirkin). Therefore, some of the commentaries will offer views as to which two particular blessings were intended.

רבי יהודה ורבי נחמיה. רי"א: ובְרַכְתִּי אוֹתָהּ, לִתֵּן לָהּ בֵּן. וּבֵרַכְתִּיהָ, לְבִרְכַּת הֶחָלָב. א"ל רבי נחמיה: וכי כבר נתבשרה בחלב, והלא עדיין לא נתעברה? אלא מלמד שהחזירה הקב"ה לימי נערותיה.

R. JUDAH AND R. NEHEMIAH DISAGREED. R. JUDAH SAID: THIS MEANS, AND I WILL BLESS HER THAT SHE SHOULD GIVE THEE A SON; YEA, I WILL BLESS HER WITH RESPECT TO MILK. SAID R. NEHEMIAH TO HIM: HAD SHE THEN ALREADY BEEN INFORMED ABOUT HER MILK, IN LIGHT OF THE FACT THAT SHE HAD NOT YET BEEN PREGNANT? THIS TEACHES, HOWEVER, THAT GOD RESTORED HER TO HER YOUTH.

Rabbi Judah and Rabbi Nehemiah are not the only ones who are engaged in a debate about our text.

רבי אבהו בשם ר' יוסי בר חנינא: נותן אני יראתה על כל עובדי כוכבים, דלא יהון מונין לה וצווחין, דא עקרתא.

R. ABBAHU EXPLAINED IT THUS IN THE NAME OF R. JOSE B. R. HANINA: I WILL INSPIRE ALL PEOPLES WITH AWE OF HER, SO THAT THEY SHOULD NOT CALL HER, "BARREN WOMAN."

What Rabbi Abbahu is saying is that in addition to being blessed with a son, the second expression *u'verakhtiha* refers to the fact that she was given the strength to overcome those who call her names such as "barren woman."

ר' יודן בשם ריש לקיש: עיקר מיטרין לא הוה לה, וגלף לה הקב"ה עיקר מיטרין.

R. JUDAN SAID IN THE NAME OF RESH LAKISH: SHE LACKED AN OVARY, BUT THE LORD FASHIONED AN OVARY FOR HER.

T he view of Rabbi Judan does not differ that much from that of Rabbi Nehemiah. One claims that the blessing was that she became youthful again, and the other specifies that her youthfulness consists of a replacement of a missing ovary.

מלכי עמים ממנה יהיו. א"ר חמא בר' חנינא: מיכן דרש אברהם והחזיר את קטורה:

AND KINGS OF PEOPLES SHALL BE OF HER. R. HAMA B. R. HANINA SAID: ABRAHAM DREW A DEDUCTION FROM THIS AND TOOK BACK KETURAH.

S ee the Seed Thoughts.

—

Seed Thoughts

The verse goes on to say, "And kings of peoples shall be of her." This section is very difficult. Rabbi Hama makes a most unusual comment: He maintains that Abraham took the blessing very seriously, especially the one that said "kings of peoples shall be of her." It does not mean that "kings of peoples" will descend directly from her, but *of* her – meaning from within her jurisdiction. It is for this reason that Abraham brought Hagar back into his life. Sarah had given Hagar to Abraham as his wife with the hope that children descended from Hagar would be looked upon as part of the inheritance of Sarah. Since Hagar herself was a princess, the daughter of Pharaoh, it seems somewhat logical that "kings of peoples" should be descended from her. Therefore, after the death of Sarah, Abraham sent for Hagar, whose name is also Keturah, to resume their marriage.

—

Additional Commentary

Sarah's Blessings

The verse says: "I will *bless* her and give her a child and I will *bless* her." Therefore, there is a dispute what the two blessings are. Rabbi Yehuda says one is a child, and the other is milk to nurse the child. Rabbi Nehemiah says one is a child, and the other is her returning to youthfulness. (Mirkin)

PARASHAH FORTY-SEVEN, *Midrash Three*

ג ויפול אברהם על פניו ויצחק. שתי פעמים נפל אברהם על פניו, וכנגדן ניטלה מילה מבניו. ב׳ פעמים, אחד במצרים ואחד במדבר. במצרים, בא משה ומלן. במדבר, בא יהושע ומלן.

3. THEN ABRAHAM FELL UPON HLS FACE (GEN. 17:17). R. PHINEHAS SAID IN R. LEVI'S NAME: ON TWO OCCASIONS DID ABRAHAM FALL ON HIS FACE. IN CONSEQUENCE, HIS CHILDREN WERE DEPRIVED OF CIRCUMCISION, ONCE IN THE WILDERNESS AND ONCE IN EGYPT. IN EGYPT, MOSES CAME AND CIRCUMCISED THEM; IN THE WILDERNESS, JOSHUA CAME AND CIRCUMCISED THEM.

This midrashic interpretation is based on the belief that whatever happened to the people of the biblical generation was a symbol of something that was going to happen to their offspring. The Midrash points to the fact that Abraham fell on his face twice. That is a symbol that something negative is going to happen to his children. The Midrash points out that what actually happened was that the Children of Israel were forced to abandon milah on two occasions. The first occasion was in Egypt, where their servitude made circumcision very difficult. The second occasion was in the wilderness, where this practice became a source of physical danger and therefore had to be abandoned. In Egypt, Moses restored milah to the entire people in order to prepare them for the Paschal offering. In the wilderness, circumcision was restored to them by Joshua to enable them to inherit the Land of Canaan.

ויאמר בלבו: הלבן מאה שנה יולד וגו׳.

AND SAID IN HIS HEART: SHALL A CHILD BE BORN UNTO HIM THAT IS A HUNDRED YEARS OLD, ETC.

The reason why Abraham laughed was because of his astonishment and also his gratitude that a person of 100 years old, namely himself, could father a child.

רבי יודן ורבי עזריה. רבי יודן אמר: הלבן מאה שנה יולד, למה ששרה הבת תשעים שנה תלד? האיש אינו מזקין והאשה מזקנת. רבי עזריה אמר: אף לזאת לא נצרך, שהרי שרה בת תשעים שנה לא הזקינה. אי זו היא זקינה? כל שקורין אותה אימא פלנית, ואינה מקפדת:

R. JUDAN AND R. AZARIAH HAVE A DIFFERENCE OF OPINION. R. JUDAN
INTERPRETED: SHALL A CHILD BE BORN UNTO HIM THAT IS A HUNDRED
YEARS OLD? WHY [THIS ASTONISHMENT]? FOR, [SAID HE], SHALL SARAH,
THAT IS NINETY YEARS OLD, BEAR? R. AZARIAH INTERPRETED: A MAN
DOES NOT GROW AGED, BUT A WOMAN DOES. WHEN IS A WOMAN TO BE
REGARDED AS AGED? SAID R. SIMEON B. LAKISH: WHEN SHE IS CALLED
"MOTHER SO-AND-SO" AND DOES NOT MIND.

According to Rabbi Judan, Abraham's feelings were not only that he
was 100, but also that Sarah was 90. Apparently, it was his belief that a
man is able to father a child even in his advanced years but that women
age in earlier years. Rabbi Azariah, however, says that although Sarah
was 90, she was not considered old. How does one decide upon age in
terms of a woman? When she is referred to by names such as "Mother
So-and-So" or "Grandmother So-and-So" and she does not have objections to this terminology. Only the attitude of a woman can determine
whether she looks upon herself as aged.

—

Seed Thoughts I

The text says that Abraham fell on his face on two occasions, Genesis
17:3, and17:17. The Midrash had built up a series of teachings on these
two falls. However, when we examine the context of the two falls, they
are really quite different. The first section in Verse 3 of Chapter 17 describes Abraham as falling on his face because of milah, whereas in the
verse quoted by our Midrash, he laughed in happiness when told of the
birth of Isaac. There seems to be quite a difference in atmosphere between the circumstances of one fall and the circumstances of the other.
This, however, did not bother midrashic writers. In general, when the
scribes of the Midrash had something they wanted to say, they put aside
all literary rules and concentrated on what bothered them. They were
concerned that Abraham fell on his face twice. The fact that he did so for
two different reasons did not bother the writers in the slightest. We can
never know the real motivation, but it does not matter. The midrashic
writers tell what they want to tell us, and do not allow such things as
literary precedence to bother them.

—

Seed Thoughts II

I am delighted to acknowledge that I have found something in the Midrash which I thought was modern teaching and which has turned out to be well-known to the Jewish community of the second century. We think that we are living in an era which uses terms like "women's liberation." But notice what this Midrash has been telling us. No one argues as to when a man is old; he knows when he old, and others know when he is old. But when is a woman old? According to our Midrash, no one has a right to say whether, or when, a woman is old; only she has that right. She can be as young as she wants to be in her attitude; she can also accept the status of old age whenever she wants to, and only she has the right to make that decision. The Midrash puts it in simpler words: All she has to do is to accept being referred to as "Grandmother So-and-So" or the various other terminologies in Yiddish or Hebrew, such as *bubbe* or *savta*. If she accepts those appellations, it means that she has made peace with being at old age; if not, she has the right to act in whatever way she wishes. Who said these things? Male scholars of *Midrash Rabbah* during the second and third centuries CE.

PARASHAH FORTY-SEVEN, *Midrash Four*

ד׳ לו ישמעאל יחיה לפניך.

4. AND ABRAHAM SAID UNTO GOD: OH THAT ISHMAEL MIGHT LIVE BEFORE THEE! (GEN. 17:18).

The Holy One, blessed be He, had just promised Abraham the blessings of a new son, and his only response has been to grant him life and that whatever blessings are required for his present son, Ishmael.

ר' יודן בשם רבי יהודה בר סימון אמר: משל לאוהבו של מלך, שהיה המלך מעלה לו אנונה.
א"ל המלך: אני מבקש לכפול אנונה שלך. א"ל: לא תמלא רוחי קריר, הלואי קדמייתא לא
תמנע. כך לו ישמעאל, יחיה לפניך. ויאמר אלהים אבל שרה אשתך:

R. JUDAN SAID IN R. JUDAH BAR SIMON'S NAME: IMAGINE A KING WHO WISHED TO INCREASE HIS FRIEND'S ALLOWANCE. "I INTEND TO DOUBLE YOUR ALLOWANCE," THE KING INFORMED HIM. "DO NOT FILL ME WITH

A FALSE HOPE," HE REJOINED; "PRAY ONLY THAT YOU DO NOT WITH-
HOLD MY PRESENT ALLOWANCE!" SIMILARLY ABRAHAM SAID, OH THAT
ISHMAEL MIGHT LIVE BEFORE THEE.

The parable seems to be very fitting. The king says to his beloved
friend: "I intend to double your salary." The friend, in all humility, responds to the king by saying: "Don't fill me with false hopes. My only
desire is that you find me worthy enough to continue my present salary,
and do not offer me that for which I may be unworthy" (*HaMidrash
HaMevo'ar*). This parable applies to Abraham in a very special way.
Abraham expressed himself as being most grateful for the birth of Ishmael. As for the prophecy of a forthcoming additional son to him, he
is sufficiently grateful to God for the birth of Ishmael and does not feel
himself sufficiently worthy to benefit from another son. He answers: "If
only Ishmael can be enabled to have a full life, the implication would
be that this is the only thing that I would want." God's answer to Abraham, however, was very forceful: "You have forgotten about Sarah, the
mistress of your house who is not the mother of Ishmael and who very
much wants the blessing of her own son (who would be a most precious
asset to his mother's life)."

~

Seed Thoughts

The scriptural text describes a wonderful conversation between God
and Abraham. One cannot always compare conversations with the
Divine with conversations between two human beings, but sometimes
one can learn much from the Divine conversation to benefit human beings. God was teaching a lesson to Abraham, a lesson which all married
couples understand. This lesson has to be repeated many times in marriage because we are human and not perfect. The most important aspect
of marriage is not only cooperation between husband and wife, but it
involves each one reaching out to the other, and on the highest level
thinking about the other before thinking about oneself. Abraham's response to God, when informed of the birth of another son yet to come,
was very moral, very humble, and very honest, but also very wrong. He
was satisfied with his son, Ishmael, and wanted only his blessing and his
protection. God's answer was very immediate and very forceful, and it
began with about four words, "but your wife Sarah." More was told to

Abraham than these four words, but these four words said everything. Abraham was reprimanded for thinking only about himself and forgetting about Sarah and her needs. It was a great lesson to him, and a great lesson to all married couples who identify not only with Abraham but with God's reprimanding him as well.

All who have experienced the blessings of marriage understand that two are better than one, and each one has to think of the other first. All married couples understand this, and when they sometimes forget these principles, they are quick to make it up with each other and thus strengthen their marriage even more deeply. Abraham's problem was not Divine, but the reprimand was, and all who share the blessings of marriage understand it very well.

PARASHAH FORTY-SEVEN, *Midrash Five*

ה ולישמעאל שמעתיך.

5. AND GOD SAID: NAY, BUT SARAH THY WIFE SHALL BEAR THEE A SON
. . . AND AS FOR ISHMAEL, I HAVE HEARD THEE, ETC. (GEN. 17:19F.).

The text refers to the fact that the blessing to Ishmael was already given in earlier parts of the Torah text. His numbers will be multiplied, and twelve princes will eventually preside over his population. He will become a great nation, but God's special covenant will be with Isaac. Much of the Midrash and its commentary would now deal with what Ishmael's blessings really were, how they compare with those of Isaac, and how and when they will take place over the years.

רבי יוחנן בשם רבי יהושע בר חנינא: בן הגבירה למד מבן האמה. הנה ברכתי אותו, זה יצחק.
והפרתי אותו, זה יצחק. והרבתי אותו, זה יצחק. ולישמעאל, כבר שמעתי אותו ע"י מלאך.

R. JOHANAN SAID IN THE NAME OF R. JOSHUA B. HANANIAH: HERE THE
SON OF THE BONDMAID MIGHT LEARN [THAT HE WOULD BE BLESSED]
FROM THE SON OF THE MISTRESS. FOR, BEHOLD, I HAVE BLESSED HIM
REFERS TO ISAAC; AND WILL MAKE HIM FRUITFUL REFERS TO ISAAC;
AND WILL MULTIPLY HIM REFERS TO ISAAC. AND AS FOR ISHMAEL, I
HAVE ALREADY INFORMED THEE [ABOUT HIS BLESSING] THROUGH AN
ANGEL.

What Rabbi Johanan is quoted as saying is completely astonishing. The text associated with this quotation, and every element of it, refers to Ishmael. He would be blessed, he would multiply, and he would be the founder of a great nation. One cannot pretend that the text says anything else or that these expressions refer to Isaac. Obviously, some of the Sages in this Midrash were unhappy with the blessings of Ishmael, and we will have to investigate the reason for this. It is not enough to say that he was already blessed when his mother felt abandoned in the wilderness after being sent away from Sarah's home. There, in her distress, she was visited by an angel, who assured her that her son would be well and do great things for her and her people. The text that we are now reading not only confirms that fact, but even expresses it in a very beautiful and majestic way. How, then, does Rabbi Johanan explain it away simply by saying that these blessings refer not to Ishmael but to Isaac? Rabbi Johanan uses expressions such as "the son of the maidservant as learned from the son of the mistress"; he also used the term *kal va-homer*, moving from the simple to the complex. If Ishmael was promised so many rewards, how much more so would these rewards apply to Isaac, who was the son of Sarah and second only to Abraham.

רבי אבא בר כהנא בשם רבי בירי: כאן בן האמה למד מבן הגבירה. הנה ברכתי אותו, זה ישמעאל. והפרתי אותו, זה ישמעאל. והרבתי אותו, זה ישמעאל. ק"ו וזאת בריתי, אקים את יצחק.

R. ABBA B. KAHANA SAID IN R. BIRYAI'S NAME: HERE THE SON OF THE MISTRESS MIGHT LEARN FROM THE SON OF THE BONDMAID: BEHOLD, I HAVE BLESSED HIM REFERS TO ISHMAEL; AND WILL MAKE HIM FRUITFUL REFERS TO ISHMAEL; AND WILL MULTIPLY HIM REFERS TO ISHMAEL. HOW MUCH THE MORE THEN WILL I ESTABLISH MY COVENANT WITH ISAAC.

Rabbi Abba bar Kahana's comment reflects exactly what the text says that we have been reading. It is pro-Ishmael, and eventually, we are going to have to examine why these two sages disagree in their interpretation.

א"ר יצחק: כתיב (בראשית מט): כל אלה שבטי ישראל שנים עשר, אלו בני גבירה. וישמעאל אינו מעמיד י"ב? אלא, אותן נשיאים. היך מה דאת אמר (משלי כה): נשיאים ורוח וגשם. אין אבל אלו מטות, כמה דאת אמר (חבקוק ג): שבעות מטות אומר סלה.

R. ISAAC SAID: IT IS WRITTEN: ALL THESE ARE THE TWELVE TRIBES (*SHIBTE*) OF ISRAEL (GEN. 49:28) – THESE WERE THE DESCENDANTS OF

THE MISTRESS [SARAH]. YET DID NOT ISHMAEL TOO PRODUCE TWELVE [PRINCES]? IN TRUTH THOSE WERE *NESI'IM* (PRINCES) IN THE SAME SENSE AS YOU READ, AS *NESI'IM* [E.V. "*VAPORS*"] *AND WIND*, ETC. (PROV. 25:14). BUT THESE WERE *MATOTH* (TRIBES) AS YOU READ: SWORN ARE THE *MATOTH* [E.V. "*RODS*"] *OF THE WORD SELAH* (HAB. 3:9).

Rabbi Isaac interprets the fact that the twelve tribes credited to Ishmael's future were referred to not as *shevatim*, which is the word for tribes described for Isaac, but rather as the twelve *nesi'im*, which means "princes." However, he discovers that a translation of *nasi* is "vapor" or "cloud," which means that the so-called princes of Ishmael's tribes were leaders who thought only of themselves and much less of the tribe under them, which eventually became weak and disappeared. Whereas in the case of Isaac, the twelve tribes of Israel created the Jewish people.

ואת בריתי אקים את יצחק. ר' הונא בשם ר' אידי: אותה השנה מעוברת היתה:

BUT MY COVENANT WILL I ESTABLISH WITH ISAAC, WHOM SARAH SHALL BEAR UNTO THEE AT THIS SET TIME (*LA-MOED*) IN THE NEXT YEAR (GEN. 16:21). R. HUNA SAID IN R. IDI'S NAME: THAT YEAR WAS INTERCALATED.

The Holy One, blessed be He, informed Abraham that at *la-mo'ed hazeh*, meaning "this Festival," Sarah would give birth. What was meant by the Hebrew term *la-mo'ed hazeh* at this time? It could not be from Passover to Shavuot, because the timespan there is only seven weeks. Nor could it be from Shavuot to Sukkot, because the timespan there is only four months. Nor could it be from Passover to Sukkot, because the timespan is six months. The conclusion has to be that it could only be from Sukkot to Passover, and if you remember that the text says that Sarah became pregnant on Rosh Hashanah, one would have to conclude that the child would be born on Passover, because that would have to be a leap year. The addition of an Adar would create a timespan of seven months, which is accepted as a normal delivery.

Seed Thoughts

See the commentary above.

Additional Commentary

How to explain the differences of opinion

Rabbi Johanan has a view which changes the text completely. He interprets every blessing to Ishmael as meaning Isaac. Rabbi Abba bar Kahana insists that the text should be taken literally, and if God is blessing Ishmael, He is blessing Ishmael. The difference is based on an earlier debate which has relevance to this discussion. Rabbi Johanan follows the view that Ishmael did not do teshuvah (repentance); that is to say, he did not change from his evil ways, and efforts should be made to lower the tributes to Ishmael. Rabbi Abba bar Kahana, on the other hand, feels that Ishmael did do teshuvah. He did repent of his evil ways, and therefore he should be protected and be given the honor and credit due to him. (*Tiferet Tzion*)

Intercalation

Rabbi Huna holds that these tidings were announced at the time of the Feast of Tabernacles (15th–22nd of Tishri), while *la-mo'ed* means at the Festival in Nisan (i.e., Passover). Since this gives an interval of only six months, we must assume that the year was prolonged by the intercalation of a month (Adar), which then gives seven months. The Jewish year is lunar, and consists of about 354 days. To make up to the 365 days of the solar year, a month was intercalated in certain years. (Soncino)

PARASHAH FORTY-SEVEN, *Midrash Six*

ו ויכל לדבר אתו. תני הנפטר מחבירו בין גדול בין קטן, צריך ליטול ממנו רשות.

6. AND HE LEFT OFF TALKING WITH HIM. IT WAS TAUGHT: HE WHO
DEPARTS FROM HIS NEIGHBOR, WHETHER HE IS GREATER OR SMALLER
THAN HE, MUST ASK LEAVE OF HIM.

We are about to learn how individuals should relate to each other,
whether one is dealing with a senior adult or a minor. Each one should
excuse himself by getting permission from the other to leave. What this
Midrash does, however, is to offer evidence from the Bible in relationship of Abraham to God as will be indicated.

ממי את למד? מאברהם. פעם אחת היה אברהם מדבר עם הקב"ה, באו מלאכי השרת
לדבר עמו. אמר להן: נפטר מן השכינה, שהיא גדולה מכם תחלה, אח"כ אני מדבר עמכם.
כיון שדבר עם הקב"ה כל צרכו, אמר לפניו: רבון העולמים! צריך אני לדבר. א"ל: הפטר
בשלום, הה"ד: ויעל אלהים מעל אברהם. אר"ל: האבות הן הן המרכבה, שנא': ויעל אלהים
מעל אברהם. ויעל מעליו אלהים. (בראשית כח) והנה ה' נצב עליו :

FROM WHOM DO WE LEARN IT? FROM ABRAHAM. ON ONE OCCASION
ABRAHAM WAS SPEAKING TO GOD, WHEN THE MINISTERING ANGELS
CAME TO SPEAK TO HIM. SAID HE TO THEM, "LET US TAKE LEAVE OF THE
SHECHINAH, WHICH IS GREATER THAN YOU, AND THEN I WILL SPEAK
WITH YOU." WHEN HE HAD SPOKEN WITH GOD ALL THAT HE NEEDED,
HE SAID TO HIM, "SOVEREIGN OF THE UNIVERSE! I HAVE NEED TO SPEAK
[WITH THE ANGELS]." "THEN LET ME TAKE LEAVE [OF THEE] IN PEACE,"
REPLIED HE. THUS IT IS WRITTEN: AND GOD WENT UP FROM ABRAHAM.
RESH LAKISH SAID: THE PATRIARCHS ARE [GOD'S] HEAVENLY CHARIOT.
THUS IT IS WRITTEN: AND GOD WENT UP FROM UPON ABRAHAM; AGAIN,
AND GOD WENT UP FROM UPON HIM (GEN. 35:13); FURTHER, AND, BE-
HOLD, THE LORD STOOD UPON HIM (28:13).

The reference in this section has to do with the three strangers who
came to visit Abraham. They were angelic messengers, but at the beginning, Abraham did not know this, and he was looking for ways to end
his congregation with the Almighty by receiving permission. As the text
indicates, he received this permission. The Almighty returned to his
heavenly abode, and Abraham returned to welcome his visitors.

—

Seed Thoughts

The *Tiferet Tzion* calls our attention to the fact that the lesson of this Midrash is incomplete. The lesson we are to learn is that not only should a minor receive permission from an elder or a senior to end their conversation, but that the reverse should also take place. There are times when the elder or the senior should receive permission from the minor. Courtesy, politeness, and mutual respect have to work in both directions. What the *Tiferet Tzion* noticed is that the Midrash offers an example of the minor needing permission to end his conversation with the elder – that is to say, Abraham in relation to God. But the Midrash does not give an example of the elder needing permission from the minor, and surely both are required. Is there a way to interpret the Midrash in such a way that the elder should also be shown as having requested permission from the minor to end their conversation? Let us now follow the explanation of the *Tiferet Tzion* as he tries to show that the Midrash does have an example of the *gadol*, a senior requesting permission from the *katan*, a minor.

In the Midrash, the first use of the word *va-yaal* seems to be superfluous, since such a word is mentioned several times in the full text. But let us go further. When God was speaking with Abraham, He realized that his angelic representatives were visiting Abraham, and therefore, He wanted to end the conversation. In terms of our teaching, however, He had to get permission from Abraham, who was the *katan* in this case. God started out by offering a hint to Abraham that He would like to leave, and that is what the word *va-yaal* is meant to convey. God ascended but did not leave, but was encircled by many angels. Finally, Abraham realized that there were visitors to his home, and he also wanted to leave. He thanked God, Whom he realized was ascending by informing him that he will now welcome his special visitors. This can be understood as God receiving permission from Abraham, which at first we thought that the Midrash did not contain. (*Tiferet Tzion*)

PARASHAH FORTY-SEVEN, *Midrash Seven*

ז ויקח אברהם את ישמעאל בנו ואת כל ילידי ביתו. א"ר אייבו: בשעה שמל אברהם אותן
ילידי ביתו, העמידן גבעה ערלות, וזרחה עליהם חמה, והתליעו, ועלה ריחן לפני הקב"ה
כקטורת סמים, וכעולה שהיא כליל לאישים. אמר הקב"ה: בשעה שיהיו בניו של זה באים
לידי עבירות, ולידי מעשים רעים, אני נזכר להם הריח הזה, ומתמלא עליהם רחמים ומרחם
עליהם:

7. AND ABRAHAM TOOK ISHMAEL HIS SON, AND ALL THAT WERE BORN
IN HIS HOUSE (GEN. 17:23). R. AIBU SAID: WHEN ABRAHAM CIRCUMCISED
THOSE THAT WERE BORN IN HIS HOUSE, HE SET UP A HILLOCK OF FORE-
SKINS; THE SUN SHONE UPON THEM AND THEY PUTREFIED, AND THEIR
ODOR ASCENDED TO THE LORD LIKE SWEET INCENSE. GOD THEN SAID:
"WHEN MY CHILDREN LAPSE INTO SINFUL WAYS, I WILL REMEMBER THAT
ODOR IN THEIR FAVOR AND BE FILLED WITH COMPASSION FOR THEM."

Seed Thoughts

See the Additional Commentary.

Additional Commentary

The hillock of flesh

In reading this text for the first time, the story of the mounds of flesh
reaching God and transforming into a beautiful, aromatic type of smell
is a very primitive description. It requires a little more sophistication
and a little more insight. Abraham circumcised all the members of his
household in whatever their capacity, whether they were full servants or
partial servants or whatever their status. Had they protested and not have
been willing to undergo the circumcision, Abraham would certainly not
have been able to do this operation with everyone together and more or
less at one time. Such, however, was the influence of Abraham. In addition was the love of the servants for their master, and all of them agreed
that milah should take place on their bodies. The beautiful aroma we

are talking about was God's appreciation of Abraham's spiritual behavior and a tribute to his servants for their wonderful cooperation with their master, Abraham. The transformation of the aroma was not only a chemical thing; it was ideological and a testament of great faith. (*Tiferet Tzion*)

Can one influence the future of one's descendants?

How could Abraham or any other father influence the behavior of children four or five generations later? At the same time, is it not most unexpected that God Himself should intervene in such a situation and forgive those who were doing evil things? The answer seems to be that the Almighty felt that such negative behavior would be caused by the Evil Inclination that sometimes takes over a person's life. He felt that Abraham's descendants would be capable of repentance, would have the strength to get rid of the Evil Inclination, and would be held by God's extension of mercy to them. (*Tiferet Tzion*)

PARASHAH FORTY-SEVEN, *Midrash Eight*

ח ואברהם בן תשעים ותשע וגו'.

8. AND ABRAHAM WAS NINETY YEARS OLD AND NINE, WHEN HE WAS CIRCUMCISED IN THE FLESH OF HIS FORESKIN, AND ISHMAEL HIS SON WAS THIRTEEN YEARS OLD, WHEN HE WAS CIRCUMCISED IN (*ETH*) THE FLESH OF HIS FORESKIN (GEN. 17:24F.).

The mention of the respective ages is important to this Midrash as we will shortly see, because their ages determine the nature of the teachings that will now follow.

הכא את אמר: בשר ערלתו, ולהלן כתיב: את בשר ערלתו?

HERE YOU SAY, *BESAR ORLATHO*, WHILE IN THE SECOND VERSE YOU SAY, *ETH BESAR ORLATHO*?

This is one of many occasions in Talmudic literature where the word את – *et*, is used as a pretext for a more unique type of interpretation of a phrase or a sentence since it is superfluous to the meaning of the text. Therefore, the assumption is that it hints to something not mentioned. In the act of circumcision of a child, both the removal of the foreskin (*milah*) and the cutting of the thin membrane below (*priah*) is done. When circumcision is done later in life after marriage, the thin membrane fades even if the foreskin remains. Thus, in the interpretation that follows, the extra word *et* concerning Ishmael means that for Abraham, at his age and having been married for years, the removal of the foreskin would be clearly achieved without the need of cutting the membrane (*priah*). Since Ishmael was a youngster, chances are that the removal of his foreskin would also involve *priah*, which is the removal of some of the thin membrane below.

אלא אברהם ע"י שנתמעך ע"י אשה כתיב: בשר ערלתו. ישמעאל שלא נתמעך ע"י אשה
כתיב: את בשר ערלתו:

THE REASON IS THIS: *BESAR ORLATHO* IS WRITTEN IN THE CASE OF ABRA-
HAM, BECAUSE HE HAD BEEN MADE FLABBY THROUGH A WOMAN; BUT
SINCE ISHMAEL HAD NOT BEEN MADE FLABBY THROUGH A WOMAN, *ETH
BESAR ORLATHO* IS WRITTEN.

———

Seed thought

See the first commentary.

PARASHAH FORTY-SEVEN, *Midrash Nine*

ט בעצם היום הזה נמול אברהם. א"ר ברכיה: (ישעיה מה) לא מראש בסתר דברתי, (אלא) אמר
הקב"ה: אלו מל אברהם בלילה, היו כל בני דורו אומרים: בכך וכך? אלו היינו רואים אותו,
לא היינו מניחים אותו לימול! אלא, בעצם היום הזה, דרגש ליה, ימלל.

9. IN THE SELF-SAME DAY WAS ABRAHAM CIRCUMCISED (GEN. 17:26). R.
BEREKIAH SAID: IT IS WRITTEN: I HAVE NOT SPOKEN IN SECRET (ISA.
45:19). THUS THE HOLY ONE, BLESSED BE HE, SAID: "HAD ABRAHAM
BEEN CIRCUMCISED AT NIGHT, ALL HIS CONTEMPORARIES MIGHT HAVE
SAID: 'WE DID NOT KNOW OF IT, BUT HAD WE KNOWN OF IT WE WOULD
NOT HAVE LET HIM BE CIRCUMCISED.'" HENCE HE WAS CIRCUMCISED IN
THE SELF-SAME DAY. [WITH THE CHALLENGE], "LET HIM WHO OBJECTS
SPEAK OUT!"

This is a very important lesson: God does not want us to observe the
Torah in secrecy, but in public. Let the world know who we are, let the
world know what are our teachings advocate. This applies to anywhere
in the world where the Jewish people have freedom. We have nothing of
which to be ashamed. Our heritage is our greatest asset.

נמול אברהם. א"ר אבא בר כהנא: הרגיש ונצטער, כדי שיכפול לו הקב"ה שכרו. א"ר לוי:
מל אברהם אין כתיב כאן, אלא נימול, בדק את עצמו ומצא עצמו מהול. א"ר ברכיה: בההיא
עיתא אקיל רבי אבא בר כהנא לרבי לוי. א"ל: שקרנא כזבנא את, אלא הרגיש ונצטער, כדי
שיכפול הקב"ה שכרו:

WAS ABRAHAM CIRCUMCISED. R. ABBA SAID: HE FELT THE SMART AND
SUFFERED PAIN, SO THAT THE LORD MIGHT DOUBLE HIS REWARD. R.
LEVI SAID: IT DOES NOT SAY, ABRAHAM CIRCUMCISED HIMSELF, BUT WAS
ABRAHAM CIRCUMCISED: THIS INTIMATES THAT HE EXAMINED HIMSELF
AND FOUND THAT HE WAS [ALREADY] CIRCUMCISED. R. BEREKIAH OB-
SERVED: IT WAS AT THAT TIME THAT R. ABBA B. KAHANA HUMILIATED
R. LEVI, SAYING TO HIM: "IT IS A LIE AND A FALSEHOOD! HE FELT THE
SMART AND SUFFERED PAIN, SO THAT THE LORD MIGHT DOUBLE HIS
REWARD."

The dispute between Rabbi Abba bar Kahana and Rabbi Levi now
takes dramatic proportions. This is the first time in the experience of
this commentator that swear words are used in rabbinic literature. They

are very powerful words: *shakrana* means "a liar," and *kazbana* means "a deceiver." For a possible explanation, please see the Seed Thoughts of this Midrash.

—

Seed Thoughts

This Midrash is the setting for what seemed to be personal attacks of one rabbinic sage upon the other. It seems quite preposterous that this should happen, since in rabbinic literature, Rabbi Abba bar Kahana and Rabbi Levi seemed to be very good friends and debated with each other with the greatest possible mutual respect. How then did this happen? The explanation that I admire most is that of the Radal (R. David Luria). He states that the two so-called swear words should be understood not as direct statements but as questions. The Hebrew word that he uses is בתמיה – *bi-temiha*. It would mean something like this: Rabbi Abba and Rabbi Levi disagreed in our Midrash on whether Abraham suffered pain in circumcision, which was the view of Rabbi Abba, or whether God removed that pain, which was the view of Rabbi Levi. The point of the criticism would be that Rabbi Levi says: "Do you really want people to believe that God would intervene in the life of Abraham so that he should not have pain?" Another argument that I saw was the charge that Rabbi Levi offered an opinion in public which differed from an opinion which he offered in private. The question that is posed to him is: Do you really want people to think of you in a different light? In other words, by interpreting these words as a question, the entire hostility is removed, and it becomes a good-natured exchange of differing opinions.

PARASHAH FORTY-SEVEN, *Midrash Ten*

י וכל אנשי ביתו יליד בית ומקנת כסף. תניא, הולכים ליריד של עובדי כוכבים בחולו של
מועד, ליקח מהם בתים שדות וכרמים ועבדים ושפחות.

10. AND ALL THE MEN OF HIS HOUSE, THOSE BORN IN THE HOUSE, AND
THOSE BOUGHT WITH MONEY OF A FOREIGNER, WERE CIRCUMCISED
WITH HIM (GEN. 17:27). IT WAS TAUGHT: YOU MAY ATTEND A NON-JEW-
ISH FAIR ON THE INTERMEDIATE DAYS OF A FESTIVAL TO BUY HOUSES,
FIELDS, VINEYARDS, AND MALE AND FEMALE SLAVES FROM THEM.

The first point of the Midrash is that there are some liberal views in
connection with buying and selling certain items on the Intermediate
Days of a Festival. The Midrash specifies what particular items can be
bought.

ר' אמי בשם ריש לקיש אמר: לא סוף דבר עבדים מהולים הן לו, אלא אפילו ערלים, מפני
שהוא מכניסן תחת כנפי השכינה.

R. AMMI SAID IN THE NAME OF R. SIMEON B. LAKISH: NOT ONLY CIR-
CUMCISED, BUT EVEN UNCIRCUMCISED SLAVES, BECAUSE YOU THEREBY
BRING THEM UNDER THE WINGS OF THE SHECHINAH.

This brings a liberal view over a much wider area, under the heading
of bringing such outsiders under the influence of God.

רבי יהושע בן לוי, בעי קומי דריש לקיש, א"ל: מהו ליקח עבדים מן עובדי כוכבים? א"ל:
אימתי את שואלני ביום טוב? תנא, אפילו בשבת. וכן הקונה חצר בא"י, א"ל: הרי למחר בכך
וכך. משום דחביבה א"י, יש לו רשות לומר כך. תני חזקיה: עד רדתה, אפילו בשבת, שכן
מצינו שלא נכבשה יריחו אלא בשבת. שלשה ירידים הם: יריד עזה, יריד עכו, יריד בטנן. ואין
לך מחוור מכולם, אלא יריד בטנן. אמר אברהם: עד שלא מלתי, היו העוברים והשבים באים
אצלי, תאמר משמלתי אינן באים אצלי? אמר לו הקב"ה: עד שלא מלת, היו בני אדם באים
אצלך, עכשיו אני בכבודי בא ונגלה עליך. הה"ד וירא אליו ה' באלוני ממרא:

R. JOSHUA B. LEVI ASKED RESH LAKISH: IS IT PERMITTED TO BUY UN-
CIRCUMCISED [HEATHEN] SLAVES FROM A GENTILE? ABOUT WHEN DO
YOU ASK ME, HE REPLIED, ABOUT A FESTIVAL? IT WAS TAUGHT: THIS IS
PERMITTED EVEN ON THE SABBATH. HEZEKIAH TAUGHT: [THOU MAYEST
BUILD BULWARKS AGAINST THE CITY THAT MAKETH WAR WITH THEE,]
UNTIL IT FALL (DEUT. 20:20): EVEN ON THE SABBATH, FOR THUS WE

FIND THAT JERICHO WAS INDEED REDUCED ON THE SABBATH. THERE
WERE THREE ANNUAL FAIRS: THE FAIR OF GAZA, THE FAIR OF ACCO, AND
THE FAIR OF BATNAN [BATANEA], AND NONE OF THEM IS SO CLEARLY
[OF AN IDOLATROUS CHARACTER] AS THE FAIR OF BATNAN. ABRAHAM
SAID: "BEFORE I BECAME CIRCUMCISED, TRAVELERS USED TO VISIT ME;
NOW THAT I AM CIRCUMCISED, PERHAPS THEY WILL NO LONGER VISIT
ME?" SAID THE HOLY ONE, BLESSED BE HE, TO HIM: "BEFORE THOU WAST
CIRCUMCISED, UNCIRCUMCISED MORTALS VISITED THEE; NOW I IN MY
GLORY WILL APPEAR TO THEE." HENCE IT IS WRITTEN: AND THE LORD
APPEARED UNTO HIM (GEN. 18:1).

Could it be that Abraham was wondering whether the usual visitors
are staying away for fear that Abraham might try to convince them to be
circumcised? This may have been the reason for his concern.

—

Seed Thoughts

Three fairs or marketplaces

The Midrash specifies that there were three important fairs – in Gaza,
Jericho, and Batnan. It should be specified that the number three is very
important. There were three such fairs and not more. There were many
other sales gatherings up and down the land, but these three fairs were
of a special quality. They had an international reputation. People came
to them from all over the world, and they bought and sold objects that
were created in many countries of the world and were brought to these
marketplaces. Furthermore, the non-Jewish leaders of these fairs had
great experience with the Jewish clientele, knew what their laws were,
and did their best to accommodate them, so that the rules of the Intermediate Days of the Festival – and even the Festival itself and sometimes
even the Sabbath – would be obeyed and respected to the satisfaction
of the Jewish client. The same rules did not apply to the other, smaller
and more regional type of sales gatherings, and the Sabbath and Festival
rules had to be obeyed in much greater strictness. The three special
fairs, however, were treated in a very different way because they were of
a higher category and a higher quality.

Abraham and his special visitors

The portion of *Lekh Lekha* includes many stories about the hospitality of Abraham. One of these stories will now be included again. It is quite appropriate that this little story should be appended to the last Midrash on *Lekh Lekha*, because that story begins the portion of *Vayera*. It is a beautiful ending for *Lekh Lekha* and an equally beautiful beginning for *Vayera*.

One of Abraham's concerns in connection with his hospitality is that he was the only one who benefited from a mitzvah. Everybody else was simply eating and drinking. This led him to see whether those who were benefiting from his food should also benefit from a mitzvah. He chose one person and said to him: "Why do you not thank God for your food?" The eater looked at him with a complete lack of comprehension; he was not sure what Abraham meant and how it could be done. Abraham, then, showed him the basic elements of a *berakha* (benediction). He said to him, in Hebrew of course: "Blessed art Thou, o Lord our God, King of the Universe, for giving us food to eat and water to drink." When Abraham realized that the person reacted with goodwill, he tried to do this with others. His policy was that whoever eats should be obligated to recite this benediction, and they would have to consent to do so. In short, everyone who benefited from Abraham's hospitality was now benefiting from a mitzvah as well. Many proselytes to Judaism were also created as the result of this new spiritual development.

PARASHAH FORTY-EIGHT, *Midrash One*

א וירא אליו ה' באלוני ממרא והוא יושב פתח האהל. כתיב (תהלים יח): ותתן לי מגן ישעך
וימינך תסעדני וענותך תרבני. ותתן לי מגן ישעך, זה אברהם. וימינך תסעדני, בכבשן האש,
ברעבון ובמלכים. וענותך תרבני, מה ענוה הרבה הקב"ה לאברהם? שהיה יושב והשכינה
עומדת, הה"ד וירא אליו ה':

1. AND THE LORD APPEARED UNTO HIM (GEN. 18:1). IT IS WRITTEN:
THOU HAST ALSO GIVEN ME THY SHIELD OF SALVATION, AND THY RIGHT
HAND HATH HOLDEN ME UP, AND THY CONDESCENSION HATH MADE ME
GREAT (PS. 18:36). THOU HAST ALSO GIVEN ME THY SHIELD OF SALVA-
TION ALLUDES TO ABRAHAM; AND THY RIGHT HAND HATH HOLDEN ME
UP – IN THE FIERY FURNACE, IN FAMINE, AND IN [MY BATTLE WITH]
THE KINGS; AND THY CONDESCENSION HATH MADE ME GREAT: WITH
WHAT CONDESCENSION DID THE LORD MAKE ABRAHAM GREAT? IN THAT
HE SAT WHILE THE SHECHINAH STOOD; THUS IT IS WRITTEN: AND THE
LORD APPEARED UNTO HIM . . . AS HE SAT.

It is one of the most interesting aspects of the Midrash to use quotations from what are known as the later Writings of the Bible (Ketuvim)
as a way of interpreting something significant about the biblical characters whose stories we read in the early biblical narratives. We thus have
a verse from the Book of Psalms, and we will now see how the Midrash
uses it as a way of adding more material to our knowledge of Abraham.

The verse from Psalms reads: "Thou hast also given me Thy shield
of Salvation." The Midrash then adds its own comment – this phrase
refers to Abraham. It then goes on to the next phrase from the same
Psalm, which is "And Thy right hand hath holden me up." It then adds its
own commentary: This phrase refers first to the fiery furnace into which
Abraham was thrown by the emperor Nimrod. It also refers to the famine, which brought Abraham to Egypt, as well as to God's protection
of Abraham in his battle with the kings who had captured his nephew
Lot. In all of these cases, God had helped Abraham. The Midrash then

continues with the last phrase of the sentence, "And Thy condescension hath made me great." With this phrase, we are told that the Holy One, blessed be He, gave Abraham a great lesson in humility. After all, Abraham was seated while presumably the Heavenly Presence was standing. What could be more humble? Who, according to another source, said to Abraham "remain seated?" What this verse from Psalms has now done is to express the praise of Israel for the wonderful things that God did to the Jewish people, starting with Abraham and eventually going way beyond Abraham. But this particular verse stresses the main challenges which started with Abraham, and were overcome by the goodness of God and His reaching out to Abraham – through whom He ultimately created the Jewish people.

~

Seed Thoughts

See the commentary above.

~

Additional Commentary

The Jewish Bible

The Hebrew word for the Bible is very expressive and helps you understand it almost immediately. It is *Tanach.* The word is an acronym that stands for:

- תורה – *Torah* – which refers to the Five Books of Moses
- נביאים – *Nevi'im* – which refers to the six books of the Prophets. These include the Early Prophets of Joshua, Judges, First and Second Samuel, and First and Second Kings. The Later Prophets include the great prophets Isaiah, Jeremiah, and Ezekiel, plus what are known as the book of the Twelve Minor Prophets. The word "minor" is used here simply to indicate that the number of chapters is shorter than what are known as the Great Prophets.
- כתובים – *Ketuvim* – which means "the Writings." Basically, it refers to eleven books which are the remainder of the 24 Books. These writings include the Books of Psalms, Proverbs, Job, the five scrolls referred to as *Megillot*, Daniel, Ezra and Nehemiah (considered one book by the Talmud), and First and Second Chronicles. (See *Bava Batra* 14b).

Abraham being seated

The *Tiferet Tzion* is bothered by the fact that Abraham remains seated while he knew that he was in the presence of God. How could Abraham have acted that way? How could he have shown even the slightest disrespect? It is not enough to say, as we will learn in a future Midrash, that God told him to be seated. He could have argued, as he had sometimes done, before actually agreeing to do something – namely, to be seated. At least we would understand that he felt uncomfortable, even though he obeyed God's request. Finally, the *Tiferet Tzion* admits that Abraham may have been suffering pain from the circumcision which he had just arranged for himself. But the pain could not have been that intense, and at least we would have understood why this was happening. Above all else, however, the lesson was outstanding that God taught Abraham the lengths that one could go to in practicing humility.

PARASHAH FORTY-EIGHT, *Midrash Two*

ב (איוב יט) ואחר עורי נקפו זאת ומבשרי אחזה אלוה. אמר אברהם: אחר שמלתי עצמי, הרבה גרים באו להדבק בזאת הברית.

2. AND WHEN AFTER MY SKIN THIS IS DESTROYED (*NIKKEFU*), THEN THROUGH MY FLESH SHALL I SEE GOD (JOB 19:26). ABRAHAM SAID: "AFTER I CIRCUMCISED MYSELF, MANY PROSELYTES CAME TO ATTACH THEMSELVES TO THIS SIGN [OF THE COVENANT]."

Job suffered more than any other person in his generation, and probably more than lots of others in other generations. It was felt that as a result of these tribulations, he would either rebel against God or stop observing the commandments or do something that would be interpreted as a protest against his condition. To the surprise of all, including those who continue throughout the generations to read the story of Job, he responded in a totally different manner. As the verse reads: "And when after my skin this is destroyed, then through my flesh shall I see God." I would translate it better as: "From my very suffering flesh, I experienced God." That is why this verse fits so meaningfully into the life story of Abraham; at this very moment, the Midrash has reached the great moment in which Abraham and his son Ishmael and his entire household were circumcised. He, too, experienced God in a much more intensive way, as the Midrash continues: "After I circumcised myself, many proselytes came to attach themselves to this sign [of the covenant]." In an earlier Midrash, Abraham had complained that many people who were his constant visitors were now staying away. This did not refer to the *gerim* – or proselytes – who had also experienced milah and therefore identified themselves with Abraham in a far more profound way than ever before.

ומבשרי אחזה אלוה, אילולי שעשיתי כן, מהיכן היה הקב"ה נגלה עלי? וירא אליו ה':

THEN THROUGH MY FLESH SHALL I SEE GOD: "HAD I NOT DONE SO, WHY SHOULD GOD HAVE REVEALED HIMSELF TO ME?" THEREFORE, AND THE LORD APPEARED UNTO HIM.

Up to the experience of milah, as it referred to Abraham himself as well as to his entire household, God had revealed Himself to Abraham in various ways – either through words, signs, or personal visions of various types – so that he could receive Divine messages. But after he had gone through the experience of milah, of circumcision, God then revealed Himself to Abraham in a much more profound way. His Heavenly Presence (*Shekhina*) completely enveloped Abraham's existence. When it says that God revealed Himself to Abraham while Abraham was sitting at the entrance of his tent, the Heavenly Presence revealed itself to him in a different way than at any time in the past, and created a new spiritual beginning in relationship to the Holy One, blessed be He. (Mirkin)

~

Seed Thoughts

See the second commentary above.

Parashah Forty-Eight, *Midrash Three*

ג ר' איסי פתח: (שם לא) אם אמאס משפט עבדי ואמתי בריבם עמדי, מה אעשה כי יקום אל
וכי יפקוד מה אשיבנו.

3. R. ISSI COMMENCED HIS DISCOURSE THUS: IF I DID DESPISE THE CAUSE OF MY MANSERVANT, OR OF MY MAIDSERVANT, WHEN THEY CONTENDED WITH ME – WHAT THEN SHALL I DO WHEN GOD RISETH UP? AND WHEN HE REMEMBERETH, WHAT SHALL I ANSWER HIM (JOB 31:13)?

T his Midrash discusses the importance of respecting those who work for us in every respect, and in particular, in terms of the payments that are owed to them for services rendered.

אתתיה דרבי יוסי הוה מכתשא עם אמתיה, אכחשה קדמא. א"ל: מפני מה אתה מכחישני
לפני שפחתי?

R. ISSI'S WIFE QUARRELED WITH HER MAIDSERVANT, WHEREUPON HE GAVE HER [HIS WIFE] THE LIES IN HER PRESENCE. "WHY DO YOU GIVE ME THE LIE BEFORE MY OWN SERVANT?" SHE COMPLAINED.

R abbi Issi's wife had quarreled with her maidservant to the point where Rabbi Issi entered the argument and criticized his wife's behavior.

א"ל: לא כך אמר איוב (שם):אם אמאס משפט עבדי.

HE REPLIED: "DID NOT JOB SAY, 'IF I DID DESPISE THE CAUSE OF MY MANSERVANT . . . WHAT THEN SHALL I DO WHEN GOD RISETH UP? AND WHEN HE REMEMBERETH, WHAT SHALL I ANSWER HIM?'"

W hat Rabbi Issi seems to mean is that even though he and his wife have complete authority over their servants, they had to be very careful in their relationship to them, because as the Book of Job says, God will not allow anyone to take advantage of His authority over employees who are as much God's responsibility as their employers.

ד"א: אם אמאס משפט, זה אברהם, ויקח אברם את ישמעאל בנו וגו'.

ANOTHER INTERPRETATION: IF I DID DESPISE THE CAUSE OF MY MANSERVANT – ALLUDES TO ABRAHAM, AS IT SAYS: AND ABRAHAM TOOK ISHMAEL HIS SON . . . AND CIRCUMCISED THEM (GEN. 17:23).

The point here is that Abraham was aware that Ishmael's mother was engaged in a quarrel with Sarah, Abraham's wife, who was her employer. Despite this, and despite the fact that he always tried to conform to what his wife Sarah wanted, in this particular case, entering his son Ishmael into the covenant of circumcision had priority.

אמר: אילולי שעשיתי כן, מהיכן היה הקב"ה נגלה עלי? וירא אליו ה' באלוני ממרא והוא יושב:

SAID HE: "HAD I NOT DONE SO, WHY SHOULD GOD HAVE REVEALED HIM-SELF TO ME?" CONSEQUENTLY, AND THE LORD APPEARED UNTO HIM, ETC.

Abraham then felt that the appearance of the Shechinah justified not only his own personal circumcision, but also the inclusion of his son Ishmael in this covenant.

—

Seed Thoughts

The Midrash quotes a difference of opinion between Rabbi Issi and his wife. Part of his argument is a quotation, from Job, to his wife: "If I despise the cause of my manservant, etc." In other words, he was quoting a verse from the Book of Job, and she obviously understood it. This is quite remarkable. There are, of course, two or three verses in the Book of Job, universally known and popular. But most of them are not known except by those who are very close to the literature of the Book of Job and others. One of the side teachings of this Midrash is that both Rabbi Issi and his wife knew Scripture very well, and there probably were others in their circle who had the same familiarity with less memorized biblical books.

—

Additional Commentary

Rabbi Issi and his wife

The first detail to note is that the name of Rabbi Issi's wife seems to have been עמדי – Imadi. The name also means "with me," referring to the verse where he mentioned the woman who lived with him as his wife, whom he referred to as Imadi. It can be seen from the story quoted by the Midrash that Rabbi Issi does not agree with his wife in connection with his wife's quarrel with her servant. She then complained why he entered the quarrel openly so that the servant should know that her employer's husband agreed with the servant. Rabbi Issi's wife complained that he showed complete disrespect for her by this behavior. After all, Jewish law is that the husband has to respect his wife even more than he respects himself. She did not quarrel with her husband's right to his opinion; she only quarreled with his public announcement of this fact, which embarrassed her very much. It simply shows that even great scholars can make mistakes. (*Tiferet Tzion*)

PARASHAH FORTY-EIGHT, *Midrash Four*

ד רבי יצחק פתח: מזבח אדמה תעשה לי וגו'. א"ר יצחק: מה אם זה שבנה מזבח לשמי,
הריני נגלה עליו ומברכו. אברהם שמל עצמו לשמי, על אחת כמה וכמה! וירא אליו ה'
באלוני ממרא:

4. R. ISAAC COMMENCED THUS: AN ALTAR OF EARTH THOU SHALT MAKE UNTO ME ... [THEN] I WILL COME UNTO THEE AND BLESS THEE (EX. 20:21). SAID R. ISAAC: IF I REVEAL MYSELF TO BLESS HIM WHO BUILT AN ALTAR IN MY NAME, HOW MUCH THE MORE TO ABRAHAM WHO CIRCUMCISED HIMSELF FOR MY SAKE! CONSEQUENTLY, AND THE LORD APPEARED UNTO HIM, ETC.

The actual text places the phrase נמלו אתו – *nimolu ito*, meaning "circumcised with him," next to the phrase "and the Lord appeared unto him." From this, the Midrash draws the teaching that the act of circumcision facilitated the Divine revelation. In addition, the Midrash here says that based on the verse which says that whoever builds an altar to God, according to His command, will be blessed – how much more so when someone like Abraham offers his own body as a sacrifice, in an act of circumcision commanded by God – that he should also be blessed in an exceptional way.

Seed Thoughts

See the commentary above.

─

Additional Commentary

Abraham's Blessings

The Midrash Tanhuma writes (Vayera 2): "Rabbi Yitzhak Nafha opened: 'An earthen alter you shall make for me,' [and it says] 'In every place where my name is mentioned I will come and bless you' (Exodus 20) The Holy One, blessed be He, said: If one who brought an *olah* or peace offering, I appear to him to bless him, Abraham who offered himself *a fortiori* that he should be blessed" (*Midrash Tanhuma*)

───

PARASHAH FORTY-EIGHT, *Midrash Five*

───

הרבי לוי פתח: (ויקרא ט) ושור ואיל לשלמים לזבוח לפני ה'. אמר: מה אם זה שהקריב שור ואיל לשמי, הריני נגלה עליו ומברכו, אברהם שמל עצמו לשמי, עאכ"ו! וירא אליו ה' באלוני ממרא:

5. R. LEVI COMMENCED: AND [TAKE] AN OX AND A RAM FOR PEACE-OFFERINGS . . . FOR TODAY THE LORD APPEARETH UNTO YOU (LEV. 9:4). [GOD] SAID: "IF I REVEAL MYSELF TO AND BLESS HIM WHO SACRIFICED AN OX AND A RAM FOR MY SAKE, HOW MUCH THE MORE TO ABRAHAM, WHO CIRCUMCISED HIMSELF FOR MY SAKE!" CONSEQUENTLY, AND THE LORD APPEARED UNTO HIM, ETC.

The presentation in this Midrash resembles very closely that of Midrash 4. If one who offers sacrifices to God on His altar receives a blessing, how much more should this apply to Abraham, who offers his own body as a sacrifice to God. Therefore, it says "and the Lord appeared unto him" immediately after the account of the circumcision.

─

Seed Thoughts

See the commentary above.

Parashah Forty-Eight, *Midrash Six*

וכתיב(ישעיהלג):פחדובציוןחטאים.אמררבייירמיהבןאלעזר:משללשניתינוקותשברחומבית
הספר, היה זה לוקה וזה מירתת. א"ר יונתן: כל חנופה שנאמר במקרא, במינות הכתוב מדבר,
ובנין אב שבכולן. פחדו בציון חטאים אחזה רעדה חנפים. אר"יי בר רבי: סימן לארכיליסטוס
שמרד במלך. אמר המלך: כל מי שהוא תופשו, אני נותן לו פרוקופי. עמד אחד ותפשו. אמר
המלך: שמרו שניהם עד הבוקר, והיה זה מתפחד וזה מתפחד. זה מתפחד לומר: איזו פרוקופי
המלך נותן לי? וזה מתפחד ואומר, אי זה דין המלך דן אותי? כך לעתיד לבא ישראל מתפחדים
ועובדי כוכבים מתפחדים. ישראל מתפחדים (הושעג):ופחדו אל ה' ואל טובו באחרית הימים.
ועובדי כוכבים מתפחדים (ישעיהלג):פחדו בציון חטאים. אר"י"ב"ר סימון:למה הוא קורא אותן
מוקדי עולם? שאילו ניתן להם רשות, היו מוקדים כל העולם כולו על יושביו לשעה קלה. (שם)
הולך צדקות, זה אברהם, ושמרו דרך ה' לעשות צדקה ומשפט, (שם) דובר מישרים מישרים
אהבוך. (שם) מואס בבצע מעשקות, שנאמר: אם מחוט ועד שרוך נעל (שם). נוער כפיו מתמוך
בשוחד, הרימותי ידי אל ה' אל עליון. הוא מרומים ישכון. ר"י בר רבי סימון בשם רבי חנין בשם
רבי יוחנן: העלה אותו למעלה מכיפת הרקיע, הדא דהוא א"ל: הבט נא השמימה אינו שייך
לומר הבט, אלא מלמעלה למטה. (שם) מצדות סלעים משגבו אלו, ענני כבוד. לחמו ניתן מימיו
נאמנים, יקח נא מעט מים. (שם) מלך ביפיו תחזינה עיניך, וירא אליו ה' באלוני ממרא:

6. IT IS WRITTEN: THE SINNERS IN ZION ARE AFRAID (ISA. 33:14). R. JER-
EMIAH B. ELEAZAR SAID: THIS MAY BE ILLUSTRATED BY TWO CHILDREN
WHO RAN AWAY FROM SCHOOL: WHEN ONE IS PUNISHED, THE OTHER
TREMBLES. R. JONATHAN SAID: WHENEVER *HANUFAH* OCCURS IN SCRIP-
TURE, IT REFERS TO HERESY, AND THE LOCUS CLASSICUS FOR ALL CASES
IS THE VERSE: THE SINNERS IN ZION ARE AFRAID, TREMBLING HATH
SEIZED THE UNGODLY (*HA-HANEFIM*). R. JUDAH B. R. SIMON SAID: THIS
MAY BE ILLUSTRATED BY A ROBBER CHIEF WHO REVOLTED AGAINST
THE KING, AND THE KING ANNOUNCED: "I WILL GIVE PREFERMENT TO
ANY MAN WHO CAPTURES HIM." A MAN AROSE AND CAUGHT HIM, AND
THE KING ORDERED THEM BOTH TO BE GUARDED UNTIL MORNING. ONE
WAS FILLED WITH ANXIETY, THINKING WHAT PREFERMENT THE KING
WOULD GIVE HIM. THE OTHER WAS FILLED WITH ANXIETY, THINKING
WHAT PUNISHMENT THE KING WOULD PRONOUNCE UPON HIM. THUS,
IN THE MESSIANIC FUTURE ISRAEL SHALL FEAR, VIZ. AND THEY SHALL
COME IN FEAR UNTO THE LORD AND TO HIS GOODNESS (HOS. 3:5); AND
THE GENTILES WILL FEAR: THE SINNERS IN ZION ARE AFRAID. R. JUDAH
B. R. SIMON SAID: WHY ARE THEY CALLED EVERLASTING BURNINGS (ISA.
33:14)? BECAUSE IF THEY WERE GIVEN FREE PASSAGE THEY WOULD BURN
UP THE WHOLE WORLD.

He that walketh righteously (33:15) – alludes to Abraham, as it is written: To the end that he [sc. Abraham] may command his children . . . that they may keep the way of the Lord to do righteousness and justice (Gen. 18:19). And speaketh uprightly (Isa. 33:15), as it is written: The upright ones do love thee (Song 1:4). He that despiseth the gain of oppressions (Isa. 33:15), as it says: I will not take a thread or a shoe latchet (Gen. 14:23). That shaketh his hands from holding of bribes (Isa. 33:15). I have lifted up my hand unto the Lord, God Most High (Gen. 14:22). He shall dwell on high (Isa. 33:16): R. Judah b. R. Simon and R. Hanin in R. Johanan's name said: He lifted him [sc. Abraham] up above the vault of heaven; hence He said to him: Look now (habbet) at heaven (Gen. 15:5): Habbet is applicable only when one looks downward from above. His place of defense shall be the munitions of rocks (Isa. 33:16): this alludes to the clouds of Glory. His bread shall be given (33:16) – And I will fetch a morsel of bread (Gen. 18:4). His waters shall be sure (Isa. 33:16). – Let now a little water be fetched (Gen. 18:4). Thine eyes shall see the King in his beauty (Isa. 33:17). – And the Lord appeared unto him.

"The sinners in Zion are afraid, trembling has seized the ungodly." Rabbi Jeremiah ben Elazar said that the text talks about the fear of the sinners, but also about the trembling of the hypocrites. This can be compared to two children who run away from school: When one was captured, the second was very fearful about being caught. The more the second child learned of the punishment of the first, the more the second child trembled. The meaning of this parable is as follows: The evildoers in Israel are very fearful of the punishment that God will mete out to them as He punishes the nations in the Time to Come. So will the hypocrites also tremble. As Rabbi Jonah's son says: wherever the word "hypocrisy" – hanufa in Hebrew – is mentioned in Scripture, it refers to apostasy – that is to say, pretending to accept the Torah but giving interpretations which include many unauthorized changes. All this is intended by the phrase "the sinners in Zion are afraid, trembling has seized the ungodly." This means that the punishment of the hypocrites will be even greater than that of the sinners.

Rabbi Judah ben Simon added a further interpretation to the phrase "the sinners in Zion are afraid, trembling has seized the ungodly." In his interpretation, this has been compared to a robber chief who rebelled against the king. The king said: "Whoever captures him will give him a preferment." Someone did capture him. The king said: "Keep the two of them until the morning." The robber was fearful the entire night, but the one who captured him was also fearful. The one who was guilty was worried about what punishment to receive, and the one who captured him was concerned about what the king meant by the use of the term "reward." By the same token, Israel worries about the End of Days and the nations also worry. Israel worries about what reward they may receive for obeying the Torah, and the nations of the world worry and are fearful as to what punishment might be meted out to them. That is another interpretation of the verse "the sinners in Zion are afraid, trembling has seized the ungodly." Israel worries that sin might have occurred which would interfere with the reward at the End of Days, and the nations of the world are worried about the extent to which God might punish them because of their sins. The prophet also mentions "everlasting burnings." If these burnings had the opportunity, they would destroy the world even though they are a small group.

The verses from the prophet now move from a consideration of the evildoers to those upon whom the world depends for doing good. The first phrase mentioned is "he that walks righteously." This refers to Abraham, for it was said about him that God trusted Abraham and was assured that Abraham would teach his children and his entire household to follow the way of the Lord and to practice only righteousness and justice.

As for the phrase "and speaks uprightly," this also refers to Abraham. The phrase "the upright ones do love you" refers to Abraham as well, but also to Isaac and Jacob, who not only loved righteousness but overcame many challenges. The prophet also mentions the phrase "he that despises the gain of oppressions, that shakes his hands from holding of bribes"; that phrase also refers to Abraham, who refused to accept a gift from the king of Sodom, because he questioned the morality of how the king of Sodom acquired his possessions. As for the phrase "he shall dwell on high," this also refers to Abraham, who is told to look to the heavens and count the stars, but the Hebrew word for "looking" is *habbet*, which is interpreted as looking downward from a higher position. Abraham was propelled by God to stand outside the present universe and look down towards the heavens, because he was looking at them from above. Finally, there is a phrase, "his place of defense shall be the munitions of rocks." This refers to Sarah, who is as moral and ethical as her husband. There is a tradition that as long as Sarah lived, clouds of honor circled her home. These clouds sometimes appear near rocks and are mistaken for them. But the expression "the munitions of rocks" refers to the clouds of honor.

⌣

Seed Thoughts

See the Additional Commentary below.

⌣

Additional Commentary

Who was the Midrash criticizing?

Sometimes it helps to relate what the Sages have said to something that took place historically in their time. It might be helpful to find evidence in various places of what the Sages of the Midrash really had in mind. It has been suggested that their concern was directed at the early Christians *minim* of their day, and more importantly, to those Jews who became interested in Christianity to the point of conversion. The phraseology that they quote from the prophet Isaiah seems to apply both to the early Christians and to the Jews who opted to become Christians by the use of terms like "hypocrisy." There does not seem to be any better verse other than the one quoted in the Midrash, "the sinners in Zion are afraid, trembling has seized the hypocrites" (Isaiah 33:14). (Mirkin)

PARASHAH FORTY-EIGHT, *Midrash Seven*

ז והוא ישב פתח האהל כחום היום. רבי ברכיה משום ר' לוי אמר: ישב כתיב, בקש לעמוד. א"ל הקב"ה: שב, אתה סימן לבניך. מה אתה יושב ושכינה עומדת.

7. AS HE SAT (*YOSHEB*) IN THE TENT DOOR IN THE HEAT OF THE DAY.
R. BEREKIAH SAID IN R. LEVI'S NAME: THIS IS WRITTEN *YASHAB* (HE
SAT): HE WISHED TO RISE, BUT GOD SAID TO HIM: "SIT, AND THOU ART
A TOKEN TO THY CHILDREN: AS THOU SITTEST WHILE THE SHECHINAH
IS STANDING, SO WILL THY CHILDREN SIT AND THE SHECHINAH STAND."

The word ישב – *yoshev* – in the verse that is quoted is defective, in the
sense that it is missing the letter *vav*, although it is pronounced *yoshev*.
That being the case, it really means that Abraham was sitting in the presence of God. But God said: "Do not be concerned about your children,
because in the future, your children will be seated and the Heavenly
Presence will be standing."

כך, בניך יושבין ושכינה עומדת על גבן. כשישראל נכנסים לבתי כנסיות ולבתי מדרשות וקורין קריאת שמע, והן יושבים לכבודי ואני על גבן, שנאמר (תהלים פב): אלהים נצב בעדת אל.

THAT IS WHEN ISRAEL ENTER THEIR SYNAGOGUES AND HOUSES OF
STUDY AND RECITE THE *SHEMA*, AND THUS THEY SIT IN MY HONOR, AS
IT SAYS: GOD STANDETH (*NIZZAB*) IN THE CONGREGATION OF GOD (PS.
82:1).

This very beautiful interpretation connects God's appearance to
Abraham with His appearance throughout history and in modern times
whenever Jews assemble in synagogues and prayer or in houses of study,
where Torah is taught. In all these places, God is present, as the verse
says that God is present in what is actually His congregation.

א"ר חגי בשם ר' יצחק: עומד אין כתיב כאן, אלא נצב, אטימוס כמה דתימא, ונצבת על הצור. כתיב (ישעיה סה): והיה טרם יקראו ואני אענה. ר' שמואל בר חייא ורבי יודן בשם רבי חנינא: על כל שבח ושבח שישראל משבחין להקב"ה, משרה שכינתו עליהם. מה טעם? (תהלים כב) ואתה קדוש יושב תהלות ישראל:

R. HAGGAI SAID IN THE NAME OF R. ISAAC: NOT *OMED* (STANDING) IS
WRITTEN HERE BUT *NIZZAB* (STATIONED AT HIS POST), WHICH MEANS

READY, AS YOU READ: AND THOU SHALT BE STATIONED (*NIZZABTA*) UPON THE ROCK (EX. 33:21). R. SAMUEL B. R. HIYYA AND R. JUDAN IN R. HANINA'S NAME SAID: EVERY TIME THAT ISRAEL PRAISE THE HOLY ONE, BLESSED BE HE, HE CAUSES HIS SHECHINAH TO REST UPON THEM. WHAT IS THE PROOF? YET THOU ART HOLY, O THOU THAT ART ENTHRONED UPON THE PRAISES OF ISRAEL (PS. 22:4).

It is to be noted that the word *omed*, which means "to stand" in Hebrew, is not used in connection with this, but rather *nitzav*. The latter is used in Scripture to mean "standing and immediately ready to do God's will." As Rabbi Judan has quoted, it is not only when the *Shema* is recited that Israel is spiritually exalted, but every time the worshipper or the student adds prayer or praise of God, God's presence is upon them, as it is written: "Yet Thou art holy, O Thou that art enthroned upon the praises of Israel."

~

Seed Thoughts

The Midrashim in this section indicate that every time human beings, and especially Jews, do something important for God, they are blessed. One Midrash makes the connection with circumcision, where it says that after Abraham circumcised himself, God blessed him. It is connected to the same development with offerings on the altar, where it says: "Whoever gives an offering to God, I will bless them." The most unusual and original of all is that when Jews recite prayers in synagogues or study Torah in the houses of study, God is present with them as a source of continuous blessing. If we were to take this seriously, it would go a long way to make us into a really spiritual community. God is in the synagogue before we come there; we cannot see the Heavenly Presence, but it is enough if our imagination tells us that it is there. That is probably why that prayer which begins *U'va le-Tziyon go'el* – "And the redeemer shall come to Zion" – is recited frequently in our service. It is because it contains the phrase *Ve-ata kadosh yoshev tehillot Yisrael* – roughly translated as "And You, the Holy One, dwells amidst the prayers and the studies of Israel and the Jewish people."

PARASHAH FORTY-EIGHT, *Midrash Eight*

ח פתח האהל. פתח טוב פתחת לעוברים ולשבים, פתח טוב פתחת לגרים, שאלולי את לא
בראתי שמים וארץ, שנאמר (ישעיה מ): וימתחם כאהל לשבת. שאלולי את לא בראתי גלגל
חמה, שנאמר (תהלים יט): לשמש שם אהל בהם. שאלולי את לא בראתי את הירח, שנאמר
(איוב כה): הן עד ירח ולא יאהיל.

8. IN THE TENT DOOR. [GOD SAID TO HIM]: "THOU HAST OPENED A
GOOD DOOR FOR TRAVELERS; THOU HAST OPENED A GOOD DOOR TO
PROSELYTES, FOR IF NOT FOR THEE I HAD NOT CREATED HEAVEN AND
EARTH,' AS IT SAYS: HE SPREADETH THEM OUT AS A TENT TO DWELL IN
(ISA. 40:22). AGAIN, BUT FOR THEE I HAD NOT CREATED THE ORB OF THE
SUN, AS IT SAYS: IN THEM HATH HE SET A TENT FOR THE SUN (PS. 19:5).
BUT FOR THEE I HAD NOT CREATED THE MOON, AS IT SAYS: BEHOLD,
EVEN FOR THE MOON HE DOTH NOT SET A TENT – YAAHIL (JOB 25:5).

The reason why the verse takes the trouble to specify the spot where
Abraham was sitting in the tent is because it is as if the Holy One,
blessed be He, were hinting to Abraham that he was doing a good thing
by sitting near the opening of the tent. Abraham thus makes sure to
invite passers-by for his hospitality. He especially includes among them
converts to the Jewish people, since he himself was the first proselyte in
Judaism. The text indicates that the word *ohel* is used in many areas of
the Torah where many aspects of the Creation were mentioned.

א"ר לוי: לעתיד לבא, אברהם יושב על פתח גיהנם, ואינו מניח אדם מהול מישראל לירד
לתוכה. ואותן שחטאו יותר מדאי, מה עושה להם? מעביר את הערלה מעל גבי תינוקות
שמתו, עד שלא מלו, ונותנה עליהם ומורידן לגיהנם, הה"ד (תהלים נה): שלח ידיו בשלומיו
חלל בריתו. כחום היום. לכשיבוא אותו היום שכתוב בו (מלאכי ג): כי הנה היום בא בוער
כתנור.

R. LEVI SAID: IN THE HEREAFTER ABRAHAM WILL SIT AT THE ENTRANCE
TO GEHENNA, AND PERMIT NO CIRCUMCISED ISRAELITE TO DESCEND
THEREIN. WHAT THEN WILL HE DO TO THOSE WHO HAVE SINNED VERY
MUCH? HE WILL REMOVE THE FORESKIN FROM BABES WHO DIED BEFORE
CIRCUMCISION AND SET IT UPON THEM [THE SINNERS], AND THEN LET
THEM DESCEND INTO GEHENNA; HENCE IT IS WRITTEN: HE HATH SENT
FORTH HIS HANDS TO THOSE THAT WERE WHOLE; HE HATH PROFANED
HIS COVENANT. IN THE HEAT OF THE DAY: [THIS IS AN ALLUSION TO

THE TIME] WHEN THAT DAY WILL COME OF WHICH IT IS WRITTEN: FOR,
BEHOLD, THE DAY COMETH, IT BURNETH AS A FURNACE (MAL. 3:19).

The expression *petah* applied to the tent is now used to apply to Gehenna, and the English translation is "Hell," as the place where those
who have been evil in this world suffer eternally. However, in this description, Abraham's goodness is illustrated in this section as well, for
he did not permit any member of the Jewish people properly circumcised to enter Gehenna. By the same token, he arranged to cover the
circumcision area of the evildoers, as a result of which they descended
into Gehenna. This section also serves as a source of introduction to the
discussion which will follow about כחם היום – *ke-hom ha-yom*, meaning
"in the heat of the day," because the prophet Malachi describes the coming of the Day of Judgement (*Yom ha-Din*) as being היום ההוא – *ha-yom
ha-hu*, meaning "that very day."

כחום היום. תני ר' ישמעאל: כחום היום, הרי שש שעות אמורות. הא מה אני מקיים? (שמות
טז): וחם השמש ונמס בד' שעות? אתה אומר ד' שעות, או אינו אלא בו' שעות? כשהוא
אומר כחום היום – הרי ו' שעות אמורות, או חילוף כחום היום – בארבע שעות וחם השמש
ונמס, בששה שעות אמרת? היך אתה יכול לקיים כחום היום בארבע שעות והלא בארבע
שעות אין חום, אלא במקום שהחמה זורחת שם בארבע שעות – טולא קריר ושמשא
שריב. בשש שעות טולא ושמשא שריבין כחדא? הא אין עליך לומר כלשון אחרון, אלא
כלשון ראשון. כחום היום בששה שעות וחם השמש ונמס. בד' שעות, שבמקום שהחמה
זורחת בלבד, שם נמס. א"ר תנחומא: בשעה שאין לבריות צל תחתיו.

IN THE HEAT OF THE DAY. R. ISHMAEL TAUGHT: AND AS THE SUN WAXED
HOT, IT MELTED (EX. 16:21) MEANS AT FOUR HOURS. YOU SAY, AT FOUR
HOURS; YET PERHAPS THAT IS NOT SO, AND IT MEANS AT SIX HOURS?
WHEN IT SAYS, IN THE HEAT OF THE DAY, THAT MUST REFER TO SIX
HOURS. YET PERHAPS IT IS THE REVERSE? AT FOUR HOURS IT IS COOL
IN THE SHADE AND HOT IN THE SUN, WHEREAS AT SIX HOURS BOTH
THE SUN AND THE SHADE ARE EQUALLY HOT. R. TANHUMA SAID: [IN
THE HEAT OF THE DAY] MEANS WHEN PEOPLE CANNOT FIND SHADE
BENEATH IT [THE SUN].

In the case of the four-hour day, the shadow is cold but the sun is hot;
in the case of the six-hour day, both the shadow and the sun are equally
hot. The point of the discussion is that when the verse in the Torah describes Abraham as being at the gate of his tent, *ke-hom ha-yom* – "in the
heat of the day," the meaning is the sixth hour after sunrise. The point

of the discussion is to indicate the difficulty that Abraham was ready to undertake by sitting at the door of his tent and by doing so in the face of the tremendous heat.

א"ר ינאי: ניקב נקב מגיהנם, והרתיח כל העולם כולו על יושביו לשעה קלה. אמר הקב"ה:
צדיקים בצער והעולם בריוח, הדא אמרת: שהחימום יפה למכה:

R. JANNAI SAID: THE HOLY ONE, BLESSED BE HE, MADE A HOLE IN GEHENNA, MAKING THE WHOLE WORLD INTOLERABLY HOT TO ITS IN- HABITANTS FOR A SHORT WHILE. "SHALL THE RIGHTEOUS," HE SAID, "BE IN PAIN WHILE THE WHOLE WORLD IS AT EASE!" [THAT IS THE IMPLICA- TION OF] IN THE HEAT OF THE DAY. FROM THIS IT FOLLOWS THAT HEAT IS BENEFICIAL TO A WOUND.

In other words, the claim is that the heat helped Abraham recover from his circumcision wounds.

—

Seed Thoughts

Our text suggests to us that heaven and earth are a sort of *ohel* (tent) to the world in the same way that Abraham's tent gave him the opportunity to do so many good things. It therefore goes on to say that were it not for the example of the tent of Abraham and its many possibilities, heaven and earth would not have been created. Furthermore, it goes on to say in the same style that the sun would also not have been created, or the moon, the stars, or the myriad other forms of creation that make up our world and the universe of which it is a part. The question that can now be asked is the following: Once heaven and earth are created, surely the sun and the moon and the various other listings are included in this pro- cess, and why therefore was it necessary to specify each one of them as indicating that the tent of Abraham was responsible for their creation? Surely, they were dependent upon heaven and earth.

The answer has to move in another direction. Let us ask the following question: Why did God create the world? Was it only so that the Jewish people might have a place where it could practice the Torah, live the Torah life, and do as much as possible of what the scriptures command? If so, all that would have been required in the act of creation would have been this earth. The entire world would not have been necessary, and certainly not the entire universe, which includes many worlds, most of which we are not even familiar with. The answer, therefore, is that God did not create the world only for the sake of the Jewish people and the Torah, but for all of humanity in all of their diversity and in all of their specialized talents and their many purposes. They always required the entire universe with all of its potential and all of its richness. We are familiar today with what research and inventions and inventiveness have revealed from the hidden resources of the earth and the world. What has been released, however, and what we have learned from medicine, science, engineering, etc., is merely the tip of the iceberg. We have not even scratched the surface of the potentiality of this universe. It is for all human beings and certainly for the Jewish people, who have been given an even greater challenge which can be expressed as the following: "The Lord shall be king over all the earth, and in that day the Lord shall be one and His name shall be one." (*Tiferet Tzion*)

PARASHAH FORTY-EIGHT, *Midrash Nine*

ט אמר: עד שלא מלתי, היו העוברים והשבים באים אצלי. א"ל הקב"ה: עד שלא מלתה, היו
בני אדם ערלים באים, עכשיו, אני ובני פמליא שלי נגלים עליך, הה"ד: וישא עיניו וירא והנה
שלשה אנשים נצבים עליו. וירא בשכינה וירא במלאכים.

9. HE [ABRAHAM] COMPLAINED: "BEFORE I WAS CIRCUMCISED TRAVELERS USED TO VISIT ME; NOW THAT I AM CIRCUMCISED, PERHAPS THEY WILL NO LONGER VISIT ME? SAID THE HOLY ONE, BLESSED BE HE, TO HIM: "HITHERTO UNCIRCUMCISED MORTALS VISITED THEE; BUT NOW I AND MY RETINUE WILL APPEAR TO THEE. THUS IT IS WRITTEN: AND HE LIFTED UP HIS EYES AND LOOKED (GEN. 18:2) – HE SAW THE SHECHINAH AND SAW THE ANGELS.

The discussion is repeated here, similar to what we read about in a previous Midrash. Abraham complained that since his circumcision people were no longer visiting him as in the past to benefit from his hospitality which he was so anxious to share with them. God's response to him is that in the past, Abraham was visited by the uncircumcised, but today, God Himself is appearing and so are several other guests who have shared the circumcision. Abraham should look upon that visit as being on a higher level. Abraham took a better look at what was happening. The text uses the Hebrew verb וירא – *vayar* – "and he saw," and it said that he saw the Heavenly Presence and he saw the angels, though at the beginning he did not know that the three visitors were angelic people.

א"ר חנינא: שמות חדשים עלו מבבל. ריש לקיש אמר: אף שמות מלאכים, מיכאל, רפאל וגבריאל. אמר רבי לוי: אחד נדמה לו בדמות סדקי, ואחד נדמה לו בדמות נווטי, ואחד בדמות ערבי. אמר: אם רואה אני ששכינה ממתנת עליהם, אני יודע שהן בני אדם גדולים. ואם אני רואה אותן חולקים כבוד אלו לאלו, אני יודע שהן בני אדם מהוגנין, וכיון שראה אותן חולקין כבוד אלו לאלו, ידע שהן בני אדם מהוגנין.

R. HANINA SAID: THE NAMES OF THE MONTHS CAME UP WITH US FROM BABYLON. R. SIMEON B. LAKISH SAID: ALSO THE NAMES OF THE ANGELS, MICHAEL, RAFAEL, AND GABRIEL. R. LEVI SAID: ONE APPEARED TO HIM IN THE GUISE OF A SARACEN, THE SECOND IN THE GUISE OF A NABATEAN, AND THE THIRD IN THE GUISE OF AN ARAB. SAID HE [ABRAHAM]: "IF I SEE THAT THE SHEKHINAH WAITS FOR THEM, I WILL KNOW THAT THEY ARE WORTHY; AND IF I SEE THAT THEY PAY RESPECT TO EACH OTHER, I WILL KNOW THAT THEY ARE DISTINGUISHED." AND WHEN HE DID SEE THEM PAY RESPECT TO EACH OTHER, HE KNEW THAT THEY WERE DIS-TINGUISHED.

At this point in our text, Abraham did not know that they were angels and seemed to get the impression that they were people from various foreign countries. For example, the term *sirki* is used as the name of a traveling salesman who peddles certain things. Another guest appeared as a *sapan*, or a sailor. Yet another guest was simply an Arab.

א"ר אבהו: אהל פלן של אבינו אברהם, מפולש היה. רבי יודן אמר: כהדין דרומילוס. אמר: אם אני רואה אותן שהפליגו את דרכם להתקרב דרך כאן, אני יודע שהן באים אצלי, כיון שראה אותן שהפליגו, מיד, וירץ לקראתם מפתח האהל וישתחו ארצה:

R. ABBAHU SAID: THE TENT OF THE PATRIARCH ABRAHAM OPENED AT BOTH SIDES. R. JUDAN SAID: IT WAS LIKE A DOUBLEGATED PASSAGE. SAID HE: "IF I SEE THEM TURN ASIDE, I WILL KNOW THAT THEY ARE COMING TO ME." WHEN HE SAW THEM TURN ASIDE, IMMEDIATELY HE RAN TO MEET THEM FROM THE ENTRANCE OF THE TENT AND THEY BOWED TO THE GROUND.

One of the things to understand from this Midrash is that Abraham's tent was very large with at least two main entrances, both of which were far away from each other. Abraham first discerned his visitors from one of the entrances and was under the impression that they would not be entering his tent. He therefore ran to meet them. Despite the fact that he was now elderly and suffering from the third day of circumcision, such was his desire to offer him hospitality that these events did not stand in his way. The Midrash also describes his own personal tests as to what kind of people they are. One test was whether the Almighty would interrupt His communication to Abraham to allow Abraham to examine his visitors. When that happened, he felt that that was a sign that they were high-class people. When he offered them water to wash themselves, none of them took advantage of their fellow leader whose name was the angel Michael, and that taught him also that they were individuals of noble bearing.

—

Seed Thoughts

The text says: "He held the Shechinah [the Heavenly Presence of God]." He also beheld the angels at the very same time. The commentators are bothered by the fact that the Hebrew word *vayar* – "and he beheld" – is mentioned twice. But there is something, it seems to me, that should bother every reader and every student of the midrashic and religious leadership. What is meant by the Shechinah? What is meant by this translation as "the Heavenly Presence of God?" Believe it or not, there is a person in my community who claims that he either beheld God or that God spoke with him. When I asked him to explain in detail what actually happened, he actually could not do so. His point was that when such a miraculous thing happened, you understand very well what it is, but it cannot be interpreted to others. We do not take this person seriously, because we do not believe that these things actually happen. It is the contention of Moses Maimonides, the Rambam, that what happens to a person in a prophetic dream is that the person's eyes are closed when this extraordinary experience happens. But it is the miracle of prophecy and the vehicle where this expression is a dream. This is probably what happened when the text says that Abraham beheld the Heavenly Presence of God, since this can last a relatively longer time. It would be possible for him to experience the Shechinah and possibly become aware of the presence of others, although at the onset he did not know that the ones who visited him were angels.

—

Additional Commentary

Babylon and the Jews

Our midrashic text branches off from its main discussion to inform us that the names of the Hebrew months and the names of the angelic beings came to us from the community of Babylon, or as written in Hebrew, *Bavel*. The Hebrew months came from the Persian Empire and many of them are mentioned for the first time in the Scroll of Esther. The names of the Angels Gabriel and Michael, even though they are in Hebrew, were mentioned for the first time in the Book of Daniel and therefore also associated with Babylonia. (*Matnot Kehuna*). The reason why this material is mentioned here is probably because the three guests of Abraham ultimately turned out to be angels, and their names according to the Midrash were Michael, Gabriel and Raphael.

In light of the tension that exists today between the Jewish people, Israel, and Iran (which is the modern name for Persia), it is somewhat surprising to note or even to have to explain that Bavel (or the expanded Babylon, which was Iraq and sometimes under Persian control) contained Jewish communities which, more than any other, kept us alive for the past 3000 years. It possessed a remarkable Jewish community. Much of what we call the Oral Torah (*Torah she-be'al peh*) was compiled in the Babylonian Jewish community. The number of great Jewish scholars who functioned in Babylon was greater than in Israel after the destruction of the Second Temple. It is they who created what is known in Hebrew as *Talmud Bavli* (the Babylonian Talmud) – probably the greatest religious work of all time. It is not, therefore, surprising that our present Midrash states that the names of the Hebrew months came from Bavel (Babylon) as did the names associated with angels, etc. The Babylonian Jewish community existed from the time of Nebuchadnezzar and the fall of the First Temple of Jerusalem through the rebuilding of the Second Temple under Cyrus, king of Persia, and for a very long time after that. The Babylonian community was a major Jewish community up until the Middle Ages and existed as a significant community until the mid-twentieth century. (W. S.)

PARASHAH FORTY-EIGHT, *Midrash Ten*

י וַיֹּאמַר אֲדֹנָי אִם נָא מָצָאתִי חֵן. תָּנֵי ר' חִיָּיא: לַגָּדוֹל שֶׁבָּהֶן. אָמַר: זֶה מִיכָאֵל.

10. AND HE SAID: MY LORD, IF NOW I HAVE FOUND FAVOR IN THY SIGHT
(GEN. 18:3). R. HIYYA TAUGHT: HE SAID THIS TO THE GREATEST OF THEM,
VIZ. MICHAEL.

The first word Abraham said to his guest was אדני – *Adonai*. It should be pointed out that this word has to be understood as plural, and the conversation later on moves to the singular: "If only I found favor in your eyes." What happened was that at the beginning he spoke to everyone together, because he did not know who their elder or their leader is. Therefore, he said *Adonai*. Usually when this happens, the real leader understands what is happening and introduces himself, as a result of which Abraham continued by directing this conversation to him. It turns out that Michael was the leader of the three, the source of which is the Book of Daniel.

According to this interpretation, the word *Adonai* is not only plural but secular, i.e., it refers to the men approaching Abraham and not to God. Even though Rabbi Levi, in the previous Midrash, felt that the word *Adonai* should be considered sacred, the view of the Midrash in this context is definitely secular. This is why the Midrash spelled out the word completely and did not use such things as the letter *heh* with an apostrophe, or the letter *yod* with an apostrophe, as representing the names of God. The rule seems to be that when the letter *nun* in *Adonai* has a *kamatz*, it is sacred, but when it doesn't, it is secular. However, in our text it is written with a *kamatz*, but from the context, it seems to refer to the men and not to God therefore there is a dispute as to whether it is sacred or secular in this text.

יֻקַּח נָא מְעַט מַיִם. ר"א בְּשֵׁם ר' סִימַאי אָמַר: אָמַר הקב"ה לְאַבְרָהָם: אַתָּה אָמַרְתָּ: יֻקַּח נָא מְעַט מַיִם, חַיֶּיךָ! שֶׁאֲנִי פּוֹרֵעַ לְבָנֶיךָ בַּמִּדְבָּר, וּבַיִּישׁוּב, וְלֶעָ"ל, הַה"ד (במדבר כא): אָז יָשִׁיר יִשְׂרָאֵל אֶת הַשִּׁירָה הַזֹּאת: עֲלִי בְאֵר עֱנוּ לָהּ, הֲרֵי בַמִּדְבָּר. בְּאֶרֶץ כְּנַעַן מִנַּיִן? (דברים ח): אֶרֶץ נַחֲלֵי מָיִם עֲיָנֹת וּתְהֹמֹת יֹצְאִים בַּבִּקְעָה וּבָהָר. לֶעָ"ל מִנַּיִן? ת"ל (זכריה יד): בַּיּוֹם הַהוּא יֵצְאוּ מַיִם חַיִּים מִירוּשָׁלַם. אַתָּה אָמַרְתָּ: וְרַחֲצוּ רַגְלֵיכֶם, חַיֶּיךָ! שֶׁאֲנִי פּוֹרֵעַ לְבָנֶיךָ בַּמִּדְבָּר, וּבַיִּישׁוּב, וְלֶעָ"ל. בַּמִּדְבָּר מִנַּיִן? שֶׁנֶּאֱמַר (יחזקאל טז): וָאֶרְחָצֵךְ בַּמַּיִם. בַּיִּישׁוּב מִנַּיִן? שֶׁנֶּאֱמַר (ישעיה א): רַחֲצוּ הִזַּכּוּ. לֶעָ"ל מִנַּיִן? שֶׁנֶּאֱמַר (שם ד): אִם רָחַץ ה' אֵת צֹאַת בְּנוֹת צִיּוֹן. אַתָּה אָמַרְתָּ: וְהִשָּׁעֲנוּ

תחת העץ, חייך! שאני פורע לבניך וכו'. (תהלים קה): פרש ענן למסך, הרי במדבר. בארץ
מנין? (ויקרא כג): בסוכות תשבו שבעת ימים. לע"ל מנין? (ישעיה ד): וסוכה תהיה לצל
יומם מחורב. אתה אמרת: ואקחה פת לחם, חייך! שאני פורע לבניך וכו'. (שמות טז): ויאמר
ה' אל משה הנני ממטיר לכם לחם מן השמים, הרי במדבר. בארץ מנין? שנ' (דברים ח): ארץ
חטה ושעורה. לע"ל מנין? (תהלי עב): יהי פסת בר בארץ. כך כתיב: ואל הבקר רץ אברהם,
חייך! שאני פורע לבניך וכו'. (במדבר יא): ורוח נסע מאת ה' ויגז שלוים מן הים, הרי כמדבר.
בארץ מנין? (שם לב): ומקנה רב היה לבני ראובן. לע"ל מנין? (ישעיה ז): והיה ביום ההוא
יחיה איש וגו'. כך כתיב: והוא עומד עליהם, חייך! שאני פורע לבניך וכו'. (שמות יג): וה' הולך
לפניהם יומם בעמוד ענן לנחותם הדרך, הרי במדבר. בארץ מנין? שנאמר (תהלים פב): אלהים
נצב בעדת אל. לע"ל מנין? שנאמר (מיכה ב): עלה הפורץ לפניהם:

LET NOW A LITTLE WATER BE FETCHED (GEN. 18:4). GOD SAID TO ABRA-
HAM: THOU HAST SAID: LET NOW A LITTLE WATER BE FETCHED. I SWEAR
THAT I WILL REPAY THY CHILDREN (IN THE WILDERNESS, IN INHABITED
COUNTRY [THE LAND – ERETZ ISRAEL], AND IN THE MESSIANIC FUTURE).
THUS IT IS WRITTEN: THEN SANG ISRAEL THIS SONG! SPRING UP, O WELL
– SING YE UNTO IT (NUM. 21:7) – THAT WAS IN THE WILDERNESS. WHERE
DO WE FIND IT IN THE LAND [SC. ERETZ ISRAEL]? A LAND OF BROOKS
OF WATER (DEUT. 8:7). AND IN THE MESSIANIC FUTURE? AND IT SHALL
COME TO PASS IN THAT DAY, THAT LIVING WATERS SHALL GO OUT FROM
JERUSALEM (ZECH. 14:8). THOU HAST SAID: AND WASH YOUR FEET: I
SWEAR TO THEE THAT I WILL REPAY THY CHILDREN. THEN WASHED I
THEE IN WATER (EZEK. 16:9) REFERS TO THE WILDERNESS. IN THE LAND?
WASH YOU, MAKE YOU CLEAN (ISA. 1:16). IN THE MESSIANIC FUTURE?
WHEN THE LORD SHALL HAVE WASHED AWAY THE FILTH OF THE DAUGH-
TERS OF ZION (4:4). THOU HAST SAID: AND RECLINE YOURSELVES UN-
DER THE TREE: BY THY LIFE, I WILL REPAY THY CHILDREN. HE SPREAD
A CLOUD FOR A SCREEN (PS. 105:39) – THAT WAS IN THE WILDERNESS.
IN THE LAND? YE SHALL DWELL IN BOOTHS SEVEN DAYS (LEV. 23:42).
IN THE MESSIANIC FUTURE? AND THERE SHALL BE A PAVILION FOR A
SHADOW IN THE DAYTIME FROM THE HEAT (ISA. 4:6). THOU DIDST SAY,
AND I WILL FETCH A MORSEL OF BREAD (GEN. 18:5): I SWEAR THAT I
WILL REPAY THY CHILDREN. THUS: BEHOLD, I WILL CAUSE TO RAIN
BREAD FROM HEAVEN FOR YOU (EX. 16:4) – THAT IS IN THE WILDERNESS.
IN THE LAND? A LAND OF WHEAT AND BARLEY, ETC. (DEUT. 8:8). IN THE
MESSIANIC FUTURE? HE WILL BE AS A RICH CORNFIELD IN THE LAND
(PS. 72:16). AGAIN, THOU DIDST RUN AFTER THE HERD: I SWEAR THAT
I WILL REPAY THY CHILDREN. THUS: AND THERE WENT FORTH A WIND
FROM THE LORD, AND BROUGHT ACROSS QUAILS FROM THE SEA (NUM.
11:27), THAT IS IN THE WILDERNESS. IN THE LAND? NOW THE CHILDREN

OF REUBEN AND THE CHILDREN OF GAD HAD A VERY GREAT MULTITUDE
OF CATTLE (32:1), IN THE MESSIANIC FUTURE? *AND IT SHALL COME TO
PASS IN THAT DAY, THAT A MAN SHALL REAR A YOUNG COW, AND TWO
SHEEP* (ISA. 7:21). AS A REWARD FOR AND HE STOOD BY THEM (GEN. 18:8),
AND THE LORD WENT BEFORE THEM (EX. 13:21) – THERE YOU HAVE THE
WILDERNESS. IN THE LAND? GOD STANDETH IN THE CONGREGATION OF
GOD (PS. 82:1). IN THE MESSIANIC FUTURE? THE BREAKER IS GONE UP,
BEFORE THEM . . . AND THE LORD AT THE HEAD OF THEM (MIC. 2:13)

T he text says: "And He stood near them to help them." In several biblical instances as mentioned in our Midrash, the Holy One, blessed be
He, so to speak, functioned as a caregiver (or *shamash*) to the Children
of Israel in those generations. For example, it says "And the Lord walked
in front of them by day by means of a cloud to show them the way." It
also says "in the congregation of God." All this means that God is ready
to help Israel, as Abraham was ready and willing to help his guests.
(Mirkin)

~

Seed Thoughts

See the Additional Commentary.

~

Additional Commentary

The leader of the guests

The text begins with *Adonai* – plural, and continues with the use of the
singular "if I found favor in *your* [i.e., thy] sight. It means that at the
beginning he addressed them altogether not knowing who their leader
was, and as usual in such cases, the leader then introduced himself.
Therefore, Abraham continued in the singular, addressing the leader in
person as the others merely listened. It should be added that according
to this system, the word *Adonai* is also secular. Some scholars, such as
Rabbi Levi, thought the name was sacred. The Midrash, however, does
not feel that way at all. The general rule seems to be that when there is
a *kamatz* in the *nun* it refers to God; otherwise, it is secular. (Mirkin)

PARASHAH FORTY-EIGHT, *Midrash Eleven*

יא ואקחה פת לחם וסעדו לבכם אחר תעבורו. א"ר יצחק: בתורה ובנביאים ובכתובים מצינו
דהדא פיתא מזוניתא דליבא. בתורה מנין? ואקחה פת לחם וסעדו לבכם. בנביאים (שופטים
יט): סעד לבך פת לחם. בכתובים (תהלים קד): ולחם לבב אנוש יסעד.

11. AND I WILL FETCH A MORSEL OF BREAD, AND STAY YE YOUR HEART
(GEN. 18:5). R. ISAAC SAID: IN THE TORAH [I.E., THE PENTATEUCH], THE
PROPHETS, AND THE WRITINGS WE FIND THAT BREAD STRENGTHENS
THE HEART. IN THE TORAH: AND I WILL FETCH A MORSEL OF BREAD,
AND STAY YE YOUR HEART. IN THE PROPHETS: STAY THY HEART WITH
A MORSEL OF BREAD (JUDG. 19:5). IN THE WRITINGS: AND BREAD THAT
STAYETH MAN'S HEART (PS. 104:15).

Each of the quotations, whether from the Torah, Prophets, or Writings, identifies food with the word לחם - *lehem*, "bread," with the understanding that bread is probably the basic food in any diet – Jewish or otherwise. What is just as interesting in these quotations is that the word *lehem* as bread is immediately identified with the word "heart," which in this case stands for the person who possesses the heart. However, another thought entered my mind in perusing these quotations: Could it possibly be that *lehem* as bread was good for the heart? Could it possibly be that *lehem* was used differently in those days? The truth of the matter is that we do not really know how bread was prepared in those days. In a later Midrash, one such recipe will be included, but we do not really know how bread was made in those days. Did the bread rise upon baking? Did they have any knowledge of how to use yeast? The only bread for which the Torah gave a recipe was the manna that fell from heaven, but as for the bread of every day, and even for Festivals, we really know nothing. The Sages of the Mishnah seem to know much more than we do about this subject, and hopefully we shall learn more.

א"ר אחא: וסעדו לבבכם אין כתיב כאן, אלא וסעדו לבכם, הדא אמרת: אין יצר הרע שולט
במלאכים. הוא דעתיה דר' חייא דא"ר חייא: שיתו לבבכם לחילה אין כתיב כאן, אלא לבכם,
הדא אמרת: שאין יצר הרע שולט לעתיד לבא.

R. AHA SAID: IT IS NOT WRITTEN: AND STAY *LE-BABEKEM*, BUT AND STAY
LIBKEM (YOUR HEART). THIS PROVES THAT THE TEMPTER HAS NO POWER
OVER ANGELS. THAT IS R. HIYYA'S VIEW TOO, FOR R. HIYYA SAID: IT IS

NOT WRITTEN: TURN *LEBABEKEM* (YOUR HEARTS) TO THE DANCE, BUT,
TURN *LIBEKEM* (YOUR HEARTS) TO THE DANCE (PS. 48:17). THIS PROVES
THAT THE TEMPTER WILL HAVE NO SWAY IN THE MESSIANIC FUTURE.

This interpretation is based on the fact that sometimes the word
"heart" in Hebrew is expressed with one *veit* and sometimes with two
veitim. As we learned in a previous Midrash, when Hebrew uses one *veit*
in the Hebrew word לב – *lev*, it refers to the heart which is a main unit in
the human body. However, when the word "heart" is לבב – *levav* – with
two *veitim*, it uses "heart" as a symbol in which the heart becomes a center for the Good Inclination – the *Yetzer HaTov*, and the Evil Inclination
– the *Yetzer HaRa*. The Torah takes great pains in establishing through
its various texts that "heart", when it refers to angels, appears with only
one *veit* because they do not possess an Evil Inclination.

כי על כן עברתם על עבדכם. א"ר יהושע: מיום שברא הקב"ה את עולמו, הייתם מזומנים
לבא אצלי, כי על כן עברתם, היך מד"א, יהי כן ה' עמכם. ויאמרו כן תעשה כאשר דברת.
אמרו: אנו אין לפנינו אכילה ושתיה, אבל אתה שיש לפניך אכילה ושתיה, כן תעשה לעצמך
כאשר דברת. יהי רצון שתזכה לעשות עוד סעודה אחרת לבר דכר דיתיליד לך:

SINCE FOR THIS PURPOSE YE ARE COME TO YOUR SERVANT. R. JOSHUA
B. R. NEHEMIAH SAID: [ABRAHAM URGED:] SINCE THE DAY WHEN THE
HOLY ONE, BLESSED BE HE, CREATED YOU, YE WERE DESTINED TO COME
TO ME. SINCE FOR THIS PURPOSE (*KI AL KEN*) YE ARE COME: [*KEN* HAS
THE SAME MEANING HERE AS IN THE VERSE] SO (*KEN*) BE THE LORD
WITH YOU (EX. 10:10). AND THEY SAID: SO DO THOU, AS THOU HAST
SAID. "AS FOR US," SAID THEY, "WE NEITHER EAT NOR DRINK; BUT THOU
WHO DOST EAT AND DRINK, SO DO THOU, AS THOU HAST SAID, [MAY YOU
MERIT ANOTHER MEAL] AND MAY THIS DAY BE REPEATED IN HONOR OF
THE SON [THAT WILL BE BORN TO THEE]."

As a way for Abraham to offer to his guests a conception of how important their visit was, he points out that the decision to arrange this visit
happened many years earlier as part of the Creation of the world. His
special guests, however, would not allow themselves to be influenced by
such thoughts. Abraham had extended to his guests a full-fledged invitation for room and board in general, and for that particular moment, an
invitation to a well-planned and luxurious afternoon meal. He was hoping that they would say נעשה – *naaseh*, meaning that "we will be glad to
participate," but instead they said תעשה – *taaseh*, "you do exactly as you

have spoken to us." This was their way of saying that eating and drinking is not a requirement for them, though it is for Abraham. Therefore, they wanted Abraham to do what he had planned to do for himself, his family, and guests other than the three spiritual visitors.

Seed Thoughts

Our text says the following: "The angels do not possess an evil inclination." It then goes on to say: "This applies to all who are involved in לעתיד לבא – *le-atid lavo* – the World to Come." There is something that I like to share with the reader in connection with concepts like the Messianic Age, the World to Come, or – as the angels are described in the Torah – not possessing an Evil Inclination. None of these concepts can be described as knowledge, since they are not based on evidence. They are, however, beliefs; beliefs do not require evidence, but they do require faith. The Jewish faith, as expressed in terms like Messianism, is that in God's creation, the best is yet to come. We can only advance little by little from the moral point of view in this world because we are mortal. The Torah text is not interested in teaching us about angels either in the Abraham story or elsewhere in Scripture. It simply uses angels as ways of interpreting the goals of Messianism, which is a better life, a pure life, and a much more moral life in the World to Come. How to get there, and who will get there, is beyond our capacity to know. The Talmud has many views, none of which are authoritative but all of which are spiritual, idealistic, moral, and with maximum faith in God and His purpose for the world and for all of us.

PARASHAH FORTY-EIGHT, *Midrash Twelve*

יב וימהר אברהם האהלה אל שרה ויאמר מהרי.

12. AND ABRAHAM HASTENED INTO THE TENT UNTO SARAH, AND SAID:
MAKE READY QUICKLY THREE MEASURES OF FINE MEAL (GEN. 18:6).

The measure we are talking about now is probably 6–7 liters. Abraham was in a hurry to have the meal prepared, so he asked Sarah also to hurry and to prepare three measures of fine flour. Fine flour meant that it would be white and clean and it would be made into dough to become cakes or *matzot*, and to be used as bread.

ר' אביתר אמר: תשע סאין אפתה. שלש לעוגות, שלש לחביץ, ושלש למיני מילוטמיה.
ורבנן אמרין: שלש. אחד לעוגות, ואחד לחביץ, ואחד למלוטמיה.

R. ABIATHAR SAID: SHE BAKED NINE MEASURES IN ALL, THREE OF CAKES,
THREE OF HABIZ, AND THREE OF PASTRIES.

According to this interpretation, Sarah prepared much more than Abraham had anticipated. She prepared nine measures – three of the measures were made from fine flour. In actual fact, all that Abraham had to request were three measures for cakes. However, in his request to Sarah, he said more than he had intended. He asked for *kemah*, which is flour, and *solet*, which is fine flour. These would be for the cakes. At the end of his request, however, he mentioned *kemah* again, which represents an additional three measures, making six measures altogether. The word *solet* was then added, which represented three more measures – altogether, nine. To summarize, three measures to make cakes of bread, three measures of *habitz* (a dough or bread crumbs rolled in honey or oil and cooked but not baked), and three further measures of fine flour to be used for the equivalent of dessert at the end of the meal. (*HaMidrash HaMevo'ar*)

The Rabbis (*Rabanan*) say that only three measures were requested and prepared at all, and they were more than enough for the three guests. Furthermore, the three measures were divided in the same way as earlier indicated – one measure for the equivalent of bread or cake, one measure for the special dish (as noted above), and one measure for the dessert.

לושי ועשי עוגות. הדא אמרת: פרס הפסח הוה.

KNEAD IT, AND MAKE CAKES (*UGOTH*). IT WAS THE SEASON OF PASSOVER.

To make the cakes as soon as possible without waiting for the dough to rise – this is what is meant when it is said that the visitors came to Abraham as angels at the beginning of the holiday of Passover. This is why instead of making cakes they made *matzot*.

רבי יונה בשם ר' חמא בר חנינא: היא מדבר סין, היא מדבר אלוש. מאיזו זכות זכו ישראל שניתן להם מן במדבר? בזכות של אברהם, שאמר: לושי ועשי עוגות:

R. JONAH AND R. LEVI IN THE NAME OF R. HAMA B. R. HANINA SAID: THE WILDERNESS OF SIN AND THE WILDERNESS OF ALUSH ARE ONE AND THE SAME. [THE CHANGE OF NAME TO ALUSH TEACHES THIS]: ON ACCOUNT OF WHOSE MERIT WERE ISRAEL PRIVILEGED TO HAVE THE MANNA GIVEN TO THEM? ON ACCOUNT OF [THE MERIT OF ABRAHAM WHO SAID]: *LUSHI* (KNEAD IT), AND MAKE CAKES.

In the travels of the Children of Israel, they moved from the wilderness of Seen to Rephidim. There are certain locations in the wilderness of Seen, such as the area of Alush, where it so happens that the original manna fell. Why did this happen? Because Abraham said to Sarah: "*Lushi*" [make dough], and she answered: "*Ani Alush*". So her answer was the same as the name of the area. Therefore, the manna fell as a tribute to Abraham and Sarah.

⌣

Seed Thoughts

See the second commentary to this Midrash.

⌣

Additional Commentary

Seen and Alush

In Exodus (12:39), it says that the Children of Israel went from the desert of Seen and then camped in Rephidim, but in Numbers (33:14) it says that they went from Alush to camp in Rephidim. The answer is that Seen and Alush are the same place. The manna fell in the desert of Seen because of the merit of Sarah's kneading dough (*lushi*). (Mirkin)

יג ואל הבקר רץ אברהם.

13. AND ABRAHAM RAN UNTO THE HERD (GEN. 18:7).

The main concern of the Midrash at this point, though not expressly stated, is why Abraham ran. After all, we are dealing with a person like Abraham who is very much advanced in age and was suffering temporarily from the pain of his recent circumcision. Why did he run? After all, he had an entire staff of people, anyone of whom could do what he was about to do. The answer is that he personally wanted to be involved in the commandment of hospitality.

א"ר לוי: רץ לקדם אותה אומה, שכתוב בה (הושע י): אפרים עגלה מלומדה אוהבתי לדוש.

R. LEVI SAID: HE RAN TO ANTICIPATE THE PEOPLE OF WHOM IT IS WRIT-TEN: EPHRAIM IS A HEIFER WELL BROKEN, THAT LOVETH TO THRESH (HOS. 10:11).

Please note that the reference to Ephraim is from a prophet who existed close to 700 years after Abraham.

ויקח בן בקר, יכול גדול? ת"ל: רך, אי רך יכול חסר? ת"ל: וטוב.

AND FETCHED A CALF. YOU MIGHT THINK THAT IT WAS FULL-GROWN; THEREFORE TENDER IS STATED. IF TENDER, YOU MIGHT THINK THAT IT WAS LACKING [IN FLAVOR]; THEREFORE AND GOOD IS STATED.

One can discern from these remarks that Abraham made every effort to provide for his guests. This included the best possible and tasty foods which were within his command, and in particular, the meat that he planned to serve.

ויתן אל הנער, זה ישמעאל, בשביל לזרזו במצוות:

AND GAVE IT UNTO THE LAD: THIS WAS ISHMAEL, [ABRAHAM'S] PURPOSE BEING TO TRAIN HIM IN GOOD DEED.

One of the explanations as to why it was thought that the young man was Ishmael was because the text did not say נער – *naar*, a youth, but rather הנער – *ha-naar*, which in Hebrew means the special young man we have known about in the biblical story, namely Ishmael, Abraham's firstborn son.

—

Seed Thoughts I

Human imagination is a tremendous asset. It helps a person to face many crises in life, and even though sometimes the human imagination is in conflict with one's rational understanding, nevertheless, a human being chooses what his imagination tells him, in preference to what his intelligence really maintains.

We have had many examples where the life of Abraham has been used as an explanation for what happened to his offspring of many generations yet to come. We were told in some Midrashim that every time Abraham offered some respect (or of eating and drinking) to his guests, in some fashion, his future generations (his children, etc.) benefited. What the Midrash tells us is usually spoken to us, and we're not always certain that Abraham himself knew about these developments. But in our present Midrash, we have a line which says that Abraham not only knew about these developments, but tried to use his powers to influence them. For example, why did he rush to the barn in order to pick a choice animal? Because he remembered being told that he would start a new nation, and part of that nation included Ephraim, who was said to remember a "heifer well broken," which probably means that he helped people as many times as he can. Why did Abraham come to these conclusions? Because he had an imagination which wanted very much to accept the wonderful happenings in the future, which justify Abraham's difficulties in the present.

—

Seed Thoughts II

As we can see from the Midrashin of the *sedrot* of both *Lekh Lekha* and *Vayera*, the Midrash loved Abraham and felt that he could do no wrong. At the same time, they cried with Abraham, and the reason why they cried is that they knew how much Abraham loved his firstborn, Ishmael, and how terrible he felt that he was not in a position to bring him up by his side as his son. We know that it was not his fault. Abraham reacted to his wife Sarah's concern for the safety and integrity of his son, Isaac, whom she thought was being badly influenced by Ishmael.

We are not sure in what respect Ishmael was leading Isaac astray. Was it because of his connections to idolatry through his mother, Hagar? Or was it some difference of opinion? At any rate, the result was that Abraham was largely excluded from the task which he would have loved, of bringing up Ishmael as his firstborn son and showing him off to the world. We know that Abraham used every opportunity of seeing his son and traveling very far in order to do so. He also tried to involve him in all kinds of work with whom he himself was associated. Thus in our Midrash, he was part of Abraham's staff, who often singled him out in order to have him do something that would bring him respect and demonstrate his character and ability. Many of the readers like the Midrash, but they too cry with Abraham, and this reader also cried when the reference was made. It was Ishmael who finally brought the banqueting arrangements to the dining room of their community. Many of us even cry when the biblical text reported that both Isaac and Ishmael looked after Abraham's burial. Why did it have to wait until he died for the two of them to be together? Why could an arrangement not have been found in Abraham's lifetime? The Midrash had much reason to cry.

PARASHAH FORTY-EIGHT, *Midrash Fourteen*

יד ויקח חמאה וחלב. א"ר חנינא: המעולה אחד מששים בחלב, והבינוני אחד מארבעים,
והקיבר אחד מעשרים. רבי יונה אמר: המעולה, אחד ממאה, בינוני אחד מששים, והקיבר
א' מעשרים.

14. AND HE TOOK BUTTER, AND MILK (GEN. 18:8). R. HANINA SAID: THE
BEST [BUTTER] IS MADE FROM A SIXTIETH PART OF THE MILK; MEDIUM
QUALITY IS FROM A FORTIETH PART; WHILE INFERIOR [BUTTER] IS FROM
A TWENTIETH. R. JONAH SAID: THE BEST [BUTTER] IS MADE FROM A
HUNDREDTH PART OF THE MILK; MEDIUM QUALITY IS FROM A SIXTIETH
PART; WHILE INFERIOR [BUTTER] IS FROM A TWENTIETH.

The text does not explain why each of the Sages had a different evaluation of how the butter could be prepared. Butter is made from a fat which
comes from milk; the less fat that is required, the better the butter seems
to taste, but it does not have a large quantity. Although Rabbi Hanina
and Rabbi Jonah differ in their interpretation of what is the content of
the best butter, neither of them give us any opinion as to what kind of
butter was given to Abraham's guests. We do not have a clear-cut interpretation as to what kind of butter was served to Abraham's guests. All
we can discern is that one version uses the expression וחמאה חלב – *halav
ve-hema*, milk and butter, and another text uses the expression חמאה
וחלב – *hema ve-halav*, as though to indicate that the expression *hema ve-
halav* seems to indicate that a better form of butter was served. The only
other interpretation found by this reader is the quotation to be found in
the Seed Thoughts below, based on the hermeneutical addition of the
Hebrew letters of *halav ve-hema*, which add up to 100.

ופת היכן היא? אפרים מקשאה, תלמידו דרבי מאיר, משום ר"מ אמר: פירסה נדה ונטמאת
העיסה.

NOW WHERE WAS THE BREAD? EPHRAIM MIKSHAAH, A DISCIPLE OF R.
MEIR, SAID IN R. MEIR'S NAME: SARAH BECAME MENSTRUOUS AND THE
DOUGH WAS DEFILED.

It so happens that bread, whether described at *pat* or *ugot*, was the main
content of the food that Abraham promised guests. The verse which we
just quoted, however, refers to milk and butter, but the bread was not

included. The text offers the interpretation of a student of Rabbi Meir: "Sarah became menstruous and the dough became defiled."

רבנן אמרי: אפילו פת הביא הביא לפניהם. מה אם דברים שלא אמר הביא לפניהם, דברים שאמר
להם על אחת כמה וכמה!

THE RABBIS SAID: HE CERTAINLY BROUGHT THEM BREAD TOO, FOR IF HE BROUGHT THEM WHAT HE HAD NOT OFFERED, HOW MUCH MORE WHAT HE HAD OFFERED!

There is no question, according to the Rabbis, that bread cakes were the major promise of Abraham to his guests, and it is not important that they were not included in a particular sentence. Did the Rabbis disagree that Sarah had a menstruation problem? They had certainly accepted the miracle that Sarah would be blessed with a youthfulness in order to give birth to Isaac, but there is no proof that this problem occurred while they were occupied with these special guests.

והוא עומד עליהם. הכא את אמר: והוא עומד עליהם, ולהלן אמר: נצבים עליו, אלא עד שלא
יצא ידיהם, נצבים עליו, כיון שיצא ידיהם. והוא עומד עליהם, אימתו מוטלת עליהם, מיכאל
מירתת גבריאל מירתת.

AND HE STOOD OVER THEM. BUT EARLIER YOU READ: THREE MEN STOOD OVER HIM (GEN. 18:2)? THE EXPLANATION IS THIS: BEFORE THEY HAD PERFORMED THEIR MISSION, "THEY STOOD OVER HIM"; BUT WHEN THEY HAD PERFORMED THEIR MISSION, HE STOOD OVER THEM: HE INSPIRED THEM WITH FEAR, AND SO HE STOOD OVER THEM, MICHAEL TREMBLED AND GABRIEL TREMBLED.

This means that Abraham was more important than his guests. This is in contrast to what was said earlier, at the beginning of the visit where it says that *they* stood over him. In other words, at the beginning of the visit, the visitors or angels looked upon themselves as superior to Abraham. But as the visit became longer, and they became more aware of who Abraham and Sarah were, they changed and accepted the fact that he was above them. Therefore, the text says "and he stood over them," not only in serving them but also in their mutual attitudes. So long as Abraham was engaged in serving them and looking after them, he acted as though they were superior. But from the moment he concluded the major part of his hospitality, they looked upon Abraham as superior to them. The commentators go on to say that Michael, who was the leader of the angelic group, was full of respect for Abraham, who he came to revere; the same held true for Gabriel and Raphael – all because they learned very quickly of Abraham's reputation in the areas of justice and mercy.

רבי תנחומא משום ר' אלעזר ור' אבון בשם רבי מאיר: מתלא אמר: עלת לקרתא, הלך
בנימוסה! למעלה שאין אכילה ושתיה, עלה משה למרום ולא אכל, שנאמר (דברים ט): ואשב
בהר ארבעים יום וארבעים לילה, לחם לא אכלתי ומים לא שתיתי. אבל למטה, שיש אכילה
ושתיה, והוא עומד עליהם תחת העץ, ויאכלו וכי אוכלין היו. אלא, נראין כאוכלין, ראשון
ראשון, מסתלק:

R. TANHUMA IN R. ELEAZAR'S NAME AND R. ABUN IN R. MEIR'S NAME SAID: THE PROVERB RUNS: "WHEN IN ROME, DO AS ROME DOES." ABOVE [IN THE CELESTIAL SPHERE] THERE IS NO EATING AND DRINKING; HENCE WHEN MOSES ASCENDED ON HIGH HE APPEARED LIKE THEM [THE ANGELS], AS IT SAYS: THEN I ABODE IN THE MOUNT FORTY DAYS AND FORTY NIGHTS; I DID NEITHER EAT BREAD NOR DRINK WATER (DEUT. 9:9). BUT BELOW, WHERE THERE IS EATING AND DRINKING, WE FIND: AND HE STOOD BY THEM UNDER THE TREE, AND THEY DID EAT. DID THEY THEN EAT? THEY PRETENDED TO EAT, REMOVING EACH COURSE IN TURN.

Abraham did not realize that his visitors do not require eating and drinking, but they pretended they were doing so. The Midrash interprets this as a lesson to all of us to try to emulate the customs of your host or host country, which will contribute to peaceful relationships on all sides.

—

Seed Thoughts

It is hard to know what motivates people; none of the Sages quoted were known as experts in the production of butter from milk. They may have heard of opinions from people who were expert in this, and this may explain the views quoted in the Midrash in the name of Rabbi Hanina and in the name of Rabbi Jonah. However, one of the commentators offered a particular interpretation of why Rabbi Jonah had a recipe for the best kind of butter in a very special way. He discovered that the words *hema ve-halav*, when the letters were added up in terms of the hermeneutical principles, added up to 100. This may have been what motivated Rabbi Jonah to suggest that the best butter is based on one-hundredth of the milk fat. (Mirkin)

PARASHAH FORTY-EIGHT, *Midrash Fifteen*

טו ויאמרו אליו איה שרה אשתך וגו'. אל"ף יו"ד וי"ו נקוד, למ"ד אינו נקוד. אמר ר"ש בן
אלעזר: בכל מקום שאתה מוצא כתב רבה על הנקודה, אתה דורש את הכתב. נקודה רבה
על הכתב, אתה דורש את הנקודה. כאן שהנקודה רבה על הכתב, אתה דורש את הנקודה.

15. AND THEY SAID UNTO HIM (*ELAW*): WHERE IS SARAH THY WIFE (GEN.
18:9)? THE *ALEF*, *YOD*, AND *WAW* ARE DOTTED, BUT THE *LAMED* IS NOT
DOTTED. R. SIMEON B. ELEAZAR SAID: WHEREVER YOU FIND THE PLAIN
WRITING EXCEEDING THE DOTTED LETTERS, YOU MUST INTERPRET THE
PLAIN WRITING; IF THE DOTTED LETTERS EXCEED THE PLAIN WRITING,
YOU MUST INTERPRET THE DOTTED LETTERS. HERE THAT THE DOTTED
LETTERS EXCEED THE UNDOTTED, YOU MUST INTERPRET THE DOTTED
TEXT.

In the word אליו - *elav*, the letters *aleph*, *yod*, and *vav* have a mark on
top of each of these letters, but the letter *lamed* does not have such a
dot. This is one of ten words in the Torah which have dots over certain
letters. Rabbi Simeon b. Eleazar explains that if in a dotted word the
undotted letters are in the majority, the word has the meaning that
follows those letters. If, on the other hand, the dotted letters are in the
majority, the word follows the meaning of those letters. Here in our text,
the dotted letters are in the majority. So it is as though the letter *lamed*
does not exist for our purposes. The new meaning is, therefore, איו – *ayo*,
which means "where is he?"

איו אברהם. א"ר עזריה: כשם שאמרו איה שרה, כך אמרו לשרה איו אברהם. ויאמר הנה
באהל.

THUS, [THE ANGELS ASKED SARAH,] "WHERE IS HE-ABRAHAM? 'R.
AZARIAH SAID: JUST AS THEY SAID TO ABRAHAM, "WHERE IS SARAH," SO
THEY SAID TO SARAH, "WHERE IS ABRAHAM?" AND HE SAID: BEHOLD, IN
THE TENT.

The meaning is, "where is Abraham." Rabbi Azariah explains that they
knew very well where Abraham was, but this was asked to make Sarah
feel good. This can be explained as a model form of human behavior,
known in Hebrew as *derekh eretz*, so that every person visiting a home
or a family should ask about the welfare of those in whose home they

find themselves. This includes the case of a husband to ask about the welfare of his wife, and in the case of a wife inquiring about the welfare of her husband,

הה"ד (שופטים ה): תבורך מנשים יעל אשת חבר הקיני מנשים באהל תבורך. רבי אלעזר ורבי שמואל בר נחמן: רבי אלעזר אמר: מנשי דור המדבר, שהן יושבות באהלים, שנאמר (במדבר יא): איש לפתח אהלו. ולמה תבורך מהם? הן ילדו וקיימו את העולם. ומה היה מועיל להם, שאלמלא היא, כבר היו אבודין. רבי שמואל בר נחמן אמר: מן האמהות, הן ילדו וכו'. שאלולי היא, כבר היו אבודין:

THUS IT IS WRITTEN: BLESSED ABOVE WOMEN SHALL JAEL BE, THE WIFE OF HEBER THE KENITE, ABOVE WOMEN IN THE TENT SHALL SHE BE BLESSED (JUDG. 5:24). R. ELEAZAR SAID: IT MEANS, ABOVE THE WOMEN OF THE GENERATION OF THE WILDERNESS. THEY GAVE BIRTH TO CHILDREN, YET BUT FOR HER [JAEL] THEY [THE CHILDREN] WOULD HAVE BEEN DESTROYED. R. SAMUEL B. NAHMAN SAID: ABOVE THE MA-TRIARCHS. THEY GAVE BIRTH TO CHILDREN, YET BUT FOR HER THEY WOULD HAVE BEEN DESTROYED.

The Midrash now turns our attention to the text about the prophetess Deborah where she says: "Blessed is Jael, the wife of Heber the Kenite, who killed Sisera, the enemy of Israel." In her blessing of Jael, Deborah said: "May she be blessed even above those women who stay in their tents as a result of their modesty." What is the reference of "women in the tents"? There are two views: One view is that it refers to the women in the wilderness who produced children and brought up a community even in the desert area. While the men sat outside crying about the manna and the meat, the women, remained in their tents and did not participate in the protests against Moses. So they were singled out as being on a higher level. A second opinion is that the expression "women in the tents" refers to the Matriarchs – Sarah, Rebecca, Rachel, and Leah – all of whom were described by various Torah texts in relation to the tents in which they lived. They are suggesting that Jael was on an even higher level than the wonderful women in the wilderness as well as the Matriarchs – women who enabled their generation to survive. The Sages that have been quoted have placed Jael above the women of these previous generations, because if she had not acted the way she did, all of Israel might have been destroyed by Sisera.

Seed Thoughts

In the commentary of *HaMidrash HaMevo'ar*, something is added to the prophecy of Deborah which is not found in the text of the prophecy. In that text, Sisera escaped from the battlefield by himself, was utterly exhausted when he entered the nearest home, which was that of Jael, the wife of Heber the Kenite. As she recognized him at once as being one of the greatest enemies of Israel, her mind was going through various possibilities of handling the situation. She gave him something warm to drink and he fell asleep. At that point, she took the nail of the tent and killed him. According to the *HaMidrash HaMevo'ar*, there either was a sexual relationship between them which actually put him to sleep, or she was prepared to do so despite her strong principles of sexual modesty, if that were the only way in which Sisera could be overcome. The commentators of *HaMidrash HaMevo'ar* may be right and they may have other sources that support them. For example, where the mother of Sisera is quoted as being worried about her son, one of the points that she mentions is that he was a womanizer, and this may account for his delay. But it is quite astonishing to have it mentioned in a text in the Midrash, since it does not mention this at all as being one of the reasons why Deborah rated Jael as being blessed above all other women because of the way she acted. Perhaps we will learn more about this subject if the matter is debated by other commentators.

Parashah Forty-Eight, *Midrash Sixteen*

טז ויאמר שוב אשוב אליך כעת חיה וגו'. והוא אחריו, זה ישמעאל. והוא אחריו, מפני היחוד.

16. AND HE SAID: I WILL CERTAINLY RETURN UNTO THEE WHEN THE SEASON COMETH ROUND ... AND SARAH HEARD IN THE TENT DOOR, AND HE WAS BEHIND HIM (GEN. 18:10). THIS REFERS TO ISHMAEL: AND HE WAS BEHIND HIM, SO THAT THEY [THE ANGEL AND SARAH] SHOULD NOT BE ALONE.

The Midrash is explaining here the position of everyone in the tent while the special news of Sarah's impending birth is being exchanged. Sarah was in a position where she could hear everything but was not to be seen. Abraham was at the entrance of the tent to prevent additional visitors who would interrupt their special proceedings. The visiting angel was seated near Abraham. Ishmael was near Sarah so that he would be in a position to do her bidding, whether there were things to be delivered or information to be conveyed.

והוא אחריו, זה המלאך שהביט לאחריו והרגיש שבאת אורה מאחריו.

ANOTHER INTERPRETATION: AND HE WAS BEHIND HIM: SHE UNDERSTOOD THAT THE GUEST HAD COME.

The other interpretation simply adds that the visiting angel was seated in such a way that he was greatly influenced by Sarah's beauty and her presence in general.

ואברהם ושרה זקנים. אמר רבי יוחנן: כבר כתיב ואברהם ושרה זקנים. מה ת"ל ואברהם זקן? אלא שהההזירו הקב"ה לימי נערותיו, צריך לכתוב פעם שנייה ואברהם זקן. רבי אמי אמר: כאן זקנה שיש בה לחלוחית, ולהלן בזקנה שאין בה לחלוחית.

NOW ABRAHAM AND SARAH WERE OLD (GEN. 18:11). R. JOHANAN SAID: SINCE IT IS NOW WRITTEN: NOW ABRAHAM AND SARAH WERE OLD, WHY IS IT AGAIN WRITTEN, NOW ABRAHAM WAS OLD (24:1)? THE REASON IS BECAUSE THE HOLY ONE, BLESSED BE HE, RESTORED HIM TO THE DAYS OF HIS YOUTH, THEREFORE: AND ABRAHAM WAS OLD MUST THEN BE WRITTEN A SECOND TIME. R. AMMI SAID: HERE OLD AGE COMBINED WITH VIRILITY IS MEANT, WHILE FURTHER ON IT MEANS OLD AGE WITHOUT VIRILITY.

In the same way that Sarah was blessed with a return to her former youthfulness in order to give birth to a child, so was Abraham returned to his youth so he could function as the father of his son eventually to be born. By the same token, after Isaac is born, some of Abraham's youthfulness will be removed, which is why he is referred to again as an elderly person, but he would still have the virility that would enable him to father the children of Keturah, whose original name was Hagar.

חדל להיות לשרה אורח כנשים. היך מה דאת אמר (דברים כג): וכי תחדל לנדור. פסק, המד"א
(במדבר ט): וחדל לעשות הפסח:

IT HAD CEASED (HADAL) TO BE WITH SARAH AFTER THE MANNER OF WOMEN. [HADAL MEANS], IT HAD FORBORNE, AS IN THE VERSE, BUT IF THOU SHALT FORBEAR (TE-HEDAL) TO VOW (DEUT. 23:23). OR, IT HAD CEASED; AS IN THE VERSE, AND FORBEARETH (WE-HADAL) TO KEEP THE PASSOVER (NUM. 9:13).

By the same token, Sarah was blessed with youthfulness to enable her to bear her eventual child. Now that this is on the way to be accomplished, those special blessings of youthfulness can be removed so that she could return to her regular self as a woman of an elderly age.

—

Seed Thoughts

The *Tiferet Tzion* is quite surprised at this Midrash. What difference does it make where a person stands or where a person sits? In general, it would have been a much stronger Midrash if the word *ve-a'harav* – meaning "and after him" – would have been completely eliminated. However, since it has not been eliminated, some reason has to be found for its inclusion. Why is it here, and what is it telling us? Let us completely remove from our minds the whole discussion of where people are standing or sitting. This word, *ve-a'harav*, should be related to Ishmael, and it has nothing to do with whether he was standing or sitting. From the point of view of Ishmael, *ve-a'harav* would refer to things that might happen after Isaac is born. Ishmael was not completely certain of what would happen, but he did feel almost instinctively that the new events would not be to his benefit. Since we know what later happened in his life, his instincts were quite strong. We should remember that at a certain stage, Sarah insisted that Ishmael and his mother, Hagar, leave her home and return to Hagar's family, because she felt that Ishmael was becoming a bad influence over her son, Isaac.

PARASHAH FORTY-EIGHT, *Midrash Seventeen*

יז ותצחק שרה בקרבה לאמר. זה אחד מן הדברים ששינו לתלמי המלך. ותצחק שרה
בקרוביה לאמר, ואדני זקן.

17. AND SARAH LAUGHED WITHIN HERSELF (*BEKIRBAH*), SAYING (GEN. 18:12). THIS IS ONE OF THE TEXTS WHICH THEY AMENDED FOR KING PTOLEMY, READING IT, AND SARAH LAUGHED BEFORE HER RELATIVES (*BI-KEROBEHAH*), SAYING ... AFTER I AM WAXED OLD, I SHALL HAVE *EDNAH* [E.V. "PLEASURE"].

King Ptolemy ordered a number of rabbinic scholars to translate the Five Books of Moses into Greek, so that he may read them and learn from them. They deliberately changed some of the words for fear they might compromise the Jewish community. See the Additional Commentary below. One of the changes they made was to remove the word *bekirba*, which meant that Sarah laughed within herself, within her heart, and changed to *bi-kroveha*, among her relatives. However, Abraham also laughed, but it was within his heart alone; in Sarah's case, in addition to laughing, she said a few things. This is what forced God to take notice in mentioning this to Abraham. They were afraid that Ptolemy would take notice and were uncertain what action it might lead him to. She said: "... after I am waxed old, I shall have pleasure, and my lord is old." In other words, after expressing a sense of wonder about herself, why did she have to express a sense of wonder about her husband?

אמרה: האשה הזו, כל זמן שהיא ילדה, יש לה תכשיטים נאים, ואני אחרי בלותי היתה לי
עדנה – תכשיטים היך מה דאת אמר (יחזקאל טז): ואעדך עדי.

SHE SAID THUS: AS LONG AS A WOMAN IS YOUNG SHE HAS FINERY, WHEREAS AFTER I AM WAXED OLD, I SHALL HAVE *EDNAH*, THAT MEANS FINERY, AS IN THE VERSE, I DECKED THEE ALSO WITH ORNAMENTS – *EDI* (EZEK. 15:11).

Sarah felt that even though she too was getting old, she still needed the finery and the various other forms of jewelry that a kept a woman young in spirit, prepared for challenges, even those of childbirth and other challenges of womanhood. Sarah admitted that even in her advanced years, she found the need for finery and other forms of decoration, and even during the ninety years, she lived like a bride every bit prepared for her wedding canopy. Even though she laughed, she was very happy until the possibility of her giving birth to her child.

האשה הזו, כל זמן שהיא ילדה, יש לה וסתות, ואני אחרי בלותי, היתה לי עדנה – עידונים. האשה הזו, כל זמן שהיא ילדה, יש לה עידויין, ואני אחרי בלותי, היתה לי עדנה – זמני, אלא, ואדני זקן. רב יהודה אמר: טוחן ולא פולט.

A WOMAN, AS LONG AS SHE IS YOUNG, HAS HER REGULAR PERIODS, WHILE AFTER I AM WAXED OLD, I SHALL HAVE *EDNAH*, I.E., MENSES. THE FACT, HOWEVER, IS THAT MY LORD IS OLD. RAB JUDAH SAID: HE IS VIRILE, YET IMPOTENT.

Sarah never wondered about herself; she tried successfully to think positively in terms of her return to youthfulness. Her only worry was about her husband, whether he would succumb to difficulties whereby old age would prevent him from becoming a father. One of the important lessons that we derive from the various texts quoted is that it is permitted to make certain changes in speech to contribute to peace between individuals and the world at large. Even in the case where the Holy One, blessed be He, complained to Abraham about Sarah's laughter, He also said to Abraham *va-ani zakanti*, meaning that she was getting old. In actual fact, she had said the very opposite – namely, that her husband was getting old. But the Holy One, blessed be He, said to Abraham: "Sarah said *va-ani zakanti*, referring to herself." If God Himself can change these words for the sake of bringing peace to husband and wife, and also to other human beings, who sometimes make slips of the tongue without meaning it, surely we could do the same and thus bless each other with the same kind of goodwill that the Holy One, blessed be He, sets as an example.

אמר רבי יהודה בר' סימון, אמר הקב"ה: אתם מילדים עצמכם ומזקינים את חבריכם, ואני זקנתי מלעשות נסים?:

R. JUDAH B. R. SIMON SAID: [THE HOLY ONE, BLESSED BE HE, SAID:] "YE
DECLARE YOURSELVES YOUNG AND YOUR COMPANIONS OLD, YET I AM
TOO OLD (GEN. 18:13) TO PERFORM MIRACLES!"

In connection to the text just quoted, it should be stated as follows:
"Am I too old to perform miracles? Of course not!" (Aryeh Mirkin)

~

Seed Thoughts

See the third commentary to this Midrash.

~

Additional Commentary

The case of King Ptolemy and the Hebrew Bible

King Ptolemy gathered 70 elders of Israel and placed them in 70 houses,
and he did not reveal to them at first for what purpose he had gathered
them. He then visited each one of them, and said to them individually:
"Write for me a Greek translation of the Torah of Moses your Teacher."
The Holy One, blessed be He, placed counsel in each of their hearts,
and all of them independently arrived at a common decision about how
to translate various words in the Torah. (This is known as The Septua-
gint – *Tirgum HaShivim.*) They wrote for him in Greek, "God created
in the beginning" rather than "In the beginning created God." They also
wrote: "I shall make man in image and form" rather than "Let us make
man in image and likeness." Relevant for this Midrash, they also wrote
"and Sarah laughed among her relatives" rather than "and Sarah laughed
inwardly." There are many other examples in Tractate *Megillah* 9a-9b.
(Artscroll, *Schottenstein Edition, Talmud Bavli*)

PARASHAH FORTY-EIGHT, *Midrash Eighteen*

יח ויאמר ה' אל אברהם למה זה צחקה שרה לאמר.

18. AND THE LORD SAID UNTO ABRAHAM: WHEREFORE DID SARAH LAUGH, SAYING . . . SEEING THAT I AM OLD (GEN. 18:13).

W hat has just been quoted is not exactly what Sarah said. She actually said: "My husband is old," but the Almighty, in speaking to Abraham, compromised her words and said to him that Sarah had added about herself that she was old.

בר קפרא אמר: גדול השלום, שאף הכתובים דברו בדאית, בשביל להטיל שלום בין אברהם לשרה. ותצחק שרה בקרבה לאמר אחרי בלותי היתה לי עדנה ואדני זקן. לאברהם אינו אומר כן, אלא למה זה צחקה שרה לאמר האף אמנם אלד ואני זקנתי, לא דיבר הכתוב כמו שאמרה שרה, ואדוני זקן, אלא ואני זקנתי:

BAR KAPPARA SAID: GREAT IS PEACE, FOR EVEN SCRIPTURE MADE A MIS-STATEMENT IN ORDER TO PRESERVE PEACE BETWEEN ABRAHAM AND SARAH. THUS, IT IS WRITTEN: WHEREFORE DID SARAH LAUGH, SAYING: SHALL I OF A SURETY BEAR A CHILD? IT DOES NOT SAY: SINCE MY LORD IS OLD, BUT SEEING THAT I AM OLD.

—

Seed Thoughts

We are all impressed the first time we read the story of how the Holy One, blessed be He, changed the contents of Sarah's speech where she added the thought that her husband being old was one of the reasons why she had had difficulty in childbirth. The Almighty changed her speech and told Abraham: "Sarah said that she herself was old." We are given the interpretation that the Almighty did this to indicate that we can change certain truths for the sake of peace. In this particular case, the peace of the household of Abraham and Sarah was at stake and God did not want to jeopardize it in any way. However, this remarkable intervention is certainly one which we accept when it comes from God. But how are we, human beings, supposed to act? Can truth be compromised? How do we know that at certain moments truthful things can be changed for the sake of peace and some other very precious ideal? On the other hand, our tradition does say ה' אלהיכם אמת – *Hashem Eloheikhem emet*, meaning "The Lord your God is true." This means that God's foremost attitude is truth. How then can it be compromised? By accepting the meaning of this beautiful Midrash, we are left with a serious problem. How can we teach truth properly and protect it properly? How can we explain our Midrash to younger children, to whom we are beginning to teach beautiful concepts like truth and peace? The Talmud seems to imply that one can say a partial truth if it is for the sake of peace (*Yebamot* 65B). However, the questions still remains. I have no real answers in posing these questions, only to state that we have much to learn and much to safeguard in order to protect the ideals by which we live.

PARASHAH FORTY-EIGHT, *Midrash Nineteen*

יט היפלא מה' דבר וגו'. רבי יודן בר' סימון אמר: משל לאחד שהיה בידו שתי קפליות,
הוליכן אצל נפח. אמר לו: יכול אתה לתקנם לי? אמר לו: לבראתן כבתחלה אני יכול, לתקנם
לך איני יכול? כן הכא, (להחזירם) לבראתן כבתחלה אני יכול, להחזירם לימי נערותן איני יכול!:

19. IS ANYTHING TOO HARD FOR THE LORD (GEN. 18:14). R. JUDAN B. R. SIMON SAID: THIS MAY BE COMPARED TO A MAN WHO HAD IN HIS HAND TWO PARTS OF A LOCK AND WENT TO A SMITH AND ASKED HIM: "CAN YOU REPAIR THESE?" "I CAN MAKE THEM FROM THE OUTSET," HE REPLIED, "AND YOU THINK THAT I CANNOT REPAIR THEM?!" SO HERE, [GOD SAID], "I CAN CREATE MAN FROM THE BEGINNING, YET [YOU WOULD SAY THAT] I CANNOT RESTORE THEM TO THEIR YOUTH!"

God's response to this parable is as follows: Granted that God created all of existence from the beginning, are you then suggesting that He could not repair something that was broken as the blacksmith explained? Surely not. He Who created everything could certainly look after this miracle as He did the other miracles of Creation.

Seed Thoughts

There is a detail in this Midrash which is not explained but which seems to be important. God is described as intervening in the argument between Sarah and Abraham, and the parable is suggesting that He may not be able to repair their lives, by which we mean their giving birth to Isaac. At this point, God responds to the problem by speaking about Himself in the third person. He doesn't say, "I created the entire universe, etc."; He says "God created the entire universe." This is with greatest possible ease, reflecting some of the past Midrashim that the world was created simply by God's word of mouth without any effort and energy on His part. At this point, God Himself moves from the first person to the third person, as though to say, "I am the God I was speaking about, and I can certainly look after the miracle of your birth as well as other miracles far beyond the capacity of the blacksmith and others with similar problems." The use of the change from the first person to the third person seems to add power to the divine intervention.

PARASHAH FORTY-EIGHT, *Midrash Twenty*

כ ותכחש שרה לאמר לא וגו'. רבי יהודה בר' סימון אמר: מעולם לא נזקק הקב"ה להשיח
עם אשה, אלא עם אותה הצדקת, ואף היא על ידי עילה. ר' אבא בר כהנא בשם רבי אידי
אמר: כמה כירכוכים כירכר בשביל להשיח עמה. ויאמר, לא כי צחקת! רבי אלעזר אומר:
והכתיב (בראשית טז): ותקרא שם ה' הדובר אליה. רבי יהושע בשם רבי נחמיה בשם רבי אידי
אמר: על ידי מלאך, והכתיב: ויאמר ה' לה. רבי לוי אמר: על ידי מלאך. רבי אלעזר בשם רבי
יוסי בר זימרא אמר: ע"י שם בן נח.

20. THEN SARAH DENIED, SAYING: I LAUGHED NOT, ETC. R. JUDAH B. R. SIMON AND R. JOHANAN IN THE NAME OF R. SIMEON B. ELEAZAR SAID: THE HOLY ONE, BLESSED BE HE, NEVER CONDESCENDED TO CONVERSE WITH A WOMAN SAVE WITH THAT RIGHTEOUS WOMAN [VIZ. SARAH], AND THAT TOO WAS THROUGH A PARTICULAR CAUSE. R. ABBA B. KAHANA SAID IN R. BIRYI'S NAME: AND WHAT A ROUNDABOUT WAY HE SOUGHT IN ORDER TO SPEAK WITH HER, AS IT IS WRITTEN: AND HE SAID: NAY, BUT THOU DIDST LAUGH. BUT IT IS WRITTEN: AND SHE [HAGAR] CALLED THE NAME OF THE LORD THAT SPOKE UNTO HER, ETC. (GEN. 16:13)? SAID R. JOSHUA IN R. NEHEMIAH'S NAME IN R. IDI'S NAME: THAT WAS THROUGH AN ANGEL. BUT IT IS WRITTEN: AND THE LORD SAID UNTO HER – REBEKAH (25:23)? R. LEVI SAID IN THE NAME OF R. HAMA B. R. HANINA: THAT WAS THROUGH AN ANGEL. R. ELEAZAR SAID IN THE NAME OF R. JOSE B. ZIMRA: THAT WAS THROUGH THE MEDIUM OF SHEM.

The main argument in the Midrash thus far is the problem of God speaking directly to a woman. At the outset it was felt that this happened only with Sarah because of her righteousness. However, as the Midrash continues, God also spoke with Hagar and with Rebecca. Some of the Sages claim that there was a difference in the character of these conversations, because only in the case of Sarah was it directly towards God, whereas in the case of Hagar and Rebecca, it was through an angel representing God. The final development is that in the case of Rebecca, the conversation was through Shem, the son of Noah, who lived long enough to reach their generation, and originally, Rebecca had gone for help because of the pain experienced in her childbearing. It was also known that Shem, the son of Noah, was a righteous man who could have been the person to direct Rebecca how to reach God by prayer.

A Special Note: The Midrash that follows this one is listed in some editions of the *Bereshit Rabbah* – *Genesis Rabbah* – as Midrash 21 that concludes Chapter 48 of *Genesis Rabbah*.

⁓

Seed Thoughts

This particular Midrash is concerned with the question of whether the Almighty did or did not converse with women in the Holy Scriptures. There is another concern which affects this reader, which is that according to the text, God intervened in a conversation and/or argument between two people, in this case Abraham and Sarah. Is there another incident in the Bible where God intervened in a human discussion? Whether or not that is so, we should be concerned with why it is happening now in this particular Midrash.

Let me share my interpretation. At the beginning of the Abraham story, we are informed of a serious problem in his household. Sarah was convinced that Ishmael, Abraham's son, was a bad influence over Isaac. Sarah felt that it would be in the best interests of their family, and in particular their son Isaac, for Ishmael and his mother Hagar to return to Hagar's family residence, keeping in mind that she was a princess, the daughter of Pharaoh. Abraham was devastated with this news, since he loved Ishmael, but he received a message from the Lord, which basically said: "Listen to Sarah and do whatever she wants to do." We are not told whether that was a temporary message or valid for all time. We now come back to our Midrash – why did God intervene in the disagreement between Abraham and Sarah? He did so to inform Sarah that He agreed with Abraham, and this was very important, since we now know that He treated both equally. At one stage already quoted, He announced that Sarah was correct this time. Now, he intervened in order to demonstrate that Abraham is correct. God does not play favorites, and that is a lesson that we should learn from.

ויקומו משם האנשים וישקיפו על פני סדום ואברהם הולך עמם, לשלחם, מתלא אמר: אכלית, אשקית, לוית. כך, ואברהם הולך עמם לשלחם:

AND THE MEN ROSE UP FROM THENCE, AND LOOKED OUT TOWARD SODOM; AND ABRAHAM WENT WITH THEM TO BRING THEM ON THE WAY (GEN. 18:16). SO RUNS THE PROVERB: WHEN YOU HAVE GIVEN YOUR GUEST FOOD AND DRINK, ESCORT HIM. HENCE, AND ABRAHAM WENT WITH THEM TO BRING THEM ON THE WAY.

It should be understood that by this time, Abraham realized that one or all of them were angels or some kind of divine character. He did not use this knowledge to suggest that they no longer had to be looked after. On the contrary, he went out of his way to escort them until they departed, at which time he was free of the obligation of *hakhnasat orhim*, which means hospitality to others, hospitality to guests. This is a lesson that all of us are expected to observe.

א וה' אמר המכסה אני מאברהם. רבי יצחק פתח: (משלי י): זכר צדיק לברכה ושם רשעים
ירקב.

1. AND THE LORD SAID: SHALL I HIDE FROM ABRAHAM (GEN. 18:17)? R.
ISAAC COMMENCED HIS DISCOURSE THUS: THE MEMORY OF THE RIGH-
TEOUS SHALL BE FOR A BLESSING (PROV. 10:7).

Although the thinking of the Almighty is expressed in the form of a
question, in the sense of "shall I or shall I not tell Abraham?", the answer
in the text is quite clear – Abraham was told, and was told in great detail.
The Midrash now tries to offer an explanation as to why God should or
should not tell Abraham. This is now what follows.

אמר רבי יצחק: כל מי שהוא מזכיר את הצדיק ואינו מברכו, עובר בעשה. מה טעמיה? זכר
צדיק לברכה. וכל מי שהוא מזכיר את הרשע ואינו מקללו עובר בעשה, מה טעמיה? ושם
רשעים ירקב.

SAID R. ISAAC: IF ONE MAKES MENTION OF A RIGHTEOUS MAN AND
DOES NOT BLESS HIM, HE VIOLATES A POSITIVE COMMAND. WHAT IS
THE PROOF? "THE MEMORY OF THE RIGHTEOUS SHALL BE FOR A BLESS-
ING" (PROV. 10:7). WHILE HE WHO MENTIONS A WICKED MAN AND DOES
NOT CURSE HIM, ALSO VIOLATES A POSITIVE COMMAND. WHAT IS THE
REASON? BUT THE NAME OF THE WICKED SHALL ROT (10:7).

This point of view is quite strict. Let us see how it is explained. Apparently, the moment you take the position that blessing the righteous is a
positive commandment, you are forced to the conclusion that cursing
an evildoer is also a positive commandment. Let us proceed further.

א"ר שמואל בר נחמן: שמותן של רשעים דומים לכלי קורייס. מה כלי קורייס כל מה שאת
משתמש בהם הם עומדים, הנחתם, הם מתרפים. כך שמעת מימיך אדם קורא שם בנו
פרעה, סיסרא, סנחריב? אלא, אברהם, יצחק, יעקב, ראובן, שמעון.

R. SAMUEL B. NAHMAN SAID: THE NAMES OF THE WICKED ARE LIKE
WEAVING IMPLEMENTS – AS LONG AS YOU USE THEM, THEY REMAIN
TAUT; IF YOU LAY THEM ASIDE, THEY SLACKEN. THUS, HAVE YOU EVER
HEARD A MAN CALL HIS SON PHARAOH, SISERA, OR SENNACHERIB? NO:
HE CALLS HIM ABRAHAM, ISAAC, JACOB, REUBEN, OR SIMEON, LEVI, OR
JUDAH.

Apparently, when the right names are chosen, it is as though the weaving machine is being used correctly. When the wrong names are chosen, it is as though the weaving machine is being used incorrectly.

רבי ברכיה ורבי חלבו, משום רבי שמואל בר נחמן ור' יונתן: כשהיה מגיע לפסוק הזה: אשר
הגלה מירושלים עם הגולה וגו', הוה אמר נבוכדנצר שחיק עצמות: ולמה לא הוה אמר כן
בירמיה? אלא שכל נ"נ שכתוב בירמיה חי הוי, ברם הכא, מת הוי. רב כי הוי מטי להמן
בפורים, אמר: ארור המן וארורים בניו, לקיים מה שנאמר: ושם רשעים ירקב. א"ר פנחס:
חרבונה זכור לטוב. א"ר שמואל בר נחמן: מצינו שהקב"ה מזכיר שמן של ישראל ומברכן,
שנאמר (תהלים קטו): ה' זכרנו יברך. ר' הונא בשם רבי אחא אמר: אין לי אלא ס' רבוא. מנין
שכל אחד ואחד מישראל שהקב"ה מזכיר שמו ומברכו? שנאמר: וה' אמר: המכסה אני
מאברהם אשר אני עושה? ואברהם היו יהיה לגוי גדול ועצום, לא היה צריך קרא למימר,
אלא, ויאמר ה' זעקת סדום ועמורה כי רבה! אלא, אמר הקב"ה: הזכרתי את הצדיק ואיני
מברכו? ואברהם היו יהיה לגוי גדול:

R. BEREKIAH, R. HELBO IN THE NAME OF R. SAMUEL B. NAHMAN AND R.
JONATHAN, WHEN THEY CAME TO THE VERSE, WHO HAD BEEN CARRIED
AWAY FROM JERUSALEM WITH THE CAPTIVES . . . WHOM NEBUCHADNEZ-
ZAR . . . HAD CARRIED AWAY (EST. 2:6) WOULD EXCLAIM, "NEBUCHAD-
NEZZAR, ROT HIS BONES!" THEN WHY DID THEY NOT SAY THIS (WHEN
THEY READ HIS NAME) IN THE BOOK OF JEREMIAH? BECAUSE WHENEVER
NEBUCHADNEZZAR OCCURS IN JEREMIAH HE WAS YET ALIVE: WHEREAS
HERE (IN THE BOOK OF ESTHER) HE WAS ALREADY DEAD. RAB [WHEN-
EVER HE MENTIONED HAMAN] WOULD SAY, "CURSED BE HAMAN AND
HIS CHILDREN." R. PHINEHAS SAID: ONE MUST SAY, "HARBONAH, BE HE
REMEMBERED FOR GOOD." R. SAMUEL B. NAHMAN SAID: WE FIND THAT
WHEN THE HOLY ONE, BLESSED BE HE, MENTIONS ISRAEL BY NAME, HE
BLESSES THEM, AS IT SAYS: THE LORD HATH BEEN MINDFUL OF US, HE
WILL BLESS . . . THE HOUSE OF ISRAEL (PS. 115:12). R. HUNA SAID IN THE
NAME OF R. AHA: I KNOW THIS ONLY OF SIX HUNDRED THOUSAND. HOW
DO WE KNOW THAT THE LORD BLESSES EVERY SINGLE ISRAELITE WHEN
HE MENTIONS HIS NAME? BECAUSE IT SAYS: AND THE LORD SAID: SHALL
I HIDE FROM ABRAHAM THAT WHICH I AM DOING; AND ABRAHAM SHALL

SURELY BECOME A GREAT AND MIGHTY NATION. NOW SCRIPTURE NEED MERELY HAVE SAID, AND THE LORD SAID: VERILY, THE CRY OF SODOM AND GOMORRAH IS GREAT (GEN. 18:20), BUT THE HOLY ONE, BLESSED BE HE, SAID: "HAVING MADE MENTION OF THIS RIGHTEOUS MAN, SHALL I NOT BLESS HIM?" HENCE, AND ABRAHAM SHALL SURELY BECOME A GREAT AND MIGHTY NATION.

~

Additional Commentary

What does it mean to curse an evildoer?

The Midrash mentions the fact that when a number of Rabbis read the book of Esther and came to the part where the Children of Israel were forced into exile by the emperor Nebuchadnezzar, they cursed him to the effect of "may his bones rot." The Midrash raises the question, however, that in the Book of Jeremiah, Nebuchadnezzar is mentioned many times without any negative swear words directed to his name. Why is that so? Because in the Book of Esther, Nebuchadnezzar had been dead for many years, whereas in the Book of Jeremiah, he was alive and active. The Rabbis, therefore, refrained from criticizing too severely so that if necessary, he might have the opportunity to repent and move himself from the list of evildoers to the list of righteous ones. There is a beautiful insight in this interpretation. No Jew really wants to engage in terrible swear words against the evildoers. We are happy to add as many blessings as possible to the righteous, but we hesitate when it comes to the evildoers for the very reason given by the Midrash. Let us give them a chance to repent, but when they are dead, these inhibitions no longer apply, and somehow to curse one when he is dead does not seem to be as bad as to curse one when he is still alive. This kind of interpretation should help all of us who deal with some of the questions listed above, where we are commanded to curse the evil in the same way that we are commanded to bless the good. We happily bless the good when they are alive, but we only curse the evil ones when they are gone. (*HaMidrash HaMevo'ar*)

ב כתיב (תהלים כה): סוד ה' ליראיו ובריתו להודיעם. איזהו סוד ה'? זו מילה שלא גלה אותה
מאדם ועד עשרים דור, עד שעמד אברהם ונתנה לו, שנאמר: ואתנה בריתי ביני ובינך.

א"ל הקב"ה: אם תמול, תטול סוד ה'. מה סוד ה'? ס' ששים, ו' ששה, ד' ארבעה, הרי
שבעים. שבעים אני מעמיד ממך, בזכות המילה, שנאמר (דברים י): בשבעים נפש ירדו
אבותיך. מעמיד אני מהן שבעים זקנים, שנא' (במדבר יא): אספה לי שבעים איש מזקני
ישראל. ומעמיד אני מהן משה, שהוא הוגה בתורה בשבעים לשון, שנאמר (דברים א): הואיל
משה באר וגו'. בזכות מי? בזכות המילה, שנאמר: סוד ה' ליראיו.

א"ל הקב"ה לאברהם: דיו לעבד שיהא כרבו. אמר לפניו: ומי ימול אותי? אמר: אתה בעצמך!
מיד, נטל אברהם סכין והיה אוחז בערלתו ובא לחתוך, והיה מתירא שהיה זקן. מה עשה
הקב"ה? שלח ידו ואחז עמו, והיה אברהם חותך, שנ' (נחמיה ט): אתה ה' האלהים אשר בחרת
באברם וגו'. וכרות לו הברית אין כתיב כאן אלא וכרות עמו, מלמד שהיה הקב"ה אוחז בו.

ד"א: סוד ה' ליראיו. בתחלה היה סוד ה' ליראיו, ואח"כ לישרים, ולישרים סודו, ואח"כ
לנביאים (עמוס ג): כי לא יעשה ה' אלהים דבר כי אם גלה סודו אל עבדיו הנביאים. אמר
הקב"ה: אברהם זה, ירא אלהים, שנאמר (בראשית כב): עתה ידעתי כי ירא אלהים אתה.
אברהם זה, ישר מן הישרים, שנא' (שיר א): מישרים אהבוך. אברהם זה, נביא, שנאמר
(בראשית כ): ועתה השב אשת האיש כי נביא הוא, ואיני מגלה לו.

2. IT IS WRITTEN: THE SECRET [E.V. "COUNSEL"] OF THE LORD IS WITH
THEM THAT FEAR HIM AND HIS COVENANT, TO MAKE THEM KNOW IT
(PS. 25:14). NOW WHAT IS THE SECRET OF THE LORD? CIRCUMCISION,
WHICH HE DID NOT REVEAL UNTIL TWENTY GENERATIONS AFTER NOAH,
I.E., UNTIL ABRAHAM AROSE AND HE GAVE IT TO HIM, AS IT SAYS: AND
I WILL GIVE [E.V. "ESTABLISH"] MY COVENANT BETWEEN ME AND THEE
(GEN. 17:7). [RADAL: BETWEEN ME AND THEE IMPLIES THAT IT WAS IN
THE NATURE OF A SECRET WHICH REMAINS AS IT WERE BETWEEN TWO.]

Now God said to him: If thou wilt circumcise thyself, thou wilt receive the secret (*sod*) of the Lord. What is the secret (*sod*) of the Lord?
Samech stands for sixty, *waw* for six, and *daleth* for four [that is the
Hebrew spelling of *sod* – סוד)], making seventy in all. [Thus God said]:
In the merit of circumcision, I will cause seventy people to spring from
thee, as it says: Thy fathers went down into Egypt with threescore and
ten persons (Deut. 10:22). From them I will set up seventy elders, as it

says: Gather unto Me seventy men of the elders of Israel (Num. 11:16). From them, I will raise up Moses, who will study the Torah in seventy languages, as it says: Moses took upon him to clarify [E.V. "expound"] this law (Deut. 1:4). [By "clarify" the Rabbis understood that it was to be intelligible to all peoples; hence it must have been explained in all languages.] For the merit of what was all this? For the merit of circumcision, as it says: The secret of the Lord is with him that fear Him, and His covenant. ["Covenant" was often understood to refer to circumcision.]

The Holy One, blessed be He, said to Abraham: "It is sufficient for a servant to be like his master." [Mah. holds that this is out of place here. Some commentators attempt to fit it in, but not very plausibly.] Then Abraham said to Him: "And who shall circumcise me?" "Thyself," He replied. Abraham took a knife forthwith and held his foreskin and was about to cut it, yet he was afraid, being an old man. What did the Lord do? He put forth His hand and held it with him, whilst Abraham cut. For it says, Thou art the Lord God, who didst choose Abram ... and didst cut [E.V. "madest"] a covenant with him (Neh. 9:7*f.*). Now it is not written: "and didst cut a covenant for him," but "and didst cut a covenant with him," which teaches that the Lord held [the foreskin] with him.

Another interpretation: The secret of the Lord is with them that fear Him. At first the secret of the Lord was with them that feared Him; later it was with the upright, as it is written: But His secret is unto the upright (Prov. 3:32); and finally with the prophets, as it says: For the Lord God will do nothing, but He revealeth His secret unto His servants the prophets (Amos 3:7). Now the Holy One, blessed be He, said: "This Abraham is God-fearing," as it says: Now I know that thou art a God-fearing man (Gen. 22:12); "this Abraham is upright," as it says: The upright love thee (Song 1:4); "this Abraham is a prophet," as it says: Now therefore restore the man's wife, for he is a prophet (Gen. 20:7): Shall I then not reveal it to him? Hence, And the Lord said: Shall I hide from Abraham, etc.

The main text of this Midrash is the verse in Genesis which reads: "Shall I hold back from Abraham that which I intend to do? God has many secrets in connection with the various individuals with whom He had communication. One of his main covenants, which was eventually transformed into the Jewish people, was the covenant that Abraham would become a numerous and powerful nation. The covenant was later dramatically transformed into the covenant of circumcision. *Brit milah*, as the Hebrew language describes circumcision, began with Abraham.

On the one hand, it was a great gift to Abraham, and on the other hand, it expressed his tremendous dedication, as it was indicated by the fact that he arranged for his entire household and military staff to undergo the ritual circumcision with all the personal sacrifice and pain that was involved in this endeavor.

אמר רבי יהושע בן לוי: משל למלך, שנתן אוסיא לאוהבו. לאחר זמן בקש המלך לקוץ מתוכה חמשה אילני סרק. אמר המלך: אילו מן פטריקון שלו הייתי מבקש לא היה מעכב, ומה בכך! ונמלך בו. כך, אמר הקב"ה: כבר נתתי את הארץ מתנה לאברהם, שנאמר: לזרעך נתתי את הארץ. וחמשה כרכים הללו בתוך שלו הם, ואילו מפטריקון שלו הייתי מבקש לא היה מעכב בידי, ומה בכך! ונמלך בו. אר"י בר' סימון: למלך שהיו לו שלשה אוהבים ולא היה עושה דבר חוץ מדעתן. פעם אחת בקש המלך לעשות דבר חוץ מדעתן, נטל את הראשון וטרדו והוציאו חוץ לפלטין, שני חבשו בבית האסורים ונתן ספרגים שלו עליו, שלישי שהיה לו חביב יותר מדאי, אמר: איני עושה דבר חוץ מדעתו. כך, אדם הראשון, ויגרש את האדם. נח, ויסגר ה' בעדו. אברהם, שהיה חביב עליו יותר מדאי, אמר: מה אני עושה דבר חוץ מדעתו? א"ר שמואל בר נחמן: משל למלך שהיה לו סנקתדרים אחד ולא היה עושה דבר חוץ מדעתו. פעם אחת בקש המלך לעשות דבר חוץ מדעתו, אמר המלך: כלום עשיתי אותו סנקתדרים שלי, אלא שלא לעשות דבר חוץ מדעתו? א"ר יודן: אמר הקב"ה: הרי יש שם לוט בן אחיו, ואיני מגלה לו? ורבנן אמרי: כבר קראתי אותו אביהם, שנאמר (בראשית יז): כי אב המון גוים נתתיך. דנים את הבן חוץ מן האב? מתן תורה גליתי לו, גיהנם גליתי לו, דינה של סדום למחר, ואיני מגלה לו?

AND THE LORD SAID: SHALL I HIDE FROM ABRAHAM THAT WHICH I AM DOING, ETC. R. JOSHUA B. LEVI SAID: IT IS LIKE A KING WHO PRESENTED AN ESTATE TO HIS FRIEND AND SUBSEQUENTLY WISHED TO CUT DOWN FIVE NON FRUIT-BEARING TREES FROM IT. SAID THE KING: "HAD I WANTED [TO CUT THEM] DOWN EVEN FROM HIS PATRIMONY, HE WOULD CERTAINLY NOT REFUSE ME: WHAT THEN CAN I LOSE?" AND SO HE CONSULTED HIM ABOUT IT. SIMILARLY, THE HOLY ONE, BLESSED BE HE, SAID: "I HAVE ALREADY MADE A GIFT OF THIS LAND TO ABRAHAM," AS IT SAYS: UNTO THY SEED HAVE I GIVEN THIS LAND (GEN. 15:18). "NOW THESE FIVE TOWNS WERE INDEED IN MY TERRITORY; YET IF I DESIRED THEM EVEN OF HIS ANCESTRAL HERITAGE HE WOULD NOT REFUSE ME: WHAT THEN DOES IT MATTER [IF I ASK HIM]?" AND SO HE CONSULTED HIM. R. JUDAH B. R. SIMON SAID: THIS MAY BE COMPARED TO A KING WHO HAD THREE FRIENDS WITHOUT WHOSE CONSENT HE DID NOTHING. BUT ON ONE OCCASION HE DESIRED TO DO SOMETHING WITHOUT THEIR CONSENT. WHEREUPON HE EVICTED ONE FROM THE PALACE; THE SECOND, HE PUT IN PRISON, AFFIXING HIS SEAL ON IT [THE PRISON DOOR]. BUT AS FOR THE THIRD, WHOM HE LOVED EXCEEDINGLY, HE

SAID, "I CANNOT DO ANYTHING WITHOUT HIS CONSENT." SIMILARLY,
ADAM – SO HE DROVE OUT THE MAN (3:24); NOAH – AND THE LORD
SHUT HIM IN (7:16). BUT AS HE LOVED ABRAHAM SO MUCH HE SAID, "I
WILL DO NOTHING WITHOUT HIS CONSENT." R. SAMUEL B. NAHMAN
SAID: IT MAY BE COMPARED TO A KING WHO HAD AN ADVISER WITHOUT
WHOSE CONSENT HE DID NOTHING. ON ONE OCCASION, HOWEVER, HE
WISHED TO DO SOMETHING WITHOUT HIS CONSENT, WHEREUPON HE
OBSERVED: "SURELY I MADE HIM MY ADVISER FOR NO OTHER REASON
THAN THAT I SHOULD DO NOTHING WITHOUT HIS CONSENT." R. JUDAN
SAID: THE HOLY ONE, BLESSED BE HE, SAID THUS: "DID I DESIGNATE HIM
THE MAN OF MY COUNSEL (ISA. 46:11) FOR ANY OTHER REASON THAN
THAT I SHOULD DO NOTHING WITHOUT HIS CONSENT? WITH THEM
[THE SODOMITES] IS LOT, HIS BROTHER'S SON, YET I AM NOT TO REVEAL
IT TO HIM [ABRAHAM]!" THE RABBIS SAID: "I HAVE ALREADY CALLED
HIM THEIR FATHER, AS IT SAYS: FOR THE FATHER OF A MULTITUDE OF
NATIONS HAVE I MADE THEE (GEN. 17:5): DOES ONE JUDGE THE SON
WITHOUT THE FATHER'S KNOWLEDGE? GEHENNA I HAVE REVEALED TO
HIM: THE GIVING OF THE TORAH I HAVE REVEALED TO HIM; SHALL I
NOT REVEAL TO HIM SODOM'S JUDGMENT!"

The various parables having to do with a king are all meant to indicate
that God did not have to consult either with Abraham or any of his
associates, since He had already given Abraham much of what He had
promised, such as the entire land of Canaan. Since he intended to do
one particular thing without their consent, it did not seem to him to be
taking advantage of his friendship. He knew that if he asked specifically
for what he wanted, everything would be granted to him by his friend.
Why, therefore, should it be a problem as to whether he should inform
his friend about his intentions or not? Transferring these thoughts to
God and Abraham, it would be merely stating the point that it did not
seem to matter whether God spoke to Abraham or not. Therefore, we
shall see some of the arguments which intended to show the Almighty
that He should definitely not consult with Abraham but rather inform
him of what lies ahead.

רבי אחא בשם רבי שמואל בר נחמן, בשם רבי נתן אמר: אפי' הלכות ערובי חצרות היה
אברהם יודע. רבי פנחס בשם רבי שמואל אמר: אפילו שם חדש שהקב"ה עתיד לקרוא
לירושלים, שנא' (ירמיה ג): בעת ההיא יקראו לירושלים כסא ה', היה אברהם יודע. רבי ברכיה
ור' חייא ורבנן דתמן, בשם ר' יהודה: אין יום ויום שאין הקב"ה מחדש הלכה בב"ד של

מעלה, מאי טעמיה? (איוב לו) שמעו שמוע ברגז קלו והגה מפיו יצא, ואין הגה אלא תורה,
שנאמר (יהושע א): והגית בו יומם ולילה, אפי' אותן הלכות היה אברהם יודע:

R. AHA SAID IN R. ALEXANDRI'S NAME, AND R. SAMUEL B. NAHMAN SAID
IN R. NATHAN'S NAME: ABRAHAM KNEW EVEN THE LAWS OF THE *ERUB*
OF COURTYARDS. R. PHINEHAS, R. HELKIAH, AND R. SIMON IN THE NAME
OF R. SAMUEL SAID: ABRAHAM EVEN KNEW THE NEW NAME WHICH THE
HOLY ONE, BLESSED BE HE, WILL ONE DAY GIVE TO JERUSALEM, AS IT
SAYS: AT THAT TIME THEY SHALL CALL JERUSALEM, THE THRONE OF GOD
(JER. 3:17). R. BEREKHIAH, R. HIYYA, AND THE RABBIS OF THAT COUNTRY
[BABYLONIA] IN R. JUDAH'S NAME SAID: NOT A DAY PASSES IN WHICH THE
HOLY ONE, BLESSED BE HE, DOES NOT TEACH A NEW LAW (HALACHAH)
IN THE HEAVENLY COURT. WHAT IS THE PROOF? HEAR ATTENTIVELY THE
NOISE OF HIS VOICE, AND THE MEDITATION THAT GOETH OUT OF HIS
MOUTH (JOB 37:2). NOW "*MEDITATION*" REFERS TO NOUGHT BUT TORAH,
AS IN THE VERSE, BUT THOU SHALT MEDITATE THEREIN DAY AND NIGHT
(JOSH. 1:8). EVEN THOSE LAWS ABRAHAM KNEW.

All of these aforementioned new laws were those which would be
created by the Sanhedrin or some other supreme religious organization
or authority. Despite the fact that they would not appear until many
generations later, they were already given to Abraham so that he would
know of them. All of this indicates that God did not need permission
from Abraham to do the destruction of Sodom and Gomorrah, but that
it was sufficient to inform him. This is precisely what the Holy One,
Blessed be He, did. Abraham was informed.

Seed Thoughts

This text contains a very beautiful episode about which more should be
known. The Holy One, blessed be He, waited twenty generations before
revealing what he called the great secret of the covenant of circumcision
to Abraham. In the conversation recorded in the Midrash, Abraham
asked God: "And who will perform my own personal circumcision?" At
this point, the Holy One, blessed be He, recognized what He surely knew
anyhow, that Abraham feared the procedure of circumcision because of
his old age. He held the knife in his hand, at which point the Holy One,
blessed be He, said to Abraham: "Have no fear; I will assist you, you will
be circumcised, and you will have no pain." We are not informed exactly

how God arranged His procedure with Abraham. The text in Nehemiah does not read in the Hebrew לו וכרות – *vekharot lo*, which means "to arrange the circumcision for him," but rather "with him," for which the Hebrew is עמו וכרות – *vekharot imo*. It does not necessarily mean what the Midrash describes as God appearing as another human being helping Abraham, as one human being would help another. The divine power is unlimited; it would have been enough for God to simply stay to say what should have happened and what would have happened. Or, he could have sent angelic beings to help Abraham. How it was done was not important. What is important is that God intervened in order to help Abraham, which is something we should all understand and appreciate.

PARASHAH FORTY-NINE, *Midrash Three*

ג ואברהם היו יהיה.

3. SEEING THAT ABRAHAM SHALL SURELY BECOME – *HAYOH YIHYEH* (GEN. 18:18).

It does not mean merely that a generation will emerge from Abraham; it also means that he himself will be a great nation.

ר' תנחום בשם רבי ברכיה: בשרו שאין העולם חסר משלשים צדיקים כאברהם.

R. TANHUM SAID IN THE NAME OF R. HUS ELAI IN R. BEREKHIAH'S NAME: HE INFORMED HIM THAT THE WORLD MUST NEVER CONTAIN LESS THAN THIRTY RIGHTEOUS MEN LIKE ABRAHAM.

Note that he does not use the term גדול גוי – *goy gadol* – or great nation, but גדול לגוי – *le-goy gadol,* and the *lamed* stands for "thirty." Therefore, this text could be used as an additional source to remind us that every generation requires thirty righteous people.

רבי יודן ור' אחא בשם רבי אלכסנדרי. מייתי לה מהכא, ואברהם היו יהיה, יו"ד עשר וה' חמש וי"ד עשר וה' חמש:

R. JUDAN AND R. AHA IN R. ALEXANDRI'S NAME DEDUCED IT FROM THIS VERSE: SEEING THAT ABRAHAM SHALL SURELY BECOME – *HAYOH YIHYEH*: YOD IS TEN, *HEH* FIVE, YOD TEN, AND *HEH* FIVE.

In other words, the word יהיה – *yihiyeh* in gematria is ten-five-ten-five.

Seed Thoughts

In this Midrash as well as in the preceding one, the *gematria* is used. *Gematria* is the term used for what some people would call numerology. In this science or study, words of the Hebrew alphabet have a numerical meaning other than their value as an alphabet letter. The numbers are closely related in the alphabet; thus, *aleph* is 1, *bet* is 2, *gimel* is 3, etc. Therefore, in the present Midrash, the word *yihiyeh*, which is translated as "will become," can be rendered in gematria as the sum total of its four letters. The *yod*, which appears twice, has a numerical value of 10, and here the total value is 20. The letter *heh* has a numerical value of 5, but since it appears twice, it adds up to 10. Twenty plus ten equals thirty, and this is used by one of the commentators as additional proof that thirty righteous people are required in every generation. Is gematria a law or part of the halakha? It is not. But some people feel that it strengthens the argument that a numerical value offers a good interpretation of a word. Looking up the word "gematria" in the *Encyclopedia Judaica* would be helpful to any reader.

Parashah Forty-Nine, *Midrash Four*

ד כי ידעתיו למען אשר יצוה.

4. FOR I HAVE KNOWN HIM, TO THE END THAT HE MAY COMMAND HIS
CHILDREN AND HIS HOUSEHOLD AFTER HIM THAT THEY MAY KEEP THE
WAY OF THE LORD, TO DO RIGHTEOUSNESS AND JUSTICE – *ZEDAKAH U-
MISHPAT* (GEN. 18:19).

This is one of the most beautiful statements in the Abraham story.
The lesson is that one of the reasons for the choice of Abraham to begin
the Jewish nation is because God was certain that he would teach his
children the ways of righteousness and justice. Although this statement
is beautiful and meaningful, the Midrash saw it as a problem. What is
meant by righteousness and justice in practical terms? These are terms
that are very fancy and idealistic, but what do they mean? People who
know English literature well would only use terms like "power" and
"glory" as referring to the Divine, not the terms of an ordinary human
blessing. How, then, are we supposed to know the practical meaning of
righteousness and justice? A discussion now emerges where individual
Sages offer their interpretation of the concepts of righteousness and
justice. This is described as *derekh Hashem*, "the way of the Lord."

רבי יודן בשם רבי אלכסנדרי: זו הובריא. ורבנן אמרי: זו ביקור חולים. ר' עזריה בשם ר"י:
מתחלה צדק, לבסוף משפט. הא כיצד? אברהם היה מקבל את העוברים ואת השבים,
משהיו אוכלים ושותים, אמר להם: ברכו! אמרו ליה: מה נאמר? א"ל: אמרו, ברוך אל עולם
שאכלנו משלו. אם מקבל עליו ובריך, הוה אכיל ושתי ואזיל, ואי לא הוה מקבל עליה ובריך,
הוה א"ל, הב מה דעלך! ואמר: מה אית לך עלי הוה? א"ל: חד קסיט דחמר, בעשרה פולרין,
וחד ליטרא דקופר, בי' פולרין, וחד עיגול דריפתא, בי' פולרין. מאן יהיב לך חמרא במדברא?
מאן יהיב לך קופר במדברא? מאן יהיב לך עיגולא במדברא? מן דהוה חמי ההיא עקתא,
דהוה עקי ליה, הוה אמר: ברוך אל עולם שאכלנו משלו, הה"ד: לכתחלה צדקה, ולבסוף
משפט.

R. JUDAN SAID IN R. ALEXANDRI'S NAME: THIS (*ZEDAKAH*) REFERS TO
HIS HOSPITALITY [TO WAYFARERS]. THE RABBIS SAID: IT REFERS TO
VISITING THE SICK. R. AZARIAH SAID IN R. JUDAH'S NAME: FIRST *ZEDA-
KAH* AND THEN *MISHPAT* (JUSTICE): HOW IS THIS TO BE UNDERSTOOD?
ABRAHAM USED TO RECEIVE WAYFARERS. AFTER THEY HAD EATEN AND
DRUNK HE WOULD SAY TO THEM, "NOW RECITE GRACE." "WHAT SHALL

WE SAY?" THEY ASKED. "BLESSED BE THE GOD OF THE UNIVERSE OF
WHOSE BOUNTY WE HAVE PARTAKEN," HE REPLIED. IF ONE CONSENTED
TO RECITE GRACE, HE WOULD [BE ALLOWED TO] EAT, DRINK, AND DE-
PART. BUT IF ONE REFUSED, HE WOULD DEMAND, "PAY ME WHAT YOU
OWE ME." "WHY, WHAT DO I OWE YOU?" HE WOULD REPLY, "ONE *XESTES*
OF WINE COSTS TEN *FOLLERA*, A POUND OF MEAT COSTS TEN *FOLLERA*;
A ROUND OF BREAD COSTS TEN *FOLLERA*. WHO WILL GIVE YOU WINE IN
THE WILDERNESS; WHO WILL GIVE YOU MEAT IN THE WILDERNESS; WHO
WILL GIVE YOU BREAD IN THE WILDERNESS?" SEEING HIMSELF THUS
DRIVEN INTO A CORNER, HE WHO WOULD SAY, "BLESSED BE THE GOD OF
THE UNIVERSE OF WHOSE BOUNTY WE HAVE EATEN." HENCE ZEDAKAH IS
WRITTEN FIRST AND THEN MISHPAT.

This can be translated as doing acts of love, either in one's personal
capacity or with one's financial assets. A second interpretation is *hov-
raya*, which has to do with a custom in ancient times of providing food
and whatever help is necessary on the first day of mourning, which is
the most difficult. The Sages (*Rabanan*) offer their interpretation of
righteousness and justice as referring to *bikur holim*, which is visiting
the sick, which in those days meant more than visiting. It meant helping the sick as a nurse would do these days. As written elsewhere in
the Talmud, visiting the sick and burying the dead are the equivalent
to walking in the ways of God. The Midrash notes that in most cases,
mishpat precedes the word *zedakah* when both are used together. It is as
though first one does what is required, and afterwards you go beyond
the Law, which is the interpretation of righteousness.

At the beginning, Abraham acted towards his guests in a spirit of
righteousness, *zedek*, offering them whatever he had available at no cost.
After that, he tried to introduce the concept of *mishpat*; he would bring
them into the house and while they were eating and drinking, he would
ask them to recite a blessing of Thanksgiving to God. They said to him:
"What should we say?" His answer, in translation, was: "Blessed be the
God of the world of whose bounty we have eaten." By reciting this blessing, everybody would understand that the real host is not Abraham but
the God of Abraham. When they refused to do so, Abraham requested
of that particular individual that he pay for what he ate and drank. That
individual would respond: "What do you have against me that you
charge me in this manner for food which I did not request but which I
was happy to receive?" Abraham would then present him with a list of

expenses which were very high based on the reality that what Abraham offered his guests was not available anywhere in the desert or in any of the deserts of the land of Canaan.

למען הביא ה' על אברהם וגו'.

TO THE END THAT THE LORD MAY BRING UPON ABRAHAM, ETC.

Although Abraham continued to offer *zedakah* before *mishpat*, that is to say, offering his guests food and drink as part of his gift, he tried to get them to understand that God was a real host and that they should acknowledge that fact by the short blessing. If they did not wish to do that, they should then pay for the food which they had eaten and which they felt was justified by Abraham. At the end of that discussion, most of Abraham's guests did agree to recite the brief prayer to the Holy One, blessed be He, and to begin following the way of the Lord to the extent that they could do so.

תני ר"ש בן יוחאי אומר: כל מי שיש לו בן יגע בתורה, כאילו לא מת, שנאמר: למען הביא ה' על אברהם את אשר דבר אליו, לא נאמר, אלא את אשר דבר ה' עליו:

R. SIMEON B. YOHAI TAUGHT: HE WHO LEAVES A SON TOILING IN THE TORAH IS AS THOUGH HE HAD NOT DIED. WHAT IS THE PROOF? – THE VERSE, TO THE END THAT THE LORD MAY BRING UPON ABRAHAM THAT WHICH HE HATH SPOKEN OF HIM. IT DOES NOT SAY SIMPLY, THAT WHICH HE HATH SPOKEN, BUT THAT WHICH THE LORD HATH SPOKEN OF HIM.

Seed Thoughts

Let us examine the beautiful statement by Rabbi Simeon bar Yohai. It does not say that if a father had given his son swimming lessons, the son would have achieved Olympic medals with the swimming lessons. It does not say that if (after the death of his father) he would have continued the swimming lessons with even greater rewards, it does not follow that it would be as though his late father never left this world. But his life has ended in the same manner that the lives of the other people have ended.

What is the difference between the teaching of Torah and the teaching of swimming lessons? Let it be said at the outset that there is no criticism here of swimming lessons or of any other worldly endeavor. The importance here is to establish the meaning of Torah – how it differs radically from any other pastime or life work that takes place in this world.

Swimming lessons are very good to have as part of the effort to live in good health in this world. They are to be commended but not overly so. They are valuable in this world but have no meaningful value in relationship to the World to Come, or in relationship to any manifestation that goes beyond the routine relationship between parents and children.

This is not so in a case of the human soul. The human soul is beyond this life and beyond this world. It is eternal; it connects individuals with each other on the highest level, and connects individuals with God, which goes way beyond this earth and way beyond the World to Come and to the manifestation of the entire universe.

The Torah is the Jewish way of speaking of the human soul. Not only it is by itself probably the single greatest value in this world, but it also creates a relationship and a connection with all human beings, with the greatest of all minds, and with all the manifestations that relate to human beings and God (and with a Jewish person and God).

For the Jewish person, the Torah is the name we give for the highest of our values. It represents the law, by which we mean the religious law, known in Hebrew as halakha, the Jewish way of life. It also represents the highest values of justice and righteousness. The one who teaches Torah in any direction and to any pupil is doing something which makes his life worthwhile. If a father teaches his son Torah, then that teaching is so successful that he continues the study of Torah as an important part of his life. The father has given himself eternal status not only in the life of his son, but in the highest value system that God has created for human beings. To quote the midrashic text itself, it is as though, in this connection, their father has not really died but has continued to live in the Torah that the son is teaching, learning, and living.

PARASHAH FORTY-NINE, *Midrash Five*

ה ויאמר ה' זעקת סדום ועמורה כי רבה. ר' חנינא אמר: רבה והולכת. רבי ברכיה משם רבי
יוחנן: שמענו בדור המבול שנדונו במים, והסדומים שנדונו באש. מנין? ליתן את האמור בזה
בזה, ת"ל: רבה רבה, לגזירה שוה:

5. AND THE LORD SAID: VERILY, THE CRY OF SODOM AND GOMORRAH IS
GREAT (GEN. 18:20). R. HANINA INTERPRETED: IT WAXED EVER GREATER.
R. BEREKIAH SAID IN R. JOHANAN'S NAME: WE KNOW THAT THE GENERA-
TION OF THE FLOOD WAS PUNISHED BY WATER, AND THE SODOMITES BY
FIRE: WHENCE DO WE KNOW TO APPLY WHAT IS STATED HERE TO THE
CASE ABOVE, AND THE REVERSE? BECAUSE "GREAT" IS MENTIONED IN
BOTH PLACES, AFFORDING AN ANALOGY.

This is a very difficult Midrash. When I, as an editor, am confronted
with a difficult text, I try to discover its motivation. Why is the text
needed? What is the goal of its teaching?

It seems to me that in this case, the goal of Midrash 5 is similar to
Midrash 6 that follows. It contains the interpretation that God wanted
to offer the Sodomites an opportunity for repentance and their ultimate
forgiveness. This opportunity was not given to the generation of the
Flood. It is based on a similarity of two texts and their interpretation.
The first text is that of the story of Sodom. In the Flood story, the text is:
"It waxed ever greater." In the Hebrew, the word רבה – *rabbah* – appears
twice; in both cases, it means "great." But it requires more interpretation. The *HaMidrash HaMevo'ar* includes a detailed interpretation of
the grammar that is involved. In the case of "great" (*rabbah*) as used in
Sodom, the letter *resh* is the one to be stressed; in Hebrew, that is known
as *mil-el*, and it means that the stress is on the syllable before the last
syllable. Thus, *rabbah* with the *resh* stressed means that their wickedness
was ongoing but not yet complete. In the case of the Flood story, the
word *rabbah* should stress the *bet* and not the *resh*, and it should be considered *mil-ra*, which means that the stress is on the last syllable. That
would mean that the word *rabbah* should be pronounced with the *bet*
syllable stressed. The interpretation is that in the Flood, the wickedness
was already complete. That is why God offered the generations of Sodom an opportunity for repentance, by saying that He would descend
and see for Himself. How bad the wickedness really was depended on

whether there was a real chance for repentance. In all other respects, both the Flood and Sodom were equally wicked, and both were punished by both water and fire.

⁓

Additional Commentary

Fire and water

This connects to an earlier Midrash (28, 9), describing that the rain of the flood was boiled in Gehenna so that the flood was water and fire. Concerning the punishment of Sodom and Gemorrah it says: God rained upon them sulfur and salt (Genesis 19:24) so you have the fire of Sodom and water (rain) hinted to as well. (Mirkin)

PARASHAH FORTY-NINE, *Midrash Six*

ו ארדה נא. תני, ר"ש בן יוחאי: זו אחת מעשר ירידות האמורות בתורה.

6. I WILL GO DOWN NOW (GEN. 18:21). R. SIMEON B. YOHAI TAUGHT: THIS IS ONE OF THE TEN DESCENTS MENTIONED IN THE TORAH.

These expressions that God descended were prompted by something that happened at the time of this saying, which God wanted the community to take much more seriously than it did.

א"ר אבא בר כהנא: מלמד שפתח להם המקום פתח של תשובה, שנאמר: ארדה נא ואראה הכצעקתה הבאה אלי עשו כלה.

R. ABBA B. KAHANA SAID: THIS TEACHES THAT THE HOLY ONE, BLESSED BE HE, GAVE THEM THE OPPORTUNITY OF REPENTING. FOR IT SAYS, I WILL GO DOWN NOW, AND SEE WHETHER THEY HAVE DONE ACCORDING TO THE CRY OF IT, THEN IT IS AN END.

We understand, of course, that God knows everything, and He certainly knew what was going on in Sodom and Gomorrah. Although the words give the impression that God expected to learn something, in actual fact, His entire desire was to offer the people of Sodom an opportunity for repentance.

כלייה הן חייבין, ואם לא אדעה, אודיע בהן מדת הדין בעולם.

THEY MUST BE COMPLETELY DESTROYED; AND IF NOT, I WILL KNOW,
I.E., I WILL TEACH THEM THAT THE ATTRIBUTE OF JUSTICE EXISTS IN
THE WORLD.

As of the moment, they deserved destruction. But if they show any sign of repentance, I will know how to handle them and will exercise the principles of justice as we understand them.

א"ר לוי: אפי' אני מבקש לשתוק, דינה של ריבה איני מניח אותי לשתוק. מעשה בשתי
נערות שירדו לשתות ולמלאות מים. אמרה אחת לחברתה: למה פניך חולניות? אמרה לה:
כלו מזונותיה, וכבר היא נטויה למות. מה עשתה? מלאה את הכד קמח, והחליפו נטלה זו,
מה שביד זו. וכיון שהרגישו בה, נטלו ושרפו אותה. אמר הקב"ה: אפי' אני מבקש לשתוק,
דינה של נערה אינו מניח אותי לשתוק!

R. LEVI SAID: [GOD SAID]: "EVEN IF I WISHED TO KEEP SILENT, JUSTICE
FOR A CERTAIN MAIDEN (*RIBAH*) DOES NOT PERMIT ME TO KEEP SILENT."
FOR IT ONCE HAPPENED THAT TWO DAMSELS WENT DOWN TO DRAW
WATER FROM A WELL. SAID ONE TO THE OTHER, "WHY ARE YOU SO
PALE?" "WE HAVE NO MORE FOOD LEFT AND ARE READY TO DIE," RE-
PLIED SHE. WHAT DID SHE DO? SHE FILLED HER PITCHER WITH FLOUR
AND THEY EXCHANGED [THEIR PITCHERS], EACH TAKING THE OTHER'S.
WHEN THEY [THE SODOMITES] DISCOVERED THIS, THEY TOOK AND
BURNT HER. [AN ANCIENT MIDRASHIC TRADITION (IN PIRKEI DE-RABBI
ELIEZER 25) ADDS THE FOLLOWING PRAYER THAT THE GIRL SAID: "LORD
OF THE UNIVERSE, PLEASE PRESENT MY CASE IN THE DIVINE COURT,
AND LET THE LAW APPLY TO THE PEOPLE OF SODOM WHO HAVE DONE
THIS TERRIBLE THING. THIS CRY WENT TO HEAVEN AND REACHED THE
THRONE OF GLORY."] SAID THE HOLY ONE, BLESSED BE HE: "EVEN IF I
DESIRED TO BE SILENT, JUSTICE FOR THAT MAIDEN DOES NOT PERMIT
ME TO KEEP SILENT."

The fact that God said the story of the two maidens is what prevents Him from being silent in terms of the punishment of Sodom. We have to understand that God suffers every time this kind of story takes place, as it does innumerable times in the world. But it is included by Him, so that the people will know this story and accept the fact that Sodom deserves the maximum type of punishment.

הה"ד: הכצעקתה, הכצעקתם, אינו אומר, אלא הכצעקתה.

HENCE IT DOES NOT SAY, WHETHER THEY HAVE DONE ACCORDING TO
THEIR CRY; BUT ACCORDING TO HER CRY – THE CRY OF THAT MAIDEN.

The fact that the Hebrew expression for the word "cry" is appropriately in the feminine as it relates to the city of Sodom (*ir* – "city" is
feminine), it can also be interpreted as relating to the story of the two
girls which the Midrash just included. It is not only the cry of Sodom in
general, but also the particular cry of the wickedness done to the young
maidens that horrified everyone, including the Almighty.

ואיזו? זו דינה של נערה. א"ר ירמיה בן אלעזר: עיקר שלוותה של סדום לא היתה אלא
חמשים ושתים שנה, ומהם עשרים וחמש שנה היה הקב"ה מרעיש עליהם הרים ומביא
עליהם זוועות, כדי שיעשו תשובה, ולא עשו, הה"ד (איוב ט): המעתיק הרים ולא ידעו ובסוף
אשר הפכם באפו:

WHAT IS THE JUSTICE OF THE MAIDEN? R. JEREMIAH B. ELEAZAR SAID:
THE REAL PROSPERITY OF SODOM LASTED FIFTY-TWO YEARS ONLY, AND
FOR TWENTY-FIVE OF THESE THE HOLY ONE, BLESSED BE HE, MADE
THE MOUNTAINS TO TREMBLE AND BROUGHT TERRORS UPON THEM IN
ORDER THAT THEY MIGHT REFORM, YET THEY DID NOT. HENCE IT IS
WRITTEN: WHO REMOVETH THE MOUNTAINS, AND THEY KNOW IT NOT,
WHEN HE OVERTURNETH THEM IN HIS ANGER (JOB 9:5).

Rabbi Jeremiah added the following thought: When the Almighty
added the phrase ארדה נא – *erda na*, "I will descend," the word *na* is spelled
in Hebrew as נא, which in gematria is 50 (the *nun*) and 1 (the *aleph*). The
total is 51. Whereas the age of the city of Sodom is sometimes based on
the difference of Abraham at the age of 48, when the city started, to his
age of 99, when it was destroyed. The total here is 52, but the last year
was incomplete, and therefore, we speak of the age of Sodom as 51 years.
This adds an interesting touch to the words of the Almighty *erda na*,
meaning: "I will descend on the fifty-first year of Sodom."

PARASHAH FORTY-NINE, *Midrash Seven*

ז ויפנו משם האנשים. הדא אמרת: אין עורף למלאכים.

7. AND THE MEN TURNED (*WAYYIFENU*) FROM THENCE (GEN. 18:22). THIS
PROVES THAT ANGELS HAVE NO BACK.

The text seems to give the impression that the angels returned along
the way they had come without turning around. This is what the text
seems to imply when they suggest that angels have no back.

וילכו סדומה ואברהם עודנו עומד לפני ה'.

AND THEY WENT TOWARD SODOM; BUT ABRAHAM STOOD YET BEFORE
THE LORD.

Abraham did not follow the visitors and/or angels; he stayed behind
in deep thought.

א"ר סימון: תיקון סופרים הוא זה, שהשכינה היתה ממתנת לאברהם:

R. SIMON SAID: THIS IS AN EMENDATION OF THE SOFERIM, FOR THE
SHECHINAH WAS ACTUALLY WAITING FOR ABRAHAM.

The Midrash has included a very astute teaching by Rabbi Simon.
Abraham, of course, was in great thoughtfulness, thinking more about
the Holy One, blessed be He, than anyone else, and worrying about
what His decision should be. In actual fact, says Rabbi Simon, the Holy
One, blessed be He, was watching Abraham, since His decisions would
affect Abraham as a leader more than anyone else. The Almighty had
many reasons to watch Abraham and wait for him to leave, but it was not
written this way because it might give the impression that Abraham, in
this instance, was as important as God, which of course was untrue. This
change in emphasis is what is known as *Tikkun Soferim*, meaning that
the Scribes had a right to influence the meaning of the text.

—

Seed Thoughts

The line in the biblical text that Abraham stayed behind was something
I remember from my earliest years that impressed me in Abraham's

story. He stayed behind – why? Because too many things have been happening to him in too rapid a fashion. He was searching for a measure of control over the events that were happening to him. One of the commentators added an insight that Abraham was worried about the future of Sodom, particularly in light of the fact that his nephew, Lot, lived there. He remained behind, thoughtful and worried, and hopeful that everything would turn out all right.

PARASHAH FORTY-NINE, *Midrash Eight*

ח ויגש אברהם ויאמר וגו'. ר"י ורבי נחמיה ורבנן. רי"א: הגשה למלחמה (ד"ה א יט): ויגש יואב
והעם אשר עמו לפני ארם למלחמה.
8. AND ABRAHAM DREW NEAR, AND SAID, ETC. (GEN. 18:23). R. JUDAH,
R. NEHEMIAH, AND THE RABBIS EACH COMMENTED. R. JUDAH SAID: HE
DREW NEAR FOR BATTLE, AS IT SAYS: SO JOAB AND THE PEOPLE THAT
WERE WITH HIM DREW NIGH UNTO BATTLE, ETC. (II SAM. 10:13).

Although the proof text that features Joab deals with an actual battle-field situation, it should be understood in the Midrash that the war, in Abraham's mind, was a war of arguments, discussion, and a sharing of views.

ר' נחמיה אמר: הגשה לפיוס, היך מד"א: (יהושע יד): ויגשו בני יהודה אל יהושע.
R. NEHEMIAH SAID: HE DREW NEAR FOR CONCILIATION, AS IN THE
VERSE, THEN THE CHILDREN OF JUDAH DREW NIGH UNTO JOSHUA
(JOSH. 14:6) – TO EFFECT A RECONCILIATION.

It could also include a search for a peaceful solution to whatever the confrontation might be.

רבנן אמרי: הגשה לתפלה, המד"א: (מלכים א יח): ויהי כעלות המנחה ויגש אליהו הנביא,
ויאמר ה' אלהי אברהם יצחק וישראל, היום יודע כי אתה אלהים בישראל וגו'. ר"א: פשט
לה, אם למלחמה אני בא, אם לפיוס, אני בא, אם לתפלה, אני בא.
THE RABBIS SAID: HE DREW NIGH FOR PRAYER, AS IT SAYS: AND IT CAME
TO PASS AT THE TIME OF THE OFFERING OF THE EVENING OFFERING,
THAT ELIJAH THE PROPHET CAME NEAR, AND SAID: O LORD, THE GOD

OF ABRAHAM, OF ISAAC, AND OF ISRAEL, LET IT BE KNOWN THIS DAY
THAT THOU ART GOD IN ISRAEL, ETC. (I KINGS 18:36). R. ELAZAR SAID:
INTERPRET IT THUS: I COME, WHETHER IT BE FOR BATTLE, CONCILIA-
TION, OR PRAYER.

It can be seen from Rabbi Elazar's view that he has eliminated just
about every possibility of argument and disagreement, since all interpretations of the expression "drawing near" are acceptable.

רבי פנחס ורבי לוי ורבי יוחנן: זה שהוא עובר לפני התיבה, אין אומרים לו בוא ועשה, בוא
קרב, בוא ועשה קרבן של ציבור, אלא בוא וקרב להתפלל. א"ר תנחומא: למה התקינו
ברכות חמש עשרה עד שומע תפלה? כנגד ט"ו אזכרות שבהבו לה' בני אלים, עד ה' למבול
ישב, שהוא מכלה את הפורעניות מלבא לעולם.

R. PHINEHAS, R. LEVI, AND R. JOHANAN, IN THE NAME OF MENAHEM
OF GALLIA, SAID: WHEN ONE PASSES BEFORE THE ARK, WE DO NOT SAY
TO HIM, "COME AND DO," BUT "COME AND DRAW NEAR", WHICH MEANS,
COME AND WAGE WAR FOR US, COME AND OFFER THE PUBLIC SACRIFICE
[I.E., PRAY]. R. TANHUMA SAID: WHY DID THEY INSTITUTE THAT THE
FIFTEENTH BENEDICTION SHOULD BE "HE WHO HEARETH PRAYER"? –
TO CORRESPOND TO THE DIVINE NAME WHICH OCCURS FIFTEEN TIMES
IN THE PSALM, ASCRIBE UNTO THE LORD, O YE SONS OF MIGHT ... AS
FAR AS THE LORD SAT ENTHRONED AT THE FLOOD (PS. 29), WHICH RE-
STRAINS PUNISHMENT FROM VISITING THE WORLD.

רב הונא בשם רבי אחא: האף תספה, אתה גודר את האף, והאף לא יגדרך. א"ר יהושע בר
נחמיה: אף שאתה מביא לעולמך, אתה מכלה בו את הצדיקים ואת הרשעים, ולא דייך
שאתה תולה הרשעים בשביל הצדיקים, אלא שאתה מכלה את הצדיקים עם הרשעים.
רבי ורבי יונתן. רבי אומר: ב"ו חימה כובשתו, אבל הקב"ה כובש את החימה, שנאמר (נחום
א): נוקם ה' ובעל חימה. רבי יונתן אמר: ב"ו קנאה כובשתו, אבל הקב"ה כובש את הקנאה,
שנאמר: אל קנוא ונוקם ה'.

[WILT THOU INDEED SWEEP AWAY THE RIGHTEOUS WITH THE WICKED?]
R. HUNA SAID IN R. AHA'S NAME: WILT THOU INDEED (HA-AF) SWEEP
AWAY (TISPEH): THOU CONFINEST ANGER, BUT ANGER CANNOT CON-
FINE THEE.

R. Joshua b. Nehemiah interpreted it: The anger (af) which Thou
bringest upon Thy world, wouldst Thou destroy therewith the righteous
and the wicked! And not enough that Thou dost not suspend judgment

of the wicked for the sake of the righteous, but Thou wouldst even destroy the righteous with the wicked!

Rabbi and R. Jonathan each commented. Rabbi said: [Abraham pleaded:] A human being is mastered by his anger, but the Holy One, blessed be He, masters anger, as it says: The Lord avengeth and mastereth wrath (Nahum 1:2). R. Jonathan said: A human being is mastered by his jealousy, but the Holy One, blessed be He, masters His jealousy, as it says: The Lord is God [i.e., master] over jealousy and vengeance (1:2).

The reader should be alerted to the fact that in the material that we are now discussing, and in the main statement, God is asked by Abraham whether He seems to be planning that the righteous suffer with the wicked. The problem is that the Hebrew word אף – *af* – has more than one meaning. The question which Abraham put to God, which begins with *ha-af*, meaning "wilt Thou," could have been replaced with other expressions that have the same meaning in the form of a question, such as the word *ha-gam*, which often is the way a question begins. The problem is that the word *af* can also be used as a noun and its meaning is "anger." The question now takes many forms as to whether God's anger will be a factor in affecting His judgment. Much of the Midrash, from this point on, will deal with this question. In the case of human beings, their anger is sometimes uncontrollable and can lead to results unforeseen, usually very negative. In the case of God, however, even when He sometimes reverts to anger because of the evildoings of man, that anger is always controllable and there can be an assurance that the word *af*, in terms of its meaning of anger, will not be the motivation that determines God's decision.

רבי שמלאי שאל לרבי יונתן: מאי דכתיב (משלי יג): ויש נספה בלא משפט?

R. SIMLAI ASKED R. JONATHAN: WHAT IS MEANT BY THE VERSE, BUT THERE IS THAT IS SWEPT AWAY WITHOUT JUDGMENT (PROV. 13:23)?'

The Midrash now moves to that part of Abraham's question dealing with the Judge of all the earth, Who should certainly do justice. The material, which is self-explanatory, deals with some of the problems connected with justice, which sometimes becomes injustice and often very accidentally.

אמר לו: בלא משפט מקומו. מעשה באחד שנשתלח לגבות בני טבריא ובני ציפורי. כשהיה גובה בטבריא, ראה אחד מציפורי עמד ותפשו. א"ל: מציפורי אני. א"ל: יש בידי כתבים

מציפורי לגבותה, ולא הספיק לגבות בני טבריא, עד שבאת רווחה לציפורי, ונמצא נספה
בלא משפט מקומו. ר' לוי אמר: לדובה שהיתה משכלת כחיה, ולא מצאת לשכל בחיה,
ושכלה בבניה. רבי סימון אמר: למגל כוסחת כובין ולא שלם לה, שושנה ולא שלם לה:

"IT MEANS WITHOUT JUDGMENT ON HIS OWN TOWN," HE ANSWERED.
THUS IT ONCE HAPPENED THAT A MAN WAS SENT TO COLLECT [A FINE]
FROM THE CITIZENS OF TIBERIAS AND SEPPHORIS. WHILST HE WAS
THUS COLLECTING IN TIBERIAS, HE SAW A CITIZEN OF SEPPHORIS,
WHEREUPON HE AROSE AND SEIZED HIM. "I BELONG TO SEPPHORIS,"
HE PROTESTED. "I HAVE WARRANTS INSTRUCTING ME TO COLLECT IN
SEPPHORIS TOO," HE REPLIED; BUT BEFORE HE FINISHED COLLECTING
IN TIBERIAS, REMISSION WAS GRANTED TO SEPPHORIS, AND THUS THIS
MAN WAS "GATHERED IN" WITHOUT THE JUDGMENT OF HIS OWN TOWN.
R. LEVI AND R. SIMON COMMENTED. R. LEVI SAID: [ABRAHAM PLEADED:
"IS THINE ANGER] LIKE A SHE-BEAR RAVAGING AMONG ANIMALS WHICH,
IF IT DOES NOT FIND ANOTHER BEAST TO DESTROY, DESTROYS ITS OWN
YOUNG!" R. SIMON SAID: [IS THINE ANGER] LIKE A SCYTHE WHICH CUTS
DOWN THORNS, BUT WHEN IT FINDS [NO MORE] CUTS DOWN ROSES!

Seed Thoughts I

This Midrash has some fascinating information about the fifteenth
benediction of the *Amidah*. The reason why it is the fifteenth prayer is
based on Psalm 29, where the expression הבו – *havu*, meaning "let us,"
in the sense that "let us do the following" appears fifteen times. It is also
significant that in the entire Psalm 29, the name of God appears eighteen
times, as do the various forms of remembrance, known in Hebrew as
azkarot. This number makes it somewhat fitting that this Psalm should
be associated with the *Amidah*, which consists of eighteen benedictions.
Why does the prayer of "He who hears prayer," or *Shome'a Tefillah*, end
with the fifteenth declaration? Because that is followed by the expression "as far as the Lord sat enthroned at the Flood." What this reminds
us is that after the Flood, God promised that the world would not be
destroyed again as a punishment to man. Therefore, this prayer has
become a universal declaration of peace, which is why its place in the
Amidah is so important. The eighteenth benediction in the *Amidah* has
to do with *shalom*, but when we read it, the content applies to the peace

of the Jewish people. Not so with *Shome'a Tefillah*, which is the clarion call of our daily prayers for the universal peace of the world.

⁓

Seed Thoughts II

The Sages who gathered in Yavneh added a nineteenth benediction, which in Hebrew is referred to as *Malshinim*, to condemn those members of the Children of Israel who betrayed their people to the Romans who destroyed the Temple. That prayer, however, as we can see, was introduced later than *Shome'a Tefillah*.

⁓

Additional Commentary

Communal prayer

Rabbi Phinehas, Rabbi Levi, and Rabbi Johanan said: The person who is about to lead prayers as *shaliah tzibur* (the representative of prayer to the congregation) should not be invited with the expression, "do what you have to do to lead the service." He should be invited as per the Hebrew expression בא קרב – *bo krav*, meaning "come and do what you are supposed to do," which basically means "do the offering of the congregation." In other words, the leader is acting, although in a distant way, as though he were equivalent to the *kohen* (the priest who presides over the offerings of the congregation). He has to be made sensitive to this role, and the same applies to the members of the congregation. If this were accepted, the entire atmosphere of the prayer service – indeed, all the prayer services which include a *minyan* (the required quorum) – would be transformed into a most important spiritual asset. If this approach were accepted, congregations would have to adopt some additional educational responsibilities. The leader of the service would have to understand the purpose of his leadership, would have to understand the prayers in a more significant way, and even his voice would have to be helped so that the words would be pronounced with accuracy and with the correct intonation.

PARASHAH FORTY-NINE, *Midrash Nine*

ט חללה לך. א"ר יודן חלילה הוא לך, ברייה הוא לך.

9. THAT BE FAR FROM THEE – *HALILAH LEKHA* – [TO DO AFTER THIS MANNER, TO SLAY THE RIGHTEOUS WITH THE WICKED; THAT BE FAR FROM THEE] (GEN. 18:25). R. JUDAN INTERPRETED: IT IS A PROFANATION (*HALILAH*) FOR THEE, IT IS ALIEN TO THY NATURE.

The point to note here is that in the word חללה – *halila*, the *yod* has been left out. That happens from time to time in many parts of the oral tradition when it wants to say something in the form of a shortcut. The letter *yod* often stands for that which is a symbol of Judaism. When it is left out, it implies that the noun or verb is stating something which could be looked upon very critically. Since the text wishes to state that the action of the Almighty appears to be out of line with Jewish thought, it is said by the texts simply by eliminating the *yod*, and a further explanation is not really necessary.

א"ר אחא: חלילה, חלילה שתי פעמים, חלול שם שמים יש בדבר. א"ר אבא: מעשות דבר אין כתיב כאן אלא מעשות כדבר, לא היא ולא דכוותה, ולא דפחותה מינה. א"ר לוי: שני בני אדם אמרו דבר אחד, אברהם ואיוב. אברהם: חלילה לך מעשות כדבר הזה, להמית צדיק עם רשע. איוב אמר (איוב ט): אחת היא, על כן אמרתי תם ורשע הוא מכלה. אברהם, נטל עליה שכר. איוב, נענש עליה. אברהם אמר: בישולה. איוב אמר: פגה אחת היא, על כן אמרתי תם ורשע הוא מכלה.

R. AHA SAID: HALILAH IS WRITTEN TWICE, IMPLYING: SUCH ACTION WOULD PROFANE (*HILAL*) THE DIVINE NAME. R. ABBA SAID: NOT "TO DO THIS" IS WRITTEN HERE, BUT TO DO AFTER THIS MANNER: NEITHER THIS NOR ANYTHING LIKE IT NOR ANYTHING EVEN OF A LESSER NATURE. R. LEVI SAID: TWO MEN SAID THE SAME THING, VIZ. ABRAHAM AND JOB. ABRAHAM: THAT BE FAR FROM THEE, TO DO AFTER THIS MANNER, TO SLAY THE RIGHTEOUS WITH THE WICKED. JOB: IT IS ALL ONE – THERE-FORE I SAY: HE DESTROYETH THE INNOCENT AND THE WICKED (JOB 9:22). YET ABRAHAM WAS REWARDED FOR IT, WHILE JOB WAS PUNISHED FOR IT! THE REASON IS BECAUSE ABRAHAM SAID IT IN CONFIRMATION, WHILE JOB SAID IT IN CAVIL: IT IS ALL ONE!

Abraham was rewarded because his views and/or his criticism came after much thinking, much meditation, and much intellectual effort. Job was punished because his views were expressed in a fit of anger without allowing enough time for him to reflect on what he was saying and his consequences. Alternatively, as some of the commentators put it, Abraham's views were like a fruit completely ripened, whereas Job's views were like a fruit that fell from a tree long before it ripened. As for Abraham's reward, there was the fact that the Almighty continued to reach out to him and look upon him as a superior type of human being. Job was punished with the severe torture and suffering we read about in his scriptural book. That, however, was in This World. In the World to Come, Job will be restored to the highest possible honor.

ר' חייא בר אבא אמר: עירבובי שאילות יש כאן. אברהם אמר: חלילה לך מעשות כדבר הזה, להמית צדיק עם רשע. והקב"ה אומר: והיה כצדיק כרשע, יתלה לרשעים בשביל צדיקים, הלואי צדיקים דהא אינם, אלא צדיקים ניבלי.

R. HIYYA B. ABBA SAID: WE HAVE HERE A MERGING OF ANSWERS. THIS ABRAHAM SAID: THAT BE FAR FROM THEE, TO WHICH GOD REPLIED: SO SHALL [THE WICKED] BE AS THE RIGHTEOUS! THOU DESIREST THAT JUDGMENT OF THE WICKED SHOULD BE SUSPENDED FOR THE SAKE OF THE RIGHTEOUS; BUT ARE THEY RIGHTEOUS? SURELY THEY ARE BUT COUNTERFEIT RIGHTEOUS.

The reverence here which is treated as a part of God's views makes the point that the righteous in Sodom were not truly righteous. One of the references of this fact is the symbol that we have already learned, that in the word צדיקם - tzaddikim, the last *yod* has been eliminated. So, you say you are helping the evildoers by referring to them as almost righteous and you are affecting the righteous by asserting that they are not far enough away from the evildoers. All this is said to us by the absence of the *yod*, the Judaic symbol, from the Hebrew word for the righteous, which is tzaddikim.

דאמר רבי יוחנן: כל צדיקים שנאמרו בסדום, צדיקם כתיב, היא דעתיה דר' יוחנן. דא"ר יוחנן (יהושע ט): ויאמרו אלינו זקינינו וכל יושבי ארצנו, זקננו כתיב, זקני אשמה, היינו סבא דבהתא.

FOR R. JOHANAN SAID: WHEREVER *ZADDIKIM* (RIGHTEOUS) OCCURS IN CONNECTION WITH SODOM, IT IS SPELLED DEFECTIVELY. THAT COR-RESPONDS WITH R. JOHANAN'S VIEW, FOR R. JOHANAN SAID: AND OUR ELDERS (*ZEKENENU*) AND ALL THE INHABITANTS OF OUR COUNTRY

SPOKE TO US (JOSH. 9:11): IT IS SPELLED *ZEKENENU* [WITH THE TWO
EXTRA *YODS*], INTIMATING THAT THEY WERE ELDERS IN WRONGDOING,
ELDERS IN WICKEDNESS.

Up to this point, the Midrash has brought for us two examples of
how the absence of the letter *yod* is meant to describe a lessening or
an absence of Jewish religious content in the word or teaching that is
discussed. Here in our present discussion, the insertion of the letter *yod*
into the word זקינינו – *zekenenu* – is meant to Judaize the concept and
guarantee the Jewish leadership of their community, which was completely false. In other words, the letter *yod* is used in both directions;
sometimes to add to the Jewish content, and most of the time to erase
the Jewish content.

א"ר יהושע בן לוי: אמר אברהם: צרף מעשי ויעלו למנין חמשים. א"ר יהודה בר' סימון: לא
את הוא צדיקו של עולם, צרף עצמך עמהם ויעלו למנין חמשים. אר"י בר' סימון: כך אמר
ליה אברהם: מלך ב"ו תולין לו אנקליטון מדוכוס לאפרכוס. מאפרכוס לאסטרליטוס, ואת
בשביל שאין לך מי שיתלה לך אנקליטון, לא תעשה משפט? אר"י בר' סימון: כשבקשת
לדון את עולמך, מסרת אותו ביד שנים, רומוס ורומילוס, שאם בקש אחד מהם לעשות
דבר, חבירו מעכב על ידו, ואת בשביל שאין לך מי שיעכב על ידך, לא תעשה משפט?

R. JOSHUA B. LEVI SAID: [ABRAHAM PLEADED,] "COMBINE THEIR GOOD
DEEDS, AND SO THEY WILL AMOUNT TO FIFTY." R. JUDAH B. R. SIMON
SAID: [ABRAHAM PLEADED:] "ART THOU NOT THE RIGHTEOUS ONE
OF THE UNIVERSE? COMBINE THYSELF WITH THEM AND THEY WILL
AMOUNT TO FIFTY." R. JUDAH B. R. SIMON SAID: [ABRAHAM PLEADED
THUS:] "EVEN IN THE CASE OF A HUMAN JUDGE, AN APPEAL CAN BE
MADE FROM THE COMMANDER TO THE PREFECT AND FROM THE PRE-
FECT TO THE GOVERNOR; BUT THOU, BECAUSE NO APPEAL CAN BE MADE
FROM THY JUDGMENT, WILT THOU NOT DO JUSTLY?" R. JUDAH SAID
FURTHER: "WHEN THOU DESIREDST TO JUDGE THY WORLD, THOU DIDST
ENTRUST IT TO TWO, ROMULUS AND REMUS," SO THAT IF ONE WISHED TO
DO SOMETHING THE OTHER COULD VETO HIM; WHILE THOU, BECAUSE
THERE IS NONE TO VETO THEE, WILT THOU NOT DO JUSTLY?

The various views that the Rabbis mentioned required the leadership
of at least two people who correlate their behavior and their leadership
with each other. The best example in the political world is the leadership
of the brothers (Romulus and Remus) who created Roman civilization
and transformed it into the world's greatest power of that generation.

אמר ר' אדא: נשבעת שאין אתה מביא מבול לעולם. מה את מערים על השבועה? מבול
של מים אין אתה מביא, מבול של אש את מביא, אם כן לא יצאת ידי שבועה. אמר רבי
לוי: השופט כל הארץ לא יעשה משפט? אם עולם אתה מבקש, אין דין. ואם דין אתה
מבקש, לית עולם. את תפיס חבלא בתרין ראשין, בעי עלמא ובעי דינא, אם לית את מוותר
ציבחר, לית עלמא יכיל קאים. א"ל הקב"ה: אברהם (תהלים מה): אהבת צדק ותשנא רשע.
אהבת לצדק את בריותי ותשנא רשע, מאנת לחייבן, ע"כ משחך אלהים אלהיך, שמן ששון
מחבריך. מהו מחבריך? מנח ועד אצלך י' דורות, ומכלם לא דברתי עם אחד מהם, אלא
עמך, ויאמר ה' אל אברם לך לך:

R. ADA SAID: [ABRAHAM PLEADED:] "THOU HAST SWORN NOT TO BRING
A DELUGE UPON THE WORLD. WOULDST THOU EVADE THINE OATH!
NOT A DELUGE OF WATER WILT THOU BRING BUT A DELUGE OF FIRE?
THEN THOU HAST NOT ACTED ACCORDING TO THINE OATH." R. LEVI
COMMENTED: SHALL NOT THE JUDGE OF ALL THE EARTH DO JUSTLY? IF
THOU DESIREST THE WORLD TO ENDURE, THERE CAN BE NO ABSOLUTELY
STRICT JUDGMENT, WHILE IF THOU DESIREST ABSOLUTELY STRICT
JUDGMENT, THE WORLD CANNOT ENDURE, YET THOU WOULDST HOLD
THE CORD BY BOTH ENDS, DESIRING BOTH THE WORLD AND ABSOLUTE
JUDGMENT! UNLESS THOU FOREGOEST A LITTLE, THE WORLD CANNOT
ENDURE. SAID THE HOLY ONE, BLESSED BE HE, TO ABRAHAM: "THOU
HAST LOVED RIGHTEOUSNESS (PS. 45:8): THOU HAST LOVED TO JUSTIFY
MY CREATURES; AND HATED WICKEDNESS: THOU HAST REFUSED TO
CONDEMN THEM. THEREFORE GOD, THY GOD, HATH ANOINTED THEE
WITH THE OIL OF GLADNESS ABOVE THY FELLOWS (45:8). FROM NOAH
TO THEE WERE TEN GENERATIONS, AND OUT OF ALL OF THEM I REMEM-
BERED BUT THEE ALONE."

T he Midrash is making a strong point at this time. We have to be aware
of extreme positions. If everything in this world has to follow an ethical
and spiritual law, the world would not be able to survive. Human beings
would not be able to accept the perfection of behavior that would be
required. If, on the other hand, we allowed human beings on their own
to create their own forms of living, then that which we call justice would
not be able to survive. It is too much to expect an ordinary world combined with perfect justice to be possible, and we have to be prepared for
the compromises necessary for the world and for humanity to survive.

Seed Thoughts

The purpose of these remarks is to record a series of reflections. I am bothered by several things that came to my attention as a result of this Midrash. Why are Remus and Romulus, the two brothers who were among the founders of the Roman Empire, mentioned in this Midrash? Could it be that despite the terrible persecution of the Jews by the Romans, highlighted by the destruction of the Second Temple, certain Jewish leaders secretly admired the Roman system – a system which started out small and ultimately ruled the entire world of that generation?

Another thought bothers me in this connection. One of the commentators (*HaMidrash HaMevo'ar*) makes the point that this development by the Roman founders took place just about the same time that Jeroboam created the government of Israel, which broke away from the Jewish state at that time. In other words, from then on, there was a northern kingdom of Israel and a southern kingdom of Judea. Israel was a small country at that time, but as the generation after King Solomon, it possessed much political power. Could it be that Romulus and Remus saw this moment as an opportunity to take over from the government of Israel, now torn in half, and build their future upon it? I hope that some scholar reading these reflections might be in the position to offer a satisfying interpretation.

PARASHAH FORTY-NINE, *Midrash Ten*

י ויאמר ה' אם אמצא בסדום. רבי יודן ורבי יהודה בר' סימון בשם ר' יהושע בן לוי אמרו:
(איוב לד) כי אל אל, האמור נשאתי לא אחבול, היינו דכתיב: ונשאתי לכל המקום בעבורם לא
אחבול, איני ממשכנם, היך מה דכתיב (שמות כב) אם חבול תחבול, והן חובלים עלי דברים
ואומרים: אינו דן כשורה. בלעדי אחזה, בר מיני זיל פשפש דינא, ואם טעיתי, אתה הוריני,
ואם און פעלתי עם הראשונים, לא אוסיף עם האחרונים.

10. AND THE LORD SAID: IF I FIND IN SODOM (GEN. 18:26). R. JUDAN B.
R. SIMON, IN THE NAME OF R. JOSHUA B. LEVI, QUOTED: "FOR IT IS FOR
GOD TO HAVE SAID: I HAVE FORGIVEN" (JOB 34:31). THUS, THEN WILL
I FORGIVE ALL THE PLACE FOR THEIR SAKE. *LO EHBOL* (34:31) MEANS,
I WILL NOT TAKE THEM IN PLEDGE, AS IN THE VERSE: IF THOU AT ALL
TAKE THY NEIGHBOR'S GARMENT TO PLEDGE – *TAHBOL* (EX. 22:25). YET
THEY [MEN] ABUSE ME WITH WORDS AND SAY: "HE DOES NOT JUDGE
WELL." APART FROM MYSELF, I WILL SEE (JOB 34:32): I.E., WITHOUT ME,
DO THOU GO AND SCRUTINIZE MY JUDGMENT. AND IF I HAVE ERRED,
TEACH THOU ME (34:32). AND IF I HAVE WROUGHT INJUSTICE (34:32) –
TO THE EARLIER GENERATIONS; I WILL DO IT NO MORE – TO THE LATER
GENERATIONS.

Abraham had spoken very strongly against the apparent intention
of the Almighty to destroy the city of Sodom in the way in which apparently both the evildoers and the righteous will be equally smitten.
With God's answer that He would save the city if fifty righteous people
could be found and even a lesser number, all of Abraham's objections
and forcefulness were immediately answered and eliminated. God was
now ready to do even more than Abraham had demanded. He was ready
to save Sodom, including all of the evildoers who were the majority, if
fifty righteous men could be found. Nor would He use the occasion to
force the evildoers to repent or to undergo other forms of submission.
His response was unilateral – the fifty righteous men would cancel the
punishment of Sodom and Gomorrah.

(איוב מא) לא אחריש בדיו, לך אני מחריש, ולבדים היוצאים ממך. לאברהם, שהוא אומר:
חלילה לך מעשות כדבר הזה. ולמשה, שהוא אומר (שמות לב): למה ה' יחרה אפך בעמך.
וליהושע, שהוא אומר (יהושע ז): למה העברת העביר את העם. ולדוד שהוא אומר (תהלים

י): לֶמֶה ה' תַּעֲמוֹד בְּרָחוֹק תַּעֲלִים לְעִתּוֹת בַּצָּרָה. (איוב מא) וְדִבֶּר גְּבוּרוֹת וְחִין עֶרְכּוֹ, חַן נִיתַן
בַּעֲרִיכוּת שְׂפָתִים, בְּשָׁעָה שֶׁבִּקֵּשׁ רַחֲמִים עַל הַסְּדוֹמִיִּים:

TO HIM WILL I KEEP SILENCE [AND] TO HIS BRANCHES (JOB 41:4):
[GOD SAID TO ABRAHAM:] TO THEE WILL I KEEP SILENCE AND TO THE
BRANCHES THAT PROCEED FROM THEE. [I WILL KEEP SILENCE] TO ABRA-
HAM, WHO SAID: THAT BE FAR FROM THEE TO DO AFTER THIS MANNER;
TO MOSES, WHO SAID: LORD, WHY DOTH THY WRATH WAX HOT AGAINST
THY PEOPLE (EX. 32:11); TO JOSHUA, WHO SAID: WHEREFORE HAST THOU
AT ALL BROUGHT THIS PEOPLE OVER THE JORDAN (JOSH. 7:7); AND TO
DAVID, WHO SAID: WHY STANDEST THOU AFAR OFF, O LORD, ETC. (PS.
10:1). OR HIS PROUD TALK, OR HIS FAIR (*HIN*) ARRAY OF WORDS (JOB
41:4): HIS [SC. ABRAHAM'S] LONG SPEECH WAS ENDOWED WITH GRACE
(*HEN*) WHEN HE BESEECHED MERCY FOR THE SODOMITES.

God admits that He has not acted this way in other crises when the
future of the Jewish people was at stake. In the case of Moses, Joshua,
David, and others, He established conditions which the people would
have to meet in order to be entitled to God's acceptance. In relation to
Sodom, however, He went far beyond His usual moral persuasion. It
is interesting to note that He did not say that He would acknowledge
various forms of repentance in the future. The Hebrew word would have
been *va'esa*; rather, he used the word *ve-nasati*, as though there were no
further forms of repentance required. This was a tremendous reaction
by God and Abraham's supposed criticism immediately evaporated.

—

Additional Commentary

Penitance

"I will not take them in pledge (*lo ahbol*)" meaning – I will not even
require that some of them repent as a sort of collateral for the others.
(*HaMidrash Hamevo'ar*)

PARASHAH FORTY-NINE, *Midrash Eleven*

יא ויען אברהם ויאמר הנה נא הואלתי. אמר: אלו הרגני אמרפל, לא הייתי עפר? ואי שרפני
נמרוד, לא הייתי אפר?

11. AND ABRAHAM ANSWERED AND SAID: BEHOLD NOW, I HAVE TAKEN
UPON ME TO SPEAK UNTO THE LORD, WHO AM BUT DUST AND ASHES
(GEN. 18:27). HE SAID: HAD AMRAPHEL SLAIN ME, WOULD I NOT HAVE
BEEN DUST, AND HAD NIMROD BURNT ME, WOULD I NOT HAVE BEEN
ASHES? [ADDED TO SONCINO TRANSLATION]

The reference to Amraphel refers to the wars in which some of the local kings of ancient Israel were engaged. Amraphel had achieved power
over all the kings of his area, and his only opponent was Abraham, who
fought against him in order to safeguard the life of his nephew, Lot, who
later on was rescued. Amraphel's main goal in fighting against Abraham
was to take Abraham's life. However, God interfered and Abraham was
miraculously saved. That is the meaning of what the text is saying: "Do
you not realize that if Amraphel had gotten his way, I would be dust and
earth now, and not a person?"

The same explanation applies to Nimrod. In an earlier decade of
Abraham's life, Nimrod had arranged for Abraham to be burned at the
stake because of Abraham's opposition to Nimrod's gods. However,
God intervened miraculously and Abraham was saved, and the text
makes reference to this by saying: "Do you not realize that if Nimrod
had had his way, I would be ashes and not a person?"

אמר לו הקב"ה: חייך! אתה אמרת ואנכי עפר ואפר, חייך! שאני נותן לבניך כפרה בהם,
שנאמר (במדבר יט): ולקחו לטמא מעפר שרפת החטאת, ואסף איש טהור את אפר הפרה.

SAID THE HOLY ONE, BLESSED BE HE, TO HIM: THOU DIDST SAY, I AM BUT
DUST AND ASHES; BY THY LIFE, I WILL GIVE THY CHILDREN ATONEMENT
THEREWITH, AS IT SAYS: AND FOR THE UNCLEAN THEY SHALL TAKE OF
THE ASHES (*AFAR*) OF THE BURNING OF THE PURIFICATION FROM SIN
(NUM. 19:17); ALSO, AND A MAN THAT IS CLEAN SHALL GATHER UP THE
ASHES OF THE HEIFER (19:9).

The nature of reward to Abraham's children can only be realized if we
put ourselves in a different framework from that of modern life. The red

heifer was an animal with a color of skin appearing as though he was a miraculous animal. Therefore, on the rare occasions when a red heifer was sacrificed on the altar, it was looked upon as one of the highest spiritual associations available in the sacrificial system. To participate in the ashes of the red heifer would be the equivalent to being given the highest possible honor in the present-day Torah reading service. From the point of view of Abraham's offspring, their participation in the sacrifice of a red heifer was looked upon as a great reward and a very high spiritual achievement. The reason why this award of the red heifer ashes was so appropriate to the descendants of Abraham was because he very often referred to himself as a person identified with ashes because of the experiences that he went through. There is, however, another area where Abraham's influence should be noted as being very important.

תנינן, סדר תעניות כיצד? מוציאין את התיבה ברחוב העיר וכו', ונותנין אפר מקלה על גבי התיבה. רבי יודן בר מנשה ור' שמואל בר נחמן: חד אמר: זכותו של אברהם. וחד אמר: זכותו של יצחק. מאן דאמר זכותו של אברהם, אנכי עפר ואפר. מאן דאמר זכותו של יצחק, אפר בלבד. מילתא דרבי יודן פליגא אהא דרבי יהודה בן פזי: דהוה מכריז בציבורא, ואמר: כל מאן דלא מטא שליחא דציבורא לגביה למיתן קיטמא ברישיה, יסב איהו קימטא ויהיב ברישיה. מילתיה דרבי יהודה בן פזי אמר: הוא עפר והוא אפר:

WE LEARNT: WHAT WAS THE RITUAL OF A FAST? THE ARK WAS CARRIED OUT INTO THE PUBLIC SQUARE OF THE TOWN AND BURNT ASHES WERE SPRINKLED ON THE ARK. R. JUDAN B. R. MANASSEH AND R. SAMUEL B. NAHMAN DISAGREED. ONE MAINTAINED: [THE ASHES WERE TO RECALL] THE MERIT OF ABRAHAM, FOR IT IS WRITTEN: I WHO AM BUT DUST AND ASHES. BUT THE OTHER MAINTAINED THAT THEY WERE TO RECALL THE MERIT OF ISAAC; HE LEARNT "ASHES" ONLY. THE FOLLOWING STATE-MENT OF R. JUDAH B. PAZZI DISAGREES, FOR HE WOULD PUBLICLY AN-NOUNCE: IF THE CONGREGATIONAL BEADLE CANNOT GET TO ANYONE [TO POUR ASHES ON HIS HEAD], LET HIM TAKE ASHES HIMSELF AND POUR THEM ON HIS OWN HEAD. [THAT IS NOT SO, FOR] R. JUDAH B. PAZZI'S ANNOUNCEMENT TEACHES THAT *AFAR* (DUST) AND *EFER* (ASHES) ARE IDENTICAL.

The Midrash now describes some of the unusual procedures of the Jewish fast days. In every community, the Ark was brought into the public square of the city. Some say that a scroll of the Law was in the Ark, although that is not in all the sources. One of the customs was that the greatest scholar and/or the greatest rabbi would place ashes on his head to be followed by every other male person as well. There are those who say that earth would be placed on their heads, and not ashes. The difference depends on those who felt that this ritual was a tribute to Abraham and others who felt that this ritual was a tribute to Isaac. Since Abraham was quoted many times as saying that he is both earth and ashes, *afar* and *efer*, it seems that all of this was actually done as a form of continuous tribute to Abraham.

―

Seed Thoughts I

It is still difficult for the modern religious Jew to identify completely with the sacrificial service where God is offered animal life as a form of prayer and getting close to Him. The whole idea of a red heifer, as being different from other animals, is that his skin is so different in color, and his appearance in animal life is so rare. Nevertheless, human beings seem to share the same unusual reaction to the phenomenon of life. I recall that several years ago, within the past 25–30 years, a red heifer was discovered in Israel, even though there is no sacrificial service today. Nonetheless, the news became tremendously prominent; Jews from all over Israel came to look at the phenomenon, and human beings of all stripes and of all religions made their way to look at that unusual animal. I come to no conclusion except that if such a reaction could take place in the twentieth century in an environment which is largely secular, how sensitive it must have been in ancient Israel to have confronted this beautiful animal and then to figure out a religious use for it that would be a form of thanking God for this phenomenon. To this day, the Jewish religious calendar has one of the Sabbaths preceding the festival of Passover, which is designated as *Shabbat Parah*, which I suppose could be translated as "the Sabbath of the Heifer."

―

Seed Thoughts II

From time to time, there are people (including scholars) who feel that an effort must be made to create a Third Temple, and therefore to revive the sacrificial system as being the authentic form of Jewish worship. The vast majority of religious Jews do not seem to feel this way, and it is very hard to know how to react to such efforts. It is not completely certain what the views of Maimonides were; one seems to have the impression that he would want a Third Temple, but that the animal service should be replaced by the services of prayers which have developed so beautifully in the world of Jewish prayer. The subject will continue to be raised until such time as there is tremendous interest by religious Jews in this phenomenon.

PARASHAH FORTY-NINE, *Midrash Twelve*

יב אולי יחסרון חמשים הצדיקים, חמשה. אמר רבי חייא בר אבא: בקש אברהם לירד לו
מחמשים לחמשה. אמר לו הקב"ה: חזור בך למפרע. א"ר לוי: לחלף סרדה מלאה מים, כל
זמן שהיא מלאה מים, הסניגור מלמד. פעמים, שהדיין מבקש שילמד סניגוריא, הוא אומר:
הוסיפו בתוכה מים:

12. PERADVENTURE THERE SHALL LACK FIVE OF THE FIFTY RIGHTEOUS.
R. HIYYA B. ABBA SAID: ABRAHAM WISHED TO DESCEND FROM FIFTY TO
FIVE, BUT THE HOLY ONE, BLESSED BE HE, SAID TO HIM: "TURN BACK."
R. LEVI SAID: THIS MAY BE COMPARED TO A CLEPSYDRA FULL OF WATER;
ONLY AS LONG AS IT CONTAINS WATER MAY THE DEFENDING COUNSEL
PLEAD; YET SOMETIMES THE JUDGE DESIRES HIM TO CONTINUE HIS
DEFENSE, AND SO HE ORDERS: "POUR MORE WATER INTO IT."

The parable is meant to show that it was perfectly in order for the Holy One, blessed be He, to request of Abraham to take more time in his presentation and not move so quickly from fifty to five. Similarly, the judge in the parable that was quoted arranged for additional water to be put into the clepsydra so that more time would be taken for the arguments.

～

Seed Thoughts I

According to Rabbi Hiyya bar Abba, Abraham wished to descend "from fifty to five" without the intermediate steps. He probably renders: "Peradventure the fifty shall be lacking, and there be but five." When God tells Abraham to turn back, what it means is that "this is too great a jump." A clepsydra, according to Jastrow, is "a water-clock used in courts of justice for measuring the time given for argument." (All quotations here are from Soncino.)

———

Seed Thoughts II

One of the remarkable achievements of the Midrash is the use of a parable to explain its teachings in a more simplified way. Some of the parables are quite extraordinary, and many have been published even independent of the midrashic text itself. The enclosed parable we have just read in connection with the water-clock is most unfortunate. It is very difficult to understand, and it does not simplify our understanding of the midrashic text. The Midrash by itself tells us more than this particular parable.

———

PARASHAH FORTY-NINE, *Midrash Thirteen*

יג ויאמר אל נא יחר לה' אולי ימצאון שם עשרה. ולמה עשרה? כדי כניסה לכולם. ד"א: למה עשרה? כבר נשתייר בדור המבול שמונה, ולא נתלה לעולם בזכותן. ד"א: למה עשרה? שהיה סבור שיש שם עשרה: לוט ואשתו, וד' בנותיו, וד' חתניו.

13. AND HE SAID: OH, LET NOT THE LORD BE ANGRY . . . PERADVENTURE TEN SHALL BE FOUND THERE (GEN. 18:32). AND WHY TEN? SO THAT THERE MIGHT BE SUFFICIENT FOR AN ASSEMBLY [OF RIGHTEOUS MEN TO PRAY] ON BEHALF OF ALL OF THEM. ANOTHER REASON, WHY TEN? BECAUSE AT THE GENERATION OF THE FLOOD EIGHT RIGHTEOUS PEOPLE YET REMAINED [SONCINO: NOAH, HIS THREE SONS, AND THEIR WIVES], AND THE WORLD WAS NOT GIVEN A RESPITE FOR THEIR SAKE. ANOTHER REASON, WHY TEN? BECAUSE HE THOUGHT THAT THERE WERE TEN THERE, VIZ. LOT, HIS WIFE, HIS FOUR DAUGHTERS AND FOUR SONS-IN-LAW [SONCINO: BUT HE WAS MISTAKEN IN THINKING THEM RIGHTEOUS].

רבי יהודה בר' סימון ורבי חנין בשם ר' יוחנן: כאן עשרה, ובירושלים אפי' אחד, הה"ד (ירמיה ה): שוטטו בחוצות ירושלים. וכאן הוא אומר (קהלת ז): אחת לאחת למצוא חשבון.

R. JUDAH B. R. SIMON AND R. HANIN IN R. JOHANAN'S NAME SAID: HERE TEN WERE REQUIRED, WHILE IN JERUSALEM EVEN ONE WOULD HAVE

SUFFICED, AS IT IS WRITTEN: RUN YE TO AND FRO IN THE STREETS OF
JERUSALEM . . . AND SEEK . . . IF YE CAN FIND A MAN, IF THERE BE ANY
THAT DOETH JUSTLY (JER. 5:1); AND THUS IT SAYS TOO: ADDING ONE
THING TO ANOTHER, TO FIND OUT THE ACCOUNT (ECCL. 7:27).

The Midrash here has added an interpretation which places Jerusalem
on a much higher level than any of the other cities so far mentioned.

א"ר יצחק: עד כמה הוא מצוי חשבון לעיר אחת? עד אחד, אם נמצא אחד בכל העיר, תולין
לה בזכותו:

R. ISAAC SAID: HOW FAR CAN AN ACCOUNT BE EXTENDED FOR ONE CITY?
AS [LONG] AS ONE MAN {CAN BE FOUND IN ALL OF THE CITY, THEY SPARE
IT IN HIS MERIT.}

As the commentator points out, in the case of Sodom, it was difficult
to find ten righteous people for whom the city can be spared, and in
the case of Jerusalem, while the Temple was being attacked, not one
righteous person could be found to save the Temple from destruction.
One would have to conclude, in light of these statements, that the evil
in Jerusalem of that day was worse than that of Sodom. (*HaMidrash
HaMevo'ar*)

―

Seed Thoughts

One of the reasons why the number ten does not help Abraham in his
attempt is that Lot's family was not sufficiently worthy to be described
as righteous. As we know from further episodes in the Torah text, Lot's
daughters were capable of very immoral behavior and were not worthy
of being rescued. The best that could have happened did happen, and
Abraham was able to save Lot and his wife and those of the family who
were willing to escape with him.

PARASHAH FORTY-NINE, *Midrash Fourteen*

יד וילך ה' כאשר כלה לדבר אל אברהם. הדיין הזה, כל זמן שהסניגור מלמד, הוא ממתין. נשתתק הסניגור, עמד לו הדיין. כך, וילך ה', כאשר כלה לדבר אל אברהם.

14. AND THE LORD WENT HIS WAY, AS SOON AS HE HAD LEFT OFF SPEAK-
ING TO ABRAHAM (GEN. 18:33). A JUDGE WAITS AS LONG AS THE ADVO-
CATE IS PLEADING; WHEN THE ADVOCATE BECOMES SILENT, THE JUDGE
RISES [TO GO]. SIMILARLY, AND THE LORD WENT HIS WAY, AS SOON AS
HE HAD LEFT OFF SPEAKING TO ABRAHAM.

What the Midrash is doing is to describe the questions and answers
between Abraham and God as though this were a court of law in which
Abraham would be the defense attorney and God would be the equivalent of the prosecution attorney. Abraham's main concern was the
welfare of Sodom and Gomorrah, and the horror that the Master of the
Universe would destroy a city even though it contained some righteous
people. However, when he received an answer that God would not
destroy the city even if he found only ten, then Abraham's concern was
lessened. He asked no more of the Almighty, and since Abraham is the
defense attorney, he had nothing more to say. God, as the prosecution attorney, had to reason to remain where he was. So the Midrash describes
that God returned presumably to Heaven, and Abraham returned to his
home.

הסניגור הזה, כל זמן שהדיין מסביר לו פנים, הוא מלמד. עמד לו הדיין, נשתתק הסניגור. כך,
וילך ה' כאשר כלה לדבר אל אברהם. וכתיב: ואברהם שב למקומו. הקטיגור הזה, כל זמן
שהסניגור מלמד והדיין מסביר לו פנים, ממתין. עמד לו הדיין, נשתתק הסניגור, והמקטרג
הולך לעשות שליחותו. כך, וילך ה'. וכתיב: ויבאו שני המלאכים סדומה בערב:

AGAIN, AN ADVOCATE GOES ON PLEADING AS LONG AS THE JUDGE IS
WILLING TO PAY ATTENTION TO HIM, BUT WHEN THE JUDGE RISES
TO GO, THE ADVOCATE BECOMES SILENT. THUS, AND THE LORD WENT
HIS WAY, AS SOON AS HE HAD LEFT OFF SPEAKING TO ABRAHAM; AND
ABRAHAM RETURNED TO HIS PLACE. AGAIN, AS LONG AS THE DEFENDER
PLEADS AND THE JUDGE SHOWS HIMSELF WILLING TO HEAR, THE AC-
CUSER WAITS; WHEN THE JUDGE RISES AND THE ADVOCATE IS SILENT,
THE ACCUSER SETS FORTH ON HIS MISSION. SIMILARLY: AND THE LORD
WENT HIS WAY, AS SOON AS HE HAD LEFT OFF SPEAKING TO ABRAHAM;

AND ABRAHAM RETURNED UNTO HIS PLACE. THIS IS FOLLOWED BY: AND
THE TWO ANGELS CAME TO SODOM AT EVEN (GEN. 19:1).

As the result of these happenings, the angels who appeared as human beings were also free to continue in their pilgrimage. As merciful
people, they were ready to wait as long as possible if Abraham could find
ways of justifying the survival of Sodom and Gomorrah. When Abraham discontinued his criticism and basically withdrew his complaints,
the angels were free to continue in their mission, which was to destroy
Sodom and Gomorrah. This motivated them to journey to Sodom and
Gomorrah, which they reached towards evening.

—

Additional Commentary

Why Abraham stopped at ten

Abraham stopped at ten since he saw that God went His way. He therefore knew that he could not continue his defense. (Mirkin)

א ויבאו שני המלאכים סדומה בערב וגו'. (יחזקאל א) והחיות רצוא ושוב כמראה הבזק.

1. AND THE TWO ANGELS CAME TO SODOM AT EVEN ETC. (GEN. 19:1). IT
IS WRITTEN: AND THE LIVING CREATURE RAN (*RAZO*) AND RETURNED AS
THE APPEARANCE OF A FLASH OF LIGHTNING (EZEK. 1:14).

The Midrash is trying to create for the reader some of the tension that
existed in Sodom and Gomorrah when it was realized by some people
that the angelic figures were there to destroy both cities. The Midrash
spends a lot of time trying to interpret the strange words for the animals
and the other living creatures. At first, the interpretation is that they are
jumping and dancing and are so energetic that it appeared that all of
them were creating flashes of lightning.

א"ר אייבו: רצות אין כתיב כאן, אלא רצוא, רצין לעשות שליחותן כמראה הבזק.

R. AIBU SAID: NOT *RAZOTH* (RUNNING) IS WRITTEN BUT *RAZO*: THEY ARE
EAGER (*RAZIN*) TO PERFORM THEIR MISSION. "AS THE APPEARANCE OF A
FLASH OF LIGHTNING" (*BAZAK*):

Rabbi Aibu uses the occasion that the Midrash is not saying the
animals were running, to use an entirely different term, which gave the
impression that they are trying to fulfill what God wanted them to fulfill. Do not read the word *ratz* as meaning "running"; it should be interpreted as the word *yirtzeh*, which means that God may approve of what
the animals are doing. They, too, were helping to create – through those
flashes of lightning – more of the tension that was being felt everywhere.

ר"י בשם רבי סימון בשם רבי לוי בר פרטא: כזה שהוא בוזק גפת בכירה. רבי חייא בר אבא
אמר: כרוחא לזיקא. רבנן אמרי, כזיקא לעננא.

R. JUDAH B. R. SIMON SAID IN THE NAME OF R. LEVI B. PARTA: [LIKE THE
FLAMES BREAKING FORTH] WHEN ONE SCATTERS (*BOZEK*) OLIVE REFUSE

IN A STOVE. R. HIYYA B. ABBA SAID: IT WAS LIKE WIND DRIVING SPARKS
(*ZIKA*). THE RABBIS SAID: LIKE A LIGHTNING-FLASH TO THE EYE.

The Midrash now quotes a number of rabbis, all of whom interpret
the behavior of the animals as their way of helping God fulfill His ruler-
ship of the world.

נפטרים מאברהם בשש שעות, ובאין סדומה בערב. אלא מלאכי רחמים היו, והיו ממתינים
וסבורים שמא ימצא להם זכות, וכיון שלא מצא להם זכות, ויבואו שני המלאכים סדומה
בערב:

NOW [RETURNING TO OUR SUBJECT,] THEY TAKE LEAVE OF ABRAHAM AT
NOON, AND ARRIVE IN SODOM IN THE EVENING! THE FACT IS, HOWEVER,
THAT THEY WERE ANGELS OF MERCY, AND THEY DELAYED, THINKING
THAT PERHAPS ABRAHAM MIGHT FIND SOMETHING IN THEIR FAVOR;
BUT WHEN HE FOUND NOTHING IN THEIR FAVOR, THE TWO ANGELS
CAME TO SODOM AT EVEN.

The Midrash goes on to say that the angelic figures were delaying their
responsibility in the hope that Abraham may yet find reason to forgive
the Sodomites. When this did not happen, the angels were ready, of
course, to do the bidding of the Eternal One.

—

Seed Thoughts

It is very difficult to find ways of responding in dealing with angelic figures. Originally, three angelic figures in the form of human beings were
intended to visit Abraham. The angel Michael had a role that was short
and sweet – all he had to do was to inform Sarah and Abraham that they
would have a child within a year. Having done that, he could return to
his angelic place. His colleagues, Raphael and Gabriel, demonstrated
that they had strong feelings of mercy, and they hoped that they would,
in some fashion, be relieved of the task of destroying Sodom and Gomorrah. This was not destined to happen, but at least it demonstrated
that it was possible to have angelic individuals to possess the qualities
of mercy.

PARASHAH FIFTY, *Midrash Two*

ב (איוב כג) והוא באחד ומי ישיבנו ונפשו אותה ויעש. תנא, אין מלאך אחד עושה שתי
שליחות, ולא שני מלאכים עושים שליחות אחת, ואת אמרת שני? אלא, מיכאל אמר
בשורתו ונסתלק, גבריאל נשתלח להפוך את סדום, ורפאל להציל את לוט. ויבואו שני
המלאכים סדומה.

2. THEN THE TWO ANGELS CAME, ETC. BUT HE IS AT ONE WITH HIMSELF,
AND WHO CAN TURN HIM? AND WHAT HIS SOUL DESIRETH, EVEN THAT
HE DOETH (JOB 23:13). IT WAS TAUGHT: ONE ANGEL DOES NOT PERFORM
TWO MISSIONS, NOR DO TWO ANGELS TOGETHER PERFORM ONE MIS-
SION, YET YOU READ THAT TWO [ANGELS CAME TO SODOM]? THE FACT
IS, HOWEVER, THAT MICHAEL ANNOUNCED HIS TIDINGS [TO ABRAHAM]
AND DEPARTED: GABRIEL WAS SENT TO OVERTURN SODOM, AND RA-
PHAEL TO RESCUE LOT; HENCE, THEN THE TWO ANGELS CAME, ETC. IT IS
WRITTEN, HE SENT FORTH UPON THEM THE FIERCENESS OF HIS ANGER,
WRATH, INDIGNATION, AND TROUBLE, A SENDING OF MESSENGERS OF
EVIL (PS. 78:49); YET YOU SAY, TWO [ANGELS]! BUT THE FACT IS THAT
MICHAEL ANNOUNCED HIS TIDINGS AND DEPARTED; GABRIEL WAS SENT
TO OVERTURN SODOM, AND RAFAEL TO SAVE LOT. HENCE, THEN THE
TWO ANGELS CAME.

The verse quoted from the Book of Job proclaims that whatever great
decisions the Almighty makes, He carries them out alone and by Himself. Only part of this behavior is carried on by those who are selected
to help God to rule the world. For example, as the Midrash says, only
one angel alone can perform one mission; no one angel is permitted
to fulfill two divine missions. How is this statement compatible with
the midrashic phrase that two angels entered Sodom in the evening?
This is how it should be understood: The verse from Job does not say
ve-hu e'had, meaning that only one person can help Him; rather, he says
be-e'had. He allows himself to be helped by one angelic figure at a time.
This angelic figure is not given more than one mission. For example,
in the Midrashim we have recently studied, it says that three human
beings appeared in Abraham's home. Only later on do we realize that
we are dealing with three angels. The first was Michael, whose mission
it was to inform Abraham and Sarah that they would be blessed with a
child within the year. Michael then disappears from that delegation. The

two remaining angels, Gabriel and Raphael, remained. Gabriel would eventually have the responsibility of destroying Sodom, and Raphael's mission would be to protect Lot and his family. So long as none of the three performed their mission, they were described as *anashim*, ordinary human beings. The moment one of them carried out his mission, everything changed and they were henceforth to be referred to as angels.

הכא את אמר מלאכים, ולהלן קורא אותן אנשים? אלא, להלן שהיתה שכינה על גביהן, קראם אנשים, כיון שנסתלקה שכינה מעל גביהן, לבשו מלאכות. אמר רבי תנחומא, א"ר לוי: אברהם שהיה כחו יפה, נדמו לו בדמות אנשים, אבל לוט, על ידי שהיה כחו רע, נדמו לו בדמות מלאכים. אמר רבי חנינא: עד שלא עשו שליחותן, קראן אנשים, משעשו שליחותן, מלאכים. א"ר תנחומא: לאחד שנטל הגמוניא מן המלך, עד שלא הגיע לבית אווריין שלו, היה מהלך כפגן, כיון שהגיע לבית אווריין שלו, היה מהלך כקאלמין. כך, עד שלא עשו שליחותן, קראן אנשים, כיון שעשו שליחותן, קראן מלאכים:

[AND THE TWO ANGELS CAME TO SODOM.] HERE YOU CALL THEM ANGELS, WHEREAS EARLIER THEY WERE TERMED MEN? EARLIER, WHEN THE SHECHINAH WAS ABOVE THEM, THEY WERE MEN; BUT AS SOON AS THE SHECHINAH DEPARTED FROM THEM, THEY ASSUMED THE FORM OF ANGELS. R. TANHUMA SAID IN THE NAME OF R. LEVI: TO ABRAHAM, WHOSE [RELIGIOUS] STRENGTH WAS GREAT, THEY LOOKED LIKE MEN; BUT TO LOT THEY APPEARED AS ANGELS, BECAUSE HIS STRENGTH WAS FEEBLE. R. HANINA SAID: BEFORE THEY PERFORMED THEIR MISSION THEY WERE CALLED MEN; HAVING PERFORMED THEIR MISSION, THEY ASSUMED THE STYLE OF ANGELS. R. TANHUMA SAID: THEY MAY BE LIKENED TO A MAN WHO RECEIVED A GOVERNORSHIP FROM THE KING. BEFORE HE REACHES THE SEAT OF HIS AUTHORITY, HE GOES LIKE AN ORDINARY CITIZEN. SIMILARLY, BEFORE THEY PERFORMED THEIR MISSION, THEY ARE CALLED MEN; HAVING PERFORMED IT, THEY ASSUMED THE STYLE OF ANGELS.

———

Seed Thoughts

Whoever reads the story of the special visitors who came to Abraham after his circumcision wonders that, at the beginning of the story, they are described as men, but at the end of the story, they are reinterpreted as angels. Everyone, young or old, who is exposed to this story reacts the same way. Why are they men in one place and angels in another?

Our Midrash adds many interpretations that try to explain this development. One interpretation is that in relationship to Abraham, who has a special relationship with God, the so-called angels appeared and were described as ordinary men. In the case of Lot, however, whose moral position in life was very low, they were immediately recognized by him as angels whom he would now have to deal with, since they were being presented as his visitors.

A second interpretation might be that if they did not perform their mission as of yet, they were men and could be so interpreted. The moment, however, a mission was fulfilled by them, their category would change immediately and they were angels. Rabbi Tanhuma's interpretation is very simple and very convincing. If the king appoints someone to be his representative in a certain town, he would be immediately accepted in that role in modern times, because we have the ability to communicate news instantaneously. Yet, in the generation of the king we are now describing, the representative would wait until he arrived in the designated city. He would enter the palace or special office prepared for him, and don the uniform of his new responsibility. At that moment, his acceptance would be assured. By the same token, when the men in Abraham's story fulfilled their mission or obligation, we no longer hear about them as men, but only as angels.

PARASHAH FIFTY, *Midrash Three*

ג סדומה.

3. SEDOMAH (TO SODOM).

The Midrash will begin with an interpretation of elementary Hebrew grammar. The motivation for this explanation is the first word in this Midrash, which is *Sedomah*. There may be certain people whose knowledge of Hebrew is so elementary that they would look upon this word *Sedomah* as being the actual name of the town. It is that possibility that brings forward the midrashic lesson in elementary Hebrew.

תני, משום ר' נחמיה: כל דבר שצריך למ"ד בתחלתו תן לה ה"א בסופו, סדומה שעירה מצרימה חרנה. אתיבון, והכתיב (תהלים ט): ישובו רשעים לשאולה? ר' אבא בר זבדא אמר: לביטי התחתונה שבשאול.

IT WAS TAUGHT IN R. NEHEMIAH'S NAME: WHEN A WORD REQUIRES A LAMED AS A PREFIX YOU ADD HEH AS A SUFFIX [INSTEAD], E.G., SEDOMAH (TO SODOM), SEIRAH (TO SEIR), MIZRAIMAH (TO EGYPT), HARANAH (TO HARAN). AN OBJECTION WAS RAISED: YET IT IS WRITTEN: THE WICKED SHALL RETURN LI-SHEOLAH - TO THE NETHERWORLD (PS. 9:18). SAID R. ABBA B. ZABDA: THAT MEANS TO THE NETHERMOST COMPARTMENT OF HELL.

Two lessons are included in this sentence. You can write the expression "to Sodom" in two ways. One way is to use the Hebrew *el Sedom*, which of course means "to Sodom." That can be replaced by adding the letter *heh* to the noun *Sedom*, and therefore, *Sedomah* now also means "to Sodom," and both ways of writing are acceptable in the Hebrew language. This applies, of course, not only to the word *Sedom*, but to any word in the Hebrew language, and the text includes certain words that are spelled that way in the biblical text, such as *Seirah* ("to Seir"), *Mizraimah* ("to Egypt"), and *Haranah* ("to Haran"). This teaching is immediately contradicted by the word *li-Sheolah*, which means "to Sheol," a parallel word for *Gehinnom* or Hell, which uses both the *lamed* at the beginning and the *heh* at the end, both meaning "to Sheol." Rabbi Abba bar Zabda informs us that the special forms used in *li-Sheolah* are meant to inform us that they have in mind the worst possible area of Hell.

בערב. בא ערבה של סדום, ושקע שמשה, ונחתם גזר דינה.

BA'EREB (AT EVENING). THE EVENING OF SODOM HAD COME, ITS SUN
HAD SET, AND ITS DOOM WAS SEALED.

The reason for a comment is because it does not say "before evening"
or "as evening approaches," but "at evening," as though they knew exactly at what particular time the world was observing evening, and that
is when they entered Sodom. The teaching is for the word *erev* itself, that
it should inform us that the end of Sodom was about to happen.

אמר רבי לוי: אין הקב"ה דן את אומות העולם, אלא בלילה בשעה שהן ישנים, ואינו דן את
ישראל, אלא ביום בשעה שהם עסוקים במצות, הה"ד (תהלים ט): והוא ישפוט תבל בצדק.

R. LEVI SAID: THE HOLY ONE, BLESSED BE HE, JUDGES THE NATIONS
AT NIGHT ONLY, WHEN THEY ARE ASLEEP FROM THEIR SINS; WHILE
HE JUDGES ISRAEL BY DAY ONLY, WHEN THEY ARE ENGAGED IN GOOD
DEEDS. HENCE IT IS WRITTEN: AND HE WILL JUDGE THE WORLD (*TEBEL*)
IN RIGHTEOUSNESS, HE WILL MINISTER JUDGMENT TO THE PEOPLES
WITH EQUITY (PS. 9:9).

This is the kind of interesting teaching that does not really matter one
way or another. It is possible for sins to take place in the daytime, and the
observance of commandments during the nighttime. So, we could look
upon this teaching as one person's opinion, and there could be others.
One of the commentators on this verse informs us that the word *tevel*
does not refer to the entire universe, but rather to that part of the world
that our text is now talking about. *Tevel* refers to the Land of Israel, and
those who dwell there occupy themselves with Torah.

ולוט יושב, ישב כתיב, אותו היום מינוהו ארכי דייינם. חמשה ראשי דיינים היו בסדום: קץ
שקר, ורב שקר, רב מסטידין, רב נבל, וקלא פנדר. לוט היה ארכי הדיינים שבכולן.

AND LOT SAT IN THE GATE OF SODOM. "SAT" IS WRITTEN DEFECTIVELY,
INTIMATING THAT ONLY THAT DAY HAD HE BEEN APPOINTED BY THEM
CHIEF JUSTICE. THERE WERE FIVE PRINCIPAL JUDGES IN SODOM: FALSE-
PRINCIPLES, LYING-SPEECH, CAD, JUSTICE-PERVERTER, AND MAN-
FLAYER, WHILE LOT WAS THEIR CHIEF JUDGE.

Commenting on the verse "And Lot sat in the Gate of Sodom," the
Midrash noticed that the word *yoshev*, meaning "to sit," has been written
without a *vav*. That means that it can be rendered in a different way, not

merely that "he sits at the gate" but rather that "he once sat at the gate." Apparently, the day of the angel's visit was the first day that Lot sat at the gate of Sodom, because he had been appointed one of the heads of their justice system.

בשעה שהיה אומר להם דברים שהם ערבים להם, הן אומרים לו: גש הלאה, סק לעיל. ובשעה שהיה אומר להם דברים שאין ערבים להם, היו אומרים לו: האחד בא לגור וישפוט שפוט:

WHEN HE TOLD THEM SOMETHING WHICH PLEASED THEM, THEY WOULD SAY TO HIM, GO FURTHER (GEN. 19:9), TAKE A HIGHER SEAT; BUT IF HE SAID SOMETHING WHICH DISPLEASED THEM, THEY WOULD SAY, THIS ONE FELLOW CAME IN TO SOJOURN, AND HE WILL NEED TO PLAY THE JUDGE! (19:9).

In other words, the new position of Lot did not make things easier for him. It made it easier for him to be exposed to the criticism of the general population of Sodom.

PARASHAH FIFTY, *Midrash Four*

ד וירא לוט ויקם לקראתם וגו'. ויאמר הנה נא אדוני. רבי יודן ורבי הונא. רבי יודן אמר: סורו נא אפילו איני כדאי, עקמו עלי את הדרך. רבי הונא אמר: עקמו עלי את הדרך, כדי שלא תהיו נראים באים אצלי, אל בית עבדכם.

4. AND LOT SAW THEM, AND ROSE UP TO MEET THEM . . . AND HE SAID: BEHOLD NOW, MY LORDS, TURN ASIDE, I PRAY YOU (GEN. 19:1F.). R. JU-DAN INTERPRETED: EVEN IF I AM NOT WORTHY, DIVERT YOUR COURSE FOR MY SAKE. R. HUNA SAID: [HE ASKED THEM:] COME TO ME BY A CIR-CUITOUS ROUTE, SO THAT YOU MAY NOT BE SEEN COMING TO ME.

We will now discover that the midrashic rabbis disagreed not only with each other but mostly in their interpretation of Lot's behavior. Why he did use a term like *suru na* – "turn around?" Why could he not simply invite him to his home? One of the rabbis states that this was Lot's way of saying that his hospitality would not reach the level of Abraham's, but he would try his best. Another rabbi points out that the people of

Sodom had blocked the usual way of going to Lot's home. He, therefore, had to take them in a roundabout way, but he was willing to do so.

ולינו ורחצו. אברהם מקדים רחיצה ללינה, ולוט מקדים לינה לרחיצה? אלא אברהם מקפיד על טינופת עבודת כוכבים, לפיכך הקדים רחיצה, ולוט אינו מקפיד על טינופת עבודת כוכבים. ויש אומרים: אף זה עשה כשורה, כדי שיצאו ויראו אבק על רגליהם, שלא יאמרו היכן לנו.

AND TARRY ALL NIGHT, AND WASH YOUR FEET. ABRAHAM ASKED THEM TO WASH FIRST AND THEN STAY WITH HIM, WHEREAS LOT FIRST IN-VITED THEM TO STAY WITH HIM AND THEN TO WASH. THE TRUTH IS THAT ABRAHAM WAS PARTICULAR ABOUT THE POLLUTION OF IDOLA-TRY, WHEREAS LOT HAD NO OBJECTION TO IT. SOME SAY: THIS TOO LOT DID WITH FORETHOUGHT, SO THAT WHEN THEY [THE ANGELS] WENT OUT, THE DUST WOULD BE SEEN ON THEIR FEET, AND THE SODOMITES SHOULD NOT ASK, "WHERE HAVE THEY SPENT THE NIGHT?"

The Rabbis made a comparison between how Lot invited the angels and how Abraham did. Apparently, washing one's feet and removing the dust has a special meaning for those engaged in the worship of idols. That is why Lot made it not the first but the second arrangement he would make for his guests. Abraham had no such fear of idolatry, and therefore he invited what seemed to be proper – first wash their feet and then spend the evening in comfort.

ויאמרו לא כי ברחוב נלין. ממאנין בקטן ואין ממאנין בגדול.

AND THEY SAID: NAY; BUT WE WILL ABIDE IN THE BROAD PLACE ALL NIGHT ... [THIS TEACHES THAT] YOU MAY REFUSE AN ORDINARY PER-SON, BUT NOT A GREAT PERSON.

Lot would not accept their refusal, and implored them almost as emo-tionally as a child would try to get his parents to do his bidding. The angels finally accepted Lot's invitation to join him at his home.

ויפצר בם מאד. הכניס בם אף וצרה. ויסורו אליו, ויבאו אל ביתו. הדא מסייעא להההוא דאמר רב הונא: עקמו עלי את הדרך, כדי שלא תהיו נראים באים אצלי. ויעש להם משתה. בביתו של אברהם אבינו היה, שהיה מקבל את העוברים ואת השבים. א"ר יצחק: מצות גדולה עמדה על המלח. דהוא אמר לה: הב לאלין אכסניא, קליל מלח. והות אמרה ליה: אף הדא סוניתא בישא את בעי מילפא הכא:

AND HE URGED (*WAYYIPZAR*) THEM GREATLY (GEN. 19:3): THROUGH
THEM HE BROUGHT ANGER (*AF*) AND TROUBLE (*ZARAH*) INTO HIS HOME.
AND THEY TURNED ASIDE TO HIM. THIS SUPPORTS R. HUNA'S CONTEN-
TION THAT HE ASKED THEM TO TAKE A CIRCUITOUS PATH TO HIM THAT
THEY MIGHT NOT BE SEEN ENTERING HIS HOUSE. AND HE MADE THEM A
FEAST. HE HAD BEEN REARED IN THE HOME OF ABRAHAM WHO SHOWED
HOSPITALITY TO TRAVELERS. R. ISAAC SAID: A FIERCE QUARREL BROKE
OUT OVER THE SALT, FOR HE [LOT] SAID TO HER [HIS WIFE], "GIVE THESE
GUESTS A LITTLE SALT," TO WHICH SHE REPLIED, "DO YOU WANT TO IN-
TRODUCE HERE THAT EVIL PRACTICE TOO?"

The text now makes a comparison to the behavior of Sarah to the
same guests and the behavior of Lot's wife to these same guests. Sarah
was delighted to help in the hospitality. Lot's wife was resentful and felt
that the leaders of Sodom would punish them. Ironically, later in the
story, she becomes transformed into a pillar of salt.

PARASHAH FIFTY, *Midrash Five*

ה טרם ישכבו. התחילו שואלים אותו: אמרו לו אנשי העיר: מה הם? אמר להון: כל אתר אית
טבין ובישין, ברם הכא, סוגייה בישין.

5. BUT BEFORE THEY LAY DOWN, THEY COMMENCED QUESTIONING HIM,
"WHAT IS THE NATURE OF THE PEOPLE OF THIS CITY?" "IN EVERY TOWN
THERE ARE PEOPLE GOOD AND BAD," HE REPLIED, "BUT HERE THE OVER-
WHELMING MAJORITY ARE BAD."

The angelic guests, immediately upon their entrance to Lot's home,
asked him many questions about the nature of the people in his community. Lot's answer was that the majority are dominated by evil ways.
Almost as though to prove his point, the people of Sodom – all of them
– had apparently gathered outside Lot's home and demanded that he
surrender his guests to them.

ואנשי העיר אנשי סדום נסבו על הבית. אין אחד מהם מעכב. ויקראו אל לוט ויאמרו לו.
רבי יהושע בן לוי בשם ר' פדייה אמר: כל אותו הלילה היה לוט מבקש עליהם רחמים, והיו
מקבלין ממנו, כיון שאמרו לו, הוציאם אלינו ונדעה אותם לתשמיש. אמרו לו: עד מי לך

פה, קרי ביה: עוד מי לך פה? ע"כ היה לך רשות ללמד סניגוריא עליהם, מכאן ואילך אין לך
רשות ללמד סניגוריא עליהם:

THE MEN OF THE CITY, THE MEN OF SODOM, COMPASSED THE HOUSE
ROUND, BOTH YOUNG AND OLD – NOT ONE OF THEM OBJECTING. AND
THEY CALLED UNTO LOT, AND SAID UNTO HIM, ETC. (GEN. 19:5). R. JOSHUA
B. LEVI SAID IN THE NAME OF R. PADIAH: LOT PRAYED FOR MERCY ON
THEIR BEHALF THE WHOLE OF THAT NIGHT, AND THEY WOULD HAVE
HEEDED HIM; BUT IMMEDIATELY THEY [THE SODOMITES] DEMANDED,
BRING THEM OUT UNTO US, THAT WE MAY KNOW THEM – FOR SEXUAL
PURPOSES – THEY SAID TO HIM: "HAST THOU HERE (POH) ANY BESIDES
(19:12)? UNTIL NOW YOU HAD THE RIGHT TO PLEAD IN THEIR DEFENCE,
BUT FROM NOW YOU HAVE NO RIGHT TO PLEAD FOR THEM."

All the while this was happening, Lot would plead with his neighbors
surrounding his house that they show mercy. After all, he had indicated
to his guests that every city has its good and bad, but that Sodom has
much more bad than good. At the same time that there was more bad
than good, at least there were some people who were good, and he
hoped that they would listen to his pleas for treating his guests with
tolerance. However, it became obvious that God would not listen to
Lot's prayers in the same manner that He was not accepting the curse of
Abraham that was referred to in an earlier Midrash. This was especially
heartbreaking when he realized that they wanted them outside in order
to use them for sexual purposes. The guests immediately changed their
form of conversation and kept asking Lot who all the members of his
family were, and whether he could get them together if necessary. The
guests then explained to Lot that Sodom was about to be destroyed:
"Up to now, you were able to defend Sodom, that there were some good
people among them, but now it should be obvious that no forms of
defense of the people could take place."

———

Seed Thoughts

The average reader must surely have some degree of sympathy for Lot
and the situation in which he found himself. He had chosen to live in
the area of Sodom and Gomorrah, which were the most fertile parts of
Abraham's possession. But it was given to him by Abraham as an act of
love, and now he finds himself in a situation where the inhabitants of

his city, or certainly the leadership of his city, were ready to perform the most obnoxious acts of human behavior against the guests who dared to visit with Lot, against the local rules of the population. Now, Lot would have to make a terrible choice. The angels were ready and willing to liberate all members of Lot's family from the terrible fate that awaited their community. But Lot had to get their agreement, which was not going to be easy. He would then have them all accompany him to the nearest safe place which would protect them. It was probably only when members of his family actually saw the beginnings of the destruction of Sodom that all of them agreed to go with Lot wherever he would take them. But this experience would be with them forever and make life most difficult for all of them.

PARASHAH FIFTY, *Midrash Six*

ו ויצא אליהם לוט הפתחה אל נא אחי הנה נא לי שתי בנות וגו'. רק לאנשים האל, הקשות.
ד"א: אלהות הם, אלו חזקים.

6. AND LOT WENT OUT UNTO THEM TO THE DOOR . . . AND HE SAID: I PRAY YOU, MY BRETHREN, DO NOT DO SO WICKEDLY. BEHOLD NOW, I HAVE TWO DAUGHTERS . . . ONLY UNTO THESE (*HA-EL*) MEN (GEN. 19:6FF.): THEY ARE POWERFUL MEN. [ANOTHER INTERPRETATION]: THEY ARE MEN OF GODLY STRENGTH.

The word האלה – *ha-eleh* – in Hebrew is used very often as a form of description. It means "these." Our Midrash uses the same word from time to time, but it leaves out the last letter, *heh*, and the word thus become *ha-el*. The short form is very often used as one of the names of God. In our Midrash, it is meant to show how powerful Lot's visitors were. Lot sometimes uses the word *ha-el* only in describing his visitors, because it sometimes refers to God and would therefore be appropriate to use the shortened form of *ha-el* in describing his visitors who were, as we shall soon see, both human and divine.

כי על כן באו בצל קורתי, לא בזכותי, אלא בזכותו של אברהם. ד"א: כי על כן באו בצל קורתי. מלמד שהטמתה את הבית עליהם. א"ל: אם בעית מקבלתון, קבל בחלקך:

FORASMUCH AS THEY ARE COME UNDER THE SHADOW OF MY ROOF: NOT
IN MY MERIT, BUT IN THE MERIT OF ABRAHAM. ANOTHER INTERPRETA-
TION IS THAT THE VERSE FORASMUCH AS THEY ARE COME UNDER THE
SHADOW OF MY ROOF TEACHES THAT SHE [LOT'S WIFE] TURNED THE
HOUSE AGAINST THEM, SAYING TO HIM, "IF YOU WANT TO RECEIVE
THEM, RECEIVE THEM IN YOUR PORTION."

As part of Lot's appeal to his fellow Sodomites to treat his guests with
respect, he mentioned in this and subsequent Midrashim that his special guests were here not at his request, but in order to respond to the
needs of Abraham. It is hard to figure out whether or not the people
of Sodom and Gomorrah had the respect for Abraham which he very
much deserved. That will probably come up, as the story becomes more
dangerous to all the inhabitants and to Lot's family as well.

Seed Thoughts

Aryeh Mirkin, in his commentary on *Midrash Rabbah*, relies a great deal
on the Yehuda Theodore–Hanoch Albeck version and commentary of
Bereshit Rabbah (Jerusalem 1963), whose comments are most unusual
in many ways. Their commentary, in this regard, is highly critical of Lot's
wife. She disagreed with him completely in terms of his special visitors.
She seemed to be more fearful of the vengeance of the people of Sodom
rather than what the men, who were considered angels, were able to ac-
complish. In order to enforce her views, she had workmen rework the
door to her home, so that one door became two doors. As she said to
her husband, "Those of you who wish to entertain will have to enter
through your door, and those who I wish to associate with will enter
through my door and into my apartment." She was consistent in her
antipathy to these guests throughout the episode of her stay in Sodom.

Parashah Fifty, *Midrash Seven*

ז ויאמרו גש הלאה. קרב להלן! ויאמרו האחד בא לגור וישפוט שפוט, דין שדנו ראשונים
אתה בא להרוס! רבי מנחמא משם רבי ביבי: כך התנו אנשי סדום ביניהם, אמרו: כל אכסניא
שהוא בא לכאן, יהו בועלים אותו ונוטלים את ממונו, אפילו אותו שכתוב בו: ושמרו דרך ה׳,
אנו בועלים אותו ונוטלים את ממונו:

7. AND THEY SAID: STAND BACK (GEN. 19:9) – OUT OF THE WAY! AND
THEY SAID: THIS ONE FELLOW CAME IN TO SOJOURN, AND HE WILL
NEED TO PLAY THE JUDGE – YOU WISH TO DESTROY THE JUDGMENTS
OF YOUR PREDECESSORS! R. MENAHEMA SAID IN R. BIBI'S NAME: THE
SODOMITES MADE AN AGREEMENT AMONG THEMSELVES THAT WHEN-
EVER A STRANGER VISITED THEM, THEY SHOULD FORCE HIM TO SODOMY
AND ROB HIM OF HIS MONEY; EVEN HIM OF WHOM IT IS WRITTEN, THAT
THEY MAY KEEP THE WAY OF THE LORD, TO DO RIGHTEOUSNESS AND
JUSTICE (GEN. 18:19), WE WOULD USE HIM BESTIALLY AND ROB HIM OF
HIS MONEY.

It is important to note that the behavior of the Sodomites, in relationship to the divine human guests of Lot, was not something exceptional.
That is the way the Sodomites greeted or welcomed (if such a term can
be used) all visitors of Sodom who wished to become a part of their
community. They would attack him sexually and, in the process, remove
whatever monetary funds he may have at the time. It is the kind of story
which lends credence to the whole thought of destroying Sodom and
Gomorrah, since they don't deserve the gift of humanity.

—

Seed Thoughts

There are two Hebrew expressions which are used very frequently by
the peoples who made up the area around the Dead Sea and the Jordan
River. They are expressions of antipathy – opposition. They might often
say *gesh hala*, which really means "leave this place," but it is made up in a
peculiar way. The word *gesh* seems to mean "come closer," and the word
hala might mean "keep your distance." However, for whatever reason,
this is the formula where individuals are directed to leave a community
if possible. There is a second expression, used by the Sodomites and

featured in this Midrash, which might be translated as "this one came to live among us and now wishes to change our laws." These are expressions that we will come across again and again as we read about the struggle for communities in that period of time to create a way of life for themselves that will be as permanent as possible.

PARASHAH FIFTY, *Midrash Eight*

ח וישלחו האנשים את ידם ויביאו את לוט אליהם וגו' ואת האנשים אשר פתח הבית. מי שהתחיל בעבירה, ממנו התחילה הפורענות, שנאמר: ואנשי סדום וגו'. לפיכך הוכו בסנורים מקטן ועד גדול. דכוותה (בראשית ז): וימח את כל היקום אשר על פני האדמה, מי שהתחיל בעבירה, ממנו התחילה הפורעניות. דכוותה (במדבר ג): ביום הכותי כל בכור בארץ מצרים, מי שהתחיל בעבירה, ממנו התחילה הפורענות. דכוותה (שם ה): וצבתה בטנה ונפלה יריכה, אבר שהתחיל בעבירה תחלה, ממנו התחילה הפורענות. דכוותה (דברים יג): הכה תכה את יושבי העיר ההיא לפי חרב, מי שהתחיל בעבירה תחלה, ממנו התחילה הפורענות.

8. BUT THE MEN PUT FORTH THEIR HAND AND BROUGHT LOT INTO THE HOUSE TO THEM ... AND THEY SMOTE THE MEN THAT WERE AT THE DOOR (*PETHAH*) OF THE HOUSE WITH BLINDNESS (GEN. 19:10). THEY WERE FIRST TO DO THE EVIL, AND THEY WERE THE FIRST TO BE PUNISHED. SIMILARLY, AND HE BLOTTED OUT EVERY LIVING SUBSTANCE, ETC. (7:23): HE WHO WAS THE FIRST TO DO WRONG WAS THE FIRST TO BE PUNISHED. [FURTHER, ON THE DAY THAT I SMOTE ALL THE FIRSTBORN IN THE LAND OF EGYPT (NUM. 3:13): HE WHO WAS THE FIRST TO DO WRONG WAS THE FIRST TO BE PUNISHED.] FURTHER, AND HER BELLY SHALL SWELL, AND HER THIGH SHALL FALL AWAY (5:27): THE LIMB THAT WAS FIRST TO SIN WAS THE FIRST TO BE PUNISHED. [FURTHER, THOU SHALT SURELY SMITE THE INHABITANTS OF THAT CITY WITH THE EDGE OF THE SWORD (DEUT. 13:16): HE WHO WAS THE FIRST TO DO WRONG WAS THE FIRST TO BE PUNISHED.]

The main teaching of this Midrash has already been stated in its opening lines. That lesson is that those who sin first deserve to be punished first. The Midrash will bring to our attention a number of places in Scripture where this point was taught, beginning immediately with events during the time of the Flood, where it was quite clear that those who began the sin which brought about the Flood were punished first.

These included, first, the human being, then the beasts in the field, then the birds above, then the crawling things. But the human being was punished first because he was the first to sin. This lesson will be taught again and again as we go through the material of this particular Midrash. In the case of the angels who brought Lot into the house and closed the door, those outside the entrance were stricken with blindness, but in the following order: They were stricken with blindness from the youngest to the old – first the children, then the youth, and finally the elders. After the *sotah* episode, similar behavior can be found in what is called "the abandoned city," where all of the people worshipped idols. In the city, the human beings were punished first, and later the animals, fulfilling the decree that those who sin first should be punished first.

There are several phrases which are repeated time and time again, and it is important that we become familiar with them. Let me first state the Hebrew, where the punishment is described as מקטן ועד גדול – *mi-katan ve-ad gadol*. In other words, no one escaped this punishment. It included even the very young (the *katan*) as well as the adult community (who were the *gedolim*). There is another phrase which repeats itself, so that we realize how deeply felt was God's anger at those who misused the blessings of being a human being. The phrase is מנער ועד זקן – *mi-naar ve-ad zaken*. It refers to the youth which presumably would be anywhere from a teenager (*naar*) to a more advanced adult, and to a *zaken*, which would be even more advanced than what was described for a *gadol*. So the young and the old, the youth and the elders – that encompasses the entire community.

וילאו למצא הפתח, אלאון, היך מה דאת אמר (ישעיה טז): והיה כי נראה כי נלאה מואב, אינסון, היך מד"א (שם א): נלאיתי נשוא, אישתטון, היך מה דאת אמר (ירמיה ד): כי אויל עמי:

SO THAT THEY WEARIED (*WAYYILE'U*) THEMSELVES TO FIND THE DOOR: [THEY WERE WEARIED, AS IN THE VERSE, AND IT SHALL COME TO PASS, WHEN MOAB HATH WEARIED HIMSELF (ISA. 16:12); THEY WERE TESTED, AS IN THE VERSE, I AM WEARY TO BEAR THEM (1:14)]; THEY WERE MAD-DENED, AS IN THE VERSE, FOR MY PEOPLE IS FOOLISH – *EWIL* (JER. 4:22). [ALL SECTIONS IN THIS MIDRASH IN PARENTHESES ADDED TO THE SONCINO TRANSLATION.]

The text notes that Lot's family belittled what the angels were doing – in the first place, the family had no knowledge of their being angels. However, the moment they saw the first fires that arose in the lower part of Sodom, they changed their tune, and watched everything happening with great disbelief.

PARASHAH FIFTY, *Midrash Nine*

ט כי משחיתים אנחנו. ר' לוי בשם רב נחמן: מלאכי השרת על ידי שגילו מסטורין של הקב"ה, נדחו ממחיצתן מאה ושלשים ושמונה שנה.

9. AND THE MEN SAID TO LOT . . . FOR WE WILL DESTROY THIS PLACE (GEN. 19:13). R. LEVI SAID IN R. NAHMAN'S NAME: BECAUSE THE MINIS-TERING ANGELS REVEALED GOD'S SECRET, THEY WERE BANISHED FROM THEIR PRECINCTS A HUNDRED AND THIRTY-EIGHT YEARS.

This Midrash is quite remarkable. The men, of course, were the angels, who we have been dealing with in the past several Midrashim. They were criticized because they said: "We will be destroying the city." How could they have said such a thing that midrashic scholars added? Surely they realized that God made these decisions which they have merely carried out. They are being accused of reciting something for no reason whatsoever; they did not have to state their objective. Furthermore, they said what they said without permission. They were angels of mercy carrying out God's will, and they were not original decision-makers. As a result of their interference, which is after all God's exclusive right, they were punished, they were eliminated from angelic responsibilities for 138 years. More will be spoken about this.

ורבי תנחומא: הוה מפיק לישנא קלה. א"ר חמא בר חנינא: על שנתגאו ואמרו כי משחיתים אנחנו את המקום הזה. וידבר אל חתניו וגו'. ארבע בנות היו לו שתים ארוסות ושתים נשואות, לקוחי בנותיו אין כתיב כאן, אלא לוקחי בנותיו. ויהי כמצחק בעיני חתניו.

R. TANHUMA EXPRESSED IT IN THE WORD *KELAH*. R. HAMA B. HANINA SAID: [THEY WERE PUNISHED] BECAUSE THEY EXPRESSED THEMSELVES BOASTFULLY, FOR *WE WILL DESTROY THIS PLACE*. AND LOT WENT OUT, AND SPOKE UNTO HIS SONS-IN-LAW [AND] THOSE WHO WERE TAKING HIS DAUGHTERS (GEN. 19:14). HE HAD FOUR DAUGHTERS, TWO BETROTHED AND TWO MARRIED, FOR IT IS NOT WRITTEN: WHO WERE MARRIED TO HIS DAUGHTERS, BUT WHO WERE TAKING [I.E., MARRYING] HIS DAUGH-TERS. BUT HE SEEMED UNTO HIS SONS-IN-LAW AS ONE THAT JESTED.

The reason why he used these two forms of expression is because two of his daughters were married, and two of them had been engaged to be married but had not yet been married. Thus, the married daughters were with their husbands; the unmarried daughters lived with their father. Sometimes, he would take a shortcut in his speech and describe them together as "those who were taking [i.e., marrying] his daughters."

אמרו לו: אדרכולין וכרבלין במדינה, ומדינה נהפכת!:

SAID THEY TO HIM: ORGANS AND CYMBALS ARE IN THE LAND AND THE LAND IS TO BE OVERTHROWN!

Musical instruments, such as organs and cymbals, are of as little importance as the messages about the punishment of Sodom and Gomorrah.

Seed Thoughts

From a certain point of view, it can be said that the ministering angels received what we sometimes call a bad press. They were accused of something of which they should not have been accused. Suppose, in the twenty-first century, that an automobile maker was to inform the public about a new automobile in the making. One of his engineers might say to the press: "It is my responsibility to produce a new car." But it was not only his responsibility; there are those above him who had appointed him. They might very well have been insulted. But this does not usually happen because it is pretty certain that the individual involved had no intention of listening to the importance of someone else. It is quite certain that the angels involved had no intention of suggesting that they, and not God, were responsible for the destruction of Sodom. They were merely describing their present role, and they did so accurately. Why, then, have they been criticized so severely? Because the Almighty was interested in conveying a message of extreme honesty, especially on the part of the angels who represented Him. This lesson became most important, and the angels had to suffer the consequences. A punishment of 138 years of isolation is very difficult for a human being, but much less so for angels, who are eternal, for whom the passage of time is not a serious matter. God had a reason for punishing His angels, and that reason was to make honesty a very important part of the angelic program.

Additional Commentary

The Serving Angels (or Malachei ha-Sharet)

In light of what we have learned about the serving angels, it would be of interest to simply note the biblical understanding of what actually happened to them. The story of Sodom and its prophetic destruction happened on the same day as the birth of Isaac to Abraham and Sarah. A number of years later, Isaac was present at the birth of Jacob. He was also present when Jacob was beginning his journey to visit his relatives in Upper Mesopotamia. This is where Jacob had his famous dream of a ladder whose foundation was on earth but which reached heaven. It also said that angels were ascending and descending the ladder in that order. How could angels ascend the ladder unless they were on earth, which is what happened? What is meant is that the angels of mercy were permitted to ascend the ladder and thus end their isolation from the other serving angels, but we do not yet know whether or not they return completely to be with their colleagues. At any rate, their function was resumed, which is why it is written in the dream that angels ascended. They were the ones who were originally punished, but their punishment apparently had now ended. (*HaMidrash HaMevo'ar*)

PARASHAH FIFTY, *Midrash Ten*

י וכמו השחר עולה ויאיצו המלאכים בלוט לאמר. א"ר חנינא: משיעלה עמוד השחר
עד שיאיר המזרח, אדם מהלך ארבעה מילין, משהאיר המזרח עד שתנץ החמה ארבע
מילין, שנאמר: וכמו השחר עלה. וכתיב: השמש יצא על הארץ. ומסדום לצוער ארבע
מילין? א"ר זעירא: המלאך היה מקדר לפניהם את הדרך. ומנין משהאיר המזרח עד
שתנץ החמה אדם מהלך ארבע מילין? כמו וכמו, מילתא דמיא למילתא. אמר רבי יוסי
בר אבין: אם יאמר לך אדם: הדא כוכבתא דצפרא, איילתא דשחרא, שקרן הוא! פעמים
פוחתת ופעמים שהיא מוספת, אלא כמין תרתין קרנין, דנהורא סלקין ממדינחא ומנהרין
לעלמא.

10. AND AS THE MORNING AROSE, THEN THE ANGELS HASTENED
LOT, SAYING (GEN. 19:15). R. HANINA SAID: A MAN CAN WALK FOUR
MILES FROM DAWN UNTIL IT BECOMES LIGHT IN THE EAST; FOR IT
SAYS: AND WHEN THE MORNING AROSE [I.E., AT EARLY DAWN] ... AND
THEN IT IS WRITTEN: THE SUN WAS RISEN UPON THE EARTH WHEN
LOT CAME UNTO ZOAR (19:23). IS IT THEN FOUR MILES FROM SODOM
TO ZOAR? SAID R. ZE'IRA: THE ANGEL LEVELED THE WAY FOR THEM.
AND HOW DO WE KNOW THAT ONE CAN WALK FOUR MILES FROM
THE TIME IT BECOMES LIGHT IN THE EAST UNTIL THE SUN BEGINS
TO SPARKLE? – AND AS IS WRITTEN, INTIMATING THAT ONE PERIOD
IS EQUAL TO THE OTHER. R. JOSE B. ABIN SAID: IF A MAN TELLS YOU
THAT THE MORNING STAR IS THE MORNING DAWN, HE IS SPEAKING
FALSELY, FOR SOMETIMES IT IS EARLIER AND SOMETIMES LATER; BUT
TWO RAYS OF LIGHT, AS IT WERE, ISSUE FROM THE EAST AND LIGHT
UP THE WORLD.

The reason why the Midrash goes into such tremendous detail about
the time in which light appears eventually to provide the light of the day
is because it attempts to differentiate between the time of the morning star and the full richness of the sun's rays during a typical day in
that region. It is hard to know whether the word "mile" means the same
thing in the midrashic literature as it does in our day. All these things are
meant to dramatize the terrible event about to take place in the utter destruction of Sodom and Gomorrah. The fact that the distance between
Sodom and Zoar, which would be the temporary resting place of Lot
and his family, also conveys a scene of great difficulty in escaping from
Sodom by foot for a period of four miles.

ואת שתי בנותיך הנמצאות וגו'. א"ר טוביה בר רבי יצחק: שתי מציאות רות המואביה ונעמה
העמונית. אמר רבי יצחק (תהלים פט): מצאתי דוד עבדי. היכן מצאתי אותו? בסדום:

ARISE, TAKE THY WIFE AND THY TWO DAUGHTERS THAT ARE FOUND. R.
TOBIAH B. R. ISAAC SAID: TWO "FINDS" [WOULD SPRING FROM THEM],
RUTH THE MOABITESS AND NAAMAH THE AMMONITESS. R. ISAAC COM-
MENTED: I HAVE FOUND DAVID MY SERVANT (PS. 89:21): WHERE DID I
FIND HIM? IN SODOM.

This Midrash will repeat several times that Ruth the Moabite and
Naamah the Ammonite are direct descendants of Lot and his daughters. That is also a reason to explain why Rabbi Tobiah b. Rabbi Isaac
said that he discovered David in Sodom. The meaning is that David
was descended from Ruth, and therefore one can understand what he
meant when he said that David was found in Sodom. The meaning is
that events in Sodom eventually produced the personality and character
of David, one of the greatest characters who ever lived.

—

Seed Thoughts

There is something in this story that reflects a mind of tremendous literary talent. What I am now going to discuss is something I discovered
many years ago when I first read the terrible story of the destruction of
Sodom and Gomorrah. Why does this story require a discussion on the
appearance of light? Why do we have to know? When the morning star
usually arises, how important is it that we know when daylight comes,
and when the sun reaches the fullness of its power? Why is this spoken of
now? In this Midrash, and in association with the destruction of Sodom
and Gomorrah, the people of Sodom and Gomorrah knew very well
that their behavior as a community was criticized over a period of years,
and they paid very little attention to that criticism. The challenge of
reality is now coming upon all of them. The presence of the angels with
Lot signaled a tremendous change in their present and future. There is a
reason for calling their attention to the remarkable phenomenon of the
coming of daylight and the tremendous power of the sun to the entire
universe. There are surely some people in Sodom and Gomorrah who
might understand that when this kind of miraculous physical phenomenon embracing our lives as human beings. Why do we allow ourselves
to cheapen our lives with the worst possible immoral behavior? It is the

contrast between the light of the universe and the darkness of Sodom and Gomorrah way of life that is the great literary achievement of this story. The impact is not only on the people of that day. It influences each one of us who reads this account, and tries his or her best to live up to the greatest of all blessings – the possibility of a good life under the spiritual leadership of the Holy One, blessed be He.

PARASHAH FIFTY, *Midrash Eleven*

יא ויתמהמה, תמהון אחר תמהון. אמר: כמה אבוד בכסף וזהב אבנים טובות ומרגליות! הדא הוא דכתיב (קהלת ה): עושר שמור לבעליו לרעתו.

11. BUT HE LINGERED – *WAYYITHMAHAMAH* (GEN. 19:16). HE KEPT ON DELAYING, EXCLAIMING, "WHAT A LOSS OF GOLD AND SILVER AND PRECIOUS STONES!" THUS IT IS WRITTEN: RICHES KEPT BY THE OWNER THEREOF TO HIS HURT (ECCL. 5:12).

The Midrash uses the text from Ecclesiastes to state a number of re-markable interpretations. The point they make is the fact that all those individuals, and sometimes more than individuals, have become impor-tant figures in the biblical story due to the fact that they had become owners of tremendous wealth in terms of gold, silver, and precious stones.

רבי יהושע בן לוי אמר: זה לוט. רבי שמואל בר נחמן אמר: זה קרח. רבי יהודה בר סימון אמר: זה נבות. רבי לוי אמר: זה המן. רבי יצחק אמר: זה שבט ראובן וגד. רבנן אמרי: זה איוב, דהוה עתיר ונתמסכן, וחזר למה דהוה.

R. JOSHUA B. LEVI SAID: THIS APPLIES TO LOT. R. SAMUEL B. NAHMAN SAID: IT APPLIES TO KORAH. R. JUDAH B. R. SIMON REFERRED IT TO NABOTH; R. LEVI, TO HAMAN; R. ISAAC, TO THE TRIBES OF REUBEN AND GAD; THE RABBIS APPLIED IT TO THE TRIBE OF LEVI [CURRENT EDI-TIONS: OR TO JOB], WHICH BECAME IMPOVERISHED BUT SUBSEQUENTLY REGAINED THEIR ORIGINAL STATE.

This applies to all of them. It is their very wealth that motivates them to challenge the great leader, Moses, and through Moses, challenges the Almighty Himself. In every case, as listed, their wealth was their ruination. I was surprised to note that the Midrash included the tribes of Reuben, Gad, and half of the tribe of Menashe, who requested that they be given land in Trans-Jordan. I and others thought that the tribe of Reuben and his associates were doing something noble by settling the land as early as possible, and then helping the rest of Israel carry on until they come home. The Midrash had an entirely different view of this behavior, claiming that the behavior of Reuben and his associates possessed tremendous flocks of sheep of various sizes and various forms of development. They chose Trans-Jordan, because its fields were excellent areas whereby their flocks could live and multiply. The Midrash also has a critical view of Job. Job did not live up to the Almighty's hopes that he would accept his poverty, at the same time retaining his faith in God. What actually happened was that Job complained bitterly that he did not deserve what was happening to him. The result was that everything that was taken from him was restored to him. The conclusion was that he was given every manner of blessing for this world but that it did not include the World to Come.

ויחזיקו האנשים בידו וביד אשתו וביד שתי בנותיו וגו'. מי היה זה? זה רפאל. אתיבון, והא כתיב: ויוציאוהו ויניחוהו, וכתיב: ויהי כהוציאם אותם החוצה? א"ל: קרון דבתריה, ויאמרו המלט על נפשך אין כתיב, אלא ויאמר המלט על נפשך. ההרה המלט פן תספה, בזכות אברהם שנקרא הר, (שיר ב): מדלג על ההרים. ואומר (מיכה ו): שמעו הרים וגו'. ואנכי לא אוכל להמלט ההרה וגו'. ויאמר לוט אליהם אל נא אדני הנה מצא עבדך חן בעיניך וגו'. ר' ברכיה ורבי לוי בשם רבי חמא בר חנינא: שני בני אדם אמרו דבר אחד, לוט וצרפית. צרפית אמרה: עד שלא באת אצלי, היה הקב"ה רואה מעשי ומעשה אנשי עירי, והיו מעשי רבים על אנשי בני עירי, והייתי צדקת בינהם, עכשיו שבאת אצלי, באת להזכיר את עוני ולהמית את בני! לוט אמר: עד שלא הלכתי אצל אברהם, היה הקב"ה רואה מעשי ומעשי בני עירי, ואני צדיק בינהם, עכשיו שאני הולך אצל אברהם שמעשיו רבים על שלי, איני יכול לעמוד בנחלתו. ואנכי לא אוכל. ר' ברכיה בשם ר' לוי: מן הן תנינן, כשם שהנוה הרעה בודק, כך הנוה היפה בודק. מן הכא ואנכי לא אוכל להמלט ההרה פן תדבקני, וסדום בעומקא היא, לפום כך הוא אומר: ואנכי לא אוכל להמלט ההרה, שרי בעומקא. ואינון אמרו ליה: פוק לטורא. והוא אמר: הכין? הדא אמרה: אפילו מנוה הרעה לנוה היפה, הרי שהנוה היפה בודק, הנה נא העיר הזאת קרובה לנוס שמה. ויאמר אליו: הנה נשאתי פניך גם לדבר הזה. א"ר חלפתא קסרייא: ומה אם לוט? על ידי שכבד את המלאך נשא לו פנים, לך לא אשא פנים מפניך ומפני אבותיך? (במדבר ו): ישא ה' פניו אליך:

AND THE MEN LAID HOLD UPON HIS HAND, AND UPON THE HAND OF HIS WIFE, AND UPON THE HAND OF HIS TWO DAUGHTERS, ETC. WHO WAS IT? RAPHAEL. A DIFFICULTY WAS RAISED: IT IS WRITTEN: AND IT CAME TO PASS, WHEN THEY HAD BROUGHT THEM FORTH? READ WHAT

FOLLOWS, HE REPLIED; IT IS NOT WRITTEN: AND *THEY* SAID, BUT AND
HE SAID: ESCAPE FOR THY LIFE. IF SO, WHY DOES IT SAY, AND THEY LAID
HOLD, ETC.? [BECAUSE IT MEANS], ABRAHAM'S MERIT TOGETHER WITH
RAPHAEL. ESCAPE TO THE MOUNTAIN, I.E., FOR THE SAKE OF ABRAHAM.
LEST THOU BE SWEPT AWAY – THROUGH THE INIQUITY OF THE CITY.
AND LOT SAID UNTO THEM: OH, NOT SO, MY LORD; BEHOLD NOW, THY
SERVANT HATH FOUND GRACE IN THY SIGHT . . . AND I CANNOT ESCAPE
TO THE MOUNTAIN, LEST THE EVIL OVERTAKE ME, AND I DIE (GEN.
19:18F.). R. BEREKIAH AND R. LEVI IN THE NAME OF R. HUNA B. HANINA
SAID: TWO PEOPLE SAID THE SAME THING, LOT AND THE WOMAN OF
ZAREPHATH. THE WOMAN OF ZAREPHATH SAID: BEFORE YOU [ELIJAH]
CAME TO ME, THE HOLY ONE, BLESSED BE HE, SAW MY [GOOD] DEEDS
AND THOSE OF MY FELLOW CITIZENS, AND MINE EXCEEDED THEIRS.
NOW, HOWEVER, THAT YOU HAVE COME HERE, YOU HAVE RECALLED MY
SINS AND SLAIN MY SON. LOT SAID: BEFORE I WENT TO ABRAHAM, THE
LORD SAW MY [GOOD] DEEDS AND THE DEEDS OF MY FELLOW CITIZENS,
AND MINE EXCEEDED THEIRS. NOW THAT I AM TO GO TO ABRAHAM, HIS
GOOD DEEDS ARE SO MUCH MORE THAN MINE, AND I CANNOT WITH-
STAND HIS BURNING COALS. HENCE, I AM UNABLE [TO ESCAPE TO THE
MOUNTAIN]. R. BEREKIAH SAID IN R. LEVI'S NAME: WHAT IS THE SOURCE
OF WHAT WE LEARNT: JUST AS A BAD DWELLING PUTS ONE TO THE TEST,
SO DOES A GOOD ONE? THIS PASSAGE: AND I CANNOT ESCAPE TO THE
MOUNTAIN; HE DWELLS IN A VALLEY AND THEY TELL HIM TO GO TO THE
MOUNTAIN AND HE REPLIES THUS! THIS PROVES THAT EVEN [IN CHANG-
ING] FROM A BAD DWELLING TO A GOOD ONE [THERE MAY BE DANGER],
BECAUSE [EVEN] A GOOD DWELLING IS A TEST. BEHOLD NOW, THIS CITY
IS NEAR TO FLEE UNTO . . . AND HE SAID UNTO HIM: SEE, I HAVE SHOWN
THEE FAVOR CONCERNING THIS THING ALSO (19:20F.). R. TAHLIFA OF
KETIREH SAID: [GOD SAID TO ISRAEL:] "IF THE ANGEL SHOWED FAVOR
TO LOT BECAUSE HE [LOT] HAD SHOWN HIM HONOR, WILL I NOT SHOW
THEE FAVOR FOR THINE OWN SAKE AND FOR THE SAKE OF THINE ANCES-
TORS?" [HENCE IT IS WRITTEN]: THE LORD LIFT UP HIS COUNTENANCE
UPON THEE, AND GIVE THEE PEACE (NUM. 6:26).

The remainder of the Midrash portrays some of the difficulties that
faced the accompanying angels in their attempt to save the lives of Lot
and his family. The most difficult situation had to do with Lot himself
and his struggle to change the direction in which the angels wished
to take them and thus save their lives. The angels – sometimes only

Raphael, and sometimes both Raphael and Gabriel – kept saying to them: "Save your lives! You have to reach the top of this hill, which is the mountainous area since Sodom is in the valley, and you have to be as far away from it as possible." It is this advice which bothered Lot, and he protested. He claimed that he could not climb the hill to reach the mountainous area. He was quite certain that the effort would end his life. He, therefore, began urging the angelic leaders to figure out a new way of going and a new way of saving their lives. In modern times, it might have been written that he may have had a heart problem, and in such cases, climbing a steep hill would be dangerous. Lot gave no reason for his objection to the hill other than the amount of energy that would be required.

I find it most interesting that some of the great scholars who offered an opinion in the Midrash gave this entire event a midrashic interpretation. They said that the top of the hill happened to be the city of Hebron, which was the area where Abraham had his home. It was this fact that dominated Lot's opinion and concern; he did not want to be Abraham's neighbor again. They had been together in Lot's early years, since he was Abraham's nephew, but Abraham asked him to leave when their staffs could not get along and were causing much trouble. Abraham asked Lot to leave, but at the same time, gave him enough gold, silver, and precious stones to protect him throughout his lifetime. Lot was afraid that living beside Abraham again would not be good for him. He could not compete with Abraham in terms of doing good deeds, and he was worried that if they should have a difference of opinion, Lot would then have to leave again and fend for himself. This was the real reason for his interfering with the leadership of the angels, although our Midrash did not as of yet reach the end of the story. We know, of course, from the biblical narrative, that the angels did discover a small village halfway to Zoar where Lot and his family were allowed to end their traveling and rebuild their home in that spot.

Parashah Fifty, *Midrash Twelve*

יב מהר המלט שמה כי לא אוכל לעשות דבר עד בואך שמה וגו'. א"ר לוי: משל למדינה
שהיו לה שני פיטרונין, אחד עירוני ואחד בן המדינה, וכעס עליהם המלך ובקש לרדותן.
אמר המלך: אם רודה אני אותם בפני, בני המדינה עכשיו הן אומרים: אלו היה עירוני כאן היה
מתקיים עלינו, ואילו היה בפני עירוני עכשיו הן אומרין: אילו בן המדינה שם, היה מתקיים
עלינו. כך לפי שהיו סדומיים מהם עובדים לחמה ומהם עובדים ללבנה. אמר הקב"ה: אם
אני רודה אותן ביום, עכשיו הם אומרין: אילו היתה לבנה שם, היתה מקיימת עלינו. אם אני
רודה אותם בלילה, עכשיו הם אומרין: אילו היתה החמה שם, היתה מקיימת עלינו. אלא,
נקם מהם בששה עשר בניסן, בשעה שהחמה ולבנה עומדים ברקיע.

12. HASTEN THOU, ESCAPE THITHER; FOR I CANNOT DO ANYTHING TILL
THOU BE COME THITHER, ETC. (GEN. 19:22). R. LEVI SAID: THIS MAY BE
COMPARED TO A GREAT CITY WHICH HAD TWO PATRONS, ONE FROM A
LARGE TOWN AND THE OTHER A PROVINCIAL TOWN. THE KING WAS AN-
GRY WITH THEM [THE CITIZENS] AND WISHED TO PUNISH THEM. SAID
THE KING: "IF I PUNISH THEM IN THE PRESENCE OF THE TOWNSMAN
ALONE, THEY WILL SAY, 'HAD THE PROVINCIAL BEEN HERE, HE WOULD
HAVE PROTECTED US'; WHILE IF I PUNISH THEM IN THE PRESENCE OF
THE PROVINCIAL THEY WILL SAY, 'HAD THE TOWNSMAN BEEN HERE
HE WOULD HAVE PROTECTED US.'" SIMILARLY, BECAUSE SOME OF THE
SODOMITES WORSHIPPED THE SUN AND OTHERS THE MOON, GOD SAID:
"IF I PUNISH THEM BY DAY THEY WILL SAY, 'HAD THE MOON BEEN THERE
IT WOULD HAVE PROTECTED US'; WHILE IF I PUNISH THEM AT NIGHT
THEY WILL SAY, 'HAD THE SUN BEEN THERE IT WOULD HAVE PROTECTED
US.'" THEREFORE [HE DESTROYED THEM] ON THE SIXTEENTH OF NISAN,
WHEN BOTH THE SUN AND THE MOON ARE VISIBLE IN THE SKY.

The remarkable thing about this Midrash is that the day of the sixteenth of Nisan, which is the second day of Passover, is described as a
day when the moon can also be visible in the daytime. Not necessarily
the entire day, but enough time to make a difference and to become
noticeable. It would be interesting to note if this situation remains the
same today as well.

הה"ד: השמש יצא על הארץ ולוט בא צוערה וגו':

HENCE IT IS WRITTEN: THE SUN WAS RISEN UPON THE EARTH WHEN LOT
CAME UNTO ZOAR (GEN. 19:23).

And at that time the moon was still visible (Soncino). If it turns out the moon is visible during the day, even if it is only left over from the night, it is still a remarkable interpretation of the parable of the patrons based entirely on movements in the sky. This would be a form of commemorating the day of the destruction of Sodom, which is really not that important to remember. But it is also a key to the solution of an interesting parable based entirely on the living reality of our heavens.

⁓

Seed Thoughts

The cities and/or communities of the ancient world or, at any rate, the world we are talking about is probably the second century of the Common Era. Cities in those days did not have what we call a "police force" to look after law enforcement in their area. Sometimes, they had branches of the military living within the bounds of their community who might have acted as police temporarily, although they had never been trained. In the absence of such resources, cities (if we can call them that) or gatherings of people who live next to each other, who could be communities or cities, had to face the problem of law and order. They thus appointed individuals described in our Midrash as being patrons. The community in our Midrash describes one leading patron who knew the city well and was trained in what we would call police work. He also had an assistant less talented than he, who helped him very much. Sometimes, the patron would appoint other people to help him depending upon the size of the community or the city, and would have the beginnings of what we would call a "police force." Our Midrash must be describing a smaller community – it refers only to one patron and an assistant. It is also important to notice that they were appointed by the king in those places which had a king and therefore a throne of authority.

א וה' המטיר על סדום ועל עמורה גפרית ואש וגו'. כתיב (תהלים נח): כמו שבלול תמס יהלך
נפל אשת בל חזו שמש וגו'. כהדין כיליי סיליי ליימצא כשלשול הזה שהוא נמחה בצואה,
כאישית זו שאינה מספקת לראות שמש, עד שהיא חוזרת לעפר, כאשת איש שזינתה
והיא מתביישת שלא תראה עוברה והיא משליכתו בלילה קודם שלא תחזנה שמש, הה"ד:
השמש יצא על הארץ ולוט בא צוערה:

1. THEN THE LORD CAUSED TO RAIN UPON SODOM AND UPON GOMORRAH
BRIMSTONE AND FIRE FROM THE LORD OUT OF HEAVEN (GEN. 19:24). IT
IS WRITTEN: LET THEM BE LIKE A SNAIL WHICH MELTETH AND PASSETH
AWAY, LIKE THE UNTIMELY BIRTHS OF A WOMAN, THAT HAVE NOT SEEN
THE SUN (PS. 58:9). LIKE A SNAIL, LIKE A SLUG WHICH DISSOLVES IN
EXCREMENTS; LIKE A MOLE WHICH SEES NOT THE LIGHT BEFORE IT
RETURNS TO THE DUST; LIKE A MARRIED WOMAN WHO HAS COMMITTED
ADULTERY, AND, BEING ASHAMED THAT HER CHILD SHOULD BE DISCOV-
ERED, CASTS IT AWAY AT NIGHT BEFORE IT SEES THE SUN. HENCE IT IS
WRITTEN: THE SUN WAS RISEN UPON THE EARTH ... AND THE LORD
[HAD] CAUSED TO RAIN UPON SODOM.

We now begin a series of Midrashim whose goal seems to be to indicate to the reader that the suffering and the hardship that came to the
inhabitants of Sodom and Gomorrah were far greater than was ever to
be expected. The first comparison is that of a snail. The life of a snail is
very short-lived, and it experiences very little of the light of the world.
The suffering in Sodom and Gomorrah was on the very difficult level
of the life of the snail. Let us go further. The second comparison was
even worse than the snail, because it deals with those who came into
the world without sight and left with either seeing little or nothing of
the light of the world. The most heart-wrenching of all is the illustration of the adulteress who is ashamed of her way of life and her fears
are concentrated on the new child she has created who would be seen

by people who know her or about her. This is an embarrassment too great for her, and she would rather put the infant to death than face the consequences of his life. What we are being told with this illustration is that there is one thing worse than physical suffering, and that is that life itself has no meaning.

PARASHAH FIFTY-ONE, *Midrash Two*

ב וה' המטיר על סדום וגו'. משל לשני מדינות שמרדו במלך. אמר המלך: תשרף אחת
משלה וא' תשרף מטמיון. כך להלן (ישעיה לד): ונהפכו נחליה לזפת ועפרה לגפרית. ברם
הכא, וה' המטיר על סדום ועל עמורה וגו'. אמר ר' אבון: לשפחה שהיתה רודה פת בתנור.
בא בן גברתה ורדת פת, ונתנה לו. בא בן בנה ורדת גחלים, ונתנה לו. כך להלן: ויאמר ה'
אל משה הנני ממטיר לכם לחם מן השמים. ברם הכא, וה' המטיר על סדום ועל עמורה
גפרית ואש. ר' חלבו בן ר' חילפי בר סמקאי בשם ר"י בר ר' סימון. וה' המטיר על סדום, זה
גבריאל. מאת ה' מן השמים, זה הקב"ה. אר"א: כל מקום שנאמר וה', הוא ובית דינו.

2. THEN THE LORD CAUSED TO RAIN UPON SODOM, ETC. THIS MAY BE COMPARED TO TWO COUNTRIES THAT REVOLTED AGAINST THE KING, WHEREUPON THE KING ORDERED ONE TO BE BURNT DOWN AT ITS OWN COST, AND THE OTHER TO BE BURNT DOWN AT THE EXCHEQUER'S COST. SIMILARLY, ELSEWHERE WE FIND: AND THE STREAMS THEREOF [SC. EDOM] SHALL BE TURNED INTO PITCH, AND THE DUST THEREOF INTO BRIMSTONE (ISA. 34:9); WHEREAS, HERE WE READ: THEN THE LORD CAUSED TO RAIN UPON SODOM AND UPON GOMORRAH, ETC. R. ABIN SAID: IT MAY BE COMPARED TO A SERVANT WHO WAS REMOVING BREAD FROM THE OVEN. HER CHILD CAME AND TOOK OUT A LOAF, WHEREUPON SHE LET HIM HAVE IT; BUT HER MISTRESS'S CHILD CAME AND TOOK OUT BURNING COALS, AND SHE LET HIM HAVE THEM. SIMILARLY, ELSEWHERE IT SAYS: THEN THE LORD SAID UNTO MOSES: BEHOLD, I WILL CAUSE TO RAIN BREAD FROM HEAVEN FOR YOU (EX. 16:4); WHEREAS HERE WE READ: THEN THE LORD CAUSED TO RAIN UPON SODOM AND UPON GOMORRAH BRIMSTONE AND FIRE. ABBA HILFI, THE SON OF SAMKAI, SAID IN THE NAME OF R. JUDAH: THEN THE LORD CAUSED TO RAIN, ETC. REFERS TO GABRIEL; FROM THE LORD (OUT OF HEAVEN, TO THE HOLY ONE, BLESSED BE HE). R. LEAZAR SAID: WHEREVER "AND THE LORD" OCCURS, IT MEANS, HE AND HIS HEAVENLY COURT.

What is the question that seems to be bothering the writers of the Midrash that so many comparisons follow? It seems to be that both fire and brimstone descended upon Sodom and Gomorrah. Why the two of them? Would not fire have done sufficient damage? Would not brimstone have done sufficient damage? It is at this point where the Midrash, in trying to answer the question, tries to answer it with various comparisons. Why the example of the two states? Because the original questions had to do with two items – fire and brimstone. The Midrash gives us this interpretation but apparently it needs more. It is in that connection that the example of the cook and the two children is also added. Both demonstrate the anger of the king and the supposed reason for his severe punishment. The king, of course, in these examples, represents the Holy One. When the same word or name being repeated in various parts of Scripture, this is meant to show how much additional energy is required in the downfall of Sodom and Gomorrah. Each of the verses require a name to be repeated twice. By the same token, God required fire and brimstone together.

א"ר יצחק: בתורה בנביאים וכתובים מצינו שההדיוט מזכיר שמו ב' פעמים: בפסוק אחד בתורה (בראשית ד): ויאמר למך לנשיו, נשי" אין כתיב כאן, אלא נשי למך האזנה וגו'. בנביאים (מלכים א א): ויאמר המלך להם קחו עמכם את עבדי אדוניכם והרכבתם את שלמה בני על הפרדה אשר לי וגו'. את בן המלך אין כתיב כאן, אלא את שלמה בני. בכתובים דכתיב (אסתר ח): כי כתב אשר נכתב בשם המלך ונחתם בטבעת המלך, ואת תמיה שהקב"ה מזכיר שמו שני פעמים בפסוק אחד?:

R. ISAAC SAID: BOTH IN THE TORAH [PENTATEUCH], IN THE PROPHETS, AND IN THE WRITINGS WE FIND A COMMONER MENTIONING HIS NAME TWICE IN ONE VERSE. IN THE TORAH: AND LAMECH SAID UNTO HIS WIVES: ADAH AND ZILLAH HEAR MY VOICE; THIS IS NOT FOLLOWED BY, "MY WIVES," BUT BY, YE WIVES OF LAMECH (GEN. 4:23). IN THE PROPHETS: AND THE KING SAID UNTO THEM: TAKE WITH YOU THE SERVANTS OF YOUR LORD, AND CAUSE SOLOMON MY SON TO RIDE UPON MINE OWN MULE, ETC. (I KINGS 1:33) – IT DOES NOT SAY, "TAKE MY SERVANTS," BUT "TAKE . . . THE SERVANTS OF YOUR LORD." IN THE WRITINGS: FOR THE WRITING WHICH IS WRITTEN IN THE KING'S NAME, ETC. (EST. 8:8). YET YOU WONDER THAT THE HOLY ONE, BLESSED BE HE, MENTIONS HIS NAME TWICE IN ONE VERSE!

Rabbi Isaac has introduced a most interesting interpretation in connection with certain names in Scripture. There are a number of places where the names of commoners are repeated in a verse without any purpose. For example, in Genesis, the Midrash quotes material in the light of Lamech, where the word "wives" is repeated twice without any special meaning the second time. From the Book of Esther, the word "king" is repeated twice for no special reason. We now turn to the original text of theMidrash, and now we read a surprising text: The word "the Lord" is mentioned twice, the second time for no reason. However, we create our own reason for us to understand how seriously God looked upon everything that was happening in Sodom and Gomorrah, and which texts are doing their best to elaborate this.

PARASHAH FIFTY-ONE, *Midrash Three*

ג גפרית ואש. הה"ד (תהלים יא): ימטר על רשעים פחים אש וגפרית וגו'. פחים, גומרים
ומצדין אש וגפרית. א"ר יודן: מפני מה אדם מריח ריח גפרית ונפשו סולדת עליו? למה
שהיא יודעת שהיא נידונת בה לע"ל, שנאמר: מנת כוסם. ר' ישמעאל בר נחמן משום ר'
יונתן: כפיילי פיטרין לאחר המרחץ. א"ר חנינא: אין דבר רע יורד מלמעלה. אתיבון, והכתיב
(תהלים קמח): אש וברד שלג וקיטור? אמר להם: רוח סערה היא שהיא עושה דברו. מילתא
דר"ש בן לקיש: פליגא אהא דא"ר חנינא בן פזי: (דברים כח) יפתח ה' לך את אוצרו הטוב,
מכאן שיש לו אוצרות אחרים. מאת ה' מן השמים, כמרתק מן גבר:

3. BRIMSTONE AND FIRE. THUS IT IS WRITTEN: UPON THE WICKED HE WILL CAUSE TO RAIN *PAHIM* [E.V. "COALS"] – THIS MEANS COALS AND SNARES – FIRE AND BRIMSTONE (PS. 11:6). R. JUDAN SAID: WHY DOES A MAN INSTINCTIVELY RECOIL WHEN HE SMELLS BRIMSTONE? BECAUSE HIS SOUL KNOWS THAT IT WILL BE PUNISHED THEREWITH IN THE FUTURE. THE PORTION OF THEIR CUP (11:6). R. ISHMAEL B. NAHMAN SAID IN R. JONATHAN'S NAME: LIKE A DOUBLE MEASURE OF *POTERION* AFTER A BATH. R. HANINA B. PAZZI SAID: NOTHING EVIL DESCENDS FROM ABOVE. THE SCHOLARS OBJECTED: YET IT IS WRITTEN: FIRE AND HAIL, SNOW AND VAPOR, STORMY WIND, FULFILL HIS WORD (148:8)? IT IS THE STORMY WIND ALONE WHICH FULFILS HIS WORD, HE ANSWERED THEM. THE FOLLOWING STATEMENT OF R. SIMEON B. LAKISH DISAGREES WITH THIS. FOR R. SIMEON B. LAKISH SAID: THE LORD WILL OPEN UNTO THEE HIS GOOD TREASURE (DEUT. 28:12): HENCE IT FOLLOWS THAT HE POSSESSES TREASURES OF A DIFFERENT KIND TOO. FROM THE LORD OUT OF HEAVEN: LIKE A BLOW FROM A POWERFUL MAN.

The question is raised in this Midrash as to whether only good things are rained down from heaven. How could that be when we are studying the fire and the brimstone that destroyed the cities of Sodom and Gomorrah? Can it be that the heavens respond with punishment when the people deserve it, and with rewards when the people deserve rewards? But there is another question: When the manna descended as bread from heaven, was it in response to Jewish high moral behavior, or was it an attempt to get the people to move in that direction? It is said that the Almighty always acts in keeping with his own Beth Din. In fact, the angel Gabriel, one of the three prophets in the Abraham story, represented the divine Beth Din in carrying out the punishment of Sodom and Gomorrah.

—

Seed Thoughts

These words are written on the day following Yom HaShoah, Holocaust Day, commemorating the attempt to end the Jewish people by the death camps of Europe. Nothing worse ever happened to the Jewish people, including the terrible punishment of Sodom and Gomorrah. Nowhere was it ever written that Sodom and Gomorrah buried an individual alive, or cremated very large numbers of people. This included non-Jews, but by far the majority were Jews. What happened in the Holocaust is probably the worst experience in the history of the Jewish people, including the destruction of the two Temples, the defeat of Bar Kokhba, and various other terrible events that we read about not only in Scripture but beyond the scriptural material. It is difficult to react to this terrible knowledge. We do not know why it was allowed to happen, and we hope and pray that someday the truth will be known to all of us, and our faith in the future can be restored. This is our hope and prayer.

PARASHAH FIFTY-ONE, *Midrash Four*

דויהפוך את הערים האל. רבי לוי בשם רבי שמואל בר נחמן: חמשת הכרכים הללו היו יושבות
על צור אחד, שלח מלאך את ידו והפכן, הה"ד (איוב כח): בחלמיש שלח ידו, הפך משרש הרים.
תרין אמוראי פליגי. חד אמר: בחלמיש של יד. וחד אמר: בחלמיש של אצבע קטנה.

4. AND HE OVERTHREW THOSE CITIES. (GEN. 19:25). R. LEVI SAID IN THE
NAME OF R. SAMUEL B. NAHMAN: THESE FIVE CITIES WERE BUILT ON
ONE ROCK, SO THE ANGEL STRETCHED OUT HIS HAND AND OVERTURNED
THEM, AS IT IS WRITTEN: HE PUTTETH FORTH HIS HAND UPON THE FLINT
ROCK, HE OVERTURNETH THE MOUNTAINS BY THE ROOTS (JOB 28:9).
TWO AMORAIM DISPUTE THIS. ONE SAYS, IT MEANS: WITH A FIFTH OF HIS
HAND; WHILE THE OTHER INTERPRETS: WITH A FIFTH OF HIS FINGER.

The dispute between the two Amoraim has to be understood in terms
of the Hebrew word חלמיש – *halamish*, which is part of the verse in Job.
There is a tradition that the letter *lamed* in *halamish* should not appear.
By removing that Hebrew letter (as well as the letter *yod*), what is left if
the Hebrew word חמש – *hamesh*, which means "five." The difference of
opinion, therefore, is that *halamish* should now be translated as "five" by
one scholar. The other scholar feels that the reference is to one-fifth of
the hand, indicating the small finger, making it very easy for the angel to
uproot the hill on which the five towns rested.

אמר רבי יהושע: וצמח האדמה, אפילו צמחי האדמה לקו. א"ר יהושע בן לוי: עד עכשיו אם
יקלוט אדם מטר מאוירו של סדום ויתן בערוגה, אינה מצמחת:

AND WHICH GREW UPON THE GROUND INTIMATES THAT EVEN THE
SPONTANEOUS PRODUCE OF THE GROUND WAS SMITTEN. R. JOSHUA
B. LEVI SAID: TO THIS VERY DAY, IF A MAN COLLECTS RAIN FROM THE
ATMOSPHERE OF SODOM AND POURS IT OVER A FURROW ELSEWHERE, IT
DOES NOT PROMOTE GROWTH.

This interpretation makes the devastation of Sodom and Gomorrah
even more difficult and injurious to the population. Of the five towns
that are spoken of, one of them is Zoar. None of the terrible developments just described applied to Zoar, because that was where Lot and
his family lived, and Lot was guaranteed the protection and survival of
his family circle.

PARASHAH FIFTY-ONE, *Midrash Five*

ה ותבט אשתו מאחריו. ר' יצחק אמר: שחטאה במלח באותו הלילה שבאו המלאכים אל
לוט. מה היא עושה? הולכת אל כל שכינותיה ואומרת להן: תנו לי מלח, שיש לנו אורחים,
והיא מכוונת שיכירו בהן אנשי העיר. על כן, ותהי נציב מלח:

5. BUT HIS WIFE LOOKED BACK FROM BEHIND HIM, AND SHE BECAME A
PILLAR OF SALT. R. ISAAC SAID: BECAUSE SHE SINNED THROUGH SALT.
ON THE NIGHT THAT THE ANGELS VISITED LOT, WHAT DID SHE DO? SHE
WENT ABOUT TO ALL HER NEIGHBORS AND ASKED THEM, "GIVE ME SALT,
AS WE HAVE GUESTS," HER INTENTION BEING THAT THE TOWNSPEOPLE
SHOULD BECOME AWARE OF THEIR PRESENCE. THEREFORE, SHE BECAME
A PILLAR OF SALT.

She asked her neighbors for salt even though everyone had more than
enough, because Sodom and Gomorrah were very close to the Dead
Sea, where salt was available to everyone in large amounts. What Lot's
wife actually tried to do is for her neighbors not only to know about the
visitors, but to realize that people like her were not willing to offer them
hospitality, which is what the authorities of Sodom wanted. In other
words, her punishment for salt was really measure for measure.

PARASHAH FIFTY-ONE, *Midrash Six*

וויהי בשחת אלהים את ערי הככר ויזכור אלהים את אברהם וישלח את לוט. מה זכירה נזכר
לו? שתיקה ששתק לאברהם, בשעה שאמר אברהם על שרה אשתו אחותי היא, היה יודע
ושותק. מתוך ההפכה. ר' שמואל בר נחמן אמר: שהיה שרוי בהן. רבנן אמרי: שהיה מלוה
להן ברבית:

6. AND IT CAME TO PASS, WHEN GOD DESTROYED THE CITIES OF THE
PLAIN, THAT GOD REMEMBERED ABRAHAM, AND SENT LOT OUT OF
THE MIDST OF THE OVERTHROW (GEN. 19:29). WHAT RECOLLECTION
WAS BROUGHT UP IN HIS FAVOR? THE SILENCE WHICH HE MAINTAINED
FOR ABRAHAM WHEN THE LATTER PASSED OFF SARAH AS HIS SISTER;
HE KNEW OF THIS, YET WAS SILENT. AND SENT LOT OUT OF THE MIDST
OF THE OVERTHROW, WHEN HE OVERTHREW THE CITIES IN WHICH LOT
DWELT (19:29). R. SAMUEL B. NAHMAN SAID: THIS MEANS THAT HE AC-
TUALLY DWELT IN [ALL] OF THEM. THE RABBIS SAID: IT MEANS THAT HE
LENT MONEY ON INTEREST THERE.

Two things are said here in support of the special treatment given to
Lot. In the first place, he was very helpful to Abraham. When Abraham
wanted to enter Egypt, he was forced to acknowledge that Sarah was his
sister and not his wife, a declaration which probably saved his life. Lot
knew, of course, that Sarah was his wife, but he acted as though sworn to
secrecy< and thus helped save Abraham's life. The second information
given to us in the Midrash was that Lot was self-supporting and that he
developed a liking for finance and for lending money on interest.

PARASHAH FIFTY-ONE, *Midrash Seven*

ז ויעל לוט מצוער וישב בהר. הה"ד (תהלים נז): למנצח אל תשחת לדוד מכתם בברחו מפני
שאול במערה. אמר לפניו: רבון העולמים! עד שלא נכנסתי למערה, עשית חסד עם אחרים
בשבילי. עכשיו שאני נתון במערה, יהי רצון מלפניך, אל תשחת:

7. AND LOT WENT UP OUT OF ZOAR, AND DWELT IN THE MOUNTAIN (GEN.
19:30). THUS IT IS WRITTEN: FOR THE LEADER; *AL-TASHHETH.* [A PSALM]
OF DAVID; MICHTAM; WHEN HE FLED FROM SAUL, IN THE CAVE (PS. 57:1).
HE [DAVID] PRAYED TO HIM: "SOVEREIGN OF THE UNIVERSE! BEFORE
I ENTERED THIS CAVE THOU DIDST SHOW MERCY TO OTHERS FOR MY
SAKE; NOW THAT I AM IN THE CAVE, O GRANT THAT THOU DESTROYEST
NOT (*AL TASHHETH*)!"

David often used the Psalms to express his feelings. In the Psalm
just quoted, we thank God for helping him protect himself in the cave
against Saul, and although not mentioned in this psalm, he was very
appreciative of the help Lot gave him in his early years. The fact that Lot
dwelled in Zoar and from time to time lived in the mountainous area
which was in the same territory as the five towns, made it much easier
for him to pursue his new financial business and give him a sense of
security in that regard.

PARASHAH FIFTY-ONE, *Midrash Eight*

ח ותאמר הבכירה אל הצעירה אבינו זקן וגו'. שהיו סבורות שנתכלה העולם כדור המבול.
לכה נשקה את אבינו יין וגו'. ר' תנחומא משום רבי שמואל: ונחיה מאבינו זרע, ונחיה מאבינו
בן, אין כתיב כאן, אלא ונחיה מאבינו זרע, אותו זרע שהוא בא ממקום אחר. ואי זה? זה מלך
המשיח.

8. AND THE FIRSTBORN SAID UNTO THE YOUNGER: OUR FATHER IS
OLD, AND THERE IS NOT A MAN IN THE EARTH. ETC. (GEN. 19:31). THEY
THOUGHT THAT THE WHOLE WORLD WAS DESTROYED, AS IN THE GEN-
ERATION OF THE FLOOD. COME, LET US MAKE OUR FATHER DRINK WINE
. . . THAT WE MAY PRESERVE SEED OF OUR FATHER (19:32). R. TANHUMA
SAID IN SAMUEL'S NAME: IT IS NOT WRITTEN, THAT WE MAY PRESERVE A
CHILD OF OUR FATHER, BUT, THAT WE MAY PRESERVE SEED OF OUR FA-
THER: VIZ. THE SEED THAT COMES FROM A DIFFERENT SOURCE, WHICH
IS THE KING MESSIAH.

This section of the story begins with an attempt to justify the behavior of the daughters of Lot. Just as in the story of the Flood whatever
inhabitants there were, felt that the entire world had become a source
of danger, so here too, the daughters of Lot felt that the entire world
around them had been destroyed. They were wrong, as they themselves
learned a little while later, but that feeling seems to have justified their
behavior. It is the main function of the creation of human beings to
populate the world. This was no longer possible for the daughters of
Lot, at least in terms of what they were thinking at the beginning. Since
there is no other way for us to provide a seed for our family in terms of
the justification of the birth of children, the only way to function (or so
they thought) was to make use of the only force left in the universe in
relation to their father, but this time, even sexually, as explained by the
text.

ותשקן את אביהן יין וגו'. נקוד על וי"ו של ובקומה, שבשכבה לא ידע בקומה ידע. ויהי
ממחרת ותאמר הבכירה אל הצעירה וגו'. מנין היה להם יין במערה? אלא ממה שהיין
מרובה להן, היו מביאין אותו במערות. א"ר יהודה בר סימון: נעשה להם מעין דוגמא של
עולם הבא, היך מה דאת אמר (יואל ד): והיה ביום ההוא יטפו ההרים עסיס:

AND THEY MADE THEIR FATHER DRINK WINE . . . AND HE KNEW NOT
WHEN SHE LAY DOWN, AND WHEN SHE AROSE – *U-BEKUMAH* (GEN. 19:33):

THIS WORD [U-BEKUMAH] IS DOTTED, INTIMATING THAT HE DID NOT
INDEED KNOW OF HER IYING DOWN, BUT HE DID KNOW OF HER ARISING.
AND IT CAME TO PASS ON THE MORROW, THAT THE FIRSTBORN SAID
UNTO THE YOUNGER ... LET US MAKE HIM DRINK WINE THIS NIGHT
ALSO (19:34). WHENCE DID THEY PROCURE WINE IN THE CAVE? SINCE
THEY [THE SODOMITES] HAD AN ABUNDANCE OF WINE, THEY STORED
IT IN CAVES. R. JUDAH B. SIMON SAID: A SPECIMEN, AS IT WERE, OF THE
MESSIANIC AGE WAS PROVIDED FOR THEM, AS YOU READ: AND IT SHALL
COME TO PASS IN THAT DAY, THAT THE MOUNTAINS SHALL DROP DOWN
SWEET WINE (JOEL 4:18).

The text goes along to inform us that the daughters agreed to continue
on the second night what they had done on the first night. The text mentions that the father had no knowledge of the fact that his daughters had
lain in bed with him. Nor did he know when it was that they left him.
The text mentions that the word *bekuma*, meaning when she arose to
leave, was punctuated in the most unusual way, with a dot in the middle
of the word on top. Does this mean that Lot was aware of what had
been happening with his daughters? It does not say so explicitly, but the
unusual punctuation that has been described is enough for the text or
the readership to start insinuations that this is what happened, although
it is pure speculation. The fact that they had wine for the second night
is not a problem; there could have been some wine left over from the
last night, but probably, it came from the very cave in which they were
living. It was the custom of the Sodomites (who had made an abundance of wine) to store them in various caves so that they would remain
somewhat cool and very safe from the possibility of damage.

—

Seed Thoughts

In the literature of the early verses in Chapter 51, the reference is made
more than once of the astounding information that Ruth the Moabite
and the people of Ammon were descended from Lot and his daughters.
The repetition of this kind of information may convince some readers
that it exonerates the daughters from the wickedness of their behavior.
It is not the intention of the Midrash to reach such a conclusion, but a
way might be found to explain to the reader that this conclusion is not
warranted.

PARASHAH FIFTY-ONE, *Midrash Nine*

ט ותהרין שתי בנות לוט מאביהן. אמר ר"א: לעולם אין האשה מתעברת מביאה ראשונה. אתיבין, והא כתיב: ותהרין שתי בנות לוט מאביהן? אמר ר' תנחומא: שלטו בעצמן והוציאו ערותן ונתעברו כמביאה שניה. א"ר נחמן בר חנין: כל מי שהוא להוט אחר בולמוס של עריות, סוף שמאכילין אותו מבשרו.

9. THUS WERE BOTH THE DAUGHTERS OF LOT WITH CHILD BY THEIR FATHER (GEN. 19:36). R. LEAZAR SAID: A WOMAN NEVER CONCEIVES BY HER FIRST INTIMACY. THE SCHOLARS RAISED AN OBJECTION: SURELY IT IS WRITTEN: THUS WERE BOTH THE DAUGHTERS OF LOT WITH CHILD BY THEIR FATHER? SAID R. TANHUMA: THEY PUT PRESSURE ON THEM-SELVES AND BROUGHT FORTH THEIR VIRGINITY AND THUS CONCEIVED AT THE FIRST ACT OF INTERCOURSE. R. NAHMAN B. HANIN OBSERVED: WHOEVER IS AFLAME WITH ADULTEROUS DESIRE IS EVENTUALLY FED WITH HIS OWN FLESH.

It is quite true that usually, a woman does not conceive from the first sexual encounter. However, the female body can be adjusted so that this development can be speeded up, and the first and second sexual encounters can be united as one. This happens in modern times as well, although this is not the proper place to discuss medical matters.

רבי יודן דמן גליו ורבי שמואל בר נחמן אמרין תרוויהון אמרי משום רבי אליהועיני: אין אנו יודעים אם לוט נתאוה לבנותיו, אם בנותיו נתאוו לו, מן מה דכתיב (משלי יח): לתאוה יבקש נפרד, הוי, לוט נתאוה לבנותיו ובנותיו לא נתאוו לו. ר' תנחומא בר רבי חייא משם ר' הושעיא תורגמנו: אין כל שבת ושבת שאין קורין בה פרשתו של לוט. מאי טעמיה? (שם): בכל תושיה יתגלע. א"ר אחא: יתגלעו אין כתיב כאן, אלא יתגלע, האנשים נתרחקו והנשים נתקרבו:

R. JUDAN OF GALLIA AND R. SAMUEL B. NAHMAN BOTH SAID IN THE NAME OF R. ELIJAH ENENEL: WE WOULD NOT KNOW WHETHER LOT LUSTED AFTER HIS DAUGHTERS OR THEY LUSTED AFTER HIM, BUT THAT IT SAYS: HE THAT SEPARATETH HIMSELF SEEKETH DESIRE (PROV. 18:1), WHENCE IT FOLLOWS THAT LOT DESIRED HIS DAUGHTERS. R. TANHUM B. R. HIYYA SAID IN THE NAME OF R. HOSHAYA, HIS INTERPRETER: NOT A SABBATH PASSES WITHOUT THIS CHAPTER ON LOT BEING READ. WHAT IS THE REASON? BECAUSE IT IS WRITTEN: AT EVERY [CONGRE-GATION OF] WISDOM HE IS REVEALED – OR, REPELLED (18:1). R. AHA COMMENTED: IT IS NOT WRITTEN: THEY ARE REPELLED, BUT *HE IS*

REPELLED: MEN WERE REPELLED [BY THIS READING], BUT WOMEN WERE
ATTRACTED.

There is a question as to whether Lot was influenced by his daughters
and whether he wanted to use them sexually, or conversely, whether the
daughters had similar thoughts in connection with their father. The Midrashim come back to this problem from time to time, but the opinions
are purely speculative, and there is no way in which one could come to
a conclusion. The general opinion, strictly from the text, is that Lot had
a stronger sexual appetite, which might or might not have included his
daughters, but that the daughters were far more modest in this regard
than their father. In fact, it is stated more than once that the goal of the
daughters was *le-shem Shamayim* – for the sake of Heaven. As indicated
above, they thought that with the destruction of Sodom and Gomorrah,
all of the world which they knew had been devastated. What they were
trying to do would be to continue the development of the world and in
particular, of the human beings and their culture.

A number of themes are touched upon in this Midrash, some of
which have been alluded to in these comments. They can be listed as
follows: What was the relationship between Lot and his daughters,
especially in the area of sexuality brought to the fore by the behavior of
Lot's daughters? A great deal of attention was paid to the personality of
Lot himself, which was traced from the moment he left his relationship
with Abraham until he finally shows Sodom to be his main residence.
The description of Lot was very negative, and not to have been expected
by one whose early years were brought up by his contact with Abraham,
who replaced his parents in Lot's life. A further theme had to do with
the relationship of the people of Ammon and Moab with those of Israel.
The view in the Torah was that male members of Moab and Ammon are
to be looked upon as having no relationship with the Children of Israel.
They would not be free to marry Israelite women without conversion
and the various other demands having to do with this kind of relationship. This was not so in terms of the women of Moab and Ammon, and
the halakha uses the expression *Ammoni ve-lo Ammonit*, meaning that
the restrictions had to do with the male members of Moab and Ammon. Insofar as the women of Ammon and Moab, they were permitted
to marry Israelite men. The story of Ruth and Boaz reveals this relationship in a very strong way.

Seed Thoughts

Some of the commentators raise the question of whether or not this was the first sexual encounter of the daughters of Lot. The reason is that usually, women do not give birth as a result of the first sexual intimacy, but only of the second and others. The Midrash reveals that there were many ways of solving this problem medically, so that both the first and the second sexual intimacies would be related to each other. It is quite remarkable that this behavior continues in modern times, and most married women have undertaken these surgical-like procedures in order to render their new sexual life painless. It is always remarkable to discover that what appears to be a modern medical procedure was known, for example, in Talmudic times (which is probably around the second century CE). If we want to project it to the lives of Lot, it was probably up to two millennia earlier.

PARASHAH FIFTY-ONE, *Midrash Ten*

י הה"ד (ירמיה מח): אני ידעתי נאום ה', עברתו ולא כן בדיו. ר' הונא בר פפא, ורבי סימון. רבי הונא אמר: מתחלת עיבורו של מואב, לא היה לשם זנות אלא לש"ש, שנא': לא כן בדיו עשו לש"ש, אלא לשם זנות, שנאמר (במדבר כה): וישב ישראל בשטים ויחל העם לזנות וגו'.

10. IT IS WRITTEN: I KNOW HIS [SC. MOAB'S] CONCEPTION, SAITH THE LORD, THAT IT WAS NOT SO (JER. 48:30). R. HANINA B. PAPA AND R. SIMON DISAGREE. R. HANINA B. PAPA SAID: THE ORIGINAL CONCEPTION OF MOAB WAS BROUGHT ABOUT NOT IN A SPIRIT OF IMMORALITY BUT WITH A NOBLE MOTIVE; BUT HIS SCIONS [LIT. "BRANCHES"] DID NOT ACT THUS (48:30), BUT WITH IMMORAL MOTIVES, AS IT SAYS: AND ISRAEL ABODE IN SHITTIM, AND THE PEOPLE BEGAN TO COMMIT HARLOTRY WITH THE DAUGHTERS OF MOAB (NUM. 25:1).

The first issue that is dealt with in this Midrash is the question of whether the children of Lot were involved in a noble endeavor, such as helping to build up a devastated world or whether they were engaged in harlotry. One of the Rabbis quoted maintained that even those who believed that the daughters of Lot were engaged in noble goals were first to acknowledge that the children and grandchildren of Lot did not maintain those noble aspirations. On the contrary, the Scripture itself acknowledges that they were engaged in immoral activities, such as in the Valley of Shittim, where they were described as trying to motivate Israel to give up their moral positions.

ר' סימון אמר: מתחלת עיבורו של מואב לא היה לש"ש, אלא לשם זנות, שנאמר: ועברתו לא כן. בדיו לא עשה כן. בדיו לשם זנות, אלא לש"ש, שנאמר (רות ג): ותרד הגורן ותעש ככל אשר צותה חמותה.

R. SIMON SAID: THE FIRST CONCEPTION OF MOAB WAS NOT WITH A NO-BLE MOTIVE BUT IN A SPIRIT OF IMMORALITY; HIS SCIONS DID NOT ACT THUS, BUT WITH A NOBLE MOTIVE, AS IT SAYS: AND SHE WENT DOWN UNTO THE THRESHING-FLOOR, AND DID ACCORDING TO ALL THAT HER MOTHER-IN-LAW BADE HER (RUTH 3:6).

The other point of view states that the offspring of the daughters of Lot were produced with immoral goals, but that their children and offspring changed their way of life so that they could be described as having noble motives. The text that is chosen to support this contention is the behavior of Ruth the Moabitess, and her well-behaved obedience to her mother-in-law, and eventually to Boaz, whom she later married.

א"ר לוי: אם תחלתו של מואב לשם זנות, גם סופו היה לשם זנות. בדיו לא כן עשו, וישב ישראל בשטים וגו'. ואם מתחלת עיבורו לשם שמים, אף סופו לש"ש. בדיו לא כן עשו, ותרד הגורן:

R. LEVI SAID: IF THE FIRST CONCEPTION OF MOAB WAS IN A SPIRIT OF IMMORALITY, THEN HIS SUBSEQUENT ACTIONS TOO WERE IN THE SAME SPIRIT, FOR DID NOT HIS SCIONS ACT THUS? AS IT SAYS: AND ISRAEL ABODE IN SHITTIM, ETC. WHILE IF HIS FIRST CONCEPTION WAS WITH A PURE MOTIVE, HIS SUBSEQUENT ACTS TOO WERE THUS: DID NOT HIS SCIONS ACT THUS? [SURELY], AND SHE WENT DOWN UNTO THE THRESH-ING-FLOOR, ETC.

Rabbi Levi is now quoted as saying that even the future generations of Lot's daughters followed ways that could only be described as immoral, such as at Shittim, as described in Scripture.

PARASHAH FIFTY-ONE, *Midrash Eleven*

יא ותלד הבכירה בן וגו'. רבי יודן משם ר' אייבו: הבכירה ע"י שביזת כבוד אביה ואמרה: שמו
מואב, מאב, אמר הכתוב (דברים ב): אל תצר את מואב ואל תתגר בם מלחמה. מלחמה אי
אתה עושה עמהן, אבל אתה מפתק הנהרות שלהן, שורף גדישים שלהן באש, אבל הצעירה
ע"י שחסתה על כבוד אביה ואמרה: ותקרא שמו בן עמי, בן מי שהיה עמי. אמר הכתוב (שם):
אל תצורם ואל תתגר בהם כל עיקר.

11. AND THE FIRSTBORN BORE A SON, AND CALLED HIS NAME MOAB (GEN.
19:37). R. JUDAN SAID IN R. AIBU'S NAME: BECAUSE THE FIRSTBORN
DISGRACED HER FATHER AND CALLED HIS NAME MOAB, WHICH MEANS,
"BY MY FATHER" (ME-'AB), SCRIPTURE COMMANDED, BE NOT AT ENMITY
UNTO MOAB, NEITHER CONTEND WITH THEM IN BATTLE (DEUT. 2:9):
THOU MAYEST NOT WAGE WAR WITH THEM, YET THOU MAYEST DIVERT
THEIR RIVERS AND BURN THEIR BARNS IN FIRE. BUT BECAUSE THE
YOUNGER SPARED HER FATHER'S HONOR, FOR SHE CALLED HIS NAME
BEN-AMMI, DECLARING, HE IS A SON (BEN) OF ONE WHO WAS WITH ME
(IMMI), SCRIPTURE ORDERED: HARASS THEM NOT, NOR CONTEND WITH
THEM (2:19) – IN ANY WAY, WHATSOEVER.

The Midrash calls our attention to some of the personal policies having to do with the naming of their children. The older daughter named
her son Moab, which literally speaking means "from my father." This was
a disgrace to her father's reputation, and she is criticized very forcefully
in the midrashic texts. The people who were descended from this birth
were the nations of Moab. The Children of Israel were warned to never
go to war against Moab, but as described in Scripture itself, lesser forms
of persuasion (even though violent) would be permitted. In the case of
the second daughter, who named her son Ben Ami ("son of my people")
without any hint whatsoever about their relationship to her father, she
was rewarded by the nation that emerged from her, the nation of Ammon. Not only were the Children of Israel not permitted to go to war
against them, but they were also prohibited from using any form of pressure against them. If there is a problem between them, let the Children
of Israel leave and travel elsewhere.

אמר ר"י ב"ר סימון ורבי חנין בשם ר' יוחנן: בנותיו של לוט הולכות לעבור עבירה, ונתפקדו.
באיזה זכות? בזכות מואב, מי אב, שנאמר באברהם (בראשית יז): כי אב המון גוים נתתיך:

R. JUDAH B. R. SIMON AND R. HANIN IN R. JOHANAN'S NAME SAID: LOT'S
DAUGHTERS WENT TO COMMIT WRONG, YET BECAME PREGNANT! IN
WHOSE MERIT WAS THIS? IN THE MERIT OF MOAB, I.E., OF ONE WHO WAS
A FATHER (MI'AB) [VIZ. ABRAHAM, OF WHOM IT SAYS], FOR THE FATHER
OF A MULTITUDE OF NATIONS HAVE I MADE THEE (GEN. 7:5).

How do you explain the fact that the children of the two daughters of
Lot ultimately became the leaders of two great nations in ancient times
– those of Moab and Ammon? One of the reasons may be that in choosing the name Moav (Moab), the oldest daughter did not mean this as a
reference to her own father, but to the father of the Jewish nation, who
was (of course) Abraham, and who received a special blessing of being
the spiritual father of all mankind.

Additional Commentary

Engaging with Moab

The Midrash is bringing to our attention now, and will explain later,
the instructions given to Moses in Scripture. Those instructions were
to be used as the Children of Israel approach the area of Moab in their
journey across the Land of Canaan. About Moab it says: "Do not incite
them to war" (Deuteronomy 2:9). Under no circumstances were they
to be engaged in war with Moab. War can sometimes destroy a people,
and the text did not want the Moabite people to be destroyed because
of their ancestry, as the people produced by the family of Lot. On the
other hand, if they faced political problems of policy with the leaders
of Moab, they could use certain methods of punishment which might
produce fear in the leadership of Moab, which would be enough to
resolve the problem between them. Some of the methods that Scripture
permitted were quite violent, such as interfering with the directions of
the rivers and their waterways, and permission if necessary to set fire to
their wheat fields. This, however, is far less dangerous than war between
them, which would not be permitted. In the case of Amon, even these
types of activities were prohibited as it says: "Do not incite them [at
all]" (2:19). This was due to the fact the Lot's daughter did not mention
directly that the child was from her father, but called him "son of my
people [ben ami]." (HaMidrash HaMevo'ar)

Parashah Fifty-Two, *Midrash One*

א ויסע משם אברהם ארצה הנגב. רבי אבון: פתח (איוב יד) ואולם הר נופל יבול וצור יעתק
ממקומו. ואולם, הר נופל, זה לוט, שנפל מהר. וצור, זה אברהם. יעתק ממקומו, פנה ממקומו,
לפי שחרב מקומה של סדום, פסקו העוברים והשבים. ואמר: מה אני מפסיק צדקה מביתי?
הלך ונטה לו אהל בגרר, הדא הוא דכתיב: ויסע משם אברהם:

1. AND ABRAHAM JOURNEYED FROM THENCE, ETC. (GEN. 20:1). R. ABIN
COMMENCED HIS DISCOURSE THUS: AND SURELY THE MOUNTAIN FALL-
ING CRUMBLETH AWAY, ETC. (JOB 14:18). AND SURELY THE MOUNTAIN
FALLING – ALLUDES TO LOT, WHO FELL [MORALLY] AT A MOUNTAIN;
AND THE ROCK IS REMOVED OUT OF ITS PLACE (14:18) – ALLUDES TO
ABRAHAM. FOR IN CONSEQUENCE OF THE DESTRUCTION OF THE REGION
OF SODOM WAYFARERS CEASED, AND HE SAID: WHY SHOULD I PERMIT
HOSPITALITY TO CEASE FROM MY HOUSE? HE THEREFORE WENT AND
PITCHED HIS TENT IN GERAR. HENCE IT IS WRITTEN: AND ABRAHAM
JOURNEYED FROM THENCE.

The verse in Job is interpreted midrashically so that the mountain is
Lot and the rock is Abraham. In the case of Lot, he fell from a lofty
position to an ordinary one, because of the immoral behavior of his
daughters. As for Abraham, he felt that his home in Hebron was too
close to the new address of Lot, and he therefore decided to go to the
western part of Canaan and reestablish his home there. Both Lot and
Abraham seem to have agreed to lessen their contacts with each other.

While living in the area of Sodom, Abraham was able to act as host
to those who were either coming or going to the area of Sodom. After
the destruction, however, that was not possible. One of Abraham's additional motivations was to find a place where he could continue his
service to the travelers to and from his new area. The Negev Desert now
became his home and the area of his outreach to all the passersby.

433

Seed Thoughts

Abraham's decision to offer hospitality to travelers in his area, whether
they were coming or going from the areas of their concern, was quite
obvious. Abraham felt that he must be doing something good with his
life, and the idea of hosting travelers who were coming or going ap-
pealed to him very much. His name continued to be associated with
altruistic behavior. His goal was to help the travelers. After a while, they
all knew about his goal and appreciated it.

PARASHAH FIFTY-TWO, *Midrash Two*

ב (משלי יח) אח נפשע מקרית עוז. אח, זה לוט, שהיה בן אחיו של אברהם. נפשע מקרית עוז,
פשעת באברהם, כפרת ביה, שקרת ביה. ומה גרם לך? ומדינים כבריח ארמון, הביא עליו
מדינים כבריחי בה"מ. מה להלן: לא יבא טמא, אף כאן לא יבא עמוני ומואבי בקהל ה' עד עולם:

2. A BROTHER OFFENDED (*NIFSHA*) IS HARDER TO BE WON THAN A
STRONG CITY (PROV. 18:19). A BROTHER – ALLUDES TO LOT, THE SON
OF ABRAHAM'S BROTHER. NIFSHA: THOU DIDST SIN AGAINST ABRAHAM,
THOU DIDST DENY HIM, THOU WAST FALSE TO HIM. AND WHOM DID HE
[AS A RESULT] STIR UP AGAINST HIMSELF? – AND JUDGES LIKE THE BARS
OF A CASTLE (18:19): HE BROUGHT JUDGES AGAINST HIMSELF [WHO
SHUT HIM OUT] LIKE THE BARS OF THE TEMPLE. AS WE READ THERE:
THAT NONE THAT WAS UNCLEAN IN ANY THING SHOULD ENTER IN (II
CHRON. 23:19), SO HERE TOO, AN AMMONITE OR A MOABITE SHALL NOT
ENTER INTO THE ASSEMBLY OF THE LORD (DEUT. 23:4). HENCE, AND
ABRAHAM JOURNEYED FROM THENCE.

When the Midrash mentions that the Moabite and the Ammonite
should not enter the community of the Lord, they are referring to marriage. According to Jewish law, neither a male Moabite nor a male Ammonite is permitted to marry a Jewish woman. As we shall see later on,
this refers only to male Moabites and male Ammonites, not the females.
According to Jewish law, a Jewish male is permitted to a female Moabite
and a female Ammonite, and in Hebrew it is *Moavi ve-lo Moavit* and *Ammoni ve-lo Ammonit*. As we shall see later on, this is derived from Ruth,
who was a Moabite and a God-fearing person. Her behavior determined
the changes in the halakha.

PARASHAH FIFTY-TWO, *Midrash Three*

ג ד"א: ויסע משם אברהם. (שם) חכם לב יקח מצוות. חכם לב, זה אברהם. יקח מצוות, לפי
שחרב מקומה של סדום, ופסקו העוברים והשבים, ולא חסר קלורין שלו כלום. אמר: מה
אני מפסיק צדקה מביתי! הלך ונטה לו אהל בגרר. ואויל שפתים ילבט, זה לוט, שהיה אויל
בשפתיו, שהיה צריך לומר לבנותיו דבר, שלקה בו העולם אנו באים לעשות? אלא, ילבט.
מה גרם לו ילבט? הביא עליו לבטי לבוטים. מה להלן: לא יבא טמא לכל דבר, אף כאן: לא
יבא עמוני ומואבי בקהל ה':

3. THE WISE IN HEART WILL TAKE GOOD DEEDS (PROV. 10:8) – THIS RE-
FERS TO ABRAHAM; WILL TAKE GOOD DEEDS: THE REGION OF SODOM
WAS NOW DESOLATE AND TRAVELERS HAD CEASED, WITH THE RESULT
THAT HIS STORES WERE NOW IN NO WAY DIMINISHED; THEREFORE HE
SAID: "WHY SHOULD I ALLOW HOSPITALITY TO CEASE FROM MY HOUSE?"
AND HE WENT AND PITCHED HIS TENT IN GERAR. BUT THE FOOLISH OF
TONGUE (10:8) – ALLUDES TO LOT WHO WAS FOOLISH WITH HIS TONGUE,
FOR HE SHOULD HAVE SAID TO HIS DAUGHTER: "SHALL WE COMMIT
THAT SIN FOR WHICH THE WHOLE WORLD WAS PUNISHED!" WHAT DID
IT LEAD TO? – HE SHALL FALL (10:8): "HE BROUGHT UPON HIMSELF FALL
AFTER FALL": AS WE READ THERE: THAT NONE THAT WAS UNCLEAN IN
ANY THING SHOULD ENTER IN (II CHRON. 23:19), SO HERE TOO, AN AM-
MONITE OR A MOABITE SHALL NOT ENTER INTO THE ASSEMBLY OF THE
LORD. HENCE, AND ABRAHAM JOURNEYED FROM THENCE.

The opening section of this Midrash offers a reason as to why Abraham left his home and wandered more deeply into the Land of Canaan
in order to reestablish his way of life. Aside from the fact that Sodom
had encouraged an immoral form of life, which ultimately led to its own
destruction, it also lessened by far those individuals who sought hospitality with Abraham, who had transformed his home into a welcoming
agent for those who were going to/from Sodom and Gomorrah. Finally,
Abraham said to himself: "Why should I allow the lessening of visitors
because of Sodom to interfere with my desire to do *tzedaka* (charitable
work)? I will therefore find a new home which will enable me to carry
on my *tzedaka* even more intensively than I did before."

The Midrash describes the expression *hakham lev* – "wise in heart" –
as referring to Abraham, who had the ability to understand why he was
being subjected to a diminishing group of visitors. One would require

that in order to rectify that situation – that explains why he moves from the area of Sodom to a less populated area of Canaan, where he reestablishes his home. His new home becomes the Negev, which was even more uninhabited than it is in modern times.

Ammon and Moab were the grandchildren of Lot, and Lot basically trampled carelessly on the way of life he had received from his uncle, Abraham. That is one of the reasons why there were restrictions in marriage between the male Ammonites and Moabites and the Children of Israel, which restricted their relationship with the Children of Israel much more dramatically than with any of the other nations of the world.

PARASHAH FIFTY-TWO, *Midrash Four*

ד ויסע משם אברהם. פנה מפני ריח רע, שהיו אומרים לוט בן אחי אברהם, בא על שתי בנותיו.

4. AND ABRAHAM JOURNEYED FROM THENCE. HE DEPARTED BECAUSE OF THE ILL-REPUTE [OF HIS FAMILY], AS PEOPLE WOULD SAY: "LOT, ABRAHAM'S NEPHEW, HAS BEEN INTIMATE WITH HIS TWO DAUGHTERS."

Abraham left Sodom because of the immorality of the total community. It should be added that what affected him most were the opinions of the scoffers, and there were many of them in the community that would make jokes out of their accusation that Lot had become sexually intimate with his daughters. This was too much for Abraham to take, and this was the real reason why he left that community and moved elsewhere in the Land of Canaan.

ארצה הנגב, שבעה שמות נקראו לו: דרום, נגב, תימן, ים, ימין, וסנינים. [נ"א וסינים] היתיבון, והכתיב (תהלים עה): ולא ממדבר הרים? אמר להם: אף הוא, דרום הוא. אמר רבי חייא בר אבא: עבר הוית קמיה כנישתא דצפורין, שמעית מינוקא יתיבין וקריין: ויסע משם אברהם, אמרתי: גדולים דברי חכמים, שאמרו: הוי זהיר בגחלתן שלא תכוה, שנשיכתן נשיכת שועל, ולחישתן לחישת שרף, וכל דבריהם כגחלי אש, שמעשה שפירש אבינו אברהם מלוט, היתה פרישתו פרישת עולם. ויגר בגרר, בגרדיקי. ויאמר אברהם אל שרה אשתו אחותי היא, ע"כ, שלא בטובתה:

TOWARD THE LAND OF THE SOUTH (NEGEB). IT HAS SEVEN NAMES: DA-ROM (SOUTH), NEGEB (THE DRY REGION), TEMAN, YAMIN (THE RIGHT),

HADAR, YAM, AND SININ. A DIFFICULTY WAS RAISED: BUT IT IS WRIT-
TEN: NOR YET FROM THE WILDERNESS, HARIM (PS. 75:7)? THE ANSWER
WAS GIVEN: THAT TOO IS DAROM. R. HIYYA B. ABBA SAID: I WAS PASSING
THE BABYLONIAN SYNAGOGUE OF SEPPHORIS, WHEN I HEARD CHILDREN
SITTING AND RECITING THE VERSE, AND ABRAHAM JOURNEYED FROM
THENCE. AT THAT I REMARKED, HOW GREAT ARE THE WORDS OF THE
SAGES, WHO SAID: TAKE HEED OF THEIR GLOWING COALS, THAT THOU
BE NOT BURNT, FOR THEIR BITE IS THE BITE OF A FOX, ETC. FOR FROM
THE MOMENT THAT OUR FATHER ABRAHAM SEPARATED FROM LOT, THE
SEPARATION WAS FOR ALL TIME. AND HE SOJOURNED IN GERAR – IN
GERADIKE. AND ABRAHAM SAID OF SARAH HIS WIFE: SHE IS MY SISTER
(GEN. 20:2) – WITHOUT HER WILL OR CONSENT.

This can be explained as implied in the fact that it is not mentioned
that Abraham asked her beforehand, as he did when approaching Egypt.
Also, she was unwilling to permit it, since on the previous occasion it
had led to her being taken to the house of Pharaoh (Rashi, M.K., Y.T.).
It is better, however, to amend the whole passage as follows (it is so in
Yalkut): And Abimelech King of Gerar sent and took Sarah (Gen. 20:2).
Is it possible that she went by her own desire? No, it was without her
will or consent (this paragraph is verbatim from Soncino).

The text includes the question as to why Abraham did not seek permission from Sarah to describe their relationship as sister and brother,
and not husband and wife. The Midrash makes the additional point
that this request by Abraham would not benefit Sarah. It would help
Abraham because of the nature of the religious practices of Abimelech's
dynasty, where the brother was on a very high level and protected, but
the sister (for example, Sarah, who was actually Abraham's wife) was not
protected. Abraham even noticed that while he was being questioned
by the authorities of the king, Sarah was being ushered into the palace of
King Abimelech. One interpretation of this question is that this episode
was a close duplication of what had happened several years before when
the couple were in Egypt and were questioned by Pharaoh's servants.
One presumes that on that occasion, Abraham and Sarah had shared
this problem with each other, and she had agreed to go ahead with it.
One can say, therefore, that Abraham already had her permission and
did not think it had to be repeated. As we have seen in the Midrash, the
Almighty warned Abimelech in a dream that under no circumstances
should he either touch Sarah or in any way inconvenience her, and in-

deed, both the king and his followers were stricken with an illness that made it impossible for them to live normally while Sarah was in their household.

—

Seed Thoughts

Abraham chose to move his home to the Negev, which in his day and for many generations to come was actually wilderness area. In modern times, Jews who were interested in creating the new State of Israel were aware that the wilderness of the Negev covered the entire south of the future Israeli state. The fact that Abraham chose to build his future in the Negev should have been a great motivation for modern Jews to do the same. Readers of the Midrash in modern times are aware that much progress has been made in developing the Negev, which today includes important cities, a great university, and many wonderful institutions. All these helped make the State of Israel a source of pride and accomplishment.

PARASHAH FIFTY-TWO, *Midrash Five*

ה ויבא אלהים וגו' בחלום הלילה. א"ר יוסי: אין הקב"ה נגלה על נביאי אומות העולם, אלא בשעה שדרך בני אדם לפרוש זה מזה, הה"ד (איוב ד): בשעיפים מחזיונות לילה ואלי דבר יגונב וגו'.

5. BUT GOD CAME TO ABIMELECH IN A DREAM OF THE NIGHT (GEN. 20:3). R. JOSE B. BIBAH SAID: THE HOLY ONE, BLESSED BE HE, APPEARS TO THE HEATHENS ONLY IN THE HOUR WHEN PEOPLE GENERALLY TAKE LEAVE OF EACH OTHER [SC. AT NIGHT], AS IT SAYS: NOW A WORD WAS SECRETLY BROUGHT TO ME ... AT THE TIME OF LEAVE-TAKING, FROM THE VISIONS OF THE NIGHT, WHEN DEEP SLEEP FALLETH ON MEN (JOB 4:12F.).

The Jewish prophets of Israel, it seems, are spoken to whenever and wherever communication is possible. The non-Jewish prophets in the Bible, however, are not spoken in this ordinary manner but only at a time when human communication is difficult and, for most people, impossible. The only time that such forms of speaking can take place is during periods of sleep.

מה בין נביאי ישראל לנביאי אומות העולם? רבי חנינא בר פפא ורבנן. רבי חנינא בר פפא אמר: משל למלך שהיה נתון הוא ואוהבו בטרקלין, וילון מונח ביניהם. כל זמן שהיה רוצה לדבר עם אוהבו היה קופל את הוילון ומדבר עמו. אבל לנביאי אומות העולם אינו מקפל אותו, אלא מדבר עמהם מאחרי הוילון. ורבנן אמרי: למלך, שהיה לו אשה ופלגש, כשהוא הולך אצל אשתו הוא הולך בפרהסיא, וכשהוא הולך אצל שפחתו הולך במטמוניות. כך, אין הקב"ה נגלה על אומות העולם, אלא בלילה, (במדבר כב:) ויבא אלהים אל בלעם לילה. (בראשית לא) ויבא אלהים אל לבן הארמי בחלום הלילה. (שם כ:) ויבא אלהים אל אבימלך בחלום הלילה. מה בין נביאי ישראל לנביאי אומות העולם? רבי חמא ב"ר חנינא ור' יששכר מכפר מנדי. ר' חמא אמר: אין הקב"ה נגלה על נביאי אומות העולם, אלא בחצי דבור, היך מה דאת אמר (במדבר כג) ויקר אלהים אל בלעם. א"ר יששכר דכפר מנדי: אין הלשון הזה ויקר, אלא לשון טומאה, היך מד"א (דברים כג) כי יהיה בך איש אשר לא יהיה טהור מקרה, אבל נביאי ישראל בדבור שלם, בלשון חיבה, בלשון קדושה, בלשון שמלאכי השרת מקלסין אותו, שנאמר (ישעיה ו) וקרא זה אל זה ואמר קדוש וגו'. א"ר יוסי בן ביבה: (משלי טו) רחוק ה' מרשעים, אלו נביאי אומות העולם. ותפלת צדיקים ישמע, אלו נביאי ישראל. ויבא אלהים אל אבימלך ויאמר לו הנך מת על האשה וגו'. מכאן שאין התראה בבני נח. והיא בעולת בעל. אמר רבי אחא: בעלה נתעטר בה, והיא לא נתעטרה בבעלה. רבנן אמרי: מרתא דבעלה, בכל מקום האיש גוזר, ברם הכא, כל אשר תאמר אליך שרה, שמע בקולה:

WHAT IS THE DIFFERENCE BETWEEN THE PROPHETS OF ISRAEL AND THE PROPHETS OF OTHER NATIONS? R. HANINA SAID: IT MAY BE COMPARED TO A KING WHO WAS WITH HIS FRIEND IN A CHAMBER (BUT SEPARATED BY A CURTAIN; WHENEVER HE DESIRED TO SPEAK TO HIS FRIEND), HE FOLDED UP THE CURTAIN AND SPOKE TO HIM. (BUT HE SPEAKS TO THE PROPHETS OF OTHER NATIONS WITHOUT FOLDING THE CURTAIN BACK BUT FROM BEHIND IT.) THE RABBIS COMPARED IT TO A KING WHO HAS A WIFE AND A CONCUBINE; TO HIS WIFE HE GOES OPENLY, BUT TO HIS CONCUBINE, HE REPAIRS WITH STEALTH. SIMILARLY, THE HOLY ONE, BLESSED BE HE, APPEARS TO THE HEATHENS ONLY AT NIGHT, AS IT SAYS: AND GOD CAME TO BALAAM AT NIGHT (NUM. 22:20); AND GOD CAME TO LABAN THE ARAMEAN IN A DREAM OF THE NIGHT (GEN. 31:24); AND GOD CAME TO ABIMELECH IN A DREAM AT NIGHT. BEHOLD, THOU SHALT DIE, BECAUSE OF THE WOMAN WHOM THOU HAST TAKEN; THIS TEACHES THAT NO FORMAL WARNING IS NECESSARY IN THE CASE OF THE NOACHIDES. FOR SHE IS A MAN'S WIFE. R. AHA SAID: HER HUSBAND WAS CROWNED THROUGH HER, BUT SHE WAS NOT CROWNED THROUGH HER HUSBAND. THE RABBIS SAID: SHE IS HER HUSBAND'S RULER. USUALLY, THE HUSBAND GIVES ORDERS, WHEREAS HERE WE READ: IN ALL THAT

SARAH SAITH UNTO THEE, HEARKEN UNTO HER VOICE (21:12). WHAT IS
THE DIFFERENCE BETWEEN THE PROPHETS OF ISRAEL AND THOSE OF
OTHER NATIONS? R. HAMA B. R. HANINA SAID: THE HOLY ONE, BLESSED
BE HE, REVEALS HIMSELF TO HEATHEN PROPHETS WITH HALF-SPEECH
ONLY, AS YOU READ: AND GOD MET (*WAYYIKKOR*) BALAAM (NUM. 23:4).
R. ISSACHAR OF KEFAR MANDI OBSERVED: THE TERM *WAYYIKKOR* SIGNI-
FIES UNCLEANNESS, AS IN THE VERSE, IF THERE BE AMONG YOU ANY
MAN, THAT IS NOT CLEAN BY REASON OF THAT WHICH CHANCETH HIM
(*MIKREH*) BY NIGHT (DEUT. 23:11). BUT TO THE PROPHETS OF ISRAEL, HE
SPEAKS WITH COMPLETE SPEECH, IN TERMS OF LOVE AND SANCTITY,
WITH LANGUAGE IN WHICH THE MINISTERING ANGELS PRAISE HIM, AS
IT SAYS: AND ONE [*SERAPH*] CALLED UNTO ANOTHER, AND SAID: HOLY,
HOLY, HOLY, IS THE LORD OF HOSTS (ISA. 6:3). R. JOSE SAID: THE LORD
IS FAR FROM THE WICKED (PROV. 15:29) – REFERS TO THE PROPHETS
OF OTHER NATIONS; BUT HE HEARETH THE PRAYER OF THE RIGHTEOUS
(15:29) – TO THE PROPHETS OF ISRAEL. R. LEAZAR B. MENAHEM SAID:
THE LORD IS FAR FROM THE WICKED – REFERS TO THE PROPHETS OF
OTHER NATIONS; BUT HE HEARETH THE PRAYER OF THE RIGHTEOUS –
TO THE PROPHETS OF ISRAEL. AND GOD APPEARS TO THE NATIONS ONLY
LIKE ONE WHO COMES FROM AFAR, AS YOU READ: THEY ARE COME FROM
A FAR COUNTRY UNTO ME (ISA. 39:3). BUT IN CONNECTION WITH THE
PROPHETS OF ISRAEL WE READ: AND [THE LORD] APPEARED (GEN. 18:1),
AND THE LORD CALLED (LEV. 1:1) – IMPLYING, FROM THE IMMEDIATE
VICINITY.

Additional Commentary

Was Balaam an exception?

There is an interesting expression in the Scripture with connection to
the prophet Balaam, ויקר אלהים אל בלעם – *vayikar Elohim el Bilam*. The
translation of this text is: "And God met Balaam." However, there is
something much more that seems to be indicated in this expression.
The word *vayikar* is sometimes used in a different grammatical way by
the words *mikreh* or *kara*, which mean something casual and incomplete happening (see Soncino). What this means is that in this instance,
God did not approach Balaam at night, but appeared to meet him in

an ordinary day and time of the week. But how does this conform to what we just learned that God appears to the non-Jewish prophets at nighttime? It appears to be somewhat of an exception; it may bother individual readers such as the present writer, but it does not seem to bother the Midrash. The midrashic writers were so clear everywhere and so demanding in interpreting even the least deviation, but they are silent in reacting to the phrase *vayikar* as interpreted as something happening accidentally and not in the usual way.

PARASHAH FIFTY-TWO, *Midrash Six*

ו ואבימלך לא קרב אליה וגו'. הגוי גם צדיק תהרוג? אמר: אם כך דנת לדור המבול ולדור
הפלגה, צדיקים, צדיקים היו! א"ר ברכיה: אי גוי זה תהרוג, צדיק תהרוג, הלא הוא אמר לי וגו'. והיא
גם היא היא וחמריה וגמליה ובני ביתא ואנשי ביתה, כולם אמרו כן, בתם לבבי הדא אמרת
משמוש ידים היה:

6. NOW ABIMELECH HAD NOT COME NEAR UNTO HER; AND HE SAID: LORD, WILT THOU SLAY EVEN A RIGHTEOUS NATION (GEN. 20:4)? IF THOU DIDST SENTENCE THE GENERATION OF THE FLOOD AND THE GENERATION OF THE SEPARATION IN THIS FASHION, HE PROTESTED, THEN THEY WERE RIGHTEOUS. R. BEREKIAH EXPLAINED IT: [ABIMELECH PLEADED]: IF THOU WOULDST SLAY THIS NATION [SC. ABIMELECH], THEN SLAY THE RIGHTEOUS ONE [ABRAHAM]. SAID HE NOT HIMSELF UNTO ME: SHE IS MY SISTER? AND SHE, SHE TOO (*GAM*) HERSELF SAID: HE IS MY BROTHER (20:5): SHE, HER ASS-DRIVERS, AND HER CAMEL-DRIVERS, HER DOMESTICS, AND ALL HER HOUSEHOLD. IN THE INTEGRITY OF MY HEART AND THE INNOCENCY OF MY HANDS HAVE I DONE THIS: THIS PROVES THAT HE MISHANDLED HER.

Many statements in the text of our scriptural portion and the Talmudic interpretations were aware that Abimelech was personally interested in every woman that entered his palace. Abraham's fear was that Sarah, too, might be mishandled. That is probably the explanation as to why God appeared to Abimelech in the dream and warned him that Sarah was not to be touched. Please see the next Midrash for additional interpretation.

PARASHAH FIFTY-TWO, *Midrash Seven*

ז ויאמר אליו האלהים בחלום גם אנכי ידעתי גם אנכי וגו' ואחשוך גם אנכי אותך מחטוא לי. ר"י
אומר: מחטוא לי, מחטונך לי. על כן לא נתתיך. משל לגבור, רוכב על הסוס, והסוס רץ וראה
תינוק אחד מושלך ומשך הסוס ולא הזיק את התינוק. למי הכל מקלסים לסוס או לרוכב?
לא לרוכב? כך, על כן לא נתתיך לנגוע אליה, מחטונך לי, יצרך המחטיאך בידי הוא מסור,
ואני מנעתיך מלחטוא, משכתיך מן החטא, והשבח שלי הוא ולא שלך:

7. AND GOD SAID UNTO HIM: YEA, I KNOW ... AND I ALSO WITHHELD
THEE FROM SINNING (*ME-HATO*) AGAINST ME (GEN. 20:6). R. ISAAC
EXPLAINED: THINE EVIL DEMON (*MAHTONEKA*) IS IN MY POWER, THERE-
FORE SUFFERED I THEE NOT TO TOUCH HER (20:6). R. AIBUN SAID: IT
IS LIKE THE CASE OF A WARRIOR WHO WAS RIDING HIS HORSE AT FULL
SPEED, WHEN SEEING A CHILD IYING IN THE PATH, HE REINED IN THE
HORSE, SO THAT THE CHILD WAS NOT HURT. WHOM DO ALL PRAISE, THE
HORSE OR THE RIDER? SURELY THE RIDER! [SIMILARLY HERE GOD SAID]:
THEREFORE SUFFERED I THEE NOT TO TOUCH HER, [AND THE CREDIT IS
MINE, NOT THINE].

Seed Thoughts

This Midrash gives a beautiful example of a certain style that it has adopted to explain serious theological concepts in a very serious way. How
does one explain how or why God entered into the sleep of Abimelech
in the form of a dream? To teach him that He – the Almighty – was
behind some of the sexual restrictions that Abimelech was forced to accept. The style is in the form of a parable. The one in our Midrash is very
simple but very convincing, and redefines the theological problem of
God and Abimelech in a simple way that most people can understand.
One might say that midrashic literature specializes in the use of the parable. It is one of many ways in which the midrashic text has become a
loveable text in the life of its readers.

PARASHAH FIFTY-TWO, *Midrash Eight*

ח ועתה השב אשת האיש כי נביא הוא. א"ל: מי מפייסו שלא נגעתי בה? א"ל: כי נביא הוא.
א"ל: מי מודיע לכל? א"ל: ויתפלל בעדך וחיה. ואם אינך משיב דע כי מות תמות, מיכן, שאין
התראה בבני נח:

8. NOW THEREFORE RESTORE THE MAN'S WIFE; FOR HE IS A PROPHET
(GEN. 20:7). WHO WILL REASSURE HIM [ABRAHAM] THAT I DID NOT
TOUCH HER? ASKED HE. [IT IS UNNECESSARY], FOR HE IS A PROPHET,
HE REPLIED. AND WHO SHALL MAKE IT KNOWN TO ALL? HE PURSUED.
AND HE SHALL PRAY FOR THEE, AND THOU SHALT LIVE (20:7), WAS THE
ANSWER. AND IF THOU RESTORE HER NOT, KNOW THOU THAT THOU
SHALT SURELY DIE (20:7): THIS PROVES THAT NO FORMAL WARNING IS
REQUIRED IN THE CASE OF THE NOACHIDES.

Seed Thoughts

In his dream to Abimelech, the Holy One, blessed be He, referred to
Abraham as a prophet. Abraham thus becomes one who has a relationship not only with Jews but also with non-Jews. The only such activity
that is described in these phrases is that Abraham prayed for Abimelech.
Abimelech's reaction, when told that Abraham was a prophet, was his
concern that the world (or at least his environment) should understand
that he did not molest Sarah in any way at all. God assured him that
Abraham would pray for him, and this would become known. In all of
their circles, the idea of Abraham praying for his secular king is a great
expansion of the responsibilities of a prophet.

PARASHAH FIFTY-TWO, *Midrash Nine*

טו וישכם אבימלך בבקר וגו'. א"ר חנין: לפי שהיו רואים עשנה של סדום עולה ככבשן האש,
אמרו: תאמר אותן המלאכים שנשתלחו לסדום באו לכאן? לפיכך, וייראו האנשים מאד:

9. AND ABIMELECH ROSE EARLY IN THE MORNING, ETC. (GEN. 20:8). R.
HANIN SAID: BECAUSE THEY HAD SEEN THE SMOKE OF SODOM ASCEND-
ING LIKE THAT OF A FIERY FURNACE, THEY SAID: PERHAPS THE ANGELS
THAT WERE SENT TO SODOM HAVE COME HITHER? ON THAT ACCOUNT,
AND THE MEN WERE SORE AFRAID (20:8).

Apparently, the followers of Abimelech, who saw the smoke and fire coming from Sodom, may have been convinced for the first time that the angels who were responsible for the event had to be taken seriously, and that they have shown their ability to destroy an entire city. It was natural that when and if the angels returned to Abimelech's kingdom, the people should have been fearful and worried about their present and future.

—

Seed Thoughts

When Abimelech (king of the Philistines) and his court saw the smoke and fire arising from the destruction of Sodom and Gomorrah, they were shocked and also filled with fear. You would think that since they shared the same moral values as Sodom and Gomorrah, and knew each other intimately, this might have been the moment for the expression of sympathy. But this was not on their mind. What concerned them most was that they might be next on the list of destruction. All of a sudden, they realized how much power the angels had who had visited them, and that made them even more concerned.

King Abimelech immediately rushed to Abraham to get his support in their problem. After all, he said to Abraham: "Surely you realized that I have been completely innocent in relationship to Sarah; I have protected her immediately." No sooner had he said these words that he was immediately rebuked by one of the angels. "Your Majesty," the angel said, "we sent one of our angels to enter your dream, and he told you that if you as much as touch Sarah, you will die." This was Sarah's real protection. "We protected her more than you did." We hear no more about this subject, but the king did lavish many gifts to Abraham and Sarah upon their departure, and these gifts may have spoken for him.

PARASHAH FIFTY-TWO, *Midrash Ten*

י ויקרא אבימלך לאברהם ויאמר לו: מה חטאתי לך? ומה עשית לנו? המד"א: הנך מת על
האשה אשר לקחת וגו'. ומה חטאתי לך, אם אינך משיב, דע כי מות תמות, כי הבאת עלי
ועל ממלכתי חטאה גדולה. כי עצור עצר ה' בעד כל רחם לבית אבימלך, מעשים אשר לא
יעשו. א"ר חלבו: בכל מקום היתה רווחה מקדמותך, וכאן קדמך רעבון. מעשים אשר לא
יעשו, ויאמר אבימלך לאברהם: מה ראית כי עשית את הדבר וגו':

10. THEN ABIMELECH CALLED ABRAHAM, ETC. (GEN. 20:9). WHAT DID
HE MEAN BY, WHAT HAST THOU DONE UNTO US? – [THIS WAS SAID IN
REFERENCE TO,] BEHOLD, THOU SHALT DIE, BECAUSE OF THE WOMAN
WHOM THOU HAST TAKEN; AND WHEREIN HAVE I SINNED AGAINST
THEE, IN REFERENCE TO, AND IF THOU RESTORE HER NOT, KNOW THAT
THOU SHALT SURELY DIE (20:7); THAT THOU HAST BROUGHT ON ME
AND ON MY KINGDOM A GREAT SIN, IN REFERENCE TO, FOR THE LORD
HAD FAST CLOSED UP ALL THE WOMBS OF THE HOUSE OF ABIMELECH
(20:18). [AS FOR HIS REBUKE], DEEDS THAT ARE NOT DONE, R. HELBO
SAID: [ABIMELECH COMPLAINED,] "IN ALL PLACES PROSPERITY WENT
BEFORE THEE, WHEREAS HERE FAMINE PRECEDED THEE. THUS, THOU
HAST DONE DEEDS UNTO ME THAT ARE NOT DONE [ELSEWHERE]."

When Abimelech complained that things that happened to him were most unique and had not occurred earlier, he was unable to find any justification for this. What Abimelech meant was that Abraham was known everywhere for his hospitality to everyone, looking after everyone in terms of their needs, and if necessary, pretending that he did not notice certain things open to criticism. But now, in terms of Abraham's harsh words and threats to him, Abraham was acting in a way quite contrary to his former behavior, and Abimelech could find no justification in this turn of events.

Seed Thoughts

Each complaint of Abimelech referred to something said or done. Thus, in "What hast Thou done unto us?", he upbraided Abraham for the threat, "Behold, thou shalt die," maintaining that it was unjustified, seeing that the position had arisen because of what Abraham himself had done. The others are to be explained in similar fashion. (Copied verbatim from Soncino)

PARASHAH FIFTY-TWO, *Midrash Eleven*

יא ויאמר אברהם כי אמרתי רק אין יראת אלהים וגם אמנה אחותי בת אבי היא, בשיטתן
השיבן.

11. AND ABRAHAM SAID: BECAUSE I THOUGHT: SURELY THE FEAR OF GOD
IS NOT IN THIS PLACE . . . AND MOREOVER SHE IS INDEED MY SISTER,
THE DAUGHTER OF MY FATHER (GEN. 20:11–12): [SAID HE <R. MEIR> TO
THEM:] HE ANSWERED THEM IN ACCORDANCE WITH THEIR OWN VIEWS,
[FOR THEY PERMIT <MARRIAGE WITH> THE DAUGHTER OF ONE'S FA-
THER, BUT INTERDICT THE DAUGHTER OF ONE'S MOTHER; THEREFORE,
HE ANSWERED THEM IN ACCORDANCE WITH THEIR PRACTICE.] (THE
WORDS IN BRACKETS IN THIS PARAGRAPH ARE FROM SONCINO.)

Midrash 11 contains the answer to the question posed by Abimel-ech in the previous Midrash. This question by Abimelech was: "Why are these threats directed against me?" They are so different from the kindness shown by Abraham in so many aspects of his life. Abraham's answer was: "First of all, I felt that in the circle of Abimelech, the fear of the Lord was not present, and that they would probably kill me in order for the king to have my wife Sarah exclusively to him. Furthermore, she actually is my sister, but only paternally and not maternally." The rule in the religion followed by the Noahide community is perfectly acceptable to be perfectly married to the paternal daughter who is also his sister. If then, it may be asked: "Was Abraham permitted to marry Sarah?" The answer is that she was, in reality, not his paternal sister, but the daughter of his brother, so that we could use the term "sister" in a much broader way. Abraham's goal was to explain things that Abimelech would accept in order to protect both Sarah and himself.

ויהי כאשר התעו אותי אלהים מבית אבי וגו'. א"ר חנין: הלואי נדרוש הדין קריא תלת אפין וניפוק ידוי. בשעה שבקשו אומות העולם ליזדווג לי, עד שאני בבית אבי נתקיים עלי הקב"ה. ובשעה שבקשו אומות העולם להתעות אותי, נגלה עלי הקב"ה ואמר לי: לך לך! ובשעה שבקשו אומות העולם לתעות מדרכיו של הקב"ה, העמיד להם שני גדולים משל בית אבא, שם ועבר והיו מתרים בהן:

AND IT CAME TO PASS, WHEN GOD CAUSED ME TO WANDER (HITHE'U) FROM MY FATHER'S HOUSE, ETC. (GEN. 20:13). R. HANIN SAID: WOULD THAT WE MAY INTERPRET THIS VERSE IN THREE WAYS, AND SO DISCHARGE OUR DUTY! (I) WHEN THE NATIONS OF THE WORLD WISHED TO FALL UPON ME WHILE I WAS YET IN MY FATHER'S HOUSE, GOD CAME TO MY HELP. (II) AGAIN, WHEN THE NATIONS OF THE WORLD WISHED TO MISLEAD ME [INTO IDOLATRY], GOD REVEALED HIMSELF TO ME AND BADE ME, GET THEE ... OUT OF THY FATHER'S HOUSE (GEN. 12:1). AND FINALLY, (III) WHEN THE NATIONS OF THE WORLD WISHED TO STRAY FROM HIS WAYS, HE RAISED TWO GREAT MEN OUT OF MY FATHER'S HOUSE [I.E., FAMILY], SHEM AND EBER, TO WARN THEM.

Additional Commentary

Sarah the Sister

One can interpret the words of Abraham as fitting in to the culture of his hosts – that Sarah was his sister paternally. In truth, however, Sarah was not actually his sister but a close member of his family (his niece). Her original name was Iscah, daughter of Haran (the brother of Abraham). He described his relative, the daughter of his brother, as "my sister." He described Sarah as the daughter of Terah (Abraham's father), and she was actually the daughter of Terah's son (Haran), and we follow the principle of *bnei banim kebanim* – that the children of our children be treated as our children. (*HaMidrash HaMevo'ar*)

PARASHAH FIFTY-TWO, *Midrash Twelve*

יב ויקח אבימלך צאן ובקר ולשרה אמר הנה נתתי אלף כסף לאחיך. א"ר יהודה בר רבי אלעאי: אזלת למצרים סחרת בה, אתית להכא וסחרת בה. אם ממון את בעי, הא לך ממון, וכסי מינה עינה, הנה הוא לך כסות עינים.

12. AND ABIMELECH TOOK SHEEP AND OXEN . . . ; AND GAVE THEM UNTO ABRAHAM . . . AND UNTO SARAH HE SAID: BEHOLD, I HAVE GIVEN THY BROTHER A THOUSAND PIECES OF SILVER, ETC. (GEN. 20:14FF.). R. JUDAH B. R. ILAI SAID: [ABIMELECH REPROACHED ABRAHAM:] "YOU WENT TO EGYPT AND MADE MERCHANDISE OF HER, AND YOU CAME HERE AND TRADED IN HER. IF YOU DESIRE MONEY, HERE IS MONEY AND COVER UP [YOUR] EYES FROM HER." THAT IS THE MEANING OF, BEHOLD, IT IS FOR THEE A COVERING OF THE EYES.

T here is a popular saying, that the best defense in life is an offense. There is much in Abimelech's behavior up to this event with which he could be charged. His way of defending himself was to accuse Abraham of using his wife first in Egypt, and now in Gerar to take advantage of her so that they would forget the charges against Abimelech himself. What Abimelech described as a cover-up which she applied to Abraham's behavior is more appropriately to be used in explaining Abimelech's background and behavior. This observation by Rabbi Judah will later on be quoted by Abimelech, which signifies his approval of it.

א"ר יוחנן: עשה לה כסות, שיהיו הכל מביטין בה ולא בנויה. כסות עינים, כסות, שהיא עשויה עינים עינים. רבי ברכיה אמר: עשאה מטרונה כסות, שהיא מכוסה מן העין. ר"ל אמר: בקש להקנותה בפני בעלה לומר: כל השנים הללו היא עמו ולא עשה לה דבר, וזה לילה אחת, עשה לה את כל הכבוד הזה. ד"א: א"ל: אתם כסיתם מני את העין, בן שאתם מעמידים יהא כסוי עינים.

BEHOLD, IT IS FOR THEE A COVERING (KESUTH) OF THE EYES. R. JOHANAN EXPLAINED IT: [ABIMELECH SAID TO ABRAHAM:] "MAKE THEE A GARMENT THAT ALL MAY LOOK AT IT," NOT AT HER BEAUTY, A COVERING OF THE EYES MEANING A GARMENT WHICH ATTRACTS THE EYES. R. BEREKIAH SAID: HE [ABIMELECH] MADE HER A NOBLE LADY, A GARMENT OF THE EYES MEANING ONE IN WHICH SHE WOULD BE COVERED FROM THE EYES. R. SIMEON B. LAKISH SAID: HE WISHED TO MAKE HER DISCONTENTED WITH HER HUSBAND, THAT SHE MIGHT COMPLAIN: ALL

THOSE YEARS HE HAD BEEN WITH HER AND HAD NOT MADE HER ANY
FINERY, YET THIS MAN DID ALL THIS FOR HER BECAUSE OF A SINGLE
NIGHT. [ANOTHER INTERPRETATION:] HE [ABIMELECH] SAID TO HIM:
"YOU COVERED MY EYES; THEREFORE, THE SON THAT YOU WILL BEGET
WILL BE OF COVERED EYES."

This is actually what happened for when Isaac reached a mature age
– his vision became dim, and he had difficulty recognizing his sons as to
which one was Jacob and which one was Esau.

ואת כל ונכחת. אמר לה: כבר תוכחתיה דההוא גברא גביה, דתנן: המורדת על בעלה, פוחתין
לה מכתובתה, שבעה דינרין בשבת. ולמה שבעה דינרין? כנגד שבעה מלאכות שהאשה
עושה לבעלה: טוחנת, ואופה, ומבשלת, ומכבסת, ומניקה את בנה, ומצעת לו את המטה,
ועושה בצמר, לפיכך שבעה. וכן המורד על אשתו, מוסיפין לה על כתובתה שלשה דינרין
בשבת. למה שלשה? כנגד שלשה דברים שהוא מתחייב לה: שאר, כסות, ועונה. לפיכך,
שלשה. אמור שהכניסה לו עבדים ושפחות אינה מתחייבת לו כלום? אמור שלא נתן לה,
לא שאר, לא כסות, לא עונה, אינה מתחייבת לו כלום? אמר רבי יוחנן: צערו של איש
מרובה מצערה של אשה, הדא הוא דכתיב (שופטים טז): ויהי כי הציקה לו בדבריה כל הימים
ותאלצהו, שהיתה שומטת עצמה מתחתיו. ותקצר נפשו למות, אבל היא לא קצרה נפשה,
שהיתה עושה צריכה ממקום אחר:

AND BEFORE ALL MEN THOU ART REPROVED. HE SAID TO HER: "THIS
MAN'S [ABRAHAM'S] REPROOF IS ALREADY WITH HIM." FOR WE
LEARNED: IF A WOMAN REVOLTS AGAINST HER HUSBAND, SEVEN *DENA-
RII* ARE DEDUCTED FROM HER SETTLEMENT WEEKLY. AND WHY SEVEN
DENARII? BECAUSE OF THE SEVEN LABORS WHICH A WOMAN OWES TO
HER HUSBAND: GRINDING CORN, BAKING, LAUNDERING, COOKING,
SUCKLING HER CHILD, PREPARING HIS BED, AND WORKING IN WOOL:
HENCE SEVEN. CONVERSELY, IF A MAN REVOLTS AGAINST HIS WIFE, HER
SETTLEMENT IS INCREASED BY THREE *DENARII* PER WEEK. WHY THREE?
BECAUSE HE OWES HER FOOD, RAIMENT, AND MARITAL PRIVILEGES:
HENCE THREE. BUT CONSIDER: IF SHE BROUGHT IN [MALE AND] FEMALE
SLAVES [IN HER DOWRY], SHE OWES HIM NOTHING AT ALL. AGAIN, IF
HE STIPULATED [AT THE TIME OF MARRIAGE] TO BE FREE FROM THE
OBLIGATION OF FOOD, RAIMENT, AND MARITAL RIGHTS, HE OWES HER
NOTHING? SAID R. JOHANAN: A MAN'S SUFFERING EXCEEDS A WOMAN'S,
AS IT SAYS [IN CONNECTION WITH SAMSON], AND IT CAME TO PASS,
WHEN SHE PRESSED HIM DAILY WITH HER WORDS, AND URGED HIM
(JUDG. 16:16). THIS MEANS THAT SHE SLIPPED AWAY FROM HIM, [AND
THE VERSE CONTINUES], THAT *HIS* SOUL WAS VEXED UNTO DEATH, BUT

HER SOUL WAS NOT VEXED. WHY? BECAUSE SHE TOOK HER PLEASURES
ELSEWHERE.

There were many interpretations in our Midrash about the meaning
of Abimelech's gift to Abraham and Sarah. Why did he do it? After all,
it was Abraham who declared, rather falsely, that Sarah was his sister,
not his wife. One interpretation is that God's appearance to Abimelech
in a dream made him realize how Abraham and Sarah were important
to him. This may be one reason for his giving out the various gifts. Resh
Lakish (Rabbi Shimon ben Lakish), however, had an entirely different
interpretation. In his view, Abimelech had his eyes on Sarah. He was
overwhelmed by her beauty and the various ways she conducted herself.
He realized that Abraham and Sarah were husband and wife, but he also
realized that Abraham was the type of husband who never gave his wife
a present or gift, whereas when she was in his palace for only one night,
Abimelech treated her as a great celebrity with a large amount of money
as a gift. It was his thinking that if Abraham and Sarah ever had a quarrel
which became even slightly serious, she would remember that there was
one person in her past, Abimelech, who treated her as a noble lady and
who would welcome her at any time. This, said Resh Lakish, is the main
reason why he donated these lavish presents to Abraham and Sarah.

―

Seed Thoughts I

Do not look at her [Sarah] to trade in her. Or: cover other people's eyes
from her, that they should not desire her. (Copied almost verbatim from
Soncino, referring to what Abimelech is telling Abraham.)

―

Seed Thoughts II

What is the meaning of the term *kesut einayim*, which in its literal translation means "the covering of the eyes?" In the commentary to the Midrash of *HaMidrash HaMevo'ar*, there is a note to all readers that many
commentators have their own special interpretations of the meaning
of that phrase. It is recommended that readers look up the meaning of
that phrase in the Concordance of the Bible, or of the Tanach. What we
have in our present Midrash are interesting opinions, but there are many

more in various aspects of the Talmudic literature. Basically, it means the effort to find a new and different meaning in what your eyes see.

PARASHAH FIFTY-TWO, *Midrash Thirteen*

יג ויתפלל אברהם אל האלהים. אמר רבי חמא בר רבי חנינא: מתחלת הספר ועד כאן לא נאמר בלשון הזה. כיון שהתפלל אבינו אברהם הותר הקשר הזה.

13. AND ABRAHAM PRAYED UNTO GOD (GEN. 20:17). R. HAMA B. R. HANINA SAID: FROM THE BEGINNING OF THE BOOK [OF GENESIS] UNTIL HERE WE DO NOT FIND THIS EXPRESSION. BUT AS SOON AS ABRAHAM PRAYED, THIS KNOT WAS UNTIED.

S ee the Seed Thoughts below.

כי עצור עצר, נאמר: עצירה בפה, עצירה בגרון, עצירה באוזן, עצירה מלמעלה, עצירה מלמטה, והכל אומרים: על דבר שרי אשת אברם. א"ר ברכיה: עלו דטולמיסין למקרב למסאנא דמטרונא, כל אותה הלילה היתה שרה שטוחה על פניה ואומרת: רבון העולמים! אברהם יצא בהבטחה ואני יצאתי באמנה. אברהם חוץ לסירה ואני נתונה בסירה. אמר לה הקב"ה: כל מה שאני עושה בשבילך, אני עושה! והכל אומרין: על דבר שרי אשת אברם. א"ר לוי: כל אותה הלילה היה מלאך עומד ומגלב בידו, והיה מתיעץ בשרה, אם אמרה ליה: מחי! מחי, ואם אמרה ליה שבוק! הוה שביק. כל כך למה? שהיתה אומרת לו: אשת איש אני, ולא היה פורש. רבי אלעזר תני לה משום רבי אליעזר: שמענו בפרעה שלקה בצרעת, ואבימלך שלקה בעיצור. מנין שהכל לקו בזה ובזה? תלמוד לומר: על דבר שרי אשת אברם, גזירה שוה:

FOR THE LORD HAD FAST CLOSED UP (GEN. 20:18). THIS "CLOSING UP" APPLIED TO THE MOUTH, THE THROAT, THE EYE, THE EAR, ABOVE, AND BELOW. AND ALL ADMITTED THAT IT WAS BECAUSE OF SARAH ABRAHAM'S WIFE. R. BEREKIAH SAID: IT WAS BECAUSE HE DARED TO APPROACH THE SHOE OF THAT LADY. AND THE WHOLE OF THAT NIGHT SARAH LAY PROSTRATE ON HER FACE, CRYING: "SOVEREIGN OF THE UNIVERSE! ABRAHAM WENT FORTH [FROM HIS LAND] ON THINE ASSURANCE, AND I WENT FORTH WITH FAITH; ABRAHAM IS WITHOUT THIS PRISON WHILE I AM WITHIN!" SAID THE HOLY ONE, BLESSED BE HE, TO HER: "WHATEVER I DO, I DO FOR THY SAKE, AND ALL WILL SAY: IT IS BECAUSE OF SARAH ABRAHAM'S WIFE." R. LEVI SAID: THE WHOLE OF THAT NIGHT AN ANGEL STOOD WITH A WHIP IN HIS HAND; WHEN SHE ORDERED, "STRIKE," HE

STRUCK, AND WHEN SHE BADE HIM, "DESIST," HE CEASED. AND WHY
SUCH SEVERITY? BECAUSE SHE TOLD HIM [ABIMELECH]: "I AM A MAR-
RIED WOMAN," YET HE WOULD NOT LEAVE HER. R. ELEAZAR SAID, AND
IT WAS ALSO TAUGHT IN THE NAME OF R. LIEZER B. JACOB: WE KNOW
THAT PHARAOH WAS SMITTEN WITH LEPROSY AND ABIMELECH WITH
THE CLOSING UP [OF THE ORIFICES]. HOW DO WE KNOW THAT WHAT IS
SAID HERE IS TO BE APPLIED THERE, AND VICE VERSA? BECAUSE "FOR
THE SAKE OF" OCCURS IN BOTH PLACES, IN ORDER THAT AN ANALOGY
SHOULD BE DRAWN.

W e might understand better if we were to interpret the Hebrew *atzor
atzar* as a form of paralysis, not only of Abimelech but of the entire
population of his palace; so long as Sarah was in his premises, they could
not function normally. In all respects, not just those of sexuality, the use
of similar Hebrew terms in the story of Pharaoh and Sarah, as well as in
the story of Abimelech and Sarah is what prompts the commentators
to feel that both monarchs were treated with the same punishment and
suffered from the same temporary paralysis of their daily life.

***

Seed Thoughts I

The Midrash mentions the fact that the use of the term תפילה – *tefillah*
– in Hebrew, translated as "prayer," appears in the Pentateuch for the
first time ever in this portion. Up to this point, the approach of man
to God was achieved by means of the sacrificial service. An animal or
bird was slaughtered for this purpose, and it was usually celebrated by
means of a feast, and sometimes, the mere slaughter of the animal was
good enough to be used as an expression of love and faith. Nowhere in
the Bible do we note that these sacrifices were accompanied by what
today we would call prayer, but commentators in the Talmudic writings are quite certain that what we call prayer, which is the expression
of devotion by means of language, accompanied almost every aspect of
the sacrificial experience. We accept the fact that this is so, even though
the evidence can be approached only with great difficulty. But even the
commentators are correct; the use of the term *tefillah* (or in English,
"Prayer," as though expressing something quite unique) has its origin in
the Midrash we are now studying. Prayer has turned out to be probably
the most important spiritual experience in Judaism and in many other

religions. It can be fixed into liturgical books or a ritual in synagogues and holy temples, and indeed it can be recited simply as the devotion of one's heart without any special preparation or ritual or authority. It can be recited by men or women, adults or children. Prayer is one of the most useful experiences of the religious act.

Seed Thoughts II

There are many emotional gradations in the entire story of Abraham, Sarah, and King Abimelech. Some of the events are positive and honorable, and some of the events are very low regarding moral and ethical significance. The high point of the entire development, however, is the sentence in our present Midrash that Abraham prayed for Abimelech. Here, we have a person like Abraham who indulged in a form of trickery by suggesting that his wife was his sister, and Abimelech tried to find some acceptance of his position and situation by giving lavish gifts to Sarah and Abraham upon their departure. However, for Abraham to pray for Abimelech places both of them in the highest possible position. What was said in Abraham's prayer? The Midrash does not contain this information. One has to assume, however, that Abraham asked for God's forgiveness to Abimelech, and he may have added his own forgiveness for Abimelech's interest in Sarah, which was never realized, and possibly some aspect of forgiveness in their relationship to each other. The fact that Abimelech looked upon himself as a member of a separate religion did not bother Abraham, who had no desire to convert him. Abraham merely accepted him as a human being with both the high qualities and the difficult challenges that affect all of us. He was also one of the first to realize that prayer could do all the things that have so far been described, and much more that could be added. Probably, Abraham's prayer for Abimelech was the highest achievement in Abimelech's life and career.

א וה' פקד את שרה כאשר אמר. זהו שאמר הכתוב (יחזקאל יז): וידעו כל עצי השדה כי אני
ה' השפלתי עץ גבוה הגבהתי עץ שפל. אמר רבי יודן: לא כדין דאמרין ולא עבדין, אלא, אני
ה' דברתי ועשיתי. אמר רבי ברכיה: אני ה' דברתי ועשיתי, והיכן דבר (שם כב): למועד אשוב
אליך ולשרה בן. ועשה. וידעו כל עצי השדה, אלו הבריות, היך מד"א: (דברים כ) כי האדם עץ
השדה. כי אני ה' השפלתי עץ גבוה, זה אבימלך. הגבהתי עץ שפל, זה אברהם. הובשתי עץ
לח, אלו נשי אבימלך. דכתיב, כי עצור עצר ה'. הפרחתי עץ יבש, זו שרה. אני ה' דברתי. היכן
דבר? למועד אשוב אליך ועשיתי, הה"ד: ויעש ה' לשרה כאשר דבר:

1. AND THE LORD REMEMBERED SARAH AS HE HAD SAID (GEN. 21:1). IT
IS THUS THAT SCRIPTURE WRITES: AND ALL THE TREES OF THE FIELD
SHALL KNOW THAT I THE LORD HAVE BROUGHT DOWN THE HIGH TREE,
HAVE EXALTED THE LOW TREE, HAVE DRIED UP THE GREEN TREE, AND
HAVE MADE THE DRY TREE TO FLOURISH; I THE LORD HAVE SPOKEN AND
DONE IT (EZEK. 17:24). R. JUDAN SAID: NOT LIKE THOSE WHO SPEAK
BUT DO NOT PERFORM. R. BEREKIAH SAID ON THE VERSE, I THE LORD
HAVE SPOKEN AND DONE IT: WHERE DID HE SPEAK IT? – AT THE SET
TIME I WILL RETURN UNTO THEE ... AND SARAH SHALL HAVE A SON
(GEN. 18:14). AND I HAVE DONE IT – AND THE LORD DID UNTO SARAH
AS HE HAD SPOKEN. AND ALL THE TREES OF THE FIELD SHALL KNOW –
REFERS TO THE PEOPLE, AS YOU READ: FOR THE TREE OF THE FIELD IS
MAN (DEUT. 20:19). THAT I THE LORD HAVE BROUGHT DOWN THE HIGH
TREE – ALLUDES TO ABIMELECH; HAVE EXALTED THE LOW TREE – TO
ABRAHAM; HAVE DRIED UP THE GREEN TREE – TO ABIMELECH'S WIVES,
AS IT IS WRITTEN: FOR THE LORD HAD FAST CLOSED UP ALL THE WOMBS
OF THE HOUSE OF ABIMELECH (GEN. 20:18). AND HAVE MADE THE DRY
TREE TO FLOURISH – ALLUDES TO SARAH. I THE LORD HAVE SPOKEN:
SAID R. JUDAN: NOT LIKE THOSE WHO SPEAK BUT DO NOT PERFORM.
R. BEREKIAH COMMENTED: I THE LORD HAVE SPOKEN: WHERE DID HE
SPEAK IT? AT THE SET TIME I WILL RETURN UNTO THEE, ETC. AND I
HAVE DONE IT: THUS IT IS WRITTEN: AND THE LORD DID UNTO SARAH
AS HE HAD SPOKEN.

Our midrashic text has shown us how the symbol of a tree can be used to simplify our knowledge of our forebearers, Abraham and Sarah, and their many adventures.

~

Seed Thoughts

The use of the tree as a symbol that can influence human behavior can be found in many literatures. The text of our Midrash is a beautiful explanation of the use of the tree as a symbol by which to interpret many of the texts that deal with Abraham and Sarah. The English language and literature has many examples of the tree as a symbol. I can remember a poem ("Trees" by J. Kilmer), which later on was set to music, and it went something like this: "I think that I shall never see a poem lovely as a tree." It also concludes in a beautiful way: "Poems are made by fools like me, but only God can make a tree." There is an immediate difference, however, when one compares this poem with what we have been reading in the Midrash. Most poems or essays about trees deal with the beauty of a tree, and a tree's growth can often be used as a comparison to human life. In the Jewish tradition, however, the tree is used not to show off its beauty but to teach us something about life and its problems, as the text that we are now reading can testify. This is based on that most unusual phrase in Hebrew, *ki ha-adam etz ha-sadeh*, which means that the human being can be compared to the ordinary tree that can be found in any garden or forest.

Parashah Fifty-Three, *Midrash Two*

ב (איוב ד) האנוש מאלוה יצדק אם מעושהו יטהר גבר, וכי אפשר לאדם להיות צדיק יותר
מבוראו? אם מעושהו יטהר גבר, וכי אפשר לאדם להיות טהור יותר מבוראו? מה אלישע
אומר לשונמית? (מלכים ב ד): למועד הזה כעת חיה את חובקת בן. אמרה לו: אל אדוני איש
האלהים, אל תכזב בשפחתך! אותן המלאכים שבשרו את שרה כך אמרו לה: למועד אשוב
אליך כעת חיה ולשרה בן. אמר לה: אותן המלאכים היו יודעים שהם חיים וקיימין לעולם,
אמרו: למועד אשוב אליך, אבל אני, שאני בשר ודם – קיים היום מת למחר – בין חי, בין
מת, למועד הזה את חובקת בן. מה כתוב שם? ותהר ותלד בן למועד הזה, כעת חיה אשר
דבר אליה אלישע, דבריו של בשר ודם מתקיים ודבריו של הקב"ה אין מתקיימין? וה' פקד
את שרה כאשר אמר וגו':

2. SHALL A MAN BE MORE JUST THAN GOD, SHALL A MAN BE PURER THAN
HIS MAKER (JOB 4:17)? IS IT POSSIBLE FOR A MORTAL TO BE MORE RIGH-
TEOUS THAN HIS CREATOR? SHALL A MAN BE PURER THAN HIS MAKER:
IS IT POSSIBLE FOR A MORTAL TO BE PURER THAN HIS CREATOR? NOW
WHAT DID ELISHA SAY TO THE SHUNAMMITE? "AT THIS SEASON, WHEN
THE TIME COMETH ROUND, THOU SHALT EMBRACE A SON." AND SHE
SAID TO HIM: "NAY, MY LORD, THOU MAN OF GOD, DO NOT LIE UNTO
THY HANDMAID" (II KINGS 4:16). FOR THE ANGELS WHO GAVE THE
GOOD TIDINGS TO SARAH SAID THUS TO HER: "AT THE SET TIME I WILL
RETURN UNTO THEE," ETC. THOSE ANGELS, KNOWING THAT THEY LIVE
FOR EVER, COULD SAY, "AT THE SET TIME I WILL RETURN UNTO THEE,"
HE REPLIED. "BUT I AM MORTAL, HERE TO-DAY AND DEAD TOMORROW;
WHETHER I AM ALIVE OR DEAD [BY THEN], AT THIS SEASON ... THOU
SHALT EMBRACE A SON. NOW WHAT IS WRITTEN THERE FURTHER? AND
THE WOMAN CONCEIVED, AND BORE A SON (4:17). NOW IF THE WORDS
OF A MERE MORTAL WERE FULFILLED, HOW MUCH MORE THOSE OF THE
HOLY ONE, BLESSED BE HE! HENCE, AND THE LORD REMEMBERED SARAH
AS HE HAD SAID, ETC.

Seed Thoughts

On what is the text based that asks the question whether a human being
can be more righteous than the Creator? It is probably based on the
experience of the prophet Elisha with the Shunammite woman whom

he assisted by his prayers that she would have a son. The Shunammite woman immediately contested his prediction, because he had left out the important fact that he would not necessarily be present when she gives birth. In the case of the Holy One, blessed be He, He assured Sarah that He would return and that elsewhere an angel affirmed that someone would be present. In the case of Elisha, he specified that he would not be present. This, therefore, is the source of the question whether a human being, such as a prophet, is not required to be present at the time that his prediction is expected to unfold, whereas the Holy One, blessed be He, assures Sarah that He would return. We now have a setting by which it might seem that a human being, such as a prophet, is treated by the text more righteously than the Holy One, blessed be He. The prophet Elisha, when he is accosted with this different set of requirements between the prophet and God, immediately explains that the angels live forever and they can be relied upon to return when Sarah needs them. Elisha, however, is a person of flesh and blood; he might die before the event. How, then, could he predict his presence? This explanation seems to remove the force of the comparison that a human being (e.g., a prophet) can be treated with more privileges than the Almighty Himself. It so happens that Elisha was probably present at the Shunammite woman's birth.

—

Additional Commentary

God's justness

"Shall a man be more just than God . . . ?" Perhaps the justification of this question is based on a particular scriptural text. The verse says: "The Lord remembered Sarah as He had spoken." Or the verse that says: "and God did for Sarah what He had promised." These additional phrases were not necessary. It would have been enough for the scriptural text to say merely "and the Lord remembered Sarah." The rest of the text was not necessary and is probably the basis for the question as posed by the Book of Job and the Midrash. (Mirkin)

Parashah Fifty-Three, *Midrash Three*

ג (חבקוק ג) כי תאנה לא תפרח ואין יבול בגפנים כחש מעשה זית ושדמות לא עשה וגו'. כי
תאנה לא תפרח, זה אברהם, היך מה דאת אמר (הושע ט): כבכורה בתאנה בראשיתה, ראיתי
אבותיכם. ואין יבול בגפנים, זו שרה המד"א (תהלים קכח): אשתך כגפן פוריה וגו'.

3. FOR THOUGH THE FIG-TREE DOTH NOT BLOSSOM, ETC. (HAB. 3:17).
THIS ALLUDES TO ABRAHAM, AS IN THE VERSE: I SAW YOUR FATHERS
AS THE FIRST-RIPE IN THE FIG-TREE AT HER FIRST SEASON (HOS. 9:10).
NEITHER IS THERE FRUIT IN THE VINES (HAB. 3:17), ALLUDES TO SARAH,
AS YOU READ: THY WIFE SHALL BE AS A FRUITFUL VINE (PS. 128:3).

This text has to be understood as trying to establish how extreme
a person's faith and hope is liable to reach. We have a listing here that
the fig tree did not blossom, and that there was no juice in the grapes.
Even the olive tree lacked its liquid, and the fields did not render its
product. Furthermore, the sheep and the cattle were not yet ready to
be of help. Nevertheless, despite all of these potential disasters, I will
rejoice and hope in the Lord, and in the God Who will deliver me. The
Midrash goes on to describe a number of interpretations that help support a person's hope and faith. As for the fig tree that did not blossom,
this is a reminder of Abraham, the most important of our Patriarchs.
After all, the verse in Scripture says, "as a fig tree ripens, do I remember
Abraham?" The reader would include Abraham, Isaac, and Jacob to
compensate for whatever evils may have occurred in other generations.
As to the expression, "there is no harvest among the grapes," this refers
to Sarah, the wife of Abraham and first among the Matriarchs in the
Bible. As Solomon says, "your wife shall be as a fruitful vine within your
home." We are talking about her as being barren but always with hope in
the Lord Who rewarded her faith with the birth of Isaac.

כחש מעשה זית, אותן המלאכים שבישרו את שרה האירו פניה כזית, כוחשים היו? אלא,
שדמות לא עשו אוכל? אותן השדים המתים לא עשו אוכל. גזר ממכלה צאן, היך מה דאת
אמר (יחזקאל לד): ואתן צאני צאן מרעיתי, אדם אתם, אלא ואין בקר ברפתים, היך מד"א:
(הושע י) אפרים עגלה מלומדה אוהבתי לדוש? חזרה שרה ואמרה: מה אני מובדה סברי מן
ברייי? אלא, (חבקוק ג): ואני בה' אעלוזה אגילה באלהי ישעי. אמר לה הקב"ה: את לא אובדית
סיברך, אף אנא איני מובדית סיברך, אלא, וה' פקד את שרה וגו'. וה' פקד את שרה. (ישעיה

מ) יבש חציר נבל ציץ. יבש חצירו של אבימלך, ונבל ציצו, ודבר אלהינו יקום לעולם. וה' פקד
את שרה כאשר אמר:

THE LABOR OF THE OLIVE FAILETH (HAB. 3:17): THE FACES OF THOSE
ANGELS WHO GAVE THE GOOD TIDINGS TO SARAH SHONE LIKE AN OL-
IVE: WERE THEY IYING? NO, BUT THE FIELDS (SHEDEMOTH) YIELD NO
FOOD, WHICH MEANS, THE WITHERED BREASTS (SHADAYIM HA-METHIM)
YIELDED NO FOOD. THE FLOCK IS CUT OFF FROM THE FOLD (HAB. 3:17)
HAS THE SAME CONNOTATION AS IN THE VERSE, AND YE MY FLOCK, THE
FLOCK OF MY PASTURE, ARE MEN (EZEK. 34:31). THERE IS NO HERD IN
THE STALLS (HAB. 3:17), HAS THE MEANING IT HAS IN THE VERSE, AND
EPHRAIM IS A HEIFER WELL BROKEN, THAT LOVETH TO THRESH (HOS.
10:11). SUBSEQUENTLY, HOWEVER, SARAH EXCLAIMED, "WHAT! AM I TO
LOSE FAITH IN MY CREATOR! HEAVEN FORFEND! I WILL NOT LOSE FAITH
IN MY CREATOR, FOR I WILL REJOICE IN THE LORD, I WILL EXALT IN THE
GOD OF MY SALVATION" (HAB. 3:18). SAID THE HOLY ONE, BLESSED BE
HE, TO HER: "SINCE THOU DIDST NOT LOSE THY FAITH, I TOO WILL NOT
GIVE THEE CAUSE TO LOSE FAITH." BUT RATHER, AND THE LORD REMEM-
BERED SARAH, ETC. THE GRASS WITHERETH, THE FLOWER FADETH (ISA.
40:8): THAT MEANS, THE GRASS OF ABIMELECH WITHERETH AND HIS
FLOWER FADETH. BUT THE WORD OF OUR GOD SHALL STAND FOR EVER
(40:8); HENCE, AND THE LORD REMEMBERED SARAH, AS HE HAD SAID.

The text now lists a number of episodes that affected Sarah. The
emptiness of the olive tree is one of the comments that interpret Sarah's
difficulties, for the olive tree represents her. On the other hand, when
the angels brought the message to her that she would give birth at the
appropriate time, her feeling of rejoicing was unlimited, despite the
challenges. She would never give up her faith in God and her confidence
that someday she would experience the great fulfillment for which her
faith had prepared her.

Thus Sarah feared that "flocks" would be cut off from her and there
would be no herd in her stalls – she could not bring up children. (Copied verbatim from Soncino, as commentary to "And Ephraim is a heifer
well broken from Hosea.)

PARASHAH FIFTY-THREE, *Midrash Four*

ד (תהלים קיט) לעולם ה' דברך נצב בשמים. הא בארץ לא? אלא, מה שאמרת לאברהם
בשמים, למועד אשוב אליך כעת חיה. ר' נחמן דיפו משם ר' יעקב דקיסרין פתח: (תהלים
פ): אלהים צבאות שוב נא הבט משמים וראה ופקוד גפן זאת, שוב ועשה מה שאמרת
לאברהם: הבט נא השמימה וספור הכוכבים. ופקוד גפן זאת, וה' פקד את שרה.

4. FOR EVER, O LORD, THY WORD STANDETH FAST IN HEAVEN (PS.
119:89) – BUT NOT ON EARTH? BUT IT MEANS, WHAT THOU DIDST SAY
TO ABRAHAM IN HEAVEN: AT THE SET TIME I WILL RETURN UNTO THEE,
ETC. HENCE, AND THE LORD REMEMBERED SARAH. R. MENAHEMA AND R.
NAHMAN OF JOPPA IN THE NAME OF R. JACOB OF CAESAREA COMMENCED
WITH THE TEXT: O GOD OF HOSTS, RETURN, WE BESEECH THEE (PS.
80:15). RETURN AND DO WHAT THOU DIDST PROMISE ABRAHAM. LOOK
FROM HEAVEN, AND BEHOLD (80:15) – AS IT SAYS: LOOK NOW TOWARD
HEAVEN, AND COUNT THE STARS, ETC. (GEN. 15:5). AND BE MINDFUL OF
THIS VINE (PS. 80:15): THUS, AND THE LORD REMEMBERED SARAH.

The Midrash states that when Abraham elevated to the heavens and
God spoke to him, many important statements were included. Abraham
was not merely told to look at the heavens and count the stars; he was
placed in the position that put him at the very top of the heavens, so that
he was looking downwards all the time. It was while in this position that
God told him to count the stars if possible, and his offspring would be
like the stars that he was able to see at close range. He was also told that
God would watch over Sarah. A year from this experience, or to be more
specific, at the appropriate time when she is able to give birth, He will
return and be present at the birth of her son. Rabbi Nahman of Joppa
broadens the influence of Abraham's presence in heaven and gives him
a heavenly role. His prayer was that the *gefen* or vine-tree, which was
a symbol of Abraham and his children, may be blessed by Abraham,
who was asked to count the stars on their behalf. The hope was that
the community and the people of Israel might profit from Abraham's
blessing forever. "Look down from heaven and count the stars and thus
will your descendants be. Watch over the vine-tree and bless Israel for
good." Israel is symbolized by the *gefen* or vine-tree in Psalm 119, and it
includes the blessings to Sarah, who is also symbolized by the vine-tree
together with her husband. In this respect, it will be established forever.

God made a promise to Abraham when he was elevated to that lofty position in the heavens.

ר' שמואל בר נחמן: פתח (במדבר כג): לא איש אל ויכזב, ובן אדם ויתנחם. א"ר שמואל: הפסוק
הזה לא ראשו סופו, ולא סופו ראשו. לא איש אל ויכזב וגו'. ההוא אמר: ולא יעשה ודבר לא
יקימנה, אלא בשעה שהקב"ה גוזר להביא טובה לעולם, לא איש אל ויכזב. ובשעה שהוא גוזר
להביא רעה, ההוא אמר ולא יעשה. בשעה שאמר לאברהם, כי ביצחק יקרא לך זרע, לא איש
אל ויכזב. ובשעה שאמר לו: קח נא את בנך את יחידך, ההוא אמר ולא יעשה. בשעה שאמר
הקב"ה למשה: (שמות ג) פקוד פקדתי אתכם, לא איש אל ויכזב. בשעה שאמר לו הקב"ה:
(דברים ט) הרף ממני ואשמידם, ההוא אמר ולא יעשה. בשעה שאמר הקב"ה לאברהם: וגם
את הגוי, לא איש אל ויכזב. ובשעה שאמר לו: ועבדום וענו אותם, ההוא אמר ולא יעשה.
בשעה שאמר לו הקב"ה: שוב אשוב אליך, לא איש אל ויכזב, אלא, וה' פקד את שרה:

R. SAMUEL B. NAHMAN COMMENCED THUS: GOD IS NOT A MAN, THAT HE SHOULD LIE, ETC. (NUM. 23:19). SAID R. SAMUEL B. NAHMAN: IN THIS VERSE, THE BEGINNING DOES NOT CORRESPOND TO THE END, NOR THE END TO THE BEGINNING. THUS IT COMMENCES: GOD IS NOT A MAN, THAT HE SHOULD LIE, ETC., WHILE IT CONCLUDES: WHEN HE HATH SAID, HE WILL NOT DO IT, AND WHEN HE HATH SPOKEN, HE WILL NOT MAKE IT GOOD. BUT THE MEANING IS THIS: WHEN THE HOLY ONE, BLESSED BE HE, DECREES TO BRING GOOD UPON THE WORLD, THEN, GOD IS NOT A MAN, THAT HE SHOULD LIE. BUT WHEN HE DECREES TO BRING EVIL UPON THE WORLD, THEN, WHEN HE HATH SAID, HE WILL NOT DO IT. WHEN HE SAID TO ABRAHAM: FOR IN ISAAC SHALL SEED BE CALLED TO THEE (GEN. 21:12), THEN GOD IS NOT A MAN, THAT HE SHOULD LIE, NEITHER THE SON OF MAN, THAT HE SHOULD REPENT. WHEN HE SAID TO HIM: TAKE NOW THY SON, THINE ONLY ONE, ETC. (22:2), THEN, WHEN HE HATH SAID, HE WILL NOT DO IT, AND WHEN HE HATH SPOKEN, HE WILL NOT MAKE IT GOOD. WHEN GOD SAID TO MOSES: I HAVE SURELY REMEMBERED YOU (EX. 3:16), THEN, GOD IS NOT A MAN, THAT HE SHOULD LIE, NEITHER THE SON OF MAN, THAT HE SHOULD REPENT. BUT WHEN HE SAID TO HIM: LET ME ALONE, THAT I MAY DESTROY THEM (DEUT. 9:14), THEN, WHEN HE HATH SAID, HE WILL NOT DO IT, AND WHEN HE HATH SPOKEN, HE WILL NOT MAKE IT GOOD. WHEN GOD SAID TO ABRAHAM: AND ALSO THAT NATION, WHOM THEY SHALL SERVE, WILL I JUDGE, ETC. (GEN. 15:14), THEN, GOD IS NOT A MAN, THAT HE SHOULD LIE, NEITHER THE SON OF MAN, THAT HE SHOULD REPENT. BUT WHEN HE SAID TO HIM: AND THEY SHALL SERVE THEM, AND THEY SHALL AFFLICT THEM FOUR HUNDRED YEARS (15:13), THEN, WHEN HE HATH SAID, HE WILL NOT DO IT, AND WHEN HE HATH SPOKEN, HE WILL NOT MAKE IT GOOD. FINALLY,

WHEN GOD SAID TO HIM, I WILL CERTAINLY RETURN UNTO THEE, ETC.
(GEN. 18:10), THEN, GOD IS NOT A MAN, THAT HE SHOULD LIE, ETC., BUT,
AND THE LORD REMEMBERED SARAH.

The Midrash now brings to our attention two verses which seem
to contradict each other. One verse reads: "God is not man, that He
should lie." The second verse is: "When He had said, He will not do
it, and when He had spoken, He will not make it good." These are not
contradictions. When God is about to do something good, He fulfills
it no matter what the difficulties may be. But when He intends to do
something with evil consequences, He may decide not to do so depending upon the circumstances. For example, God ordered Abraham to
take his favorite son, Isaac, and prepare him for an offering. At the very
same time, He had prepared an angel so that if Abraham misinterpreted
the message and looked upon the offering as his slaughter, God had an
angel in reserve. God called to Abraham not to harm the young man
under any circumstances because the desire of the Almighty is that Isaac
be saved, but also that the world be redeemed from its evil behavior.

$$\sim$$

Seed Thoughts

This Midrash makes several references to Abraham being in heaven and
God asking him to count the stars. In fact, he was elevated to the top-
most point of the heavens, so that he would have to look down in order
to count the stars. The problem is that this episode has been interpreted
by the Midrash time and time again as referring to numbers, and that
we have never had such numbers. In fact, either during the time of the
Second Temple or some other ancient time period, we probably had
more Jews than today, but it did not last very long. It would seem that
the blessing of numbers was not really fulfilled. Maybe the intention
and the lesson are somewhat different. Looking at the stars, one would
not have the intention of quantity but quality. Each star was magnificent, and it might be the message that the Jewish people would have
righteous people or scholars or leaders who might be the equivalent of
stars to their communities. This might be a much greater blessing than
numbers. Furthermore, it would be a blessing already fulfilled many
times over the centuries and is probably valid today as well. It is the
blessing of Jewish quality and not quantity.

PARASHAH FIFTY-THREE, *Midrash Five*

ה וה' פקד את שרה. (מלכים א ח) אשר שמרת לעבדך דוד אבי את אשר דברת לו. אשר
שמרת לעבדך, זה אברהם. את אשר דברת לו, למועד אשוב אליך. ותדבר בפיך ובידך
מלאת כיום הזה, וה' פקד את שרה.

5. AND THE LORD REMEMBERED SARAH. WHO HAST KEPT WITH THY SER-
VANT DAVID MY FATHER, ETC. (I KINGS 8:24). WHO HAST KEPT WITH THY
SERVANT – ALLUDES TO ABRAHAM. THAT WHICH THOU DIDST PROMISE
HIM, VIZ. AT THE SET TIME I WILL RETURN UNTO THEE, ETC. (GEN.
18:14). YEA, THOU SPOKEST WITH THY MOUTH, AND HAST FULFILLED IT
WITH THY HAND, AS IT IS THIS DAY (I KINGS 8:24), VIZ. AND THE LORD
REMEMBERED SARAH.

The quotation by King Solomon is meant to indicate that Abraham
was the first person to be described by the Holy One, blessed be He,
as God's servant. That condition of service and being a servant of the
Lord was followed by others over several generations, until it reached
the time of King David (Solomon's father). Only in David's case was the
expression repeated that he was a servant of God.

(תהלים קיג) מושיבי עקרת הבית אם הבנים שמחה. מושיבי עקרת הבית, זו שרה, ותהי שרי
עקרה, אם הבנים שמחה, שנאמר: הניקה בנים שרה. וה' פקד את שרה, כאשר אמר.

WHO MAKETH THE BARREN WOMAN TO DWELL IN HER HOUSE (PS. 113:9).
THIS ALLUDES TO SARAH, AS IT IS WRITTEN: AND SARAI WAS BARREN
(GEN. 11:30); AS A JOYFUL MOTHER OF CHILDREN, AS IT SAYS: SARAH
HAS GIVEN CHILDREN SUCK (21:7) AND THE LORD REMEMBERED SARAH
AS HE HAD SAID.

The various verses that begin with God remembering Sarah conclude
with a near-repetition of the first phrase, with the meaning that the Almighty fulfilled for Sarah what He had promised her. At the same time,
the Midrash mentions many beautiful things about Sarah's behavior,
even when she was barren. She befriended and encouraged all other
women who were barren, assuring them that sooner or later, they would
be helped by the Almighty. At the same time, she was always available to
help children who required help, including those whose mothers were
barren but not anymore, of course. She herself was formerly a barren

woman, but with the birth of Isaac, that status was changed. She became
a very happy mother – not only of her son, but of all children. In fact,
she was known as the mother of all the Children of Israel.

רבי יהודה אמר: כאשר אמר, מה שאמר לה, הוא באמירה, ויעש ה' כאשר דבר. מה שדבר
לה, על ידי מלאך. רבי נחמיה אמר: וה' פקד את שרה כאשר אמר, מה שאמר לה על ידי
מלאך. ויעש ה' לשרה כאשר דבר, מה שאמר לה הוא. רבי יהודה אמר: כאשר אמר ליתן
לה בן, כאשר דבר לברכה בחלב. א"ל רבי נחמיה: והלא כבר נתבשרה בחלב? אלא, מלמד
שהחזירה הקב"ה לימי נערותיה.

R. JUDAH SAID: AND THE LORD REMEMBERED SARAH AS HE HAD SAID
REFERS TO THE PROMISES WHICH WERE PREFACED WITH THE TERM
"SAYING" (*AMIRAH*); AND THE LORD DID UNTO SARAH AS HE HAD SPO-
KEN REFERS TO THE PROMISES PREFACED WITH THE TERM "SPEAKING"
(*DIBBUR*). R. NEHEMIAH SAID: AND THE LORD REMEMBERED SARAH AS
HE HAD SAID REFERS TO WHAT HE SAID TO HER THROUGH THE ANGEL,
WHILE AND THE LORD DID UNTO SARAH AS HE HAD SPOKEN REFERS TO
WHAT HE HIMSELF SAID TO HER. R. JUDAH EXPOUNDED: AND THE LORD
REMEMBERED SARAH – TO GIVE HER A SON; AND THE LORD DID UNTO
SARAH AS HE HAD SPOKEN – TO BLESS HER WITH MILK. SAID R. NEHE-
MIAH TO HIM: HAD SHE THEN ALREADY BEEN INFORMED ABOUT MILK?
THIS TEACHES, HOWEVER, THAT GOD RESTORED TO HER THE DAYS OF
HER YOUTH.

One of the interesting by-products of Sarah's birth to Isaac is the fact
that she was blessed with the most unusual large supply of breast milk.
This has been interpreted as though Sarah was returned to her youthfulness. She tried to supply and help those children whose mothers felt
that they had this need.

רבי אבהו אמר: נותן אני יראתה על כל אומות העולם, דלא יהון מונין לה וצווחין לה:
"עקרתא". ר' יהודה בשם ריש לקיש: עיקר מטרין לא היה לה, וגלף לה הקב"ה עיקר מטרין.
אמר רבי אדא: בעל פקדונות אני! עמלק הפקיד אצלי חבילות של קוצים, והחזיר לו הקב"ה
חבילות של קוצים, שנאמר (שמואל א טו): פקדתי את אשר עשה עמלק לישראל. שרה
הפקידה אצלי מצוות ומעשים טובים, החזיר לה הקב"ה מצוות ומעשים טובים, וה' פקד
את שרה:

R. ABBAHU SAID: HE INSPIRED ALL PEOPLE WITH FEAR OF HER, SO THAT
THEY SHOULD NOT CALL HER A "BARREN WOMAN." R. JUDAN SAID: SHE
LACKED AN OVARY, WHEREUPON THE LORD FASHIONED AN OVARY FOR
HER. R. ADDA SAID: THE HOLY ONE, BLESSED BE HE, IS LIKE A TRUSTEE

FOR AMALEK WHO DEPOSITED WITH HIM BUNDLES OF THORNS [WRONG-
DOINGS]; THEREFORE HE RETURNED TO HIM BUNDLES OF THORNS
[PUNISHMENT], AS IT SAYS: I REMEMBER THAT WHICH AMALEK DID TO
ISRAEL (I SAM. 15:2). SARAH LAID UP WITH HIM A STORE OF PIOUS ACTS
AND GOOD DEEDS; THEREFORE THE LORD RETURNED HER [THE REWARD
FOR] THESE, AS IT SAYS: AND THE LORD REMEMBERED SARAH.

The nation of Amalek is described as producing a way of life that can
be compared to thorns. This means that Amalek's way of life continued
to produce troubles and idolatrous ways of living. Since Amalek produced a way of life described as thorns, God evaluated Amalek's life in
the same spirit – namely, that of bundles of thorns, meaning negative
experiences. Sarah, on the other hand, produced commandments and
good deeds. Her reward, therefore, was a life of commandments and
good deeds.

―

Seed Thoughts

In the early days of their marriage, Abraham appeared to be the dominat-
ing figure. God spoke to him, and he was appointed to do many things.
Sarah, on the other hand, seemed to be interested merely in domestic
issues. She arranged for her husband to marry Hagar in order to relieve
her of what she thought was the shame of being barren. Ultimately, she
became critical of Hagar and of the bad influence that their son Ishmael
had over Isaac. She ultimately sent both mother and son from her home.
As the years went by, we suddenly discover that God speaks to Sarah
sometimes by means of an angel. Presented in various forms, the consistent message was that she would give birth to a son in the year that
followed. This was repeated many times and used as an indication that
God fulfills the hopes and expectations of those who listen to His rules.
Ultimately, she ends up as the symbolic mother of all the Children of
Israel.

PARASHAH FIFTY-THREE, *Midrash Six*

ו וה' פקד את שרה. אמר רבי יצחק: כתיב (במדבר ה): ואם לא נטמאה האשה וטהורה היא
ונקתה ונזרעה זרע, זו שנכנסה לביתו של פרעה ולביתו של אבימלך ויצאת טהורה, אינו דין
שתתפקד? אמר רבי יהודה ברבי סימון: אע"ג דאמר רבי הונא: מלאך הוא שהוא ממונה על
התאוה, אבל שרה לא נצרכה לדברים הללו, אלא הוא בכבודו. וה' פקד את שרה ותהר ותלד
שרה לאברהם בן לזקוניו, מלמד שלא גנבה זרע ממקום אחר. בן לזקוניו, מלמד שהיה זיו
איקונין שלו דומה לו.

6. AND THE LORD REMEMBERED SARAH. R. ISAAC SAID: IT IS WRITTEN:
AND IF THE WOMAN BE NOT DEFILED, BUT BE CLEAN; THEN SHALL
SHE BE CLEARED, AND SHALL CONCEIVE SEED (NUM. 5:28). THEN THIS
WOMAN [SARAH] WHO HAD ENTERED THE HOUSES OF PHARAOH AND
ABIMELECH AND YET EMERGED UNDEFILED – SURELY IT WAS BUT RIGHT
THAT SHE SHOULD BE REMEMBERED. R. JUDAH B. R. SIMON SAID: AL-
THOUGH R. HUNA SAID THAT THERE IS AN ANGEL APPOINTED OVER DE-
SIRE, SARAH HAD NO NEED FOR SUCH, BUT HE IN HIS GLORY [MADE HER
CONCEIVE]; HENCE, AND THE LORD REMEMBERED SARAH. AND SARAH
CONCEIVED, AND BORE ABRAHAM A SON. (GEN. 21:2). THIS TEACHES
THAT SHE DID NOT STEAL SEED FROM ELSEWHERE. A SON IN HIS OLD
AGE: THIS TEACHES THAT HIS [ISAAC'S] FEATURES WERE LIKE HIS OWN.

When a husband suspected his wife of immoral behavior (usually means having contact with another male), she went to the Temple in Jerusalem. During the special *sotah* ritual, she was given bitter waters to drink. If they caused her great distress, it was a sign of her guilt. If she drank the water normally and carefully, it was a sign of her innocence. Nothing like this was done with Sarah, except that her being with Pharaoh and Abimelech was against her will, and therefore, she is pronounced pure and ready to continue her marriage to Abraham. Although Sarah was accepted as being pure despite her being in the palaces of Pharaoh and Abimelech, Sarah was not satisfied by being defined as pure because of the special relationship she had with Abraham and with the kings who motivated her and indeed forced her to spend some time in their palaces. Sarah wanted to be treated in the same way as other women and wanted to go through the difficult procedure of the *sotah*, the woman whose behavior is suspect. Only when that procedure pronounced her as pure, was she satisfied.

למועד אשר דבר אתו אלהים. רבי יודן ור' חמא. רבי יודן אמר: לט' חדשים נולד, שלא יהיו
אומרין: גרוף מביתו של אבימלך. רבי חמא אמר: לשבעה, שהם תשעה מקוטעים. רבי הונא
בשם רבי חזקיה: בחצות היום נולד. נאמר כאן מועד ונאמר להלן (דברים טז) כבוא השמש
מועד צאתך ממצרים:

AT THE SET TIME OF WHICH GOD HAD SPOKEN TO HIM. R. JUDAN SAID:
HE WAS BORN AT NINE MONTHS [OF PREGNANCY], SO THAT IT MIGHT
NOT BE SAID THAT HE WAS A SCION OF ABIMELECH'S HOUSE. R. HAMA
SAID: HE WAS BORN AT SEVEN MONTHS, WHICH WERE NINE INCOMPLETE
MONTHS. R. HUNA SAID IN HEZEKIAH'S NAME: HE WAS BORN AT MIDDAY.
FOR "SET TIME" (MO'ED) IS SAID HERE, WHILE ELSEWHERE IT SAYS, AT
THE SEASON (MO'ED) THAT THOU CAMEST FORTH OUT OF EGYPT (DEUT.
16:6).

The Midrash now includes a discussion as to how many months were
required for Sarah's pregnancy to end with the delivery of Isaac. Rabbi
Judan said that the length of her pregnancy was nine months, which is
the usual way for most women. Rabbi Hama, on the other hand, felt bad
that the pregnancy was seven months, which is acceptable in the lives
of many women. He came to this conclusion because the year of Isaac's
birth was a Jewish leap year, which meant that the months were intercalated. Basically, that means that there were two months of Adar, since
Sarah's pregnancy was from Sukkot (which is between the 15th and 22nd
of Tishrei) and ended with the festival of Passover. So the count is seven
months, which the Midrash sort of pronounced as breaking up the nine-
month syndrome. However, both opinions have their supporters.

There is a third element that is also part of the discussion. God's message to Sarah was that she would deliver at the heat of the day, which
probably meant either midday or close to midday. There are several
verses which include expressions such as *ke'hom hayom*, as the day was
getting warm.

Seed Thoughts

There was some concern in the various discussions as to why Abraham
was referred to as becoming a father. In the first place, old age in those
days may not be the same as old age in the modern world. Chances
are that one would have to be much older than Abraham to be defined
as זקן – *zaken*. It is sometimes interpreted as proving that the birth of

Isaac was an even greater miracle than anticipated, since both husband and wife lacked certain biological requirements. However, one of the commentators in this Midrash suggests that we need not take the term זקוניו – *zekunav* literally. It should be looked upon as the combination of two Hebrew words – זיו – *ziv* and איקוניו – *ikunav*, which means that the bright appearance of Isaac, even from his birth, imitated his father. It was quite obvious that we are dealing with father and son unquestionably.

PARASHAH FIFTY-THREE, *Midrash Seven*

ז ויקרא אברהם את שם בנו יצחק. יצא חוק לעולם, ניתן דורייה לעולם. אמר רבי יצחק
חפושית: יו"ד, עשרה, כנגד עשרת הדברות. צד"י, תשעים, ואם שרה הבת תשעים שנה
תלד? קו"ף, מאה, הלבן מאה שנה? חי"ת, כנגד המילה, שניתנה לשמונה, וימל אברהם את
יצחק וגו'. הדא הוא דכתיב (בראשית יי): ובן שמונת ימים ימול לכם כל זכר לדורותיכם:

7. AND ABRAHAM CALLED THE NAME OF HIS SON THAT WAS BORN UNTO
HIM, WHOM SARAH BORE TO HIM, ISAAC – YITZHAK (GEN. 21:3). [THE
NAME SIGNIFIES] LAW HAD GONE FORTH (*YATZA HOK*) TO THE WORLD, A
GIFT WAS MADE TO THE WORLD. R. ISAAC HIPUSHITH SAID: *YOD* IS TEN,
CORRESPONDING TO THE TEN COMMANDMENTS. *TZADDI* IS NINETY:
AND SHALL SARAH, THAT IS NINETY YEARS OLD, BEAR? (GEN. 17:17). *KUF*
IS HUNDRED: SHALL A CHILD BE BORN UNTO HIM THAT IS A HUNDRED
YEARS OLD (17:17)? *HETH* [IS EIGHT], IN REFERENCE TO CIRCUMCISION,
AS IT SAYS: AND ABRAHAM CIRCUMCISED HIS SON ISAAC WHEN HE WAS
EIGHT DAYS OLD (21:4).

There are many interpretations that can be found in this Midrash regarding the name יצחק – *Yitzhak* (Isaac). For example, it could be understood as rendering two words into one, the explanation being יצא חוק - *yatza hok*, which means that the Law emerged from the name. The interpretation would be that from the birth of Yitzhak, the concept of law entered the world with great power. It was from this origin that the Children of Israel received the Torah, which has also been called *Hok*, meaning Law. Furthermore, it can be attributed to Yitzhak and to his descendants that they initiated the practice of circumcision, which has been called by the name *hok* in many biblical sources. As a result of Isaac's birth, the entire universe was blessed with the concept of a righteous law, on the basis of which many good things came to the world. Indeed, the world was blessed by the righteous people and by Israel itself who blessed the world with *hok*, meaning law. Many concepts that emerged from Law are also included in this blessing, such as freedom from the intellectual point of view, and much healing from the point of view of circumcision (which has many medical advantages). Many of these advantages can be attributed to Israel, and were motivated by these interpretations of the name Yitzhak.

The Midrash also includes an interpretation of the name by means of gematria. For example, the letter *yod* (which means ten) represents the Ten Commandments, which were received by Israel (the children of Yitzhak). The letter *tzaddi*, which represents 90, is a reminder that Sarah gave birth to Isaac at the age of 90. The letter *kuf* is, numerically speaking, 100 – which was the age of Abraham, the father of Isaac, at the time of the latter's birth. As for the letter *heth*, whose numerical translation is eight, is a reminder of circumcision. Isaac was the first to be circumcised on the eighth day of his life, and this continues forever.

Seed Thoughts

The name Yitzhak lends itself to many interpretations, some of which are included in this Midrash. The ones that are included in this Midrash can be listed as follows: Yitzhak as one of the sources of law, Yitzhak as a reminder of the ages of his parents, and the fact that they were dedicated to the Ten Commandments and to ritual circumcision throughout the life of their descendants.

However, the name Yitzhak has been discussed elsewhere in biblical sources. In one particular section, there is an actual difference of opinion between Sarah and the Holy One, blessed be He. At the birth of Isaac, Sarah called out: "The whole world will *tzohek* with me." The question is, what does that word mean? God said to Abraham: "Why did Sarah laugh?" Did she not believe that God would fulfill what He had promised to do? Sarah replied that she had not laughed, but the text did say that she laughed. One has to interpret it as meaning that she did not laugh in the spirit of rebellion, but rather as part of her emotion of happiness, feeling that the whole world would join with her in her joy. At the same time, despite all these interpretations or maybe because of them, the child's name was given as Yitzhak. It means to laugh or to

enjoy. It is written grammatically in the future tense as though it is the
hope that Isaac and the generations that emerged from him would be a
source of joy and happiness.

PARASHAH FIFTY-THREE, *Midrash Eight*

ח ותאמר שרה צחוק עשה לי אלהים. ר' ברכיה בר' יהודה ברבי סימון, בשם רבי שמואל,
ברבי יצחק: ראובן בשמחה, שמעון מה איכפת ליה? כך שרה נפקדה. אחרים, מה איכפת
להם?

8. AND SARAH SAID: GOD HATH MADE JOY FOR ME; EVERY ONE THAT
HEARETH WILL REJOICE WITH ME (GEN. 21:6). R. BEREKIAH, R. JUDAH
B. R. SIMON, AND R. HANAN IN THE NAME OF R. SAMUEL B. R. ISAAC
SAID: IF REUBEN HAS CAUSE TO REJOICE, WHAT DOES IT MATTER TO
SIMEON? SIMILARLY, IF SARAH WAS REMEMBERED, WHAT DID IT MATTER
TO OTHERS?

When Sarah said "God had made joy for me," she felt that everyone
who heard the news would rejoice with her. Some of the rabbis protested this observation. If you don't know who a person is, why would
you rejoice at his/her celebration? Why, therefore, should Sarah have
felt that this does not apply in her case?

אלא, בשעה שנפקדה אמנו שרה, הרבה עקרות נפקדו עמה, הרבה חרשים נתפקחו, הרבה
סומים נפתחו, הרבה שוטים נשתפו.

BUT WHEN THE MATRIARCH SARAH WAS REMEMBERED [GAVE BIRTH],
MANY OTHER BARREN WOMEN WERE REMEMBERED WITH HER; MANY
DEAF GAINED THEIR HEARING; MANY BLIND HAD THEIR EYES OPENED,
MANY INSANE BECAME SANE.

What the Midrash is saying here is that the happy moment of Isaac's
birth was shared by many people who had suffered from serious disabilities, such as barrenness, deafness, and blindness. These people
were healed. In many respects, this corresponds to the fact that when
King Ahasuerus married Esther, he removed some of the taxes that his
government had instituted in order to have the recipients rejoice with

Esther, just as those who had recovered from their disabilities rejoiced with Sarah.

נאמר כאן עשייה, ונאמר להלן (אסתר ב) והנחה למדינות עשה. מה עשייה שנא' להלן, ניתן דורייה לעולם, אף עשייה שנא' כאן, דורייה לעולם. ור' לוי אמר: הוסיפו על המאורות. נאמר כאן עשייה, עשה לי, ונאמר להלן ויעש אלהים את שני המאורות:

FOR "MAKING" [HATH MADE] IS MENTIONED HERE, AND ALSO ELSE-
WHERE, VIZ. AND HE MADE A RELEASE TO THE PROVINCES (EST. 2:18).
AS THE MAKING MENTIONED THERE MEANS THAT A GIFT WAS GRANTED
TO THE WORLD, SO THE MAKING MENTIONED HERE MEANS THAT A GIFT
WAS GRANTED TO THE WORLD. R. LEVI SAID: SHE INCREASED THE LIGHT
OF THE LUMINARIES: "MAKING" IS MENTIONED HERE, VIZ. GOD HATH
MADE FOR ME, WHILE ELSEWHERE IT SAYS: AND GOD MADE THE TWO
LIGHTS (GEN. 1:16).

The tradition tells us that when Adam and Eve sinned by eating the fruit of the tree that had been prohibited to them, the universe suffered in the sense that the sun and the moon (the two main luminaries of the universe) had their powers of light affected and lessened. However, when Sarah gave birth to Isaac, God restored the light to the two luminaries, and therefore, the entire universe was brightened again. That is why in this connection, the word *aseh* – to make, in connection with the luminaries – is used.

PARASHAH FIFTY-THREE, *Midrash Nine*

ט ותאמר: מי מלל לאברהם היניקה בנים שרה. ר' פנחס משום רבי חלקיה: מי אמר מי דבר
אין כתיב כאן אלא מי מלל, רמזו שהוא מוליד למאה שנה. מנין מל"ל.

9. AND SHE SAID: WHO WOULD HAVE SAID (*MILLEL*) UNTO ABRAHAM
THAT SARAH SHOULD SUCKLE CHILDREN (GEN. 21:7)? R. PHINEHAS SAID
IN R. HELKIAH'S NAME: NOT *AMAR* (SAID) OR *DIBBER* (TALKED) BUT *MIL-
LEL* (SPOKE) IS WRITTEN: THUS SHE INDIRECTLY DREW HIS ATTENTION
TO THE FACT THAT HE HAD BEGOTTEN A CHILD AT THE AGE OF ONE
HUNDRED YEARS.

The amount of 100 is derived by gematria from the word מלל – *millel*,
where the *mem* stands for 40 and the *lamed* stands for 30, of which there
are two. The total, therefore, is 100.

ר' פנחס אמר: קומתו של אברהם אבינו היתה יבשה ונעשה מלילות.

R. PHINEHAS SAID IN R. HELKIAH'S NAME: [MILLEL SIGNIFIES THAT]
THE STANDING CROP OF OUR FATHER ABRAHAM HAD BEEN DRIED UP,
BUT IT NOW TURNED TO RIPE EARS OF CORN (*MELILOTH*).

In other words, Abraham's youthfulness was restored.

היניקה בנים שרה. היניקה בן אין כתיב כאן, אמנו שרה היתה צנועה יותר מדאי. אמר לה
אבינו אברהם: אין זו שעת הצניעות, אלא גלי את דדיך כדי שידעו הכל, שהתחיל הקב"ה
לעשות נסים! גלתה את דדיה והיו נובעות חלב, כשני מעיינות והיו מטרוניות באות ומניקות
את בניהם ממנה, והיו אומרות: אין אנו כדי להניק את בנינו מחלבה של צדקת. רבנן ורבי
אחא. רבנן אמרי: כל מי שבא לשם שמים, נעשה ירא שמים. רבי אחא אמר: אף מי שלא
בא לשם שמים, ניתן לו ממשלה בעוה"ז, כיון שהתפליגו עצמן בסיני ולא קבלו את התורה,
נטלה מהם אותה הממשלה:

THAT SARAH SHOULD HAVE SUCKLED CHILDREN: SHE SUCKLED BUILD-
ERS. OUR MOTHER SARAH WAS EXTREMELY MODEST. SAID ABRAHAM TO
HER: "THIS IS NOT A TIME FOR MODESTY, BUT UNCOVER YOUR BREASTS
SO THAT ALL MAY KNOW THAT THE HOLY ONE, BLESSED BE HE, HAS BE-
GUN TO PERFORM MIRACLES." SHE UNCOVERED HER BREASTS AND THE
MILK GUSHED FORTH AS FROM TWO FOUNTAINS, AND NOBLE LADIES
CAME AND HAD THEIR CHILDREN SUCKLED BY HER, SAYING, "WE DO
NOT MERIT THAT OUR CHILDREN SHOULD BE SUCKLED WITH THE MILK

OF THAT RIGHTEOUS WOMAN." THE RABBIS SAID: WHOEVER CAME FOR
THE SAKE OF HEAVEN BECAME GOD-FEARING. R. AHA SAID: EVEN ONE
WHO DID NOT COME FOR THE SAKE OF HEAVEN WAS GIVEN DOMINION
[I.E., GREATNESS] IN THIS WORLD. YET THEY DID NOT CONTINUE TO
ENJOY IT, FOR WHEN THEY STOOD ALOOF AT SINAI AND WOULD NOT
ACCEPT THE TORAH, THAT DOMINION WAS TAKEN FROM THEM. THUS IT
IS WRITTEN: HE LOOSETH THE BONDS OF KINGS, AND BINDETH THEIR
LOINS WITH A GIRDLE (JOB 12:18).

—

Seed Thoughts I

Orthodox readers might be somewhat taken aback in reading that
Abraham would request Sarah to reveal her breasts in public. The entire
episode could have been carried out in closed doors with the same results although taking a little bit longer. One would have to conclude, at
least judging by this Midrash, that some of the sexual attitudes differed
somewhat in those days from those that are practiced in Orthodox
circles today. However, one might also point out that from the Midrash,
it seems that only women came to bring their infants to Sarah to be
suckled.

—

Seed Thoughts II

By a play on words *banim* (children) being read as *bana'im* (builders).
Those who were suckled by her (as explained in the text) became God-
fearing and were granted dominion, and they built up the world, as it
were. This can be supported by the fact that the Torah does not say
"She suckled a son," but rather "She suckled sons (children)." (See the
Soncino commentary.)

—

Seed Thoughts III

One gets the impression from our Midrash that even the infant children
of non-Jews were brought to be suckled by Sarah. They were described
as being people who gained power, and this may help us complete that

reference. It then says that since they did not accept the revelation at Sinai, which included the Ten Commandments and many other things, they no longer shared the experience of the Children of Israel, and did not merit their power any more.

PARASHAH FIFTY-THREE, *Midrash Ten*

י ויגדל הילד ויגמל. ר' הושעיה רבה אמר: נגמל מיצר הרע. רבנן אמרי: נגמל מחלבו.

10. AND THE CHILD GREW, AND WAS WEANED (GEN. 21:8). R. HOSHAYA THE ELDER SAID: HE WAS WEANED FROM TEMPTATION. THE RABBIS SLID: HE WAS WEANED FROM HIS MOTHER'S MILK.

The Hebrew word *gomel* has the meaning that he had completed the necessity for his mother's milk. In those days, it lasted a much longer time than today.

ויעש אברהם משתה גדול. רבי יודא ב"ר סימון אמר: גדול עולמים היה שם. רבי יודן בר
מספרתא אמר: (אסתר ב) ויעש המלך משתה גדול, גדולי עולם היו שם, הדא הוא דכתיב
(דברים ל): כי ישוב ה', לשוש עליך לטוב בימי מרדכי ואסתר, כאשר שש על אבותיך, בימי
אברהם יצחק ויעקב. אמר רבי יהודה בר' סימון: משתה גדול, משתה גדולים, עוג וכל גדולים
עמו היו שם. אמרו לעוג: לא היית אומר אברהם פרדה עקרה ואינו מוליד? אמר להם: עכשיו
מתנתו מה היא, לא שפופה! אין יהיב אנא אצבעי עליה, אנא פחיש ליה. אמר ליה הקב"ה:
מה! אתה מבזה על מתנתו, חייך! שאת רואה אלף אלפים ורבי רבבות יוצאים מבני בניו, ואין
סופו של אותו האיש ליפול אלא בידו, שנא' (במדבר כא): ויאמר ה' אל משה אל תירא אותו,
כי בידך נתתי וגו'. דאמר רבי לוי: לא נדנדה עריסה תחלה, אלא בביתו של אברהם אבינו.
דאמר רבי יהושע בן מנחמה: אותן ששים ושנים מלכים שהרג יהושע, כולם היו במשתה
של אברהם אבינו, ולא שלשים ואחד היו, אלא כי ההיא דאמר: רבי ברכיה ורבי חלבו ורבי
פרנך משום רבי יוחנן, מלך יריחו אחד. מה תלמוד לומר אחד? אלא, הוא ואנטקיסור שלו:

AND ABRAHAM MADE A GREAT FEAST. R. JUDAH SAID: THE GREAT ONE OF THE UNIVERSE WAS THERE. R. JUDAN SAID IN THE NAME OF R. JOSE B. R. HANINA: THEN THE KING MADE A GREAT FEAST (EST. 2:18) MEANS THAT THE GREAT ONE OF THE WORLD WAS THERE. THUS IT IS WRITTEN: FOR THE LORD WILL AGAIN REJOICE OVER THEE FOR GOOD (DEUT. 30:9) – IN THE DAYS OF MORDECAI AND ESTHER; AS HE REJOICED OVER THY FATHERS (30:9) – IN THE DAYS OF ABRAHAM, ISAAC, AND JACOB. R. JUDAH SAID: A GREAT FEAST MEANS A FEAST FOR GREAT PEOPLE, FOR

OG AND ALL THE GREAT MEN WERE THERE. SAID THEY TO OG, "DID YOU NOT SAY THAT ABRAHAM IS LIKE A BARREN MULE AND CANNOT BEGET A CHILD?" "EVEN NOW WHAT IS [THE VALUE OF] HIS GIFT," REPLIED HE, "IS HE [ISAAC] NOT PUNY? I CAN CRUSH HIM BY PUTTING MY FINGER ON HIM." SAID THE HOLY ONE, BLESSED BE HE, TO HIM: "WHAT MEAN-EST THOU BY DISPARAGING MY GIFT! BY THY LIFE, THOU WILT YET SEE COUNTLESS THOUSANDS AND MYRIADS OF HIS DESCENDANTS, AND THINE OWN FATE WILL BE TO FALL INTO THEIR HANDS," AS IT SAYS: AND THE LORD SAID UNTO MOSES: FEAR HIM NOT; FOR I HAVE DELIVERED HIM INTO THY HAND (NUM. 21:34). (R. LEVI SAID: THE CRADLE WAS ROCKED FOR THE FIRST TIME IN THE HOUSE OF OUR FATHER ABRAHAM.) FOR R. JOSHUA B. MENAHAMA SAID: THE THIRTY-ONE KINGS SLAIN BY JOSHUA WERE ALL PRESENT AT ABRAHAM'S BANQUET. YET THERE WERE NOT THIRTY-ONE ONLY, BUT AS R. BEREKIAH AND R. HELBO AND R. PAR-NAK IN R. JOHANAN'S NAME SAID: THE KING OF JERICHO, ONE (JOSH. 12:9): WHY STATE "ONE"? BECAUSE IT MEANS, HE AND HIS REGENT.

What is meant by the great feast that Abraham arranged? One view is that God Himself was present as He was present at the feast of Queen Esther, and since God is the greatest, that feast was called *mishteh gadol*.

─

Seed Thoughts I

The text says that Isaac was weaned from the evil inclination. How did Rabbi Hoshaya understand that? In order to explain his opinion, it should be noted that Isaac was 13 years old at the time of this great celebration. At the age of 13, it is possible to watch a young boy and his behavior. It could be seen in Isaac that he was a good boy, and that he kept away from anything that can be described as evil or delinquent or antisocial. At the same time, the *Tiferet Tzion* makes the point that Isaac was bar mitzvah – this was his bar mitzvah celebration. It should not be concluded that this resembles in any way how we celebrate bar mitzvahs today. However, it does affirm the fact that a life of mitzvot has now begun for him. It looked to Rabbi Hoshaya that he would definitely fulfill his life with God's commandments.

─

Seed Thoughts II

This Midrash provides an insight to a major difference in how children
were brought up. In ancient times, children were treated as though they
were small adults. They were looked after carefully from the moment
they could walk or run. They were even dressed as adults. According
to the Midrash, it was only around the time of Abraham that the cradle
and all other forms of helping infants was used on a daily basis. Children
were made to sit in the cradle and, when necessary, they were rocked in
the cradle and were also taught to play with the cradle. This became the
instrument of their little playroom, bedroom, and kitchen. It was quite
easy to place a miniature near the cradle or as part of the cradle, so that
the children could be fed and taught to eat by themselves in their own
furniture, which was their cradle. Of course, this was used in Abraham's
time. It was used more in the ancient world after Abraham.

PARASHAH FIFTY-THREE, *Midrash Eleven*

יא ותרא שרה את בן הגר המצרית. אמר רבי שמעון בן יוחאי: רבי עקיבא היה אומר בו
דבר לגנאי, ואני אומר בו דבר לשבח. דרש רבי עקיבא: (בראשית כא) ותרא שרה וגו', אין
מצחק אלא גלוי עריות, היך מד"א: (שם לט) בא אלי העבד העברי, אשר הבאת לנו לצחק
בי, מלמד שהיתה אמנו שרה רואה אותו לישמעאל מכביש גנות, וצד נשי אנשים ומענה
אותן. תני, רבי ישמעאל אומר: אין הלשון הזה של צחוק, אלא עבודת כוכבים, שנאמר (שמות
לב): וישב העם לאכול ושתו ויקומו לצחק, מלמד שהיתה אמנו שרה רואה את ישמעאל
בונה בימוסיות, וצד חגבים ומקריב עליהם. רבי אלעזר בנו של רבי יוסי הגלילי אומר: אין
הלשון הזה צחוק, אלא לשון שפיכות דמים, היך מה דאת אמר (שמואל ב ב): יקומו נא הנערים
וישחקו לפנינו. רבי עזריה משום רבי לוי אמר: אמר ליה ישמעאל ליצחק: נלך ונראה חלקינו
בשדה, והיה ישמעאל נוטל קשת וחצים ומורה כלפי יצחק, ועושה עצמו כאילו מצחק, הדא
הוא דכתיב (משלי כב): כמתלהלה היורה זקים וגו'. כן איש רמה את רעהו ואומר הלא מצחק
אני. ואומר אני בו דבר לשבח, אין לשון הזה של צחוק, אלא לשון ירושה, שבשעה שנולד
אבינו יצחק, היו הכל שמחים. אמר להם ישמעאל: שוטים אתם, אני בכור ואני נוטל פי
שנים, שמתשובת אמנו שרה לאברהם, כי לא יירש בן האמה הזאת עם בני, אתה למד כי
לא יירש עם בני, אפי' שאינו יצחק, ועם יצחק אע"פ שאינו בני, קל וחומר עם בני עם יצחק:

11. AND SARAH SAW THE SON OF HAGAR THE EGYPTIAN, ETC. (GEN. 21:9).
R. SIMEON B. YOHAI SAID: R. AKIBA USED TO INTERPRET THIS TO HIS
[ISHMAEL'S] SHAME. THUS R. AKIBA LECTURED: AND SARAH SAW THE

SON OF HAGAR THE EGYPTIAN, WHOM SHE HAD BORNE UNTO ABRAHAM, MAKING SPORT. NOW MAKING SPORT REFERS TO NOUGHT ELSE BUT IM- MORALITY, AS IN THE VERSE: THE HEBREW SERVANT, WHOM THOU HAST BROUGHT UNTO US, CAME IN UNTO ME TO MAKE SPORT OF ME (GEN. 39:17) [ED.: THIS IS PART OF THE JOSEPH STORY.]. THUS THIS TEACHES THAT SARAH SAW ISHMAEL RAVISH MAIDENS, SEDUCE MARRIED WOMEN AND DISHONOR THEM. R. ISHMAEL TAUGHT: THIS TERM SPORT RE- FERS TO IDOLATRY, AS IN THE VERSE: AND ROSE UP TO MAKE SPORT (EX. 32:6). THIS TEACHES THAT SARAH SAW ISHMAEL BUILD ALTARS, CATCH LOCUSTS, AND SACRIFICE THEM. R. ELEAZAR SAID: THE TERM SPORT REFERS TO BLOODSHED, AS IN THE VERSE: LET THE YOUNG MEN, I PRAY THEE, ARISE AND SPORT BEFORE US (II SAM. 2:14). R. AZARIAH SAID IN R. LEVI'S NAME: ISHMAEL SAID TO ISAAC, "LET US GO AND SEE OUR PORTIONS IN THE FIELD"; THEN ISHMAEL WOULD TAKE A BOW AND ARROW AND SHOOT THEM IN ISAAC'S DIRECTION, WHILST PRETENDING TO BE PLAYING. THUS IT IS WRITTEN: AS A MADMAN WHO CASTETH FIRE-BRANDS, ARROWS, AND DEATH; SO IS THE MAN THAT DECEIVETH HIS NEIGHBOR, AND SAITH: AM NOT I IN SPORT (PROV. 22:18F.)? BUT I SAY: THIS TERM SPORT [MOCKERY] REFERS TO INHERITANCE. "FOR WHEN OUR FATHER ISAAC WAS BORN ALL REJOICED, WHEREUPON ISH- MAEL SAID TO THEM, 'YOU ARE FOOLS, FOR I AM THE FIRSTBORN AND I RECEIVE A DOUBLE PORTION.'" YOU MAY INFER THIS FROM SARAH'S PROTEST TO ABRAHAM: FOR THE SON OF THIS BONDWOMAN SHALL NOT BE HEIR WITH MY SON, WITH ISAAC (GEN. 21:10). WITH MY SON, EVEN IF HE WERE NOT ISAAC; OR WITH ISAAC, EVEN IF HE WERE NOT MY SON; HOW MUCH THE MORE, WITH MY SON WITH ISAAC!

There are two approaches that various Talmudic scholars have taken in this Midrash. One of them is that Ishmael was guilty of something of great significance that merited his being eliminated from Abraham's household. The other view, though not necessarily specified by particu- lar examples, is that Ishmael was brought up in Abraham's home, and he would not have been taught immoral activities. The Tosefta says, "Heaven forbid that a son who received training from Abraham should have engaged in idolatry, adultery, or bloodshed." Therefore, what is regarded by the Midrash as "making sport" simply refers to games and various types of exercises that they shared together. The Midrash finally concludes that which would have been very obvious from the outset, that Sarah herself interpreted the word *tzehok* as referring to their inheritance. Ishmael was explaining to Isaac and the world that as a firstborn, he was entitled to a double share of the inheritance from his father. This bothered Sarah very much, as she felt that since Isaac was her firstborn, and indeed a miraculous firstborn, he should be regarded as the true successor. This was the reason for her protest, and it was important enough to justify asking Ishmael and his mother to leave their household. One might add that Ishmael was the son of Hagar who was a servant in the household, whereas Isaac was the son of a mother whose social class was equal to that of a notable in their community.

～

Seed Thoughts

When Sarah made her request to Abraham that Hagar and her son be eliminated from their household, Abraham looked upon this as a most unfortunate development. Ishmael, after all, was Abraham's firstborn and indeed, the latter had married Hagar at the request of Sarah. This could have been the setting for a serious quarrel between Abraham and Sarah. What happened, however, was that the Holy One, blessed be He, intervened. He said to Abraham: "Whatever Sarah demands, I recommend that you fulfill them." Immediately, this stopped Abraham from engaging in any quarrel or any public disagreement with Sarah. As a matter of fact, the tradition tells us that Abraham made every effort to maintain contacts with Ishmael and indeed to visit him from time to time. One of the most meaningful experiences is that when Abraham died, both Ishmael and Isaac together arranged for their father's burial with great love and great appreciation.

～

Additional Commentary

What's in a game?

One of the interpretations suggests that the behavior between Ishmael and Isaac was harmless despite the fact that they appeared to be engaged in the worship of false gods. One of the procedures in this kind of worship was the placing of locusts on an altar. However, there were many children's games based on this idolatrous practice. The children, as they played the game, had no idea that this was idolatry; they simply had a good time. This was the kind of game that Ishmael and Isaac were playing, and therefore, Rabbi Ishmael suggested that the behavior need not be taken seriously. (Mirkin)

PARASHAH FIFTY-THREE, *Midrash Twelve*

יב וירע הדבר מאד בעיני אברהם. הדא הוא דכתיב (ישעיה לג): עוצם עיניו מראות ברע. ויאמר
אלהים אל אברהם אל ירע בעיניך וגו'. א"ר יודן: יצחק אין כתיב כאן, אלא ביצחק. ר' עזריה
בשם בר חטייא: בי"ת תרין. במי שהוא מודה בשני עולמות. א"ר יודן ברבי שלום: כתיב
(תהלים קה): זכרו נפלאותיו אשר עשה מופתיו ומשפטי פיו, מופת נתת למי שהוא מוציא
מתוך פיו, כל מי שהוא מודה בב' עולמות, יקרא לך זרע. וכל מי שאינו מודה בשני עולמות,
לא יקרא לך זרע:

12. AND THE THING WAS VERY GRIEVOUS IN ABRAHAM'S SIGHT (GEN. 21:11). THUS IT IS WRITTEN: AND SHUTTETH HIS EYES FROM LOOKING UPON EVIL (ISA. 33:15). AND GOD SAID UNTO ABRAHAM: LET IT NOT BE GRIEVOUS IN THY SIGHT ... FOR IN ISAAC SHALL SEED BE CALLED TO THEE (21:12): R. JUDAN B. SHALUM SAID: NOT "ISAAC," BUT IN ISAAC IS WRITTEN HERE. R. AZARIAH SAID IN THE NAME OF BAR HUTAH: THE *BET* (IN) DENOTES TWO, I.E., [THY SEED SHALL BE CALLED] IN HIM WHO RECOGNIZES THE EXISTENCE OF TWO WORLDS; HE SHALL INHERIT TWO WORLDS. R. JUDAN B. R. SHALUM SAID: IT IS WRITTEN: REMEMBER HIS MARVELOUS WORKS THAT HE HATH DONE, HIS SIGNS [E.V. "WONDERS"], AND THE JUDGMENTS OF HIS MOUTH (PS. 105:5): [GOD SAYS]: "I HAVE GIVEN A SIGN [WHEREBY THE TRUE DESCENDANTS OF ABRAHAM CAN BE KNOWN], VIZ. HE WHO EXPRESSLY RECOGNIZES [GOD'S JUDGMENTS]: THUS WHOEVER BELIEVES IN THE TWO WORLDS SHALL BE CALLED 'THY SEED', WHILE HE WHO REJECTS BELIEF IN TWO WORLDS SHALL NOT BE CALLED 'THY SEED.'"

Seed Thoughts

Abraham was very bothered by the turn of events whereby Ishmael would have to leave his home. The Midrash uses this occasion to explain the teaching that Abraham's descendants will emerge from Isaac and not from anyone else, including Ishmael. The text goes on to offer an interesting definition. The verse that is quoted reads ביצחק – *be-Yitzhak*. The letter ב – *bet*, which translates as the number two and is made to refer to the belief in two worlds. The letter *bet* is added to the word יצחק – *Yitzhak*. This is meant to prove that we are not dealing with anything racial. It does not mean that every descendant of Isaac will automatically be a representative of Abraham. Only those who believe in the World to Come in addition to This World, which are the two worlds that form the interpretation of the letter *bet*, will become Abraham's representatives. Only those who share the spiritual philosophy, which in terms of the present Midrash is described as the belief in the two worlds, will become Abraham's representatives.

PARASHAH FIFTY-THREE, *Midrash Thirteen*

יג וישכם אברהם בבקר ויקח לחם וחמת מים ויתן אל הגר. ביתו של אבינו אברהם ותרנים היו, שנאמר: וישכם אברהם בבקר ויתן אל הגר, שכן דרך עבדים שיהיו ממלאים כדים על שכמם. על שכמה ואת הילד, בן כ"ז שנים, ואת אמרת שם על שכמה? אלא, מלמד שהכניסה בו שרה עין רעה, ונכנסה בו חמה ואכאבית. תדע לך שכן דכתיב: ויכלו המים מן החמת, שכן דרך החולה להיות שותה הרבה ובכל שעה.

13. AND ABRAHAM AROSE UP EARLY IN THE MORNING, AND TOOK BREAD AND A BOTTLE OF WATER (GEN. 21:14). ABRAHAM'S HOUSEHOLD WAS LIBERAL, YET IT SAYS: AND ABRAHAM AROSE UP EARLY IN THE MORNING ... AND GAVE IT UNTO HAGAR? THE REASON IS THAT SUCH WAS THE CUSTOM OF SLAVES, TO CARRY WATER IN THEIR PITCHERS. PUTTING IT ON HER SHOULDER AND THE CHILD: HE WAS TWENTY-SEVEN YEARS OLD, YET YOU SAY, PUTTING IT ON HER SHOULDER AND THE CHILD! THIS, HOWEVER, TEACHES THAT SARAH CAST AN EVIL EYE ON HIM, WHEREUPON HE WAS SEIZED WITH FEVERISH PAINS. THE PROOF LIES IN THE VERSE, AND THE WATER IN THE BOTTLE WAS SPENT (21:15), A SICK PERSON DRINKING FREQUENTLY.

The question here is: Why did Abraham act this way? Not only was he known as a generous person, his generosity extended to anyone and everyone that came into contact with him. One of the commentators asserted that this proved that Abraham was hostile to Ishmael, because the latter wanted to become his chief heir. We have other sources, however, that assert that Abraham loved Ishmael and from time to time went to visit him in the mountains of Seir, where he was active. Furthermore, after Abraham's death, his funeral arrangements were looked after jointly by Ishmael and Isaac, which indicates that the relationship was a positive one. Was his behavior motivated by the advice of the Almighty for Abraham, always to listen to the advice of Sarah? Who was hostile to Ishmael? We still do not know the real explanation for Abraham's behavior.

ותשלך את הילד תחת אחד השיחם. אמר ר' מאיר: שכן דרך הרתמים להיות גדלים במדבר. א"ר אמי: תחת אחד השיחם, ששם השיחו עמה מלאכי השרת. ותלך ותשב לה מנגד. נאמר כאן ותשב לה מנגד, ולהלן הוא אומר (במדבר ב): מנגד סביב לאהל מועד. הרחק הכא, את אומר: הרחק כמטחוי קשת ולהלן את אמר (יהושע ג): אך רחוק יהיה ביניכם וביניו כאלפים אמה במדה. הא למדנו, נגד מנגד, ורחוק מרחוק. א"ר יצחק: כמטחוי קשת, שני טווחים בקשת, מיל. א"ר ברכיה: כמטחת דברים כלפי מעלה אמרה: אתמול אמרת לי: הרבה ארבה את זרעך וגו', ועכשיו הוא מת בצמא:

AND SHE CAST THE CHILD UNDER ONE OF THE SHRUBS – *SIHIM* (GEN. 21:15). R. MEIR SAID: IT WAS A JUNIPER TREE, THESE USUALLY GROWING IN THE DESERT. R. AMMI SAID: [UNDER ONE OF THE SIHIM IS AN INTIMATION] THAT THERE THE MINISTERING ANGELS SPOKE (*HESIHU*) TO HER. AND SHE WENT AND SAT HER DOWN OVER AGAINST HIM (*MI-NEGED*) A GOOD WAY OFF (21:16). HERE YOU SAY, AND SAT DOWN OVER AGAINST HIM – *MI-NEGED* (WHILST ELSEWHERE IT SAYS, OVER AGAINST IT (*MI-NEGED*), ROUND ABOUT THE TENT OF MEETING (NUM. 2:2). A GOOD WAY OFF: HERE YOU SAY, A GOOD WAY OFF (*HARHEK*), AS IT WERE A BOW-SHOT), WHILST ELSEWHERE YOU READ: YET THERE SHALL BE A SPACE (*RAHOK*) BETWEEN YOU AND IT, ABOUT TWO THOUSAND CUBITS BY MEASURE (JOSH. 3:4). THUS WE LEARN THE MEANING OF *NEGED* FROM *NEGED* AND *HARHEK* FROM *RAHOK*. R. ISAAC OBSERVED: THE PHRASE AS THE SHOTS OF A BOW [SHOWS THE DISTANCE, FOR] TWO BOWSHOTS COVER A MILE. R. BEREKIAH SAID: THE PHRASE CONNOTES, AS A WOMAN WHO IMPUGNED GOD'S JUSTICE, SAYING, "YESTERDAY THOU DIDST PROMISE ME, I WILL GREATLY MULTIPLY THY SEED, ETC. (GEN. 16:10), AND NOW HE IS DYING OF THIRST!"

Hagar remembered her experience with the angel when her son was very little and they were escaping from the wrath of Sarah. At that time, the angel promised Hagar that she would be a mother of one of the world's greatest families. She saw no evidence of this prophesy in her present situation and was very pessimistic about her son's recovery. That is why she moved away from him, not wishing to experience his probable death, which would tear her apart emotionally.

PARASHAH FIFTY-THREE, *Midrash Fourteen*

יד הה"ד (תהלים נו): נודי ספרת אתה שימה דמעתי בנאדך, כאותה בעלת נוד. כשם שכתוב בספר תהלים (שם לט): שמעה תפלתי ה' ושועתי האזינה וגו'. אל דמעתה של הגר לא החרשת, אל דמעתי אתה מחריש! ואם תאמר ע"י שהיתה גיורת היתה חביבה, אף אנכי, כי גר אנכי עמך תושב ככל אבותי. ויקרא מלאך אלהים אל הגר, בזכותו של אברהם. באשר הוא שם, בזכות עצמו. יפה תפלת החולה לעצמו יותר מכל.

14. THUS IT IS WRITTEN: THOU HAST COUNTED (*NUDI*) (PS. 56:9): WHICH MEANS, THOU HAST COUNTED MY WANDERINGS. PUT THOU MY TEARS INTO THY BOTTLE (56:9). [ESTIMATE THEM BY] THAT WOMAN OF THE BOTTLE (*NOD*). ARE THEY NOT IN THY BOOK (56:9)? AS IT IS WRITTEN IN THE BOOK OF PSALMS: HEAR MY PRAYER, O LORD, AND GIVE EAR UNTO MY CRY; KEEP NOT SILENCE AT MY TEARS (39:13): THOU DIDST NOT KEEP SILENCE AT HAGAR'S TEARS; WILT THOU KEEP SILENCE AT MINE! AND SHOULDST THOU REPLY, "BECAUSE SHE WAS A STRANGER SHE WAS MORE BELOVED," THEN I TOO AM THUS, FOR I AM A STRANGER WITH THEE, A SOJOURNER, AS ALL MY FATHERS WERE (39:13). AND THE ANGEL OF GOD CALLED TO HAGAR (GEN. 21:17) – FOR ABRAHAM'S SAKE; WHILE [GOD HATH HEARD THE VOICE OF THE LAD] WHERE HE IS CONNOTES FOR HIS OWN SAKE, FOR A SICK PERSON'S PRAYERS ON HIS OWN BEHALF ARE MORE EFFICACIOUS THAN THOSE OF ANYONE ELSE.

Our Rabbis are stating an important truth. The best pleader for the health of a sick person is the sick person himself. No outsider can understand or appreciate the tension of the one who suffers as much as he himself. That is why the verse says, "And God heard the prayer of the lad," meaning Ishmael, who is suffering from a sickness of fever.

באשר הוא שם. אמר רבי סימון: קפצו מלאכי השרת לקטרגו. אמרו לפניו: רבון העולמים! אדם שהוא עתיד להמית את בניך בצמא, אתה מעלה לו באר? אמר להם: עכשיו מה הוא,

צדיק או רשע? אמרו לו: צדיק! אמר להם: איני דן את האדם, אלא בשעתו. קומי שאי את
הנער.

WHERE HE IS. R. SIMON SAID: THE MINISTERING ANGELS HASTENED TO
INDICT HIM, EXCLAIMING, "SOVEREIGN OF THE UNIVERSE! WILT THOU
BRING UP A WELL FOR ONE WHO WILL ONE DAY SLAY THY CHILDREN
WITH THIRST?" "WHAT IS HE NOW?" HE DEMANDED. "RIGHTEOUS," WAS
THE ANSWER. "I JUDGE MAN ONLY AS HE IS AT THE MOMENT," SAID HE.
[THEREFORE, SCRIPTURE CONTINUES], ARISE, LIFT UP THE LAD, ETC.

The point that is made here is that individuals have to be judged by
what they themselves say and do, and not by what their descendants say
and do. It is always possible for their descendants to eliminate their bad
forms of behavior and to not be committed to a sinful life, which they
can eliminate by returning to a moral way of life. God does not judge
them many generations before their arrival, but He waits to see how
they will behave in their generation.

ויפקח את עיניה. אמר רבי בנימין: הכל בחזקת סומין, עד שהקב"ה מאיר את עיניהם, מן
הכא ויפקח אלהים את עיניה. ותלך ותמלא את החמת, הדא אמרת מחוסרת אמנה היתה:

AND GOD OPENED HER EYES, ETC. (GEN. 21:18F.). R. BENJAMIN B. LEVI
AND R. JONATHAN B. AMRAM BOTH SAID: ALL MAY BE PRESUMED TO BE
BLIND, UNTIL THE HOLY ONE, BLESSED BE HE, ENLIGHTENS THEIR EYES.
THAT FOLLOWS FROM THIS VERSE: AND GOD OPENED HER EYES AND SHE
SAW, ETC. AND SHE WENT AND FILLED THE BOTTLE WITH WATER. THIS
PROVES THAT SHE WAS LACKING IN FAITH.

There are two possibilities here. One is that the well was there all the
time, and Hagar simply did not notice it. The other possibility is that
the well was created in order to help Hagar in her present predicament.
Since she did not really know which procedure was correct, she feared
that in the same way that the well appeared, it could simply disappear
from her sight. That is why she filled the bottle with water, not because
she was lacking in faith.

PARASHAH FIFTY-THREE, *Midrash Fifteen*

טו ויהי אלהים את הנער ויגדל. רבי ישמעאל שאל את ר"ע: א"ל: בשביל ששימשת נחום
איש גם זו עשרים ושתים שנה, אכים ורקים מיעוטים, אתין וגמין ריבוים, הדין את דכתיב
הכא מהו? א"ל: אילו נאמר: ויהי אלהים הנער, היה הדבר קשה, אלא את הנער. א"ל: כי
לא דבר רק הוא מכם, ואם רק מכם, שאין אתם יודעים לדרוש, אלא את הנער הוא וחמריו
וגמליו ובני ביתו.

15. AND GOD WAS WITH (*ETH*) THE LAD, AND HE GREW (GEN. 21:20). R.
ISHMAEL ASKED R. AKIBA: SINCE YOU HAVE STUDIED TWENTY-TWO
YEARS UNDER NAHUM OF GIMZO [WHO INTERPRETED EVERY] *AKH* (SAVE
THAT) AND *RAK* (EXCEPT) AS LIMITATIONS, AND *ETH* AND *GAM* (ALSO) AS
EXTENSIONS, TELL ME WHAT OF THE *ETH* WRITTEN HERE? IF THE TEXT
STATED: "AND GOD WAS THE LAD," IT WOULD BE UNINTELLIGIBLE, HE
REPLIED; HENCE, WITH (*ETH*) THE LAD MUST BE WRITTEN. THEREUPON
HE CITED TO HIM, FOR IT IS NO EMPTY THING FROM YOU (DEUT. 32:47),
AND IF IT IS EMPTY, IT IS SO ON YOUR ACCOUNT, BECAUSE YOU ARE UN-
ABLE TO INTERPRET IT RIGHTLY: ETH THE LAD, HOWEVER, MEANS WITH
HIM, HIS ASS-DRIVERS, AND HIS CAMEL-DRIVERS, AND HIS HOUSEHOLD.

What is involved here is the importance of the conjunction in understanding the meaning of a language. In the English language, articles
such as "the" are very important in adding understanding to the language. The Hebrew language requires many more such articles such as
eth, and they are indispensable. The Torah asserts the indispensability
by quoting the verse, "For it is no empty thing from you." The principle
is that every verse in the Bible has a meaning of significance, and that
meaning has to be researched if it is not obvious. Only when a meaning
is found has the verse fulfilled its function.

ויהי רובה קשת, רבה וקשיותו עמו [נ"א רבה וקשיותו אמו] רבה מתלמד בקשת. רבה על
כל המורים בקשת.

AND BECAME AN ARCHER – *ROBEH KASHATH* (GEN. 21:20). EVEN AS HE
GREW (*RABBAH*), SO DID HIS CRUELTY (*KASHIUTH*) GROW WITH HIM.
[ANOTHER VERSION]: WHILE A LAD (*ROBEH*), HE TRAINED HIMSELF IN
THE USE OF THE BOW. [ANOTHER INTERPRETATION]: MASTER (*RABBAH*)
OF ALL ARCHERS.

What is involved in these verses is to indicate that Ishmael was not an ordinary archer. He was an expert in the use of the bow, whether as a performer, as a coach, or as a military person; he was a master of the bow and arrow in all respects.

וישב במדבר פארן. אמר רבי יצחק: זרוק חוטרא לאוירא ועל עיקריה הוא קאים. כך, לפי
שכתוב: ולה שפחה מצרית ושמה הגר, לפיכך, ותקח לו אמו אשה מארץ מצרים:

AND HE DWELT IN THE WILDERNESS OF PARAN, ETC. (GEN. 21:21). R. ISAAC SAID: THROW A STICK INTO THE AIR, AND IT WILL FALL BACK TO ITS PLACE OF ORIGIN [THE GROUND]. THUS, BECAUSE IT IS WRITTEN: AND SHE HAD A HANDMAID, AN EGYPTIAN, WHOSE NAME WAS HAGAR (16:1), THEREFORE IT IS WRITTEN: AND HIS MOTHER TOOK HIM A WIFE OUT OF EGYPT.

The interesting thing here is that you might have expected that the wife she might have chosen for her son had a relationship to the home of Abraham, one of whose wives she had become. But because she had been forced to leave that household, she had returned to Egypt, where she had the status of a princess and felt that her son should now be related to her former family where they had been living at the time.

—

Seed Thoughts

In order to support the appearance of the word *et* in connection with Ishmael, and that the word *eth* gives meaning to the sentence, other sources are used to justify that interpretation. The verse is "For it is no empty thing from you." One of the Midrashim goes on to say that the word *mikem*, meaning "from you," is interpreted as meaning that if the verse seems to be empty, it is because of you, not the verse. In other words, you do not know enough to explain the verse. However, in our Midrash, the statement goes a little farther, because it is "your life." What is the expression "it is your life?" The nature of life is that we are called upon not only to work, but to give our maximum energy at all times. First we learn to walk, then we learn to talk, then we go to school to learn, and then we do our best to earn a livelihood, which sometimes demands the maximum of our energy, our time, and our devotion. Every aspect of human life demands great effort, and it produces great results. And so, just as in life maximum energy is demanded, so when we come upon a commandment in the Torah that is hard to understand, it demands our maximum of research, study, discussion, and a major effort. My daughter, Elizabeth, of blessed memory, used to say when her pupils would ask her to explain a difficult commandment, "You have to figure it out." She would then suggest to the questioner that they sit down together immediately and try to figure it out. That is what all of us have to do in order to render the Torah meaningful.

א ויהי בעת ההיא ויאמר אבימלך ופיכל שר צבאו. (משלי טז) ברצות ה' דרכי איש גם איביו
ישלים אתו.

1. AND IT CAME TO PASS AT THAT TIME, THAT ABIMELECH AND PHICOL
THE CAPTAIN OF HIS HOST, ETC. (GEN. 21:22). IT IS WRITTEN: WHEN A
MAN'S WAYS PLEASE THE LORD, HE MAKETH EVEN HIS ENEMIES TO BE AT
PEACE WITH HIM (PROV. 16:7).

The verse quoted has, as its motivation, the hostility that took place
between Abraham and Abimelech, the leader of the Philistines, which
lasted for many years. Finally, the servants of both Abimelech and Abraham came to an agreement about the ownership of the well, which each
side thought belonged to them. Finally, an agreement was reached that
the well belonged to Abraham, but that the servants of Abimelech had
a right to use it. This agreement had a very important effect upon both
Abraham and Abimelech, who arranged many covenants of friendship
and peace between them. This behavior motivated the verse in Proverbs: "When a man's ways please the Lord, etc."

רבי יוחנן אמר: זו אשתו, שנאמר (מיכה ז): אויבי איש אנשי ביתו. מעשה באשה, שקבלה על
בעלה לשלטון והתיז את ראשו, וי"א אף התיז את ראשה.

R. JOHANAN SAID: "HIS ENEMIES" REFERS TO HIS WIFE, AS IT SAYS: A
MAN'S ENEMIES ARE THE PEOPLE OF HIS OWN HOUSE (MICAH 7:6). IT
ONCE HAPPENED THAT A WOMAN BROUGHT A CHARGE AGAINST HER
HUSBAND TO THE GOVERNOR, AND HE BEHEADED HIM. SOME SAY, HE
EXECUTED HER TOO.

Who are the enemies that the verse in Proverbs talks about? It is here
that the answers of the text appear to be unsatisfactory. The first enemy
is a wife; is she supposed to represent all wives or only herself? She is
described as arranging the arrest of her husband, who was later on put

to death by the authorities. Apparently, the same thing happened to her later on in her life. This was a most unfortunate choice, and women of the world do not deserve this type of treatment.

רבי שמואל אמר: זה הנחש. תנא ר' חלפתא אומר: הנחש הזה להוט אחר השום. ומעשה בנחש אחד, שירד מן ההר לבית ומצא קערה של שום ואכלה והקיא בתוכה, וראה נחש שבבית ולא הוה יכול לעמוד לו, כיון שיצא אותו הנחש יצא הנחש של בית ומילא אותה עפר.

R. SAMUEL B. NAHMAN SAID: THE VERSE REFERS TO THE SERPENT. THE SCHOOL OF HALAFTA B. SAUL TAUGHT: A SERPENT IS VERY FOND OF GARLIC. IT ONCE HAPPENED THAT A SERPENT WENT DOWN INTO A HOUSE, WHERE HE FOUND A DISH OF GARLIC, OF WHICH HE ATE, AND HE THEN SPAT [HIS POISON] INTO IT. NOW THERE WAS A SNAKE IN THE HOUSE, WHICH COULD NOT FIGHT AGAINST IT; BUT AS SOON AS THE FIRST DEPARTED, IT WENT AND FILLED THE DISH WITH EARTH.

The second enemy is the serpent. Beginning with the Garden of Eden story, the serpent was described as the permanent enemy of the human being. This may apply to those countries where serpents abound. Certainly, this does not include those countries that are included as part of Western civilization – Europe, parts of Africa, North and South America. The serpent, there, as an enemy, is actually limited to certain countries where that particular kind of animal is there with a large population.

רבי יהושע בן לוי אמר: זה יצר הרע. בנוהג שבעולם אדם גדל עם חבירו שתים ג' שנים בכרך והוא קושר לו אהבה, וזה גדל עם אדם מנערותו ועד זקנותו, אם מצא בתוך שבעים הוא מפילו, בתוך שמונים הוא מפילו, הוא שדוד אומר (תהלים לה): כל עצמותי תאמרנה ה' מי כמוך, מציל עני מחזק ממנו ועני ואביון מגוזלו. אמר רבי אחא: וכי יש גזלן גדול מזה? ואמר שלמה (משלי כה): אם רעב שונאך, האכילהו לחם, ואם צמא, השקהו מים. מלחמה של תורה, היך מה דאת אמר (שם ט): לכו לחמו בלחמי. ומימה של תורה, היך מה דאת אמר (ישעיה נה): הוי כל צמא לכו למים. א"ר ברכיה: אויביו, גם אויביו, לרבות מזיקי ביתו, כגון: יתושים ופרעושים וזבובים. ד"א: (משלי טז) ברצות ה' דרכי איש, זה אברהם שנקרא איש, דכתיב ביה (ישעיה מו) מארץ מרחק איש עצתי. גם אויביו, זה אבימלך:

R. JOSHUA B. LEVI SAID: IT REFERS TO THE EVIL INCLINATION. GENER-ALLY SPEAKING, IF ONE IS BROUGHT UP ALONG WITH ANOTHER FOR TWO OR THREE YEARS, HE BECOMES CLOSELY ATTACHED TO HIM; BUT THIS ONE [THE EVIL INCLINATION] GROWS WITH MAN FROM HIS YOUTH

UNTIL OLD AGE, AND YET IF HE CAN, HE STRIKES HIM DOWN EVEN IN HIS SEVENTIES OR IN HIS EIGHTIES. IT WAS THIS THAT DAVID SAID: ALL MY BONES SHALL SAY: LORD, WHO IS LIKE UNTO THEE, WHO DELIVEREST THE POOR FROM HIM THAT IS TOO STRONG FOR HIM, YEA, THE POOR AND THE NEEDY FROM HIM THAT SPOILETH HIM (PS. 35:10). R. AHA OB-SERVED: IS THERE A GREATER DESPOILER THAN HE [THE EVIL INCLINA-TION]? AND OF HIM SOLOMON SAID: IF THINE ENEMY BE HUNGRY, GIVE HIM BREAD TO EAT, ETC. (PROV. 25:21): [RESIST HIM] WITH THE BREAD OF THE TORAH, AS YOU READ: COME, EAT OF MY BREAD (9:5); AND IF HE BE THIRSTY, GIVE HIM WATER TO DRINK (9:25) – THE WATER OF THE TORAH, AS IN THE VERSE: HO, EVERYONE THAT THIRSTETH, COME YE FOR WATER (ISA. 55:1). R. BEREKIAH SAID: "EVEN (GAM) HIS ENEMIES," INSTEAD OF SIMPLY "HIS ENEMIES," INCLUDES THE PESTS OF HIS HOUSE, SUCH AS INSECTS, VERMIN, AND FLIES. ANOTHER INTERPRETATION: "WHEN A MAN'S WAYS PLEASE THE LORD," ETC. (REFERS TO ABRAHAM, WHO IS CALLED A MAN, AS IT IS WRITTEN: CALLING . . . THE MAN OF MY COUNSEL FROM A FAR COUNTRY [ISA. 46:11]; "EVEN HIS ENEMIES" REFERS TO ABIMELECH, AS IT IS WRITTEN): AND IT CAME TO PASS AT THAT TIME, THAT ABIMELECH AND PHICOL THE CAPTAIN OF HIS HOST SPOKE, ETC.

Is there a third enemy that the text brings to our attention? It is obvious from these many quotations that the Evil Inclination of the human being is the real enemy of mankind and of the world. In this connection, our knowledge of what the Evil Inclination is, is no greater today than it was at the time of King Solomon and of the various others who have been quoted. If there is an Evil Inclination, there should also be a Good Inclination. That is what is intended in saying that only the Torah and the ways of the Torah can oppose the Evil Inclination and make life worth living for everyone else.

—

Seed Thoughts

What is the Evil Inclination? Is it something that is part of the human body, so that one could look at it, operate it, remove it, or whatever one does with parts of the body that interfere with the good life? So far, nothing has been found. The outstanding scientists of many generations have tried to find an Evil Inclination which can be defined as part of the human body, but they failed to do so. We know that something is happening when a human being does things which are evil and continues to do them. The response, however, has nothing to do with a change in the human body, but only with a change in human behavior. The moral life demands that we oppose the Evil Inclination wherever it may be. That is the challenge of all good people everywhere. That is one of the main teachings of the Torah, and those who teach that the Torah is the real answer to the Evil Inclination have something to tell us of the most importance. The Evil Inclination is the real enemy of all the good people of the world. All the good people of the world should find a way to resist all the evildoers, the terrorists, the killers of people, and all who do those things which contribute to the destruction of the world and not to its rebuilding.

PARASHAH FIFTY-FOUR, *Midrash Two*

ב ויהי בעת ההיא ויאמר אבימלך ופיכול. רבי יהודה אמר: פיכול שמו. רבי נחמיה אמר: פה
שכל צבאותיו נושקים לו על פיו.

2.... AND PHICOL. R. JUDAH AND R. NEHEMIAH DISAGREE. R. JUDAH SAID: PHICOL WAS ACTUALLY HIS NAME. R. NEHEMIAH SAID: [PHICOL IS AN ATTRIBUTIVE, MEANING] THE MOUTH (*PEH*) RESPONSIBLE FOR THE PROVISIONING OF ALL (*KOL*) HIS TROOPS.

The name Phicol, literarily speaking, was derived from the fact that everyone was forced to kiss him, which was a way of establishing his authority. In this sense, Phicol was a name used by the Philistine king to describe the person whom they elevated to the highest position in their country and who was responsible for carrying out all the business of the country, and especially the policy of the king. Briefly, Abimelech was the name used by all the Philistine kings, while Phicol was the name used by each of their executive assistants.

אלהים עמך. לפי שהיו אומות העולם אומרין: אילו היה צדיק, לא היה מוליד, אתמהא?

GOD IS WITH THEE IN ALL THAT THOU DOEST. NOW THE PEOPLE OF THE WORLD HAD SAID: IF HE WERE A RIGHTEOUS MAN, WOULD HE NOT HAVE BEGOTTEN CHILDREN?

This section indicates that it was very difficult to be considered a righteous person. All kinds of issues and criticisms were raised which had no basis in reality. Our text mentions some of them as they applied to Abraham, and which gradually disappeared as his life and his actions proved the validity of his being a righteous person.

כיון שהוליד אמרו לו: אלהים עמך. ואילו היה צדיק, לא היה שומע לקול אשתו, וכיון שנאמר לו: כל אשר תאמר אליך שרה שמע בקולה. אמרו לו: אלהים עמך! ואילו היה צדיק, לא היה דוחה את בנו בכורו? כיון שראו את מעשיו, אמרו לו: אלהים עמך בכל אשר אתה עושה.

HENCE WHEN HE DID BEGET A CHILD, THEY SAID TO HIM: GOD IS WITH THEE IN ALL THAT THOU DOEST. AGAIN, IF HE WERE A RIGHTEOUS MAN, WOULD HE HAVE HEEDED HIS WIFE? BUT WHEN, IN ALL THAT SARAH SAITH UNTO THEE, HEARKEN UNTO HER VOICE (GEN. 21:12), WAS SAID TO HIM, THEY ADMITTED, GOD IS WITH THEE IN ALL THAT THOU DOEST. FURTHER, IF HE WERE A RIGHTEOUS MAN, WOULD HE HAVE THRUST AWAY HIS FIRSTBORN SON? BUT WHEN THEY SAW HIS BEHAVIOR, THEY SAID TO HIM, GOD IS WITH THEE, ETC.

The reference to his behavior was that Abraham was very critical of the moral behavior of his son Ishmael.

ד"א: לפי שחרבו מקומות של סדום, ופסקו העוברים והשבים, ולא חסר קלרין שלו כלום, לפיכך אלהים עמך בכל אשר אתה עושה, הואיל והאלהים עמך. ועתה השבעה לי באלהים הנה אם תשקור לי ולניני ולנכדי, עד כאן רחמי האב על הבן.

ANOTHER INTERPRETATION: BECAUSE THE REGION OF SODOM WAS NOW DESOLATE AND TRAVELERS HAD CEASED, WITH THE RESULT THAT HIS STORES WERE NOW IN NO WAY DIMINISHED, [HE SAID: WHY SHOULD I ALLOW HOSPITALITY TO CEASE FROM MY HOUSE? THEREFORE, HE WENT AND PITCHED HIS TENT IN GERAR]. IN CONSEQUENCE [ALL EXCLAIMED], GOD IS WITH THEE IN ALL THAT THOU DOEST, ETC. NOW THEREFORE SWEAR UNTO ME HERE BY GOD THAT THOU WILT NOT DEAL FALSELY WITH ME, NOR WITH MY SON, NOR WITH MY SON'S SON (21:22F.): THUS FAR IS A FATHER'S COMPASSION FOR HIS SON.

Please note that these words end after the third generation.

א"ר אבא: עד כאן לאחים השותפין. א"ר יוסי בר חנינא: כתיב (תהלים לח) ואויבי חיים עצמו. מה שניתן לאברהם לשבע דורות, ניתן לאבימלך לשלשה. למה לא נחם אלהים דרך ארץ פלשתים? שעדיין נכדו קיים?

R. ABBA B. KAHANA SAID: THUS FAR FOR BROTHERS IN PARTNERSHIP. R.
JOSE B. HANINA SAID: IT IS WRITTEN: BUT MINE ENEMIES ARE STRONG
IN HEALTH (PS. 38:20). WHAT WAS GIVEN TO ABRAHAM FOR SEVEN GEN-
ERATIONS WAS GIVEN TO ABIMELECH FOR THREE. WHY WAS IT THAT
GOD LED THEM NOT BY THE WAY OF THE LAND OF THE PHILISTINES (EX.
8:17)? BECAUSE HIS [ABIMELECH'S] GRANDSON WAS STILL ALIVE THEN.

This last sentence is very interesting. When the Children of Israel left
Egypt, the Torah text says that they did not take the short route lest the
Children of Israel become demoralized and rush back to Egypt. Here
you have another interpretation: They did not take the short route because the children of Abimelech were living in that part of Canaan and
their covenant between each other motivated the Children of Israel not
to harm the part of the land they were occupying.

כחסד אשר עשיתי עמך. מה חסד עשה לו? אלא, שאמר לו: הנה ארצי לפניך, ואעפ"כ לא
קבל עליו:

BUT ACCORDING TO THE KINDNESS THAT I HAVE DONE UNTO THEE
(GEN. 21:23). WHAT KINDNESS THEN HAD HE SHOWN HIM? BY SAYING TO
HIM, BEHOLD, MY LAND IS BEFORE THEE: DWELL WHERE IT PLEASETH
THEE (20:15). YET EVEN SO, ABRAHAM HAD NOT ACCEPTED THIS OFFER.

The Midrash closes by referring to the kindness Abimelech showed
Abraham. That kindness involved making available to him almost all of
the Philistine territory if Abraham should ever want it. Abraham never
made use of this offer. Had it been given to Joshua in his generation, a
good part of the biblical story would have had to be changed. Joshua
would have accepted this offer with open arms.

ג והוכיח אברהם את אבימלך וגו'. א"ר יוסי בר חנינא: התוכחת מביאה לידי אהבה, שנאמר
(משלי ט): הוכח לחכם ויאהבך. היא דעתיה דרבי יוסי בר חנינא דאמר: כל אהבה שאין
עמה תוכחה, אינה אהבה. אמר ריש לקיש: תוכחה מביאה לידי שלום, והוכיח אברהם את
אבימלך, היא דעתיה, דאמר: כל שלום שאין עמו תוכחה, אינו שלום.

3. AND ABRAHAM REPROVED ABIMELECH, ETC. (GEN. 21:25). R. JOSE B. R.
HANINA SAID: REPROOF LEADS TO LOVE, AS IT SAYS: REPROVE A WISE
MAN, AND HE WILL LOVE THEE (PROV. 9:8). SUCH INDEED IS R. JOSE
B. HANINA'S VIEW, FOR HE SAID: LOVE UNACCOMPANIED BY REPROOF
IS NOT LOVE. RESH LAKISH SAID: REPROOF LEADS TO PEACE; HENCE,
AND ABRAHAM REPROVED ABIMELECH. SUCH IS HIS VIEW, FOR HE SAID:
PEACE UNACCOMPANIED BY REPROOF IS NOT PEACE.

The entire discussion of the relationship of love and disagreement,
or of peace and disagreement, is based on what happened between
Abimelech and Abraham. Their servants had a disagreement. Each
one claimed that the freshwater well belonged to them. After much
discussion, they came to an agreement that the well actually belonged
to Abraham, but that the servants of Abimelech should have complete
access to it. This agreement between the servants of both parties led
to the ultimate agreement between Abimelech and Abraham. The disagreement over the well eventually resolved the dispute between the
two parties and made it possible for the various scholars in the Midrash
to discuss the relationship between love and some disagreements during the love relationship.

על אודות באר המים אשר גזלו עבדי אבימלך. ואי זהו גזלן? בר קפרא אמר: זה שהוא גזול
בפרהסיא, היך מה דאת אמר (שופטים ט): ויגזלו את כל אשר יעבור עליהם בדרך. מה דרך
בפרהסיא, אף גזל בפרהסיא. ר' שמעון בן יוחאי: מייתי לה מהכא, (מלאכי א): והבאתם גזול
את הפסח ואת החולה. מה פסח וחולה מומין בגלוי, אף גזל בגלוי. רבי אבהו בשם ריש
לקיש אמר: לפני ט' גנב, ולפני עשרה גזלן. רבי תנחומא בשם ר' הונא: לעולם אינו גזלן, עד
שיגזלה מידו, שנאמר (שמואל ב כג): ויגזול את החנית מיד המצרי. ויאמר אבימלך לא ידעתי
מי עשה את הדבר הזה וגם אתה לא הגדת לי, על ידי מלאך. וגם אנכי לא שמעתי, בלתי היום:

BECAUSE OF THE WELL OF WATER, WHICH ABIMELECH'S SERVANTS HAD
VIOLENTLY TAKEN AWAY – *GAZLU* (GEN. 21:25). WHO IS CALLED A ROB-
BER (*GAZLAN*)? R. LEAZAR, THE SON OF KAPPARA, SAID: ONE WHO ROBS

OPENLY, AS IN THE VERSE, AND THEY ROBBED (*WAYYIGZELU*) ALL THAT
CAME ALONG THAT WAY BY THEM (JUDG. 9:25): AS THE WAY IS PUBLIC,
SO DOES A *GAZLAN* ACT OPENLY. R. SIMEON B. YOHAI QUOTED THIS
VERSE: AND YE HAVE BROUGHT THAT WHICH WAS TAKEN BY VIOLENCE
(*GAZUL*), AND THE LAME (MAL. 1:13): AS THE LAME SUFFERS FROM AN
OPEN DEFECT, SO THE *GAZLAN* ACTS OPENLY. R. JOSE IN R. ABBAHU'S
NAME, AND R. HEZEKIAH REPORTING R. ABBAHU IN THE NAME OF RESH
LAKISH, SAID: [HE WHO STEALS] IN THE PRESENCE OF NINE PEOPLE IS
A THIEF (*GANAB*); IN THE PRESENCE OF TEN, IS A ROBBER (*GAZLAN*). R.
TANHUMA SAID IN R. HUNA'S NAME: ONE IS NOT A ROBBER (*GAZLAN*)
UNLESS HE ACTUALLY SNATCHES THE ARTICLE FROM THE VICTIM'S
HAND, AS IT SAYS: AND PLUCKED (*WAYYIGZOL*) THE SPEAR OUT OF THE
EGYPTIAN'S HAND (II SAM. 23:21). AND ABIMELECH SAID: I KNOW NOT
WHO HATH DONE THIS THING; NEITHER DIDST THOU TELL ME – BY A
MESSAGE.

There is an agreement in the Midrash that the name *gazlan* is one who
steals openly and in public. The name *ganav* applies to one who steals
secretly in whatever way he finds successful. One of the problems that
the Midrash tries to deal with is what is or is not the public. For example, if the crime is committed in the presence of nine, does that make
the person a *gazlan* or does it require at least ten? These are the issues.

—

Seed Thoughts I

The relationship between love and disagreement has many angles. It
should certainly be possible for people in love to handle minor disagreements. What happens when issues become very serious, having to do
with the education of children or their marriage, or many other fundamental aspects of human behavior? It should be possible for people
in love to handle such matters. We know, however, in many cases, that
many disagreements lead to the breakup of many marriages. The problem is that there is an element in human life which is very hard to define.
That element is called personality. Very often, personality changes how
a person might act in the presence of difficulty. Furthermore, we could
never know in advance how that could happen. The only advice that can
be offered is that in the case of those who love each other, they think
first how their loved one will react before reacting too strongly about

their views on the issue at hand. There are no real laws in this regard, only experience and a little bit of *mazal* (good luck) will go a long way!

—

Seed Thoughts II

How do we happen to have a discussion on the difference between a *ganav* (a certain type of thief) and a *gazlan* (a different type of thief)? It is based on the fact that Jewish law differentiates between these types of delinquents, and Jewish law, of course, has its origin in the Bible. Is there a way in which we could describe this division in more modern terms?

It could be said that the person who is a *ganav* and goes about his stealing secretly and privately does not really wish to be such a person. He would rather be a good fellow, but either his salary is not high enough or food is lacking for the table, and he lacks other resources. This forces him to make a decision which he may not like, but it includes stealing, even though it is done secretly. The person who is called a *gazlan* and who functions in public is of an entirely different sort. He has discovered a new profession. Why work when as a result of good thinking you could acquire another major source of income without doing any real work? These situations exist in modern times without giving them any special names, but the world recognizes the phenomenon, and we do whatever we can to oppose these developments.

Parashah Fifty-Four, *Midrash Four*

ד ויקח אברהם צאן ובקר ויתן לאבימלך ויאמר אבימלך לאברהם מה הנה שבע כבשות. אמר
לו הקב"ה: אתה נתת שבע כבשות בלי רצוני, חייך! שאני משהה בשמחת בניך ז' דורות.

4. AND ABRAHAM SET SEVEN EWE-LAMBS OF THE FLOCK, ETC. (GEN.
21:28). THE HOLY ONE, BLESSED BE HE, SAID TO HIM [ABRAHAM]: "THOU
GAVEST HIM SEVEN EWE-LAMBS; AS THOU LIVEST, I WILL DELAY THE JOY
OF THY CHILDREN FOR SEVEN GENERATIONS!"

The main point of this Midrash is that the Holy One did not approve
of establishing intimate relationships between Israel and the heathen
nations, meaning those who were worshippers of the stars, as in the
Hebrew *ovdei kokhavim*. At the same time, He had a special criticism
of Abraham, who had access to God as nobody before ever had, and
he did not discuss the possibility of this new covenant and therefore
ask for divine approval. Each time this Midrash lists some of the suffering of the descendants, it is preceded by an expression "you entered
this covenant without my permission." The entire Midrash consists of
a listing of those who suffered in the next seven generations. It did not
stop until after the third generation of Abimelech, since apparently, the
third generation of Abimelech was in the same time range as the seventh
generation from Abraham.

אתה נתת לו ז' כבשות בלי רצוני, חייך! כנגד כן, הורגים מבניך שבעה צדיקים, ואלו הן: חפני
ופנחס ושמשון ושאול וג' בניו. אתה נתת לו ז' כבשות בלי רצוני, כנגד כן, בניו מחריבין מבניך
ז' משכנות, ואלו הן: אוהל מועד וגלגל נוב וגבעון ושילה ובית עולמים תרין. אתה נתת לו
ז' כבשות בלי רצוני, כנגד כן, ארוני חוזר בשדה פלשתים ז' חדשים, הה"ד (תהלים עח): ויתן
לשבי עזו, זה ארון ברית, וכתיב (ש"א ו) ויהי ארון ה' בשדה פלשתים ז' חדשים.

THOU GAVEST HIM SEVEN EWE-LAMBS; AS THOU LIVEST, HIS DESCEN-
DANTS WILL SLAY SEVEN RIGHTEOUS MEN OF THY DESCENDANTS, VIZ.
HOFNI, PHINEHAS, SAMSON, AND SAUL WITH HIS THREE SONS. THOU
GAVEST HIM SEVEN EWE-LAMBS; ACCORDINGLY, THY DESCENDANTS'
SEVEN SANCTUARIES SHALL BE DESTROYED, VIZ. THE TENT OF APPOINT-
MENT, [THE SANCTUARIES AT] GILGAL, NOB, GIBEON, AND SHILOAH,
AND THE TWO TEMPLES. THOU GAVEST HIM SEVEN EWE-LAMBS; MY ARK
WILL SPEND SEVEN MONTHS IN PHILISTINE TERRITORY, (AS IT SAYS:
AND HE DELIVERED HIS STRENGTH INTO CAPTIVITY (PS. 78:61), WHICH

REFERS TO THE ARK OF THE COVENANT, AS IT IS WRITTEN: AND THE
ARK OF THE LORD WAS IN THE COUNTRY OF THE PHILISTINES SEVEN
MONTHS (I SAM. 6:1).

The Midrash lists seven righteous individuals who lost their lives as
they battled with the Philistines. It then continues to list the various
holy places (in Hebrew, *mishkanot*) that were used by the people either
to pray or communicate with God or His representatives. There were
seven such holy places, including the First and Second Temples.

ותפארתו ביד צר, אלו בגדי כהונה, כמה דאת אמר (שמות כח) ועשית בגדי קדש לאהרן וגו'
ולתפארת.

[CONTINUING THE VERSE]: AND HIS GLORY INTO THE ADVERSARY'S
HAND (PS. 78:61) REFERS TO THE PRIESTLY GARMENTS, AS IT SAYS: AND
THOU SHALT MAKE HOLY GARMENTS FOR AARON THY BROTHER, FOR
SPLENDOR AND FOR GLORY (EX. 28:2).

The list also includes the priestly garments that were originally worn
by Eli and his sons and were taken over by the Philistines.

רבי ירמיה בשם רבי שמואל בר רב יצחק, בשם ר' אבא: למה לקו אנשי בית שמש? על ידי
שהיו מליזין בארון. אמר הקב"ה: אילו תרנגולתו של אחד מהם אבדה, היה מחזיר עליה
כמה פתחים להביאה, וארוני בשדה פלשתים שבעה חדשים, ואין אתם משגיחים בו? אם
אין אתם משגיחים עליו, אני אשגיח עליו, (תהלים צח): הושיעה לו ימינו וזרוע קדשו. הה"ד
(שמואל א ו): וישרנה הפרות בדרך, מהלכות בישרות הפכו פניהם כלפי ארון ואמרו שירה,
והיינו דכתיב: וישרנה ואמרו שירה בפה. אי זו שירה אמרו? רבי מאיר אומר: שירת הים
אמרו. נאמר כאן, הלכו הלוך וגעו, ונאמר להלן, כי גאה גאה. רבי יוחנן אמר: שירו לה' שיר
חדש. רבי אליעזר אמר: הודו לה' קראו בשמו. רבנן אמרי: ה' מלך תגל הארץ. רבי ירמיה
בשם רבי שמואל בר יצחק אמר: תלת: שירו לה' שיר חדש, שירו לה' כל הארץ, ה' מלך ירגזו
עמים. תני אליהו, רומי השיטה, התנופפי ברוב הדרך המחושקת ברקמי זהב, המהוללה
בדביר ארמון, המעולפת מבין שני כרובים. אמר רבי שמואל בר נחמן: כמה יגיעות יגע בו בן
עמרם, עד שלימד שירה ללוים, ואתם אומרות שירה מאליכם? יישר חילכם:

R. JEREMIAH SAID IN THE NAME OF R. SAMUEL B. R. ISAAC: (WHY WERE
THE PEOPLE OF BETH SHEMESH SMITTEN? BECAUSE THEY MADE MERRY
OVER THE ARK. THE HOLY ONE, BLESSED BE HE, SAID): "IF A FOWL
HAD BEEN LOST, WOULD NOT ITS OWNER HAVE GONE IN SEARCH OF IT
THROUGH MANY HOUSES TO RECOVER IT? YET MY ARK HAS BEEN SEVEN
MONTHS IN THE COUNTRY OF THE PHILISTINES AND YE CARE NOUGHT
FOR IT. I MYSELF WILL CARE FOR IT," HENCE, HIS RIGHT HAND, AND HIS

HOLY ARM, HATH WROUGHT SALVATION FOR HIM (PS. 98:1). THUS IT IS
WRITTEN: AND THE KINE TOOK THE STRAIGHT WAY – *WAYYASHARNAH*
(I SAM. 6:12): THEY WENT A STRAIGHT PATH, TURNED THEIR FACES TO
THE ARK AND BROKE FORTH INTO SONG. WHAT SONG DID THEY SING?
R. MEIR SAID: THE SONG OF THE SEA, FOR HERE IT IS STATED: THEY
WENT ALONG . . . IOWING (*GA'U*) *AS THEY WENT* (6:12), WHILE THERE IT
SAYS: FOR HE AS HIGHLY EXALTED – *GA'OH GAAH* (EX. 15:1). R. JOHANAN
SAID: O SING UNTO THE LORD A NEW SONG (PS. 98:1). R. LEAZAR SAID:
O GIVE THANKS UNTO THE LORD, CALL UPON HIS NAME (PS. 105:1). THE
RABBIS SAID: THE LORD REIGNETH, LET THE EARTH REJOICE (PS. 97:1).
R. JEREMIAH SAID: THEY SANG THREE [SONGS]: O SING UNTO THE LORD
A NEW SONG; SING UNTO THE LORD, ALL THE EARTH (PS. 96:1) AND, THE
LORD REIGNETH, LET THE PEOPLES TREMBLE (PS. 99:1). ELIJAH TAUGHT:
[THEY SANG THUS:] "RISE, O RISE, THOU ACACIA, SOAR, YEA SOAR, IN
THINE ABUNDANT GLORY, BEAUTIFUL IN THY GOLD EMBROIDERY, EX-
TOLLED IN THE INNERMOST SHRINE OF THE SANCTUARY, ENCASED BE-
TWEEN THE TWO CHERUBIM." R. SAMUEL B. R. ISAAC SAID: HOW MUCH
TOIL DID THE SON OF AMRAM EXPEND BEFORE HE TAUGHT THE SONG
TO THE LEVITES, WHILE YE [COWS] RECITE SONG SPONTANEOUSLY! ALL
STRENGTH TO YOU!

The list concludes with a remarkable story of the Ark, which contained the sacred documents of Judaism. The Ark was captured during
the generation of Eli and it was desecrated by the Philistines in many
ways. The divine wrath was extended to the Israelite people, especially
those of Beth Shemesh, where the Ark eventually found some type of
resting place. Despite the fact that the Ark was in the presence of the
people of Beth Shemesh, it was completely ignored. Granted that they
could not capture the Ark from the Philistines, it would still have been
possible for them to make a deal with them either through money or
through various other ways of negotiating, in order that the Ark would
be in Jewish hands. The Midrash even goes so far as to quote the Almighty as saying that if any one of the members of Beth Shemesh lost
a fowl, they would do everything possible to look for it and to find it.
However, they did nothing for the Ark.

Not only were the people of Beth Shemesh punished, but the remarkable end of the story is that God Himself entered this world and He
Himself rescued the Ark. The Philistines were unsure of what was happening to the Ark, since it seemed to move in various directions. They

placed the Ark on two cows when necessary. The Midrash describes that somehow or another, these animals seemed to realize that they were pulling something belonging to God. So they carried themselves on in an atmosphere of reverence, looking at the Ark from time to time to make sure that it was being handled in a reverential way. Ultimately, the Midrash describes these animals as singing; their singing consisted of praise to the Lord. Many rabbis offered their opinions as to what tunes the animals were singing. All of them quoted the various verses from Psalms, all of which were meant to show that the animals were able to show the kind of reverence that the people of Beth Shemesh were not able to emulate. Of course, these were miracles, but the lessons that they were teaching could not have been lost on the people of Beth Shemesh or even in the generations that followed.

PARASHAH FIFTY-FOUR, *Midrash Five*

ה ויאמר כי את שבע כבשות וגו'. רבנן ורבי יצחק בן חקורה. רבנן אמרי: רועיו של אברהם
היו מדיינים עם רועיו של אבימלך. רועי אברהם אומרים: לנו הבאר! ואלו אומרים: לנו
הבאר! אמרו להם רועי אברהם: כל מי שהמים עולים להשקות את צאנו, שלו היא הבאר!
כיון שראו המים צאנו של אברהם אבינו, מיד עלו. אמר לו הקב"ה: את סימן לבניך, מה את,
כיון שראו המים את צאנך מיד עלו, אף בניך, כיון שהבאר רואה אותן מיד יהא עולה, הה"ד
(במדבר כא): אז ישיר ישראל את השירה הזאת וגו'.

5. AND HE SAID: VERILY, THESE SEVEN EWE-LAMBS SHALT THOU TAKE OF MY HAND (GEN. 21:30). THE RABBIS SAID: ABRAHAM'S SHEPHERDS QUAR-RELED WITH ABIMELECH'S SHEPHERDS, EACH CLAIMING, "THE WELL IS OURS." SAID ABRAHAM'S SHEPHERDS TO THEM: "IT BELONGS TO HIM FOR WHOSE FLOCKS THE WATER WILL RISE WHEN IT SEES THEM." WHEN THE WATER SAW ABRAHAM'S FLOCKS, IT IMMEDIATELY ASCENDED. SAID THE HOLY ONE, BLESSED BE HE, TO HIM: "THOU ART AN AUGURY, FOR THY CHILDREN, THAT THE WELL WILL RISE FOR THEM"; THUS IT IS WRIT-TEN: SPRING UP, O WELL – SING YE UNTO IT (NUM. 21:17).

We see from this account that the hostility of the servants of Abimel-ech and the servants of Abraham was longstanding. This quarrel was resolved through a miracle, when the water rose up from the well when the servants of Abraham were about to make use of it. That miracle was proof that the servants of Abimelech accepted, and they agreed that they now understand that the well belongs to Abraham. This agreement changed the entire social structure of Abimelech and Abraham. The hostility was replaced by a covenant, as we saw earlier, which lasted for seven generations on Abraham's side and three generations on Abimelech's side.

אמר להם ר' יצחק בר חקורה: עוד מן אתרה לית היא חסירה, בעבור היתה לי לעדה אין כתיב כאן אלא, בעבור תהיה לי לעדה:

R. ISAAC B. HAKORAH SAID: IN THIS VERY PASSAGE THERE IS NO LACK OF PROOF. IT IS NOT WRITTEN: THAT IT WAS A WITNESS UNTO ME, BUT, THAT IT WILL BE A WITNESS [I.E., A SIGN] UNTO ME (GEN. 21:30).

The Midrash questions why the text begins with a reference to the seven ewes that Abraham had given to Abimelech, and not the usual method of announcing ownership in the future generations (like with Jacob) by a combination of iron, wood, and metal. What happened here was that the well water recognized the rams and rose up in response to their presence, which is what Abraham thought might happen in some miraculous way.

—

Seed Thoughts

One of the lessons that this text is trying to teach is that just as the quarrel between Abraham and Abimelech was solved by a miracle of the well water rising up on its own accord, so did God assure them that their children would be helped in a similar manner. If they suffer sin and persecution, they will ultimately be rescued and protected. The quotation in our Midrash is from a similar well situation in the time of Moses. What are we to learn from such a story, since we did not live in an age of miracles? Is there something we can learn in a more modern way that we can identify with this teaching? Allow me to make a suggestion: The first principle is that a Jew has the right to live in any place in the world so long as he observes the laws of the country. At the same time, however, every Jew should remember that his goal, wherever he may be, is to create a Jewish community. When you are dealing with only one Jew in a community of other traditions, it is hard to expect a community in this situation, although there are remarkable stories of individual Jews who heroically led a Jewish life in a community of strangers who respected their development and even helped them. When there are more Jews in a certain area, the goal should be the creation of a Jewish community. That community will create a place for worship, a place for study, organizational arrangements to make kosher food available, and a *tzedaka* (charity) fund to help those who are not able financially to fulfill their share. The existence of this community with its many blessings is almost identical with the well water rising up and fulfilling the thirst of the needy. A good Jewish community is one of the blessings of being a Jew.

PARASHAH FIFTY-FOUR, *Midrash Six*

ו ויטע אשל בבאר שבע וגו'. רבי יהודה ורבי נחמיה. רבי יהודה אמר: אשל, פרדס! שאל מה תשאל, תאנים, וענבים, ורמונים. ר' נחמיה אמר: אשל פונדיק, שאל מה תשאל, עיגולא, קופר, חמר, ביעין. רבי עזריה בשם ר' יהודה בר סימון: אשל, סנהדרין, היך מה דאת אמר (שמואל א כב): ושאול יושב בגבעה תחת האשל ברמה.

6. AND ABRAHAM PLANTED AN ESHEL (E.V. "TAMARISK") TREE (GEN. 21:33). R. JUDAH SAID: ESHEL MEANS AN ORCHARD, THE WORD MEANING ASK (SHE'AL) FOR WHATEVER YOU WISH, FIGS, GRAPES, OR POMEGRANATES. R. NEHEMIAH SAID: ESHEL MEANS AN INN, THE WORD CONNOTING, ASK WHATEVER YOU DESIRE, MEAT, WINE, OR EGGS. R. AZARIAH SAID IN THE NAME OF R. JUDAH: ESHEL MEANS A COURT OF LAW, AS IN THE VERSE, NOW SAUL WAS SITTING IN GIBEAH, UNDER THE ESHEL (E.V. "TAMARISK TREE") IN RAMAH (I SAM. 22:6).

What the verse in I Samuel is to prove is that King Saul, as a monarch, was in charge of the entire judicial system of his day. He, therefore, headed a court. The fact that the area he chose was next to a well-known *eshel* tree was the reason why it was suggested by Rabbi Azariah that *eshel* refers to a court of law.

על דעתיה דרבי נחמיה: דאמר אשל פונדיק, אברהם היה מקבל את העוברים ואת השבים ומשהיו אוכלין ושותין אמר לון: בריכו! והן אמרין: מה ניגמור? ואמר להון: ברוך אל עולם שאכלנו משלו, הה"ד, (בראשית כא) ויקרא בשם ה' אל עולם ויגר אברהם בארץ פלשתים ימים רבים, רבים מאותן שעשה בחברון. בחברון עשה עשרים וחמש שנה, וכאן עשה עשרים ושש שנים:

ACCORDING TO R. NEHEMIAH'S VIEW THAT IT WAS AN INN, ABRAHAM
USED TO RECEIVE WAYFARERS, AND AFTER THEY HAD EATEN AND DRUNK
HE WOULD SAY TO THEM, "NOW SAY GRACE." WHEN THEY ASKED WHAT
TO SAY, HE WOULD REPLY: "BLESSED BE THE EVERLASTING GOD, OF
WHOSE BOUNTY WE HAVE EATEN." HENCE IT IS WRITTEN: AND CALLED
THERE ON THE NAME OF THE LORD, THE EVERLASTING GOD (GEN. 21:33)
AND ABRAHAM SOJOURNED IN THE LAND OF THE PHILISTINES MANY
DAYS (21:34) – MORE THAN THE TIME HE SPENT IN HEBRON. IN HEBRON
HE STAYED TWENTY-FIVE YEARS, WHILE HERE HE STAYED TWENTY-SIX
YEARS.

Seed Thoughts

Three interpretations are given of the word *eshel*. The first is that it was
an orchard, which contained fruit trees that produced figs, grapes, and
pomegranates. The second term was that of a dining room or inn, which
served the fruits that the *eshel* orchard provided. The third term, court
of law, appears to be on a different level, except for the fact that in every
community, the supreme court was given one of the finest accom-
modations. In our story, the orchard must have been very beautiful, its
perfume must have captivated all visitors, and it would have given the
members of the supreme court a great pride in their community. One
can imagine that all three of these descriptions can exist next to each
other, though it did not necessarily need to be that way. It should also
be remembered that there is a folk saying that each letter of אשל – *eshel* –
has a particular meaning. The *aleph* (א) stands for אכילה – *akhila*, meaning "eating"; the *shin* (ש) stands for שתיה – *shetiya*, meaning "drinking";
and the letter *lamed* (ל) stands for לויה – *levaya*, meaning "socializing."
All these interpretations merge with each other, and can be used indis-
criminately to replace each other.

Parashah Fifty-Five, *Midrash One*

א ויהי אחר הדברים האלה והאלהים נסה את אברהם. כתיב (תהלים ס): נתתה ליראיך נס
להתנוסס מפני קושט סלה. נסיון אחר נסיון וגידולין אחר גידולין, בשביל לנסותן בעולם,
בשביל לגדלן בעולם, כנס הזה של ספינה. וכל כך למה? מפני קושט בשביל שתתקשט
מדת הדין בעולם, שאם יאמר לך אדם, למי שהוא רוצה להעשיר, מעשיר! למי שהוא רוצה,
מעני! ולמי שהוא רוצה, הוא עושה מלך! אברהם כשרצה עשאו מלך, כשרצה עשאו עשיר.
יכול את להשיבו ולומר לו: יכול את לעשות כמו שעשה אברהם אבינו? והוא אומר: מה
עשה? ואת אומר לו: ואברהם בן מאת שנה בהולד לו, ואחר כל הצער הזה נאמר לו: קח נא
את בנך את יחידך ולא עיכב, הרי, נתת ליראיך נס להתנוסס:

1. AND IT CAME TO PASS AFTER THESE THINGS, THAT GOD DID PROVE
(*NISSAH*) ABRAHAM (GEN. 22:1). IT IS WRITTEN: THOU HAST GIVEN A
BANNER (*NES*) TO THEM THAT FEAR THEE, THAT IT MAY BE DISPLAYED
(*LE-HITHNOSES*) BECAUSE OF THE TRUTH. SELAH (PS. 60:6): THIS MEANS,
TRIAL UPON TRIAL, GREATNESS AFTER GREATNESS, IN ORDER TO TRY
THEM IN THE WORLD AND EXALT THEM IN THE WORLD LIKE A SHIP'S
ENSIGN [FLYING ALOFT]. AND WHAT IS ITS PURPOSE? BECAUSE OF THE
TRUTH. SELAH: IN ORDER THAT THE EQUITY OF GOD'S JUSTICE MAY BE
VERIFIED IN THE WORLD. THUS, IF ONE SAYS, "WHOM HE WISHES TO
ENRICH, HE ENRICHES; TO IMPOVERISH, HE IMPOVERISHES; WHOM HE
DESIRES, HE MAKES A KING; WHEN HE WISHED, HE MADE ABRAHAM
WEALTHY, AND WHEN HE WISHED HE MADE HIM A KING," THEN YOU CAN
ANSWER HIM AND SAY, "CAN YOU DO WHAT ABRAHAM DID? ABRAHAM
WAS A HUNDRED YEARS OLD, WHEN HIS SON ISAAC WAS BORN UNTO HIM
(GEN. 21:5); YET AFTER ALL THIS PAIN IT WAS SAID TO HIM, TAKE NOW
THY SON, THINE ONLY SON (22:2), YET HE DID NOT REFUSE." HENCE,
THOU HAST GIVEN A BANNER TO THEM THAT FEAR THEE, THAT IT MAY
BE DISPLAYED; SO IT IS WRITTEN: THAT GOD DID PROVE ABRAHAM.

God had already signified His approval of Abraham in the scriptural
texts. There, He said: "I have known Abraham well enough to understand that he will teach his children and his other descendants the law

of the Torah and the spiritual world of the commandments." Since this was already known by the Holy One, blessed be He, why did he need to give Abraham another challenge? The answer, as explained by the present Midrash, is that God wanted the world to know about Abraham, to know that such a person could exist, and others may possibly follow. As a result of this tremendous achievement, in the binding of Isaac, Abraham received just as many important awards as anyone can hope for. Of all the challenges of his life, none were as daring and demanding so much sacrifice as the binding of Isaac, which gave Abraham and Isaac a special place in the world.

PARASHAH FIFTY-FIVE, *Midrash Two*

ב (שם יא) ה' צדיק יבחן ורשע ואוהב חמס שנאה נפשו. א"ר יונתן: הפשתני הזה, כשפשתנו לוקה, אינו מקיש עליו ביותר, מפני שהיא פוקעת, וכשפשתנו יפה הוא מקיש עליו ביותר, למה? שהיא משתבחת והולכת. כך הקב"ה, אינו מנסה את הרשעים. למה? שאין יכולין לעמוד דכתיב (ישעיה נז): והרשעים כים נגרש. ואת מי מנסה? את הצדיקים, שנא' (תהלים יא): ה' צדיק יבחן. (בראשית לט) ויהי אחר הדברים האלה ותשא אשת אדוניו וגו'. ויהי אחר הדברים האלה. אמר רבי יונתן: היוצר הזה, כשהוא בודק את הכבשן שלו, אינו בודק את הכלים המרועעים, למה? שאינו מספיק להקיש עליו אחת עד הוא שוברו. ומה הוא בודק? בקנקנים ברורים, שאפילו הוא מקיש עליו כמה פעמים, אינו שוברו. כך, אין הקב"ה מנסה את הרשעים, אלא את הצדיקים. א"ר אלעזר: לבעל הבית שהיה לו שתי פרות, אחת כחה יפה, ואחת כחה רע. על מי הוא נותן את העול, לא על אותה שכחה יפה? כך, אין הקב"ה מנסה אלא הצדיקים שנאמר: ה' צדיק יבחן:

2. THE LORD TRIETH THE RIGHTEOUS, ETC. (PS. 11:5). R. JONATHAN SAID: A POTTER DOES NOT EXAMINE DEFECTIVE VESSELS, BECAUSE HE CANNOT GIVE THEM A SINGLE BLOW WITHOUT BREAKING THEM. WHAT THEN DOES HE EXAMINE? ONLY THE SOUND VESSELS, FOR HE WILL NOT BREAK THEM EVEN WITH MANY BLOWS. SIMILARLY, THE HOLY ONE, BLESSED BE HE, TESTS NOT THE WICKED BUT THE RIGHTEOUS, AS IT SAYS: THE LORD TRIETH THE RIGHTEOUS. R. JOSE B. R. HANINA SAID: WHEN A FLAX WORKER KNOWS THAT HIS FLAX IS OF GOOD QUALITY, THE MORE HE BEATS IT THE MORE IT IMPROVES AND THE MORE IT GLISTENS; BUT IF IT IS OF INFERIOR QUALITY, HE CANNOT GIVE IT ONE KNOCK WITHOUT IT SPLITTING. SIMILARLY, THE LORD DOES NOT TEST THE WICKED BUT ONLY THE RIGHTEOUS, AS IT SAYS: THE LORD TRIETH

THE RIGHTEOUS. R. ELEAZAR SAID: WHEN A MAN POSSESSES TWO COWS, ONE STRONG AND THE OTHER FEEBLE, UPON WHICH DOES HE PUT THE YOKE? SURELY UPON THE STRONG ONE. SIMILARLY, GOD TESTS NONE BUT THE RIGHTEOUS, AS IT SAYS: THE LORD TRIETH THE RIGHTEOUS.

This Midrash and the one that follows will offer several interpretations of the verse that God tests only the righteous. In what we have just read, the example identifies the righteous with those aspects of life which render a person capable, responsible, and sufficiently strong to carry out important work. It is, however, a very limited form of comparison. As between an ox that is capable of pulling a plow and an ox that is not capable of pulling a plow, obviously, the owner and/or farmer would choose the ox that is capable of doing the work. In this respect, the parable makes a comparison that a righteous person is capable of handling certain challenges without complaint, but the unrighteous do not have this capacity. However, this responsibility is a very limiting definition; others will follow.

PARASHAH FIFTY-FIVE, *Midrash Three*

ג ד"א: ה' צדיק יבחן, זה אברהם. ויהי אחר הדברים האלה והאלהים נסה את אברהם. רבי אבון פתח: (קהלת ח) באשר דבר מלך שלטון ומי יאמר לו מה תעשה. א"ר אבין: לרב שהיה מצוה לתלמידו ואומר לו (דברים טז): לא תטה משפט! והוא מטה משפט. לא תכיר פנים! והוא מכיר פנים. לא תקח שוחד! והוא לוקח שוחד. לא תלוה בריבית! והוא מלוה בריבית. א"ל תלמידו: רבי! אתה אומר לי: לא תלוה בריבית! ואת מלוה בריבית, לך שרי ולי אסירא? א"ל: אני אומר לך: אל תלוה בריבית לישראל, אבל תלוה בריבית לעובד כוכבים, דכתיב (דברים כג): לנכרי תשיך ולאחיך לא תשיך! כך אמרו ישראל לפני הקב"ה: רבון העולמים! כתבת בתורתך (ויקרא יט): לא תקום ולא תטור, ואת נוקם ונוטר? שנאמר (נחום א): נוקם ה' ובעל חימה. נוקם הוא לצריו, ונוטר הוא לאויביו. א"ל הקב"ה: אני כתבתי בתורה: לא תקום ולא תטור את בני עמך! אבל נוקם ונוטר אני לעובדי כוכבים, נקום נקמת בני ישראל. כתיב (דברים ו): לא תנסו את ה'. והאלהים נסה את אברהם:

3. ANOTHER INTERPRETATION: THE LORD TRIETH THE RIGHTEOUS – ALLUDES TO ABRAHAM, AS IT SAYS: THAT GOD DID PROVE ABRAHAM. R. ABIN COMMENCED HIS DISCOURSE THUS: FORASMUCH AS THE KING'S WORD HATH POWER; AND WHO MAY SAY UNTO HIM: WHAT DOEST THOU (ECCL. 8:4)? SAID R. ABIN: THIS MAY BE COMPARED TO A TEACHER

WHO INSTRUCTED HIS DISCIPLE: (THOU SHALT NOT WREST JUDGMENT
[DEUT. 16:19], YET HE HIMSELF WRESTED JUDGMENT; THOU SHALT NOT
RESPECT PERSONS [16:19], YET HIMSELF RESPECTED PERSONS; NEITHER
SHALT THOU TAKE A GIFT [16:19], YET HIMSELF TOOK GIFTS;) DO NOT
LEND MONEY ON INTEREST, YET HIMSELF LENT ON INTEREST. SAID HIS
DISCIPLE TO HIM: "MASTER, YOU TELL ME, 'DO NOT LEND MONEY ON
INTEREST,' YET YOU YOURSELF LEND ON INTEREST!" HE REPLIED: "I
TELL YOU NOT TO LEND ON INTEREST TO AN ISRAELITE, BUT YOU MAY
LEND ON INTEREST TO OTHER NATIONS, FOR IT IS WRITTEN: UNTO A
FOREIGNER THOU MAYEST LEND ON INTEREST; BUT UNTO THY BROTHER
THOU SHALT NOT LEND UPON INTEREST" (23:21). SIMILARLY, ISRAEL
SAID TO THE HOLY ONE, BLESSED BE HE: "SOVEREIGN OF THE UNIVERSE!
THOU DIDST WRITE IN THY TORAH: THOU SHALT NOT TAKE VENGEANCE,
NOR BEAR ANY GRUDGE (LEV. 19:18), YET THOU DOEST SO THYSELF, AS IT
SAYS: THE LORD AVENGETH AND IS FULL OF WRATH, THE LORD TAKETH
VENGEANCE ON HIS ADVERSARIES, AND HE RESERVETH WRATH FOR HIS
ENEMIES (NAHUM 1:2). SAID GOD TO THEM: "I WROTE IN MY TORAH,
'THOU SHALT NOT TAKE VENGEANCE, NOR BEAR ANY GRUDGE' AGAINST
ISRAEL; BUT IN RESPECT OF THE NATIONS – AVENGE THE CHILDREN OF
ISRAEL, ETC." (NUM. 31:2). SIMILARLY IT IS WRITTEN: YE SHALL NOT TRY
THE LORD YOUR GOD (DEUT. 6:16), YET GOD DID PROVE ABRAHAM.

This Midrash brings to our attention a most remarkable and a most
difficult comparison. It is making the claim that the great moral and
ethical principles of Judaism apply to the Children of Israel and to the
Jewish nation as described in the biblical text. But how can this comparison be maintained? It is opposed to the great doctrines of prophetic
Judaism. The prophet Micah says: "What does the Lord require of thee
but to do justice, to love mercy, and to walk humbly with God" (Micah
6:8). This applies, according to the prophets, to all nations, and to all
people who aspire to the good life. This issue has to become a major
teaching, a major discussion, and a major controversy that cannot be
averted. It must be faced and stated with full agreement by all religious
leaders of Judaism.

—

Seed Thoughts

The way that the Midrash is presently stated, it is as though the Holy Scriptures, the Talmud, and Jewish thought itself appear to be self-centered, anti-democratic, and in need of a stronger philosophical inter-pretation. One way of approaching this subject is to examine the verses literally. The comparison in our text is between Israel, on the one hand, and those who believe that the stars in heaven are gods and religious authorities, on the other hand. Such followers do not regard themselves as obligated to the moral and ethical positions of Judaism, and indeed, if they are excluded, they amount to a small percentage of the popula-tion in the twenty-first century. Furthermore, enough spiritual material and interpretations have been printed and studied over the past several hundred years about Judaism's message to the world. The Messiah, in whose coming we believe, will redeem not only the Jewish people, but all the people of the world. We are a world people. The most that can be said about the Midrashim that we are studying now is that the purpose of Judaism and the Torah is to lift up our souls as high as possible in the world, and ideally speaking, we could produce a people that would be an example to the world. The Torah would thus have fulfilled its mission.

PARASHAH FIFTY-FIVE, *Midrash Four*

ד אחר הדברים האלה. אחר הרהורי דברים שהיו שם. מי הרהר? אברהם הרהר ואמר: שמחתי ושמחתי את הכל, ולא הפרשתי להקב"ה, לא פר אחד ולא איל אחד! אמר לו הקב"ה: ע"מ שנאמר לך, שתקריב לי את בנך ולא תעכב. על דעתיה דר"א: דאמר אלהים: והאלהים הוא ובית דינו. מלאכי השרת אמרו: אברהם זה שמח ושימח את הכל, ולא הפריש להקב"ה לא פר אחד ולא איל איל ולא אחד! אמר להן הקב"ה: על מנת שנאמר לו שיקריב את בנו ולא יעכב.

4. AFTER THESE THINGS – MISGIVINGS WERE EXPERIENCED ON THAT OCCASION. WHO THEN HAD MISGIVINGS? ABRAHAM, SAYING TO HIM-SELF: "I HAVE REJOICED AND MADE ALL OTHERS REJOICE, YET I DID NOT SET ASIDE A SINGLE BULLOCK OR RAM FOR THE HOLY ONE, BLESSED BE HE." SAID GOD TO HIM: "I KNOW THAT EVEN IF THOU WAST COMMANDED TO OFFER THINE ONLY SON TO ME, THOU WOULDST NOT REFUSE." AC-CORDING TO R. LEAZAR WHO MAINTAINED THAT THE EMPLOYMENT OF

WA-ELOHIM WHERE ELOHIM WOULD SUFFICE INTIMATES, HE AND HIS
COURT, IT WAS THE MINISTERING ANGELS WHO SPOKE THUS: "THIS
ABRAHAM REJOICED AND MADE ALL OTHERS REJOICE, YET DID NOT
SET ASIDE FOR GOD A SINGLE BULLOCK OR RAM." SAID THE HOLY ONE,
BLESSED BE HE, TO THEM: "EVEN IF WE TELL HIM TO OFFER HIS OWN
SON, HE WILL NOT REFUSE."

The question that bothered the Rabbis of the Midrash was that the
phrase says "after these words" or "after these happenings." Usually when
this phrase occurs, happening took place; this is what the Midrash means
when it says "after these things." It so happens that the only happenings
that were described were those between Abraham and Abimelech. That
had nothing to do with the events that followed. This somewhat
innocuous phrase was to interpret the thoughts that bothered Abraham
at this particular time. The Midrash then goes on to describe the main
thought that bothered Abraham. At the birth of Isaac, he was overcome
by joy, and he wanted the world to celebrate with him. He organized a
very elaborate feast to which he invited all who were associated with
him. But he forgot one thing: He should have offered a sacrifice of an ox
or ram, as was the custom of his day, to acknowledge his appreciation of
God. This omission bothered Abraham very much, and made him feel
that he had sinned against the most important influence in the world.
The Holy One, blessed be He, who had transformed Abraham into what
he was on that day, comforted him by saying that Abraham did not have
to prove anything. God was certain that no matter what further challenge He presented to Abraham, including even offering his son on the
altar, that Abraham would accept to do whatever he was ordered to do
by God.

יצחק וישמעאל היו מדיינים זה עם זה זה. אומר: אני חביב ממך, שנמלתי לשלש עשרה
שנה. וזה אמר: חביב אני ממך, שנמלתי לח' ימים. אמר ליה ישמעאל: אני חביב ממך.
למה? שהיה ספק בידי למחות ולא מחיתי. באותה שעה, אמר יצחק: הלואי היה נגלה עלי
הקב"ה ואומר לי שאחתך אחד מאיברי ולא אעכב, מיד! והאלהים נסה את אברהם. נ"א א"ל
ישמעאל: אני חביב ממך, שנמלתי לשלש עשרה שנה, אבל אתה נמלת בקטנך ואי אפשר
למחות. א"ל יצחק: כל מה שהלויתה להקב"ה, שלשה טפים דם הם, אלא, הריני עכשיו
בן ל"ז שנה, אילו מבקש לי הקב"ה להשחט איני מעכב. אמר הקב"ה: הרי השעה! מיד,
והאלהים נסה את אברהם:

ISAAC AND ISHMAEL WERE ENGAGED IN A CONTROVERSY: THE LATTER
ARGUED, "I AM MORE BELOVED THAN THOU, BECAUSE I WAS CIRCUM-

CISED AT THE AGE OF THIRTEEN"; WHILE THE OTHER RETORTED: "I AM
MORE BELOVED THAN THOU, BECAUSE I WAS CIRCUMCISED AT EIGHT
DAYS." SAID ISHMAEL TO HIM: "I AM MORE BELOVED, BECAUSE I COULD
HAVE PROTESTED, YET DID NOT." AT THAT MOMENT ISAAC EXCLAIMED:
"O THAT GOD WOULD APPEAR TO ME AND BID ME CUT OFF ONE OF MY
LIMBS! THEN I WOULD NOT REFUSE." SAID GOD: "EVEN IF I BID THEE
SACRIFICE THYSELF, THOU WILT NOT REFUSE." (ANOTHER VERSION:
SAID ISHMAEL TO HIM: "I AM MORE BELOVED THAN THOU, SINCE I WAS
CIRCUMCISED AT THE AGE OF THIRTEEN, BUT THOU WAST CIRCUMCISED
AS A BABY AND COULDST NOT REFUSE." ISAAC RETORTED: "ALL THAT
THOU DIDST LEND TO THE HOLY ONE, BLESSED BE HE, WAS THREE DROPS
OF BLOOD. BUT LO, I AM NOW THIRTY-SEVEN YEARS OLD, YET IF GOD
DESIRED OF ME THAT I BE SLAUGHTERED, I WOULD NOT REFUSE." SAID
THE HOLY ONE, BLESSED BE HE: "THIS IS THE MOMENT!" STRAIGHTWAY,
GOD DID PROVE ABRAHAM.)

In this debate between Ishmael and Isaac, there does not seem to be a winner. Both are correct: Ishmael was circumcised at the age of 13, which eventually became an important age in the life of a Jewish boy. For it began the Jewish boy's commitment to the commands of the Jewish religion. In Isaac's case, his circumcision became the pattern that followed by all Jewish male infants to this day and the future.

⁓

Seed Thoughts

One of the fascinating things about this Midrash is that Ishmael and Isaac were involved with each other and this seemed to be a natural and frequent occurrence. The Midrash actually explains that Ishmael was coming to visit his father, and apparently, this was a routine which happened from time to time. In the scriptural text itself, we do not have any references to such meetings. The only event that is described was that Ishmael and Isaac were present at the burial of their father, Abraham. When we associate this incident with what this Midrash describes, we come to the realization that Isaac and Ishmael continued to have a life together with frequent visits and frequent conversations.

PARASHAH FIFTY-FIVE, *Midrash Five*

ה (מיכה ו) במה אקדם ה' אכף לאלהי מרום. רבי יהושע דסכנין בשם רבי לוי אמר: אף על
פי שהדברים אמורין במישע מלך מואב, שעשה מעשה והעלה את בנו לעולה, אבל אינו
מדבר אלא ביצחק, שנאמר: במה אקדם ה' אכף לאלהי מרום וגו'. הירצה ה' באלפי אילים,
ברבבות נחלי שמן, האתן בכורי פשעי, פרי בטני, חטאת נפשי? ביצחק, אע"פ שלא נעשה
מעשה, קבלו כגומר מעשה, ובמישע לא נתקבל לפניו:

5. WHEREWITH SHALL I COME BEFORE THE LORD, AND BOW MYSELF
BEFORE GOD ON HIGH (MICAH 6:6)? R. JOSHUA OF SIKNIN SAID IN R.
LEVI'S NAME: THOUGH THIS PASSAGE WAS [APPARENTLY] SAID ABOUT
MESHA, KING OF MOAB, YET IT REFERS TO NONE BUT ISAAC. FOR IT
SAYS: WHEREWITH SHALL I COME BEFORE THE LORD, AND BOW MYSELF
BEFORE GOD ON HIGH ... SHALL I GIVE MY FIRSTBORN FOR MY TRANS-
GRESSION, THE FRUIT OF MY BODY FOR THE SIN OF MY SOUL? (NOW IN
THE CASE OF ISAAC THE DEED WAS NOT ACTUALLY DONE, YET HE AC-
CEPTED IT AS THOUGH IT WERE COMPLETED, WHEREAS IN THE CASE OF
MESHA IT WAS NOT ACCEPTED.)

—

Seed Thoughts I

Mesha was the king of Moab, and as will be described later on, he offered
his son as a sacrifice while engaged in a war with Israel. He hoped the
sacrifice would change the war from defeat to victory, but that did not
happen. The opening phrase of the Midrash, "Wherewith shall I come
before the Lord, and bow myself before God on high," was intended to
be for Mesha, who did not accept it. It did, however, apply to Isaac, and
the prophet Micah continued his quoted verse with the phrase, "What
does the Lord require of thee but to do justice, to love mercy, and to
walk humbly with God?"

—

Seed Thoughts II

In the midrashic text, God said to Abraham: "I never intended that you
slaughter your son. I did not mean *shahtehu*, meaning 'slaughter him.' I

meant *haalehu le-olah*, meaning 'place him on the altar for the purpose of a burnt offering.'" This was a puzzle to some of the midrashic writers, because the prophet Micah spoke with derision of offering a burnt offering to God, an *olah*. Do you think that God wanted a burnt offering rather than justice and mercy? Of course not. But we have to understand what God said to Abraham: "What I really meant was not merely offer an offering, but to tell the world what a terrible thing it was to offer your son or your children as burnt offerings to the Lord."

—

Additional Commentary

Wanted: The right attitude

An English proverb says: "Actions speak louder than words." In this Midrash, however, there is something either more important than action, or what kind of action it ought to be. In Hebrew, what we are talking about is called *kavanah*, which can be rendered either as "the right attitude" or "the right intention." In Isaac's situation, not only was he properly prepared by Abraham to the terrible fact that he would be the one offered on the altar. Isaac accepted with a full heart, and even though it was never really consummated, he was given every consideration as though it had already happened. He and Abraham together shared the most extreme of all sacrifices in terms of offering their lives to God. Mesha, king of Moab, was an entirely different type. Isaac acted for the sake of Heaven; Mesha acted for the sake of power. Mesha drew the wrong lesson from the example of the binding of Isaac; he thought that he would be favored because of his physician, but he failed in this effort. His son was slaughtered, and no good came to Mesha from this terrible sacrifice. (*HaMidrash HaMevo'ar*)

PARASHAH FIFTY-FIVE, *Midrash Six*

ו והאלהים נסה את אברהם. ר' יוסי הגלילי אומר: גדלו כנס הזה של ספינה. רבי עקיבא
אומר: נסה אותו בוודאי, שלא יהיו אומרין: הממו, ערבבו ולא היה יודע מה לעשות. ויאמר
הנני. אמר רבי יהושע בן קרחה: בשני מקומות דימה משה עצמו לאברהם. א"ל הקב"ה:
(משלי כה): אל תתהדר לפני מלך ובמקום גדולים אל תעמוד. אברהם אמר: הנני, הנני לכהונה,
הנני למלכות, זכה לכהונה וזכה למלכות. זכה לכהונה (תהלים קי): נשבע ה' ולא ינחם, אתה
כהן לעולם. למלכות, נשיא אלהים אתה. משה אמר: הנני, הנני לכהונה, הנני למלכות. א"ל
הקב"ה: אל תקרב הלום, אין קרב אלא כהונה, היאך מד"א: (במדבר א): והזר הקרב יומת. ואין
הלום, אלא מלכות, המד"א: (שמואל ב ז): כי הביאותני עד הלום:

6. THAT GOD DID PROVE (*NISSAH*) ABRAHAM. R. JOSE THE GALILEAN
SAID: HE EXALTED HIM LIKE A SHIP'S ENSIGN (*NES*). R. AKIBA SAID: HE
TESTED HIM UNEQUIVOCALLY, THAT PEOPLE MIGHT NOT SAY THAT HE
CONFUSED AND PERPLEXED HIM SO THAT HE DID NOT KNOW WHAT TO
DO. AND SAID UNTO HIM: ABRAHAM; AND HE SAID: HERE AM I (GEN.
22:1). R. JOSHUA SAID: ON TWO OCCASIONS MOSES COMPARED HIMSELF
TO ABRAHAM, AND GOD ANSWERED HIM: GLORIFY NOT THYSELF IN THE
PRESENCE OF THE KING, AND STAND NOT IN THE PLACE OF GREAT MEN
(PROV. 25:6). NOW ABRAHAM SAID: HERE AM I – READY FOR PRIESTHOOD,
READY FOR KINGSHIP – AND HE ATTAINED PRIESTHOOD AND KINGSHIP.
HE ATTAINED PRIESTHOOD, AS IT SAYS: THE LORD HATH SWORN, AND
WILL NOT REPENT: THOU ART A PRIEST FOR EVER AFTER THE MANNER
OF MELCHIZEDEK (PS. 110:4); KINGSHIP: THOU ART A MIGHTY PRINCE
AMONG US (GEN. 23:5). MOSES TOO SAID: HERE AM I (EX. 3:4) – READY
FOR PRIESTHOOD, READY FOR KINGSHIP – BUT GOD ANSWERED: DRAW
NOT NIGH HITHER – *HALOM* (3:5); NOW "DRAWING NIGH" REFERS TO
PRIESTHOOD, AS IN THE VERSE: AND THE COMMON MAN THAT DRAWETH
NIGH SHALL BE PUT TO DEATH (NUM. 1:51), WHILE *HALOM* CONNOTES
KINGSHIP, AS IN THE VERSE: THAT THOU HAST BROUGHT ME THUS FAR
– *HALOM* (II SAM. 7:18).

Seed Thoughts

One of the most beautiful words in the Hebrew language is the word
hineni. It is used just as often in modern times as it was in the biblical
story. *Hineni* is a response to what a teacher or employer or colleague

may ask of a person who is ready to do his bidding. He would not answer with a complicated response, but he would merely say *hineni*. The word means either "here I am" or "I am ready" or "I am prepared to do your bidding." *Hineni* does not mean that what one requests will happen. In our Midrash, Abraham was able to fulfill God's commandment. On the other hand, Moses was not able to do so, which does not lessen his importance, but merely shows how carefully God asserts His desires even upon those who are close to him. *Hineni* is a short word for what could be a very long experience, but a great word in the Hebrew language as to the spiritual messages that come from the *Midrash Rabbah* – let us hope we can all say and pray *hineni*.

—

Additional Commentary

What is a miracle?

The word *nes* is usually translated as "miracle." It can also be used as a verb. Very often, that verb is used in connection with God. Here, He challenges Abraham in a certain direction and uses a miracle to save him if necessary. There are two interpretations of miracles. There is the miracle in which God does something spectacular in terms of His children, the best example of which is the binding of Isaac. God also uses miracles to protect His honor or to defend and proclaim His majesty. Probably the destruction of Sodom and Gomorrah might be considered a miracle of the second kind. Abraham was very saddened by the destruction of Sodom and Gomorrah, but he had to acknowledge the decision of God, Whose majesty was being compromised. This is probably what is meant by Rabbi Akiva, who said that God does perform miracles similar to the ensign on the top of a ship. Every ship has a flag or a pole or some form of identification so that smaller boats and ships can learn from the ship either their position on the map or the strength of the wind and weather. This can also be looked upon as an explanation as to what God's miracles are intended to teach us. (*Tiferet Tzion*)

Parashah Fifty-Five, *Midrash Seven*

ז ויאמר קח נא את בנך וגו'. אמר לו: בבקשה ממך, קח נא את בנך! א"ל: תרין בנין אית לי,
אי זה בן? א"ל: את יחידך! א"ל: זה יחיד לאמו, וזה יחיד לאמו. א"ל: אשר אהבת! א"ל: אית
תחומין במעיא? א"ל: את יצחק! ולמה לא גלה לו מיד? כדי לחבבו בעיניו וליתן לו שכר על
כל דבור ודבור.

7. AND HE SAID: TAKE, I PRAY THEE, THY SON, ETC. (GEN. 22:2). SAID HE
TO HIM: "TAKE, I PRAY THEE – I BEG THEE – THY SON." "WHICH SON?"
HE ASKED. "THINE ONLY SON," REPLIED HE. "BUT EACH IS THE ONLY ONE
OF HIS MOTHER?" –"WHOM THOU LOVEST." –"IS THERE A LIMIT TO THE
AFFECTIONS?" "EVEN ISAAC," SAID HE. AND WHY DID HE NOT REVEAL IT
TO HIM WITHOUT DELAY? IN ORDER TO MAKE HIM [ISAAC] EVEN MORE
BELOVED IN HIS EYES AND REWARD HIM FOR EVERY WORD SPOKEN.

One should add, in connection with this beautiful interpretation, that
it was not only to make Isaac more beloved to Abraham, but it was also
a great tribute to Abraham himself. God wanted to add words to His
speaking to Abraham, because although for Abraham to speak with God
was a great occurrence, experienced more than once, God made the
present message have more words and more hidden meanings. In this
way, His speech to Abraham should be lengthened more than necessary.

היא דעתיה דר' יוחנן, דא"ר יוחנן: לך לך, זו אפרכיה שלך. וממולדתך, זו שכונתך. מבית
אביך, זו בית אביך. אל הארץ אשר אראך. ולמה לא גלה לו מיד? כדי לחבבה בעיניו, וליתן
לו שכר על כל דבור ודבור, ועל כל פסיעה ופסיעה. א"ר לוי בר חייתא: שני פעמים כתיב לך
לך, ואין אנו יודעים אי זה חביבה אם הראשונה אם השניה. מן מה דכתיב: ולך לך אל ארץ
המוריה, הוי שניה חביבה מן הראשונה. ולך לך אל ארץ המוריה. רבי חייא רבה ורבי ינאי: חד
אמר: למקום שהוראה יצאה לעולם. ואוחרנא אמר: למקום שיראה יצאה לעולם. דכוותה
דביר: ר' חייא ורבי ינאי: חד אמר ממקום שהדיברות יוצאות לעולם. וחד אמר: ממקום
שהדיבור יוצא לעולם. דכוותה ארון: ר' חייא ור' ינאי: חד אמר: למקום שהאורה יוצאה
לעולם. וחד אמר: מקום שיראה יוצא לעולם. אמר ריב"ל: שמשם הקב"ה מורה לאומות
העולם, ומורידם לגיהנם. ר"ש בן יוחאי אמר: למקום שהוא ראוי, כנגד בה"מ למעלה. רבי
יודן אמר: למקום שיהא מראה לך. ר' פנחס אמר: לאתר מרוותא דעלמא. רבנן אמרי:
למקום שהקטורת קריבין, המד"א: אלך לי אל הר המור, ואל גבעת הלבונה.

THIS AGREES WITH THE DICTUM OF R. JOHANAN, WHO SAID: GET
THEE OUT OF THY COUNTRY (GEN. 12:1) MEANS FROM THY PROVINCE;
AND FROM THY KINDRED (12:1) – FROM THE PLACE WHERE THOU ART

SETTLED; AND FROM THY FATHER'S HOUSE – LITERALLY THY FATHER'S
HOUSE. UNTO THE LAND THAT I WILL SHOW THEE (12:1). WHY DID HE
NOT REVEAL IT TO HIM THERE AND THEN? IN ORDER TO MAKE IT MORE
BELOVED IN HIS EYES AND TO REWARD HIM FOR EVERY STEP. R. LEVI
B. HAYYATHA SAID: "GET THEE" IS WRITTEN TWICE, AND WE DO NOT
KNOW WHICH WAS MORE PRECIOUS [IN THE EYES OF GOD], THE FIRST
OR THE SECOND. BUT WHEN IT IS WRITTEN, AND GET THEE INTO THE
LAND OF MORIAH (22:2), IT FOLLOWS THAT THE SECOND OCCASION
WAS MORE PRECIOUS THAN THE FIRST. AND GET THEE INTO THE LAND
OF MORIAH. R. HIYYA THE ELDER AND R. JANNAI DISCUSSED THIS. ONE
SAID: TO THE PLACE WHENCE INSTRUCTION (HORAAH) WENT FORTH TO
THE WORLD. WHILE THE OTHER EXPLAINED IT: TO THE PLACE WHENCE
RELIGIOUS AWE (YIRAH) WENT FORTH TO THE WORLD. SIMILARLY, THE
WORD ARON (THE ARK); R. HIYYA AND R. JANNAI – ONE SAID: THE PLACE
WHENCE ORAH (LIGHT) GOES FORTH TO THE WORLD; WHILE THE OTHER
EXPLAINED IT: THE PLACE WHENCE YIRAH (RELIGIOUS REVERENCE)
GOES FORTH TO THE WORLD. SIMILARLY, THE WORD DEBIR; R. HIYYA
AND R. JANNAI DISCUSSED THIS. ONE SAID: THE PLACE WHENCE [GOD'S]
SPEECH (DIBBUR) WENT FORTH TO THE WORLD; WHILE THE OTHER EX-
PLAINED IT: THE PLACE WHENCE RETRIBUTION (DEBER) GOES FORTH
TO THE WORLD. R. JOSHUA B. LEVI SAID: IT MEANS THE PLACE WHENCE
THE HOLY ONE, BLESSED BE HE, SHOOTS (MOREH) AT THE OTHER NA-
TIONS AND HURLS THEM INTO GEHENNA. R. SIMEON B. YOHAI SAID:
TO THE PLACE THAT CORRESPONDS (RA'UI) TO THE HEAVENLY TEMPLE.
R. JUDAN B. PALYA SAID: TO THE PLACE THAT HE WILL SHOW (MAREH)
THEE. R. PHINEHAS SAID: TO THE SEAT OF THE WORLD'S DOMINION
(MARWETHA). THE RABBIS SAID: TO THE PLACE WHERE INCENSE WOULD
BE OFFERED, AS YOU READ: I WILL GET ME TO THE MOUNTAIN OF MYRRH
– MOR (SONG 5:6)

Whereas entering the Land of Canaan is a commandment, it can be
understood that by not revealing specifically the name and place of the
land intended as the Jewish homeland – the reward is not only for the
commandment, but rather for each step taken in that direction.

והעלהו שם לעולה. ר' יודן בר סימון אמר אמר לפניו: רבון העולמים! יש קרבן בלא כהן?
א"ל הקב"ה: כבר מניתיך שתהא כהן, הה"ד (תהלים ק') אתה כהן לעולם. על אחד ההרים
אשר אומר אליך. א"ר הונא משום ר"א בנו של ר' יוסי הגלילי: הקב"ה מתהא ומתלה
בעיניהם של צדיקים, ואח"כ הוא מגלה להם טעמו של דבר. אל הארץ אשר אראך על אחד

ההרים וגו'. דכוותה (יונה ג): וקרא אליה את הקריאה אשר וגו'. דכוותה (יחזקאל ג): קום צא אל
הבקעה ושם אדבר אתך:

AND OFFER HIM THERE FOR A BURNT-OFFERING (GEN. 22:2). R. JUDAN
B. R. SIMON SAID: HE [ABRAHAM] SAID TO HIM: "SOVEREIGN OF THE
UNIVERSE! CAN THERE BE A SACRIFICE WITHOUT A PRIEST?" "I HAVE
ALREADY APPOINTED THEE TO BE A PRIEST," REPLIED THE HOLY ONE,
BLESSED BE HE: THUS IT IS WRITTEN: THOU ART A PRIEST FOR EVER
(PS. 110:4). UPON ONE OF THE MOUNTAINS WHICH I WILL TELL THEE OF
(GEN. 22:2). FOR R. HUNA SAID ON THE AUTHORITY OF R. ELIEZER: THE
HOLY ONE, BLESSED BE HE, FIRST PLACES THE RIGHTEOUS IN DOUBT
AND SUSPENSE, AND THEN REVEALS TO THEM THE REAL MEANING
OF THE MATTER. THUS, TO THE LAND THAT I WILL SHOW THEE (12:1);
UPON ONE OF THE MOUNTAINS WHICH I WILL TELL THEE OF; AND MAKE
UNTO IT THE PROCLAMATION THAT I BID THEE (JONAH 3:2); SIMILARLY,
ARISE, GO FORTH INTO THE PLAIN, AND I WILL THERE SPEAK WITH THEE
(EZEK. 3:22).

Seed Thoughts

Moriah

This Midrash will include a number of possible definitions for many of
the sacred areas and the sacred objects that were connected with the
Temple in Jerusalem. The fact that one rabbi interpreted Moriah as
coming from the word *horaah*, which means "teaching" or "education,"
and another rabbi interpreted it as coming from the root *yirah*, meaning "piety" or "religious reverence." We should understand that both of
these interpretations are correct. We are dealing with a spiritual process
which manifests itself in many directions. Two of them are mentioned
in this Midrash but many more are possible, and we will come to them
eventually. Similarly, in the case of the word *aron*, you have one interpretation which says that it refers to *orah*, meaning the spiritual light
that comes from the Torah, while another says that it comes from *yirah*.

The problem with the word *devir* is much more complicated. It was
first used in King Solomon's Temple as the place where the High Priest
would stand and bring them as close as possible to the Ark. However,
the problem is, as our Midrash would state, that many of the interpretations and translations of *devir* are completely opposite to each other.

There is no conclusion in this respect. The reader should do as much thinking as possible simply to note the various opinions. Someday, a better interpretation may occur which we then cherish.

PARASHAH FIFTY-FIVE, *Midrash Eight*

ח וישכם אברהם בבוקר ויחבוש את חמורו. אר"ש בן יוחai: אהבה מקלקלת את השורה
ושנאה מקלקלת את השורה. אהבה מקלקלת את השורה, דכתיב: וישכם אברהם בבוקר
וגו', ולא היה לו כמה עבדים? אלא, אהבה מקלקלת את השורה. ושנאה מקלקלת את
השורה, שנא' (במדבר כב): ויקם בלעם בבוקר ויחבוש את אתונו, ולא היה לו כמה עבדים?
אלא שנאה מקלקלת את השורה. אהבה מקלקלת את השורה, שנאמר (בראשית מו): ויאסור
יוסף מרכבתו ויעל לקראת ישראל אביו, וכי לא היה ליוסף כמה עבדים? אלא, אהבה
מקלקלת את השורה. שנאה מקלקלת את השורה, דכתיב (שמות יד): ויאסור את רכבו, ולא
היה לו כמה עבדים? אלא, שנאה מקלקלת השורה. אר"ש בן יוחai: תבא חבשה ותעמוד
על חבשה. תבוא חבשה, שחבש אברהם אבינו לילך ולעשות רצונו של מקום, של מי שאמר
והיה העולם, שנאמר: וישלח אברהם את ידו וגו'? ותעמוד על חבשה, שחבש בלעם לילך
ולקלל את ישראל. תבא אסרה שאסר יוסף לקראת אביו, ותעמוד על אסרה של פרעה,
שהיה הולך לרדוף את ישראל. תני רבי ישמעאל: תבא חרב יד. שעשה אברהם אבינו,
שנאמר: וישלח אברהם את ידו ויקח את המאכלת לשחוט את בנו. ותעמוד על חרב יד,
שאמר פרעה (שם טו): אריק חרבי ויקח את שני נעריו אתו. א"ר אבהו: שני בני אדם נהגו
בדרך ארץ: אברהם ושאול. אברהם, שנאמר: ויקח את שני נעריו. שאול, (ש"א כ"ח): וילך הוא
ושני אנשים עמו. ויבקע עצי עולה. ר' חייא בר יוסי בשם ר' מיאשא, ותני לה בשם ר' בניה:
בשכר ב' בקיעות, שבקע אברהם אבינו עצי עולה, זכה להבקע הים לפני בני ישראל, שנא':
ויבקע עצי עולה ונאמר להלן (שם יד): ויבקעו המים. אמר ר' לוי: דייך עד כה! אלא, אברהם
לפי כחו, והקב"ה לפי כחו. ויקם וילך אל המקום. ניתן לו שכר קימה ושכר הליכה:

8. AND ABRAHAM ROSE EARLY IN THE MORNING, AND SADDLED HIS ASS
(GEN. 22:3). R. SIMEON B. YOHAI SAID: LOVE UPSETS THE NATURAL OR-
DER, AND HATE UPSETS THE NATURAL ORDER. LOVE UPSETS THE NATU-
RAL ORDER: AND ABRAHAM ROSE EARLY IN THE MORNING, ETC.: SURELY
HE HAD PLENTY OF SLAVES? BUT THE REASON WAS THAT LOVE UPSET
THE NATURAL ORDER. HATE UPSETS THE NATURAL ORDER: AND BALAAM
ROSE UP IN THE MORNING, AND SADDLED HIS ASS (NUM. 22:21): SURELY
HE HAD PLENTY OF SLAVES? HATE, HOWEVER, UPSETS THE NATURAL
ORDER. LOVE UPSETS THE NATURAL ORDER: AND JOSEPH MADE READY
HIS CHARIOT, ETC. (GEN. 46:29): YET SURELY JOSEPH HAD PLENTY OF
SLAVES? BUT LOVE UPSETS THE NATURAL ORDER. HATE UPSETS THE

NATURAL ORDER: AND HE MADE READY HIS CHARIOT (EX. 14:6): YET
SURELY HE HAD PLENTY OF SLAVES? THUS HATE UPSETS THE NATURAL
ORDER. R. SIMEON B. YOHAI SAID: LET SADDLING COUNTERACT SAD-
DLING. LET THE SADDLING DONE BY OUR FATHER ABRAHAM IN ORDER
TO GO AND FULFILL THE WILL OF HIM AT WHOSE WORD THE WORLD
CAME INTO EXISTENCE COUNTERACT THE SADDLING DONE BY BALAAM
IN ORDER TO GO AND CURSE ISRAEL. LET PREPARING COUNTERACT
PREPARING. LET JOSEPH'S PREPARING [OF HIS CHARIOT] TO MEET HIS
FATHER COUNTERACT PHARAOH'S PREPARING TO GO AND PURSUE IS-
RAEL. R. ISHMAEL TAUGHT: LET THE SWORD OF THE HAND COUNTERACT
THE SWORD OF THE HAND. LET THE SWORD TAKEN IN THE HAND OF
OUR FATHER ABRAHAM, AS IT SAYS: AND ABRAHAM STRETCHED FORTH
HIS HAND, AND TOOK THE KNIFE TO SLAY HIS SON (GEN. 22:10), COME
AND COUNTERACT THE SWORD GRASPED BY PHARAOH'S HAND WHEN
HE SAID: I WILL DRAW MY SWORD, MY HAND SHALL DESTROY THEM (EX.
15:9). AND TOOK TWO OF HIS YOUNG MEN WITH HIM, AND ISAAC HIS SON.
R. ABBAHU SAID: TWO PEOPLE BEHAVED WITH PROPRIETY, ABRAHAM
AND SAUL: ABRAHAM, AS IT SAYS: AND TOOK TWO OF HIS YOUNG MEN
WITH HIM; SAUL, AS IT SAYS: AND SAUL . . . WENT, HE AND TWO MEN
WITH HIM (I SAM. 28:8). AND HE CLEAVED THE WOOD FOR THE BURNT-
OFFERING. R. HIYYA B. R. JOSE SAID IN THE NAME OF R. MIASHA, AND
IT WAS ALSO REPEATED IN THE NAME OF R. BANNAIAH: AS A REWARD
FOR THE TWO CLEAVINGS WHEREWITH OUR FATHER ABRAHAM CLEAVED
THE WOOD OF THE BURNT-OFFERING, HE EARNED THAT GOD SHOULD
CLEAVE [DIVIDE] THE SEA BEFORE HIS DESCENDANTS, AS IT SAYS: AND
THE WATERS WERE DIVIDED (EX. 14:21). SAID R. LEVI: ENOUGH OF THIS!
IN TRUTH ABRAHAM ACTED ACCORDING TO HIS POWERS AND THE HOLY
ONE, BLESSED BE HE, ACCORDING TO HIS POWERS. AND ROSE UP, AND
WENT UNTO THE PLACE. HE WAS REWARDED FOR RISING UP AND FOR
GOING.

Seed Thoughts

Sometimes, one wonders as to whether the Midrash should be taken
seriously or simply ignored. Since when is a so-called natural order of
things so important? If Joseph had not acted in a very personal way to
look after his chariot in preparation for visiting his father for the first
time in twenty-two years, should not his associates have wondered

whether he took his visit seriously? Was it supposed to be just an ordinary visit? Was it not the most emotional moment in Joseph's own recent history? Should not the reader and those of his/her generation be upset if he/she had not upset the natural order of things? That applied not only to those who do good things, but also to people like Balaam whose intentions are evil. To become active and enthusiastic is far more important than being subject to the natural order of things. That applies both to good intentions and bad intentions. It is interesting to read this Midrash, but it should not be taken too seriously. Furthermore, what is the purpose of saying that one good action compensates for one bad action? They seem to have no connection with each other either in the Midrash or in life itself.

On the other hand, the fact that both Abraham and Saul each took two young men with him was very good advice. It is not only a question that the young men would serve them in many ways as caregivers, but that Abraham and Saul would also influence them in many ways by means of Abraham's and Saul's actions. That two such men are more valuable than one in each situation is perfectly alright as explained in the Midrash itself, but one could also do very well even when only one helper is available. It probably is of interest and value that the Midrash takes the time to leave the reader simple messages on how to do things to make one's life more livable. Only people of noble means or with high incomes are usually the ones to look for such personal helpers, but people of a lesser rank can find such help among their many friends who would gladly support them.

—

Additional Commentary

Abraham's Power

The Midrash concludes with a beautiful thought. It says that Abraham did whatever was in his power, and that God also did whatever was in His power. Rabbi Levi says that one should not be imagine that the verb which describes Abraham's cutting of a tree for the altar resembles the word used to describe the division of the waters of the Red Sea where the Egyptians were in difficulty. It was not the action used by Abraham that brought about the victory over the Egyptians at the Sea, but rather, God's power, which brought about Israel's victory rather than defeat.

א ביום השלישי וישא אברהם את עיניו. כתיב (הושע ו) יחיינו מיומים ביום השלישי יקימנו
ונחיה לפניו. ביום השלישי של שבטים, כתיב (בראשית מב): ויאמר אליהם יוסף ביום השלישי.
ביום השלישי של מרגלים, שנאמר (יהושע ב): ונחבתם שמה שלשת ימים. ביום השלישי של
מתן תורה, שנאמר (שמות יט): ויהי ביום השלישי. ביום השלישי של יונה, דכתיב (יונה ב):
ויהי יונה במעי הדגה שלשה ימים ושלשה לילות. ביום השלישי של עולי גולה, דכתיב (עזרא
ח): ונשב שם ימים שלשה. ביום השלישי של תחיית המתים, דכתיב: יחיינו מיומים. ביום
השלישי יקימנו. ביום הג' של אסתר (אסתר ה): ויהי ביום השלישי ותלבש אסתר מלכות
לבשה מלכות בית אביה. באיזה זכות? רבנן ורבי לוי, רבנן אמרי: בזכות יום השלישי של
מתן תורה, שנאמר: ויהי ביום השלישי בהיות הבקר. ור' לוי אמר: בזכות של יום שלישי של
אברהם אבינו, שנאמר: ביום השלישי וירא את המקום מרחוק. מה ראה? ראה ענן קשור
בהר. אמר: דומה שאותו מקום שאמר לי הקב"ה להקריב את בני שם:

1. ON THE THIRD DAY. ETC. (GEN. 22:4). IT IS WRITTEN: AFTER TWO DAYS
HE WILL REVIVE US, ON THE THIRD DAY HE WILL RAISE US UP, THAT WE
MAY LIVE IN HIS PRESENCE (HOS. 6:2). E.G., ON THE THIRD DAY OF THE
TRIBAL ANCESTORS: AND JOSEPH SAID UNTO THEM THE THIRD DAY:
THIS DO, AND LIVE (GEN. 42:18); ON THE THIRD DAY OF REVELATION:
AND IT CAME TO PASS ON THE THIRD DAY, WHEN IT WAS MORNING (EX.
19:16); ON THE THIRD DAY OF THE SPIES: AND HIDE YOURSELVES THERE
THREE DAYS (JOSH. 2:16); ON THE THIRD DAY OF JONAH: AND JONAH
WAS IN THE BELLY OF THE FISH THREE DAYS AND THREE NIGHTS (JO-
NAH 2:1); ON THE THIRD DAY OF THOSE RETURNING FROM THE EXILE:
AND WE ABIDED THERE THREE DAYS (EZRA 8:32); ON THE THIRD DAY
OF RESURRECTION: *AFTER TWO DAYS HE WILL REVIVE US, ON THE THIRD
DAY HE WILL RAISE US UP*; ON THE THIRD DAY OF ESTHER: NOW IT CAME
TO PASS ON THE THIRD DAY, THAT ESTHER PUT ON HER ROYAL APPAREL
(EST. 5:1) – I.E., SHE PUT ON THE ROYAL APPAREL OF HER ANCESTOR.
FOR WHOSE SAKE? THE RABBIS SAY: FOR THE SAKE OF THE THIRD DAY,
WHEN REVELATION TOOK PLACE. R. LEVI MAINTAINED: IN THE MERIT
OF WHAT ABRAHAM DID ON THE THIRD DAY, AS IT SAYS: ON THE THIRD
DAY, ETC. AND SAW THE PLACE AFAR OFF (GEN. 22:4). WHAT DID HE SEE?

HE SAW A CLOUD ENVELOPING THE MOUNTAIN, AND SAID: "IT APPEARS
THAT THAT IS THE PLACE WHERE THE HOLY ONE, BLESSED BE HE, TOLD
ME TO SACRIFICE MY SON."

We have here a listing of many times in which the third day appears
in Scripture. Making allowance for the various grammatical changes
that are made from time to time, I counted eighteen or nineteen times
in which the third day appears in Scripture. Is there a meaning to all
of this? Sometimes, the concept of the third day comes as a result of a
celebration. At other times, it refers happily to the end of a difficult period, either in a person's life or in the life of a community. Probably, this
may account for the Jewish tradition of many centuries that the third
day of the week is a good luck day. If it is your intention to start either
a new business or a new project, it is suggested that you begin it on the
third day, and the decision will be justified by a happy event. If there are
deeper meanings to the use of the third day so often, it may be hoped
that such new meaning will be realized as soon as possible.

PARASHAH FIFTY-SIX, *Midrash Two*

ב אמר ליצחק: בני! רואה את מה שאני רואה? א"ל: הין! אמר לשני נעריו: רואים אתם מה
שאני רואה? אמרו לו: לאו! אמר: הואיל וחמור אינו רואה, ואתם אין אתם רואים, שבו
לכם פה עם החמור! ומניין שהעבדים דומין לבהמה? מהכא, שבו לכם פה, עם החמור, עם
החמור. רבנן מייתי ליה מהכא, ממתן תורה שנאמר (שמות כ): ששת ימים תעבוד ועשית
כל מלאכתך וגו', אתה ובנך ובתך ועבדך ואמתך ובהמתך. א"ר יצחק: עתיד המקום לירחק
מבעליו ולעולם, תלמוד לומר (תהלים קלב): זאת מנוחתי עד, עד פה אשב, לכשיבא אותו
שכתוב בו (זכריה ט): עני ורוכב על חמור. ואני והנער נלכה עד כה. א"ר יהושע בן לוי: נלך
ונראה מה יהיה בסופו של כה, ונשתחוה ונשובה אליכם, בשרו שהוא חוזר מהר המוריה
בשלום. א"ר יצחק: הכל בזכות השתחויה, ואברהם לא חזר מהר המוריה בשלום, אלא
בזכות השתחויה.

2. HE THEN SAID TO HIM [ISAAC]: "ISAAC, MY SON, SEEST THOU WHAT
I SEE?' 'YES,' HE REPLIED. SAID HE TO HIS TWO SERVANTS: "SEE YE
WHAT I SEE?" "NO," THEY ANSWERED. SINCE YE DO NOT SEE IT, ABIDE
YE HERE WITH THE ASS,' (GEN. 22:5), HE BADE THEM, FOR YE ARE LIKE
THE ASS, WHENCE IT FOLLOWS THAT SLAVES ARE LIKE AN ASS. THE RAB-
BIS PROVED [IT FROM THIS VERSE SPOKEN AT] THE REVELATION: SIX

DAYS SHALT THOU LABOR, AND DO ALL THY WORK . . . THOU, NOR THY
DAUGHTER, NOR THY MAN-SERVANT, NOR THY MAID-SERVANT, NOR
THY CATTLE (EX. 20:10). R. ISAAC SAID: THIS PLACE SHALL ONE DAY BE
ALIENATED FROM ITS OWNER. FOR EVER? [NO], FOR IT IS STATED: *THIS IS
MY RESTING-PLACE FOR EVER; HERE WILL I DWELL FOR I HAVE DESIRED
IT;* (PS. 132:14) – WHEN HE COMES OF WHOM IT IS WRITTEN: LOWLY, AND
RIDING UPON AN ASS (ZECH. 9:9). AND I AND THE LAD WILL GO YONDER
– AD KOH. SAID R. JOSHUA B. LEVI: WE WILL GO AND SEE WHAT IS TO BE
THE EVENTUAL OUTCOME OF *KOH.* AND WE WILL WORSHIP, AND WE WILL
COME BACK TO YOU. HE THUS INFORMED HIM THAT HE [ISAAC] WOULD
RETURN SAFELY FROM MOUNT MORIAH. R. ISAAC SAID: EVERYTHING
HAPPENED AS A REWARD FOR WORSHIPPING. ABRAHAM RETURNED IN
PEACE FROM MOUNT MORIAH ONLY AS A REWARD FOR WORSHIPPING.

The main point here is that the two young men who accompanied
Abraham were not worthy of being present while Abraham was at the
altar of his son. Some unfortunate remarks are made at this point to suggest that the servants were like animals and could be treated as such. We
should remember that this was a time of slavery, which existed all over
the world and even in the new Americas until the nineteenth century.
What is quite important, however, is to examine the legal position of
servants in those days, having to do with family status. For example, the
fourth commandment of the Decalogue is quoted – everyone must observe the Sabbath, including male and female servants and the convert
or stranger that is in your community. All these categories have an equal
legal position. The *hamor,* or donkey, is mentioned here only because
it is specified in the story of the binding of Issac. The text also says
that Abraham said to the young man: "You wait here, and when we are
through with our worship, we shall return." Please note that the plural
"we" is used, which is a sort of mystical message that both Abraham and
Isaac would return in good health. This section indicates that Abraham
and his group would leave Mount Moriah, the holy place, but only temporarily. His people would eventually return under the leadership of the
Messiah, about whom it is said that he would be like a poorer person
riding upon a donkey. The key connection is the appearance of the word
hamor again.

ונשתחוה ונשובה אליכם. ישראל, לא נגאלו אלא בזכות השתחויה, שנאמר (שמות ד):
ויאמן העם וגו' ויקדו וישתחוו. התורה, לא נתנה אלא בזכות השתחויה, שנאמר (שם כד):

והשתחויתם מרחוק. חנה, לא נפקדה אלא בזכות השתחויה, שנאמר (שמואל א): וישתחו
שם לה'. הגליות, אינן מתכנסות אלא בזכות השתחויה, שנאמר (ישעיה כז): והיה ביום ההוא
יתקע בשופר גדול וגו'. והשתחוו לה' בהר הקדש בירושלים. בהמ"ק, לא נבנה אלא בזכות
השתחויה, שנאמר (תהלים צט): רוממו ה' אלהינו והשתחוו להר קדשו. המתים, אינן חיין
אלא בזכות השתחויה, שנאמר (שם צה): באו ונשתחוה ונכרעה נברכה לפני ה' עושנו:

AND WE WILL WORSHIP AND WE WILL COME BACK TO YOU. ISRAEL WAS
REDEEMED ONLY AS A REWARD FOR WORSHIPPING: AND THE PEOPLE
BELIEVED . . . THEN THEY BOWED THEIR HEADS AND WORSHIPPED (EX.
4:31). THE TORAH WAS GIVEN ONLY AS A REWARD FOR WORSHIPPING:
AND WORSHIP YE AFAR OFF (24:1). HANNAH WAS REMEMBERED ONLY
AS A REWARD FOR WORSHIPPING: AND THEY WORSHIPPED BEFORE THE
LORD (I SAM. 1:19). THE EXILES WILL BE REASSEMBLED ONLY AS A RE-
WARD FOR WORSHIPPING: AND IT SHALL COME TO PASS IN THAT DAY,
THAT A GREAT HORN SHALL BE BLOWN; AND THEY SHALL COME THAT
WERE LOST . . . AND THAT WERE DISPERSED . . . AND THEY SHALL WOR-
SHIP THE LORD IN THE HOLY MOUNTAIN AT JERUSALEM (ISA. 27:13). THE
TEMPLE WAS BUILT ONLY AS A REWARD FOR WORSHIPPING: EXALT YE
THE LORD OUR GOD, AND WORSHIP AT HIS HOLY HILL (PS. 99:9). THE
DEAD WILL COME TO LIFE AGAIN ONLY AS A REWARD FOR WORSHIP-
PING: O COME, LET US WORSHIP AND BEND THE KNEE; LET US KNEEL
BEFORE THE LORD OUR MAKER (95:6).

The Midrash, at this point, brings to our attention how some of the
most beautiful events in Scripture took place as a result of the serious-
ness and sincerity of the worship of God.

Seed Thoughts

In this Midrash and in many other places, it is stated that as a result of a
person kneeling before God (in Hebrew, השתחוה – *hishtahaveh*), many
good things happened in the religious life of a person. This kneeling, or
hishtahaveh, is mentioned so often and in such a convincing fashion that
we sometimes wonder why we are not doing the same, or perhaps we
are doing the same without knowing it. The Soncino, in its translation of
the Talmudic literature, has translated the Hebrew *hishtahaveh* as worship. This translation helps us very much because we can identify with it
more than with the concept of kneeling. By the same token, it should be
mentioned that when the Temple (Beit HaMikdash in Hebrew) existed,

kneeling was part of the religious practice, not only by the priestly clan, but by all who came to offer sacrifices at the altar. While the First and Second Temples existed, kneeling was definitely part of the worship. This, we know definitely from our practice on Yom Kippur at various points during the *Musaf* service and also on Rosh Hashanah at *Aleinu*, where the congregation kneels, thus reproducing the religious practice at the Temple. While the Temple existed, kneeling was practiced only there, and not elsewhere in the world. This is probably why it is no longer part of Jewish religious worship except on the High Holidays as indicated. When the Third Temple is established, and may it be soon, the practice of kneeling will probably be introduced again in the religious services of the Third Temple.

PARASHAH FIFTY-SIX, *Midrash Three*

ג ויקח אברהם את עצי עולה. כזה שהוא טוען צלובו בכתפו.

3. AND ABRAHAM TOOK THE WOOD OF THE BURNT-OFFERING (GEN. 22:6) – LIKE ONE WHO CARRIES HIS STAKE ON HIS SHOULDER.

According to Soncino, this is referring to "the stake on which he is to be executed."

ויקח בידו את האש ואת המאכלת. אמר ר' חנינא: למה נקראת סכין מאכלת? לפי שמכשר אוכלים. ורבנן אמרי: כל אכילות שישראל אוכלים בעוה"ז, אינם אוכלים אלא בזכות אותה המאכלת.

AND HE TOOK IN HIS HAND THE FIRE AND THE KNIFE (*MA-AKHELETH*). R. HANINA SAID: WHY IS A KNIFE CALLED *MAAKHELETH*? BECAUSE IT MAKES FOOD (*OKHLIM*) FIT TO BE EATEN. WHILE THE RABBIS SAID: ALL EATING (*AKHILOTH*) WHICH ISRAEL ENJOY IN THIS WORLD, THEY ENJOY ONLY IN THE MERIT OF THAT MA-AKHELETH (KNIFE).

Apparently, the word *maakhelet* was used in those days in connection with whatever food was eaten on the table of Jewish people, whereas the word *sakin* was used for whatever other purpose a knife would be used for.

וילכו שניהם יחדו. זה לעקוד וזה ליעקד, זה לשחוט וזה לישחט:

AND THEY WENT BOTH OF THEM TOGETHER (GEN. 22:6): ONE TO BIND
AND THE OTHER TO BE BOUND, ONE TO SLAUGHTER AND THE OTHER TO
BE SLAUGHTERED.

—

Seed Thoughts

One of the most beautiful expressions is "and they both walked together."
The reference is to Abraham and his son Isaac, as they prepared for the
most important moment of the binding of Isaac. One has to understand
that Abraham could not carry the wood for the altar by himself. The
donkeys were too far away for them to carry the burden. But Isaac was
young enough so that he carried whatever was necessary for that special
event. In this respect, he received additional rewards for his cooperation
and help.

As we go further in the discussion of this event, we realize that Isaac
was eventually informed that in the absence of a ram, he would be the
person who was offered as a sacrifice. Despite this news, he accepted
this role in the same spirit as did his father, Abraham. So it could be said
safely of both of them, that the two walked together – one to slaughter
and one to be slaughtered. The idea of a father and son working together, believing together, thinking together, and struggling together, is
a tremendous ideal. We have seen this happen many times in modern
society; the difference is that the father and son are cooperating in a
different fashion. The goals of many of them are to prepare for a more
successful livelihood or a better place in society or a higher monetary
income, all of which have their place in life. What seems to be absent,
however, is a dedication to God, a commitment to the Torah, a love of
the moral and religious life, and commitment to each other to share and
stand for the highest ideals of human society. To motivate fathers and
sons in this direction could indeed be one of the greatest tasks in the
human experience. What a wonderful thing it would be if we could say
of any father and son that they walked together for God, for the Torah,
for Israel, and for the highest ideals of the Jewish religious experience.

PARASHAH FIFTY-SIX, *Midrash Four*

ד ויאמר יצחק אל אברהם אביו ויאמר אבי. בא לו סמאל אצל אבינו אברהם אמר ליה:
סבא סבא! אובדת לבך, בן שניתן לך לק' שנה, אתה הולך לשחטו? א"ל: ע"מ כן! א"ל: ואם
מנסה אותך יותר מיכן, את יכול לעמוד? (איוב ד) הנסה דבר אליך תלאה! א"ל: ויתר על דין!
א"ל: למחר אומר לך שופך דם, את חייב ששפכת דמו של בנך? א"ל: ע"מ כן! וכיון שלא
הועיל ממנו כלום בא לו אצל יצחק. אמר לו: ברא דעלובתא, הולך הוא לשוחטך! א"ל: ע"מ
כן! א"ל: א"כ כל אותן הפרגזיות שעשת אמך לישמעאל שנאיה דביתה ירותא, ואתה אינך
מכניס בלבך? כד לא תיעול מילא תיעול פלגא, הה"ד: ויאמר יצחק אל אברהם אביו, הה"ד:
למה אבי אבי פ' פעמים? כדי שיתמלא עליו רחמים. ויאמר הנה האש והעצים. א"ל: יצף
להההוא גברא דיגער ביה, מכל מקום, אלהים יראה לו השה בני, ואם לאו, אתה השה לעולה
בני!

4. AND ISAAC SPOKE UNTO ABRAHAM HIS FATHER, AND SAID: MY FA-
THER (GEN. 22:7). SAMAEL CAME TO THE PATRIARCH ABRAHAM AND
UPBRAIDED HIM SAYING: "WHAT MEANS THIS, OLD MAN! HAST THOU
LOST THY WITS? THOU GOEST TO SLAY A SON GRANTED TO THEE AT
THE AGE OF A HUNDRED!" "EVEN THIS I DO," REPLIED HE. "AND IF HE
SETS THEE AN EVEN GREATER TEST, CANST THOU STAND IT?" SAID HE,
AS IT IS WRITTEN: IF A THING BE PUT TO THEE AS A TRIAL, L WILT
THOU BE WEARIED (JOB 4:2)? "EVEN MORE THAN THIS," HE REPLIED.
"TOMORROW HE WILL SAY TO THEE, 'THOU ART A MURDERER, AND ART
GUILTY,'" "STILL AM I CONTENT," HE REJOINED. SEEING THAT HE COULD
ACHIEVE NOUGHT WITH HIM, HE APPROACHED ISAAC AND SAID: "SON
OF AN UNHAPPY MOTHER! HE GOES TO SLAY THEE." "I ACCEPT MY FATE,"
HE REPLIED. "IF SO," SAID HE, "SHALL ALL THOSE FINE TUNICS WHICH
THY MOTHER MADE BE A LEGACY FOR ISHMAEL, THE HATED OF HER
HOUSE?" IF A WORD IS NOT WHOLLY EFFECTIVE, IT MAY YET AVAIL IN
PART; HENCE IT IS WRITTEN: AND ISAAC SPOKE UNTO ABRAHAM HIS
FATHER, AND SAID: MY FATHER: WHY HIS FATHER ... MY FATHER? SO
THAT HE SHOULD BE FILLED WITH COMPASSION FOR HIM. AND HE SAID:
BEHOLD, THE FIRE AND THE WOOD. "MAY THAT MAN BE DROWNED WHO
HAS THUS INCITED HIM," EXCLAIMED HE. AT ALL EVENTS, GOD WILL
PROVIDE HIMSELF THE LAMB, O MY SON; AND IF NOT, THOU ART FOR A
BURNT-OFFERING, MY SON.

The story of Samael is probably a dream which Isaac had. However,
very often, a dream includes some of the issues about which the dreamer

is concerned. Out text, of course, mentions those areas which Isaac realized was a serious problem that, on the one hand, he was promised to be the founder of a nation and, on the other hand, he was about to be slaughtered. The same concerns were part of Abraham's thinking, though he also decided that under no condition would he inform God that these questions occupied his own mind as well. He would obey God exclusively without any reference to any doubts he may have had. Isaac also informs Samael that whatever the risks to his life with which he may be confronted, he would accept whatever God wanted him to accept.

וילכו שניהם יחדו. זה לעקוד וזה ליעקד, זה לשחוט וזה לישחט:

SO THEY WENT BOTH OF THEM TOGETHER – ONE TO SLAUGHTER AND THE OTHER TO BE SLAUGHTERED.

T o quote the text again, one went to slaughter (the father) and one went to be slaughtered (the son).

Additional Commentary

Hospitality likened to an offering

One of the questions raised by some of the commentators was why Abraham did not bring an offering at the conclusion of the story of the binding of Isaac. Of course he was relieved, and of course he was thankful to God, but he always advocated that one should give a sacrifice at such a moment to commemorate the occasion and one's gratitude to God. It has been said that after the passing of a certain amount of time, even Abraham began to feel that he should have done so, but it really is not the case. Not only did Abraham show that he was prepared to sacrifice his dearest possession for the sake of God. He was prepared to sacrifice his entire charitable life, by which we mean making his home available to all persons, traveling from one area of the country to another, who would be invited to stop at his home to eat and drink whatever was available. The ability to resume his hospitality was certainly as altruistic as the giving of an offering, and surely, Abraham's behavior did not require that something more would have to be added. (*Tiferet Tzion*)

PARASHAH FIFTY-SIX, *Midrash Five*

ה ויבאו אל המקום אשר אמר לו האלהים ויבן שם אברהם את המזבח. ויצחק היכן היה?
אמר רבי לוי: נטלו והצניעו. אמר: דלא יזרוק ההוא דיגער ביה אבן, ויפסלנו מן הקרבן.

5. AND THEY CAME TO THE PLACE WHICH GOD HAD TOLD HIM OF; AND
ABRAHAM BUILT THE ALTAR THERE (GEN. 22:9). AND WHERE WAS ISAAC?
SAID R. LEVI: HE HAD TAKEN AND HIDDEN HIM, SAYING: "LEST HE WHO
SOUGHT TO SEDUCE HIM THROW A STONE AT HIM AND DISQUALIFY HIM
FROM SERVING AS A SACRIFICE."

Even at this difficult moment, Abraham reacted in terms of what God
wanted of him and not in terms of protecting his son. He hid Isaac temporarily lest others decide to do something such as throwing a stone at
him that would create an injury, therefore disqualifying him from being
a candidate for a sacrifice.

ויבן שם אברהם את המזבח וגו' ויעקד את יצחק בנו. רבי חפני בר יצחק אמר: כל מה שהיה
אבינו אברהם עוקד את יצחק בנו מלמטן, היה הקב"ה כובש שריהם של עובדי כוכבים
מלמעלן, ולא עשה אלא, כיון שהפליגו ישראל עצמן בימי ירמיהו, אמר להם הקב"ה: מה
אתם סבורים דאלין כפתיא קיימין? שנא' (נחום א): כי עד סירים סבוכים וכסבאם סבואים.
כי עד שרים סבוכים אלא כסבאם סבואים? אשתרון יתהון כפתיא, דכתיב (שם) אכלו כקש
יבש מלא.

AND BOUND ISAAC HIS SON. R. HAFNI B. ISAAC SAID: EVEN AS ABRA-
HAM BOUND HIS SON ISAAC BELOW, SO THE HOLY ONE, BLESSED BE HE,
BOUND THE PRINCES OF THE HEATHENS ABOVE. YET THEY DID NOT
REMAIN [THUS BOUND]. FOR WHEN ISRAEL ALIENATED THEMSELVES
[FROM GOD] IN THE DAYS OF JEREMIAH, THE HOLY ONE, BLESSED BE
HE, SAID TO THEM: "WHAT THINK YE: THAT THOSE FETTERS STILL EX-
IST?" AS IT SAYS: FOR SHALL THEY BE LIKE TANGLED THORNS (SIRIM)
FOR EVER (NAHUM 1:10), WHICH MEANS: FOR ARE THE PRINCES (SARIM)
TO BE ENTANGLED [I.E., BOUND] FOR EVER? NO, FOR WHEN THEY [THE
ISRAELITES] ARE DRUNKEN ACCORDING TO THEIR DRINK (1:10), THEIR
FETTERS ARE BROKEN, FOR IT IS WRITTEN: THEY SHALL BE DEVOURED
AS STUBBLE FULLY DRY (1:10).

God does not act merely in terms of one individual – even one as great
as Abraham. He watches things and for Him, the World to Come and

the present world comprise one unit. Thus, He kept a firm hand on the Princes of the nations, of those who followed a different religion, and He handicapped them so that the Jewish people should be protected from their onslaughts. When, however, Israel rebelled against God, all those fetters were removed and the persecutors did just about as they pleased. The prophet Jeremiah was one of those who interpreted this lesson to his community, urging them to return to God, but the prophets did not always succeed. The Midrash uses the drama of Abraham sacrificing Isaac as a way to open up this historical discussion. More will follow.

בשעה ששלח אבינו אברהם את ידו ליקח את המאכלת לשחוט את בנו, בכו מלאכי השרת
הה"ד (ישעיה לג): הן אראלם צעקו חוצה. מהו חוצה? רבי עזריה אמר: חוצה חיצה הוא בריה,
למיכס ית בריה! ומה היו אומרים? (שם): נשמו מסלות, אין אברהם מקבל את העוברים ואת
השבים? שבת עובר אורח, היך מה דאת אמר: חדל להיות לשרה. הפר ברית, ואת בריתי
אקים את יצחק? מאס ערים, וישב בין קדש.

WHEN THE PATRIARCH ABRAHAM STRETCHED FORTH HIS HAND TO TAKE THE KNIFE TO SLAY HIS SON, THE ANGELS WEPT, AS IT SAYS: BE-HOLD, THEIR VALIANT ONES [THE ANGELS] CRY WITHOUT – *HUZAH* (ISA. 33:7). WHAT DOES *HUZAH* MEAN? R. AZARIAH SAID: IT IS UNNATURAL. IT IS UNNATURAL THAT HE SHOULD SLAY HIS SON WITH HIS OWN HAND. AND WHAT DID THEY SAY? THE HIGHWAYS LIE WASTE (33:8)? DOES NOT ABRAHAM SHOW HOSPITALITY TO TRAVELERS? THE WAYFARING MAN CEASETH *SHABATH* (33:8) – AS IN THE VERSE, IT HAD CEASED (*HADAL*) TO BE WITH SARAH (GEN. 18:11). HE HATH BROKEN THE COVENANT (ISA. 33:8), VIZ. BUT MY COVENANT WILL I ESTABLISH WITH ISAAC (GEN. 17:21). HE HATH DESPISED THE CITIES (ISA. 33:8), VIZ. AND [ABRAHAM] DWELT BETWEEN KADESH AND SHUR (GEN. 20:1).

We can see from this discussion that not only leaders of idolatrous religions were involved by God in Abraham's actions, but even the good angels reacted in a completely opposite direction, crying for what they saw, remembering the wonderful merit of Abraham, hoping that something would be done to not allow what was happening to happen. The Midrash lists so many of the wonderful things that happened to Abraham and Isaac, who spent their lives offering hospitality and food to all who came and went by their home, always situated in a place where travelers could be invited and helped. Furthermore, Sarah was blessed with the return of her feminine youthfulness, so that both Abraham and Sarah in their old age could be blessed with the birth of Isaac. For that matter, the Holy One, blessed be He, promised that a great covenant would be made between Him and Isaac. The angels hoped that these wonderful events might persuade the Almighty to change what seemed imminent.

לא חשב אנוש לא עמדה זכות לאברהם אתמהא? ומי יאמר לך שאין הפסוק מדבר אלא במלאכי השרת? נאמר כאן ממעל, ונאמר להלן ממעל (שם ו): שרפים עומדים ממעל לו:

HE REGARDETH NOT MAN (ISA. 33:8) – HAS ABRAHAM NO MERIT IN HIS FAVOR? AND WHO SAYS THAT THIS VERSE REFERS TO THE ANGELS? HERE IT SAYS, UPON (*MI-MAAL*) THE WOOD, WHILE IN ANOTHER PASSAGE IT SAYS: ABOVE (*MI-MAAL*) HIM STOOD THE SERAPHIM (ISA. 6:2).

The use of the Hebrew term ממעל – *mi-maal*, instead of the term *maal*, both of which mean the very same in Hebrew, has been connected by the Midrash to the use of the similar word in God's revelation to Isaiah. In the scene where Isaiah was declared to be a prophet, in that context, the word *mi-maal* referred to all the extraordinary angels in the Heavenly Court. Therefore, says the Midrash, it would not only be the ministering angels (in Hebrew letters, *malakhei ha-sharet*) that cried in connection to the binding of Isaac, but all the angels in the Heavenly Court shared this great distress.

ו וישלח אברהם את ידו ויקח את המאכלת. רב בעא קומי רבי חייא רבה: מנין לשחיטה
שהיא בדבר המטלטל? מן הכא, וישלח אברהם את ידו. א״ל: אין מן ההגדה, אמר לך חזר
הוא ביה, ואין מן אולפן אמר לך, לית הוא חזר ביה. דתני לוי: היו נעוצים מתחלתן, הרי אלו
פסולים. תלושין ונעצן, הרי אלו כשרים. דתנן: השוחט במגל יד, במגל קציר, ובצור ובקנה,
שחיטתו כשרה.

6. AND ABRAHAM STRETCHED FORTH HIS HAND, AND TOOK THE KNIFE.
RAB ASKED R. HIYYA THE ELDER: REGARDING RABBI'S TEACHING, IN
WHICH HE SAID: HOW DO WE KNOW THAT RITUAL SLAUGHTERING
MUST BE WITH A MOVABLE OBJECT? FROM THIS VERSE: AND ABRAHAM
STRETCHED FORTH HIS HAND, AND TOOK THE KNIFE – DID HE TELL YOU
THIS AS *HAGGADAH*, IN WHICH CASE HE MIGHT RETRACT; OR DID HE
STATE IT AS A TRADITION, IN WHICH CASE HE WOULD NOT RETRACT
FROM IT? FOR R. LEVI TAUGHT: IF THEY [E.G., SHARP FLINTS] WERE FAS-
TENED [TO THE GROUND OR ROCKS] FROM THE VERY BEGINNING, THEY
ARE UNFIT; BUT IF THEY HAD BEEN ORIGINALLY DETACHED BUT SUB-
SEQUENTLY FIXED IN THE GROUND, THEY ARE FIT. FOR WE LEARNED:
IF ONE SLAUGHTERS WITH A HAND-SICKLE, A FLINT, OR A REED, THE
SLAUGHTERING IS FIT.

Basically, the question they are debating is whether or not a knife or
any other instrument used for slaughter can be attached to the ground
or to some aspect of the ground, such as a rock. The point was later
made that if an object that was connected from the beginning with the
earth but was later detached and appeared that way for a long time, the
instrument could then be used for kosher slaughter. The question that
was then raised was whether Rav's opinion was halakha (law) or Aggadah (merely Jewish thought). If it were Aggadah, he might change his
mind in the future, and that change would be acceptable. If, however, he
looked upon it as halakha, meaning his interpretation of Jewish law, that
would not ever be changed.

אמר רבי יוסי: חמשה דברים נאמרו בקרומיות של קנה: אין שוחטין בה, ואין מוהלין בה,
ואין חותכין בה, בשר ואין מקנחין בה את הידים, ולא מחצין בה את השנים, מפני שרוח
רעה שוכנת עליו:

R. JOSE [B. ABIN] SAID: FIVE THINGS WERE SAID OF A REED STALK: YOU
MAY NOT SLAUGHTER, CIRCUMCISE, CUT MEAT, WIPE YOUR HANDS, NOR
PICK YOUR TEETH WITH IT, BECAUSE AN EVIL SPIRIT RESTS UPON IT.

The Midrash concludes with the following statement: "Five things
were said of a reed stalk: You may not slaughter, circumcise, cut meat,
wipe your hands, nor pick your teeth with it, because an evil spirit rests
upon it." Even though the *Talmud Bavli* says that the reason a reed stalk
cannot be used to clean teeth or wipe your hands or cut meat is due
to the physical danger of splinters, the Midrash should not be changed
here since it follows the text of the Jeruslam Talmud (Etz Yosef).

—

Seed Thoughts

This Midrash brings to our attention the two main classifications of Talmudic literature. These divisions are described in Hebrew as halakha,
meaning Jewish law, and Aggadah, meaning Jewish thought. The latter
covers all aspects of Jewish thought with the exception of those that are
involved in the creation of law. The source of Jewish law is, of course, the
Bible, and it is the function of the Talmud to interpret that law so it could
be functional in the various future generations of Jewish life. If ever it
were changed, it would only be in the way that might be either more
purified or more relevant to a new generation. The Aggadah, which I
have described as Jewish thought, covers all elements of that thought
with the exception of law. In the area of halakha, there can only be one
Jewish law. For example, the various laws that interpret the Sabbath are
not changeable, but various customs that do not have the power of Jewish law can be introduced into the Sabbath to make it more enjoyable or
more practical or even more philosophical. The Midrash we are reading
and all other Midrashim which cover a vast amount can be interpreted
in many directions and by many people. All of the Midrashim can be
understood as part of the world of Aggadah – Jewish thought. In our
own work, we have come across many Midrashim which have four or
five great rabbis offering opinions which differ from each other. All of
those opinions are acceptable, can be followed or not followed. There
is a certain amount of freedom in midrashic literature, and indeed, in
many aspects of the Aggadah (which is part and parcel of the Talmud).
It can be looked upon as a freedom of expression for those Jewish schol-

ars who have strong opinions on many subjects. On any average page of the Talmud, you will find views in connection with halakha (meaning law) and Aggadah (meaning thought). In the discussion in the Talmud, and in whatever yeshiva in which the Talmud is studied, great attention is paid to the law which, when accepted, is independent, and to Jewish thought, which is privileged with as many opinions as the scholars are able to pronounce. Both halakha and Aggadah, together, make the Talmud one of the greatest forms of literature that the intellectual world has ever seen.

PARASHAH FIFTY-SIX, *Midrash Seven*

ז ויקרא אליו מלאך ה' מן השמים אברהם אברהם. תני רבי חייא: לשון חיבה, לשון זירוז. ר' אליעזר בן יעקב אמר לו ולדורות: אין דור שאין בו כאברהם, ואין דור שאין בו כיעקב, ואין דור שאין בו כמשה, ואין דור שאין בו כשמואל.

7. AND THE ANGEL OF THE LORD CALLED UNTO HIM OUT OF HEAVEN, AND SAID: ABRAHAM, ABRAHAM (GEN. 22:11). R. HIYYA TAUGHT: THIS IS AN EXPRESSION OF LOVE AND ENCOURAGEMENT. R. LIEZER SAID: [THE REPETITION INDICATES THAT HE SPOKE] TO HIM AND TO FUTURE GENERATIONS: THERE IS NO GENERATION WHICH DOES NOT CONTAIN MEN LIKE ABRAHAM, AND THERE IS NO GENERATION WHICH DOES NOT CONTAIN MEN LIKE JACOB, MOSES, AND SAMUEL.

There are two opinions to explain the repetition of the name. The first opinion is an expression of love. In other words, "Abraham, Abraham" is written as though it were "I love you, Abraham." The same holds for Jacob, Moses, and Samuel. The second interpretation is that the repetition of the word has to do with future generations. A point of view is expressed that there is no generation in the future that is without individuals like Abraham, Jacob, Moses, and Samuel. We do not know who they are, but their influence is very great without our knowing who they are individually.

ויאמר אל תשלח ידך. וסכין היכן היה? נשרו שלש דמעות ממלאכי השרת, ושחת הסכין. א"ל: אחנקנו! אמר לו: אל תשלח ידך אל הנער! א"ל: אוציא ממנו טפת דם! אמר לו: אל תעש לו מאומה, אל תעש לו מומה. כי עתה ידעתי. הודעתי לכל שאת אוהבני. ולא חשכת

וגו'. שלא תאמר כל החלאים שחוץ לגוף אינן חלאים, אלא מעלה אני עליך כאילו אמרתי
לך, הקרב עצמך לי, ולא עיכבת:

AND HE SAID: LAY NOT THY HAND UPON THE LAD, ETC. (GEN. 22:12).
WHERE WAS THE KNIFE? TEARS HAD FALLEN FROM THE ANGELS UPON IT
AND DISSOLVED IT. "THEN I WILL STRANGLE HIM," SAID HE [ABRAHAM]
TO HIM. "LAY NOT THY HAND UPON THE LAD," WAS THE REPLY. "LET
US BRING FORTH A DROP OF BLOOD FROM HIM," HE PLEADED. NEITHER
DO THOU ANY THING TO HIM, HE ANSWERED: "INFLICT NO BLEMISH
UPON HIM. FOR NOW I KNOW – I HAVE MADE IT KNOWN TO ALL – THAT
THOU LOVEST ME, AND THOU HAST NOT WITHHELD, ETC. AND DO NOT
SAY, 'ALL ILLS THAT DO NOT AFFECT ONE'S OWN PERSON ARE NOT ILL,'
FOR INDEED I ASCRIBE MERIT TO THEE AS THOUGH I HAD BIDDEN THEE
SACRIFICE THYSELF AND THOU HADST NOT REFUSED."

Apparently, Abraham wanted to do a few things that would not injure
Isaac but would prove to the world that it was indeed his intention to do
what God wanted him to do, even to the extent of slaughtering his son.
"Is it alright," he said to the angel, "if I let out of him a drop of his blood
or that I use a pin to cause a slight pain?" These requests, however, were
completely forbidden, and Abraham was assured that the entire world
would understand that he was ready to do God's bidding without the
additional things he was prepared to do at this moment.

PARASHAH FIFTY-SIX, *Midrash Eight*

ח ד"א. א"ר יצחק: בשעה שבקש אברהם לעקוד יצחק בנו אמר לו: אבא! בחור אני, וחוששני שמא יזדעזע גופי מפחדה של סכין ואצערך, ושמא תפסל השחיטה ולא תעלה לך לקרבן אלא, כפתני יפה יפה.

8. ANOTHER COMMENT: R. ISAAC SAID: WHEN ABRAHAM WISHED TO SACRIFICE HIS SON ISAAC, HE SAID TO HIM: "FATHER, I AM A YOUNG MAN AND AM AFRAID THAT MY BODY MAY TREMBLE THROUGH FEAR OF THE KNIFE AND I WILL GRIEVE THEE, WHEREBY THE SLAUGHTER MAY BE RENDERED UNFIT AND THIS WILL NOT COUNT AS A REAL SACRIFICE; THEREFORE BIND ME VERY FIRMLY."

What Isaac said to his father was his concern that because of Abraham's age, his hand holding the knife might shake, and that would cause additional pain to Isaac. He asked, therefore, that his father should make sure that he is tied comfortably to prevent anything from happening that might add to his pain and possibly disqualify the whole sacrifice from being accepted, which would be a terrible development. He would, then, not only lose his life, but also for no purpose. Abraham immediately tried his best to fulfill Isaac's request.

מיד, ויעקד את יצחק. כלום יכול אדם לכפות בן שלשים ושבע? [נ"א בן עשרים ושש שנה] אלא לדעתו? מיד, וישלח אברהם את ידו, הוא שולח יד ליטול את הסכין, ועיניו מורידות דמעות, ונופלות דמעות לעיניו של יצחק מרחמנותו של אבא, ואעפ"כ, הלב שמח לעשות רצון יוצרו.

FORTHWITH, HE BOUND ISAAC: CAN ONE BIND A MAN THIRTY-SEVEN YEARS OLD (ANOTHER VERSION: TWENTY-SIX YEARS OLD) WITHOUT HIS CONSENT? PRESENTLY, AND ABRAHAM STRETCHED FORTH HIS HAND – HE STRETCHED FORTH HIS HAND TO TAKE THE KNIFE WHILE THE TEARS STREAMED FROM HIS EYES, AND THESE TEARS, PROMPTED BY A FATHER'S COMPASSION, DROPPED INTO ISAAC'S EYES. YET EVEN SO, HIS HEART REJOICED TO OBEY THE WILL OF HIS CREATOR.

See the Seed Thoughts.

והיו המלאכים מתקבצין כתות כתות מלמעלן. מה הוון צווחין? (שם לג) נשמו מסלות שבת עובר אורח הפר ברית מאס ערים. אין רצונו בירושלים ובבית המקדש, שהיה בדעתו להוריש לבניו של יצחק?

THE ANGELS ASSEMBLED IN GROUPS ABOVE. WHAT DID THEY CRY?
THE HIGHWAYS LIE WASTE, THE WAYFARING MAN CEASETH; HE HATH
BROKEN THE COVENANT, HE HATH DESPISED THE CITIES (ISA. 33:8).
HAS HE NO PLEASURE IN JERUSALEM AND THE TEMPLE, WHICH HE HAD
INTENDED GIVING AS A POSSESSION TO THE DESCENDANTS OF ISAAC?

The text is referring to Abraham's practice of making his home available to all travelers coming and going along the highways leading to his house. He invited all to remain for dinner or for any type of rest as needed. This is why Abraham's house and the road that led to his house are mentioned by the angels, because in Abraham's absence, they are completely absent of people. The implication is that the Almighty did not necessarily appreciate the hospitality that Abraham offered. This surprised the angels, who were also astonished that Abraham seemed to have abandoned so many of the promises that he had made to Isaac and to people in Israel in general, not to speak of the Almighty who had made promises in connection with Jerusalem and the Holy Temple.

לא חשב אנוש, לא עמדה זכות לאברהם? לית לכל בריה חשיבות קדמוי! א"ר אחא: התחיל אברהם תמיה, אין הדברים הללו אלא דברים של תימה. אתמול אמרת: כי ביצחק יקרא לך זרע, חזרת ואמרת: קח נא את בנך! ועכשיו את אמר לי: אל תשלח ידך אל הנער, אתמהא? אמר לו הקב"ה: אברהם! (תהלים פט) לא אחלל בריתי ומוצא שפתי לא אשנה. כשאמרתי לך: קח נא את בנך! לא אמרתי: שחטהו! אלא, והעלהו! לשם חיבה אמרתי לך אסיקתיה וקיימת דברי, ועתה אחתיניה. נ"א משלו משל למלך שאמר לאוהבו העלה את בנך אל שלחני! הביאו אותו אוהבו וסכינו בידו. אמר המלך: וכי העלהו לאכלו אמרתי לך, העלהו אמרתי לך! מפני חיבתו. הדא הוא דכתיב (ירמיה יט): ולא עלתה על לבי זה יצחק:

HE REGARDETH NOT MAN (ISA. 33:8): IF NO MERIT HAS STOOD IN ABRA-
HAM'S FAVOR, THEN NO CREATURE HAS ANY VALUE BEFORE HIM. R.
AHA SAID: [ABRAHAM WONDERED]: SURELY THOU TOO INDULGEST IN
PREVARICATION! YESTERDAY THOU SAIDEST, FOR IN ISAAC SHALL SEED
BE CALLED TO THEE (GEN. 21:12); THOU DIDST THEN RETRACT AND SAY,
TAKE NOW THY SON (22:2); WHILE NOW THOU BIDDEST ME, LAY NOT THY
HAND UPON THE LAD! SAID THE HOLY ONE, BLESSED BE HE, TO HIM: "O
ABRAHAM, MY COVENANT WILL I NOT PROFANE (PS. 89:35), AND I WILL
ESTABLISH MY COVENANT WITH ISAAC (GEN. 17:21). WHEN I BADE THEE,
'TAKE NOW THY SON,' ETC., I WILL NOT ALTER THAT WHICH IS GONE

OUT OF MY LIPS (PS. 89:35). DID I TELL THEE, SLAUGHTER HIM? NO! BUT,
'TAKE HIM UP.' THOU HAST TAKEN HIM UP. NOW TAKE HIM DOWN."

God concludes this discussion by repeating what He has said in many
of the previous Midrashim. His point was that Abraham misunderstood
His command. He never said "slaughter your son." He said "lift him up
to the altar." His goal was for us to prove to the world that the slaughter
of children and young people is a sin. The problem with this interpretation is that if Abraham misunderstood the commandment, the same
charge can be laid to all who offer animal sacrifices that were prevalent
in ancient times. In no case was a person told to slaughter an animal. He
was told to offer the animal as a sacrifice, and everyone understood that
slaughter was to be done. If Abraham misunderstood the command,
that was because the vast majority of those who offered animal sacrifices
would have been guilty of the same misunderstanding. It is this reality
which makes the readers of the world sympathize with Abraham.

—

Seed Thoughts

The *Midrash Rabbah*, which we are now studying, has given us an
entirely new conception of Isaac. In the Torah text, Isaac is quoted as
saying to his father: "We have everything arranged for the sacrifice,
but where is the ram which is to be offered?" Abraham's response was
that God would provide a ram for them in due course. The Midrash,
however, adds much more to that response. It says in more than one
place that God would provide the ram, but if He does not, then Isaac
himself would be offered as the sacrifice. Isaac accepted this interpretation without any question. He was ready to serve God on the same level
as his father did. When the quotation in both the text and the Midrash
says that the two of them walked together, it should be understood that
both did and accepted God's command to Abraham, which Isaac also
accepted even though it was his life that was going to be offered. We
now have a new conception of the leadership of Israel at that time. It was
Abraham and Isaac, and both of them were blessed with characters of
the highest spiritual quality.

Parashah Fifty-Six, *Midrash Nine*

ט וישא אברהם את עיניו וירא והנה איל אחד. מהו אחר? אמר רבי יודן: אחר כל המעשים,
ישראל נאחזים בעבירות ומסתבכין בצרות וסופן ליגאל בקרנו של איל, שנאמר (זכריה ט):
וה' אלהים בשופר יתקע וגו'. אמר רבי יהודה בר סימון: אחר כל הדורות, ישראל נאחזים
בעבירות ומסתבכין בצרות, וסופן ליגאל בקרנו של איל, הה"ד: וה' אלהים בשופר יתקע.
א"ר חנינא ב"ר יצחק: כל ימות השנה ישראל נאחזים בעבירות ומסתבכין בצרות, ובראש
השנה, הן נוטלין שופר ותוקעין בו, ונזכרים לפני הקב"ה והוא מוחל להם, וסופן ליגאל בקרנו
של איל, שנאמר: וה' אלהים בשופר יתקע.

9. AND ABRAHAM LIFTED UP HIS EYES, AND LOOKED, AND BEHOLD
BEHIND HIM (*AHAR*) A RAM (GEN. 22:13). WHAT DOES *AHAR* MEAN?
SAID R. JUDAN: AFTER ALL THAT HAPPENED, ISRAEL STILL FALL INTO
THE CLUTCHES OF SIN AND [IN CONSEQUENCE] BECOME THE VICTIMS
OF PERSECUTION; YET THEY WILL BE ULTIMATELY REDEEMED BY THE
RAM'S HORN, AS IT SAYS: AND THE LORD GOD WILL BLOW THE HORN,
ETC. (ZECH. 9:14). R. JUDAH B. R. SIMON INTERPRETED: AT THE END
OF [AFTER] ALL GENERATIONS ISRAEL WILL FALL INTO THE CLUTCHES
OF SIN AND BE THE VICTIMS OF PERSECUTION; YET EVENTUALLY THEY
WILL BE REDEEMED BY THE RAM'S HORN, AS IT SAYS: AND THE LORD GOD
WILL BLOW THE HORN, ETC. R. HANINA B. R. ISAAC SAID: THROUGHOUT
THE YEAR ISRAEL ARE IN SIN'S CLUTCHES AND LED ASTRAY BY THEIR
TROUBLES, BUT ON NEW YEAR THEY TAKE THE SHOFAR AND BLOW ON
IT, AND EVENTUALLY THEY WILL BE REDEEMED BY THE RAM'S HORN, AS
IT SAYS: AND THE LORD GOD WILL BLOW THE HORN.

What happened in the text is that Abraham saw this ram caught in
a thicket, and after a while, he noticed that the ram had freed himself.
That would have ended the story except that he noticed that it was the
same ram that God Himself caught in another thicket, and apparently,
this was going to continue. That made Abraham feel that what he was
seeing was a vision that required interpretation. He was then told that
what happened with the ram is a symbol of the Jewish people. Their sins
will ultimately lead them into servitude and persecution, but after all
of it, they will be redeemed, as it is written: "God will blow the shofar."
Individual Jews blow the shofar on Rosh Hashanah to ask forgiveness,
but when God will blow the shofar, that will be the beginning of Messianism and the complete redemption of Israel.

רבי לוי אמר: לפי שהיה אברהם אבינו רואה את האיל ניתוש מן החורש הזה, והולך ומסתבך
בחורש אחר, אמר לו הקב"ה: כך עתידין בניך להסתבך למלכיות מבבל למדי, מן מדי ליון,
ומיון לאדום, וסופן ליגאל בקרנו של איל, הה"ד: וה' אלהים בשופר יתקע. וילך אברהם
ויקח את האיל ויעלהו לעולה תחת בנו. רבי בנאי אמר: אמר לפניו: רבון העולם! הוי רואה
דמיו של איל זה כאילו דמו של יצחק בני אימוריו כאילו אימוריו דיצחק ברי כהדא דתנן
הרי זו תחת זו הרי זו תמורת זו הרי זו חלופי זו הרי זו תמורה רבי פנחס אמר אמר לפניו
רבון העולמים הוי רואה, כאלו הקרבתי את יצחק בני תחלה, ואח"כ הקרבתי את האיל
הזה תחתיו, היך מה דאת אמר (מלכים ב טו): וימלוך יותם בנו תחתיו. כהדא דתנן: כאימרא
כדירים. רבי יוחנן אמר: כאימרא תמידא. ריש לקיש אמר: כאילו של יצחק. תמן אמרי: כולד
החטאת. תני, בר קפרא: כאימור דלא ינק מן יומי:

R. ABBA B. R. PAPPI AND R. JOSHUA OF SIKNIN IN R. LEVI'S NAME SAID:
BECAUSE THE PATRIARCH ABRAHAM SAW THE RAM EXTRICATE HIMSELF
FROM ONE THICKET AND GO AND BECOME ENTANGLED IN ANOTHER,
THE HOLY ONE, BLESSED BE HE, SAID TO HIM: "SO WILL THY CHILDREN
BE ENTANGLED IN COUNTRIES, CHANGING FROM BABYLON TO MEDIA,
FROM MEDIA TO GREECE, AND FROM GREECE TO EDOM; YET THEY WILL
EVENTUALLY BE REDEEMED BY THE RAM'S HORN," AS IT IS WRITTEN:
AND THE LORD GOD WILL BLOW THE HORN . . . THE LORD OF HOSTS WILL
DEFEND THEM (ZECH. 9:14F.). AND ABRAHAM WENT AND TOOK THE
RAM, AND OFFERED HIM UP FOR A BURNT-OFFERING IN THE STEAD OF
HIS SON (GEN. 22:13). R. JUDAN SAID IN R. BANAI'S NAME: HE PRAYED TO
HIM: "SOVEREIGN OF THE UNIVERSE! LOOK UPON THE BLOOD OF THIS
RAM AS THOUGH IT WERE THE BLOOD OF MY SON ISAAC; ITS *EMURIM*
(INNER PARTS) AS THOUGH THEY WERE MY SON'S *EMURIM*," EVEN AS WE
LEARNED: WHEN A MAN DECLARES: THIS ANIMAL BE INSTEAD OF THIS
ONE, IN EXCHANGE FOR THAT, OR A SUBSTITUTE FOR THIS, IT IS A VALID
EXCHANGE. R. PHINEHAS SAID IN R. BANAI'S NAME, HE PRAYED: "SOVER-
EIGN OF THE UNIVERSE! REGARD IT AS THOUGH I HAD SACRIFICED MY
SON ISAAC FIRST AND THEN THIS RAM INSTEAD OF HIM," [IN THE STEAD
BEING UNDERSTOOD] AS IN THE VERSE, AND JOTHAM HIS SON REIGNED
IN HIS STEAD (II KINGS 15:7). IT IS EVEN AS WE LEARNED: [WHEN ONE
DECLARES I VOW A SACRIFICE] LIKE THE LAMB OR LIKE THE ANIMALS
OF THE TEMPLE STALLS, R. JOHANAN SAID: HE MEANT, LIKE THE LAMB
OF THE DAILY BURNT-OFFERING: RESH LAKISH SAID: HE MEANT, LIKE
ISAAC'S RAM. THERE [IN BABYLON] THEY SAY: LIKE THE OFFSPRING OF
A SIN-OFFERING. BAR KAPPARA TAUGHT: HE MEANT, LIKE THE LAMB
WHICH HAS NEVER GIVEN SUCK.

In offering the ram, Abraham is trying to establish that the ram would be a replacement for the intended slaughter of Isaac. The Midrash then quotes many interpretations of what was meant by this intention of Abraham. In all respects, the exchange of one sacrifice for another is looked upon as being legally acceptable in the halakha.

—

Seed Thoughts

The commentators, from time to time, express the view that the people of Israel are guilty of sinful behavior from time to time, but every year on Rosh Hashanah, they blow the ram's horn and seek forgiveness. Most of the interpretations explain that when Jews blow the shofar, they hope that God will remember the binding of Isaac and the heroic behavior of father and son in that remarkable story. It would seem to this reader that God does not have to be reminded, but that the Jewish people do require this reminder. Every Jew should realize that when they listen to the sound of the Rosh Hashanah shofar, it is meant to remind them of the ethical heroism of Abraham and the equally dedicated self-sacrifice of Isaac. The Midrash maintains that Isaac understood that he would be the sacrificial offering. If that was God's will, Isaac was prepared to accept it unconditionally. He actually helped his father in setting up the altar for his own slaughter and felt a sense of fulfillment, if this is what God required of him. The Holy Scriptures, from time to time, use the expression "they walked, the two of them, together." One was walking as the slaughterer; the other was walking to be slaughtered. Both of them were only interested in one thought – *Kiddush Hashem*, sanctifying the name of God.

Parashah Fifty-Six, *Midrash Ten*

י ויקרא אברהם שם המקום ההוא ה' יראה. ר' יוחנן אמר: אמר לפניו: רבון העולמים! בשעה
שאמרת לי קח נא את בנך את יחידך היה לי מה להשיב, אתמול אמרת כי ביצחק וגו',
ועכשיו קח נא את בנך וגו', וחס ושלום לא עשיתי כן, אלא כבשתי רחמי לעשות רצונך. יהי
רצון מלפניך ה' אלהינו, בשעה שיהיו בניו של יצחק באים לידי עבירות ומעשים רעים, תהא
נזכר להם אותה העקידה ותתמלא עליהם רחמים. אברהם קרא אותו יראה, שנאמר: ויקרא
אברהם שם המקום ההוא ה' יראה.

10. AND ABRAHAM CALLED THE NAME OF THE PLACE ADONAI-JIREH –
THE LORD SEETH (GEN. 22:14). R. BIBI RABBAH SAID IN R. JOHANAN'S
NAME: HE SAID TO HIM: "SOVEREIGN OF THE UNIVERSE! WHEN THOU
DIDST ORDER ME, 'TAKE NOW THY SON, THINE ONLY SON' (22:2), I COULD
HAVE ANSWERED, 'YESTERDAY THOU DIDST PROMISE ME, FOR IN ISAAC
SHALL SEED BE CALLED TO THEE (21:12), AND NOW THOU SAYEST, "TAKE
NOW THY SON," ETC.' YET HEAVEN FORFEND! I DID NOT DO THIS, BUT
SUPPRESSED MY FEELINGS OF COMPASSION IN ORDER TO DO THY WILL.
EVEN SO IT MAY BE THY WILL, O LORD OUR GOD, THAT WHEN ISAAC'S
CHILDREN ARE IN TROUBLE, THOU WILT REMEMBER THAT BINDING IN
THEIR FAVOR AND BE FILLED WITH COMPASSION FOR THEM." ABRAHAM
CALLED IT JIREH:

It should be mentioned that when Abraham discussed the fact that he
was aware of the contradictions in God's command to him, he had in
mind what seemed to be the changeability of God's opinion moving
from a declaration that the descendants of Isaac would form a great
people to the other prophecy ordering Abraham to sacrifice his son and
finally, the third changeable view where the angel said: "Do not hurt
your son." It should be understood that Abraham thought all about this
while he was preparing himself for the terrible act of slaughter, but he
refused to debate this with God, Who knew all the answers. Instead,
he carried out everything that God apparently told him to do. This,
by itself, is a tremendous demonstration of the strength of Abraham's
belief in God.

שם קרא אותו שלם, שנאמר (בראשית יד): ומלכי צדק מלך שלם. אמר הקב"ה: אם קורא אני
אותו יראה, כשם שקרא אותו אברהם, שם אדם צדיק מתרעם. ואם קורא אני אותו שלם,

אברהם אדם צדיק מתרעם, אלא הריני קורא אותו ירושלים, כמו שקראו שניהם, יראה שלם
ירושלים.

AND ABRAHAM CALLED THE NAME OF THAT PLACE ADONAI-JIREH. SHEM
CALLED IT SALEM [SHALEM]: AND MELCHIZEDEK KING OF SALEM (GEN.
15:18). SAID THE HOLY ONE, BLESSED BE HE: "IF I CALL IT JIREH AS DID
ABRAHAM, THEN SHEM, A RIGHTEOUS MAN, WILL RESENT IT; WHILE IF
I CALL IT SALEM AS DID SHEM, ABRAHAM, THE RIGHTEOUS MAN, WILL
RESENT IT. HENCE I WILL CALL IT JERUSALEM, INCLUDING BOTH NAMES,
JIREH SALEM."

This is one of the many interpretations we will find in the Oral Torah
as to how Jerusalem got its name.

ר' ברכיה בשם רבי חלבו אמר: עד שהוא שלם, עשה לו הקב"ה סוכה והיה מתפלל בתוכה,
שנאמר (תהלים עו): ויהי בשלם סוכו ומעונתו בציון. ומה היה אומר? יהי רצון שאראה בבנין
ביתי.

R. BEREKIAH SAID IN R. HELBO'S NAME: WHILE IT WAS YET SALEM, THE
HOLY ONE, BLESSED BE HE, MADE HIMSELF A TABERNACLE AND PRAYED
IN IT, AS IT SAYS: IN SALEM ALSO IS SET HIS TABERNACLE, AND HIS
DWELLING-PLACE IN ZION (PS. 76:3). AND WHAT DID HE SAY: "O THAT I
MAY SEE THE BUILDING OF THE TEMPLE!"

For more, see the Seed Thoughts.

ד"א: מלמד שהראה לו הקב"ה בית המקדש חרב ובנוי, חרב ובנוי, שנא': שם המקום ההוא
ה' יראה, הרי בנוי, היך מה דאת אמר (דברים טז): שלש פעמים בשנה יראה. אשר יאמר היום
בהר ה', הרי חרב, שנאמר (איכה ה): על הר ציון ששמם. ה' יראה, בנוי ומשוכלל לעתיד לבא,
כענין שנאמר (תהלים קב): כי בנה ה' ציון נראה בכבודו:

ANOTHER INTERPRETATION: THIS VERSE TEACHES THAT THE HOLY ONE,
BLESSED BE HE, SHOWED HIM THE TEMPLE BUILT, DESTROYED AND RE-
BUILT. FOR IT SAYS, AND ABRAHAM CALLED THE NAME OF THAT PLACE
ADONAI-JIREH (THE LORD SEETH): THIS ALLUDES TO THE TEMPLE
BUILT, AS IN THE VERSE: THREE TIMES IN A YEAR SHALL ALL THY MALES
BE SEEN . . . IN THE PLACE WHERE HE SHALL CHOOSE (DEUT. 16:16). AS
IT IS SAID TO THIS DAY: IN THE MOUNT REFERS TO IT DESTROYED, AS IN
THE VERSE: FOR THE MOUNTAIN OF ZION, WHICH IS DESOLATE (LAM.
5:18); WHERE THE LORD IS SEEN REFERS TO IT REBUILT AND FIRMLY ES-
TABLISHED IN THE MESSIANIC ERA, AS IN THE VERSE: WHEN THE LORD

HATH BUILT UP ZION, WHEN HE HATH BEEN SEEN IN HIS GLORY (PS. 102:17).

The intention of these verses is to indicate that the Third Temple will be built by God. We are not sure exactly what this means, except to interpret that the Third Temple will be built but not destroyed, because God will have a role to play in its development and survival. Individual Jews try from time to time to organize a campaign for the Third Temple. Such a campaign will only succeed if God wants it to.

—

Seed Thoughts

This Midrash contains a remarkable teaching. It claims that God prays, but how does that happen? To whom does He pray? For an answer, let us see what the Midrash says in terms of the content of this particular prayer at this particular time. Its content was "O that I may see the building of the Temple!" From this anecdote, we learn two things. On the one hand, prayer consists of an appeal to a higher power – in most cases, to God. There is, however, another form of thought which is designated as prayer, and that is to review one's moral values and to renew them as best as possible. One is also able to make a request and consider it as prayer as defined in the Midrash we are now studying. If God can pray, surely all of us can pray. This gives us much scope for enriching prayers in the spirit of what is now being defined as prayer.

PARASHAH FIFTY-SIX, *Midrash Eleven*

יא ויקרא מלאך ה' שנית ויאמר בי נשבעתי. מה צורך לשבועה זו? א"ל: השבע לי, שאין אתה
מנסה אותי עוד מעתה ולא את יצחק בני! משל לאחד ששמר את אגינו שבולת נהר והקפיץ
גם בנו עמו. ד"א: מה צורך לשבועה זו? רבי חמא ב"ר חנינא: א"ל: השבע לי שאין אתה
מנסה אותי עוד מעתה! משל למלך, שהיה נשוי למטרונה, ילדה ממנו בן ראשון וגרשה, שני
וגרשה, שלישי וגרשה, וכיון שילדה ממנו בן עשירי, נתכנסו כולם ואמרו לו: השבע לנו, שאין
אתה מגרש את אמנו מעתה! כך, כיון שנתנסה אברהם אבינו נסיון עשירי, א"ל: השבע לי,
שאין אתה מנסה אותי עוד מעתה! א"ר חנן: כי יען אשר עשית את הדבר הזה נסיון עשירי,
הוא ואתה אומר: כי יען אשר עשית הדבר הזה, אלא זה נסיון האחרון, שהוא שקול כנגד
הכל, שאילולי לא קבלו עליו אבד את הכל.

11. AND THE ANGEL OF THE LORD CALLED UNTO ABRAHAM A SECOND
TIME OUT OF HEAVEN, AND SAID: BY MYSELF HAVE I SWORN (GEN.
22:15F.). WHAT WAS THE NEED OF THIS OATH? HE HAD BEGGED HIM:
"SWEAR TO ME NOT TO TRY ME AGAIN HENCEFORTH, NOR MY SON
ISAAC." R. LEVI IN THE NAME OF R. HAMA B. R. HANINA GAVE ANOTHER
REASON FOR THIS OATH: HE HAD BEGGED: "SWEAR TO ME NOT TO TEST
ME AGAIN HENCEFORTH." THIS MAY BE LIKENED TO A KING WHO WAS
MARRIED TO A NOBLE LADY. SHE GAVE BIRTH TO HER FIRST SON BY HIM,
AND HE DIVORCED HER; A SECOND, AND HE DIVORCED HER; A THIRD,
AND HE DIVORCED HER. WHEN SHE HAD GIVEN BIRTH TO A TENTH SON
BY HIM, THEY ALL ASSEMBLED AND DEMANDED OF HIM: "SWEAR TO US
NOT TO DIVORCE OUR MOTHER AGAIN." SIMILARLY, WHEN ABRAHAM
HAD BEEN TRIED FOR THE TENTH TIME, HE SAID TO HIM: "SWEAR TO
ME NOT TO TEST ME AGAIN." R. HANAN COMMENTED: BECAUSE THOU
HAST DONE THIS THING (22:15) – IT WAS THE TENTH TRIAL, YET YOU
SAY, BECAUSE THOU HAST DONE THIS THING! THE FACT, HOWEVER, IS
THAT THIS WAS THE LAST TRIAL, WHICH WAS AS WEIGHTY AS ALL THE
REST TOGETHER, AND HAD HE NOT SUBMITTED TO IT, ALL WOULD HAVE
BEEN LOST.

Abraham's request for a new covenant was not meant to belittle
his former agreement with the Almighty. Abraham merely sought to
guarantee that he would not be tested again. The binding of Isaac
was not only the tenth such test but the most difficult of them all,
and he wanted an assurance that he would not have to go through
this again.

[נ"א כל מה שעשה] כי ברך אברכך וגו'. ברכה לאב, ברכה לבן. והרבה ארבה. רבות לאב,
רבות לבן.

THAT IN BLESSING I WILL BLESS THEE, ETC. (GEN. 22:17): A BLESSING
FOR THE FATHER AND A BLESSING FOR THE SON; AND IN MULTIPLYING
WILL I MULTIPLY: AN INCREASE FOR THE FATHER AND AN INCREASE FOR
THE SON.

The descendants of Isaac will be the real creators of the Jewish people,
particularly under the leadership of Jacob.

ויירש זרעך את שער שונאיו. רבי אומר: זו תרמוד, אשריו כל מי שהוא רואה במפלתה
של תרמוד שהיתה שותפת בשני חרבנות. רבי יודן ורבי חנינא: חד מנהון אמר: בחרבן בית
ראשון העמידה פ' אלף קשתים [נ"א קשטים], ובחרבן בית שני, העמידה ח' אלפים קשתים.

AND THY SEED SHALL POSSESS THE GATE OF HIS ENEMIES (GEN. 22:17).
RABBI SAID: THIS ALLUDES TO TADMOR. HAPPY IS HE WHO WILL SEE THE
DOWNFALL OF TADMOR WHICH TOOK PART IN BOTH DESTRUCTIONS. R.
JUDAN AND R. HANINA — ONE OF THEM SAID: AT THE DESTRUCTION OF
THE FIRST TEMPLE SHE SUPPLIED EIGHTY THOUSAND ARCHERS, AND AT
THE DESTRUCTION OF THE SECOND, EIGHT THOUSAND ARCHERS.

The Rabbis interpreted "'the gate of your enemies" as meaning that
an enemy of Israel has the equivalent of a gate through which they allow
attackers of Israel to enter the Land of Israel. Not only do they allow
free access, but they also provide many thousands of soldiers who are
capable of shooting deadly arrows with great accuracy. These enemy
advantages were provided to help destroy the First Temple and the
Second Temple.

וישב אברהם אל נעריו. ויצחק היכן הוא? רבי ברכיה בשם רבנן דתמן: שלחו אצל שם ללמוד
ממנו תורה. משל לאשה שנתעשרה מפלכה, אמרה: הואיל ומן הפלך הזה התעשרתי, עוד
אינו זז מתחת ידי לעולם. כך, אמר אברהם: כל שבא לידי אינו אלא בשביל שעסקתי בתורה
ובמצוות, לפיכך אינו רוצה שתזוז מזרעו לעולם. רבי חנינא אמר: שלחו בלילה מפני העין,
שמשעה שעלו חנניה מישאל ועזריה מכבשן האש, עוד לא נזכרו שמותן. ולהיכן הלכו? ר"א
אמר: מתו ברוק. ר' יוסי אמר: מתו בעין. ר' יהושע בן לוי אמר: שינו את מקומם והלכו להם
אצל יהושע בן יהוצדק, ללמוד ממנו תורה, הה"ד (זכריה ג): שמע נא יהושע הכהן הגדול, אתה
ורעיך היושבים לפניך. ר' חנינא אמר: על מנת כן ירדו חנניה מישאל ועזריה לכבשן האש, על
מנת שיעשה בהן מופת:

SO ABRAHAM RETURNED UNTO HIS YOUNG MEN (GEN. 22:19). AND
WHERE WAS ISAAC? R. BEREKIAH SAID IN THE NAME OF THE RABBIS OF

THE OTHER PLACE: HE SENT HIM TO SHEM TO STUDY TORAH. THIS MAY
BE COMPARED TO A WOMAN WHO BECAME WEALTHY THROUGH HER
DISTAFF. SAID SHE: "SINCE I HAVE BECOME WEALTHY THROUGH THIS
DISTAFF, IT WILL NEVER LEAVE MY HAND." (THUS SAID ABRAHAM: "ALL
THAT HAS COME TO ME IS ONLY BECAUSE I ENGAGED IN TORAH AND
GOOD DEEDS; THEREFORE I AM UNWILLING THAT IT SHOULD EVER DE-
PART FROM MY SEED.") R. JOSE B. R. HANINA SAID: HE SENT HIM [HOME]
AT NIGHT, FOR FEAR OF THE [EVIL] EYE. FOR FROM THE MOMENT THAT
HANANIAH, MISHAEL, AND AZARIAH ASCENDED UNSCATHED FROM THE
FIERY FURNACE THEY ARE NO MORE MENTIONED. WHITHER THEN HAD
THEY GONE? R. LEAZAR SAID: THEY DIED THROUGH THE SPITTLE; R. JOSE
B. R. HANINA SAID: THEY DIED THROUGH AN [EVIL] EYE. R. JOSHUA B.
LEVI SAID: THEY CHANGED THEIR LOCALITY AND WENT TO JOSHUA, THE
SON OF JEHOZADAK, TO STUDY TORAH; THAT IS MEANT BY THE VERSE,
HEAR NOW, O JOSHUA THE HIGH PRIEST, THOU, AND THY FELLOWS THAT
SIT BEFORE THEE; FOR THEY ARE MEN THAT ARE A SIGN (ZECH. 3:8). R.
TANHUMA B. ABINA COMMENTED IN R. HANINA'S NAME: FOR THIS VERY
PURPOSE DID HANANIAH, MISHAEL, AND AZARIAH DESCEND INTO THE
FIERY FURNACE, THAT A SIGN SHOULD BE WROUGHT THROUGH THEM.

Everything in life comes to an end. Hananiah, Mishael, and Azariah
became tremendous symbols of how God can save those who love Him.
That, however, was their entire story. We do not hear about them again.

Abraham spent the last years of his life studying Torah and performing the commandments. However, at his request, God did not challenge
him again.

———

Seed Thoughts

Abraham was tired. He was probably not tired spiritually, but he was
tired physically. He had gone through ten difficult challenges, and the
tenth was the most difficult of all. He has left behind for us one of the
greatest stories that ever happened in the world. I am referring to the
challenges where he was called upon, he thought, to sacrifice his son
on the altar. Not only was his faith in God a tremendous example to
the world, but in his son Isaac, he discovered a spiritual follower of
whom it could be said that he dedicated his life in the same spirit as
did his father, Abraham. God granted his request, although it doesn't

say so specifically, but He did not call upon Abraham again. Abraham became a private citizen. He married again after the death of Sarah, and he had other children but none of them were called upon by the Holy One, blessed be He, for any sacred purpose. We hear about Abraham again only at the time of his death, where we are informed of his age, and that his burial was looked after by Ishmael and Isaac working together, which is something for which Abraham hoped and prayed.

א ויהי אחרי הדברים האלה ויגד לאברהם לאמר הנה ילדה מלכה וגו' בנים, כתיב (משלי יד):
חיי בשרים לב מרפא ורקב עצמות קנאה, שעד שהוא בהר המוריה, נתבשר שנולד זוגתו של
בנו, שנאמר: הנה ילדה מלכה. (שם ג) רפאות תהי לשרך ושקוי לעצמותיך, שעד שהוא בהר
המוריה, נתבשר שנולדה זוגתו של בנו, שנאמר: הנה ילדה מלכה גם היא בנים:

1. AND IT CAME TO PASS AFTER THESE THINGS, THAT IT WAS TOLD TO
ABRAHAM, SAYING: BEHOLD, MILCAH, SHE ALSO HATH BORNE CHIL-
DREN, ETC. (GEN. 22:20). IT IS WRITTEN: A TRANQUIL HEART IS THE
LIFE OF THE FLESH (PROV. 14:30): THUS, WHILE HE WAS YET ON MOUNT
MORIAH HE WAS INFORMED THAT HIS SON'S MATE [REBEKAH] HAD BEEN
BORN, AS IT SAYS: BEHOLD, MILCAH, SHE ALSO HATH BORNE, ETC. IT
SHALL BE HEALTH TO THY NAVEL, AND MARROW TO THY BONES (3:8).
R. BEREKIAH SAID IN R. ISAAC'S NAME: IF THOU HEALEST, IT WILL BE
FOR THYSELF. WHAT IS THE PROOF? IF THOU HEALEST, IT WILL BE FOR
THINE OWN FLESH, FOR WHILE HE WAS YET ON MOUNT MORIAH HE WAS
INFORMED THAT HIS SON'S MATE HAD BEEN BORN, AS IT SAYS: BEHOLD,
MILCAH, SHE ALSO HATH BORNE CHILDREN.

The Midrash is concerned with the fact that the information about
Milcah giving birth to children, plus Bethuel being described as Rebekah's father, appears immediately after the *Akeida* (binding). Why is
this so? It seems to be the concern of the Midrash. Apparently, Abraham
was deeply worried about the fact that at the age of 37 (some sources
read 26 and not 37), his son Isaac was not yet married. If the slaughter
of the Akeida had actually taken place, Isaac would have left this world
without any children or any followers. The purpose of the addition of
the verse about Milcah was not only to give information to the reader,
but to inform Abraham directly that the spouse who would be the wife
of his son Isaac has just been born, and therefore, is his daughter-in-law.
This kind of a news would provide Abraham with tremendous relief
and gratitude. In the verse that is quoted, the Hebrew word *besarim* is

translated as being related to the word *besora*, meaning a message. The verse would mean that a good message is tremendous healing of the human heart.

PARASHAH FIFTY-SEVEN, *Midrash Two*

ב (שם כה) מים קרים על נפש עיפה ושמועה טובה מארץ מרחק. תמן תנינן: על הגשמים ועל בשורות טובות הוא אומר: ברוך הטוב והמטיב. מה ראו לסמוך בשורות טובות לירידת גשמים? רבי ברכיה בשם רבי לוי אמר: על שם מים קרים על נפש עיפה, שמועה טובה מארץ מרחק, מה שמועה טובה, ברוך הטוב והמטיב, אף מים קרים, ברוך הטוב והמטיב. ד"א: כמים קרים על נפש עיפה כן שמועה טובה מארץ מרחק, זה אברהם, שעד שהוא בהר המוריה, נתבשר שנולדה זוגתו של בנו, הה"ד הנה ילדה מלכה וגו':

2. AS COLD WATERS TO A FAINT SOUL, SO IS GOOD NEWS FROM A FAR COUNTRY (PROV. 25:25). WE LEARNED ELSEWHERE: AS FOR GOOD TIDINGS ONE RECITES THE BLESSING: "BLESSED BE HE WHO IS GOOD AND DOETH GOOD," SO FOR COLD WATER [I.E., RAIN] ONE RECITES THE BLESSING, "BLESSED IS HE WHO IS GOOD AND DOETH GOOD." AND, AS COLD WATER TO A FAINT SOUL, SO IS GOOD NEWS FROM A FAR COUNTRY; WHILE HE [ABRAHAM] WAS STILL ON MOUNT MORIAH, HE WAS INFORMED THAT HIS SON'S MATE HAD BEEN BORN, IN ACCORDANCE WITH THE VERSE, BEHOLD, MILCAH, SHE ALSO HATH BORNE, ETC.

The main lesson in this Midrash is that timing is a very important element in life. Abraham could have been informed several days later, or even several weeks later, about the birth of Rebekah, who was meant to be the spouse of Isaac. This would have been very important to him. However, Abraham was informed while still on Mount Moriah, after both of them had been saved miraculously. Abraham was worried about the future of his son, so the news about this birth was overwhelming. Abraham was completely relieved of his worries and very grateful for the information. Timing is very important in life.

PARASHAH FIFTY-SEVEN, *Midrash Three*

ג ויהי אחרי הדברים האלה. אחר הרהורי דברים שהיו שם. מי מהרהר? אברהם, אמר:
אילו מת בהר המוריה, לא היה מת בלא בנים? עכשיו, מה אעשה אשיאנו מבנות ענר אשכל
וממרא, שהן צדקניות. וכי מה איכפת לי מיוחסים? א"ל הקב"ה: אין אתה צריך, כבר נולד
זוגו של יצחק, הנה ילדה מלכה גם היא. היא, גם היא, מה זו בני גבירה שמונה, ובני פילגשים
ארבעה, אף זו, בני גבירה שמונה, ובני פילגשים ארבעה:

3. AND IT CAME TO PASS AFTER THESE THINGS: MISGIVINGS WERE
ENTERTAINED ON THAT OCCASION. BY WHOM? BY ABRAHAM. HE RE-
FLECTED: HAD HE DIED ON MOUNT MORIAH, HE [ISAAC] WOULD SURELY
HAVE DIED WITHOUT CHILDREN! THEREFORE, NOW I MAY INDEED GIVE
HIM IN MARRIAGE TO ONE OF THE DAUGHTERS OF ANER, ESHCOL, OR
MAMRE, WHO ARE RIGHTEOUS WOMEN; FOR WHAT DOES THEIR BIRTH
MATTER TO ME? SAID THE HOLY ONE, BLESSED BE HE, TO HIM: "YOU DO
NOT NEED THIS, FOR ISAAC'S MATE HAS ALREADY BEEN BORN"; HENCE,
BEHOLD, MILCAH, SHE ALSO HATH BORNE. WHY STATE SHE ALSO? TO
TEACH THAT JUST AS IN HER CASE THERE WERE EIGHT CHILDREN
FROM THE MISTRESS [I.E., THE LEGAL WIFE] AND FOUR FROM THE CON-
CUBINES, SO IN THIS CASE THERE WERE EIGHT CHILDREN FROM THE
MISTRESS AND FOUR FROM THE CONCUBINES.

Seed Thoughts

While still on Mount Moriah, after the deliverance of both Abraham
and Isaac from the threat of extinction at the Akeida, Abraham was
concerned with two problems. The first, we have already discussed – he
worried that his son Isaac, at the age of 37, was not yet married. He partially blamed himself for waiting until a girl of noble ancestry occurred.
This worry was abolished the moment he was told that Rebekeh, who
had just been born, would be the future wife of Isaac. However, he had
one additional concern. He wanted his spiritual challenges on behalf
of God to be curtailed now that the Akeida was the tenth (and last) of
the spiritual challenges to Abraham which God requested. He had now
asked for some assurance that his concern would be looked after and
was grateful for God's message that Abraham need not worry. Someone

else was found, a most righteous human being and outstanding Jew. His name was Job – and in Hebrew, איוב – Iyov. He would turn out to be most capable to face suffering, on the one hand, and accept whatever happy opportunities might develop, on the other hand. Milcah mentions that she had given birth to someone whose name was אוץ – Utz. It could only have referred to Job, because the book that contains his story describes him as living in the country known as Utz. No one else is so described, and God was very confident that Job would be another Abraham, so to speak, and that Abraham need not worry that his absence may make life difficult for God. The Midrash ends on this note, that the arrival of Job as Iyov makes it possible for Abraham to leave the limelight and become a private citizen, so to speak.

PARASHAH FIFTY-SEVEN, *Midrash Four*

ד ד"א: נתירא מן היסורין. א"ל הקב"ה: אין אתה צריך, כבר נולד מי שיקבלם, את עוץ בכורו, ואת בוז אחיו. איוב אימתי היה?

4. ANOTHER INTERPRETATION: [ABRAHAM ENTERTAINED MISGIVINGS,] BEING AFRAID OF SUFFERING. SAID THE HOLY ONE, BLESSED BE HE, TO HIM: "THOU NEEDST HAVE NO FEAR, FOR ALREADY HE HAS BEEN BORN WHO IS TO RECEIVE THEM, VIZ. UZ HIS FIRSTBORN, AND BUZ HIS BROTHER" (GEN. 22:21). WHEN DID JOB FLOURISH?

God had already assured Abraham in a special covenant that He would not call upon him again to carry the suffering of the entire generation. However, when the angel said, "Now I know that you could be relied upon," Abraham was afraid that this would be a new opening requesting him to undertake a new spiritual challenge. That is why God assured him not to worry. He had found a truly righteous individual who would carry on the sacred responsibilities that Abraham had borne. This person, whom we call Job (or Iyov), in which generation did he live? What now follows is the series of interpretations by some of the Talmudic scholars as to the above question.

ריש לקיש בשם בר קפרא אמר: בימי אברהם היהף שנאמר את עוץ בכורו, וכתיב (איוב א): איש היה בארץ עוץ.

R. SIMEON B. LAKISH SAID IN BAR KAPPARA'S NAME: IN THE DAYS OF ABRAHAM, FOR HERE IT SAYS, UZ HIS FIRSTBORN, WHILE IT IS WRITTEN: THERE WAS A MAN IN THE LAND OF UZ (JOB 1:1).

Rabbi Simeon b. Lakish offers his interpretation based directly on the biblical text that is included in the story of Abraham when he is informed about the birth of Utz, whose name is Job (Iyov). According to this interpretation, Iyov would have been the nephew of Abraham.

רבי אבא בר כהנא אמר: בימי יעקב היה, דאמר רבי אבא בר כהנא: דינה אשתו של איוב היתה, דכתיב: באשת איוב (שם ב) כדבר אחת הנבלות, וכתיב בדינה (בראשית לד): כי נבלה עשה בישראל.

R. ABBA B. KAHANA SAID: IN THE DAYS OF JACOB, FOR R. ABBA B. KA-HANA SAID: DINAH WAS JOB'S WIFE (FOR IN THE CASE OF JOB'S WIFE IT IS WRITTEN: THOU SPEAKEST AS ONE OF THE FOOLISH WOMEN (*NEBA-LOTH*) SPEAKETH (JOB 2:10), WHILE WITH RESPECT TO DINAH, IT SAYS: BECAUSE HE HAD WROUGHT A VILE DEED (*NEBALAH*) IN ISRAEL (GEN. 34: 7).

The main proof of this contention is the fact that Dinah was Iyov's wife. Dinah, of course, was the daughter of Jacob, and that is a direct connection to the view of Rabbi Abba b. Kahana that Job lived in the time of Jacob. It is also based on a proof text that the Hebrew word *naval* appears in the Dinah story in the time of Jacob as well as in the Dinah story as the wife of Iyov.

ר' לוי אמר: בימי שבטים היה, הה"ד (איוב טו): אשר חכמים יגידו ולא כיחדו מאבותם. זה ראובן ויהודה. ומה שכר נטלו על כך? להם לבדם נתנה הארץ.

R. LEVI SAID: HE [JOB] FLOURISHED IN THE DAYS OF THE TRIBAL ANCES-TORS, AS IT IS WRITTEN: WHICH WISE MEN HAVE TOLD, AND HAVE NOT HID IT FROM THEIR FATHERS (JOB 15:18). THIS ALLUDES TO REUBEN AND JUDAH. AND WHAT REWARD DID THEY RECEIVE FOR THIS? THAT UNTO THEM ALONE THE LAND WAS GIVEN (15:19).

See the Additional Commentary.

רבי לוי בשם ר' יוסי בר חלפתא אמר: בירידתן למצרים נולד ובעלייתן מת. אתה מוצא עיקר שניו של איוב לא היו, אלא מאתים ועשר שנים, ועשו ישראל במצרים מאתים ועשר שנים, ובא שטן לקטרג וגירה אותו באיוב. רבי חנניא בריה דרבי אחא אמר: לרועה, שהוא עומד

ומביט בצאנו. בא זאב אחד, נזדווג לו. אמר: תנו לו תיש אחד, שיתגרה בו. ורבי חמא אמר:
לאחד שהיה יושב בסעודה, בא כלב אחד ונזדווג לו. אמר: תנו לו ככר א', שיתגרה בו. כך,
בא שטן לקטרג, גירה אותו באיוב, הה"ד (איוב טז) : יסגירני אל אל עויל, ועל ידי רשעים ירטני,
והלואי בני אדם צדיקים, אלא בני אדם רשעים.

R. LEVI IN THE NAME OF R. JOSE B. HALAFTA SAID: HE WAS BORN WHEN
THEY WENT DOWN INTO EGYPT, AND DIED WHEN THEY WENT UP OUT
OF EGYPT. YOU WILL FIND THAT IN ESSENCE HIS LIFE'S SPAN WAS TWO
HUNDRED AND TEN YEARS, WHILE ISRAEL SPENT TWO HUNDRED AND
TEN YEARS IN EGYPT. NOW WHEN SATAN CAME TO DENOUNCE [ISRAEL],
HE [GOD] INCITED HIM AGAINST JOB [INSTEAD]. R. HANANIAH, THE SON
OF AHA, AND R. HAMA, THE SON OF R. HANINA, DISCUSSED THIS. R. HA-
NANIAH, THE SON OF AHA, SAID: IT MAY BE COMPARED TO A SHEPHERD
WHO STOOD WATCHING HIS FLOCKS, WHEN A WOLF CAME TO ATTACK
HIM, WHEREUPON HE ORDERED: "THROW HIM A HE-GOAT ON WHICH
TO VENT HIS RAGE." R. HAMA B. R. HANINA SAID: IT MAY BE COMPARED
TO A KING SITTING AT HIS MEAL WHEN A DOG CAME AND ATTACKED
HIM, WHEREUPON HE ORDERED, "GIVE HIM A BONE TO WORRY." THUS
IT IS WRITTEN, GOD DELIVERETH ME TO THE UNGODLY, AND CASTETH
ME INTO THE HANDS OF THE WICKED (JOB. 16:11) AND WOULD THAT THE
PEOPLE WERE RIGHTEOUS, BUT THEY ARE INDEED WICKED!

It was the sad fate of Iyov to have to suffer on behalf of the wickedness
of the people. The fact that he did so marked him as a tremendously
righteous personality.

ר' יוסי בר יהודה אומר: בימי שפוט השופטים היה, הה"ד (שם כז) : הן אתם כולכם חזיתם
ולמה זה הבל תהבלו. חזיתם מעשי ומעשי דורי, חזיתם מעשי מצות ומעשים טובים. מעשה
דורי, שהן מבקשין ליתן שכר לזונות מן הגרנות, ואין דרכן של צדיקים להיות נותנין שכר
לזונות מן הגרנות, הה"ד (הושע ט) : אהבת אתנן על כל גרנות דגן. ר' שמואל בר נחמן אמר:
בימי כשדים היה שנאמר, (איוב א) : כשדים שמו, שלשה ראשים. ר' נתן אמר: בימי מלכות
שבא היה, שנאמר (שם) : ותפול שבא ותקחם: ר' יהושע בן קרחה אמר: בימי אחשורוש
היה, דכתיב ביה (אסתר ב) : יבקשו למלך נערות בתולות טובות מראה, וכתיב (איוב מב) : ולא
נמצא נשים יפות כבנות איוב. ריש לקיש אמר: איוב לא היה ולא נהיה! מחלפיה שיטתיה,
דריש לקיש, דתמן: אמר ריש לקיש, בשם בר קפרא: בימי אברהם היה, והכא אמר, איוב לא
היה ולא נהיה! מאי לא היה ולא נהיה ביסורים שנכתבו עליו, ולמה נכתבו עליו? אלא שאילו
באו עליו, היה יכול לעמוד בהן.

R. JOSE B. R. JUDAH SAID: HE FLOURISHED IN THE DAYS WHEN THE JUDGES
JUDGED. HENCE IT IS WRITTEN: BEHOLD, ALL YE YOURSELVES HAVE
SEEN IT; WHY THEN ARE YE BECOME ALTOGETHER VAIN? (JOB. 27:12):

YE HAVE SEEN MY DEEDS, YE HAVE SEEN THE DEEDS OF MY CONTEMPO-
RARIES: YE HAVE SEEN MY DEEDS – PIETY AND NOBLE ACTS; YE HAVE
SEEN THE DEEDS OF MY CONTEMPORARIES, WHO SEEK TO PAY HARLOTS
OUT OF THE GRANARIES, BUT RIGHTEOUS MEN DO NOT PAY HARLOTS
OUT OF THE GRANARIES; THUS IT IS WRITTEN: THOU HAST LOVED A
HARLOT'S HIRE OUT OF EVERY CORN-FLOOR (HOS. 9:1). R. SAMUEL B.
NAHMAN SAID: HE LIVED IN THE DAYS OF THE CHALDEANS, FOR IT SAYS:
THE CHALDEANS SET THEMSELVES IN THREE BANDS (JOB 1:17). R. NA-
THAN SAID: IN THE DAYS OF THE QUEEN OF SHEBA, AS IT SAYS: AND THE
SABEANS MADE A RAID, AND TOOK THEM AWAY (1:15). R. JOSHUA SAID:
IN THE DAYS OF AHASUERUS, IN CONNECTION WITH WHOM IS WRITTEN:
LET THERE BE SOUGHT FOR THE KING YOUNG VIRGINS FAIR TO LOOK
ON (EST. 2:2), WHILE IT IS WRITTEN: AND . . . WERE NO WOMEN FOUND
SO FAIR AS THE DAUGHTERS OF JOB (JOB 42:15). R. SIMEON B. LAKISH
(RESH LAKISH) SAID: JOB NEVER EXISTED AT ALL AND WILL NEVER BE.
THIS VIEW OF RESH LAKISH IS SELF-CONTRADICTORY, FOR ELSEWHERE
HE SAID IN THE NAME OF BAR KAPPARA: HE FLOURISHED IN THE DAYS
OF ABRAHAM, WHILE HERE HE MAINTAINS THUS? HE MEANS, HOWEVER,
THAT HE WAS NEVER EXPOSED TO THE SUFFERINGS ASCRIBED TO HIM.
WHY THEN WERE THEY ASCRIBED TO HIM? BECAUSE HAD THEY COME
UPON HIM, HE WOULD HAVE BEEN ABLE TO WITHSTAND THEM.

Resh Lakish commented that there never was a person whose name
was Iyov, but that everything about such a person was included in the
Book of Job which, from time to time, can help individuals. Those who
suffer severe affliction can learn about a person in this book who was
able to withstand this pain and suffering, and it could be an important
element to help others survive as well.

ר' יוחנן אמר: מעולי גולה היה, וישראלי היה, ומדרשו בטבריה. לפיכך היו למדים ממנו
קריעה וברכת אבלים, הה"ד (שם א): ויקם איוב ויקרע את מעילו, מכאן שצריך אדם לקרוע
מעומד. ר' חנינא אמר: עובד כוכבים היה. תני ר' חייא: עובד כוכבים צדיק אחד עמד לי
באומות העולם, ונתתי לו שכרו ופטרתי. ואיזה? זה איוב. את עוץ בכורו. ר' יהושע בן לוי
אמר: הוא לבן, הוא קמואל, ולמה נקרא שמו קמואל? שקם כנגד אומתו של אל. ופילגשו
ושמה ראומה. א"ר יצחק: כולהון לשם מרדות: הן טבח טבחון, גחם גמחון, תחש תחשון,
מעכה מעכון:

R. JOHANAN SAID: HE WAS ONE OF THOSE WHO RETURNED FROM THE
[BABYLONIAN] EXILE, AN ISRAELITE. THEREFORE HE [R. JOHANAN]
LEARNED FROM HIM THE LAWS OF MOURNERS, AS IT IS WRITTEN: THEN

JOB AROSE, AND RENT HIS MANTLE (JOB. 1:20), WHENCE WE DERIVE THAT A MAN MUST REND HIS GARMENTS STANDING. R. HANINA SAID: HE WAS A HEATHEN. R. HIYYA TAUGHT: [GOD SAID:] "ONE RIGHTEOUS MAN AROSE AMONG THE NATIONS OF THE WORLD, AND I GAVE HIM HIS REWARD AND LET HIM GO"; AND WHO WAS THAT? JOB. UZ HIS FIRSTBORN, AND BUZ HIS BROTHER, AND KEMUEL THE FATHER OF ARAM (GEN. 22:21). R. JUDAN AND R. JUDAH B. R. SIMON IN R. JOSHUA'S NAME SAID: KEMUEL WAS LABAN; AND WHY WAS HE CALLED KEMUEL? BECAUSE HE AROSE (*KAM*) AGAINST THE PEOPLE OF GOD (*EL*). AND HIS CONCUBINE, WHOSE NAME WAS REUMAH, SHE ALSO BORE TEBAH, AND GAHAM, AND TAHASH, AND MAACAH (22:24). R. ISAAC SAID: ALL THESE NAMES SIGNIFY CHASTISEMENT: TEBAH MEANS THEY SLAUGHTER (*TABHIN*): GAHAM, THEY BURN (*GAMHIN*): TAHASH, THEY SILENCE (*TAHSHIN*), MAACAH, THEY CRUSH (*MAAKIN*).

—

Additional Commentary

Job flourishing at the time of the tribal ancestors

Reuben and Judah are mentioned here because, according to Tractate *Sotah* (7b), they confessed their sins to Jacob. The preceding verse in Job states: "That which I have seen I will declare." Job was thus their contemporary. Furthermore, according to a comment by Rashi in *Sotah*, royalty descended from Judah while Reuben was the first tribe to receive his territory. (Soncino)

I am now about to conclude my commentaries on the fourth book of Midrash that I have interpreted. The names of the previous volumes are: *The Creation; The Garden of Eden and the Struggle to be Human,* and *Noah, the Flood and the Failure of Man.* This fourth book, *Abraham and the Challenge of Faith,* has to do with the life and times of Abraham.

Let me begin with a comment on the subject which has to do not only with the present Midrash with which I have been concerned, but with a phenomenon which includes not only all of midrashic literature but all of the Talmudic literature as well. I am referring to the phenomenon of the detailed names referred to in Talmudic and midrashic literature. When I use the expression "all of the Talmudic literature," not all readers will understand just how awe-inspiring the question is. The Talmud was recently completed in a beautiful English translation, known as the Schottenstein Talmud. The Talmud, for those not fully acquainted, includes, in addition to halakha, numerous Aggadic-midrashic commentaries, and there are many volumes to the Talmud. I counted 82 volumes of the Schottenstein Talmud, which means that the Hebrew section alone must comprise about 40 volumes. I would not be surprised if one thousand names or more are included in this remarkable body of literature.

The rabbis, whose names are included in the Mishna, are known as the Tannaim, which means "the teachers." The rabbis whose names are quoted in the Gemara are described as Amoraim, which also means "the speakers." What impressed me, from the moment I saw my first page of Talmud until the present day, is that names in the Talmudic literature are treated with a holiness that I never experienced anywhere else, nor have I ever heard that names are given that prominence in other famous literatures of the world.

Let me give you one example: "Said Rabbi Zrika in the name of Rabbi Ami [who said] in the name of Rabbi Joshua Ben Levi" (*Berak-*

hot 3b). As we can see, only rabbinic scholars are included by name in the Talmud, but only because they have an opinion on a subject matter being discussed. But to continue, "Rabbi Zrika, derived this opinion from his teacher, Rabbi Ami, who in turn, derived this opinion from his teacher, Rabbi Joshua Ben Levi." Not all names are given this kind of detailed background, but only when the discussion is helped by this kind of knowledge.

I am amazed with this detailed transmission of our tradition. This is something which we find in later rabbinic works as well, and even in the Chassidic tradition. It is certainly a theme which future scholars should research and maybe they, in their studies, will help us understand how remarkable this phenomenon is.

Let us consider a few themes that relate to the Midrash just completed. Can a biblical character criticize God? In the early chapters of *Midrash Rabbah*, Abraham asks God whether Sodom and Gomorrah can be spared: "Will you save the cities if fifty righteous people live there?" The answer is yes. Abraham continues this question descending to 45, and then 40, and then going all the way down to 10. It is a magnificent literary form in addition to the question-and-answer subject matter. Abraham asks the same question that if there are ten righteous people living there, would God spare the region, and God answers yes. The discussion ends at this point. One has to assume that God did not find ten such righteous people there; otherwise, the cities would have been saved. However, we can see from the story that Abraham was not satisfied. He looked and acted as a person in mourning. We do not know what went through his mind. Probably something to the effect that one can be partially righteous and not deserve to die. Most cities do not have completely righteous people, but they are not punished for that reason. During the days that Sodom and Gomorrah were being destroyed, Abraham sat in one place just outside the city and would go nowhere and do nothing throughout the days in which those two cities were destroyed. Nowhere does it say that Abraham criticized God. He would never say such a terrible thing. But all one has to do is read his story and follow his behavior, and we would understand that he was truly in mourning for Sodom and Gomorrah. He remained in that position for the several days in which the destruction was taking place, and he did not move until God called to him and told him that He wanted him to move away from that area and to enter the Land of Canaan, which is to be the permanent homeland of his descendant.

Having gone over this part of *Genesis Rabbah*, and having followed the route through which the last chapter in this book took Job (Iyov) as they were struggling to discover the generation in which he lived, I should like to suggest another question: Why does this particular part of *Genesis Rabbah* end with Job (Iyov)? There had been no connection with it in all the chapters – all of the sudden, it emerges front and center, and this section of *Genesis Rabbah* ends with a discussion of Job (Iyov). The truth of the matter is that the more we think about it, the more relevant it appears to be. Our particular section of *Genesis Rabbah*, which centers on the personality of Abraham, has taught us to see in Abraham not only the first Jew, but the ideal representative of the moral character of a human being. But what is the lesson of Abraham for all the future generations? One of the answers is that human beings with moral character are available. They emerge, they live, they function, they sacrifice, and they honor God. Job was one of these remarkable individuals. Granted, that in the Book of Job, Satan was challenged to get Job to change his way of life, but he did not succeed. In the Book of Job, when his children died, presumably as the result of Satan's work, Job's wife said to him: "Isn't it time to criticize God?" Job's answer was: "The Lord has given, the Lord has taken. Blessed be the name of the Lord." That is the heritage of Job (Iyov), whether or not he lived in reality. His book taught us that personalities of moral character have a place in this world and are our greatest blessing.

This volume will be published soon after I have completed seventy years of rabbinical leadership at Congregation Shaar Hashomayim. I was active as Rabbi of the congregation for 47 years, after which I retired with the title of Rabbi Emeritus. My retirement package simply stated that I could involve myself in any synagogue activity, so long as it was mutually accepted. I never made use of this permission, but I was also requested to deliver the *Kol Nidre* sermon for as long as I was able to do so. I have delivered this sermon for the past 23 years. It has been a beautiful challenge and something that gave me an opportunity to plan from one year to another. All good things, however, must come to an end, and it appears as though this particular experience will now be coming to an end. I thought, therefore, that it would be appropriate to include the 23rd sermon as a replica of all the others. I hope that the readers of this volume, and the members of Shaar Hashomayim, will be pleased to have it included. The text of the sermon will now follow.

Forgiveness Is Peace

One of my most precious experiences has to do with the *Siddur*, the Jewish prayer book. I regard the *Siddur* as a tremendous achievement, a source of Judaism, almost as close as the Bible and Talmud. My interest in the prayer book was not merely a translation of some of the difficult words, but rather a search for meaning. The scholars who prepared the Jewish prayer book were great believers in a meaningful life, especially in Judaism. Everything in the prayer book deserves to be tested in what it offers for a meaningful experience. Whenever I found a text that did not meet this criterion, I spent a lot of time trying to decipher it and to search for the meaning which I knew was there, although I had not as of yet experienced it. I should like to share one such prayer with you. At the very beginning, I knew that there was a meaning in this program, although I had not as of yet experienced it. I ultimately discovered this meaning and I should like to share it with you how I went about it.

The nature of the Jewish prayer book is such that every morning service begins with a series of Psalms. Its completion – what we call *Shacharit* (morning prayer), which begins with *Barchu* (which calls upon all of us to bless God and at the same time calls upon God to bless us) – is a powerful introduction and applies to every morning service – daily, Sabbath, and Festival. What bothered me was that in the text of the *Siddur*, another blessing immediately followed the *Barchu*. Why? Was the *Barchu* not strong enough to achieve all the spiritual rewards? In order to answer this question, it was necessary to study and discuss the new benediction and understand its meaning. This is what it says: "Blessed art Thou, o Lord, our God and the God of our forefathers, *Yotzer ohr* (Creator of light)." Of course God is the Creator of light; we know that from the Creation story. The light which our benediction is speaking about is the earthly light, which appears in our life every day, which covers almost half of the earth in every nook and cranny and does so day by day without interruption, unless some calamity occurs in the natural world, such as an earthquake or storm or some other such terrible event. The blessing goes on to say *u-Voreh hoshech* ("And [also] creates darkness"); the darkness covers more or less the same area as the light but at a different time of the day.

Both of these expressions are easily understandable. The expression that follows is more difficult. It says *Oseh Shalom*, that God is the Creator of Peace. What in the world is the connection between light and darkness on the one hand, and the creation of peace on the other hand? It took me a long time to develop an interpretation. Ultimately, I used a midrashic development – not a Midrash, but the technique often used by the Midrash. I refer to the fact that very often, the Midrash assigns human characteristics to some of the phenomena of the natural world. In this respect, it is as though light would have the ability to speak to darkness and would say something to this effect: "I cover almost half the world, and you – as darkness – also cover almost half of the world. If I promise never to encroach upon your area, you also promise never to encroach on my area." Darkness agreed, and now we have the expression *Oseh Shalom*, Creator of Peace. In other words, darkness and light have shared their experience with each other, and they have become a model of what *Shalom* is all about. There is an English word which expresses what I am now writing about. It is called "compromise"; both light and darkness gave up a little bit of their independence in order to achieve peace, and they compromised. The blessing goes on to say *u-Voreh et ha-kol*, that God created everything, not just light and darkness. Therefore, compromise is the way to go for every aspect of the human experience.

This reminds me of a story. In actual fact, the story was told to me by one of our members who may actually be reading this article and would probably be pleased to notice it in print. He was eating in a restaurant, and a couple came and sat beside him. He knows that they were quarrelling. He did not know the content of the quarrel, but it did not matter to him, since it was their private business. Eventually, they left the restaurant and so did he. However, when he came outside, he noticed that they were still quarrelling, but not quietly – in a very loud voice. They were actually screaming the words to each other, and many passersby stopped and watched what was happening. A large group eventually gathered, and my friend was hoping that a policeman would come by and put an end to this kind of demonstration which should not take place in our public domain. However, when after a while a policeman did not appear, he thought to himself that it may be time to become a hero. He, therefore, went to the quarrelling couple and apologized for intervening, but said that he had a message for both of them. They asked what the message was. He answered that forgiveness is peace. The woman said to him: "What was that which you just said?" He answered: "Forgiveness is peace." he then began to cry, and he asked her why she cried. She answered that a year ago, she visited the Lubavitcher Rebbe, and when she left him, he said to her: "Forgiveness is peace." She then said: "The reason that I am crying is because he asked me to do one or two small things in my life which I neglected to do, and that is why I feel so terrible." She then opened her purse and took out a dollar and said to him: "He also gave me this dollar." She said to him that she never had the intention to spend the dollar. However, she said to him: "Since you were so kind to us, we want to give you the dollar." My friend never wanted her to know that he had many of those dollars, but he thanked her anyway. As he walked away, he reminisced that sometimes, the kind of intervention that he did produces even more fighting, but he turned around to look at them, and they were shaking hands. So he felt good about it as though he were probably doing a mitzvah. I learned one thing from this story, which has influenced me very much.

What is that form of behavior which has produced more compromise than anything else in the world? I'm not going to wait for others to answer the question, but let me tell you my conclusion. That aspect of life, which uses compromise more than any other aspect of life, is the search for forgiveness. Forgiveness is related to compromise. If one of the participants in a quarrel says to his companion "I forgive you," if the second person says "I accept your forgiveness," forgiveness has happened because compromise has happened. If the second person did not say "I accept your forgiveness," it does not matter how many times he says "I forgive you"; it accomplishes nothing. Forgiveness involves compromise or it is nothing, and it is still probably the most important aspect of life which uses compromise in the situation where most people don't know that it is even being used. I do not wish to pretend that compromise is some kind of new value that the world never experienced before. On the contrary, it is one of the oldest values not only within the Western tradition but within the tradition of any civilization. Whether we are dealing with family problems or with business relationships or with political interests, compromise is known by everyone and anyone. Not only is it known intellectually, but it is also opposed with full vigor. So many people in the world are not interested in compromise, but rather in victory. They are so certain of the rightness of their cause that they allow nothing to stand in their way. What does it matter that sometimes they have to face embittering experiences? It is only temporary. Even if it is not temporary, the ultimate victory will be easily adjusted, but this is not the way of the prayer book. Insofar, as the prayer book is concerned and the particular benediction is concerned, we are confronting compromise, and compromise becomes the most important value. Its importance can be asserted in many directions, but for our particular interest at the present time, compromise is directly achieved by forgiveness, and forgiveness makes peace possible. Can there be anything more important than this?

There is another area that should be looked at while we are dealing with compromise as the main theme. The prayer book, known as the *Machzor*, deals with the liturgy of the Day of Atonement and is replete with documents of forgiveness. There is one particular prayer where our supposed sins are listed in the order of the Hebrew alphabet and are familiar by the opening words *Ashamnu* – we are guilty, and *Bagadnu* – we have been treacherous. The same prayer book contains a litany of sins known in Hebrew as the *Al Het*, which includes all the possible sins. For the worshipper on the Day of Atonement, this litany (which contains approximately 64 levels of sinfulness, 90% of which the average worshipper is completely innocent) is often memorized by the many thousands of people who attend the Day of Atonement service. I have only scratched the surface of so many compilations of the same material. The important point to understand, however, is that we are dealing with divine forgiveness and divine justice. After every section of this litany of sinfulness, the phrase occurs: "For all these things, o Lord, forgive us, pretend that the sins never occurred, and finally help us transform our lives to become better people." All of this is divine justice; God alone will decide who will be forgiven and who will not be forgiven.

In the light of these presentations, which appear in the prayer book of the Day of Atonement, do we have the right, as human beings, to create our own policies of forgiveness? Does it really matter that compromise can help create a just forgiveness when we know that the real forgiveness will be decided by God and God alone? The Rabbis of the Talmud differentiated between sins between Man and God that God alone forgives, and sins between Man and Man that without the other's forgiveness God cannot forgive. The Rabbis taught us that the kind of forgiveness that relates to compromise is a very important spiritual development when successful, and even when only partially successful. It raises the spiritual index of every human being that undertakes the forgiveness program, makes of that person a better human being, and eventually more acceptable to the Lord, our God, Who will ultimately decide our spiritual merits and our spiritual standing on the ladder of forgiveness.

Let me remind our readers that this entire presentation began as a search for meaning in one particular part of our prayer book. We ask ourselves: "Why should something as tremendous as the call of worship by *Barchu*, which calls upon God to bless us, be followed by the particular blessing which we have been trying to interpret. That blessing reads "Blessed art Thou, o Lord our God, King of the Universe, Who created light in the world and darkness in the world," but as explained above, there is *Oseh Shalom*, "Creator of Peace," because compromise was possible between lightness and darkness. It is then followed as *u-Voreh et ha-Kol*, which means that the search for peace through forgiveness transforms the entire universe. Let us always remember that genuine compromise relates to forgiveness, and forgiveness brings with it the blessing of peace. Amen.

HaMidrash HaMevo'ar – Under the general editorship of Rabbi Abraham Steinberger presiding over a faculty of scholars, the first four volumes, comprising *Bereishit Rabbah,* were published in 1984 in Jerusalem. The final volume of the *Midrash Rabbah* was completed fifteen years later. This commentary leaves nothing undone or unexplained. Every new interpretation is traced to its source. The use of different type styles (bold, italics, etc.) helps the reader follow the various levels of interpretation. Every volume ends with from a plethora of sources.

Matnot Kehuna – This commentary is the work of Rabbi Issachar Ber ben Naftali of the town of Mishbershin in Poland. The work first appeared in the Cracow edition (1587) of the *Midrash Rabbah* and has appeared in every compilation ever since. This commentary sparkles with brevity and has been used by all who study Midrash.

Mirkin – This commentary by Moshe Aryeh Mirkin was the first of the Modern Hebrew commentaries. Published in Tel Aviv in 1968, the author emphasizes the plain meaning of the text. He leans heavily on the edition of Theodore and Albeck, then great textual scholars, and bases many of his interpretations on manuscript emendations and corrections they suggested. He has a great talent for brevity without compromising the meaning, and this is a most valuable contribution of understanding Midrash.

Rashi – Rabbi Solomon Yitzhaki (1040–1105) is the great interpreter of the Bible and Talmud. According to the Vilna Edition, Rashi also wrote a commentary to *Bereishit Rabbah,* but authorities disagree and feel that the commentary is culled from his views as written in his other commentaries. There are even some scholars who argue that the commentary to *Bereishit Rabbah* was written by someone else. However, Rashi's name is associated with these ideas and probably always will be.

RZWE – These are the initials of Rabbi Zev Wolf Einhorn. His Hebrew commentary is titled מהרז"ו, which are his Hebrew initials. His commentary is a very large work and appears also in abridged form; both forms are presented side by side in the Vilna Edition. His interpretation tries to apply the thirty-two hermeneutical principals of Rabbi Elazar ben Azariah. Our quotations are from the Vilna Edition.

Soncino – The Soncino Press, from its headquarters for many years in London, England, pioneered the translation of the great classics of Judaism into English, including the Bible, the Talmud, the Zohar, and the *Midrash Rabbah*. The *Midrash Rabbah* was translated in 1939, and in the 1980s, the rights to Soncino Press were acquired by Judaica Press in New York, through whose permission their translation has been used. In addition to the translation, the Soncino editions include explanatory notes.

Tiferet Tzion – The author of *Tiferet Tzion*, Rabbi Yitzhak Zev Yadler, passed away in 1917 and his great work, *Tiferet Tzion*, was not published until 1958. It is a tremendous work by one person, who, according to his own testimony, spent fourteen years of unremitting work, night and day, to produce this monumental commentary on the *Midrash Rabbah*. A pious scholar and mystic by belief, upbringing, and conviction, he was able to relate to many of the difficult mystical passages of the *Midrash Rabbah* as no one else has been able to do. The present work relies heavily on his insights.

ABOUT THE AUTHOR

Rabbi WILFRED SHUCHAT has been an active rabbi for over 50 years, and has studied and taught the Midrash Rabbah during his tenure as Rabbi of Shaar Hashomayim Synagogue in Montreal, Canada. His groundbreaking work in the interpretation and analysis of Midrash has made these psychological and philosophical rabbinic perspectives accessible to laymen and clergy alike.